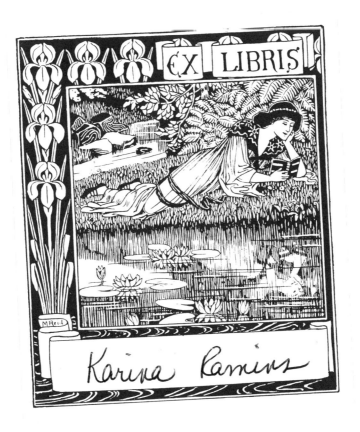

EX LIBRIS

Karina Ramins

THE SYMBOLISM OF THE BIBLICAL WORLD

THE SYMBOLISM OF THE BIBLICAL WORLD

ANCIENT NEAR EASTERN ICONOGRAPHY AND THE BOOK OF PSALMS

OTHMAR KEEL

TRANSLATED BY TIMOTHY J. HALLETT

A CROSSROAD BOOK
THE SEABURY PRESS   NEW YORK

For Hildi, my wife,
whose understanding and cooperation
made this book possible

1978
The Seabury Press
815 Second Avenue
New York, N.Y. 10017

Originally published as *Die Welt der altorientalischen Bildsymbolik und das Alte Testament: Am Beispiel der Psalmen*
© Copyright 1972 by
Benziger Verlag Zürich Einsiedeln Köln
und Neukirchener Verlag Neukirchen

English translation from the first German edition with additions
and corrections by the author

Printed in the United States of America

Library of Congress Cataloging in Publication Data

Keel, Othmar.   The symbolism of the Biblical world.
Translation of Die Welt der altorientalischen Bildsymbolik und das
Alte Testament.
"A Crossroad book."   Bibliography: p.   Includes index.
1. Bible. O.T. Psalms—Criticism, interpretation, etc.
2. Art—Near East. 3. Near East—Antiquities. 4. Symbolism
in the Bible. I. Title.
BS1430.5.K4313   223'.2'064   77-21056
ISBN 0-8164-0353-8

CONTENTS

INTRODUCTION

(Italicized numbers refer to the illustrations. Biblical quotations are given according to the RSV unless otherwise noted. Italics in biblical quotations are the author's.)

The Old Testament and the Ancient Near East

The nineteenth century rendered the service of rediscovering the long-forgotten world of ancient Egypt and the ancient empires of Mesopotamia. The vast expansion of the historical horizon occasioned by that rediscovery is reflected in wider circles today. The tendency to devote to the ancient Near East* two or three volumes of series treating world or art history is but one instance of this enlarged horizon. The ancient Near East now constitutes an integral part of our historical dimension.

In consequence of these discoveries the Bible, once thought to be "mankind's oldest book," has proved to be a relatively recent phenomenon. The bulk of its content is as far removed from the beginnings of the high cultures of the ancient Near East as it is from us (ca. 2,500 years). We now see the Bible imbedded in a broad stream of traditions of the most diverse kind and provenance. Only when this rich environment has been systematically included in the study of the OT do OT conventionalities and originalities clearly emerge. It then becomes evident where the biblical texts are carried by the powerful current of traditions in force for centuries, and where they give an intimation of a new energy inherently their own.

* As used here and elsewhere in this book, the terms "ancient Near East" and "ancient Near Eastern" are understood to include Egypt, except where otherwise noted.

Two Approaches to the World of the Ancient Near East

No contemporary scholarly work dispenses with at least occasional comparison of OT evidence with other evidence from the ancient Near East. But because the languages in which these literary witnesses exist are numerous (Sumerian, Akkadian, Egyptian, Hittite, etc.) and difficult to master, most professors of the OT and nearly all their students must content themselves with translations.

It has long been recognized in the abstract that, unlike our orthography and graphics, most ancient Near Eastern orthographic systems are—or at least once were—connected with relative closeness to their respective pictorial arts. This applies to the Sumerian-Akkadian and Hittite systems, but it applies in unique measure to the Egyptian system.[1] Egyptian paintings, even in the late period, were often a kind of calligraphically fashioned, monumental hieroglyphics. They were not intended to be viewed, like paintings of nineteenth- or twentieth-century European art *(Sehbild),* but rather to be read *(Denkbild).*[2] Unlike texts, however, these "calligraphs" markedly simplify the intended meaning. Like a monument, they tend to summarize a particular concept in one or two grand "gestures." This has enormous pedagogical advantages, especially in an era with heightened sensibility for all that is visual. Of course, this simplifying, iconographic description of the ancient Near East can itself be criticized as a simplification. But every description, including the literary, implies simplification, and every simplification results in vagaries and ambiguities. As opposed to the scholarly, literary simplification, the iconographic simplification has the advantage of having been produced by the ancient Near East itself. With powerful and emphatic strokes that

7

world has drawn its own main lines. The iconographic approach can claim the advantage of originality and authenticity; no translation of ancient Near Eastern texts can.

For the serious student, iconography can in no way replace the study of written sources. But by no means does this render iconography superfluous. We are dealing here with two related, yet different methods, each with its own distinctive characteristics. The differentiated, linguistic approach will undoubtedly remain the *via regia* into the world of the ancient Near East. Still, the iconographic approach presents its own particular and unique advantages.

The Iconographic Approach

Iconography has long been recognized as a significant factor in our understanding of those so-called biblical *realia* that are products of human creativity. We frequently know from context and from the tradition of translation that a particular phoneme must denote some weapon, cult object, musical instrument, or architectural element. In most cases, however, only archaeology can instruct us concerning the exact appearance of these man-made objects. Detailed descriptions of such artifacts are extremely rare.

Iconography is also important—perhaps even more important—when one considers entities which in themselves remain unchanged, such as the sun, moon, storms, earth, and trees. We assume far too easily that these phenomena held the same meaning for the ancient Near East as they do for us. The merism "heaven and earth," for example, sounds quite natural to us; it has no strange connotation. But when we look at illustrations from the Egyptian Book of the Dead, in which the sky in the figure of Nut is arched over the extended figure of the earth god (cf. *25, 27, 28–30, 32–33),* it becomes quite startlingly clear that in ancient Egypt the concepts "heaven and earth" were associated with ideas and feelings very different from ours. Faced with words and ideas, the individual hearer conceives their meaning in terms supplied primarily by his own preunderstanding. It is considerably more difficult for that preunderstanding to prevail when a concept is visually rendered.

Iconography allows our preunderstanding considerably less latitude than does the abstract phoneme. It can therefore make evident more quickly and effectively than written records a number of very common peculiarities of ancient Near Eastern reasoning and imagination. Iconography compels us to see through the eyes of the ancient Near East.

The term "peculiarities" does not imply that ancient Near Eastern thought was completely different from ours—prelogical or something of the sort. There may have been no fundamental difference at all.[3] The "peculiarities" are to be understood as placements of stress or emphasis.

The widespread use of ideogram and symbol is the first of these means of emphasis. In this usage, ideogram and symbol signify a concrete dimension; but to this concrete dimension is attached a significance larger than that which it inherently possesses. In an ideogram this meaning is artistically defined; in a symbol it is drawn rather more from nature and is thus less precisely fixed.[4] We tend to work almost exclusively with concepts either concrete (tree, door, house) or abstract (being, kingship, mentality). The ancient Near East, on the other hand, has a preference for concepts which are in themselves concrete, but which frequently signify a reality far larger than their concrete meaning. To the ancient Near East, similar forms, colors, movements, and sounds readily suggest a deeper coherence. The red of the evening sky signifies blood and the battle waged by the sun against the powers of darkness. Invasion by hostile peoples evokes associations with Chaos, which formerly ruled the earth (cf. *142, 144).*[5] The powerful associative capacity of the ancient Near East is able to transform any concrete incident into a portentous happening (cf. the importance of omen and dream interpretation, *251–52*).

We constantly run the risk of reading these pictures too concretely, or having avoided that risk, of treating them too abstractly. Depending on their context or on the attitude of the observer, their significance can range from the historical, concrete event to the universal, eternal world order.

When Pharaoh is shown striking down his enemies (Nubians, Libyans, Canaanites; cf. *144, 397–403, 451*), the representation may commemorate the specific, historical execution of one or more insurgent princes. It is thus to be taken quite concretely. But the picture may also serve to portray the conquest of a hostile nation. In that case, such an execution may never have occurred. The context of the scene or very nearly allegorical variations on it (cf. *399a, 132a*) reveal that the scene is frequently to be viewed without historical reference. Rather, it symbolically represents that Egyptian kingship which *ex natura sua* successfully defends the borders of Egypt against every neighboring nation, destroys every threat, and is able in every circumstance to subject the enemies of the land to its dominion. The pictures evidence a tendency to place their subjects in stereotyped, increasingly unrealistic attitudes. Contexts are fluid, ranging from the realm of the historical to the magical-mythical.

The Bible shares the mentality of the ancient Near East. Every student of the Bible knows that certain expressions are not to be understood "literally." But it is not at all easy, given specific instances, to follow the peculiarities of ancient Near Eastern thought. The study of iconography is very well suited to heighten our consciousness in these areas. Every OT scholar undoubtedly understands "horn of the wicked" (Ps 75:4, 10) as an ideogram for "power of the wicked." But consideration of ancient Near Eastern modes of thought and expression is only too easily forgotten in the face of figures of speech which may be construed more

concretely. An instance is the horror usually aroused by the imprecation over Babylon: "Happy shall he be who takes your little ones and dashes them against the rock!" (Ps 137:9). We need to consider, however, whether these "little ones" ought not to be understood just as symbolically as "Mother Babylon." The inhabitants of the oppressor-city or the children of the ruling dynasty concretize the continuation of the unrighteous empire (cf. *341–42*). In this vein, one might translate: "Happy is he who puts an end to your self-renewing domination!" Stated thus, the sentence would presumably offend no one, though it too implies brutal consequences. Its brutality, however, is cloaked in the broad mantle of abstract formulation. Such a (often dangerous) dissociation of concrete reality from idea is as foreign to the ancient Near Eastern mode of perception as the dissociation of body and spirit. Ancient Near Eastern perception usually preserves the continuity between the *concretum* and its related abstract.

A second characteristic of ancient Near Eastern perception and thought likewise comes to light more quickly and clearly in iconography than in texts: It is "the characteristic tendency of pre-Hellenistic thought not to seek a comprehensive view cast in perspective (H. Schäfer), but to be content—even in important areas of thought—with a grouping of aspects (H. Frankfort: multiplicity of approaches)."[6] This peculiarity is apparent in the characteristic Egyptian rendering of a standing man. Each part of the subject's body is presented to the viewer in such a way that its most typical aspect stands out: the face in profile, the eyes in front view, the shoulders in front view, the rest of the body and the legs in profile (e.g., *442*).[7]

The effect is rather more surprising when, by the same principle, the gates of the temple are shown from the front, but the forecourt with the altar *(196)* from the side; or when different aspects of heaven and earth are grouped in such a way that the ship of the sun, instead of traveling the heavenly ocean, traverses the body of the lady of heaven *(32)*. In such pictures, each part must be viewed first from the standpoint from which it was conceived; then the composition as a whole must be *read* as a thought-picture, not merely viewed.[8] Even so, the attempt to bring widely diverse aspects into systematic relation presupposes the beginnings of a comprehensive view. More frequently, however, quite different images stand unrelated side by side: the sky as a fixed cover *(15, 17–18, 20–21)*, the sky as a pair of wings *(19, 21–24)*, the sky as a woman *(25–26, 28–30, 32–33)*, the sky as ocean *(32, 34, 36)*. In each of these renderings, a different aspect of the sky is represented in symbol.

The multiplicity of approaches so evident in ancient Near Eastern iconography is similarly found in the psalms. The region beneath the inhabited earth is understood to be ruled by water (e.g., Ps 24:2) because water is found in the abyss and on every side. The region beneath the inhabited, sunlit earth is also the realm of the dead (e.g., Ps 63:9) for the simple reason that they are buried there. These two aspects stand side by side in ancient Near Eastern views of the nether world. They are not brought into perspective with each other, as is attempted in modern presentations of "The Ancient Near Eastern View of the World" *(56–57)*. To be sure, the two aspects are connected, or better, mixed in the conceit of a dying man fallen into the reach of the primeval flood (e.g., Ps 18:4-5). But this does not imply an attempt to achieve a unified view of what is beneath the earth. It is difficult to penetrate the peculiar, ancient Near Eastern character of these patterns of thought, where diverse, yet equally valued conceptions stand side by side (as do various working hypotheses in the modern world).

From a European standpoint one might say that each conceit or hypothesis seems suited to explain a specific aspect of the subject under consideration. On this view, it would be natural, having critically examined the various hypotheses, to attempt to place them in relation and to arrive finally at a systematic understanding of the whole. But that process is not undertaken in the ancient Near East, for it accommodates a European concern, not the concern of the ancient Near East.[9] There the various images do not—at least not primarily—serve to explain what they portray, but to *re-present* it. While the endeavor to explain is not always entirely absent, only rarely would it have been the motivating force. In the ancient Near East, the usual purpose in literary or visual representation of an event or object is to secure the existence of that event or object and to permit him who represents it to participate in it. The above-mentioned scene of the striking-down of enemies does not usually function as the portrayal of an historical event, still less as an explanation of why Pharaoh and not his enemies triumphed. Rather, the picture is intended to represent and secure the power of the Pharaoh in all its varied forms. Even the Genesis account of the origin of the world and man "did not arise out of an intellectual question concerning the source of that which is present or that which exists, but out of concern for the security of that which exists."[10] The magical-evocative, poetic word and the symbolic, monumental picture are better suited to this task than an explanatory fact-book or a naturalistic drawing.

The evocative representation is determined primarily by the requirements of the evocator, and only secondarily by the autonomy of what is evoked. Thus slight significance attaches to the compatibility or incompatibility of different aspects. If the deceased, like the sun god, is to be regenerated every morning by the sky, the sky is pictured as a woman. If he is to arch protectively over the royal palace, he is represented as a pair of wings. The ancient Near East is seldom troubled—out of scientific curiosity—about a subject in and of itself.

Ancient Near Eastern thought and discourse are, as a rule, intensely engaged and thoroughly determined by their objective. The multiplicity of aspects standing unrelated side by side corresponds to a multiplicity of approaches determined by various objectives. Consideration of this peculiarity is of the utmost importance to the exegesis of the psalms.[11]

The Present Work

The present work represents, to the best of my knowledge, the first attempt to compare systematically the conceptual world of a biblical book with that of ancient Near Eastern iconography. The choice of the Psalter for this comparison is not fortuitous, though the study will also include portions of other books, such as Job or Jeremiah, which bear the impress of the language of the psalms.

The close relation of the hymns and prayers of Israel to those of neighboring cultures has been demonstrated, for Mesopotamia, in the studies of Begrich, Castellino, Cumming, Gamper, Stummer, Widengren, and others; for Egypt in studies by Gunkel, Nagel, and especially in the monumental work by Barucq; and for the Canaanite-Phoenician sphere in the studies of Jirku, de Liagre-Böhl, and in the great commentary by Dahood (cf. the bibliography).

A number of themes which play a very special role in the psalms are also among the favorite subjects of ancient Near Eastern iconography. They include, among others, the cosmic system,[12] the temple, the king,[13] and the cultus.

The studies mentioned above are concerned almost exclusively with texts. Subsequent to Gunkel's commentary (1929), most commentaries on the psalms have indeed made occasional reference to the iconography of the ancient Near East. Gunkel himself did so with some frequency, but even he did not undertake such reference systematically. In the work of his successors, such as Kraus, reference is still less systematic, even though a great deal of new pictorial material has become available.

A very extensive selection of pictorial material is easily accessible in James B.

Pritchard's work, *The Ancient Near East in Pictures Relating to the Old Testament (ANEP),* which appeared in 1954, and in its supplemental volume (882 illustrations), which followed in 1969. This collection is indispensable to anyone engaged in study of our theme. Of the 556 illustrations in the present work, approximately 130 are also found in *ANEP.* A noticeable shortcoming of *ANEP,* however, is its failure fully to live up to the second part of its title. The work is indeed organized with regard for the relation of the individual illustrations to the OT. Nevertheless, the task of actually discovering the relation between the OT and the given illustrations is left, almost without exception, to the user. Moreover, the collection is rather one-sidedly planned from a perspective of objective, historical knowledge. Thus illustrations most important to the world of concepts and ideas are wanting. Cases in point are the most significant ancient Near Eastern representations of the world *(8, 33–34),* cycles pertaining to the birth and infancy of the Pharaoh *(332–33, 335–40),* and many others.

In Hugo Gressmann's *Altorientalische Bilder zum Alten Testament* (678 illustrations), which appeared in a second edition in 1927, the establishment of connections with the OT remains, almost without exception, the reader's task. Beyond that deficiency, *AOB* naturally lacks everything which has been discovered since 1927. Thus *AOB* and the present work have only about 70 illustrations in common. *AOB* continues, however, to be an excellent resource for the findings of the earlier excavations.

The concern of this book coincides most closely with that of the great five-volume work, *Views of the Biblical World,* which was produced by Israeli scholars under the direction of Benjamin Mazar and appeared in 1958–1961. It offers a wealth of material in the form of maps, pictures of the landscape, and photographs of archaeological discoveries. Illustrations are provided for verses from every book of the Bible, both OT and NT. In most cases, care is taken to make evident the connection between picture and biblical text. One drawback of the series is its allotment of comparatively few pictures to the individual books of the Bible (e.g., 20 for the psalms). More serious is its failure to group the illustrations thematically. Thus it is necessary to search out from all four OT volumes the illustrations relating, for example, to "king." As a result, the individual illustrations can provide only a limited measure of mutual explication, and it is difficult to obtain any reasonably compact (visual) view. Technical data are supplied only in rudimentary degree; bibliographical information may as well be lacking entirely. The selection of materials, like that of *ANEP,* has been determined in the main by considerations of objective knowledge and historical fact. Here too, one searches in vain for pictures related to the birth-narrative of the Pharaoh—pictures which would undoubtedly provide apt illustration of (and contrast to) the "sonship" of the king in Pss 2, 89, and 110. An extreme, but not altogether atypical example is the illustration chosen for Ps 132:2–5, which refers to David's endeavors concerning a dwelling for Yahweh ("I will not enter my house or get into my bed . . . until I find a place for the LORD . . ."). The passage is illustrated by the picture of an Assyrian bed in a camp tent. The accompanying text discusses the significance of the tabernacle in ancient Israel. A reader interested in the subject of the psalm would hardly consult this section first, and the five volumes have no index. More appropriate, and more expressive in the context, would have been one of the many pictures which exemplify the king's pains on behalf of the habitation of the deity (cf. *361–72*).

The present book differs from *AOB* and *ANEP* in its concern not only to offer illustrative material, but also to confront this material, picture by picture, with the texts of a biblical book. In doing so we intend not merely to present objective facts, but to make every effort to explore fundamental orders and religious propositions. In contrast to the procedure employed in *Views of the Biblical World,* material is grouped thematically. The arrangement is open to question in several particulars. A problem arises the moment one examines the psalms from a thematic point of view, for each psalm represents a whole which is fragmented by systematic-thematic treatment. The same often holds true of ancient Near Eastern pictures and their context. Our procedure requires a double fragmentation. At the conclusion of this repeated process of decomposition and reconstruction, there will of course be room for argument regarding the placement of particular details. Nevertheless, the advantages of this procedure are obvious: in a thematic arrangement, one picture or one psalm verse can illustrate another, and a positive overall impression can be obtained. The treatment of individual psalm verses in their specific context is the concern of commentaries. The advantage of the arrangement employed in *Views of the Biblical World* lies in the easy access it affords to pictures corresponding to specific Bible verses. The present book, however, compensates for that advantage by providing an index of biblical references, which often affords access to not just one, but several illustrations for a single psalm verse.

A reading of the text should make clear the sense of the juxtaposition of psalm texts with particular illustrations. Even should this not be the case, it makes little difference, for the present work intends above all to suggest a particular approach. It is not primarily concerned with the clarification of every detail. It assumes instead the task of making easily accessible, in a kind of survey, the broadest possible range of pictorial material, and of indicating, in the text, similarities between the problems and conceptions presented by the pictures and those presented by the psalms. The dependence of a psalm verse on ancient Near Eastern art, though possible (historically conceivable) in itself, is very rarely considered. The object is rather to exhibit identical, similar, or even diametrically opposed apprehensions of the same phenomenon (e.g., of the heavens, of death, of the king) in ancient Israel and its environs. In so doing, differences generally receive less emphasis than points of contact. The former are, after all, more readily apparent to the observer—especially to one not intimately acquainted with ancient Near Eastern pictorial works. As already indicated, the writer knows only too well how undeveloped many points remain. This is difficult to avoid in a survey. It is to be hoped, however, that this survey, like so many others, may prove a rich resource to those who wish to investigate the conceptual world of the OT, and in particular that of the psalms.

Many persons have had a hand in the making of this book. I can thank here only those whose contribution was determinative.

In 1964–1965, when I was still a student, my parents made it possible for me to encounter for the first time the impressive evidences of the high cultures of Egypt and Asia Minor. During this stay in the Near East, Jean-Georges Heinz, now a member of the theological faculty of the University of Strasbourg, directed my attention to the importance of ancient Near Eastern iconography to the understanding of the OT.

At a week-long conference on the psalms in Einsiedeln in August 1966, I was able to present a first draft of this work as a slide-lecture to a group of young biblical scholars. The participants in the seminar on "Psalms and Ancient Near Eastern Iconography" (1970–1971) and the understanding and interest of my colleagues from the Biblical Institute of the University of Fribourg have contributed to the clarification of many issues. Professor Werner Vycichl has advised me in questions of Egyptology.

Library conditions at the University of Fribourg, which has no long-standing tradition of oriental studies, are less than ideal for a project of this sort. The willingness of the personnel of the Canton and University Library to make full use of the possibilities of interlibrary loan was therefore highly important. In cases where the *editiones principes* were not accessible, I have tried to make use of reliable secondary sources.

The Swiss National Fund made possible a residence at the University of Chicago during the academic year 1971–1972. This enabled me to make a number of improvements and supplementations after the manuscript had been set. The *a*-numbers (e.g., *63a*) attached to some illustrations date back to this revision.

Odo Camponovo, Max Küchler, and Urs Winter assisted the completion of the manuscript in many ways. Odo Camponovo contributed much in compiling the bibliography and the index of biblical references.

Publication of the work would have been utterly impossible without the unflagging and active help of my wife. Since the time of our first meeting in the spring of 1968, she has prepared, with perseverance, exactitude, and sensitivity, approximately 225 of the 524 line drawings. Many details can be recognized more quickly and positively in drawings than they could be in the average photographic reproduction. Five hundred high quality reproductions of high quality photographs would have made the book prohibitively expensive.

The drawings contained in the book apply various techniques suited to portray the several sources. Sculptures and reliefs are generally drawn with natural or artifically enhanced shadowing. In contrast to older methods, such as that of Lepsius, shading has been dispensed with in rendering paintings. Because a number of pictures have been taken from other works, however, these principles have not been consistently applied (cf. the two murals *341* and *342*). This inconsistency would of course have a very negative effect on a work oriented toward art history. Here, where the stated concern is primarily iconographic and not stylistic, it is of minor importance. The reader interested in art history is directed to the photo-reproductions regularly cited in the catalogue of illustrations.

A book does not spring into being upon the completion of its text. During my absence in the United States, my father energetically undertook the difficult task of supervising the still-growing manuscript and acting as liaison between the publishers and the technical workshops. The latter treated the manuscript with all the care one could wish, patiently receiving and quickly including the various addenda. The publishers deserve thanks for their willingness to risk publication of the book. Let us hope that in this instance, as in so many others, their customary sensitivity to the needs of the book-buying public is not wanting.

Our times have been characterized as the era of the visual man. For some, a visual approach to the Book of Psalms may make evident anew its unsentimental power and beauty.

I conclude this preface with a practical hint: the first chapter, which deals with ancient conceptions of the cosmic system, is for various reasons the most demanding and difficult. Anyone who is easily discouraged will do well to begin with the second or third chapter. That approach is possible because each chapter constitutes a relatively complete unit.

Fribourg, August 1971
Chicago, June 1972

OTHMAR KEEL

CHAPTER I
CONCEPTIONS OF THE COSMOS

The subject matter of this chapter is divided into two main sections,[1] one dealing with technical, the other with mythical conceptions of the cosmic system. This division has special relevance when technical conceptions are related to empirical ones, and when mythical conceptions are related to the fantastical. Of course, the ancient Near East attached the weight of certainty to notions we term mythical. These understandings were no less grounded in the experience of men of that time than understandings valued by us for their empirical basis. The sky goddess Nut was to the ancient Egyptian a reality of the same order as the mountains between whose peaks the sun god appeared every morning (9–13).[2] The difference lay only in the fact that the ancient Egyptian possessed less well-defined notions of the distant, impenetrable reality of earth's frontiers than he did of the manifest, everyday world which was shaped, at least in part, by him. There was nothing to prevent him from understanding these mysterious regions on the strength of conscious or unconscious analogies, drawn as much from the biological (birth, death) or psychological (hate, love) sphere as from the technical realm. Thus the morning sunrise was understood in Egypt sometimes as birth, sometimes as entrance through a gate. To the Egyptian, one was as real as the other. The scanty data he possessed (or thought he possessed) concerning the remote, fringe regions of the world left room for numerous intuitive and speculative interpretations. These in turn were often understood—even by their authors, and all the more by the culture at large—not as mere interpretations, but as data in themselves. They in turn occasioned new intuitions and speculations, leading finally to concepts which seem at first glance to lack any basis whatsoever in experience. That apparent lack of empirical basis, however, is noticeable only to us. In many Egyptian pictures, conceptions we would term technical stand undifferentiated beside conceptions we would characterize as mythical (cf., e.g., 26). Classification of such pictures under the headings "technical" or "mythical" is an essentially extrinsic concern. It can be made only on the basis of the predominance of one or another aspect, and is often simply a matter of judgment.

1. TECHNICAL CONCEPTIONS

Technical understanding of the world—the ability to render it intelligible and manageable—is closely connected with the ability to quantify it. In Egypt and Mesopotamia, a thoroughgoing quantification of the environment was under way no later than the beginning of the third millennium B.C. Monumental architecture and the construction of irrigation canals required measurements of all kinds.[3] There are extant almost thirty drawings of the plans of ancient Mesopotamian temples, palaces, city districts, and cities.[4] They range from diagrams of large, private houses (1–2) to outlines of complex palace and temple installations. Substan-

1. and 2. Fragment of a clay tablet from Nippur, outlining the housekeeping chambers of a large house. The function of four of the rooms is given in writing, that of the other three by picture (vertical section of a mill).

3. "Unless the LORD builds the house, those who build it labor in vain" (Ps 127:1).

4. "Walk about Zion, . . . consider well her ramparts, go through her citadels; that you may tell the next generation that *this is God, our God for ever and ever*" (Ps 48:12–14).

tial amounts of technical data are often appended to them. Even more effectively than the ruins of the buildings they represent, the drawings present the men of that time as masters and fashioners of their world.

The portrait statue of Gudea of Lagash as architect (3) demonstrates, however, that it would be incorrect to view this man, for all his apparent technical skill, as the conscious executor of his own autonomous will, secure in his competence and power. The portrait of Gudea, his plan on his knees, was made for the temple of Ningirsu, lord of Lagash. Gudea sits humbly before his god. The statue and its inscription are intended to remind the god of all Gudea had done in order to secure the necessary wood, stones, copper, and gold for the building of the temple (cf. Ps 132:1–5). As a faithful servant, Gudea accomplished it all at the express command of the god Ningirsu.[5] In a dream, Ningirsu had permitted Gudea to see the god Ninduba, lord of the tablets: "He had bent his arms, held a slab of lapis lazuli in his hand, fixed upon it the plan of the house."[6] Ningirsu commissioned the building; Ninduba is the architect. Gudea is only the executive agent. The

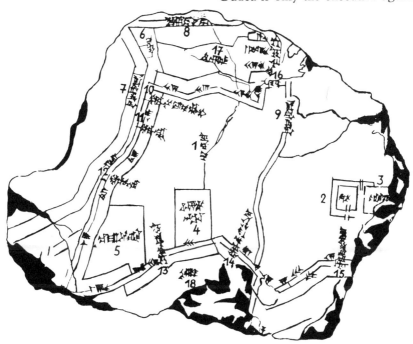

stylus lying next to the plan clearly indicates that it was drafted by him, but it was done at the direction of another (cf. Exod 25:9, 40;1 Chron 28:19). The edifice does not manifest Gudea's glory; rather through it "all foreign lands will come to recognize Ningirsu's victorious power."[7]

It is not only in the building of a temple that the deity is vitally involved. A Sumerian hymn to Nisaba, goddess of grain and of the art of writing, reads: "Nisaba, unless you ordain it, man builds no house, he builds no city, he builds no palace. . . ."[8] (cf. Ps 127:1).

Technical mastery of the world occupies a limited place in the totality of the ancient Near Eastern experience of the cosmos. Figs. 4 and 5 show two plans of the city of Nippur, located 150 kilometers southeast of Baghdad. Fig. 4, inscribed on a clay tablet (approximately 17 × 20 cm.), dates from about 1500 B.C. Fig. 5 reproduces the plan drawn up in this century by the American excavators of the city. The ancient plan is remarkably accurate. Walls, canals (7, 8, 9, 17, 18), gates (10–16), and temple (2, 3) can be easily identified by the reference numbers, which correspond to those of the modern plan. The ancient name for Nippur stands beside the number one (1). The inhabitants of Mesopotamia in 1500 B.C. could thus record with relative accuracy an area approximately 900 by 800 meters. Man's world, the city, was thought out, planned, and built by him, and he was responsible for its maintenance;[9] but it was the god who made it "rise in splendor."[10]

Like Nippur, Jerusalem of the first millennium B.C. was a fully intelligible entity. Ezekiel, in the Babylonian manner, incised its plan on a clay tablet (Ezek 4:1). But its walls, bulwarks, and towers proclaim the glory of Yahweh (Ps 48:12–13`. It is Yahweh who established Jerusalem (Ps 87:1, 5b); he made fast the bars of its gates (Ps 147:13). Should its walls be laid low, it is he who is asked to rebuild them (Ps 51:18; cf. 147:2). It was no different in Egypt. Even a city as

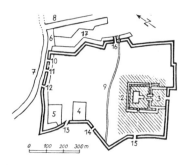

5. Plan of Nippur (4) as it appeared to the archaeologists of the 19th and 20th centuries.

new and traditionless as Pi-Ramses is said to have been founded by the sun god Re.[11]

The ancient Near East had considerable difficulty in forming a technically accurate picture of uneven terrain, particularly if the area was larger than a few square kilometers. That difficulty is evident in an Egyptian papyrus from the 19th Dynasty (6), a document slightly less ancient than the city plan of Nippur. It depicts a mining district in the Wadi Hammamat. Even in antiquity, a road led through the region from Koptos, near the Great Bend of the Nile, to Kosseir on the Red Sea (7). The area shown measures approximately 10 by 15 kilometers.

The numbers in Fig. 6 correspond to brief hieratic notes in the original. From them we learn that the two bands (numbered 1 and 3 in Fig. 6) correspond to two roads (broken lines) in Fig. 7. The connecting road, with a typical bend to the right (east) begins at the spring (Bir Hammamat, number 7). Because the two roads follow deep, dry valleys, their course cannot have changed over the millennia. The rather inexact indication of route may be attributed to the sketchy nature of the plan. But it is evident from the treatment of the mountains which skirt the roads that uneven terrain presented an insurmountable obstacle to ancient cartographers. While the roads are drawn from a bird's-eye view, the mountains are depicted in vertical section, as more or less regular cones. Numbers 4, 5, and 11 indicate the mountains where gold is mined. Number 5 (streaked) corresponds to the *"Montagne de l'or"* in Fig. 7; number 12 corresponds to the mountain of silver and gold (*"Montagne de l'argent et de l'or"*).

The draftsman sometimes uses cross-section, sometimes vertical section to portray a given object. The city plan of Nippur is consistently drawn in cross-section, even though the front elevation of certain buildings would have afforded a more characteristic view. Temples, palaces, and other man-made structures were clearly understood in every re-spect, for man knows and controls what

6. and 7. "Before the *mountains* were brought forth . . . from everlasting to ever-lasting thou art God" (Ps 90:2).

"The *mountains* melt like wax before the LORD, before the LORD of all the earth" (Ps 97:5).

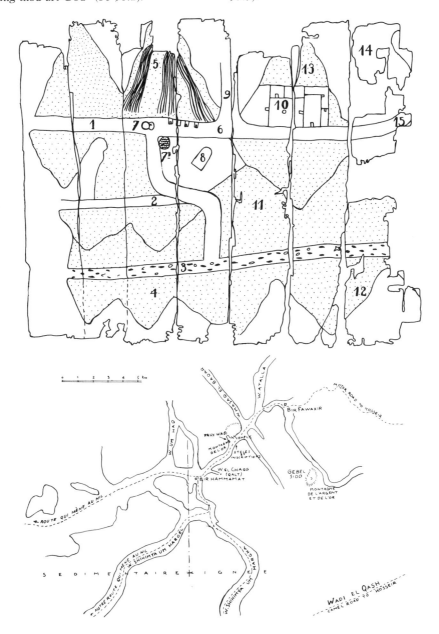

he has created (cf. Pss 33:13–15; 94:9–11; 139:15). But a mountainous terrain like that of the Wadi Hammamat, with its complex, irregular shapes, was not to be mastered in like manner. Both the city plan of Nippur and the sketch of the mining district attempt to present the parts of a specific whole in relation to each other. But in the latter, unlike the former, man no longer dominates a world transparent to him. Instead, the complex phenomena dominate him. He is forced, in order to comprehend them at all, to approach these phenomena from ever-changing points of view. As a result, isolated details dominate his field of vision. The organic coherence is lost.

We do not maintain that ancient Near Eastern man was incapable of portraying larger areas from a unified viewpoint, whether that view be technical-artificial (as in the city plan of Nippur or in modern cartography) or perspective-natural (as in European art governed by perspective). It is almost certainly not a matter of technical incapability, but rather of an intuitive reluctance to render things as seen from a single, random viewpoint. Positively stated, this tendency reflects the deep-seated necessity to show things as they have been experienced by all the senses and internalized through long association (Denkbild). At the great moment when painting in perspective first appeared, Plato protested that it reproduced only the appearance, and not the reality.[12] Two factors separate ancient Near Eastern and modern man: Plato's aversion to the subjective, momentary impression, and a disposition to view things in their peculiarity and independence.

Ancient Near Eastern man saw "houses" in cross-section, as foundation trenches and walls. But because he was incapable of flight, he experienced mountains with his eyes and feet, as peaked or blunted cones. If he wished to avoid doing violence to that basic experience, he was compelled to render mountains in two dimensions, as triangles or similar forms (cf. 6).

Ancient Near Eastern man experi-enced the arbitrariness of things more strongly than manipulating man of the twentieth century, nor was this experience of arbitrariness limited to the visual realm. A mountain, for example, could effectively impede communication. On the other hand, it could provide protection for a settlement, since it presented attackers with an almost insuperable barrier.

The arbitrary character of the mountains made them seem, like many other entities, to be spheres of the divine, even gods in their own right. The tendency of ancient Near Eastern man to view reality in such a way manifests the arbitrarily creative subjectivism inherent in naive objectivism.[13]

The mountain designated number 13 in Fig. 6 is the "pure mountain"; according to the notation at number 14, Amon resides on it. The note at number 10 reads: "the chapel of Amon of the pure mountain." The ruins of the chapel have been found.[14]

There survives from the Theban sepulchral city a hymn of thanksgiving to a goddess (Mertseger) who bears the epithet "Mountaintop." The hymnist advises his associates:

> Beware the Mountaintop,
> for there is a lion in the pinnacle;
> she strikes, like a wild lion strikes,
> and pursues whomever sins against her.[15]

The text provides a sense of the way in which the numinous power of the mountains assumed concrete form for the men of the time.[16]

When the psalms speak of mountains, they emphasize Yahweh's superiority over them (Pss 89:12; 90:2; 97:4–5; 104:32; 121:1–2). The experience of the uniqueness of Yahweh has dethroned the mountains as gods. Still, they retain some degree of their independence, and it is more than a poetic flourish when the mountains "praise Yahweh" or "tremble before him."

Ancient Israel seems to have held a view of the cosmic system quite similar, at least in its technical aspects, to that of the so-called Babylonian Map of the

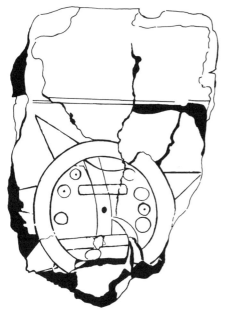

cf. 89:25; 93:3), as do "Prince Sea" *(zbl ym)* and "Judge River" *(tpṭ nhr)* in Ugaritic texts.

A famous passage from the psalms expresses a wish of world domination for the Israelite king:

> May he have dominion from sea to sea, and from the River to the ends of the earth! (Ps 72:8)

Even the more recent commentaries on the psalms[18] continue to interpret "River" in this passage as the Euphrates, with reference to 1 Kgs 4:21 [MT 5:1]. But in adopting this geographical interpretation, they are all hard put to explain what the verse is intended to mean, for it makes little sense either geographically or cosmographically to say ". . . from the Persian Gulf (sea) to the Mediterranean (sea) and from the Euphrates (river) to Gibraltar (ends of the earth)." If, on the other hand, we assume that the psalmist had notions of cosmography similar to those expressed in the Babylonian Map of the World, then we have an instance of strict parallelism which states twice that the king is to rule from one end of the earth to the other (from sea to sea and from the bitter flood to the edge of the round earth). This is completely in accord with a wish or promise to the king of Israel as Yahweh's agent on earth (cf. Pss 2:7; 89:25).

The earth in Fig. 8 is surrounded by ocean. A mountain range is shown to the north (above). In the OT too, *ṣāpôn* denotes the north in the sense of "above." Depending on the context, the word can signify an elevated part of the earth (Ps 48:1–2) or the cloudy sky (e.g., Job 26:7–8).

The Euphrates, indicated by two parallel lines, rises from the mountain range. It empties in the south (below), partly into the marshes, partly into a narrow branch of the bitter flood (Persian Gulf). The absence of the Tigris is evidence of the sketchy nature of the composition as a whole. Babylon, situated slightly above the center of the circle, is shown as a broad rectangle. The small circles to its left and right represent cities or prov-

8. ". . . from sea to sea and from the [bitter] River to the ends of the earth!" (Ps 72:8; Zech 9:10b; cf. Pss 2:7 and 89:26!).

"In his [God's] hand are the [impenetrable] depths of the earth; the heights of the mountains are his also. The sea is his, for he made it; for his hands formed the dry land" (Ps 95:4–5).

World *(8)*. In a sketch only 8 by 8 centimeters in size, the "map" attempts to represent the cosmos as a whole. The earth (in the wider sense) is shown in the drawing itself; the heavens are treated principally in the accompanying text.

The small clay tablet dates from the sixth century B.C. It may derive, however, from much older models, for the cosmic horizon of sixth-century Mesopotamia was substantially larger than what is represented here.[17] In any case, the essential features of the conception prevailed with little change.

Although the tablet is badly damaged, it clearly shows that the earth was envisioned as circular. Fig. 8 suggests that it was understood as a flat disc, but in other renderings *(22, 23)* it appears as a mountain. It is surrounded by a similarly circular band, the bitter flood *(nâr marratu)*, the ocean. In the psalms, "sea" and "river" (or "rivers") often appear in parallelism (Pss 24:2; 66:6; 80:11; and

inces. The circle to the right of Babylon is Assur.

The entities shown on the earth disc correspond to concrete geographical realities. The circular shape of the earth and its surrounding ocean is, however, the result of an intuitive-speculative process. Nonetheless, it may have had some basis in experience, for a number of seas are to be found within a radius of approximately 700 kilometers of Babylon (the Persian Gulf, Red Sea, Mediterranean Sea, Lake Van and Lake Urmia, Caspian Sea, Indian Ocean). But even this meager basis in experience is lacking in the case of the entities shown as seven isosceles triangles (partly destroyed) situated on the far side of the bitter flood.

What is represented by these triangles with their bases resting in the bitter flood? The accompanying text terms them *nagû*, "districts, regions." The marginal note pertaining to the fifth district (upper right) is preserved, though the triangle itself has been destroyed. The note indicates that the height of the district is 60 *ṣubban* (1598.4 meters). The considerable elevation and the shape suggest a mountain.[19] That combination of cross-section and vertical section, already encountered in Fig. 6, may also be present here: the earth disc is shown from a bird's-eye view, in cross-section; the mountains are shown in vertical section. Because the bases of these mountains rest in the sea, one must think of them as islands. *nagû* can in fact mean "island."[20]

The OT also locates the islands alongside the earth disc (Ps 97:1; cf. 72:10). These islands constitute the "ends of the earth" (Isa 41:5), the extreme of the circular horizon (Job 26:10) formed by the huge mountains which support the vault of heaven. When in the battle with Chaos, God churns up the sea to its very depths, the foundations of the mountains and of the earth are laid bare (Ps 18:7, 15). The parallel to Ps 18:7 in 2 Sam 22:8 reads "foundations of the heavens" instead of "foundations of the mountains." The two are identical.

The boundary between light and darkness is at the extreme horizon of the mountains which form the foundations of the heavens (Job 26:10). There are to be found the gates of the morning brightness and the evening gloom (Ps 65:8). According to the Babylonian Map of the World, the seventh district (lower right, destroyed) is "where the morning shines from its habitation." Ps 19 speaks of the portal through which the sun, portrayed as a young hero, enters the earthly regions. This scene figures frequently on the cylinder seals of the Akkadian Period (2350–2150 B.C.) (9). The model for our map of the world may also date from that period.

The sun god rises from the mountains with a powerful leap (9). The mountains from which he emerges are mythically represented by two gates, opened wide and adorned with lions (cf. the connection between mountaintop and lion in the previously cited prayer from the Theban sepulchral city (p. 20); cf. also the lions of the horizon in Figs. *16–18* and *39*). On the cylinder seal, the empirical reality (the mountains between which the sun rises) and its intuitive-speculative interpretation (the two gates) stand unrelated side by side. Similarly, the Egyptian Book of the Dead shows the gate of the world located above two mountains called *ḫ.t,* signifying that radiant place where the sun rises and sets *(10–13)*.

According to a number of psalms, the islands which constitute the ends of the earth are inhabited by ordinary men (cf. Ps 72:10). But that does not prevent cosmographical speculation from identifying the islands with the beginning of the heavens. In Ps 65:8, the inhabitants of the ends of the earth stand in parallelism with the gates of the sun. But according to Ps 19:4c–6, the gate of the sun is located at the end of the heavens. We learn from the text of the Babylonian Map of the World that only two mythical kings, Nurdagan and Gilgamesh, ever passed across the floods of death to the region of the island-mountains and the heavenly fields beyond them. The Gilgamesh epic relates how its hero, before reaching the island-mountains, had to travel from Uruk across the steppe, then over a great mountain range infested with lions, then over the bitter flood. Finally he arrived at the mountain range which keeps watch over the daily rising and setting of the sun. The vault of heaven ranges above the mountain; the breasts of the mountain reach to the nether world below.[21]

Geographical awareness of islands gave rise to the concept of the cosmic island-mountains, but closer horizons (for Mesopotamia, and Zagros Mountains in the east, the Taurus in the north, and the Mediterranean Sea in the west) may have been a more important factor in reifying the concept than the little-known islands themselves.

This experiential horizon may have been operative in Ps 139:8–10, which celebrates the omnipresence of God:

If I ascend to *heaven,* thou art there!
If I make my bed in *Sheol,* thou art there!
If I take the wings of the *morning*
  [dawn]
and dwell in the uttermost parts of the
  sea,
even there thy hand shall lead me,
and thy right hand shall hold me.

As in Amos 9:2–3, which cites in the same order *heaven* and *Sheol,* the *top of Carmel* and the *bottom of the sea,* we have here two cosmographical concepts (heaven and the world of the dead) followed by two predominantly geographical concepts (the locus of the dawn and the remotest part of the sea). These conceptual pairs in Ps 139:8–10 and Amos 9:2–3 may be taken as designations of "above" (heaven, dawn, top of Carmel) and "below" (bottom of the sea, uttermost part of the sea, Sheol) (cf. Ps 68:22). The same is true in Ps 107:3, where we find the conceptual pairs, rising-*ṣāpôn* and setting-sea [RSV: east and west; north and south]. Without any text-critical justification, the more recent commentators[22] emend *yām* (sea) to *yāmîn* (south). But if *ṣāpôn* is understood as "mountaintop" (cf. p. 20) and *yām* as a paraphrase of "below" (cf. Ps 107:23 MT: *ywrdy yām* [RSV 107:23: "some went down to the sea"]), then we have in Ps 107:3 a statement parallel to Amos 9:2–3 and Ps 139:8–10. In the light of Job 11:7–9, we can see described in Pss 107:3 and 139:8–10 lines both vertical (heaven, *ṣāpôn*—Sheol, *yām*) and horizontal (rising, dawn—setting, remotest sea). The horizontal line would incline slightly downwards from east to west.

9. ". . . he has set a tent for the sun, which comes forth like a bridegroom leaving his chamber, and like a strong man runs its course with joy. Its rising is from the end of the heavens, and its circuit to the end of them" (Ps 19:4c–6b).

". . . thou makest the outgoings [gates] of the morning and the evening to shout for joy" (Ps 65:8).

10.–13. Fig. *10* shows the closed gate of the sun over the mountains of the horizon. These also appear in Fig. *11.* A servant is about to open the gate, which is delimited above by the sign for "sky" *(p.t).* In Fig. *12,* the sun is seen entering through the opened gate. In Fig. *13,* the sun is replaced by the ideogram for "god" (a venerable sitting figure). As a strictly visual image, the deity sitting in the gate makes little sense.

14. Two representations of a threshing floor (cf. *129*).

An analogy is found in the Egyptian notion of the declivitous course of the sun from east to west (cf. *19, 33, 36, 348*), indicated in drawings by a slight inclination from east to west.[23] The loftier east, with its mountaintop, the dawn, the rising sun, and the heavens, is the realm of life; the low-lying west, with the setting sun, the sea, and the nether world, is the domain of death. Thus we can understand why Yahweh bows the heavens when he comes to earth (Ps 18:9).

Fig. *8,* however, does not evidence this polar view, but rather a concentric one. The circle of the island-mountains leads in every direction to the heavenly regions; the bitter river which surrounds the earth leads to the regions of the nether world. At the point of death, a man finds himself at the edge of the earth (Ps 61:2). Its antipole is the earth's center, against which the waters of Chaos rage in vain (Pss 61:2; 95:1). In some representations, this place of security is occupied by a mountain equivalent to the island-mountains (cf. *22–23*). On the Babylonian Map of the World, it is occupied by Babylon, or perhaps more precisely, by the ziggurat of Esagila. In the psalms, it is Jerusalem, the holy mountain, Zion; in the Egyptian picture from Dendera, it is the local sanctuary *(36).*

Fig. *15* depicts the earth as a great

15. "There is nothing hid from its [the sun's] heat" (Ps 19:6c). The scarab (*ḫpr* = "becoming") signifies the morning sun; the ram-headed man signifies the day or evening sun.

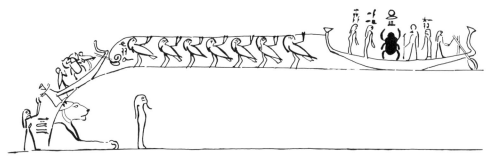

16. The edge of the earth is often delineated by lions (8, 17–18, 39). It is a dangerous region. In Egypt, however, the lion, like the night (90), was understood not only as a destructive power ("yesterday"), but also as a power of rebirth ("tomorrow") (C. de Wit, *Le rôle*, pp. 91–188). For that reason, the frames on which mummies were laid (cf. 74) were often made in the form of a lion.

trough. The picture could be a cross-section of an extended valley fringed, like Egypt, by valleys on both sides;[24] but the two renderings of threshing floors in Fig. 14 make it clear that the picture could also depict a round basin. This view will find reinforcement below (p. 37).

In Fig. 15, the sun disc rather than the temple/mountain occupies the center. The disc encloses the scarab and the ram-headed man, which portray two aspects of the sun. Its glory fills the whole earth, as does the glory of the name of Yahweh in the psalms (Ps 72:19). As in Fig. 11, the sky is flat. It rests at either end on the mountaintops (2 Sam 22:8).

In Fig. 16, the mountaintops are replaced by the forequarters of a lion. The frontier mountains which support the sky also appear as lions in Figs. 17 and 18.[25] In Fig. 17, the lion on the right is designated *sf*, "yesterday"; the lion on the left is *m dw*³, "tomorrow." "Yesterday" is thus the east, "tomorrow" the west, an unusual but understandable concept: the sun cannot in fact travel from "tomorrow" to "yesterday."[26]

As we have already seen, the concepts of mountain, horizon, and lion are readily connected one with another.[27] The lion is well suited to embody the fearsome nature of the mountains. The ends of the earth are full of deadly perils (16; cf. Ps 61:2).

In Fig. 16, treatment of both the frontier mountains and of the sky is different from that in Fig. 15. The latter shows the sky as a flat roof or an inverted box; Fig. 16 shows it as a basket-shaped arch. The length of the picture makes the middle part of the sky appear as a straight line.[28] Above this straight line, seven soul-birds convey the bark of the sun. In it is the scarab (= *ḫpr*, "becoming"), the waxing sun, together with five other deities. At the outer left, the evening sun god (scarab with ram's head) is received by the "land, which rises." The ship of the sun is thus shown twice, suggesting the progression of the sun's journey across the sky and its descent in the west.

Though the ship of the sun, as ship, represents a technical-mechanical entity, almost no one would consider the concept of the sun ship any less mythical than the concept of the sun god. If we question further why the concept of the vault of heaven should be considered less mythical than that of the ship of the sun, the answer will be equally difficult to discover. Of the two ideas, that of the vault of heaven seems to us to be better grounded in experience (the rising and setting of the sun). It is consequently a much more widespread notion than that of the ship of the sun, although even the latter is not limited to Egypt.[29] Such considerations, however, are not important to the perception of the ancient Egyp-

17. and 18. In identical contexts the sky is shown once straight, once curved. The physical configuration of distant regions such as the sky or the nether world was not well defined to the mind of the Egyptians.

tian. The ship of the sun seems to have held for him a much greater essential significance than the vault of heaven. In like contexts he can therefore quite arbitrarily portray the sky as either flat (17) or arched (18). But he clings tenaciously to the ship of the sun, even in contexts where it seems to us completely out of place, as when the sky is depicted as a pair of wings (19) or as a woman (32).

The ship of the sun was essential to the vital journey of the sun god (and to the journey of the deceased who hoped to accompany him). For that reason, it was a reality more significant than the flatness or curvature of the sky. Such indifference to fact considerably complicates the question of the technical picture of the world.

2. SYMBOLIC-MYTHICAL CONCEPTIONS

a. The Bipartite World

Leaving aside the uncertainty which prevailed in the ancient world, the notion of a vaulted sky does not necessarily derive from more adequate conceptions of cosmic structure than the idea of a flat sky. It may be traced to the idea of a heavenly bird whose giant wings spread protectively over the earth (19), or to the concept of the uplifted body of the lady of heaven (25–27, 28–30, 32–33). Both are ideas of a decidedly archaic nature.

Fig. 19 is interesting for a number of reasons. Two huge *was*-scepters appear as pillars of the heavens, replacing the border mountains or lions of the horizon. *was*-scepters are found in the hands of gods in many pictures (cf. 287, 366, 371). Occasionally the heavens were thought to be supported by great forked brackets (cf. 28). What is portrayed here, however, is not the technical arrangement, but the certainty that the gods have made the heavens unshakeably fast (cf. Pss 89:2, 29; 119:89). The space between the two pillars and the sky is filled, not by the sun god (as in Fig. 15), but by the facade of the royal palace, with the king's name ("Serpent") inscribed on it. The king stands in the place of the sun god: in the composition of the picture, the sun god is represented by the king. This representation is reinforced by the presence of the heavenly and royal falcons, one of which appears on the palace, the other in the bark of the sun. In the psalms too, the king represents Yahweh on earth, and is responsible for the maintenance of Yahweh's ordinances (Pss 2; 72; 101). Yahweh himself, however, can also be simulta-

26

neously present in heaven and in his palace (temple) (Ps 11:4).

In Fig. *20,* the sky appears as a slab, and the earth is shown as a thin band terminating at either end in a man's head. Here too, the expanse between earth and sky is dominated by the palace facade. Around it are grouped the names which constitute the titles of King Sahure. The psalms repeatedly assert that the whole earth is full of the glory of the divine name (Pss 8:1, 9; 48:10; 72:19; cf. 57:11). God's action and order dominate the space between heaven and earth. This concept has close parallels in Egyptian iconography.

As evidenced in Fig. *21,* the king himself can appear in place of his name or

19. "My grace is established for ever, my faithfulness stands fast as the heavens" (Ps 89:3 MT; translation after Kraus [cf. Ps 89:2 RSV]).

"Your word, Yahweh, is for ever, as firmly fixed as the heavens" (Ps 119:89 [author's translation]).

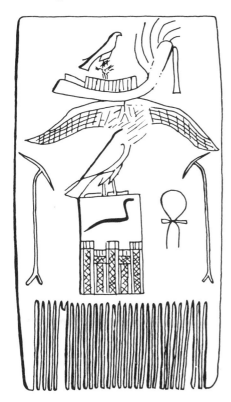

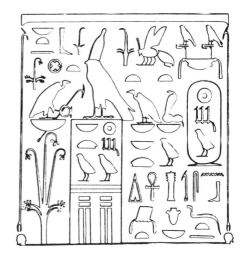

20. "As thy *name,* O God, so thy praise reaches to the ends of the earth" (Ps 48:10).

"Blessed be his glorious *name* for ever; may his glory fill the whole earth!" (Ps 72:19).

palace. It is he, rather than the slender pillars, who supports the sky. As ritual, support of the temple ceiling represents support of the heavens. The temple represents a little cosmos maintained by the king, in order that the gods may maintain the actual cosmos. In Fig. *26,* the air god fulfills that function. Lam 4:20 refers to the king as "breath of life" [RSV: "breath of our nostrils"]; in Fig. *19* the sign for "life" stands beside the royal palace. It is possible that the psalmist's reference to the destruction of the pillars [RSV: "foundations"] by the wicked (Ps 11:2–3) is an expression of concern for the pillars of the heavens and for the king who guarantees that order without which life cannot exist.

In Fig. *21,* the sky, supported by the king, is shown twice, once as a flat roof, once as the sun with a pair of wings. Two cobras (uraei), embodiments of the sun's bright rays and scorching breath, are attached to the sun (cf. Pss 19:6c; 121:6). The most probable interpretation of Fig. *19* identifies the curved wings with the sky. This identification suggests in turn that the wings in Fig. *21* also represent the sky. But the sun fixed between the two wings (in Fig. *19,* the falcon sitting in the sun-boat) soon became the central

27

feature, and the wings of the sky came to be understood as a winged sun. In that form the image spread from Egypt throughout the whole of Asia Minor (cf. Mal 4:2 [MT 3:20]).

As a rule, wings appear in Egyptian iconography as means of shelter rather than as instruments of flight (cf. 260–62). In the psalms, too, they are linked with "refuge" and similar concepts (Pss 61:4; 36:7; 57:1; 91:4). Ps 61:2–4 may be understood in a cosmic frame of reference: the ends of the earth represent the realm of death; the rock to which the suppliant desires to be led is the earth- and temple-mountain. There he finds shelter under the wings of God, signifying the (near) sky. The temple ceiling or the winged sun over the temple gate frequently represents the sheltering sky (cf. 221–22).[30]

Fig. 22 shows a Hittite version of Figs. 19–21. Though its derivation from Egypt is unmistakable, much has been

22. In this picture, the Hittite king is shown in close relation to the cosmic mountain. This is faintly reminiscent of Ps 2: "I have set my king on Zion, my holy hill" (Ps 2:6).

21. "If the pillars are torn down, what [then] can the righteous do?" (Ps 11:3 [author's translation]).

changed. The was-scepters have been replaced by the hieroglyphs for "great one" (volute) and "king" (triangles). The winged sun may represent the Hittite royal title, "my sun." The crescent moon and the eight-beamed star of Venus appear beneath the sun. Their absence in other, similar pictures makes their presence here problematic. Perhaps in this instance, the sky with its stars is intended to represent simply the royal title, "my sun." At any rate, the "dagger above the blossom" almost certainly represents the name of Labarnas, the founder of the dynasty. "Labarnas" has become an honorific title. The boot and the mountain god which occupy the center of the picture are to be read as the royal name, "Tudhaliyas." It is interesting to note that the second part of the name (the boot stands for tu) is signified here by the mountain god rather than by the conventional hieroglyph "mountain." This may evidence a certain tendency, already seen in the portrayal of the sky, to forsake purely hieroglyphic composition in favor of a more concrete image. The idea of a mountain (replaced in some pictures by a pillar or a tree: cf. 23–24) which rises in the center of the earth to support the heavens is a concept

23. "From thy lofty abode thou waterest the mountains, the earth is satisfied with the fruit of thy work" (Ps 104:13).

"Thou openest thy hand, thou satisfiest the desire of every living thing" (Ps 145:16).

of Indo-European origin. The mountain is also common in Semitic circles, but not as bearer of the heavens. It functions instead as a connecting link between heaven and earth (cf. chap. 3.1).

This cosmic mountain is the locus of life *(23)*. On its summit rises the tree of life. The pole which supports the heavens on Mitannian seals is replaced in Assyrian examples by the tree of life. The tree rises from a water vessel rather than from the earth-mountain itself. This detail emphasizes the close connection between water and (plant) life—a factor often stressed in the psalms (Pss 1:3; 65:9–13; 104:10–12; 147:8). Two vessels similar to that on the mountaintop stand at the right and left (destroyed) of the mountain. They are reminiscent of the fountain deities which flank the mountain god in Fig. *153* (cf. also *42*). The "springs" are fed in a remarkable manner by the hands of the winged disc, which thus appears as source of all life ("Thou openest thine hand . . . " Pss 104:28; 145:16). Here the winged disc is primarily a symbol of the heavens, less so of the sun. The conjuring priests at right and left secure the process by their gestures and words, detracting somewhat from the sovereignty of the sky

god. The fish costume links the figure at the left to Ea, mysterious god of the depths (cf. *43, 285*). The plaited pattern and the triangles which border the picture are not directly related to the bitter flood and the island-mountains (cf. *8*) as has sometimes been thought. They are instead an imitation in stone of a precious metal frame.[31]

Even more clearly than Fig. *23*, Fig. *24* shows that the sun disc is primarily representative of the sky god. The three male heads can only be those of the lord of the heavens, the sun god, and the moon god (2 Kings 23:5).[32] The two scorpion-men, who appear in the Gilgamesh epic as guardians of the horizon,[33] pertain to the heavens. The space between the sky and the scorpion-men is filled by a highly stylized tree of life. Two worshippers flank the scene.

For all its new features, Fig. *24* cannot conceal its Egyptian influence. In *Plate I B,* however, no such influence is discernible, either in the treatment of the cosmic mountains or of the sky, which is fashioned as a protective bird.

Figs. *19–24* show the world as a composite of earth and sky, with the sky protectively spreading its wings over the earth and (especially in Fig. *23*) ensuring its prosperity. The harmonious relation between heaven and earth is represented and guaranteed by the king (Egypt, Hit-

24. "Our God is in the heavens; he does whatever he pleases" (Ps 115:3).

The region beneath the heavens is symbolized by the tree of life. This is the "land of the living" (Ps 142:5; cf. 116:9).

tite Empire) or by the tree of life and the cultus (Mesopotamia). In them the world is set forth in its salutary order, and through them this order is ensured. The differing conceptions of the forces of order and life (in one case the king, in the other the tree of life and the cultus) are the more remarkable because the underlying framework (heaven and earth) penetrated into Assyria from Egypt via the Mitannian Empire.

If we compare the evidence of the psalms with the world-pictures of Figs. 19–24, it is evident that the psalms also understand the world as a composite of two (or more) parts. It is not a unified entity like the Greek "cosmos" or our "universe."

It is further noteworthy that in Figs. 19–24, as in analogous formulae in the psalms, the world as an ordered and prosperous whole is composed of heaven and earth. It has been maintained that the formula "heaven and earth" fails to illuminate the question of world view because, in accordance with a typical mode of thought, it divides a single totality (the universe) into two corresponding parts. The tripartite expression, "the heaven above, the earth beneath, and the water under the earth" (Exod 20:4) is held to demonstrate, to the contrary, that the world was understood as consisting of three parts.[34] As a form of thought and speech, however, merism can consist not only of two parts, but of three or more.[35] The tripartite figure "heaven, earth, and sea," or forms of four parts, such as "heaven, earth, seas, and primeval floods" [RSV: ". . . all deeps"] (Ps 135:6), are just as much formulae as the expression "heaven and earth." Moreover, it is no accident that the element omitted in the shorter form is precisely the sea (respectively, the world of the dead). With respect to the whole, it is a far less necessary, independent, and positive element than the other two. When the world of the dead does constitute the third element, it can be placed, as we shall see, in the earth or (like the Duat in early Egypt) in the sky. But where the third element is the ocean

(Tehom, primeval flood), it is more often perceived as a threat to the fixed and ordered world of heaven and earth than as an integral part of the same (42–52). Sometimes seas and floods, like the world of the dead, are simply reckoned with the "earth" (Ps 148:1, 7).

The bipartite formula illuminates very well the conception and perception of the world in the ancient Near East and in the OT. It is at least as significant as the longer tripartite formula. From a purely quantitative point of view, the bipartite formula occurs with considerable frequency in the psalms (cf. Pss 50:4; 57:11; 73:25; 78:69; 79:2; 89:11; 97:4–6; 102:25; 113:6; 148:13). More important, God as creator appears as the one "who made heaven and earth" (Pss 115:15; 121:2; 124:8; 134:3). In so doing, he reserved the heavens for himself (Ps 115:16–17). He has entrusted the earth to men; but he remains entirely aloof from "silence" (Ps 115:17), the world of the dead. The world of the dead accordingly possesses a degree of reality essentially inferior to that of other regions.

A quite similar sense prevails in Mesopotamia and Egypt. In the Akkadian sphere, the world is almost always described by the merism šamu u irṣitim, which corresponds to the fact that a dyad of Anu and Enlil or Anu and Ea frequently appears in place of the triad, Anu, Enlil, and Ea. Strictly speaking, both Enlil and Ea are lords of the earth (cf. the Sumerian name of Ea, "Enki," meaning the "lord of the earth"). Enlil is more closely associated with the air and the mountains, Ea with the flat, marshy land to the south. The world of the dead does not emerge as a distinct region.

In Egypt, the bipartite formula (p.t, t ꜣ) seems to be considerably older than the tripartite. It appears quite frequently, as early as the Pyramid Texts. In them, the earth is the region of men and of the (common) dead. The heavens are the region of the gods and of the dead kings.[36] The Duat (world of the dead) is thus localized at one place or another. Not until the Middle Kingdom does it emerge as a

25. This picture dramatically illustrates the manner in which earth and sky formerly constituted the universe (the "all"). The world in which the ancient Egyptian lived and moved came into being by the separation of the two (cf. Gen 1:7: "God . . . separated the waters").

definite, independent region. By the time of the New Kingdom, its existence as such is understood as a matter of course.

The dominant position of the heavens and the earth is mythologically expressed in Egypt. According to one of the principal Egyptian myths, the great royal gods Osiris, Isis, and Horus sprang from the union of the earth god Geb with the sky goddess Nut. Among most peoples, the earth is regarded as mother, and is thus considered feminine, while the rain-giving sky is accorded a fecundating, masculine nature. The Egyptians are an exception to this rule. The term *p.t,* "sky," is feminine. The sky was experienced as a motherly, sheltering, protective expanse. The masculinity of the earth may be related to the fact that Egypt was made fertile by the Nile, not by the sky.

Egypt shares with other cultures its view of the world as a composite of the polar sexual forces. In the primeval age, Nut and Geb were united *(25)* until separated by the air god Shu (their son?).[37] Ever since, the sky has been arched above mankind at an incomprehensible height.

In Egyptian iconography, the "wonder of the heavens" finds no clearer expression than in the various forms and attributes of the bearer of the heavens. In a relief (more than 10 meters long) from the cenotaph of Seti I *(26),* the bearer of the heavens appears without name or attributes. In the tomb of the same king,

however, he is identified, again without attributes, as Shu.[38] We may accordingly assume that the cenotaph also portrays the god of the air and lord of the space between heaven and earth. In Fig. *27* he wears a cord looped about his head;[39] above it is a sign meaning "year" *(rnpt).* This sign usually appears on the head or in the hand of Heh, as an attribute of the god of endless time *(27a;* cf. *336, 352).* In the hieroglyphic system, Heh signifies the numeral "million." Figure *32* shows that the boundless expanse of the heavens was also identified with endless time: the attitude assumed by Shu in Fig. *32* approximates that of Heh. It is an understandable association.

In the psalms, the sky is also perceived to be spatially and temporally endless: "as the days of the heavens" (Ps 89:29) is parallel to "for ever" (Ps 89:28). The statement that Yahweh's steadfast love and faithfulness extend to the heavens means that the psalmist considers them to be infinite (Ps 36:5; cf. 57:10–11; 89:2; 103:11).

The infinite expanse of the sky and the sure stability with which it abides in its lofty height made a profound impression on the ancient Near East. That impression is further reflected in the concept of the eternal permanency of the heavens. The four miniature supports of heaven in Fig. *28* indicate how thoroughly the artist was engaged by the question of the power which supports the sky. He was evidently not quite satisfied with the traditional concept of four supports which hold the heavens like a tent roof (cf. Ps 104:2). Nor was he content with the action of Shu, for he furnished the god with a novel attribute, thus giving him a new dimension: the hindquarters of a lion appear on the head of the traditional sky-bearer. In Egyptian orthography, a standard with the hindquarters of a lion signifies *ḥk₃,* "magic power."

In Fig. *32,* the god Heka sits with Maat and the sun god in the heavenly bark. It has now been shown, however, that the hindquarters of a lion, even without the standard, can signify "magic

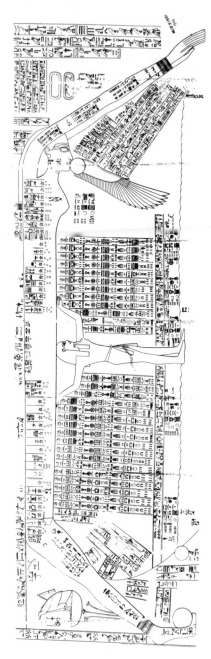

similar legend marks her mouth as the western horizon. The rising sun is seen as a scarab (Egyptian *ḫpr* = "becoming") on the upper thigh of the goddess, while the winged sun, grown old, enters her mouth in order to be born anew in the morning. The ten short vertical lines to the right of the globe of the sun read as follows: "The majesty of this god [the sun god] enters the world of the dead through her mouth. The world of the dead is open when he enters into it. The stars follow him into her and come out again after him, and they hasten to their place" (cf. Qoh 1:5). The deceased, like the stars, is not destined to remain locked in the world of the dead. He will participate in the regenerative power of the sky, which is manifested in the ever new illumination of the stars. It is for this reason that the picture of Nut is placed on the cover of the sarcophagus. The bearer of the heavens thus has the function of raising the dead to eternal rebirth.

The names and positions of a number of constellations are written on the body of Nut. The tables under her body state the days and months on which the respective constellations may be observed rising at morning, midnight, or in the evening.

These tables were intended to provide the deceased with precise knowledge of the heavenly phenomena, and to enable his effective entry into and participation in the eternal circuits. As demonstrated by the illustration, our modern separation of mythical conceptions and scientific observations was entirely foreign to the ancient Near East. Such separation and selection were of no consequence to the Egyptian.

Like many similar pictures, this one shows traces of two distinct conceptions of the world of the dead. In one view, it is located in the heavens, in the body of Nut. In the other, it is set in the earth. In the latter conception, the sun traverses the subterranean waters by night (cf. 55). The orb of the sun comes to light again at the feet of the goddess.

26. Unlike Fig. *25*, this illustration does not treat heaven and earth as primal generative forces. The earth is indicated only by an undulating line. A god supports Nut. At the right of his feet appears the word "sand." The bearer of the heavens is not identified by attributes of any kind. Interest is concentrated entirely on the sky goddess. A little epigraph labels her pudenda as the eastern horizon; a

27. "For as the heavens are high above the earth, so great is his steadfast love toward those who fear him" (Ps 103:11; cf. 57:10 = 108:4).

27a. The god Heh, the power of infinite quantity.

power."[40] Thus the artist regards neither the four supports (which suggest the question rather than providing its answer) nor the conventional air god as upholder of the heavens. Rather it is Shu, as magic power, who fulfills that function.[41] In the psalms, the heavens are similarly perceived as a mysterious, incomprehensibly marvelous phenomenon. There, however, the heavens proclaim no anonymous magic power, but the wonders of Yahweh (Ps 89:5; cf. 8:1; 19:1; 97:6).

For the Egyptians, magic power is closely linked to writings and papyrus scrolls. Thus it is not surprising that in Figs. 27 and 29 a looped cord worn upon the head appears as an attribute of the bearer of the heavens. The looped cord underlies the hieroglyphic symbols for "papyrus" and "papyrus scroll." The divine scribe and lord of all magical texts is Thoth. He appears in Figs. 329 and 478a

in the form of a baboon. That representation may be the underlying reason why the bearer of the heavens in Fig. 29 appears with a baboon's head: there, as on other occasions, Shu is equated with Thoth.[42] In Fig. 29, however, the mountains of the horizon, and not the magical writings, as is occasionally the case, provide the immediate support of the sky. This satisfies the notion that the vault of the heavens rests on earth's frontier mountains (e.g., 15). The latter, however, are held in place by Thoth's magical texts.

In the psalms, the heavens are kept in their lofty height, not by magical words and writings, but by the wisdom and command of Yahweh—by his entirely personal power. Not only does he hold them fast; he created them. As the work of his hands (Ps 102:25), indeed, of his fingers (Ps 8:3), the heavens bear witness to Yahweh's unfathomable skill and

29. "By the *word* of the LORD the heavens were made" (Ps 33:6a).

"Yahweh secures the heavens by his *wisdom*" (Prov 3:19 [author's translation]).

28. "Yahweh, the heaven praises your wondrous power!" (Ps 89:6a MT [author's translation]; cf. Ps 89:5a RSV).

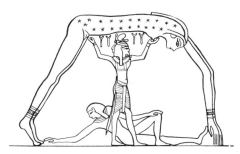

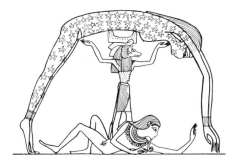

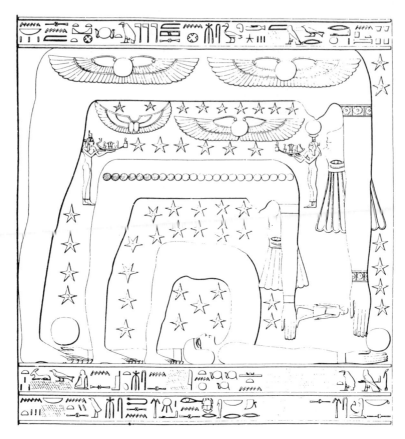

30. "Yahweh, our Lord, how wonderful is your fame in all the earth, because you have spread your majesty over the heavens" (Ps 8:2 MT [author's translation]; cf. Ps 8:1 RSV).

"The heavens are telling the glory of God" (Ps 19:1a).

The Nubian feather ornament worn here by Nut was taken over from Anuket, mistress of the cataract region near Aswan, the place of origin of this illustration (Philae).

boundless wisdom (Pss 96:5; 97:6; Prov 3:19).

The fixity of the heavens creates a considerable impression. The stars contribute further to its impressive aspect (Ps 8:1–3). In Figs. 28, 29, and 32, the body of Nut is studded with stars; and in Fig. 30, Nut appears to have been drawn twice so that special heavens can be reserved, one for the sun and one for the moon. The psalms are also aware of a plural number of heavens (e.g., Ps 148:4). The lower of the two ladies of heaven represents the heaven of the moon; the upper, as indicated by the two winged suns on her body, is the heaven

of the sun. The rising sun, in the (rudimentary) form of the scarab (cf. 16), issues in the morning from the womb of the heaven of the sun. To it belongs the ship of the sun, held by the goddess Isis (left). The noonday sun is shown twice, once as a winged disc, once as a disc on the head of Nephthys (right). The setting sun, in the figure of a man, walks across the hand of the lady of heaven, into the nether world. The recumbent, strangely bent figure is the earth god, Geb. He receives the evening sun with his right hand and thrusts it with his left to the sky. His arms form the earth's surface. Five stars are to be found within the curve of his body (cf. the innermost circle in Fig. 33). His curved body, like that of Osiris in Fig. 37 may enclose the nether world with the night sky.

In Fig. 30, Geb (the earth) fulfills the functions divided in Fig. 32 between Osiris, god of the nether world (receiving the evening sun), and Geb (representing the surface of the earth). In Fig. 30, Geb not only represents the surface of the earth, but also encompasses the Duat. Osiris, too, is not merely the "first among the dead" (and consequently a god of the nether world), but as successor of Geb and possessor of mysterious powers, he also bestows fertility on the earth (37).

The close association of the earth and the world of the dead is not surprising. The dead are buried within the earth. Thus in a very simple sense, the world of the dead is located in the earth. The Hebrew 'rṣ, "earth," like the Egyptian t } [43] or the Akkadian erṣetu, can therefore designate not only the upper surface, but also the interior of the earth as well (cf. Pss 7:5; 44:25; 63:9; 71:20; 95:4; 106:17; 141:7; 143:3; 147:6; 148:7).[44]

31. The kneeling sky goddess Nut gives birth (cf. 337) to the sun, which is identified here as the morning sun by the hieroglyph "child."

This observation, coupled with illustrations such as Figs. 30, 32, 33, and 37, indicates that the world of the dead does not possess the independence characteristic of the heavens or the earth.

Not only in Egypt, but also in Asia Minor and in the West Semitic sphere, heaven and earth are worshipped as gods and invoked as witnesses, especially upon the conclusion of covenants (Ps 50:4).[45] The earth can tremble; the heavens can declare the divine order and power (Pss 50:6; 97:4–6). Such expressions are the final echo of the concept of heaven and earth as the primeval pair.

b. The Multipartite World

As indicated above, the world can be described not only as the sum of two parts, but of three or more as well. The triad of heaven, earth, and sea appears quite frequently (Pss 8:7–8; 33:6–8; 36:5–6; 69:34; 96:11; 104:1b–2b; 135:6; 146:6). In the triad, the world of the dead may replace the sea via the concept of the primeval flood (thm) inherent in the ocean (Ps 115:15–17). This threefold division is also common in Egypt, at least from the time of the New Kingdom (p.t, t }, dw }t). In the OT, the third place is normally taken by the sea (ym), and not by the primeval ocean (thm) or the world of the dead (š'wl). The reverse is generally true in Egypt, where the Duat, the world of the dead, appears in place of the Nun (nw? nnw?: "primeval ocean"), or even in place of the sea. In Akkadian myth, however, the third place is taken by the primeval ocean (apsû), represented by the god Ea (Enki). Enlil (Ellil) controls the earthly region, and Anu (An) is the sky god. Compared to the apsû, the sea (tāmtu) and the world of the dead (arallū) play a rather limited role in this context.

Fig. 32 shows the characteristically Egyptian triad: Nut, Geb, and the Duat. Osiris, who receives the ship of the evening sun, embodies the Duat. A mat (in other representations a costly carpet) is affixed to the bow of the boat. In the marginal note, Osiris is given a mysteri-

35

ously vague title: "the great god who is in the Duat, the great god, lord of the Duat." The surface of the earth is represented by the recumbent figure of the earth god Geb. His body is covered with panicles of reed and rush (cf. Ps 104:14 and Gen 1:11–12). In a similar representation he bears the note: "Geb, prince of the gods, prince of the lords of the Duat."[46] The title demonstrates once more the close association of "earth" and "world of the dead."

In Fig. 32, both the sky and the earth appear in double form. Side by side with the concept of the sky as a woman stands another, unrelated concept: the sky as a sea traversed by the sun god. The idea of a heavenly ocean (cf. 16) probably had its origin in the observation that sky and water have the same color (in Egyptian iconography it is usually blue-green), and that water falls from above.

The concept of the heavenly ocean is also found in the OT and in Mesopotamia. In the OT it is called *mabbûl* (Ps 29:10; cf. 104:13; 148:4). There is, however, no notion of an invisible ship in which the sun traverses the *mabbûl* in majestic calm. Shipping traffic did

not play the role in Palestine that it did in Egypt.

In Egypt, where travel by boat was the easiest and most comfortable means of transportation, it was natural, once the sky was perceived as ocean, to envision the sun crossing it in an invisible ship. The same reasons may underlie the presence of the idea, independent of Egyptian influence, in Mesopotamia (cf. *Plate I A*).

In the ship, Maat, a feather on her head, sits before the falcon-headed sun god, who appears with the sun disc. Maat embodies world order, which is maintained by the ordering (light) and vivifying (warmth) action of the sun. Maat or her feather appears wherever order and justice are at stake: for example, on the scales in Fig. 83.

The sun god is considered to be the author of world order. Expressed in ancient Near Eastern terms, world order (Maat) is the daughter of the sun god. Just as world order sits before Re in the sun-bark, so in Ps 85:13, righteousness (in the sense of world order)[47] goes before Yahweh. Ps 19 suggests an association between the sun and world order

32. "The *heavens* are the LORD's heavens, but the earth he has given to the sons of men. The *dead* do not praise the LORD, nor do any

that go down into silence. But we will bless the LORD from this time forth and for evermore" (Ps 115:16–18).

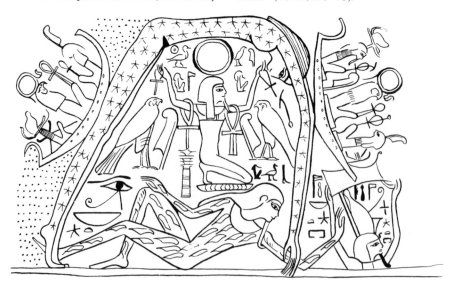

(law) when it celebrates the sun (vv. 4c–6), then moves abruptly to praise the law of Yahweh (vv. 7–10), which enlightens the eyes (v. 8).

Like the sky, the sun in Fig. 32 appears in double form: as falcon of the heavens (in the sun-bark), and as son of the lady of heaven. The newborn sun, seen near the pudenda of Nut, is identified by the goose-sign (s¡, "son") as the child of the lady of heaven.

The sun appears a second time, at full strength, above the head of Shu. Thus closely connected with the sun, Shu becomes the "breath of life" (Ps 104:29). In each hand and on his arm he bears the sign, "life." It is worth noting that Shu does not touch the body he supports. Touching is of no importance, for we are presented with a thought-picture, not a visual one. Shu's function is deduced from his position in the composition as a whole, and from his uplifted arms. That function is not graphically portrayed.

The three entities heaven, earth, and what is under the earth appear in an extremely interesting Egyptian sarcophagus relief (33). The relief itself dates from the fourth century B.C., but its antecedents may be traced to the New Kingdom (cf. 34).[48] The circular earth disc, characteristic of both Figs. 33 and 34, accords little with the realities of the narrow, extended Nile Valley. H. Schäfer has attempted to attribute this lack of correspondence to foreign influences.[49] The fact, however, that the so-called cartouche (which later enclosed the royal name) was originally circular in form (35) undermines Schäfer's suggestion. The circular cartouche is called šn. šn wr, "great ring," but that is also a frequent and ancient designation for the ocean. This fact suggests that in Egypt, visualization of the earth as a circular disc was from very ancient times at least an option. This conclusion is supported by evidence, as early as the fourteenth century B.C., of circular representations of the figure of Osiris or Geb (37). The impression produced by the line of the horizon—together with archetypal experiences—could have given rise to the concept of the earth disc.

Thus, as in the Babylonian Map of the World (8), the outermost ring in Fig. 33 may signify the ocean, the "great ring," or as it is also called in Egypt, the "great green [expanse]."

Two rings appear in Fig. 34. The innermost may signify the sea, the outermost the mountains of the horizon. The text outside the circle informs us that the heavenly ocean begins beyond the outer ring. The heavenly ocean is called ḳbḥw-Ḥr, the "cool" or "upper waters of Horus," the sky god. The surrounding wall may represent the "firmament" which contains the upper waters. The Egyptian knew no more about the nature of the celestial vault than did the Israelite. He knew only that it had to be capable of restraining the waters of the heavenly ocean, and that it must therefore have had a structure similar to a wall or dam (Ps 33:7). The structure deduced from the function of the sky is represented by the ideogram "wall-ring." Modern representations of the ancient Near Eastern world view (56 and 57) err in portraying the upper regions too concretely, as if they were as well understood by the men of that time as was the earthly environment.

Two female figures emerge from the inside of the outermost ring in Fig. 33. The figure on the right wears on her head the Egyptian sign for "west"; that on the left bears the sign for "east." The "eastern" figure conveys the ship of the sun from the subterranean ocean, which it has traversed by night, to the heavenly ocean, which it travels by day. The "western" figure conveys it downwards. The sun at its zenith is shown with wings.

The adjacent ring portrays the foreign lands, which in Egyptian eyes are generally coextensive with the desert. These lands are characterized by the gods Ha (right; shown in his temple in Fig. 34) and Sopdu (left), lords respectively of the western and eastern deserts. The lands are further characterized by the

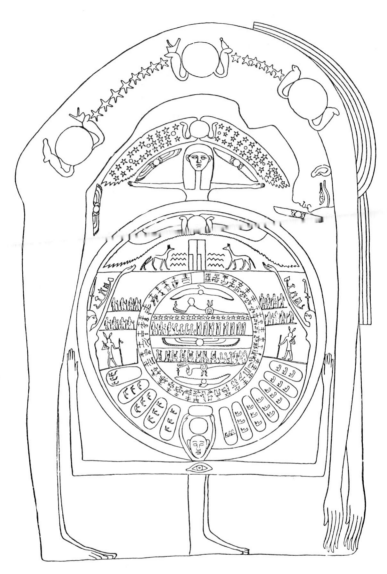

33. ". . . [Thou] who hast stretched out the *heavens* like a tent. . . , Thou didst set the *earth* on its *foundations*. . . . Yonder is the *sea,* great and wide . . ." (Ps 104:2b, 5a, 25a).

"The earth is the LORD'S and the fulness thereof, the world and those who dwell therein; for he has founded it upon the seas, and established it upon the rivers" (Ps 24: 1–2).

si, n for "chief" (appearing sixteen times) and by the carelessly executed sign of the sitting man (repeated thirty times, enclosed in twelve ovals). The latter sign is more clearly recognizable in Fig. *34,* where the figures hold, on their knees or in their hands, either a feather or a branch. In battle, the feather is worn in

the hair. Held in the hand or on the knee it signifies submission. The foreign lands and peoples surrounding Egypt have therefore been subdued.

To Israel, just as to Babylon *(8)* and Egypt *(33* and *34*), it is self-evident that *it* inhabits the center of the earth, while other nations dwell at earth's edges (Pss

22:27; 59:13; 65:8; 67:5-7; 98:3). The limits of the inhabited earth thus came to be associated with the realm of the dead (Ps 61:2; cf. 42:6-7 with 43:3). In the day of salvation, all nations of the earth will turn toward Jerusalem to worship Yahweh.

There appears in Fig. 33 a section separated from the upper portion of the second ring. It is identified as the western horizon by the two jackals (animals of the jackal-headed Anubis, god of funerary rites), by the twice-repeated sign for "water" (three wavy lines), and by the twice-repeated sign for "great building" (e.g., "tomb"; enclosure in cross-section, entrance in vertical section). It may have been placed above, instead of at the right (beside the "western" figure), for purely aesthetic reasons. On the west bank of the Nile, at the edge of the desert, lay the great necropoleis (Thebes, Sakkarah, etc.); in the west, the sun descended into the Nun, the primeval ocean, and into the realm of the dead.

The second ring (33) treats foreign realms. The terms "foreign," "ends of the earth," "waters," and "realm of the dead" are repeatedly related in the psalms. The realm of the dead is present in darkness and in the depths of the grave (cf. Ps 88:4, 6, 11); in the bottomless, dark waters which surround the earth and flow underneath the earth disc (cf. Pss 18:4-5, 16; 69:2, 15; 107:23-28); and in the outer perimeters of the inhabited earth, the desert (Pss 61:2; 107:4-7). In these places the realm of the dead is present, not as a sphere, nor as in a picture, but inasmuch as they are in fact the regions through which one enters the actual realm of the dead. Due to the strongly speculative nature of the subject, that realm, for all its reality, is not to be definitively localized.

The third ring in Fig. 33 is filled with the forty-one signs (standards) of the Egyptian nomes. It therefore signifies Egypt. The figures shown within the center circle identify it as the world of the dead (Duat); the stars identify it as night. After its setting, the winged sun (shown

three times) passes through the night. In Fig. 34, the twice-repeated, serrated water line also appears.

In the psalms too, the primeval ocean (thm) and the world of the dead (š'wl) are repeatedly merged. Because the dead are buried in the earth, Sheol is beneath the earth's surface; because water is found under the earth, there too is Tehom. The relation of the two to each other, however, remained unclear.

It is noteworthy that in Fig. 33, a passage leads from the two signs for "tomb" (in the second ring) through the third ring (Egypt) to the innermost circle, characterized by night, water, and the dead. In this representation, the "gates of death" (Pss 9:13; 107:18) are none other than the gates of the necropolis.

In Fig. 33, the whole world is upheld by the sign whose feet and eye identify it as a personal power, "ka." The two bent arms, which at an early stage come to embody "life force," may have originally (and more precisely) denoted "uplifting power." This, "as a cosmic entity, had to lift up, out of the darkness of night and into the light of day, first the globe of the sun, later the king and all mankind."[50]

In the outermost ring (sea), above the feet of the ka, is a figure consisting only of head and arms. With its head it upholds a disc (Duat?), and with its arms an oval (earth?). Because the figure rises out of the ring of ocean, it may, like the human figure in Fig. 37, embody the ocean in its mythical, primeval form. Even less clear to the ancient Near East than the relation between Tehom (primeval ocean) and Sheol (realm of the dead) was the problem of how the inhabited earth is kept from sinking into the Chaos-waters. Figs. 33 and 37 solve the problem by adopting an upholding power, which represents a purely speculative postulate. Sometimes, more graphically, there is reference to beams which support the earth disc.[51] According to one Babylonian solution of the problem, Marduk plaited reed mats, threw earth on them, and thus created a dry place.[52] This technique is still employed by the marsh-dwellers of south-

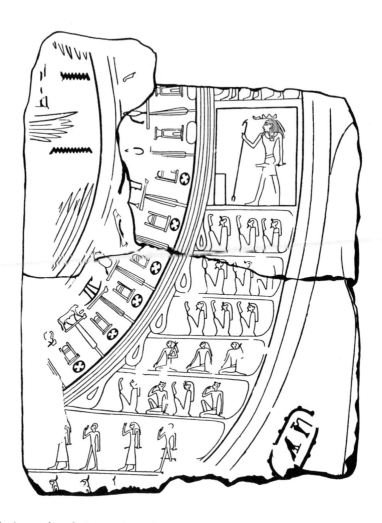

34. "All the ends of the earth shall remember and turn to the LORD; and all the families of the nations shall worship before him" (Ps 22:27).

For the circuit of wall at the lower right: "He holds the waters of the ocean as with a dam, he keeps the primeval waters in store" (Ps 33:7 [author's translation]; cf. 23).

ern Iraq. The OT postulates pillars (Ps 75:3; I Sam 2:8; Job 9:6), foundations (Pss 18:7; 82:5), or supports (Ps 104:5) [RSV: "foundations"] on which the earth disc rests. These conceptions may have an experiential basis in the mighty rock walls, articulated like pillars, of the deep-cut wadis (Plate I); but no man knows where they themselves rest (Job 38:6). The crucial factor is that Yahweh, a personal power, keeps the earth out of the Chaos-waters (Pss 24:1-2; 93:1; 96:10; 136:6). The technical means by

which that is accomplished remain unclear (contra 56 and 57; cf. 33 and 37 and the sky in 26-29).

If we regard Fig. 33 as a unified composition, it is evident that its world is basically constructed of two components: the earth, bounded by the sea and the nether world, and the heavens (Pss 148:1, 7). The importance of the bipartite formula is again apparent. It is instructive to note in this connection that the portrayal of the earth, the sea, and the nether world bears the impress of experiences of a fairly obvious nature. Such experiences are similarly common to Babylonia (cf. 8). The representation of the heavens—at least in its double form (pair of wings and Nut)—presents features which are absolutely mythical and specifically Egyptian (birth of the sun).

In Fig. 34, the two water lines are the only suggestion of the presence of water under the earth. In Fig. 36, the primeval ocean (indicated by zigzag lines) quite literally constitutes the basis of the cosmic system. On it rest the hands and feet of the lady of heaven. Here, then, the pillars of the heavens rest in the waters of Nun, and not on a range of frontier mountains somehow connected with the earth. According to Ps 104:3, 13, God constructs his upper chambers over the primeval ocean.

In Fig. 36, the sun leaps forth from between the thighs of the lady of heaven and disappears again at her mouth. The zigzag lines on Nut's garment indicate the heavenly ocean, which is nothing but a Nun raised up to heaven.[53] Here the concepts of the lady of heaven and the heavenly ocean are very closely linked. The high trough of the earth lies beneath the sky goddess and above the primeval ocean. The trees of the horizon stand on earth's border mountains; the temple stands at the center. The temple here is that of Hathor of Dendera.[54]

The tripartite world is shown more clearly on the sarcophagus of Seti I in Abydos (37) than on the sarcophagus relief in Fig. 33. The elements of Fig. 37 are considerably more clear than those of Fig. 33 because the individual parts are labelled. The background is formed by a surface whose zigzag lines show it to be water. This is surrounded by a dotted band representing the frontier mountains.

The large expanse effectively illustrates the role of the primeval waters as the source of all being (cf. Ps 104:6). The composition is adapted here to the rectangular surface which it covers; normally it is drawn in a circle.[55] The composition as a whole is surrounded by

(dotted) border mountains, into which the sun sets and out of which it rises again (cf. the sun-ball at the right of the picture). In the "background" of the composition stands Nun (primeval ocean) in human form, holding aloft the morning-bark. The scarab characterizes the sun as the "waxing," morning sun. It is held by Isis (left) and Nephthys (right), the two great tutelary goddesses. Together with the sun god, Isis, and Nephthys, there is a suite of additional gods aboard the sun-bark. The heavens belong to God and his royal household (Pss 2:4; 115:16; 123:1; 148:1–2; cf. 287). In the Egyptian mind, the divine life exists in an eternal circuit, of which the evening plunge into the (regenerating) world of the dead is as much a part as the new ascent to the heavens every morning.[56] In the OT, on the other hand, the heavens remain the sphere of God, but the world of the dead is a region utterly remote from the divine.

The scarab propels the globe of the sun. The sun is at its zenith, for the next figure is opposite. The notation tells us that it represents the sky goddess Nut, "who receives the sun." Her feet stand on the head of "Osiris, who encompasses the Duat (world of the dead)." As often, Nut here signifies the evening sky. One is struck by the forced, acrobatic posture

35. The development of the *šn*-ring from a circular cord without beginning or end. The *šn*-ring is a symbol of eternal return (cf. W. Barta, "Der Königsring," and Figs. 71, 352), concretized above all in the course of the sun (cf. Qoh 1:5). Beginning in the Fourth Dynasty, the name and given name of the Egyptian king were inscribed in the somewhat elongated *šn*-ring (cf. 351).

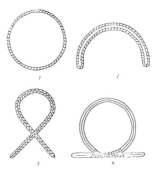

of Osiris, whose body describes a circle. The circular Osiris may represent a variant of the earth-circle of Fig. 33, which, like Osiris here, surrounds the Duat (cf. also 30).

The earth and the world of the dead are surrounded by Nun. In Hebrew, the ends of the earth are called 'psy 'rṣ (Pss 2:8; 22:27; 59:13; 67:8; 72:8; 98:3). 'ps means "end" in the sense of cessation, discontinuation of existence.

The 'psy 'rṣ are found at that point beyond which no habitable land exists. Egyptian iconography lends impressive form to this idea in the negative characterization of the serpent which bites its own tail and consumes itself (38).[57] It encircles the earth as evil Apophis (ʾpp, "great serpent"), embodying the sea. This is shown in Fig. 38 by a double figure with serpent heads. Geb, the earth god, and Osiris also appear frequently with serpent-heads. The double body is reminiscent of the hieroglyph "mountain," which represents the earth in Figs. 15, 17–18 and 36. In the iconography of the Near East, the earth is often conceived of as a mountain (22–23, 42). In the psalms as well, earth and mountains sometimes stand in parallelism (Pss 97:4–5; 98:7–8).

36. "Thy steadfast love, O LORD, extends to the heavens, . . . Thy righteousness is like the mountains of God, thy judgments are like the great deep; man and beast thou savest, O LORD" (Ps 36:5–6).

The "earth" of Fig. 38 holds in each hand a lizard, the hieroglyph for "much" (cf. the expression, "the earth and its fulness" (Pss 24:1; 50:12; 89:11). The entire composition is covered by the hieroglyph for "sky" (p.t), studded with stars. This is a very compact representation of the tripartite world (heaven, earth, sea), in which the third element represents a delimitation of the second rather than an independent entity in itself. The roughly square shape of the picture is attributable to its placement within the narrow confines of a coffin, rather than to any concept of a rectangular earth. We have already seen that little concern was wasted over the flatness or curvature of the sky. Figures 37 and 38 demonstrate that it was also relatively easy to depart from the circular form in depictions of the earth.

In Fig. 39 the self-consuming serpent, the Uroboros, is shown in circular form. The drawing comes from a papyrus of the Egyptian Book of the Dead. The two lions represent the earth-trough (cf. 16–18). The head of Mehueret, the

38. ". . . heaven and earth, the sea, and all that is in them" (Ps 146:6).

Like language, iconography too has its formulae: the heavens with the stars; the earth, represented by a double figure holding in its hands the hieroglyph for "much, numerous" (a lizard); and the sea, the serpent consuming itself. The latter may represent primarily the end of the mainland.

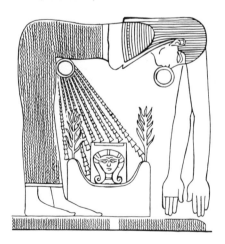

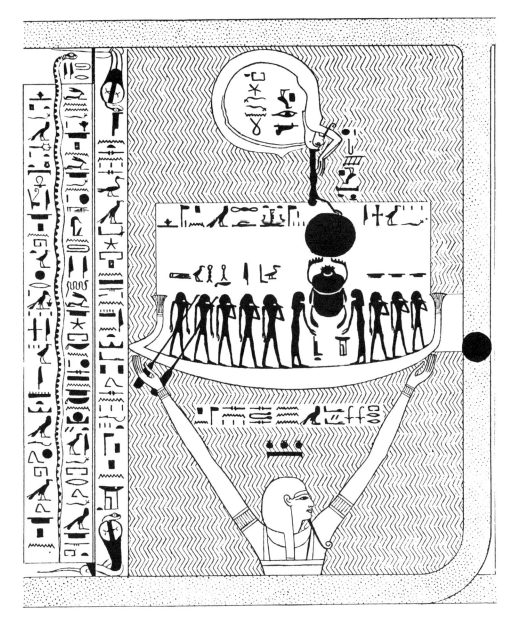

37. "Thou didst cover it [the earth] with the deep as with a garment; the waters stood above the mountains" (Ps 104:6).

"Be exalted, O God, above the heavens! Let thy glory be over all the earth!" (Ps 57:11 = 108:5).

"great flood," appears here in the space occupied in Figs. 17 and 18 by the mountain of the rising or setting sun. Mehueret upholds the sun disc (cf. 37).

Fig. 39 shows the youthful sun god with the prince's lock, his finger in his mouth (cf. 31). The eye of the sun is associated with the sun disc (God looks

down from heaven; cf. Pss 14:2; 33:13; 80:14; 102:19). A baboon and the female owner of the papyrus worship the rising sun. The arms of Nut reach down from above to take up the globe of the sun. Here, as in Fig. 37, Nut can be interpreted as the western sky. In that case, the picture would represent not only the rising of the sun, but its full daily course. The serpent would then be interpreted not as the earthly ocean, but as the heavenly. In Ps 33:7 it is likewise unclear whether reference is to the upper or lower waters. Perhaps in this instance an attempt to decide is not only impossible, but also off the mark, for in the final analysis both upper and lower waters are one (cf. 36 and 37).

As Fig. 40 shows, a clear distinction can also be made between the upper and lower oceans, and both can be represented as coiled serpents. On either side of the head of the central figure appears the mysterious sign, *imn wnwt,* "he who conceals the hours."[58] The context indicates that the figure represents one who arrests time for an instant at midnight. For this instant he takes up into himself all the hours of the day and night, in order to release them again as a new creation. This function, the mummy-form, and a passage from the Berlin hymn to Ptah suggest that the god Ptah was the model for this peculiar creation. Ptah is the primeval god, creator-god, and god of the universe:

> Your feet are on the earth, your head is in the heavens
> in your form, which is in the nether world.
> You exalt the work which you have created.
> You rely on your own power.
> You exalt yourself by the strength of your arms.
> The heaven is above you, the earth is beneath you.
> Geb [the earth god] is consolidated because of what you have concealed [the nether world?],
> and no one knows what has come into being from your body.[59]

The serpent which encircles the head of the god bears the sign *mḥn,* "the coiled one," "the coiler." It is an antitype of Apophis and protects the sun god at his setting against the monstrous, evil serpent.

39. This illustration shows exactly the same proceeding as Fig. 37. The range of frontier mountains is represented, as in Figs. 17 and 18, by two lions. Here the serpent coiling round the sun replaces the great expanse of water (in Fig. 37). The two representations demonstrate that the earthly and heavenly oceans essentially constitute a pair. In Fig. 39, the horns of the cow "of the great flood" (holding aloft the orb of the sun) appear in place of the outstretched arms of Nun. In-stead of a scarab, a child identifies the sun as the early morning sun. In Fig. 37, Nut receives the sun; here only her arms are seen.

Just as in iconography, so too in the psalms the same set of givens can be described with two completely different vocabularies. Conceptual studies are consequently a very limited resource in the investigation of the ancient Near Eastern world, with its predilection for parallelism and its multiplicity of approaches.

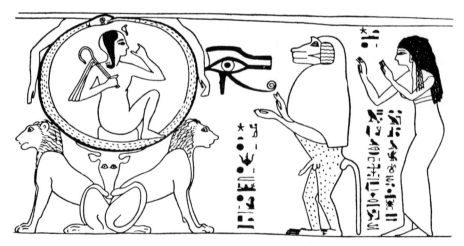

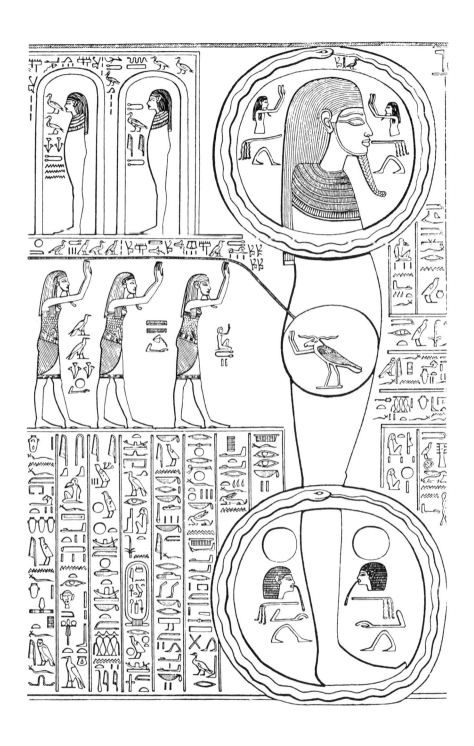

40. "The earth is full of the steadfast love of the LORD" (Ps 33:5b). In Israel, the love (ḥsd), the righteousness (ṣdqh), the glory (kbwd), and the name (šm) of Yahweh appear in place of the Egyptian and Mesopotamian deities who fill heaven and earth (cf. the texts accompanying Figs. 20, 28, 36).

From Mesopotamia we possess far fewer representations of the "world" than we do from Egypt. The reason lies in the fact that the Egyptian hoped, after death, to enter the eternal circuit of the sun. He attempted to further the realization of this hope by means of magical manipulations, such as picture-magic. The deceased desired to be taken up into the circular course of the sun-bark. That course is therefore represented countless times. Alternatively, Nut is portrayed inside the sarcophagus cover. She is to receive the deceased like the evening sun and bear him again to new life (cf. 31).

Such ideas are foreign to Mesopotamia. One reason may lie in the fact that at a very early stage there existed in Mesopotamia a stronger distinction than in Egypt between the cosmic phenomena themselves and the powers which were manifested in them. This is evident, at any rate, in iconography. In Egypt, Osiris appears, his body unnaturally twisted, as the earth circle (30 and 37); and the sky goddess appears in a most difficult posture as the vault of heaven (cf. 25, 26, 28–30, 32–33, 36). When cosmic powers appear as persons in Mesopotamian iconography, their posture generally bears no resemblance to those parts of the cosmic system which they represent. They are envisioned as free agents, whose individual attributes render them more or less recognizable to us as representatives of specific cosmic forces (cf. 9 or 43).

Inasmuch as Yahweh is One, and is altogether separate from the cosmic system, Israel again assumes an essentially different attitude (cf. chap. 4.2).

The divergent development of orthographic systems in Egypt and Mesopotamia offers a kind of analogy to their differences in the iconography of the cosmic gods. While the Sumerian-Akkadian system radically broke from its pictographic background, and that at an early stage, Egyptian hieroglyphics remained closely linked to iconography.

With the exception of a few cylinder

41. ". . . thou . . . liftest me up from the *gates of death*, that I may recount all thy praises, that in the gates of the daughter of Zion I may rejoice in thy deliverance" (Ps 9:13–14).

seals, primarily from the Akkadian (43, 44) and Late Syrian periods (23, 24), and some memorial or boundary stones (*kudurru*) from the Middle Babylonian-Kassite period (41; cf. 125, 126), Mesopotamia yields little material on the theme of symbolic-mythical conceptions of the world.

Fig. 41 is very interesting. Approximately two-thirds of the *kudurru* is taken up by a massive, fortlike structure. A serpent-dragon coils about its foundation. A similar serpent encircles the top of the stone, which is formed by the figure of the heavenly bull (not visible here). As in Fig. 40, the two serpents may represent the lower and upper oceans. The register beneath the heavenly serpent is filled with the symbols of the high gods, who were believed to have been revealed in the constellations. In Fig. 239 too, some of the stars are fixed below on the heavenly ocean. The mighty citadel represents not the earth,[60] but the city of the nether world. Its dreadful gates are also referred to in the psalms (Pss 9:13; 107:18; Jonah 2:6). The city is surrounded by the waters of Chaos (serpent). Its towers constitute the pillars (Ps 75:3) or the foundations (Pss 18:7; 82:5) of the earth.

In the next register, men and women, making music, march in procession between large potted plants. The men and women are followed by various kinds of animals. This register must represent the earth. Its inhabitants are created for the service of the gods (cf. Ps 148:9–13). The animals do not necessarily refer to the Orpheus motif:[61] they could be tame animals, which were popularly kept in courts (and probably also in temples). They were led along in processions of all kinds (468).[62]

Figure 41 demonstrates that the world can be conceived in terms of four or five parts as well as in terms of three. In this picture, the city of the dead and the waters of Chaos are clearly distinguished, to say nothing at all of the various regions of the heavens.

3. DUALISTIC FEATURES

Cosmic forces come more strongly to the fore in the world structure of Fig. 42 than in Fig. 41. The dominant figure in the cylinder seal from Mari (42) is the god seated on the mountain. His scepter identifies him as king of the gods. In Mesopotamia, An (Akkadian: Anu) is "the heavens," "king of kings," "the mountain of pure, divine powers," "he who is seated on the great throne," "to whom all bow in heaven and on earth."[63]

The two stars before the enthroned god might be read as phonotypes for AN, and as an ideogram for "god," which would yield "god An(u)." Mari, however, is situated at the edge of several cultural regions. The god on the mountain could therefore be taken as the Canaanite El or some related figure.[64] El too is king of the gods and dwells on a mountain "in the midst of the sources of the two oceans."[65] This

42. For the deity on the mountain: "O Lord, how manifold are thy works! In wisdom hast thou made them all . . ." (Ps 104:24).

For the deity with the spear: "Was thy wrath against the rivers, O Lord?" (Hab 3:8).

43. "If I ascend to heaven, thou art there! If I make my bed in Sheol, thou art there! If I take the wings of the morning and dwell in the uttermost parts of the sea, even there . . . thy right hand will hold me" (Ps 139:8–10).

In Ps 139, the regions ruled (in Fig. 43) by various Mesopotamian deities stand under the absolute control of Yahweh.

For the deity holding down the dragon, cf. Job 7:12: "Am I the sea, or a sea monster, that thou settest a guard over me?"

last feature is particularly important in relation to Fig. 42: in Mesopotamia, it is Ea who sits enthroned "in the midst of the mouth of the two rivers."[66] El, like the god on the mountain (in Fig. 42), unites in himself aspects both of Anu and Ea. Even the two stars are no impediment to interpretation of the figure as El. They can be understood as "the stars of El" [RSV: "God"], the highest stars (mentioned in Isa 14:13). The scope of El's dominion reaches from the profoundest depths to the highest heavens (Ps 95:4–5). El is the embodiment of that unity which lies behind all the strife of the prominent gods (Baal = lord of the earth, Yam = sea, Mot = realm of the dead). He embodies the cosmic order and harmony governing and pervading all things;[67] he is their wise creator. Yahweh assumed many features of El (cf. the text accompanying Figs. 283–84).

Two goddesses rise out of the two rivers which originate at the foot of the mountain (42). The boughs projecting from the goddesses identify them as embodiments of vegetation. The goddess on the left holds a tree in her hand; the one on the right holds a vessel.

The waters welling up from the mountain are no harmless brooklets, but the waters of Tehom, the primeval flood. That is made clear by the god at the outer left, who combats the waters with his spear ("Was thy wrath against the rivers, O LORD?" Hab 3:8). He may represent the storm god Baal-Hadad, who fertilizes the land with his showers and defends his realm against every aspect of threatening Chaos. Without water, life cannot exist, but water can also destroy all life. This dual nature of water is often evident in the psalms. In the psalms, the violent power of the waters of Chaos is broken and subdued by Yahweh, who in this respect has taken over the function of Baal (cf. 290–94). The waters gladden the earth and quench the thirst of plants and animals (Pss 46:3; 65:7–9; 74:15; 104:6–12).

In the world picture of Fig. 42, the primeval waters, the earth-mountain, and the heavens (represented by stars) appear as constitutive elements. The area thus delimited is ruled by the ordering power of El. He guarantees the often precarious balance between the deadly powers of Chaos and the life-force of Baal. Through the identification of

Yahweh with El, and by Yahweh's assumption of certain functions of Baal, the forces of order and life are concentrated into *one* power and set against the forces of Chaos. As a result, the Chaos powers achieved a certain independence, and the dualism of the ancient Near East was somewhat strengthened. But because the power of Yahweh was seen to be all-encompassing and overwhelming, that independence could no longer imperil the world (Pss 93:3–4; 109:9). The sea, having lost all its threatening power, is demythologized. Its dark, salt floods and its flashing foam are nothing more than water. Once Yahweh, with his mighty, sovereign word, has displaced the hard-fighting Baal, the sea loses every representative aspect (Pss 46:2–3; 65:6–7; 77:16–19; 93; 104:5–6).

A further means of overcoming the innate dualism was found in a historical understanding of the forces of Chaos. Such an understanding was already current in Israel's environment *(142, 144),* but in Israel it was more consistently followed through. The transfer of evil from the cosmic sphere to the realm of anthropology and ethics is a perceptive shift, for the dragon, the principal figure among the forces of Chaos, owes its existence more to psychological factors than to a careful observation of the outside world.

In contrast to Fig. *42,* Fig. *43* is unambiguously Mesopotamian. At the right of the picture is Ea, god of the deeps. He appears in his chamber, which is surrounded on all sides by water. Two brooks spring from his shoulders; above them are three fish (cf. *285*). To the right of Ea's underwater abode is a kneeling servant, holding a gatepost. This gate apparently seals off from Chaos the depths of the earth, with their reservoirs of fresh water (cf. Jonah 2:6). Ea is lord of these deeps. Chaos appears in the form of a winged lion, forceably restrained (in Fig. *43* at the extreme right and left). The little kneeling god who is holding down the monster may be Ninurta. A hymn describes Ninurta as

victor over the *ušumgal,* a creature with lion-paws and wide-spread wings from the retinue of Tiamat, the dragon of the primeval age.[68]

The sun god emerges from between the two wings of the conquered monster. In a quite similar posture, another god of sun and light ascends the mountain, which has at its summit the gate of heaven. He deferentially greets Ea, who is seated in his chamber. This god may be Ea's son, Marduk.[69] The sun god Shamash, with his saw, embodies the sphere of the heavens. He uses the saw to execute his verdicts. Ninurta-Ningirsu, who is often equated with Enlil (both have the symbolic number "fifty"), and Marduk, who with the rise of the Semitic element largely superseded them, represent (like the Canaanite Baal) the storm and the fruitful farm land. Ea is the god of the ground-waters. These three gods are often jointly invoked to avert calamity. Ea is the wise lord of the depths, Marduk is the battler against primeval Chaos, and Shamash drives away all darkness. Yahweh's activity embraces all these aspects (cf. Ps 139). The Chaos monster, Leviathan, embodying the destructive raging of the sea, is reduced to an object of divine amusement in the face of Yahweh's concentrated power (Ps 104:26).

To men of the ancient Near East, primeval Chaos is present in the sea. In Ugaritic myth, *yām,* "the sea," is the great antagonist of Baal. In Pss 74:13 and 89:9, *yām* appears at the forefront of the Chaos monsters. In Fig. *43,* the sun god emerges from between the wings of the Chaos dragon, as elsewhere he emerges from between the mountains *(9).* The cylinder seal *(43)* comes from southern Mesopotamia, where it was understood that the sun god could rise from the sea as well as from the mountains. The pinned-down dragon in Fig. *43* may thus represent the sea.

The more or less domesticated Chaos dragon was understood to be at work in the raging of the tempest. In Fig. *44,* the storm god Adad, in a heavy, four-wheeled chariot, travels thundering across the vault of heaven (Ps 77:18). His whip is the lightning, which rends the whirling dust clouds. His wagon is drawn by the very monster that represents the sea in Fig. *43*. It is half lion (head, forequarters), half eagle (wings, tail, hind legs).

The primeval Chaos appears, albeit in tamed form, in the sea *(43)* and in the raging of the storm *(44)* (cf. Job 7:12; Gen 9:14). But the thought that Chaos might break loose and re-establish its dreadful dominion filled men with horror. We may still sense something of that horror in the following evocative expression of hope: "Thou [Yahweh] didst set a bound which they [Chaos powers] should not pass, so that they might not again cover the earth" (Ps 104:9; cf. 93:3–4). (A goddess with streams of rain in each hand stands over the Chaos monster in Fig. *44*. She embodies the fruitful rain, the friendly aspect of the storm.)

Until it was conquered by a god (Ps 104:7–8), the dynamic Chaos harnessed in the sea and tempest was free *(45; cf. 419)* and ruled the earth (Ps 104:6). The conquering god *(45)* is shown to be a heavenly being by the stars which form his bow. In these sharply dualistic conceptions, creation is undergirded by the (provisional) victory of the god, who embodies light and order (cf. Ps 104:9; Job 7:12; Jer 5:22). Pss 74:12–17 and 89:5–14 touch on this myth. The dragon is variously named in the two passages, and a number of completely different descriptions of Leviathan indicate that there was no exact conception of its appearance.[70] In Ps 74:13–14, for example, it has several heads; in Isa 27:1 it is a twisting serpent; in Job 41:1 it is a crocodile [RSVm] which exhibits some rather fantastic features, such as spitting fire (Job 41:19).

Ancient Near Eastern pictures show a similar variety in representation of the Chaos monster. In Figs. *42–44* the Chaos dragon is depicted as a composite creature, half lion and half eagle; in Figs. *46–50* it appears in the form of a serpent; and in Figs. *51* and *52* it is a seven-headed monster. In inquiring after the origin of these ideas, we must assume an interaction between everyday experiences and the dreamlike processing of these experiences by the unconscious mind. This processing, for its part, must have further affected the experience. The monsters take the form of particular zoological species, or are at least composed of elements of them. The interdependence of zoological and mytho-

44. "Your pealing thunder was in the dome of heaven, your lightning bolts lit up the world, the nether world quaked and shook" (Ps 77:19 MT [translation of M. Dahood, *Psalms,* vol. 2, p. 224, cf. 232]; cf. Ps 77:18 RSV).

45. "Out of his [Leviathan's] mouth go flaming torches; sparks of fire leap forth" (Job 41:19).

"At thy rebuke they [the waters of Chaos] fled; at the sound of thy thunder they took to flight" (Ps 104:7).

46. ". . . who . . . treads on the heights of the earth . . ." (Amos 4:13).

"Thou didst crush Rahab like a carcass" (Ps 89:10a).

Rahab, the oppressor, is here the name for a Chaos monster. In Ps 87:4 it is a symbolic name for Egypt. On the historical interpretation of Chaos, cf. Figs. *142, 144*.

and sky is shown more clearly in Fig. *46*. There the tree of life is simultaneously the tree of the world, supporting the constellations. A female deity, related to Ishtar by the eight-pointed star, holds her hand protectively over the tree. The Chaos serpent, who was apparently about to attack the tree, is killed by Baal-Hadad, who strides over the mountains brandishing a mace (cf. *290–91*). It is uncertain whether the griffin (upper right) is supposed to be the guardian of the tree of life, and whether the three men (lower right), in the face of the impending danger, have turned in supplication to the goddess.

The dragon of Fig. *47* also has a serpent's body, but with a horned head (cf. Ps 75:4–5; cf. *41*). The figure at the left attacks the monster with bow and arrow. A little tree (tree of life?), which the archer seems to be defending, stands between the two. The tree, as in Fig. *46*, may symbolize the fruitful land, the "land of life" [RSV: "land of the living"] (Pss 142:5; 116:9).

logical elements is also evident in the linguistic sphere. In Ugarit, Leviathan *(ltn)* is described as a malicious *(brḥ)*, coiled *('qltn)* serpent-dragon *(bṯn)* with seven heads *(šb't r'šm)* (cf. Isa 27:1).[71] In Pss 58:4 and 91:13 the etymologically related *ptn* appears as a poisonous and dangerous, but quite ordinary snake.

In Fig. *45*, the tree of life, as a stylized palm, rises beside the rampant Chaos monster. The relation between the dragon, the tree of life, and the god of storm

The serpent is also driven out of the plant realm in Fig. *48*. It is difficult to say what meaning is attached to the two figures at the right of the battling hero. The kneeling figure may be handing missiles to the warrior, which the latter uses in addition to the sword. The figure at the extreme right may be celebrating the victory on the tambourine (cf. *451*). These conjectures are questionable.

The serpent-dragon of Fig. *49* possesses not only horns, but also front

47. "Thou didst set a bound which they [the Chaos waters] should not pass, so that they might not again cover the earth" (Ps 104:9; cf. Jer 5:22).

assaults Illuyankas, the coiled, fiery dragon. In the later version of the myth, the dragon is identified with the sea. His body calls to mind the breaking of mighty waves.

The monster of Fig. 51 has seven heads. Flames rise from its back. Except for its serpent-neck and thick tail, however, its heads and figure are quite clearly those of a panther. The god appears to be waging his battle with a throwing stick. At any rate, the lowest head of the monster has been hit by one.[72] The monster's many heads may be traced to the impression produced by the extreme agility of the snake's or panther's head, which seemingly multiplies itself, or to the impression created by the ever-rolling, ever-swelling breakers (cf. Ps 93:4; cf. 42:7; 88:7).

In Fig. 52, three of the dragon's seven heads already lie limp; the god with the horned crown has just put his lance to the fourth. The remaining three still hiss dangerously. A second god, exactly the same in appearance as the first, attacks from the rear. As in Fig. 51, flames shoot up from the monster's back. The serpent-dragon can simultaneously symbolize searing heat and destructive masses of water. The remaining two figures might be interpreted as onlookers, not as helpers.[73] They are men, not gods, and their presence makes it unlikely that the picture is treating a creation event in the strict sense: men were created only after the conquest of Chaos. The contexts of Pss 74 and 89 and Figs. 142 and 144

paws. His conqueror, with a sheaf of lightning in one hand and arrows in the other, is clearly the thunder god (cf. 294). He has two crossed quivers on his back. The second figure appears to be bringing forward the scepter which, as a symbol of mastery, befits the conqueror of the dragon. We may gather that the third figure is attempting to exorcize the dragon. In Ps 74:12–13, the royal name of Yahweh also appears to be connected with the victory over the dragon.

In Fig. 50, the two personae seem to represent the equivalent Hittite god of storm, weather, and fertility. With the assistance of the celestial rain gods, he

48. "As the mountains rose, they [the waters of Chaos] went down the valleys to the place you had fixed for them" (Ps 104:8 NAB).

49 "Yet God my King is from of old, working salvation in the midst of the earth" (Ps 74:12).

"Thou dost rule the raging of the sea; when its waves rise, thou stillest them" (Ps 89:9).

demonstrate, however, that the primeval event is by no means separable from the saving acts performed by the deity in the battle against evil "in the midst of the earth" (Ps 74:12).

There exists antagonism not only between the threatening, raging, bottomless sea and the fruited land, but also between the "light of life" (Ps 56:13) and the darkness (Ps 88:12).

In Mesopotamia and Egypt, the darkness is the domain of demons. Fig. 53 reproduces twice a figure identified as a god of light by the beams which radiate from his shoulders. The subject is apparently Shamash, the sun god (9, 286). The

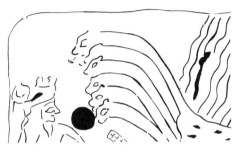

51. ". . . who dost still the roaring of the seas, the roaring of their waves, the tumult of the peoples" (Ps 65:7).

demon on the right has the paws and mouth of an animal. Demons are popularly embodied in the dangerous animals who work their mischief at night and are banished to their dark lairs by the rising sun (Ps 104:20–22; cf. 90a–99). The sun disc of Fig. 54, identified by the scarab and the ram-headed man (cf. 15) as the morning or daytime sun, drives away serpent, crocodile, and gazelle, which are considered dangerous animals and enemies of the sun (cf. Plate XXVIII). In Job 38:13, the sun drives

50. "The floods have lifted up, O LORD, the floods have lifted up their voice, the floods lift up their roaring. Mightier than the thunders of many waters, mightier than the waves of the sea, the LORD on high is mighty" (Ps 93:3–4).

52. "Thou didst divide the sea by thy might; thou didst break the heads of the dragons on the waters. Thou didst crush the heads of Leviathan, thou didst give him as food for the creatures of the wilderness" (Ps 74:13–14).

away not demons, but (in accordance with the OT demythologization of the world) the wicked. The night and the darkness are domains of danger and distress; the morning and the rising light signify help and salvation (cf. Ps 143:3, 8). In the darkness, the earth begins to falter; in the morning light it stabilizes itself again (cf. Pss 46:5; 82:5; 88:12–13; 92:2).

In Egypt, the evening darkness is above all the domain of the monstrous serpent Apophis (ʒpp). Apophis is the embodiment of the dark sea, the evening clouds, and the morning haze—in a word, those forces which can endanger the sun at its setting in the evening and on its rising in the morning. Fig. 55 dramatically portrays the threat encountered by the sun god upon his entrance into the ocean and the nether world. The sun god, with his bark, is just at the point of leaving the sky (hieroglyphic p.t; cf. 11, 15, 17–18). The serpent, whose body is stylized as wild, sheer waves (cf. 50), pits himself against the attempt to leave the sky. Seth, as helper of Re (the sun god), renders the serpent harmless.

53. "Have you commanded the morning since your days began, and caused the dawn to know its place, that it might take hold of the skirts of the earth, and the wicked be shaken out of it?" (Job 38:12–13).

active there. The heavens are his domain (Ps 115:16). The heavens are envisioned as utterly secure. With their light, they are an incomparable witness to the glorious splendor of God. The earth, on the one hand, receives the light of the heavens, and is consequently a region of life;[74] it ends, on the other hand, in dark, bottomless Chaos. One of Yahweh's great deeds was his establishment of the earth over the abyss of the floods of Chaos. On occasion it is even said that he established it over the void (Job 26:7). He has set a bound which the waters of Chaos (the void) may not pass (Ps 104:9). Should they succeed now and again in shaking the foundations of the earth, Yahweh immediately intervenes and establishes it anew (cf. Pss 11:3; 46:3; 75:3; 82:5). Since he has established it and maintains it, the earth, with all that moves on it, belongs to Yahweh (Pss 24:1; 78:69; 89:11; 93; 96:10; 104:5).

The sea, the abyss, and the darkness are the domain of the forces of Chaos.

54. "When the sun rises, they [the dangerous animals] get them away and lie down in their dens [again]" (Ps 104:22).

55. "To you belongs the day and the night as well; you have securely fixed the light of the sun" (Ps 74:16 [author's translation]).

Helpful jackal- and cobra-demons draw the ship of the sun across the sluggish floods of the nether world.

It is true that the nether world is not in principle withdrawn from the scope of Yahweh's power (cf. Ps 139:8). But Yahweh does not dwell there and is not

Where the demythologization described above (p. 49) is far advanced, the sea can be viewed as an integral part of the cosmic whole. This process of demythologization had not reached conclusion even in the latest books of the NT. In Lk 21:25, the intensified raging of the sea

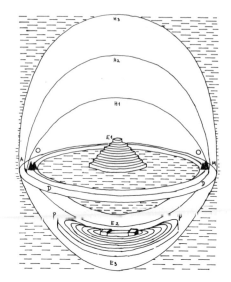

56. E_1: Earth (Upper World); E_2, E_3: Second and Third Earth (Underworld); H_{1-3}: First-Third Heaven; A: Evening (West, the two Mountains of the Sunset); M: Morning (East, the two Mountains of the Sunrise); D: Dam of the Heavens; P: Palace of the Realm of the Dead.

announces the final battle; and the seer of the Johannine Apocalypse foresees a new heaven and a new earth after the cosmic catastrophe. The author of the Apocalypse expressly notes, however, that there will be no sea in this new, imperishable world (Rev 21:1).

Concluding Note

It should have become evident, in the course of this chapter, that within the world view of the ancient Near East (including that of the psalms), empirical-technical and speculative-mythical statements and conceptions are not susceptible to consistent separation. To the ancient Near East, the empirical world, as manifestation and symbol, points beyond its superficial reality. A continuous osmosis occurs between the actual and the symbolic, and conversely, between the symbolic and the actual. This openness of the everyday, earthly world to the spheres of divine-intensive life and of bottomless, devastating lostness is probably the chief difference between ancient Near Eastern conception of the world and our own, which views the world as a virtually closed mechanical system. The principal error of conventional representations of the ancient Near Eastern view of the world (cf. 56 and 57) lies in their profantiy, transparency, and lifelessness. In the biblical and ancient Near Eastern conception, the world is open and transparent to things above and beneath the earth. It is not a lifeless stage. "The universe is thoroughly alive, and, therefore, the more capable of sympathy with man and of response to the rule of its creator, on whom both man and universe directly depend. Certainly we have here more than a poetical personification of the cosmos, when it is invited to rejoice (Ps 96:11)."[75]

Yet another fundamental error of these contemporary representations lies in their failure to suggest the extent to which the question of the foundations of the universe—of the ultimate basis and security of the sphere of existence—remained a problem. The ancient Near East was not conscious of any answer to this question. Again and again, ciphers and symbols were employed (cf. 28, 33), expressing nothing other than awe in the face of divine, magical power or divine wisdom and grace.

4. THAT WHICH FILLS HEAVEN AND EARTH

In addition to the great expanses such as heaven and earth, sea and world of the dead, the universe also includes the innumerable things which inhabit and adorn the expanses of the cosmos: "all that is in them" (Pss 69:34; 96:11;

57. Modern representations of the so-called ancient Near Eastern picture of the world overlook the fact that the ancient Near East never regarded the world as a closed, profane system. Rather, the world was an entity open at every side. The powers which determine the world are of more interest to the ancient Near East than the structure of the cosmic system. A wide variety of diverse, uncoordinated notions regarding the cosmic structure were advanced from various points of departure.

146:6). In the postexilic period, the term "all things" is occasionally used to denote heaven and earth and all that is in them (Ps 119:91). The ancient Sumerians, with the aid of huge lists, attempted to inventory and order the vast profusion of phenomena.[76]

Similar lists, albeit far less extensive, are also preserved from the period of the New Kingdom in Egypt. Their origin was apparently not without Sumerian-Babylonian influence, but their further development was independent. A. Alt has suggested[77] that Solomon was not ignorant of this science when he spoke "of trees, from the cedar that is in Lebanon to the hyssop that grows out of the wall, . . . also of beasts, and of birds, and of reptiles, and of fish" (I Kgs 4:33). G. von Rad has shown[78] that at least some of the OT hymns which refer to the above-mentioned phenomena show a marked similarity to the well-known Egyptian catalogue of Amen-em-Opet. As in that list, so too in Ps 148 the earthly phenomena (lightning, hail, snow, mist, storm, mountains, hills, plants, animals, men) follow the

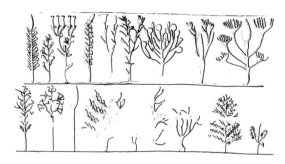

58. Section from the catalogue of plants which were brought from Syria by Thutmose III.

heavenly phenomena (the gods—depotentized as servants of Yahweh—sun, moon, stars, and heavenly ocean). The twofold division into heavenly and earthly phenomena is striking. Among the earthly phenomena are included even the sea monsters and deeps, which stand before the various meteorological manifestations. These in turn are followed by mountains, plants, animals, and men. A sequence similar to that in Ps 148 is found in Ps 104, and later in Sir 43 and in the Song of the Three Young Men (insertions to Dan 3:29–68). In these texts, empty inventories have become hymns to Yahweh's creative power. Even Amen-em-Opet's inventory contains in its superscription a hymnic accent: "the beginning of the teaching . . . concerning all that is, which Ptah [cf. 40] created and Thoth recorded [287, 349–50, 478a]."

This delight in cataloguing was also reflected in iconography. Thut-mose III had carved on the temple walls of Kar-

nak an entire catalog of plants (by no means all unusual, exotic varieties) which he brought with him from Syria.

S. Morenz has shown[79] that the allocation of specific *biotopoi* to individual species of animals is an aspect of the interest in the animal kingdom evidenced by wisdom literature as a whole. We find traces of it in Ps 104:14, 17–18, where there is reference to the maintenance of men and animals, and to the environments of small birds, storks, wild goats, and badgers. An Akkadian cylinder seal with an especially lively impression shows how the high mountains serve as a living space for the wild goats. There they can find protection from the clutches of man and lion (59). The entire animal kingdom is subject to man (Ps 8:6–8), but this dominion is not for purposes of willful destruction. Certainly the "beasts of the field" are for man to hunt, but Ps 8:7a shows that "dominion over the beasts" means primarily dominion over domestic animals. In their case, man is as much protector as usufructuary, a fact made very evident by Figs. 60 and 61. The foot placed upon the weaker animal expresses "dominion" (cf. Ps 8:6). As in the case of the king, however, this dominion consists not only in holding subject, but also in defense of the weaker animal against the attacking lion. The double pair of wings in Fig. 61 exalts the man to the level of the mythical. In 1 Sam 17:34–36, the young David appears in the role of the hero of Figs. 60 and 61 (cf. Judg 14:5–6).

59. "The high mountains are for the wild goats" (Ps 104:18a).

60. "Thou has given him dominion over the works of thy hands; . . . all sheep and oxen, and also the beasts of the field, the birds of the air, and the fish of the sea, whatever passes along the paths of the seas" (Ps 8:6a–8).

In a vase (more than a meter in height) from Uruk, plants, animals, men, and the deity appear in a wonderful order *(62)*. In registers arranged one over another there appear a river, plants (stylized ears of grain and shoots of the date palm), small livestock, oblation-bearers. On the topmost register, the prince of the city (almost completely destroyed) stands before Inanna, the goddess of love and fertility, from whom life proceeds and here, as it were, returns (cf. *180, 187, 192, 442–43*). In the psalms, praise repeatedly takes the place of sacrifice (Pss 40:6–10; 50; 51:15–17; 69:30–31). Consequently, in Ps 148:9–12, the earth, trees, animals, rulers, and common men do not appear in an offertory procession, but are summoned instead to praise.

The notion that the whole creation praises the sun god was particularly vital in Egypt in the Amarna Period. In a great hymn to the sun god, Amenophis IV [Akhenaton] sings: "When the earth grows bright, you rise again in the mountains of light . . . the birds fly up from their nests, their wings sing your praises"[80] *(289)*. The concept of praise from all creatures is pictorially expressed not only in the Amarna Period, but even earlier on sarcophagi and later in papyri from the Book of the Dead.

In Fig. *63*, the heavenly falcon, sun disc on its head, sits on the sign for "west" (cf. *25, 33*). He is worshipped (from bottom to top) by the dead (two soul-birds), the gods (Isis on the right and Nephthys on the left), the animals (four baboons, whose morning chatter was interpreted as praise), kings (four, on the right), common Egyptians (four, on the left), and (at the top) lower-class Egyptians or perhaps foreigners (left and right, one *rḫj.t*).[81] In the psalms, gods (or angels; Pss 29:1–2; 148:2), Israelites and non-Israelites (Ps 117:1), and animals (Ps 148:10) are summoned to praise. Praise from the dead, however, is characteristically Egyptian.[82] In Israel, the notion that the dead praise God is consistently challenged (Ps 115:17 etc.). Even Ps 22:29 is no exception.[83] Yahweh is a God of life and of the living. All that lives and moves praises him. Everything that has breath praises the Lord who gave that breath and daily gives it anew (Ps 104:29–30).

61. ". . . thou hast put all things under his feet" (Ps 8:6b).

62. "Praise the LORD . . . , fruit trees and all cedars, beasts and all cattle, creeping things and flying birds, kings of the earth and all peoples, . . . old men and children . . ." (Ps 148:7a, 9b, 10, 11a, 12b).

63. "Let everything that breathes praise the LORD!" (Ps 150:6).

CHAPTER II
DESTRUCTIVE FORCES

1. SPHERES OF DEATH

Ps 107 calls upon four groups of the redeemed to sing the praises of Yahweh. In their distress, they had promised sacrifice to Yahweh in the event of deliverance. Now they are expected to offer that sacrifice in the temple, where they have arrived for the great autumn festival. They will sing of Yahweh's saving act, or they will employ the Levites to do so.

Those summoned in the psalm cried out to Yahweh from four regions: the desert, where vitality was utterly sapped by hunger and thirst; prison, where strong gates and bars prevented access to the light; sickness, which brought its victims close to the gates of death; and the storm-tossed sea, which drained the physical and mental vigor of those caught in distress.

Fig. 33 showed that the gates to the world of the dead lie in the region of the desert and the sea. Ps 107 indicates very clearly what these two regions have in common with imprisonment and sickness: in all four, man's life is endangered. Their commonality lies not in their external aspects, but in man's experience. All four destroy his life, his vital power (npš [RSV: "soul"]; Ps 107:5, 18, 26), and his reasoning ability (lb, "heart"; ḥkmh, "wisdom"; Ps 107:12, 27). The Hebrew word for "sickness" (ḥly) in fact signifies simply a condition of exhaustion and weakness (ḥlh, "to be weak"). Consequently, it is sometimes difficult to determine the extent to which the word relates to sickness in the narrow sense.[1]

In the psalms, sickness is closely linked with sin (Pss 41:4; 107:17–20). The sick man is stricken because of the divine wrath: he no longer has any appetite (Ps 107:18a); he lies on his couch (Ps 41:8), waters his bed with his tears (Ps 6:6), and groans in entreaty to God (cf. 90a, 91, Plate III) that he might forgive and heal him. Severe sickness, misfor-

tune, and need bring a man "to the gates of death" (Ps 107:18; cf. 88:3). This expression corresponds quite closely to our phrase, "to be on death's doorstep." To the ancient Near East, however, pictures are rarely "only" pictures. Instead, as chapter 1 has shown, they are "exemplary reality," which, insofar as it is "exemplary," encompasses realms larger than the realm of concrete appearance. Inasmuch as it is "reality," how-

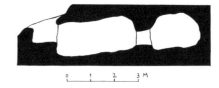

64. "I am . . . like one forsaken among the dead, like the slain that lie in the grave" (Ps 88:4b, 5).

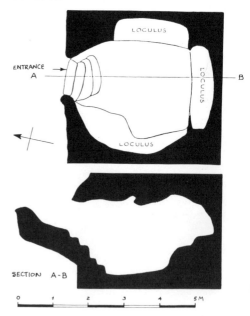

65. "And when he came to the other side, to the country of the Gadarenes, two demoniacs met him, coming out of the tombs, so fierce that no one could pass that way" (Mt 8:28 parr.).

62

ever, it can also be concretely understood.

The suppliant of Ps 88, who is apparently very ill, complains that he is already reckoned among the dead, in whose midst he lives. Like death, certain sicknesses made one unclean. We learn from the NT that persons thus rendered unclean were made to live outside the villages among the tombs (Mark 5:1–5 parr.). The type of tomb most frequently attested in Palestine of the first and second centuries B.C. is the natural or man made cave-tomb, accessible either diagonally or vertically from above (64–68). When a natural cave was used (64, 65), it appeared very much like a simple living space, particularly when it was equipped with the appropriate furniture. There are a number of well-preserved examples of such tombs from the Middle Bronze period at Jericho[2] and a few from the Iron Age at Ein Shem.[3] A tomb is occasionally described as the home of the dead (Ps 49:11; Eccl 12:5). It differs from a house, however, in its *depth,* its *darkness,* its accumulated dust, and its *decay;* in the *silence* which prevails within it; and in the impression of *forgetfulness.* All these characteristics are ascribed in the psalms to the realm of the dead (*š'wl, mwt*). In Fig. 33, two tombs comprise the entrance to the world of the dead. In Ps 88:11, "grave" stands parallel to "abyss" [RSV: "Abaddon"] in a context where "realm of the dead" ["Sheol"] is to be found in other passages (cf. Ps 6:5; Isa 38:18). Every grave is a little "Sheol."

a. The Grave

As a land from which no one has ever yet returned (cf. Ps 88:10; Job 7:9–10; 10:21; Akkadian *erṣet lā tāri,* "land of no return"), the actual realm of the dead is a speculative entity. Its concrete features are derived from empirical observation of the grave. Beyond that, very little can be said about the world of the dead. For that reason, it appears as a prototypical grave raised to gigantic proportions. Israelite speculations, compared with those of Mesopotamia and Egypt es-

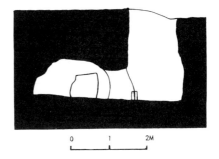

66. ". . . I call; my rock, be not deaf to me, lest, if thou be silent to me, I become like those who go down to the Pit [*bôr,* "cistern"]" (Ps 28:1).

In the Baal myth from Ugarit, Baal is addressed as follows: "Climb down into the house of uncleanness (?), the earth! You shall be reckoned among those who go down into the earth" (*UT* 67.V.14ff.).

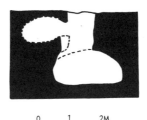

67. "Hide not thy face from me, lest I be like those who go down to the Pit [*bôr*]" (Ps 143:7; cf. 88:4).

"Is thy steadfast love declared in the *grave,* or thy faithfulness in *Abaddon* [the abyss]?" (Ps 88:11; cf. Isa 38:18).

pecially, are rather temperate and stay quite close to experience. In Mesopotamia, one could give an account of the city of the dead, with its walls, towers, and gates (cf. *41*) from which there was no escape. This city was one of unrelieved desolation and gloom. Egypt, on the other hand, attempted to lighten the darkness by means of magical precautionary measures and an enormous number of audacious myths and speculations. Yet time and again, the Egyptians too experienced death as the extremity of powerlessness (Ps 88:4) and weakness (68a).

The sketch in Fig. 69 shows an Egyptian tomb. Above it and to the right are seen four mourners. At the left of the entrance, a priest presents an offering of incense and drink. The shaft of the tomb descends vertically, as in Fig. 68. In the shaft below are a man and a priest wearing the mask of Anubis. The latter is responsible for the burial rites. Together, the two men bring the mummy to its resting place. Two mummies already lie in the room at the right. A stairway leads to a lower room, as shown also in Fig. 68.

Fig. 70 shows the full configuration of an Egyptian tomb, not at the time of burial, but as it functions for the dead. The above-ground portion of the tomb, with its portal, is crowned by the sign for "west" (cf. 63), a term frequently used for the world of the dead. The tomb here, like those of Fig. 33, is thus understood as an entryway into the realm of the dead. A vertical shaft (or stairway?) leads from the building above to the depths of the tomb below. There, through a portal shown in vertical section, one enters the first antechamber, then through another portal, the second. Through a door shown only in cross-section one reaches the main chamber, with the mummy and a number of funerary gifts. A quantity of gifts is also found in the rear chamber, which is accessible through another portal.

The deceased goes *down* to his resting-place (Pss 22:29; 28:1; 30:3, 9; 88:4; 115:17; 143:7). His realm is the depths, the abyss (Ps 88:11), the uttermost depth (Pss 63:9; 88:6). He who cries to God from the depths cries out of a situation much like death (Ps 130:1). The deceased is banished to the depths as to a prison (Ps 88:8c; cf. 107:10). The soul-bird with the human head (*ba*-bird), which flies down the grave-shaft in Fig. 70, escapes these depths. In the New

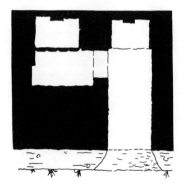

68. ". . . before I go *whence I shall not return*" (Job 10:21; cf. Ps 39:13).

"I am shut in so that I cannot escape" (Ps 88:8c).

". . . he who goes down to Sheol does not come up" (Job 7:9b).

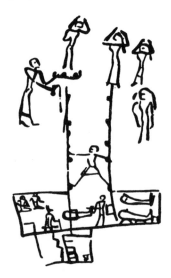

69. ". . . he has crushed my life to the ground; he has left me *dwelling* in the dark, like those long dead" (Ps 143:3 NAB; cf. Lam 3:6).

Insofar as possible, graves were provided with everything found in the dwellings of the living.

Kingdom, the Egyptian dead were accompanied by certain magical texts. Among them is a section which bears the title: "Of being transformed into a living soul" (Book of the Dead, chap. 85). The sarcophagus texts of the Middle Kingdom had already asserted that a "soul," independent of the body, emerges for

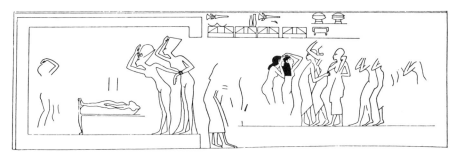

68a. The Egyptian culture strove mightily to understand and present death as a process of metamorphosis and transfiguration (cf. *26, 69–76, 90*). Even so, this attempt at comprehension was unable to exclude the experience of human powerlessness in the face of the phenomenon of death (cf. *428*). That experience is movingly expressed in the picture of Akhenaton's dead daughter. The anguish of the grief-stricken father is betrayed by the hand grasping the queen's arm.

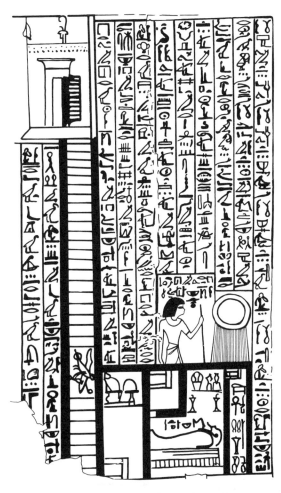

70. ". . . *you* have rescued me from the depths of the nether world" (Ps 86:13 NAB).
". . . [the dead] will never more see the light" (Ps 49:19b; cf. 58:8).

the deceased "out of the effluences of his flesh." The soul cares for the dead body. It can leave the grave-shaft; it has abundance on earth and provides the corpse, which remains in the depths, with every good thing.[4]

A second characteristic, closely related to the "depths," is impenetrable *darkness*. Occasionally the psalms use the plural to express the intensity of the gloom which prevails in the grave and in the realm of the dead (Pss 88:6 [MT 88:7]; 143:3). Whoever has once "gone down" will never again see light (Ps 49:19). In the Book of the Dead, therefore, a whole series of chapters is concerned with enabling the release of the *ba* (the soul) into the full light of day (chaps. 3, 64, 66, 68, 69). Fig. *71* shows how the *ba*-bird leaves the grave and is fed; Fig. *72* shows how it sees the sun—something not granted to the corpse. Statues which the *ba* could enter, placed outside the tomb, also served for "seeing the sun" (Ps 58:8!).

Fig. *70* shows a statue above the burial chamber gazing upon the light of the sun. In the Theban tombs of the New Kingdom, these statues often bore little stelae which carried a greeting to the rising sun.[5] It was believed that by such magical measures the deceased could be rescued from the darkness of the grave and could be enabled further to share in the "light of life" (Ps 56:13).

In Israel, Yahweh was asked not to take away the light of the eyes prematurely (Ps 13:3; cf. 38:10). Beyond that, however, one submitted to hard fact: once a man died, there was no hope left. In this condition of utter weakness (Ps 88:4), his only desire was to be able to rest with his "fathers" (Ps 49:19), of whose good will he was certain. In death, nothing was worse than to lie exposed on the field (Pss 79:2; 63:10; *135*)—a prey to animals—or in a strange land. So long as the bones are intact, even a dead man retains a minimal existence. It is therefore a great crime to destroy the bones of an innocent man (cf. Amos 2:1). The "bones" are man's most durable part—his core, so to speak. As such, they frequently stand parallel to "strength" (Ps 31:10) or "vitality" (Ps 35:9–10); elsewhere they simply replace the personal pronoun (Pss 51:8; 53:5). In Phoenician and Hebrew funerary inscriptions, the deceased asks, sometimes imploringly, sometimes threateningly, that his bones be left undisturbed.

With the exception of the bones, man is left to return to the *dust* from which he came (Pss 90:3; 104:29). The dying go down into the dust (Ps 22:29). Indeed, the suppliant of Ps 22, describing how his strength melts (vv. 14–15), already lies in the "dust of death," even before he is actually dead (v. 15c; cf. Ps 44:25).[6] The expression *šḥt* apparently connotes not only the pit (from *šwḥ*), but also decay.[7] Ps 30:9, for example, apparently requires this interpretation when its suppliant argues with Yahweh: "What profit is there . . . if I go down to decay [RSV: "to the Pit"]? Will the dust praise thee? Will it tell of thy faithfulness?" (cf. also Ps 55:24 MT: "the pit of decay" [RSV: 55:23: "the lowest Pit"]).

While individual psalmists expected Yahweh to save them from Sheol and not to let them (prematurely?) "see corruption" (Pss 16:10; 49:10 MT [RSV: Pss 16:10; 49:9: "see the Pit"]), in Egypt one relied on mummification *(74)*. This constituted a complicated process requiring over two months' time. First of all, the brain was drawn out through the nostrils by means of an iron hook.[8] The man wearing the Anubis mask (upper half of Fig. *74*) appears to be readying himself for this task. Next, the viscera were removed and the corpse was laid in natron powder (not lye). After sixty days, it was washed (lower left of Fig. *74*), then treated with coniferous resins (especially of cedar) and wrapped (lower right). This process was further reinforced by magical means. Two chapters of the Book of the Dead contain sayings intended "to prevent the decomposition of the corpse in the underworld" (chaps. 45 and 154). As is frequently the case in the Book of the Dead, in these chapters magical formulae, which of their own

71. "Because *you* will not abandon my soul to the nether world" (Ps 16:10 NAB).

72. "For you have rescued me from death, . . . that I may walk before God in the light of the living" (Ps 56:14 NAB [cf. Ps 56:13 RSV]; cf. Pss 13:3; 38:10; 49:19; 58:8).

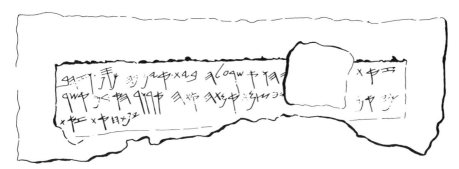

73. Translation of the inscription: "¹This is the (grave of . . .) JHW, the steward. Here is no silver and gold, ²(for) only (his bones) and the bones of his slaves are with him. Cursed be the man who ³opens *this*" (*KAI*, no. 191).

power effect the desired result, alternate with prayers, which appeal to a god. Here the god invoked is Osiris, lord of the realm of the dead:

> Hail to you, Osiris, my divine father,
> may my body not fall victim to the worms!
> Rescue me from this danger! Save me, as you saved yourself!
> May every decay be unknown to me after my death!"

In the midst of the prayer, however, the suppliant, by virtue of magical identification, appears again as Osiris.

In addition to the depth, darkness, decay, and dust, *silence* was designated as a further characteristic of the world of the grave: "If the LORD had not been my help, I [RSV: "my soul"] would soon have dwelt in the land of silence" (Ps 94:17). The dying go down into "si-

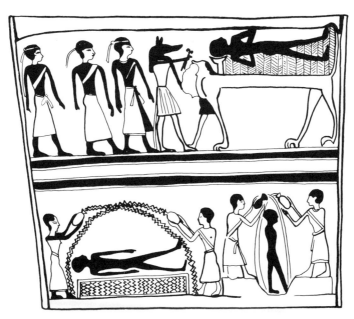

74. ". . . *you* will not . . . suffer your faithful one to suffer corruption" (Ps 16:10 NAB; cf. Ps 55:23).

"What does it profit you if I go down to decay? Would the dust praise you? Would it proclaim your faithfulness?" (Ps 30:10 MT [author's translation]; cf. Ps 30:9 RSV).

75. The dead are those ". . . that go down into silence" (Ps 115:17).

"If the LORD had not been my help, my soul would soon have dwelt in the land of silence" (Ps 94:17).

lence" (Ps 115:17). This has a very precise meaning in the psalms. It represents the antithesis of the praise of God: "The dead do not praise the LORD. . . . But we will bless the LORD" (Ps 115:17a, 18a). "Thou hast loosed my sackcloth and girded me with gladness, that glory [life fully regained] may praise thee and not be silent (Ps 30:11–12 RSVm)." In the face of death, the psalmist turns to Yahweh, and he is so fixed on Yahweh that life itself seems to consist of the praise of Yahweh, who created life and enables it.

The strong creaturely feeling which underlies this attitude is foreign to the Egyptian "mouth-opening ritual." It originally served the purpose of animating statues, but by the third century B.C. it was applied also to the animation of mummies. As its name indicates, the ritual revolved around the opening of the mouth (and also the eyes) of the deceased.[10] No doubt the mouth originally

76. The realm of the dead is the "land of forgetfulness" (Ps 88:12). The grave-stele is among the measures the Egyptians directed against forgetfulness.

". . . [those] that lie in the grave, . . . thou [God] dost remember no more, for they are cut off from thy hand" (Ps 88:5).

". . . I have passed out of mind like one who is dead" (Ps 31:12).

". . . in death there is no remembrance of thee [God]; in Sheol who can give thee praise?" (Ps 6:5).

played the central role as the organ of food intake (the ritual itself says nothing about it). In chapters 22 and 23 of the Book of the Dead, however, the ability to speak is mentioned in sayings intended to restore the "power of the mouth." In these texts, concern is certainly not with the ability to praise, but rather with the ability "to give utterance to the magical sayings in the presence of the princes of the world beyond." Wearing the mask of the funereal god Anubis, a priest opens the mummy's mouth with an adze (cf. also 76). The goddesses Isis and Nephthys stand protectively at the feet and head of the deceased. It is not certain which goddess is Isis and which is Nephthys because the usual attributes are absent. One holds a vessel with fragrant oil, the other holds the sign of life.

The silence of the world of the dead, where weakness and darkness rule, is the consequence of Yahweh's remoteness from it. The dead are cut off from his powerful arm. He remembers them no more (Ps 88:5b).

The dead are the forgotten (Ps 31:12). The realm of the dead is the land of *forgetfulness* (Ps 88:12). The dead no longer experience anything—a fact which bears constant repetition (Ps 6:5). When an ancient Israelite felt wretched and weak, he was sooner or later seized by the conviction that Yahweh had abandoned and forgotten him (Pss 13:1; 22:1; 42:9). That meant, sooner or later, certain death. In Egypt, the forgottenness and the forgetting of the dead was as keenly felt as it was in Israel. The Book of the Dead contains two chapters "Of restoring the memory of the deceased by magical means" (chaps. 25 and 90). Chapter 25 expresses the wish:

May the memory of my name always
    remain with me
when I dwell there in the night,
walled in by the fiery walls of the
    underworld.

From the most ancient times in Egypt, stelae erected beside the graves further assisted the recollection of the dead.

Originally, they bore only the name and title of the deceased. Later, biographical data, prayers, and pictorial representations were added. These showed the deceased how he should worship Osiris, lord of the realm of the dead. In Israel and Egypt alike, death was viewed as a state of weakness, as surrender to the realm of the depths, of darkness, of decay and silence. The means of facing this phenomenon, however, were entirely different.

b. Prison, Cistern and Pitfall

In the psalms, in wisdom literature, and quite generally in the OT and the ancient Near East there prevailed a strong preference for clear-cut standards—for seeing things in black and white. This tendency manifested itself in the administration of justice (76a), as well as in other areas. There was an inclination to consider the guilty party to be completely evil. Compassion for him was entirely out of place because he had offended not only against man, but against God (Ps 107:10–16). The manner in which prisoners were treated was correspondingly severe.

It is apparent from a number of documents that empty cisterns were not infrequently used as prisons (Exod 12:29; Isa 24:22; Zech 9:11; Lam 3:53). The same appears to have been the case in Egypt.[11] The use of *bôr* in Gen 40:15 and 41:14 indicates that the actual prisons, where captives were left to rot (cf. Gen 41:14), were holes as dark as cisterns (cf. Ps 107:10, 16). In addition, prisoners were often bound by iron fetters on the hands, neck, or feet (Pss 105:18; 107:10; 77, 134). Under such conditions, escape from misery was inconceivable.

The most famous men imprisoned in cisterns are Joseph "the Egyptian" (Gen 37:20–29; 40:15; 41:14) and Jeremiah (Jer 37:16; 38 pass.): "So they took Jeremiah and cast him into the cistern of Malchiah, the King's son, which was in the court of the guard, letting Jeremiah down by ropes. And there was no water in the cistern, but only mire, and Jeremiah sank in the mire" (Jer 38:6). In

76a. A rare pictorial account of a trial. The four scenes show, from left to right: (1) Four seated men (an additional four to six are broken off), designated by the accompanying text as a "court of justice" (qnbt sḏmiw). (2) The clerk, who records the testimony of a witness. A servant of the court obliges the witness to bow profoundly. (3) The splendidly attired winner of the proceedings, lifting his hand in greeting. He is accompanied by three men. As a sign of joy, the second attendant holds in his hand a cluster of plants. (4) A servant of the court striking (or driving away?) the ill-clad losers. The one partially recognizable figure of the group holds his hands before his face in lamentation. Like the psalms, the relief depicts a clear-cut separation between the innocent (ṣdyq) and the guilty (rš').

Ps 40:2 also, the miry bog into which the supplicant has sunk (cf. Ps 69:2) is parallel to the cistern. Authorship of this psalm and others similar to it (Ps 88) need not necessarily be attributed to Jeremiah. Cisterns frequently served as prisons, and one need not think of actual cisterns in every case where there is mention of miry darkness.

The psalms refer four times to the *dying* as those who go down to the pit, or more precisely, the cistern (ywrdy bwr). Sheol (Pss 30:3; 88:3) and "realm of the dead" (mwt) (Isa 38:18) frequently stand parallel or in close proximity to bôr. bôr in this context has been construed, probably correctly, as the entrance to Sheol. This is not at variance with the fact that in specific passages, such as Isa 14:19,[12] bôr denotes the grave.[13] Indeed, the grave can also be understood as an entrance to Sheol (cf. 33). As is demonstrated by a comparison of Figs 64–68 and 78–79, a cistern is quite similar in appearance to a grave. The fundamental differences are as follows. Firstly, the cistern, as distinct from the cave-tomb, has no lateral access; rather it drops precipitously from above, like a shaft-tomb. No one could extricate himself from such a cistern. Secondly, cisterns, in accordance with their purpose, are usually designed in

77. "His feet were hurt in fetters, his neck was put in a collar of iron" (Ps 105:18; cf. 134).

"Some sat in darkness and gloom, prisoners in affliction and in irons" (Ps 107:10).

such a way that rain water flows into them and remains there. Seepage is prevented by means of a lime plaster. Because a great deal of dust and earth naturally enters the cistern along with the water, the cistern floor is generally covered with sediment. The depth of sediment depends on the length of time since the last cleaning.

This concrete phenomenon becomes in the psalms a symbol of that conception of Sheol which combines Sheol with the Tehom. Sinking into the water has a more dramatic character than being carried to the grave. The Israelite had daily opportunity to observe the sinking of the leather bucket *(dly)* *(80;* cf. Num 24:7; Isa 40:15) into the mouth of the cistern and the return of the bucket to the light of day. To the suppliant of Ps 30, his deliverance seems like being drawn up *(dlh,* v. 2 MT [v. 1 RSV]) out of a cistern (cf. v. 3 RSV; v. 4 MT).

In Ps 40, the suppliant speaks of the roaring *(š'wn,* v. 3 MT [v. 2 RSVm: "tumult"])* which he heard in the cistern. This may pertain less to any real cistern than to cistern become symbol for the world of the dead and the realm of the floods of Chaos (cf. *š'wn* in Ps 65:8 MT; 65:7 RSV). The same holds true when there is reference to surging waves (Ps 88:6–7; cf. 42:6–7) and floods (Ps 69:2, 15). The cistern as symbol merges with the symbol of the Chaos dragon, which seeks to drown the suppliant in its masses of water and mire and to enclose him

78. In Hebrew, the precise meaning of *bôr* is "cistern" (see illustration). Its similarity to the grave *(66–68)* explains the application of the term to the realm of the dead. In individual psalms, dying can be described by analogy to sinking into a cistern (cf. Pss 28:1; 30:3; 88:4).

"He brought me also out of the horrible pit [cistern], out of the mire and clay" (Ps 40:2 BCP).

in its monstrous maw (Ps 69:14–15; *81;* cf. *43–45*).

In Egypt too, the realm of the dead can be portrayed as a great-mouthed monster *(82)*. With the aid of magic, death was reduced in Egypt to a passage which did not destroy man, but rather transfigured him. From the end of the third millennium (First Interim Period), however, there is evidence to support a conception of judgment of the deceased,[14] in which his worthiness for transfiguration is examined *(83)*. The heart of the deceased (outer right), as the center of his thought and action, is weighed by Anubis against Maat (world order, truth, justice; cf. *32*).[15] Thoth, the

79. "Save me, O God! For the waters have come up to my neck. I sink in deep mire, where there is no foothold; I have come into

deep waters, and the flood sweeps over me" (Ps 69:1–2).

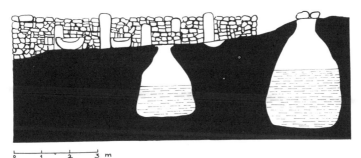

80. "I will extol thee, O LORD, for thou hast drawn me up [like a bucket]" (Ps 30:1).

81. "Let not the flood sweep over me, or the deep swallow me up, or the pit close its mouth over me" (Ps 69:15; cf. Jer 51:34).

fession of sins ("I have not. . .") is intended to help the deceased pass unmolested by the judge of the dead.

Israel, on the other hand, knew nothing of manipulative measures for escaping the miry, dark, disintegrative power of the realm of the dead (Ps 18:4–5). Only Yahweh, the Rock (Pss 18:2; 28:1), is able to provide a sure foundation (Ps 40:2).

In addition to grave and cistern, *šaḥat* occasionally appears as the place to which the dead "go down" (Pss 30:9; 55:23; Job 33:24). Whatever its etymology, *šaḥat* means in a number of passages the deliberately dug pitfall (Pss 7:15; 9:15; 35:7; 94:13). In Ezek 19:4, 8, a young lion is caught in one. *šaḥat* as

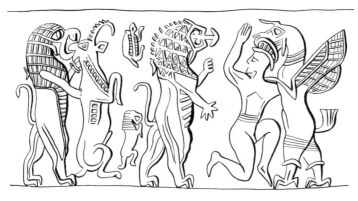

divine scribe (with the ibis head), reports to Osiris, judge of the dead and lord of "eternity" (outer left). The crocodile-headed monster waits at the feet of Osiris to devour the dead who have not satisfied Maat. Thus it is the lot of the wicked to be swallowed up by the Chaos monster. In Egypt, this second death was consistently represented by the devouring Chaos monster. To be sure, hardly anyone ran the risk of becoming his prey, for the ethical gravity of the judgment of the dead was diluted by all kinds of magical manipulations. Thus the deceased in Fig. 83 (outer right), for example, wears a heart amulet, which is supposed to impart the correct weight to his heart at its weighing. Chapter 125 of the Book of the Dead, with its negative con-

pitfall stands parallel to net (*ršt;* Pss 9:16 MT [9:15 RSV]; 35:7). However, *bôr,* the cistern which sometimes functions as a pitfall,[16] appears once in the same position (Ps 7:15). In Ps 5:9, the mouth of the slanderer is described as an "open sepulchre." That means it is a place "which continually takes up into itself new dead."[17] Cistern, prison, and pitfall are well suited in form to entrap and swallow up every living thing (cf. Belial, "the devourer," in Ps 18:5 MT [RSV Ps 18:4: "perdition"]). On the basis of their external form, all three are associated with the grave.

In any given psalm of lament, it is generally futile to inquire whether the suppliant, as a sick, unclean man, dwelt in a cave-tomb outside the village;

82. "Therefore the nether world enlarges its throat and opens its maw without limit" (Isa 5:14 NAB; cf. Ps 73:9).

"The rivulets of the devourer terrify me" (Ps 18:4 MT [author's translation; cf. Ps 18:5 RSV]; cf. N. J. Tromp, *Primitive Conceptions of Death,* pp. 125–28).

whether he was imprisoned in a cistern; or whether everything is to be understood symbolically. The realm of the dead, in all its many, similar forms, confronted the Israelite in the midst of his everyday world. The realm of the dead was truly and really manifested in these realities, yet at the same time transcended them. Even these realities could function only as ciphers for the narrowness and lostness which beset the Israelite at all times and in all places, pressing him toward Yahweh who alone could furnish sure support in the face of such deadly perils.

c. Torrent and Sea

The power of the realm of the dead is experienced not only in the depth and darkness of graves, cisterns, prisons, and pitfalls, but also (as has been shown in chapter 1) in the mighty waters which rush along the surface of the earth (cf. *42*) or storm against the mainland. The inhabitants of Palestine had special opportunity—lacking in Mesopotamia and Egypt—to experience the destructive power of the proud floods of Chaos: the numerous dry wadis can in the space of a single hour become engorged with water. The rain itself often falls somewhere in the mountains or far out in the desert. The waters gather in the dry beds; then suddenly, perhaps even under a fair sky, the flood appears in a place remote from the area of precipitation and carries off with it both man and beast (cf. Pss 124:4–5; 126:4; Job 6:15–17; Sir 40:13). On 8 April 1963, a sweeping torrent (three meters deep) filled the canyon (1.5 km. long) which leads into Petra *(Plate II),* killing twenty-two pilgrims on their way to the

83. The "devourer of the dead" lies in wait for the heart of the evil-doer, which has been found too light in the balance. In Egypt, the first death is a passage into the radiant Beyond. Consequently, this picture represents the "second death" (Rev 2:11; 20:6, 14; 21:8) at the hands of the Chaos monster (on the weighing of man, cf. Ps 62:9). In Egypt, as in Israel, the *heart* is the seat of thought and volition, and is therefore a decisive factor in judging a man.

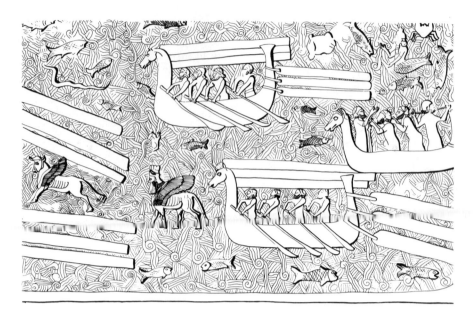

84. "Some went down to the sea in ships, doing business on the great waters; they saw the deeds of the LORD, his wondrous works in the deep" (Ps 107:23–24).

"Yonder is the sea, great and wide, which teems with things innumerable, living things both small and great" (Ps 104:25).

Nabatean capital with the Abbé J. Steinmann.

The classic manifestation of the Chaos waters is, however, the sea (cf. chap. 1.3). Since man's primary environment is the land, navigation of the "deadly salt-flood" was regarded in antiquity as inherently dangerous. This was particularly the case among the Israelites, as they were a people who had come out from the steppes into the arable land, preserving strong ties to their past. Moreover, they had no major harbor at their disposal. Due to the flimsy construction of ships (84–86), grievous disasters at sea were in fact not uncommon (Pss 48:7; 107:23–29; Jonah 1:3–16; Acts 27).

To the Israelites, ships are something as strange and awe-inspiring as the various, fabulous sea beasts (Pss 104:25–26; 8:8). The bows of ships, fashioned as animal heads (84) suggested an association between the two.

Fig. 84 depicts shipment of wood

85. ". . . I will bring them back from the depths of the sea" (Ps 68:22b).

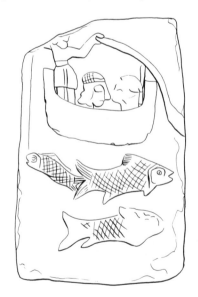

along the Phoenician coast. The waves, which run irregularly in all directions and are liberally interspersed with whirlpools, indicate the uncertainty which prevails upon the vast waters. All sorts of unexpected, fabulous creatures emerge between the fish, turtles, and prawns: a man with the body of a fish, a bull-man with wings, and a winged bull. They were as real to the ancient Near East as the zoologically certifiable fish and prawns. They concretize the uncertainty and anxiety evoked by the mysterious sea, as well as the confidence mustered against it. The latter is evident, for example, in the bull with a man's head, a tutelary genius which usually watches over palace and temple entrances (cf. *Plate VIII*).

When the Israelite horror in the face of the mythical Chaos-power receded, the sea and its denizens were numbered among the most marvelous works of God. Sir 43:24–25, sounding like an echo of Ps 104:25, describes the sea in almost hymnic tones:

> Those who sail the sea tell of its dangers,
> and we marvel at what we hear.
> For in it are strange and marvelous works
> [of God], all kinds of living things, and
> huge creatures of the sea.

Almost nowhere was creaturely feeling more strongly experienced than in this dreadful realm. Only with difficulty could it be conceived as Yahweh's work. One never felt quite secure on the water *(85)*, and the deity was thanked when one had again reached solid ground *(86)*.

86. "He made the storm be still, and the waves of the sea were hushed. Then they were glad because they had quiet, and he [God] brought them to their desired haven" (Ps 107:29–30).

Seven Canaanite ships have just put in at an Egyptian harbor. Two similar vessels, shown in larger scale, are still on the high sea. On the bow of the vessel in the foreground stands its pilot. Above him, a bird proclaims the nearness of the mainland. A thank offering for the happy conclusion of the voyage is apparently being made in the area immediately forward of the mast (cf. *162, 198–99*, and Jon 1:16). The men in the crow's nest atop the mast lift their hands in worship (cf. *422*). Similar gestures are shown, however, on the two ships which have already docked.

Because these gestures are all made in the same direction and are continued even on the land, there is some question whether the lifting up of hands and the burning of incense on the ships is in fact connected with a thank offering. It may rather be a gesture of homage before the Egyptian king or his representative. The Canaanite cities sometimes greeted the triumphant Pharaoh with incense, upraised hands, and the offering of their children (cf. uppermost row, right; cf. *132a* and *199*). The ships in this picture are obviously engaged in bringing tribute (cf. *408–10*). Apparently some petty trading of goods pilfered from the tribute is being conducted with the Egyptian dealers crouched in their stalls (cf. the description of L. Klebs, *Die Reliefs und Malereien des Neuen Reiches*, pp. 231–33).

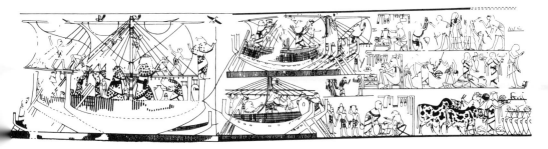

87. "O God, . . . my soul thirsts for thee; my flesh faints for thee, as in a dry and weary land where no water is" (Ps 63:1).

d. The Desert

Because the desert could not yet be mastered with fast, safe means of transportation, it, like the sea, was not a place of romantic associations, but rather a region of danger and death.

In the Near East, where there is only a limited amount of arable land, the inhabitants tended to locate necropoleis in the desert beyond the arable land. Often the desert lies immediately "on the doorstep." Two date palms and a sycamore, the last trees of the fruitful land, are seen at the right in Fig. 87. Beneath them appear an offering-table and a basin with water for ablutions. To the left, already within the scope of the stony, red desert, are three tombs. A grieving woman sits before them. The zone of transition between arable land and des-

ert is the domain of jackals and other scavengers. Dying animals were thrown to them for disposal (cf. Ps 44:19; Jer 9:11; Isa 13:22; 34:13; Ps 63:10). The edges of the desert are characterized by *death*.

Rebels and asocial elements (Ps 68:6c) roam the desert and take the fast-moving caravans by surprise. Roads are very poorly marked, if at all. Lack of roads is a characteristic common to the desert (Ps 107:4,7; cf. 142:6), the sea (Ps 77:19), and the darkness (Job 12:24–25). Perhaps for that reason, Jeremiah describes the desert not only as a land of pits and drought, where no man dwells, but also as a land of darkness (Jer 2:6, 31). He may, however, have in mind the black basalt deserts of Transjordan.

If one loses one's way, as is quite possible given the bad road conditions, one is delivered up to *hunger and thirst* (Ps 107:5; 63:1). Within a very short time, a man is exhausted to the point of death (Ps 61:2; 142:3). The prostrate man is as lonely and insignificant as a desert bird (Ps 102:6). Hunger is sometimes depicted as a demonic being (Ps 105:16). In Ps 33:19, it stands parallel to the

88. "Some wandered in desert wastes, finding no way to a city to dwell in; hungry and thirsty, their soul fainted within them" (Ps 107:4–5).

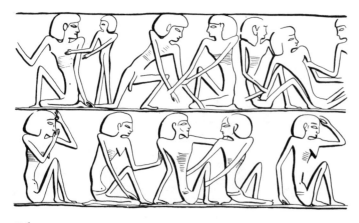

89. As in Fig. 87, the desert floor is strewn with rocks. Here and there appears a little, dry shrub. In this illustration, the strangeness and danger of the desert are concretized in all sorts of fabulous creatures (cf. the sea creatures of Fig. 84).

realm of the dead. The Egyptian relief in Fig. 88 shows starving nomads, reduced by hunger to skin and bones. Even today, many inhabitants of the Near Eastern deserts are chronically undernourished. As Fig. 88 demonstrates, the complete absence of the already scanty rainfalls would spell catastrophe were it not for help from outside. The effect of famine is drastically illustrated, not just by the emaciated bodies, but also by the woman at the lower left: with her left hand she picks vermin from her hair, conveying them to her mouth with her right. Graves, cisterns, prisons, pitfalls, ravines with suddenly descending waters, seas churned up by storm, and trackless, parched deserts are regions from which man can indeed be rescued by Yahweh's encompassing power. But Yahweh is only marginally present in these regions. They can therefore serve to represent the misery which afflicts man in any godforsaken situation.

e. The Night

Realms bordering on the world of the dead are defined not only by space, but also by time. To be sure, disaster and death can befall a man by day, but their primary sphere remains the night and darkness. At night, sickness and every evil seem far worse than they do by day. The poets of the psalms of lamentation relate how, amid fears and groans, they have lain awake all the night long (Pss 6:6; 30:5; 77:6). The world is, as it were, lost, and the suppliant is alone with his immeasurably increasing pain. At night too, scavengers come out of their lairs and, howling, seek their spoils (Ps 104:20). In the darkness, the wicked fall upon their innocent victims (Ps 11:2). Fig. 90 shows the close linkage of darkness and death. The composite figure is made up of two pairs of human legs, the body of a serpent with the head of a man, a sniffing jackal's head as tail (jackal = beast of the necropoleis; cf. 33), and a pair of vulture's wings. The broken cord about its neck suggests the wildness of this creature which stalks the night (signified by countless stars). The sun, which

90. Annotation underneath the neck of the beast: "Death, the great god, who made gods and men."

has set (or the moon?), appears beneath the serpent-body. The two vulture-wings hold the nascent sun. To the right of the creature appears the curious legend: "Death, the great god who made gods and men." The dual character of the god at first seems rather strange. It may be explained by his identification with the primeval waters of Chaos (cf. the serpent's body with Figs. 38–41 and 55), which signify on the one hand darkness and death, on the other the source of all life.

It is worthy of note that gods and men are fundamentally subject to the same process of creation. That is not the case in Israel. God stands outside all becoming. Death is not a way to life; it has no regenerative power. In Israel, what is said of death and its kingdom (weakness, darkness, decay, oblivion) remains within the bounds of ordinary verification. Consequently, the statements made concerning death in Ps 88, for example, affect us much more directly than the picture-world of the Egyptian Book of the Dead, which is difficult for us to decipher.

2. THE ENEMIES OF THE INDIVIDUAL

Man of the ancient Near East, like man throughout the ages, had his own entirely personal enemies. There is reference to enemies in the most diverse documents (letters, wisdom writings, prayers, and similar documents). These references create the impression that under the cramped housing conditions and close communal ties which prevailed in the period, enmities were rather more frequent and intense than is the case with us.[18] Besides the entirely private enemy (enmity based on rivalry) arising out of some specific personal affair (dispute over an inheritance, over a woman, over an honorary post, etc.), every community knows a type of enemy which represents, as it were, the antipole to what the community recognizes as good and desirable and continuously threatens the same (e.g., to the Communists, the capitalists, and vice versa). Even in purely private enmities, projection plays a significant role, as in the case in which someone is my enemy because I am hostile toward him (subjective), and not only because he is hostile toward me (objective). This is all the more strongly the case with that type of enemy which constitutes the antipole to one's own (good) world. Enemies of this sort are by their very nature carriers of all that is subversive and evil. The view which a particular group or culture holds of its enemies is crucial to an understanding of that group or culture.

a. Demons and Offenders

In the polytheism of Mesopotamia and Egypt, the powers of both good and evil are found in the worlds above and below. The gulf between god and man is generally greater in Mesopotamia than in Egypt, where it is bridged by the divine king (cf. chap. 5).

As is shown in the Gilgamesh epic, there exists no hope at all for man to share in the eternal, blessed life of the gods. The highest to which he can attain is a happy, secure life on this earth. However, this highest good is constantly threatened by a host of baleful powers (90a–94). Fig. 91 shows a small bronze tablet; Plate III shows the impression of a cylinder seal. Both served as amulets against these hostile powers. The popu-

90a. ". . . my body wasted away through my groaning all day long. For day and night thy hand was heavy upon me" (Ps 32:3–4; cf. 38:3; 39:11).

With his hands, a winged demon presses down upon two helpless, naked creatures, while trampling upon a third with his feet, which are those of a bird of prey (cf. 92, Plate IV). His probable manifestations are various kinds of sicknesses. An attendant of the sun god is hauling one of the demon's helpers before the lord Shamash (outer right) (cf. 53). This cylinder seal attributes sickness and healing to two distinctive powers. In the OT, however, both sickness and healing are attributed to Yahweh. In the psalms, it is Yahweh who apportions sickness or health according to the circumstances of man's religious-ethical conduct. Man is not the plaything of various competing powers. Therefore man himself bears the primary responsibility both for his own health and for the healthy condition of the world, and he bears this responsibility before a God who requires righteousness.

larity of such small tablets is demonstrated by the fact that approximately sixty of them have been found to date, some preserved entire, some only in part.[19]

The doglike head of a composite creature peers out from the reverse of the tablet in Fig. 92. The creature is endowed with two pairs of wings, a scaly body, a phallus and a tail (both ending in serpent heads), and the feet of a bird of prey. A quite similar figure is seen at the lower left of the obverse (91). Indeed, it appears there to be driving away the (female) chief demon, Lamashtu. The creature of Fig. 93 also had a protective function. The ring on its head indicates that it was used as a pendant. It bears on

the back of its wings the inscription: "I am Pazuzu, the son of Chanpa; the king of the evil spirits of the air, who bursts forth in might from the mountains and goes forth raging; I am he."[20] Pazuzu, the "running dog, . . . makes yellow the body of man, makes his face yellow and black, makes black even the root of his tongue."[21] Properly speaking, Pazuzu is an evil demon who manifests himself in the hot, oppressive, southwest wind which blows out of the Arabian desert bearing all kinds of sickness in its train.

The wings of the wind are as familiar in the psalms (Pss 18:10; 104:3; cf. 27) as the searing wind which withers both man and vegetation (Pss 6:2; 102:3–4, 11) within the space of a few hours (Ps 103:16; cf. 90:5–6). In the psalms, however, this wind is not an independent entity, but rather a manifestation of Yahweh's judgment (Pss 11:6; 18:10; 83:15) or an image for the machinations of the wicked (Ps 55:8). In Mesopotamia, on the other hand, the hot desert wind is understood as a manifestation of the king of the evil spirits of the air. His image was hung about the neck of the sick in order to ward off the attacking Pazuzu by sudden confrontation with his own image.

As is indicated in the scene at the lower left of Fig. 91, the Pazuzu-figure wards off not only Pazuzu, but also other demons, such as Lamashtu (earlier Labartu). The latter is more clearly seen in Fig. 94. Her head resembles that of a lion, her body that of a woman. At one breast she suckles a dog, at the other a pig; in each hand she holds a two-headed serpent. In the psalms, as we shall see, the wicked and the godless are likened to lion, dog, serpent, and pig—animals considered in the ancient Near East to be particularly susceptible to demons.

In Fig. 91, Lamashtu is put to flight by Pazuzu. Lamashtu is shown in a boat, kneeling on a horselike animal (an ass?). The boat is to convey her through the marshy thicket of reeds (cf. the two plants to the right of the boat) from which she has come. Lamashtu is a fever-demon who attacks mothers in

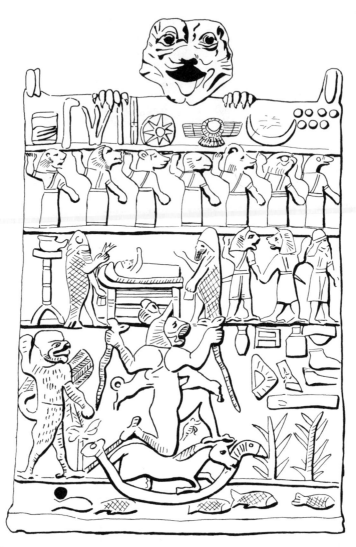

91. The sick man in his bed: "I am weary with my moaning; every night I flood my bed with tears; I drench my couch with my weeping" (Ps 6:6).

"Gladden the soul of thy servant, for to thee, O Lord, do I lift up my soul" (Ps 86:4).

"I call for help by day; I cry out in the night before thee. . . . For my soul is full of troubles, and my life draws near to Sheol. . . . I am a man who has no strength" (Ps 88:1, 3–4).

childbirth and newborn infants. She can, however, endanger anyone. In Fig. 91, she is about to leave a bearded man who lies on his bed, one hand extended in entreaty toward heaven. *Plate III* shows essentially the same scene. The man there lies on a mattress without bedstead, as was usual. He prays to the three great gods Shamash (sun), Sin (moon), and Ishtar (star).

The psalms attribute the sick man's fever, parched mouth, and thirst (Pss 6:2; 38:7; 69:21; 102:3–4, 11) not to one or more demons, but to Yahweh's blazing wrath (*ḥmh*) (Pss 6:1; 38:1–3; 102:10), which burns like fire (Ps 89:46). In at least some of the texts, the suppliant has provoked the divine wrath by his own sins (Pss 38:3, 5: 41:4).

Offenses against the deity also play a

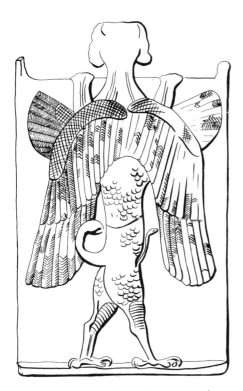

obviously sprinkling something over the sick man (cf. Ps 51:7: "Purge me with hyssop, and I shall be clean"). To his left is an oil lamp *(Plate XIV)* set on a tall stand. The lamp is a symbol of the fire god Nusku (cf. Pss 18:28; 27:1; 43:3), whose light drives away the lurking demons (cf. *53–55*). To the right of Lamashtu are a number of objects used in exorcism. Some of them may be gifts intended to persuade Lamashtu to withdraw. To the right of the Ea priest at the sick man's feet, two lion-headed demons attack each other. This result seems to have been achieved by the display of a picture showing two fighting demons.[22] At the outer right is a god with upraised arm who appears to be fending off still more demons.

92. Israel was familiar with the hot desert wind that sweeps over the foliage "and it is gone" (Ps 103:15). In Mesopotamia, the wind was attributed to the action of a winged demon.

In the register second from the top, there appear seven (probably good) demons or seven priests with animal masks. Their function is to put to flight the seven evil spirits frequently mentioned in the texts. From left to right, they wear the heads of a panther, lion, dog (?), ram, goat, falcon, and serpent. In the topmost register are the symbols of the great gods, especially of those helpful in exorcism. From left to right are the horned cap (Anu), the ram's head on a stake (Ea), the lightning bolts (Adad), the digging-stick (Marduk), the writing implements (Nabu), the eight-beamed star (Ishtar), the winged sun (Shamash), the moon (Sin), and the seven circles (the Pleiades). The beneficial forces are thus represented in the upper registers, the harmful ones in the lower. This polarization of the world links the little bronze tablet with the illustrations of chapter 1.3, "Dualistic Features" *(42–55)*. Sooner or later, every man finds himself at the frontier between those powers which benefit life and those which are bent on its destruction. The primary spheres of the demons are tombs, cisterns, pits, and the desert.[23] From there they press forward, especially under the cover of darkness, into the "land of the living."

role in this context in Mesopotamia. In polytheism, however, these offenses are less absolutely defined, and demons can assail a man without any cause. Prophylactic measures are accordingly abundant.

A priest of Ea, recognizable by the fish costume, stands at the head and feet of the sick man *(91, middle register)*. Ea was the god of the fresh-water ocean (cf. *43*) and was considered to be particularly adept in magic. The priests hold in their hands vessels filled with purificatory water. Fig. *185*, from a holy-water font of the temple of Assur in Assur, shows priests of Ea consecrating water for purifications, even as it flows forth from the vessel of the water god. The Ea priest at the head of the bed in Fig. *91* is

The earthly life of the Egyptian seems to have been less troubled by fear of

93. Ps 91 addresses the man who trusts in Yahweh rather than in amulets of the kind pictured above: "You will not fear the terror of the *night,* nor the arrow that flies by *day,* nor the pestilence that stalks in *darkness,* nor the destruction that wastes at *noonday*" (Ps 91:5–6).

94. The head of the female demon Lamashtu resembles that of a lion. At one breast she suckles a pig, at the other a dog. It was believed that these animals were particularly susceptible to demonic possession, and that demons manifested themselves in them.

demons than that of the Mesopotamian. Mesopotamia, with its marshes, irregular and dangerous inundations, and powerful dust storms, features a rather unhealthy climate. Egypt, on the other hand, enjoys a healthy, dry desert air, and the annual inundations come regularly in amounts which benefit the land in every way. Thus the great concern of the Egyptian was not so much to maintain life in this world, which was by and large secure, but to preserve life in the next world. Here, however, it proved extremely difficult to safeguard the body, necessary for the life beyond, so that it would not be despoiled for all time, either by water or animals or grave robbers (cf. 69–76). Concern and anxiety over the corpse found concrete expression in a great many demons. In the New Kingdom especially, their number becomes boundless. There is the red-eyed demon, the blind demon, the white-toothed demon, the far-striding demon, the demon who snatches the crown of the head, the bone-breaker, and many others which threaten the deceased at every juncture. In representations they appear rather harmless, considering their dreadful names *(95).*[24] Some are quite human in form; others have the head of a lion, crocodile, serpent, or other animal. In their hands they hold long knives propped on their knees.

We know very little about Canaanite demons. A cylinder seal from Tell el-'Ajjul shows a winged demon who has attacked a man *(96).* A winged demon threatening to attack a bullock appears on a cylinder seal from Beth-Shan.[25] A similar representation appears on one of the ivories found at Megiddo *(97):* a composite creature consisting of a human head, eagle's wings, and the body of a predatory animal has fallen upon an ibex, which collapses under the assault. The posture of the composite being indicates that it is to be interpreted as a demon rather than a cherub. The picture suggests to O. Eissfeldt the demon Azazel of Lev 16,[26] to whom a goat is annually sent out into the wilderness. On

95. Egyptian demons of the world beyond. These should be viewed as hieroglyphs rather than as concrete depictions of the grisly beings described in the texts.

96. Flinders Petrie interpreted the figure on the lion as a representation of north Syria, the winged creature as the representative of Egypt, and the man on the ground, assailed by both, as "Palestine" (*Ancient Gaza IV*, pp. 4f.). More probably, the goddess on the lion is Ishtar/Astarte (cf. *191; ANEP*, nos. 470–74), who was celebrated in Egypt and Palestine as a savior-goddess (*270a;* R. Stadelmann, *Syrisch-palästinensische Gottheiten*, pp. 106–8). The man on the ground may be a sick man, vexed by a demon, to whom the goddess appears as deliverer.

the basis of Lev 16:8–10 and Fig. *97* (since the ibex inhabits barren mountains), Eissfeldt posits the existence of steppe-demons. The OT also mentions elsewhere demons who inhabit the wasteland (Deut 8:15; Isa 13:21; 30:6; 34:14). They may have been distinguished by a certain bloodthirstiness, for Ps 106:37–38 compares them to the gods of Canaan to whom children were offered in sacrifice (cf. *320*).

The small plaster tablet in Figs. *97a–b* is several centuries less ancient than Fig. *97,* but it appears to be part of the same tradition. The upper of the two demons in Fig. *97a* appears, like that of Fig. *97,* in the form of a cherub; the lower provides a grisly example of the bloodthirstiness mentioned earlier. The inscription on the tablet confirms what the iconography suggests. The inscription presents translators with a number of difficulties. There is not even agreement on its language. Some argue for Canaanite, others Phoenician. Torczyner believes it to be a "particularly pure biblical Hebrew."[27] In any case, it is in a northwest Semitic idiom, and the inscription contains an exorcism directed against demons who endanger by night the newborn and women in childbirth; or perhaps it is an exorcism of night-demons in general. The pictorial representations are intended to reinforce the protective power of the formulae.

The god swinging the axe in Fig. *97b* is to be identified, on the basis of the accompanying text, as Assur or Baal. He is intended, like the symbols of the luminous gods in Fig. *91,* to put the demons in their place. Just as in Fig. *91,* however, the representation of the dreaded demons also has apotropaic significance.

97. "The goat on which the lot fell for Azazel shall be . . . sent away into the wilderness to Azazel" (Lev 16:10). The wilderness is a domain of demons.

The upper demon (female) in Fig. 97a is called simply "the flying one." It cannot be decided with certainty whether the appellations "plundering one," "(bone-) breaker" (cf. Ps 34:20), and "Lilith" (cf. Isa 34:14 [RSV: "the night hag"]), which also appear in the text, are merely sobriquets of "the flying one" or whether they signify other demons not shown in the picture. The female wolf, jackal, or dog (the lower of the two demons in Fig. 97a), shown devouring a child, is named in the text "strangler of the lamb." Undoubtedly the newborn of every kind are meant by "lamb." The other-worldly demons of Egypt evoke no echo in the psalms. There are at least traces, however, of Canaanite demons and of the sickness-demons typical of Mesopotamia (Pss 78:49c; 91:5–6). In neither passage, to be sure, have they any independence whatsoever. In Ps 78:49c they appear as emissaries of Yahweh, descending on the Pharaoh who will not let Israel go. In Ps 91:5–6 they are denied any power over anyone who trusts in Yahweh. The "pack [*not* "terror"] of the night"[28] in Ps 91:5 is reminiscent of the horrible figures rep-

97a. "(Bone-) crusher" and "strangler of the lamb," female demons, the "terror of the night" (Ps 91:5).

97b. "He [Yahweh] keeps all his [the just man's] bones; not one of them is broken" (Ps 34:20).

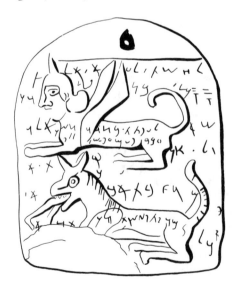

98. (Left) From the earliest times, demons have been depicted with leonine features.

99. (Right) "Do not deliver the soul of thy dove to the wild beasts" (Ps 74:19).

resented in the picture and referred to in the text of Fig. 97a. The wolf or dog of Fig. 97a calls to mind the howling, demon-possessed street dogs of Ps 59:6, 15. The "arrow that flies by day" might denote one of the sickness-bearing arrows (cf. Ps 38:2) of Reshef, the god of war and pestilence. Here the "lord of the arrows" (cf. Ps 76:3; 300–303) is depotentized to the status of a demon. deber and qeteb (Ps 91:6–7) are names of diseases. In the Canaanite sphere, the appellatives seem to have had a particularly tenacious hold in regard to the names of gods and demons.[29]

Apart from Ps 91:5–6, ordinary men, rather than malignant natural forces, appear in the psalms as enemies of the individual. The world as a whole derives from Yahweh and is good. Whatever good or evil occurs within it is brought about either by men or by Yahweh (cf. Amos 3:6). Magic is forbidden to the Israelite in his strife against his enemies. He consequently turns to Yahweh with the entire burden of his need. The suppliant accordingly attempts to demonstrate to Yahweh that his enemies are guilty (rš'ym), notoriously guilty—transgressors whom Yahweh must hate as much as does the suppliant himself. The outrageous and unscrupulous conduct of these persons supports the suppliant's belief that they live and act convinced that there is no God. This "picture of the enemy" demonstrates that the psalmists found their ideal in the preservation of Yahweh's order and in community of faith with him. The enemies, in contrast, are persons brutally and recklessly bent on riches and power. Their conduct arouses the suspicion that there is no god to judge them. The psalms depict them with almost demonic features. By and large, they take the place occupied by demons and magicians in Mesopotamian prayers.

b. Animal Comparisons

From the most ancient times, demons have been portrayed in the form of lions (94, 98; cf. also the figures second and third from the left in Fig. 95). The adversaries of the psalmists are repeatedly compared to lions (Ps 7:2).[30] Like lions, they lie in ambush (100), then suddenly fall upon the unsuspecting victim (Pss 10:9–10; 17:12; cf. 100–102). The

100. ". . . he lurks in secret like a lion in his covert . . ." (Ps 10:9a; cf. 17:12b).

101. "The hapless is crushed, sinks down, and falls by his might" (Ps 10:10).

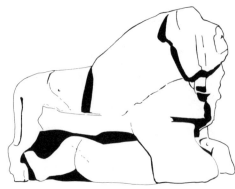

102. ". . . save me . . . lest like a lion they rend me, dragging me away, with none to rescue" (Ps 7:1–2).

mighty paws of the lion (102; cf. 98) illustrate the merciless, irresistible grasp of tyrants (Pss 7:2; 10:10); the lion's open maw denotes their dangerous, insatiable greed (Pss 17:12; 22:13–21; 58:6; 165); the lion's fearsome roaring matches their invincible pride (Pss 22:13; 35:17; 103). The lion was feared, and therefore demons were endowed with its features; but the lion was also admired, as evidenced by its appearance in the decoration of combs and seals.[31] The lion often served to represent victorious power (102–3; cf. 135). What holds true of the lion is also true of the unscrupulous rāšā' who is compared to him. On the one hand he is feared; on the other hand he is admired for his success (Ps 73:2–12).

Like the lion, the aggressive *bull* can represent the victorious ruler trampling down his enemies (104–5).[32] The bull's horns are widely used as a symbol of power in the ancient Near East (cf. Pss 75:4, 6, 10; 92:10; etc.) The Mesopotamian gods wear horned caps as a head-covering. Up to four sets of horns may be arranged on top of each other (390). Certain features of the bull, however, serve as well to illustrate the mighty powers attributed to a number of evil demons (cf. 95). Both usages should be kept in mind when the suppliant of Ps 22 (vv. 12 and 21) compares his adversaries to bulls. The wild bull (v. 21 [RSV:

103. In a bold and not infrequent metaphor, kings are portrayed as lions (102, 135, 163). In the New Kingdom in Egypt, the Pharaoh is often (less boldly) *compared* to a lion by placing the representation of a lion beside that of the triumphant king. The new symbol may be traced to the custom of certain kings (e.g., Ramses II) who went about accompanied by a tame lion (B. van de Walle, "Les rois sportifs," p. 250, n. 1).

104. "Save me . . . from the horns of the wild oxen!" (Ps 22:12).

105. "Many bulls encompass me, strong bulls of Bashan surround me" (Ps 22:12).

"ox"]), may represent an intensification of the ordinary bull (v. 12).[33]

The ambiguous nature of the lion and the bull is even more marked in the case of the *serpent*. The serpent incorporates the most manifold and contradictory significances. In Egypt it appears as protectress of Re *(55)* and of the king, who generally wears a serpent on his forehead (cf. *103*). The serpent is thus a savior-deity, (Mertseger) but also the embodiment of the primeval evil (Apophis; cf. *55*). The psalms speak most frequently of its venom (Pss 58:4; 91:13; 140:3), which makes it one of the most feared of all animals. Fig. *106* shows two men being bitten by serpents. A third stretches forth his hands in entreaty toward heaven. Since disaster seldom strikes singly, a threatening lioness appears at the right.

The ambivalence characteristic of the attitude toward the lion, the wild bull, and the serpent is generally absent with respect to the *dog*. Even so, the Egyptian king, in striking down his enemies, can be attended by a dog instead of a lion (cf. *Plate XVII*).[34] The half-wild pariah dogs, however, were undoubtedly possessed of greater affinity with dangerous demons than with triumphant rulers. Even today, they roam in packs at the outskirts of Near Eastern villages (Ps 59:6, 14). They were often considered to be possessed by demons (cf. *97a,* bottom). By night, the Babylonian Alu demon roams the streets like a dog, and the evil "seven" howl like a pack of dogs.[35] In an Egyptian sarcophagus text, the deceased implores Re-Atum to rescue him from the dog-headed demon who feeds on corpses.[36] If in any psalm the adversaries of the suppliant bear demonic features, it is in Ps 59, where they are twice compared with pariah dogs (vv. 6, 14). Ps 22 may have in mind hunting dogs rather than street dogs. The story of Sinuhe [37] attests the use of hunting dogs in Palestine at the beginning of the second millennium B.C. The representation of hunting dogs in hunting scenes from Assyria *(107)*, Syria-Palestine,[38] and Egypt *(108)* indicates how highly they were valued. Their use in war (as in *Plate XVII*) was unusual.

However differently the lion, bull, serpent, and dog (with whom the psalmist compares his adversary) were assessed, they shared the potential to endanger a man's life, and indeed, they repeatedly did so. That fact hardly needs to be emphasized with regard to the lion and the snake. As for the bull (leaving aside Figs. *104* and *105*), a Sumerian adage says: "When I had escaped the wild bull, I stood before the wild cow" (cf. Exod 21:29).[39] An Egyptian official refers in one of his reports to a grievous plague of dogs.[40] The laws of Eshnunna reckon with dogs that can bite a man so severely that he dies.[41]

The animal comparisons underscore a characteristic of the wicked and godless (*rš'ym*) which is also conspicuous in other respects: they do not want the complainant's goods and chattels; they do not want to rob him of office or of some other quantity; they seek his life and that alone (Pss 10:8; 14:4; 37:14; 94:6). We have already emphasized that the animal comparisons also illustrate the ambiguous character of the adversary: compelling and regal (lion, bull; cf. Ps 73:3–12); demonic and murderous (lion, serpent, dog.)

Strangely, the *bear* is completely absent from the animal comparisons of the

108. "Deliver . . . my only one [RSVm] from the power of the dog!" (Ps 22:20).

psalms. Elsewhere it is considered to be as dangerous as the lion (2 Kgs 2:24; Prov 17:12), and in the OT it is frequently mentioned with the lion (1 Sam 17:34–37; Prov 28:15; Isa 11:7; Hos 13:8; Amos 5:19; Lam 3:10). Bears were widespread in Syria-Palestine, and Egyptians on campaign in Syria were struck by their ferocity *(109)*.[42] The complete absence of bears in the psalms may be coincidental, but there is probably more to it than that. The psalms, more than any other book of the OT, move in a world of conception and form which is generally common to the ancient Near East. Because the bear is absent from the

106. "They have venom like the venom of a serpent, like the deaf adder that stops its ear" (Ps 58:4).

107. "Yea, dogs are round about me" (Ps 22:16; cf. *Plates XVI* and *XVII*).

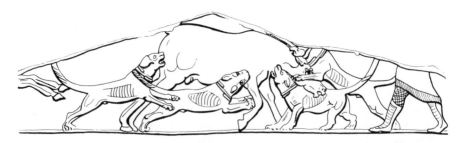

109. There is no reference to bears in the psalms. Their absence is striking, for elsewhere in the OT the bear is often mentioned, together with the lion, as a particularly dangerous animal. As the illustration indicates, the ferocity of the Syrian bear was also well known to the Egyptians.

flat river valleys of Mesopotamia and Egypt, it is also absent from their representations of demons and from their royal imagery. That may be the reason for its absence from the animal comparisons of the psalms.[43]

c. Comparisons Based on the Hunt

In the ancient Near East, hunting was practiced avidly and by many methods. Pitfalls, into which the victim falls (as into a cistern) have already been discussed (p. 72), as has hunting with dogs (pp. 87–88).

One may conjecture from the close association of net and pitfall (Pss 9:15–16; 35:7–8; 57:6) that pits were covered with camouflaged nets which entangled the prey in its fall.[44] In ancient Sumerian, the hunt was indicated by the sign ⊔⊔⊔ , designating an enclosed space. It originally meant "to surround." It is evident

from the choice of this sign that the hunt was originally conducted by entrapment in nets or pits.[45] This kind of hunting was so widespread that the Mesopotamian kings of the earliest period, who describe battle scenes as hunting scenes, represent the capture of enemies as a successful cast of the hunting net. Eannatum reports of a military success against the inhabitants of Umma: "Over the people of Umma, I, Eannatum, threw the net of the god Enlil." In the illustration which accompanies the text (110), Ningirsu, the city god of Lagash, is identified with Enlil as he holds a huge net in his left hand.[46] The enemies floundering in the net are doomed to death. Their fate is indicated by the lion-headed bird of death, Imdugud, who closes the net (cf. 164), and by the mace with which the god smites his enemies trapped inside the net. On the basis of this picture, J. G. Heintz has attempted to link ḥrm, "net" and ḥrm, "ban."[47]

In Fig. 111, the absolute mastery of the gods and of Pharaoh is shown by the net which they draw over everything that lives on the earth (the band bulged at either end; cf. 20): the net encloses fish and fowl, wild and domestic animals (gazelles and stags; bulls), and men.[48]

When the psalms refer to the hunt, it is hunting carried out by means of pits, traps, nets, and snares. In open battle with the javelin or in the chase there is an element of contest between man and beast. But in other methods of hunting, man's cunning comes to the fore. Against it the animal has no chance of survival. It is a weapon of the gods (110 and 111).

Nets and snares play a major role in magic (Ezek 13:17–21 [RSV: "veils"; "bands"]).[49] Wherever they are evident, they spread uncertainty, anxiety, and sudden, inescapable disaster. Again and again, the psalms insist that the suppliant's adversaries have *concealed* pitfalls, snares, and drawnets (Pss 9:15; 31:4; 35:7–8; 64:5; 140:5; 142:3).

môqēš and *paḥ* primarily denote the trap used for catching birds (112). The

110. Yahweh concerning Zedekiah: "I will spread my net over him, and he shall be taken in my snare . . . for the treason he has committed against me" (Ezek 17:20; cf. 12:13; 19:8; 32:3; Hos 7:12; Job 19:6).

The net is a symbol of absolute sovereignty and control, and of ultimate world dominion (cf. *SAHG,* p. 230; H. Prinz, *Altorientalische Symbolik,* p. 135).

111. "For thou [God] makest men like the fish of the sea, like crawling things that have no ruler. . . . He [Necho? Nebuchadnezzar?] drags them out with his net, he gathers them in his seine; so he rejoices and exults" (Hab 1:14–15).

In these words, Habukkuk describes the tyranny of Pharaoh Necho, who ruled over Syria-Palestine for the brief period of 609–606 B.C. (F. Horst, "Habakkuk," p. 168); or perhaps the reference is to another tyrant, Nebuchadnezzar, who superseded Necho in dominion over Syria-Palestine (K. Elliger, *Das Buch der zwölf Kleinen Propheten,* vol. 2, p. 24).

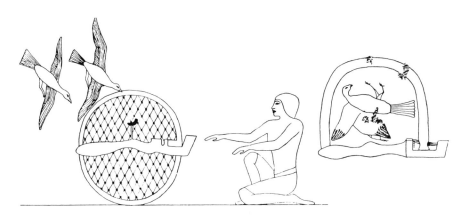

112. "Let their own table before them become a snare, let their sacrificial feasts be a trap" (Ps 69:22).

For "table" as an outspread mat, cf. Fig. 76.

"Keep me from the [arms of] the trap which they have laid for me" (Ps 141:9).

"Does a snare spring up from the ground, when it has taken nothing?" (Amos 3:5b).

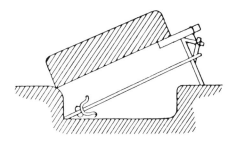

113. Modern trap from Palestine (pit and rock).

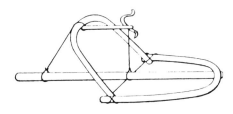

114. Modern trap from Palestine (wooden frame with net).

open trap is seen at the left; at the right, one is shown closed upon a bird enticed by the bait. Grdseloff, on the basis of remnants of such a snare found at Sakkarah, has succeeded in a detailed explanation of its mechanism.[50] Its complicated nature prevents us from going into details here; we must be content with a few particulars necessary to understanding the psalms: the "arms of the trap" (141:9 [RSV: "trap"]) are to be understood as the two bows which hold the net. These spring up (Amos 3:5b) as the trap snaps shut. The wooden trigger of Fig. 112 resembles a throwing stick (cf. 120). That may explain why *môqēš* can on the one hand signify a throwing stick (Amos 3:5a [RSV: "trap"]), on the other hand the trigger, and finally (as *pars pro toto*) the snare as a whole.[51] The form of the snare in Fig. 112 also explains the

strange curse of Ps 69:22: "Let their own table become a snare *(paḥ)*, let their sacrificial feasts be a trap *(môqēš)*." The "table," consisting of an outspread mat, might very well be compared to an open snare, as shown in Fig. *112,* and the foods placed on it could be compared to the trigger ("trap") which holds the bait.[52]

It is logical to assume that in antiquity, as today (*113* and *114*),[53] many local varieties of traps were in use, and that all were called *paḥ* (respectively, *môqēš*), just as they are presently called *faḥḥ* in Arabic.

The same may hold true in the case of the larger net (*rešet,* from the root *yrš,* "to cast down; to subdue; to take possession"). According to Ps 10:9, this net must be drawn closed. That suggests a device related to the hexagonal net fre-

115. "He lurks that he may seize the poor, he seizes the poor when he draws him into his net" (Ps 10:9b).

"Take me out of the net which is hidden for me" (Ps 31:4; cf. 35:7).

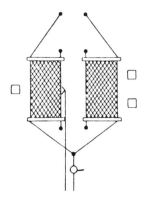

116. Modern dragnet from Galilee.

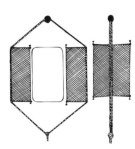

117. Reconstruction of an Egyptian dragnet by P. Montet.

quently shown in Egyptian pictures *(115).* A similar net was still being used in northern Galilee in Dalman's time *(116).* The reconstruction of the ancient Egyptian net by Montet *(117)* demonstrates the close relationship between the two. The net was deployed, as is shown in Fig. *115,* in a clearing in terrain otherwise overgrown with thick vegetation. A wall made of rushes and papyrus was often used to keep the hunters hidden from the birds. The leader of the hunt lay in wait behind the wall. The moment a flock of birds, attracted by the

bait, had settled down between the vanes of the net, the leader signaled his comrades who were standing farther apart, and they quickly began to draw the net. Because one's feet can become entangled in the *rešet* (Pss 25:15; 31:4), the term was probably used not only to denote the drawnet referred to above, but also to describe any hidden net placed slightly above ground or over a hole. With luck, an animal could free itself from such a net, provided that the hunters were not there to throw the net over their quarry or to kill it. J. D.

Barthélemy has suggested (by personal communication) that *rešet* may not refer to a net at all, but rather to a trap. Consideration must be given to the close connection between *rešet* and pit, and to the fact that the victim is almost always caught in this hidden object by the feet. It may perhaps be a trap like that described by Xenophon in his *Cynegeticus:* it consists of a shallow pit covered with camouflaged spikes arranged in concentric circles. Should a deer, stag, or similar animal step into the trap, it is impossible for it to escape.[54] Such an understanding of *rešet* would undoubtedly be appropriate in certain passages, but in others, such as Hos 7:12, it presents considerable difficulty.

mikmār (from *kmr,* "to ensnare") is used to describe yet another type of net. It may be a net erected vertically, into which the quarry is driven. It was held up by men *(118),* and was used in Egypt for catching quail. Isa 51:20 and Fig. *119* indicate, however, that it could also serve for the capture of larger animals. It

appears only once in the psalms (Ps 141:10). In order to arouse Yahweh's compassion, suppliants sometimes compare themselves to defenseless, little birds (Pss 11:1; 102:7; 124:7).

The anchored net applies to a different type of hunt than that conducted with treacherous traps and pits. The stag hunt shown in Fig. *119* is a great chase in mountainous terrain. The psalmists, however, do not compare the machinations of their adversaries to such strenuous undertakings. The trap snaps shut in the midst of an apparently peaceful countryside, and one suddenly finds oneself in a predicament from which there is no escape.

Ps 119:61 (and perhaps Ps 140:5) mentions cords. In Pss 18:4–5 and 116:3, death uses them in the hunt. The cords referred to may be cleverly concealed nooses. Such noose-snares were a widespread and popular hunting implement in Palestine, even in prehistoric times *(119a).*

The lasso, as opposed to the treacher-

118. "By the wayside they have set snares . . ." (Ps 140:5).

ous noose-snare, is not mentioned in the psalms. The lasso is usually thrown only after a long, wild chase.[55]

It is possible that even in the psalms (as in Amos 3:5a [RSV: "trap"]) *môqēš* occasionally denotes a throwing stick (e.g., Ps 141:9 [RSV: "snares"]) of the type hurled suddenly into an unsuspecting flock of birds. In Fig. *120*, an Egyptian in a papyrus boat is about to throw such a stick. Another stick has just broken the neck of one of the long-necked waterfowl. Since the herons held by the hunter appear to be alive, they may represent decoys rather than an earlier catch.[56]

In the OT, the bow and arrow are much more commonly used than the throwing stick. In wooded areas, the hunter stalks his prey, then at an opportune moment kills it with an arrow shot from ambush *(121)*. This method aptly characterizes the treacherous, unpredictable conduct of the *rš'ym* (Pss 11:2; 64:3–4).

The bow is not only a weapon of the hunter, but of the warrior as well. Often it is not possible to determine which of the two the psalmist has in mind (Pss 37:14; 64:3–4). The suppliant sometimes individualizes the predicament of the nation under attack by foreign powers (Pss 3:6; 27:3), summoning Yahweh to holy war against his adversaries (Ps 35:1–3) (cf. chaps 2.3 and 4.3).

The hunting imagery of the individual laments makes it clear that the situation is not one of open combat. Rather, the suppliant is involved in contests which are conducted by stealth and with the insidious means so abundantly at the disposal of his adversaries. Comparison with animals characterizes the adversaries as regally powerful and demonically unscrupulous. Like the forces presented in chapter 4, they encroach upon the just dominion of God and shake the confidence of the suppliant, thus threatening to separate him from

119a. "Arrogant men have hidden a trap for me" (Ps 140:5a).

119. "Your sons have fainted, they lie . . . like an antelope in a net" (Isa 51:20).

94

120. "Does a bird fall to the earth when no throwing stick has hit it?" (Amos 3:5a [author's translation]).

God and subject him to death, or even worse, to draw him to their side (Ps 125:3).

d. The Mortality and Instability of the Wicked

When the suppliant considers his adversary, he feels helpless and abandoned. If, however, he succeeds in freeing himself from anxiety, despair, and their attendant "profanity," he can turn to Yahweh, and everything will be changed. Only that which conforms to Yahweh's holy will has standing before the godhead. The ultimate instability of self-reliant, godless persons can become suddenly apparent in the cultus (Ps 73:17). Their transiency and instability is evident in the fact that they are faithful to no covenant and no alliance (Ps 55:20; cf. 41:9). Alliances and covenants were made before the deity *(122)*. In Fig. *122,* deeds of contract are set out on a small table before two men. The small stele

121. "How can you say to me, 'Flee like a bird to the mountains; for lo, the wicked bend the bow, they have fitted their arrow to the string . . .'" (Ps 11:1–2).

122. "He has violated his covenant. . . . May God cast him down into the pit of corruption" (Ps 55:20, 23 [author's translation]).

scepter symbolized the immovability of the pillars of the heavens (19 and 20). In Fig. 124, the was-scepter held by the person taking the oath may illustrate the stereotyped saying: "I have set such and such a boundary stone as firmly as the heavens are established."[58] The earthly order emulates the heavenly, and like the heavenly, it is guaranteed by the deity.

The man who does not swear falsely and who unconditionally upholds his oath will receive blessing and will never be moved (Pss 15:4–5; 24:4). But he whose right hand (the handshake was made with the right hand; cf. 123) is "a right hand of falsehood" (Ps 144:8, 11; cf., however, Ps 44:17) is without standing, and Yahweh will destroy him whose word is void (Pss 5:6; 12:3; 10:7; 12:2; 17:1; etc.). Because Yahweh was constantly involved as witness and guarantor, it is he himself who requires faithfulness to the given word.

which depicts the scene may have stood in a temple as a reminder to the deity of the conclusion of the contract and of the guarantees undertaken in it (cf. Gen 31:44–54). In Fig. 124, a qualified village elder, or perhaps the owner of the field himself,[57] takes the following oath while holding the was-scepter: "As surely as the great god endures in the heavens, this boundary stone is properly erected." From ancient times, the was-

Whenever human means of safeguard fell short of providing the necessary certainty—a frequent situation in the ancient Near East—God was brought into play. There were oaths and curses. Both measures are an expression of human powerlessness (on the curse, cf. Prov 11:26; 29:24; 30:10; 73). The same sense of powerlessness is also noticeable

123. ". . . whose mouths speak lies, and whose right hand is a right hand of falsehood"

(Ps 144:8, 11; cf. 2 Kgs 10:15; Ezra 10:19; Ezek 17:18; Prov 6:1).

in the curses, or more precisely, the imprecatory prayers of the psalms. They are not so much the expression of malignant vengefulness as of the terrible anxiety to which the suppliant was reduced (Ps 55:4–8). He calls down God's destruction on its cause (Ps 55:9). Tormenting fear cries out in the descriptions of the exquisitely relentless, remorseless conduct of the enemy and the offender. It is following such descriptions that imprecations are generally found (Pss 5:9–10; .17:14; 28:3–4; 56:5–7; 58:2–9; etc.) These are quite similar to the curses found in Middle Babylonian boundary stones *(kudurru)*. Such boundary stones constitute official documents, in the form of stones, of land investiture or donation. One finds expressed on them the fear, evidenced by a series of imprecations, that the land transfer might someday be contested: "If ever at a later time anyone should say: 'The land was not given away! . . . No seal was sealed!' . . . or if anyone should displace this boundary or this boundary stone, . . . then may all the gods who appear on this stone and all those whose names are mentioned on it curse him with a curse that cannot be broken. . . . May Anu and Enlil [*125,* horned crowns on cult pedestals], the great gods . . . destroy his offspring. May Sin [*126,* crescent moon], who abides in the bright sky, cover his body with leprosy [?] like a garment, and may Shamash [*126,* sun disc with undulating rays], the judge, . . . the greatest in heaven and earth, decree rejection of his claim. . . !" (cf. Pss 69:27–28; 109:7a).[59] Innumerable similar imprecations were voiced in ancient Israel and Mesopotamia. Sooner or later they were bound to have an effect on anyone who displaced the boundaries (cf. Deut 27:17; Hos 5:10) or otherwise violated the claim. On the kudurrus (*125* and *126*), dangerous animals such as the dog, serpent, and scorpion often appear side by side with astral symbols (sun, moon, Ishtar-symbol) and abstract ideograms (horned crown, spade). In particular, the serpent and scorpion appear on almost all the more than one hundred

124. "He who . . . does not swear deceitfully . . . will receive blessing from the LORD" (Ps 24:4–5).

". . . [he] who swears to his own hurt and does not change . . . shall never be moved" (Ps 15:4–5).

known kudurrus. Their presence is surprising, because these symbolic animals represent relatively minor deities (viper = Sataran; scorpion = Ishhara). These gods were widely understood to be guarantors of oaths. The dangerous character of their symbolic animals may have contributed considerably to this view. One can easily understand the hope that the wicked might be specially afflicted by the serpent's bite and the scorpion's sting. Furthermore, such an imminent and deadly visitation might be more fearsome than the judgment of the remote astral deities (Ps 121:6). The psalms boast that the man who trusts in Yahweh need fear neither the sun nor the moon (Ps 121:6); serpents and lions cannot harm him (Ps 91:13). The wicked and the godless, on the other hand, are even more endangered in the view of the psalms than they are in the Mesopotamian view. They have no stability (Pss 1:4–6; 9:3, 15–16; 14:5; 34:21; 37:13, 15, 17, 20–21, 28, 34–38). Either their own crimes destroy them, or God's judgment prepares an end to their doings (Pss 37:22; 11:5–6; 26:9; 28:3; etc.). For all their desperate attempts and temporary

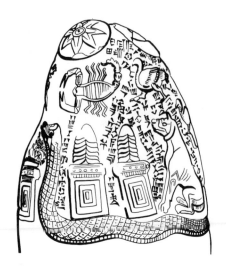

125. Instrument of land transfer in the form of a boundary stone *(kudurru)*. The stone is inscribed with curses intended to afflict any party who violates the contract, and is filled with the (dangerous) symbols of the deities who have undertaken to guarantee the contract.

126. Ps 121, in its argument against unnecessary anxieties, indicates measures the gods could take in their function as guarantors of oaths:

"The sun shall not smite you by day, nor the moon by night. The LORD will keep you from all evil; he will keep your life" (Ps 121:6–7).

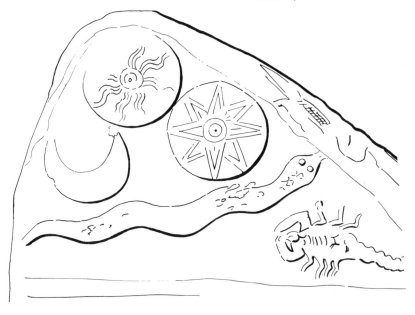

successes, God will not suffer their works to endure. Ps 129, for example, vividly portrays the failure of the efforts of the *rš'ym*. They have abused the nation like a draft animal whose back, like a plowed field, is deeply furrowed from the cuts of the draw-lines and the lash *(127)*. But Yahweh has cut the cords and freed the afflicted animal (Ps 129:3–4).

The psalms often attribute the failure of the wicked not to the direct interven-

tion of Yahweh, but to the operation of the order established by God at creation. The evil which originates with the wicked creates a fateful chain of events[60] which ultimately turns against the offender himself (Pss 7:16; 34:21; 37:15). This conviction is linked with various prudential observations and considerations. Like the sparse grass on a mud-covered roof, the wicked have no real roots. Their life therefore bears no

127. "The plowers plowed upon my back; they made long furrows. The LORD is righ-teous; he has cut the cords of the wicked" (Ps 129:3–4).

fruit (Ps 129:6); there is nothing to reap *(128)*. At winnowing time *(129)*, they scatter like chaff (Pss 1:4; 35:5); not a trace of them is left. The righteous, on the other hand, like mature grains, fall into place on the threshing floor. Reasonings such as these provide a sense of the strong influence of rural life in the ancient Near East. The Egyptian was loath to leave behind the rustic life, even in the world beyond, and consequently had it depicted many hundreds of times in tombs. Indeed, he could not envision even the life beyond without agriculture *(127–28):* there the dead, wearing festive garments, tend wonderfully productive fields.

It was known from agriculture that plants cannot thrive without good earth and water. A bad tree cannot bring forth good fruit. But these natural ordinances were never detached from their author. God ceaselessly watches over the order he has established. Just as he upholds the man who submits to it, so too he destroys the man who violates it, for that

128. With that which the wicked bring forth, ". . . the reaper cannot fill his hand, nor the gatherer of sheaves the folds of his garment" (Ps 129:7 [author's translation]).

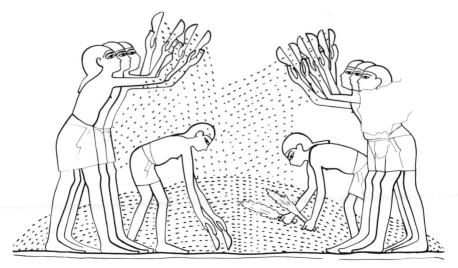

129. The wicked are ". . . like the chaff which the wind drives away" (Ps 1:4; cf. 35:5).

order which prevails throughout heaven and earth is none other than the will and work of Yahweh who ordains all things. Even for Israel, the powers portrayed on the kudurrus are not merely natural forces: they are Yahweh's creatures, and at his behest they overwhelm the wicked (Pss 78:45–46; 105:30–31, 34–35).[61]

3. ENEMIES OF THE NATION

In view of the belief that Yahweh causes all things, it comes as no surprise that in the national laments he is made responsible even for the invasion of hostile armies. To be sure, the national laments (Pss 40; 60; 74; 77; 79; 80; 83; 137; etc.) occasionally refer to those sins of the nation which have brought down the wrath of Yahweh (Pss 79:8–9; 85:1–3); but there can also be vigorous denial of any guilt in misfortune (Pss 44:17–22; 80:18). A large part of the laments is devoted to description of the crisis (Pss 44:9–16; 60:1–3; 74:3–8; 77:7–10; 79:1–4; 83:1–8), recollection of Yahweh's previous saving acts, and petition for aid. Crisis consists primarily in the fact that the right hand of Yahweh has changed (Ps 77:7–10): the people have been abandoned and rejected by him (Pss 44:9; 60:1, 10; 74:1; 89:38); they have been handed over to the violence (Pss 44:11; 79:2–3, 10–11; 83:4) and scorn of the enemy (Pss 44:13–16; 79:4; 89:41) to such an extent that no end is in sight (Ps 74:9–11). Moreover, the laments deliberately emphasize that Yahweh, no less than his people, is affected by violence and ridicule. It is *his* temple which has been destroyed (Pss 74:3–8; 79:1); *his* name is blasphemed (Pss 74:18; 79:10); *his* flock is slaughtered (Ps 44:11–12, 22); *his* vineyard is laid waste (Ps 80:8–13).

God's earlier saving acts are recalled in order to move him to intervention. More or less explicit entreaties are linked with re-presentations of the past: God is to demonstrate his superiority over Chaos, as he did in the primeval age

130. "Thou hast made us turn back from the foe; and our enemies have gotten spoil" (Ps 44:10).

131. "Though a host encamp against me, my heart shall not fear; though war arise against me, yet I will be confident" (Ps 27:3).

(Pss 74:12–17; 89:8–12); he is to prove his power, as in the Exodus from Egypt (Ps 77:11–20); he is to drive out the nations, as in the settlement of the land (Pss 44:1–3; 80:8), and to beat back all oppressors, as in the time of the judges (Ps 83:9–12; cf. also 44:4–8). He is called upon to fulfill the promises by which he opened up a future for his people (Ps 60:6–8; 89:19–37). That future now appears to be in total jeopardy. Explicit entreaties are usually couched in general terms: "Rouse thyself! Awake!" (Ps 44:23). "Grant us help!" (Ps 60:11). "Let the avenging of the outpoured blood of thy servants be known!" (Ps 79:10). "Let them know that thou alone, whose name is the LORD, art the Most High over all the earth" (Ps 83:18).

It is interesting to note that, except for one case in which the catastrophe is imminent, the national laments portray catastrophe as having already struck. Nowhere, for example, is there evidence of a state of siege (but cf. Isa 37:16–20 and its context). Humiliating circumstances generally appear to have prevailed for some time (Ps 74:9–11). Only the beginning and then (above all) the result of the catastrophe are described. The national laments were undoubtedly texts which were regularly recited over a long period of time.

The catastrophe usually began with a defeat in pitched battle. Yahweh did not go out with the army (Ps 60:10), and in consequence it had to retreat (Ps 44:10a). As a result, the unprotected land lay open to pillaging (Ps 44:10b). The Egyptian relief in Fig. 130 shows the troops of a Canaanite city (Mutir) in retreat (cf. 245). The herdsman with his cattle flees not to the city, but to the woods (cf. Judg 5:6–7): the cities were too cramped to accommodate the herds. After the battle had been lost (if indeed a battle had been fought), the fortified cities were besieged. There is no reference to sieges in the national laments, for the siege, unless it lasted an unusually long time, was not the worst of it. The brutality of the adversary could be given full reign only after the fall of the city.

In contrast to the national laments, which lack the siege motif, individual laments and hymns of confidence employ the siege motif with relative frequency. The motif was well suited to portray the uncertainty and fear which seized the individual in the face of his underhanded, treacherous foe, and also to depict the confidence instilled in him by the presence of Yahweh (Pss 3:6; 27:3; 62:3; cf. also Job 16:14; 19:12; 30:13–14).

The monuments of the pharaohs of the Ramses period and of the kings of the Neo-Assyrian period have provided us with a great many siege scenes. The host of the besiegers is shown not by a great number of figures, but by proportional miniaturization of the city and enlargement of the attackers. This is particularly true of the earlier representations of the Neo-Assyrian period (131). In later representations (132), the

132. "How long will you set upon a man to shatter him, all of you, like a leaning wall, a tottering fence?" (Ps 62:3).

132a. "Why should the nations say, 'Where is their God?'" (Ps 115:2). Here, as is typical in Egyptian representations (chap. 5) of the storming of Syro-Palestinian cities, the army plays a minor role or none at all. The relief below is basically no more than a variation of the ancient symbol of the Egyptian king's triumph over his enemies, supplemented by a depiction of the city (cf. *103, 395, 397– 401, 417a*). The inhabitants on the city walls receive the Pharaoh as a god. They burn incense to him (cf. *162*) and present their very children as propitiatory offerings (O. Keel, "Kanaanäische Sühneriten"). The prince of the city extols him with these words: "I believed that there was none other like Baal, but the king is his true son for ever." The broken bows indicate the futility of any resistance to the Pharaoh's divine epiphany (Ps 46:9; cf. *245, 328*). Given this understanding of war and victory, the triumph of an enemy power could present a severe challenge to the ancestral religion.

133. They have poured out the blood of the faithful followers of Yahweh ". . . like water round about Jerusalem, and there was none to bury them" (Ps 79:3).

134. "Let the groans of the prisoners come before thee; according to thy great power preserve those doomed to die!" (Ps 79:11).

disproportion is generally not so great.

The city on the hill (132) is hard pressed on the one side by the king,[62] accompanied by his shield-bearer, and by a wheeled battering-ram, which is operating with obvious success. These especially large figures are situated in the "foreground." Assyrian soldiers armed with spears and shields storm the citadel from the left. On the left side of the citadel a defender, struck by an arrow, falls headlong to the ground. The dead are stripped of their clothing (cf. Ps 22:18). At the center of the picture an Assyrian warrior is shown cutting off the head of a dead (or severely wounded) man. Decapitated corpses are to be seen at the extreme left of the scene and to the left of the ram. Three men have been impaled. The defenders are at the point of surrender. They lift up their hands in entreaty or (on the second tower from the left) raise hand to brow in a gesture of mourning. On the second tower from the right, an Assyrian is about to dispatch a defender who is begging for mercy. In conformity with the Egyptian concept of kingship, Egyptian siege scenes exhibit fundamental differences in composition (132a; cf. chap. 5).[63]

Upon the capture of a city, the vanquished were utterly at the mercy of their conquerors. In the course of the capture and immediately subsequent to it, large numbers of the population were often indiscriminately massacred. The captive in Fig. 133 holds in his right hand the little branch of one who implores protection (cf. the row of "foreign peoples" second from the top in Fig. 34). The vanquished were regarded as beasts for slaughter (cf. Ps 44:11a). Those who were not killed were imprisoned. The leaders of the opposing forces, if captured, were usually executed. In Fig. 134, an Elamite prince, fettered at the neck and hands, is executed by Assyrian soldiers. Much blood was shed, especially after a hard-won victory (Pss 79:3, 10–11; 83:4). The bodies of those fallen, slaughtered, and executed were often left to lie as food for jackals, ravens, and other scavengers (Ps 79:2–3; cf. 63:10; 68:23; 83:10). The dead were thus deprived of the last vestiges of their existence (cf. 73). The lion in Fig. 135 may represent not a scavenger, but the triumphant king as he overwhelms the foe. The figure under attack by the lion is drawn almost twice

135. "They have given the bodies of thy servants to the birds of the air for food, the flesh of thy saints to the beasts of the earth" (Ps 79:2).

the size of the five corpses (one of them shackled) descended upon by the two vultures and five ravens. At the upper right, a goddess (?) leads away a naked prisoner (the upper portion is broken off). A written character appeared beneath his head.

Anyone who escaped death was sold as a slave (cf. Ps 44:12) or deported. Fig. 136 shows an Assyrian warrior on foot and another on horseback driving three naked men, two women, and a girl out of the burning city of Qarqar. The Assyri-

ans apparently adopted the practice of deportation from the Hittites, but they enormously enlarged its scale. The Babylonians (cf. 137) carried it even further.

Prisoners of war were often condemned to hard labor, such as the building of fortifications (137). In addition to external miseries, prisoners suffered the scorn of their oppressors (Pss 44:13–16; 74:21; 79:4; 80:6; 89:41). Assyrian reliefs are especially rich in the portrayal of exquisitely brutal cruelties.[64] Egyptian

136. "Thou hast . . . scattered us among the nations. Thou hast sold thy people for a trifle, demanding no high price for them" (Ps 44:12–13).

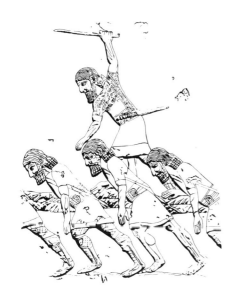

137. "Why is light given to him that is in misery, and life to the bitter in soul, who long for death but it comes not . . . ? There the wicked cease from troubling, and there the weary are at rest. There the prisoners are at ease together; they hear not the voice of the taskmaster" (Job 3:20–21, 17–18).

138. "Thou hast made us the taunt of our neighbors, the derision and scorn of those about us. Thou hast made us a byword among the nations, a shaking of the head [RSVm] among the peoples. All day long my disgrace is before me, and shame has covered my face" (Ps 44:13–15).

art, on the other hand, was inexhaustible in the invention of humiliating means of mockery and scorn.[65] Mockery and scorn, like the curse, served to weaken the enemy and, once conquered, to keep him weak. The thought which unites every representation of this theme is the symbolic-magical realization of mastery over every foe. Fig. *138* is exemplary of many similar representations: Amenophis III, triumphant victor over the Nubians, has set four of their champions between the reins of his horses. Another serves as the Pharaoh's foot rest, and a sixth kneels on the chariot-shaft at the rear of the horse.

The sack of a city was part and parcel of its capture. Apart from the royal palaces, the most rewarding sites of plunder were the temples with their rich oblations. The famous picture of Fig. 139[66] (cf. 317) shows the sack of the temple of Muzazir in Uratu (northwest of Assur). The soldiers have sought out above all the shields which adorned the temple. Some shields are shown in lateral view, others in front view (cf. 2 Sam 8:7; 1 Kings 10:16ff, especially 1 Kings 14:26–28; 2 Kings 11:10; 1 Mac 4.57). At the upper left, two scribes appear before a high official (seated) to inventory the pieces of booty. Ps 79:1 bemoans the fact that foreigners have broken into the temple and desecrated it; Ps 74:4–8 laments that they have even destroyed it. To this writer's knowledge, the destruction of the temple is nowhere depicted in iconography. It is frequently described in literature.[67] The plunder of statues of deities, however, is not infrequently shown on Assyrian reliefs (316), and one relief even shows the destruction of such a statue (317). When the entire acropolis was destroyed by fire (Plate V), the temple was naturally not spared. In Plate V, four soldiers carry plundered objects out of the city, while a fifth drives two prisoners before him. Five engineers are engaged in demolishing the city walls. The gate is consumed by fire. The destruction of the acropolis and the city wall with its gates rendered the city an open, utterly defenseless place, exposed to every band of marauders (Ps 89:40). It is like a vineyard without walls (Ps 80:12). If the enemies are not content with rendering the city defenseless, but instead completely destroy it, together with its surrounding groves of palm or olive and its orchards and other plantations (140; Ps 79:7; Deut 20:19–20; Jer 10:25),[68] then the city becomes no more than a heap of stones (Pss 79:1c; 102:14). Such heaps are numerous in the desert, and the Nomads enjoy pointing them out as the remains of long-vanished cities (cf. Ps 9:6).[69] The devastation of the cities (141) means, however, that yawning, deadly Chaos has invaded the "land of the living," for the desert is

139. "O God, the heathen have come into thy inheritance; they have defiled thy holy temple" (Ps 79:1).

"The enemy has destroyed everything in the sanctuary! Thy foes have roared in the midst of thy holy place. . . . At the upper entrance they hacked the wooden trellis with axes. And then all its carved wood they broke down with hatchets and hammers" (Ps 74:3b, 4–6).

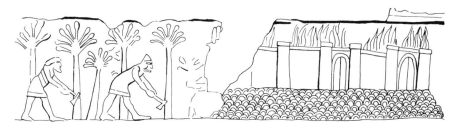

140. "For they have devoured Jacob, and laid waste his habitation" (Ps 79:7).

part of the world of Chaos (cf. chap 2.1.d).[70]

In the national laments, the ravaging of the countryside is seen as an event of cosmic proportions. The earth begins to quake (60:2). The clamor of foes resounds like the surging of the floods of Chaos (cf. Ps 74:23 with Pss 65:7; 89:9 cj.). Pss 74 and 89 contrast the raging of the national enemies with the power of Yahweh, by which in primal times he conquered the Chaos dragon (43–52). In Dan 7:4, the dragon has the body of a lion and the wings of an eagle. In Figs. 43–45, the dragon embodies a cosmic power, as the symbolic animal of Babylon's destructive world domination. In Jer 51:34, the king of Babylon is compared to a dragon which devours Jerusalem as a monster swallows a man (cf. 81). According to the inscription above the Chaos serpent's head in Fig. 142, the serpent represents the Aramean city of Laqē. An insurrection which originated there threatened to destroy the empire of Tukulti-Ninurta II. The latter, in the role of the storm god, subdued the threatening Chaos. There is a tendency to regard such instances as historicization of myth. It should not be forgotten, however, that this process simultaneously represents a mythicization of history.

Ps 80:13 compares the land to a vineyard ravaged by wild boars. The boar hunt shown in Fig. 143 appears on the

141. "They have laid Jerusalem in ruins" (Ps 79:1c). ". . . have pity on Zion; . . . for thy servants hold her stones dear, and have pity on her dust" (Ps 102:13–14).

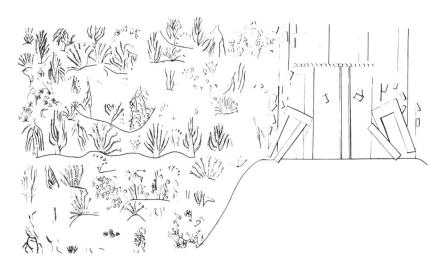

142. "How long, O God, is the foe to scoff?
Is the enemy to revile thy name for ever?
Why dost thou hold back thy hand, why dost
thou keep thy right hand in thy bosom? Yet
God my king is from of old, working salvation in the midst of the earth. . . . Thou
didst crush the heads of Leviathan. . . . Remember this, O LORD, how the enemy scoffs,
and an impious people reviles thy name" (Ps
74:10–12, 14a, 18).

entrance gate of the Hittite city of Alaça
Hüyük, beside the sacrificial scene of
Fig. 318. The thought which may underlie this combination of scenes is more
clearly expressed in the Late Hittite reliefs of Malatya. There we see, on the

one hand, how sacrifice is made to the
storm god, who travels along in a chariot
drawn by two bulls; on the other hand
we see the same god conquering the
Chaos dragon (50). The combination of
scenes may mean "thanksgiving for the
conquering of Chaos," or "supplication
for the conquering of Chaos," or both. In
any case, the juxtaposition is not fortuitous. Neither is it coincidental that sacrifice is combined sometimes with
scenes of the hunt, sometimes with
scenes of the battle against Chaos, and
finally with scenes of war.[71] Inimical
forces are manifest in all three instances,
and these forces can be overcome only
by a positive relation with the god of life
and with his salutary order (ritual).

The wild boar seems to have been a
fairly widespread symbol of Chaos in the
ancient Near East. In Egypt, it was the
animal of Seth, the evildoer among the
gods and lord of the desert. Fig. 144 (cf.
451) equates Pharaoh, who is stabbing
an enemy, with Horus, who kills the
boar of Seth. In the illustration, Horus is
assisted by Isis, the mother goddess and
goddess of love, here closely identified
with Hathor (cow's horns) (cf. 46).
Pharaoh's battle against the enemies of
the land is only another aspect of the
battle waged by Horus, god of the
heavens and of order, against the powers
of darkness and destruction. The powers
of Chaos and of death can manifest
themselves in many varied forms: in
darkness, in the watery deep, in the dust
of the grave, in the fever of demonic
possession, in wild animals, and in invasions by hostile peoples. They find their
strongest expression in the realm of the
dead and in the waters of Chaos, which
assume concrete form in the sinister dragon. The conquering of the dragon is one
of the predominant themes of the ancient Near East. The strongest guarantee
against its dominion is the presence of
God in his temple.

143. "The boar from the forest ravages it [the vineyard of Yahweh]" (Ps 80:13a; on the boar as a figure of Chaos, cf. H. Frankfort, *Cylinder Seals,* p. 132, pl. 23h.).

144. With a lance, the royal god Horus pierces the pig (cf. *143*), which represents his adversary Seth, god of the desert and opponent of salutary order. In an analogous action, the king pierces a human enemy. The power of Horus is active in the king and in the two spears, both of which terminate in falcon-heads. So too, both *adversaries* manifest one and the same power *inimical* to life (cf. H. W. Fairman, *The Triumph of Horus*).

CHAPTER III
THE TEMPLE: PLACE OF YAHWEH'S PRESENCE AND SPHERE OF LIFE

(In the following discussion, reference to the temple in Jerusalem is to the Solomonic temple. The majority of the psalms probably emerged during the span of its existence or in the early postexilic period. The postexilic temple corresponds closely to the Solomonic temple and was considered to be a restoration of it.)

The rock (Ps 61:2; cf. 27:5) is the antipole of the bottomless world of Chaos. The gates of Zion are the antipole of the gates of death (Ps 9:13–14). Zion with its temple was the symbol and sacrament of the presence of the living, life-creating God. By and large, Israel adopted this symbol from surrounding cultures. It is reasonable to suppose that the Phoenicians not only supplied the building materials for the temple (cf. 1 Kings 5:1–18), but actually built the temple as well. In any case, the entire furnishing of the interior was done under the direction of a Tyrian (1 Kings 7:13–45).

All the archaeological evidence from Palestine goes to show that the Israelites themselves lacked any skill as masons and craftsmen. Evidence of the skill of the Phoenicians in working stone from the second millennium onwards comes from sites such as Ras Shamra and Byblos and from the remains of Tyre itself. . . . Evidence of their skill as craftsmen in ivory and bronze comes from a wide area stretching from North Syria to Cyprus. Still more revealing in relation to Jerusalem is the evidence from Samaria. Here, some eighty years later (c. 880 BC), Omri, ruler of the Northern Kingdom of Israel, built himself a new capital. Omri's contacts with Phoenicians are shown by the marriage of his son Ahab to the Phoenician princess Jezebel [1 Kgs 16:31]. Excavation has shown that the masonry of the buildings of Omri and Ahab is Phoenician. The masonry is truly exquisite, the heavy walls bold and forceful, the interior walls with stones dressed to a beautifully tooled smooth face and fitted together with minute precision. We can imagine that the walls of Solomon's Temple and palace were of the same fine masonry, and that the platform was constructed of stones with the bolder type of dressing. Though so much of this has to be deduced from the mere statement that

145. Proto-Ionic (or proto-Aeolian) capital from Jerusalem, bearing witness to Phoenician influences.

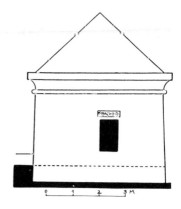

146. Reconstruction of a tomb at Silwan, the most important necropolis of Jerusalem in the period of the monarchy. The tomb is constructed in a pure Egyptian style (cf., e.g., 76).

Phoenician masons were employed in the work, one link in architectural style can be based on the evidence of the excavations [in Jerusalem]. Against the foot of the summit scarp on the eastern side . . . excavations disclosed a tumble of ashlar blocks with the fine, smooth faces of Omri's building at Samaria, and amongst them two halves of a pilaster capital of Proto-Ionic type [cf. 145]. This is precisely the type of capital found at Samaria and at other sites that have architectural links with Samaria. This tumble of masonry, obviously from an important building which had stood on top of the scarp, may be the one architectural relic of Solomon's Jerusalem so far found.[1]

Besides the Phoenician influence, there is also archaeological evidence of Egyptian influence, perhaps mediated by Phoenicians, for Jerusalem of the early monarchic period. In the present village of Silwan, within the precincts of the necropolis of pre-exilic Jerusalem, there are ruins of a tomb (146)² which is clearly of Egyptian derivation (cf. 76).

While the institution of the temple as such was undoubtedly of Canaanite-Phoenician origin, and while its craftsmanship was certainly the work of Phoenician artisans, it does not follow that the plan of the structure as a whole was without specifically Israelite features. No doubt Solomon himself, as the builder, ultimately and authoritatively determined the design of the building, and he himself had to give at least minimal consideration to the sentiments of various conservative circles (cf. 2 Sam 7:4–7). That fact is evident, for example, in the design of the holy of holies.

1. TEMPLE AND MOUNTAIN

Holy places in the ancient Near East were usually holy "by nature." Almost all the great Egyptian sanctuaries claimed to house within their courts the primeval hill, the "glorious hill of the primordial beginning," which had first emerged from the floods of Chaos (147; cf. 40).³ The great wall which surrounds the huge temple enclosure of Karnak is laid out in an undulating design. This unusual form is intended to represent the primeval waters which formerly lapped around the temple hill.⁴ The primeval hill substantiated the claim of particular temples and cities to antedate all other holy places.⁵ The creator-god made his appearance on the primeval hill; the ordered world had its origin from it. It was filled with prodigious energies and vital forces. The dead were portrayed on the primeval hill (148) so that they might be regenerated by its powers. The pyramids represent huge primeval hills (149), but that is not their only significance. Like so many Egyptian symbols, the pyramids are ambiguous. The step-pyramids had the shape not only of a hill, but (at least in their most ancient form) of a staircase. Spell 267 of the Pyramid Texts reads: "A staircase to heaven is laid for him [i.e., the king] so that he may climb up to heaven thereby."⁶

In Mesopotamia, as in Egypt, every temple has its *du-ku,* its "pure hill."⁷ And in Mesopotamia too, the sanctuary constituted a part of the primordial beginnings. The construction of the Esagila, the principal temple of Babylon, is described within the framework of the creation epic *Enuma elish.*⁸ Construction took place after Marduk, the principal Babylonian deity, had vanquished the powers of Chaos (Tiamat, Kingu) (cf. 240). The gods then raised the summit of Esagila against the Apsu: they built the temple tower (150).⁹ It is called the "house of the foundation of heaven and earth."

In step-temples, the character of staircase generally dominates that of the primeval hill. It is obvious where the huge stairs lead. The ziggurat of Larsa bears the beautiful name, "house of the bond between heaven and earth"; that of Kish is the "exalted house of Zababa and Ininna, whose head is as high as the heavens" (cf. Gen 11:4; Ps 78:69). The step-tower of Nippur bears the title, "house of the mountain"; that of Assur is the "house of the great mountain of the nations."¹⁰ Ziggurat, like "step-tower," can mean "mountaintop." In the Gilgamesh epic, Utnapishtim, on the ziggurat, pours out a libation after the flood.¹¹ Here the "ziggurat" is the top of the mountain Nisir, on which Utnapishtim's "ark" has come to land.

In the Ugaritic sphere, the conquest of Chaos is also closely related to mountain (hill) and temple. After his victory over the sea god Yam, Baal receives a temple

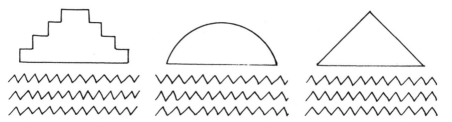

147. Various Egyptian representations of the primeval hill, the first entity to rise from the water of Chaos. The world evolved from the primeval hill.

on Zaphon, the mountain of the gods located in the northern portion of the city of Ugarit.

The abyss is a dimension of Chaos and of death, but the high place, the mountain, belongs to the temple. In the psalms, the location of the temple is Jerusalem, or more precisely, Zion. One goes *up* to Jerusalem (Ps 122:4), and at the temple gates one asks who may (further) ascend the mountain of Yahweh (Ps 24:3).

The staircases which connected the various parts of the temple structure in Jerusalem *(174–75)* are not to be compared with the monumental staircases of the Mesopotamian temple towers. We must not overlook the fact, however, that at Bethel the stairs and gate of heaven were believed to be actually present without that belief having found, insofar as we know, any expression in cultic architecture. Thus Zion could bear the title "mountain" even though there is no appreciable rise of terrain in the area immediately surrounding the gates of the temple enclosure. Temples, as such, are situated on a mountain. Ramses III, addressing Ptah-Tatenen, can say of the temple of Medinet Habu, which is located on an entirely flat plain: "I have made great thy temple on the mountain 'Lord of Life' "[12] (cf. Jer 21:13). Pss 87:1 (MT) and 133:3 even mention "mountains" in the plural with reference to Zion. The plural is probably to be taken as a plural of majesty—intensive rather than extensive. It expresses the potency of the locality marked by Yahweh's presence.[13]

Many passages which mention "mount Zion" (Pss 48:2, 11; 74:2; 78:68; 125:1; 133:3), the "holy mountain" (Pss 2:6; 3:4; 15:1; 43:3; 48:1; 99:9 [RSV: usually "holy hill"]), or the "mountain of Yahweh" (Ps 24:3 [RSV: "hill of the LORD"]) may refer not only to the immediate precincts of the temple, but to the entire hilltop on which the temple stood. Even regarded in that way, Zion, with its rise of 743 meters, is in and of itself a modest hill. Its top is not as high as the tops of the surrounding

148. The deceased was portrayed on the primeval hill in order that his life might be regenerated by the powers inherent in the hill. Ps 103, which views sin and sickness in close relation, makes the renewal of youth dependent on Yahweh's forgiveness.

149. The pyramids have the form and thus also (in the understanding of the ancient Near East) the character of the primeval hill. In the pyramid of Djoser, these aspects coincide with that of a double staircase, which is probably intended to enable the ascent of the deceased into the heavenly world. The Egyptian words for "climb" and "ascent" are determined by a double stair.

mountains: it lies 66 meters below that of the Mount of Olives, 76 meters below that of Mount Scopus, 33 meters below that of the hill to its west (the Christian Zion), and 53 meters below that of *rās el-mekkaber* (cf. Ps 125:1–2 and *Plate VI*). Ancient Jerusalem was centered on Ophel (the eastern hill) *(151)*, and Zion may indeed have seemed like a mountain to its inhabitants: they had to negotiate a difference in elevation of some 100 meters from the south end of their city wall to the top of Zion *(152; Plate VII)*. From En-rogel, the difference in elevation was even greater (130 meters). Nonetheless, it was evident that there were a number of more important mountains. There was, for instance, the

150. The title of the step-temple of Babylon is "house of the foundation of heaven and earth" (cf. Ps 78:69). The temple is the center and mainstay of creation.

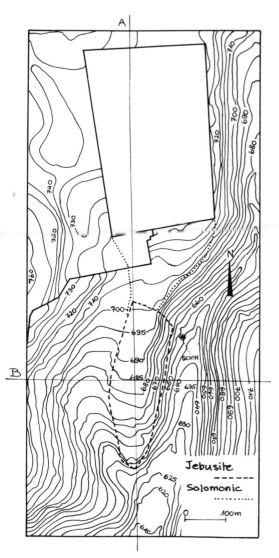

151. The situation and dimensions of Jerusalem in the time of David (Jebusite) and Solomon.

152. Section along line A (151). One ascended to the temple from Solomon's Jerusalem.

wonderful dome of Tabor towering mightily over its surroundings, and the powerful, lofty mass (elevation: 2,814 meters) of Hermon (ḥrm, "ban"; Hermon: "mountain of the ban"; cf. *Plate VII A*). In North Syria, Zaphon, the ancient Canaanite mountain of the gods, rises precipitously from the sea to an imposing height (*Plate VII B*); and in the south lies Sinai (or Horeb), the famous holy mountain of Israel's early epoch. In Ps 89:12, all are depotentized to the status of creations of Yahweh.[14] The suppliant is to await his salvation from Yahweh, who dwells on Zion, and not from any holy mountain (Ps 121:1–2). Yahweh has chosen Zion in preference to all of them. The high mountains of the region look down on it, glowering and jealous (Ps 68:15–16), for despite its modest appearance it is the true mountain of the gods, the real Zaphon (Ps 48:2). At the end of time, it will rise above all other mountains (Isa 2:2 = Mic 4:1).

Yahweh has already given to Zion the dew of Hermon, embodying its fruitfulness and life (Ps 133:3). Zion possesses all the prerogatives of the cosmic mountain.[15] Fig. *153* (cf. *42*) shows a mountain god (identified by the scale-pattern on his robe and cap) who embodies at one and the same time vegetation, fertility, and life. Two fruit-bearing stalks spring forth from his hips. In his hands he holds two more, from which mountain goats eat their fill. The mighty mountain god is flanked by two fountain goddesses (cf. *42*). Each holds in both hands an aryballos-shaped vessel, from which water rises in a high arc (cf. *191, 256*). Trees and water identify the mountain as a sphere of life.

In Fig. *153a*, the mountain god him-

116

153. ". . . with the finest produce of the ancient mountains, and the abundance of the
everlasting hills . . ." (Deut 33:15; cf. Ps
133:3).

153a. The four streams flowing from the vessel of the mountain deity are reminiscent of the four branches of the *river* of paradise (Gen 2:10; cf. *185*).

self holds the water vessel (cf. *Plate I B*). The four streams emanating from the god are reminiscent of the four rivers of paradise.

Brushwood is found on the mountains of Palestine and Syria, but there is very little water. The concept that the mountain (the height) is a sphere of life may have been motivated less by geographical considerations than by the psychological association of "being happy" (as an expression of the fulness of life) with "being high" (as an expression of heightened vital consciousness). *śmḥ*, "to be happy," and *rwm*, "to be high," are synonymous (cf. Ps 89:16 RSVm).[16] The interpretative sign for the Egyptian *ḥ'j*, "to be happy," is a man with uplifted arms (cf. *21*). Paradise was thought to be located on a high mountain (cf. Ezek 28:13–16); it was densely forested (Gen 2:8–9) and the source of mighty rivers (Gen 2:10–14). The temple site, as locus of God's presence, was very closely related to paradise. In Mesopotamian creation myths, the foundation of the temple replaces the creation of paradise.

The hill Zion is identified with the primeval hill, paradise, the cosmic mountain and mountain of the gods. But this identification depends less on Zion's relative merits as a mountain than on its

Holy Rock. The rock, with its solidity and strength, constitutes the antipole to the bottomless, slimy, sluggish (cf. *55*) floods of Chaos, which threaten the ends of the earth (Pss 18:2–5; 61:2; Isa 28:15–16; Mt 16:18). At the temple site in Jerusalem is a rock which has been venerated at least since the seventh century of the Christian era. At that time the Caliph 'Abd al-Malik ibn Marwan (A.D. 687–691) built the exquisitely beautiful central structure whose dome dominates the site to this very day (cf. *Plate IX*). It is not likely that 'Abd al-Malik arbitrarily declared the rock holy. Rather, he carried forward an older tradition. As early as A.D. 333, a pilgrim from Bordeaux records seeing a *lapis pertusus* (a stone or rock full of holes)[17] which was the object of cultic veneration by the Jews and was annually anointed in commemoration of the destruction of the temple. This rock was located not far from two statues of Hadrian, one of which (according to Jerome)[18] is said to have stood on the site of the former holy of holies. Thus, according to traditions current in the fourth century this Holy Rock had not served as the foundation of the holy of holies. This *lapis pertusus* may nevertheless be the same rock enclosed by 'Abd al-Malik's dome. That rock too is pierced by a circular hole *(154 s)* which leads down to a rectangular cavity *(154 l, m, n, o)*. The rock also displays a great many other holes and basinlike recesses.

T. A. Busink has recently evaluated the various arguments concerning the location of the temple.[19] He concludes that the temple was probably situated to the north of the Holy Rock. Without reference to Busink's opinion, E. Vogt harks back to the view of C. Warren, locating the temple to the south of the Holy Rock.[20] Busink and Vogt agree, at any rate, that the Holy Rock cannot have served as the foundation for either the altar of burnt offering or the holy of holies. If it had held the altar of burnt offering, the holy of holies would have to have been built over a substructure of some kind, for the hilltop drops off quite sharply just west of the Holy

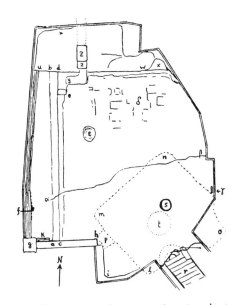

154. The Holy Rock in Jerusalem (*eṣ-ṣaḥra*): "a–b: Corner line of the lower west terrace. c–d: Line of the upper west step. e: The cleft hewn in the rock eastward from the step. f.: The cavity on the west face. g, h, i: The southwesterly cut in the rock. g: The relic shrine. k: The two small marble columns on the south side of the great west step. l, m, n, o: The cave. p: The niche in the cave. r: Cave stairs. s: The round hole in the ceiling of the cave. t: The marble slab on the floor of the cave. u–w: The northern wall of the rock. x: Northeast corner of the rock. y: High-point of the northern stairway to the rock. z: Slabs over the subterranean passage leading toward the north. α–β: The natural cleft in the rock. γ: The footprint of Idris. δ: Traces of excavations and cuts. ε: Basin cavity" (H. Schmidt, *Der heilige Fels*, key to Fig. 1). The dates of the various traces of workmanship cannot be determined with certainty. It is known that the Crusaders sent altar stones hewn from the Holy Rock to Europe.

Rock. The use of substructures is quite unlikely.[21] Just as unlikely, however, is the use of a Holy Rock as the foundation of a building (the holy of holies). For in order to use the rock as a foundation, it would undoubtedly have been necessary to cut into it. That was forbidden even in the case of ordinary altar stones (". . . for if you wield your tool upon it you profane it." Exod 20:25), let alone in the case of a Holy Rock. In all probability, the Holy Rock lay exposed at the south side of the temple (*355*), as did Golgotha in Constantine's building of a later date.

In its externals, the Holy Rock closely resembles the holy rocks which have been found at Gezer (*155*), Megiddo

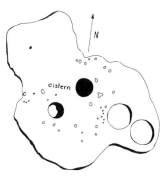

155. The "Holy Rock" at Gezer.

(*156*), and elsewhere. The common characteristics all point to cultic functions:[22] each rock has a number of basins and a cistern or cave. The latter, apart from its practical uses, may have represented the world of Chaos (cf. *78* and *79*), to which is opposed the unshakeable solidity of the rock. At the same time, the rock may have served as a manifestation of the deity (cf. "Yahweh, my rock") and as an altar (cf. *193*). (On rocks and stones as representations of the deity, cf. chap. 4.1.a).

Despite the unmistakable presence in the Jerusalem temple of components reminiscent of the Chaos-cosmos conception prevalent in ancient Near Eastern sanctuaries, no attempt was made to trace the foundation of the Jerusalem sanctuary back to the time of the primal beginnings. In the Yahwistic creation narrative (Gen 2), there appears instead of a temple a garden made for men; in the Priestly version (Gen 1) there is no special area at all. In the course of his history with Israel, Yahweh chose Zion. Yahweh is not, as it were, elementally or eternally linked with Zion. Ps 132 relates, in the context of the story of the ark (1 Sam 4–6; 2 Sam 6), how he moved to Zion. Yahweh loved (Pss 78:68; 87) and desired (Ps 132:13b) Zion, and chose (Ps 132:13a) it over all other mountains (Ps 68:16), over all the sanctuaries of Jacob (Ps 87:2). Yahweh's dwelling on Zion is thus a free act of grace. In it the exodus from Egypt and the settlement of the land find their full completion. The object of the exodus is the sovereignty of Yahweh, which produces life and salvation. That lordship will extend from Zion to include all nations (Ps 87; Isa 2:2–4; Mic 4:1–3).[23] In the free election of Zion as an act of divine condescension lie the essence and the specifics of all Zion-theology, all Davidic theology, and finally, of the whole biblical theology of incarnation.[24]

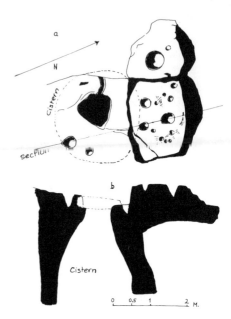

156. The "Holy Rock" at Megiddo: (a) bird's-eye view; (b) section. In the sanctuary, Chaos (the cistern) is harnessed and becomes a source of fertility.

2. THE TEMPLE GATES

As a holy precinct, the temple area, like paradise, is safeguarded by extraordinary measures. Moses had to set a boundary around Sinai (Exod 19:12). Zion was surrounded by a wall suitable for military service (Ps 48:12–13). In Jerusalem, as in the Egyptian (157) and Assyrian (158) representations of a Canaanite city, one must distinguish the outworks (158), the city wall itself, with its towers and salients (157 and 158), and the acropolis, with its fortified palaces and the temple (157 and 158). It is not quite clear whether "Zion" in Ps 48:12–13 includes at least some part of the city of Jerusalem. Jerusalem and Zion are sometimes virtually synonymous (Pss 51:18; 102:21; 147:12). According to Ps 116:19, the forecourts of the temple lie "in the midst of Jerusalem." Acropolis and city, as Figs. 157 and 158 suggest, were understood as a unity.

The gates were the most vulnerable points of an ancient Near Eastern city. Attempt was made to secure them by special fortifications (cf. 159–61) and by all kinds of magical or religious measures (158a).

Because the gate, flanked by two mighty towers, formed a most impressive representation of the city, it could stand as pars pro toto for "city" (cf. Fig. 162, where the temple gate represents the temple; cf. "gates of death" in Ps

9:13; 107:18; Mt 16:18 RSVm; and "gates of righteousness" in Ps 118:19). When in Ps 122:1–3 the pilgrim expresses his desire to stand in the gates of Jerusalem, he does not have in mind merely the moment of arrival, but also his entire sojourn in Jerusalem. Arrival at the holy place was of course a longed-for moment (Ps 84:2, 7), and passage through the several gates was a significant occasion. It was indeed possible to stand "in the gates," because in most instances there were two or three gates staggered one behind another, forming two or three chambers. 1 Kgs 9:15 reports that Solomon enlarged the walls of Gezer, Megiddo, and Hazor. Tenaille gates dating from the time of Solomon have been unearthed in all three cities (Hazor: *159;* Megiddo: *160;* Gezer: *161*). In 1 Kgs 9:15, Jerusalem is

157. Egyptian representation of the city of Ashkelon (cf. *132a*).

158. Assyrian representation of the city of Ashtartu, apparently the same city as the Ashtaroth situated east of Lake Gennesaret.

"Jerusalem, built as a city which is bound firmly together. . . . Peace be within your walls and security within your towers!" (Ps 122:3, 7).

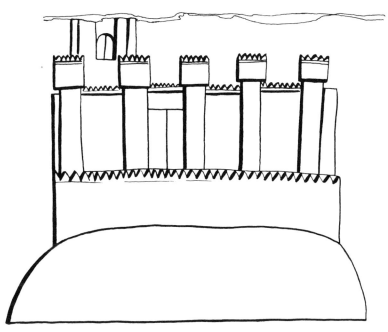

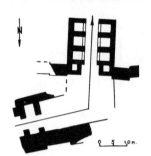

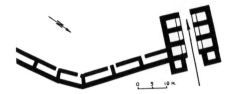

159. The Solomonic gate at Hazor.
"Our feet have been standing in your gates, O Jerusalem!" (Ps 122:1).

160. The Solomonic gate at Megiddo.
"Enter his gates with thanksgiving" (Ps 100:4a).

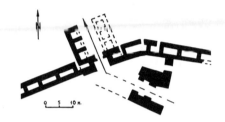

161. The Solomonic gate at Gezer.
"I am the talk of those who sit in the gate" (Ps 69:12).
"Happy is the man who has [many sons]! He shall not be put to shame when he speaks with his enemies in the gate" (Ps 127:5).

158a. "Praise the LORD, O Jerusalem! Praise your God, O Zion! For he strengthens the bars of your gates; he blesses your sons within you" (Ps 147:12–13).

The Sed festival (cf. 352) was celebrated to renew the vital powers of the Egyptian king after thirty years' reign. In the course of that festival, another vital institution was also renewed. The king walked around the capital city, carrying a sacred mace and touching each of the gates with it. This touch was intended to reestablish the defensive strength of the gates, and to prepare them to protect the sphere of blessing which surrounded the king. Ps 147 attributes this function to Yahweh. Ps 48:12–14 alludes to a circuit around Zion; but the purpose of that circuit was different from that of the Egyptian king at the Sed festival (cf. 4).

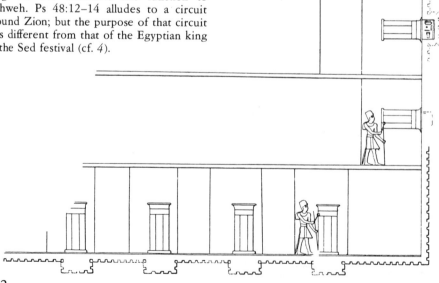

mentioned together with these three cities. We may therefore postulate the existence of such gates at Jerusalem as well. W. Zimmerli[25] finds further evidence to support this assumption in the use of tenaille gates in Ezekiel's temple plan (Ezek 40). The temple enclosure was guarded not only by the city walls and by location on the acropolis, but by its own additional walls as well.

The temple is a sphere of highly intensified life and blessing. In Fig. *162*, the life-signs and *was*-scepters (cf. *19–20*) point to the powerful, wholly other energy active within the temple (Ps 133.3). The worshipper who has fulfilled the necessary requirements participates in that energy (Ps 24:5). The flags (cf. *162a, 167a*) displayed in front of the gate-towers (pylons) also signal the presence of deity.

That which is holy must be protected from profanation. All manner of guardians safeguarded the outside entrance of the massive gate-towers. Emplaced in pair in the form of a lion *(163)*, "the king [cf. *135*] himself assumed the function of guardian of the temple. With his head raised at right angles to his body, he looked straight at anyone who approached, and that gaze was in itself apparently sufficient to repulse any impious intruder."[26] The king often guarded the temple entrance in the alternate form of a human-headed lion (cf. *434*). [27] Amenemhet III sent two sphinxes to Ugarit, where they were installed at the entrance to the temple of Baal.[28]

In Sumer, it was Imdugud, the lion-headed eagle, who guarded the temple gates *(164)*.[29] A Sumerian hymn to Enlil praises the gate complex of Ur-Nammu (ca. 2050 B.C.): "The shepherd Ur-Nammu raised up to the heavens the lofty 'House of the Mountain' [temple of Enlil] in Duranki ['Bond between Heaven and Earth' = the temple district of Nippur], set it down to the astonishment of many. With refined gold he richly adorned the front of the 'High Gate,' the 'Great Gate,' the 'Gate of Salvation of the Step-Mountains,' the 'Gate of the Unharvested Grain.' There the

Imdugud-bird killed many [foes]; no wicked one assails the eagles which stand there. The doors [of the temple] are lofty, clothed with dreadful radiance, vast in foundation, inspiring great fear."[30]

The entrances of Assyrian temples and palaces are often guarded by mighty bulls with human heads and eagle's wings *(Plate VIII)*. They are sometimes called *lamassu,* sometimes *shêdu* (cf. Ps 106:37, where *šdym* are evil demons), and sometimes *kuribu.* The latter term is related to the biblical "cherub." The best-known function of the cherubim was to guard the entrance to paradise (Gen 3:24; Ezek 28:16).

Composite figures such as those mentioned above were not the only guardian-figures in use. In Assyria and Babylonia, animals in unmixed form often appear as guardians of the gate. The two lions from Tell Harmal in the vicinity of Baghdad *(165)* guarded the entrance of the temple of Nisaba and Hani. Emplacement of gate guardians was also current in Syria-Palestine. The lion in Fig. *166* was discovered at the entrance of Temple H (cf. *208*) in Hazor.

The emplacement of guardian genii was motivated by the belief that they would repel, or even kill the wicked, and thus protect the holy precincts from defilement. There were, however, further means of ensuring the undiminished holiness of the place: lustrations and sprinklings with consecrated water (cf. *167* and *Plate VIII*).

The model of a temple from Gezer *(167)* shows two fonts of holy water, one at either side of the entrance. In them, everyone who visited the temple could "wash his hands in innocence" (Ps 26:6; cf. 24:4; 73:13; *168*), then go about the altar in the forecourt (Ps 26:6b). The crudely modelled little man on the left in Fig. *167* may be the custodian of the sanctuary. In Assyria, the priests used bronze *situlae* to ladle holy water from the basins. Those who dared pass by the guardian demons were sprinkled with the water *(Plate VIII)* as a

162. "Open to me the gates of the realm of salvation; I will enter through them and give thanks to Yahweh" (Ps 118:19 [author's translation]).

A number of life-signs and *was*-scepters appear above the great pylon of the temple at Karnak, with its eight flags. The signs and scepters characterize the temple as a sphere of life and of divine dominion. A procession has just passed from the temple through the gate. The sacred vessel of Amon is carried in the midst. The cover of the vessel is in the form of a ram's head. The ram is the animal of Amon of Karnak. Amon himself is occasionally portrayed with ram's horns *(256a)*. On either side of the vessel stands a statue of the king (cf. *397a*). The statue on the left side shows him presenting the wine offering. A huge bouquet of flowers towers in front of the vessel. It is not clear who is carrying the bouquet. At the upper left, Nebsunuennet, the governor of the palace, carries two censers *(198–99);* a priest follows him with another type of censer. These fill the air with fragrance. Nebsunuennet is the only layman in the procession. The rest of the party consists exclusively of priests, recognizable by their attire and by their shorn heads, a requirement of the code of priestly purity. The picture adorns the tomb of Panhesi, the "director of the singers of the table of Amon." Panhesi is also a priest. He leads the procession in the lower register. Together with a colleague, he is clapping out the cadence for the procession. Its progress brings the blessings of the temple into the realm of men (cf. other depictions of processions in Figs. *307a, 433a–34a, 450*).

163. In Egypt, the king himself, in the form of a lion, is sometimes the guardian of the temple gates.

164. "The Imdugud-bird killed many adversaries there . . ." (*SAHG*, p. 88).

124

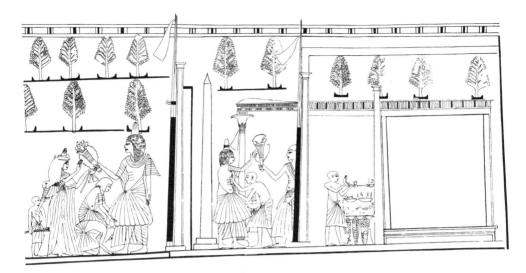

162a. A scene in the Amon Temple at Karnak, from the period of Pharaoh Ay (1349–1345 B.C.). The picture simplifies the complex structure, but preserves all its essential features. The temple fabric surrounds a park with carefully tended trees (cf. Pss 52:8; 92:13; *191, 202*) set in troughs *(10–15)* to facilitate watering. At the left, the park terminates in a pool (not shown here). The temple buildings begin at the left with the great gate installation (shown in profile) of Amenophis III. Flags adorn the facade. The gate is opened inwards. A rose-colored, painted obelisk, apparently of Aswan granite, stands in the court. A baldachin, probably used only on special occasions, is propped against the second pylon. Through the second gate, one passes from the courtyard into the roofed sanctuary, which contains an offering table. The holy of holies lies behind yet another pylon. The holy of holies rests on a socle which equalizes its height with that of the sanctuary.

The axial alignment of chambers, typical to Egypt (cf. *176–77, 238a*), is clearly evident. The successive chambers are accessible to an increasingly smaller circle. In the sanctuary, a priest is offering incense. The high priest,

with an assistant, stands in the sanctuary gate. Neferhotep, a chief overseer of the great livestock herds of Amon, is permitted to enter the courtyard, but his family waits for him outside the first pylon. The high priest rewards Neferhotep's service with a sacred bouquet from Amon's table. The scene at the left shows Neferhotep presenting the bouquet to his wife. The gift must have made a strong impression on Neferhotep, for he had it pictured in his tomb. A scene of similar content from the early Middle Kingdom is found at El Bersheh in the tomb of Ananakht (F. L. Griffith and P. E. Newberry, *El Bersheh,* vol. 2, pls. 17 and 35).

The custom of affording visitors a share in the blessings of a sanctuary was widespread in Byzantine times. The custodians of a shrine sent departing pilgrims on their way with *eulogiai,* "gifts of blessing," in the form of flowers and fruits. Perhaps the "blessing" in Pss 24:5; 67:7; 133:3 and elsewhere should be construed more concretely than is usually done (cf. Isa 65:8; on flowers in the Egyptian cultus and in the OT, cf. A. de Buck, "La fleur au front," and S. Mowinckel, *Psalmenstudien,* vol. 4, pp. 29f.).

165. A stone guardian lion from Til-Barsib (Tell 'Ahmar) bears the following inscription: "[This is] he who rushes against rebellion and purges the enemy country, who bids the evil go and the good come" (A. Parrot, *Assur,* p. 77).

means of purification from any possible impurity.

According to the information provided by the psalms, the pilgrim addressed the priest (or priests) sitting at the temple gates (cf. 1 Sam 1:9), asking who might set foot on the mountain of Yahweh (cf. Pss 15:1; 24:3). The gates of the Jerusalem temple, as "Gates of Righteousness," were open only to the "righteous" (Ps 118:19–20). *ṣdq,* however, connotes not only righteousness, but the salvation which is associated with it. Thus, the "Gates of Righteousness" are at the same time the "Gates of the Realm of Salvation." According to Pss 15 and 24, this salvation can be attained only under certain specific conditions. These conditions may be summarized under the wider category of "conformity with communal conduct."[31] He who professes fulfillment of the conditions (cf. Deut 26:13–14; Job 31) is pronounced righteous (*ṣdyq*) and may pass through the temple gates confident of receiving blessing from Yahweh (Ps 24:5; cf. 15:5). Surprisingly, the subject of these two psalms is not simply cultic impurity. In analogous texts from Egypt[32] and Mesopotamia,[33] cultic impurity always plays an important role. In Pss 24 and 15 (cf. also Ps 50), however, the chief wall which separates God and man is (ethical) misconduct toward one's coreligionists. This wall cannot be overcome by magical-elemental means (guardian spirits, holy water). One can only attempt to reduce the wall by heeding the prophetic advice that under such conditions a temple visit is futile (cf. Ps 50:16–21; 24:5; Amos 5:21–24; Isa 1:10–17; etc.). The suppliant of Ps 73 is aware that only by preserving his purity of heart (Ps 73:1, 13) can he maintain his relation to God, and only thus can he stand on firm ground (cf. Pss 73:15; 15:5c). Those who participate in the cultus without fulfilling the condition of purity proceed on slippery, shaky ground (Ps 73:17–20).

166. Guardian lion from Temple H at Hazor (cf. *208*).

167. At Jerusalem, the following question was asked of the gatekeepers: "Who can ascend the mountain of the LORD? or who may stand in his holy place?" (Ps 24:3 NAB; cf. 15:1).

167a. In Egypt, the king was *the* priest (cf. chap. 5.3). As such, he sat (or stood) in the form of colossal statues at the entrance to the temple, as shown by the relief from the great outer court of Ramses II at Luxor and by numerous finds of similar statues *in situ*. The king's function may have been not only to guard the sanctuary, but also to mediate between the deity and those who were not permitted to enter into the sanctuary proper (cf. P. Barguet, *Le Temple d'Amon-Rê*, pp. 107, 231, 300; W. S. Smith, *Art and Architecture*, p. 151; 1 Sam 1:9).

168. "I wash my hands in innocence . . ." (Ps 26:6).

3. THE FORECOURTS AND THEIR FURNISHINGS

Throughout the entire OT period in Palestine, the larger residential structures of a relatively complete nature are houses of the courtyard type. The individual rooms are grouped around an inner court (169).[34] The courtyard contains one or more cisterns and the baking oven. The wide, main room (broadroom) generally occupies the entire side of the house opposite the entrance. The Yahweh temple at Arad (30 kilometers south of Hebron), in use from the tenth to the eighth century B.C. and excavated in 1963, is essentially a courtyard house with a broad-room (170). The inner court was equipped with a large cistern. The altar of burnt sacrifice assumed, in a sense, the role of the oven. The broadroom contained a niche, which took on the significance of the holy of holies. The symbol of the god was kept within this niche (248). A Hellenistic temple at Lachish (171),[35] shows an arrangement quite similar to that of the temple at Arad. The absence of side chambers in a position lateral to the axis results in a somewhat more accentuated axis than at Arad. The courtyard temples of Arad and Lachish evidence a certain relationship to the temples with broadrooms known from the Ur III period (ca. 2050–1950 B.C.) in southern Mesopotamia. The Enki temple of Amarsin in Ur, which dates back to approximately 1980 B.C., is a fine example of this type of temple (172). The type prevailed into the Neo-Babylonian period, as is evidenced by the ground plan of the Ninmach temple (173) from Nebuchadnezzar's Babylon (604–562 B.C.). The gate structure, as well as the courtyard house, had a formative influence on the Babylonian temple. This is particularly obvious in the protruding towers which flank the broad-room.[36]

The *single* central court is characteris-

169. Typical houses constructed around an inner courtyard, from the period of the Israelite monarchy (S = side room). The courtyard is an integral part of the house.

tic of the four temple installations in Figs. 170–73, as it is in the residential houses of Fig. 169. The court is the heart of the entire design. Whoever stands in the court stands in the midst of the god's house. He is very near to the deity. He can easily catch a glimpse of the god's image; or in other words, the god can appear to him at any moment.

The psalms mention several courts in connection with the Jerusalem temple (Pss 65:4; 84:2, 10; 100:4; etc.). They constitute as integral a part of the Yahweh temple as does the single court of the courtyard house (Ps 65:4). In a number of instances, the term "house of Yahweh" clearly includes the forecourts (Pss 5:7; 135:2; 2 Kgs 11:3–4; Ezek 40:5). It is conceivable that the plural

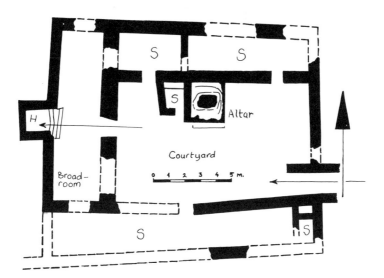

170. Ground plan of the Yahweh Temple at
Arad (10th–8th century B.C.). It exhibits all
the features typical to Israelite residential
houses. Thus, the house of Yahweh is distinguished from other houses only by its occupant (S = side room; H = holy of holies).

"forecourts" [RSV: usually "courts"] is
an intensive plural, as is the case with the
"holy mountains" (Ps 87:1 [RSV: "holy
mount"]), the "mountains of Zion" (Ps
133:3), or the "habitations" or
"dwellings of the Most High" (Pss 46:4;
43:3; 84:1; 87:2; 132:5 [RSV reflects the
Hebrew plural only at Ps 87:2]). There
are in fact a number of pre-exilic passages which speak of the forecourt of the
Yahweh temple in the singular (Jer
19:14; 26:2; Ezek 8:7). But because
there is reference to the "inner
forecourt" [RSV: "inner court"] in the
same chapter of Ezekiel (8:16), and
elsewhere in Jeremiah of the "upper forecourt" [RSV: "upper court"]
(36:10), there must have existed even in
the pre-exilic period a number of
forecourts. 2 Kgs 21:5 and 23:15 enum-
erate two courts in the time of Manasseh
and Josiah. The temple plan in the book
of Ezekiel also reflects knowledge of two
courts (174; Ezek 40–42). There, however, the "inner" court must be identical
to the "upper," since the house of
Yahweh and the altar in front of it were

probably located on the highest point of
the terrain (175).

While there were undoubtedly at least
two forecourts in the pre-exilic period, it
is possible that this was not originally the
case. There is in fact evidence that the
"inner" or "upper" forecourt was subsequently detached from the forecourt
and not extended in front of it.[37] 2 Chr
20:5 refers to a "new forecourt" [RSV:
"court"]. Jehoshaphat faces this "new
court" when leading the people in
prayer. Because one always turned toward the temple for prayer (Pss 28:2;
138:2), the "new forecourt" must mean
the "inner" or "upper" forecourt. It was
not, therefore, originally separate from
the common forecourt.

The later subdivision of the inner
forecourt into a priests' court and an Israelites' court indicates an increasing
emphasis on varying degrees of holiness
(175 I). It is possible that this subdivision
already existed in the Chronicler's time.
In that case, the "new court" would
correspond to the court of the Israelites
in the Herodian temple. In the waning

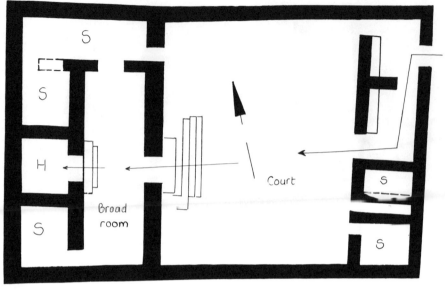

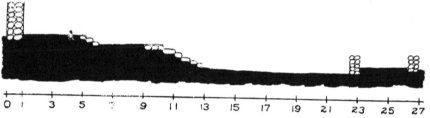

171. Ground plan (a) and section (b) of the foundations of the Yahweh (?) Temple at Lachish. Although the Yahweh Temple at Jerusalem was not built along the lines of a courtyard house, its outer courts were nevertheless regarded as part of the house of Yahweh:

"But I through the abundance of thy steadfast love will enter thy house [*byt*], I will worship toward thy holy temple [*hykl*] in the fear of thee" (Ps 5:7 RSV; Ps 5:8 MT).

Here the *hykl* is part of the *byt*.

days of the monarchy, however, the forecourt (cf. Jer 19:24; 26:2; Ezek 8:7) may have had a general correspondence in function and design to the later "women's court" (*175* W), while the "inner," "upper," or "new" court corresponded to the later court of the Israelites and priests. The area which originally comprised the one court, and was later divided into three courts, probably possessed approximately the same dimensions throughout the course of its history. Hecataeus (350–290 B.C.) states its dimensions as 155 × 50 meters.[38]

The so-called "outer court" or "court of the Gentiles" existed from the very first, inasmuch as a great enclosure wall surrounded the acropolis with its temple and royal palaces (1 Kgs 7:12). Herod, by means of a huge retaining wall (*Plate IX*), developed this enclosure into a splendid plaza. In pre-exilic times, however, it was hardly considered a forecourt of the temple. We have it directly from the psalms that the forecourts were the scene of intense cultic activity. One entered them with songs of praise (Ps 100:4), there to pay one's vows (Ps

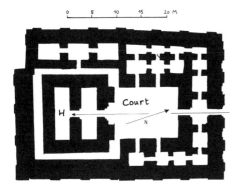

172. The Enki Temple of Amarsia in Ur (ca. 1980 B.C.). Although the entire plan is much richer than those of the courtyard houses and the temples of Arad and Lachish, the common basic concept (interior courtyard, broad-room and side rooms) is nonetheless unmistakable.

173. The Ninmach Temple of Nebuchadnezzar in Babylon (604–562 B.C.). Anyone standing in the courtyard was near the deity, however much the double broad-room may have diminished the nearness. A ziggurat was frequently extended in front of this temple type. In that case, the broad-room assumed the function of a gate in which the deity appeared to men after descending upon the ziggurat. Thus, though the form changes little, the concept changes greatly. In the simple courtyard temple, the god dwells with men; in the courtyard-gate temple he *only appears* to men, while his dwelling remains far from men in heaven.

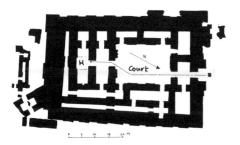

116:18–19) and to rejoice in the presence of Yahweh (Ps 84:10). The priests, who could linger there always, were called blessed. The forecourts belonged to the temple and not to the more distant palace area. In later times that area, as the court of the Gentiles, assumed more of the character of a market place than of a temple court. Only in the temple plan of Ezek 40–42 (which was never realized) was the area of the outer court incorporated into the holy space itself (Ezek 42:20).

The inner court of the temples outlined in Figs. *170–73* almost certainly derives from residential construction. That is hardly the case with regard to the forecourts of the Jerusalem temple. The forecourt extended in front of the temple building. After one building had become several, the courts, strung out on an axis, formed a series of increasingly holier precincts. In this respect, the Jerusalem temple bears a certain resemblance to the plan of Egyptian temples *(162a, 176–77)*.[39] The temple of Amenhotep III (1404–1366 B.C.) at Luxor is a superlative example of the Egyptian temple plan.[40] Essentially, the plan consists of an open forecourt, a covered hall of columns, and the holy of holies, which is surrounded by various chapels. All these elements are arranged on an axis. Particular elements can appear in double form. Fig. *176,* for example, shows two holies of holies; Fig. *177* has two covered halls of columns. In the main, however, there is no notable difference between the Khons temple of Ramses III (1197–1165 B.C.) at Karnak *(176)* and the Horus temple at Edfu *(177)*. The latter is approximately 1,000 years less ancient than the former, having been built between 237 and 57 B.C. The differentiated chambers formed a series of precincts of increasing holiness. The forecourt stands open to common worshippers. The covered vestibule, where all kinds of important ceremonies took place, was reserved to a narrower circle of cult personnel, and only the officiating priest, representing the king, dared enter the holy of holies with its

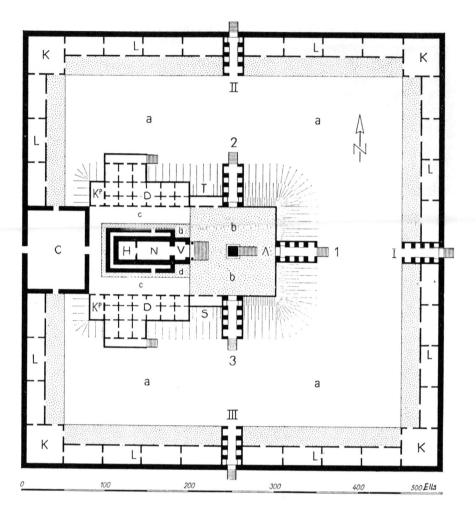

174. Ezekiel's temple plan (Ezek 40:1— 42:20; 43:13–17; 46:19–24). "I. II. III. Gateways of the Outer Court, 1. 2. 3. Gateways of the Inner Court, a. Outer Court, b. Inner Court, c. Enclosure, d. Temple Terrace, HNV, Temple House (H. Holy of Holies, N. Nave, V. Vestibule), A. Altar of Burnt Sacrifice, S. Chamber for the Sacrificial Priests, T. Chamber for the Temple Priests, D. Priests' dressing and dining Rooms, K^P. Kitchens for sacrifices consumed by the Priests, K. Kitchens for sacrifices consumed by the People, L. Halls of the Laity, C. Courtyard, apparently serving as a depository of sacrificial offal.

"The reconstruction is hypothetical in many particulars. The only assured dimensions are those of the temple proper, the altar, the gates, the courts, the retaining wall, and the Parbar. The number of steps in the stairways provide definite information concerning differences in elevation; the stairways themselves are overdrawn" (BHH, vol. 3, cols. 1943f.).

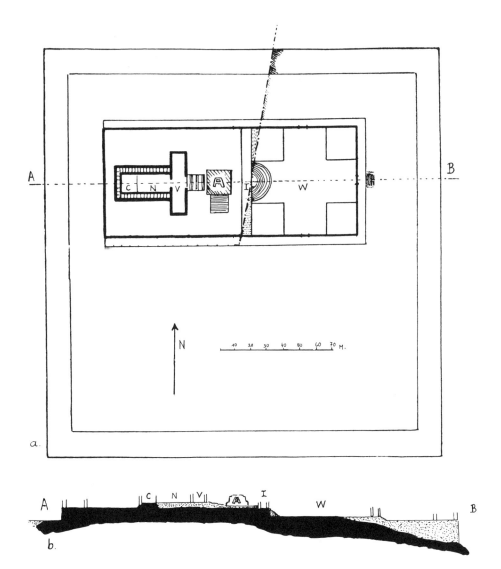

a.

b.

175. Ground plan (a) and section A-B (b) of the Herodian temple according to the reconstruction of H. Schmidt. CNV: Temple proper, C. *Cella* (Holy of holies), N. Nave, V. Vestibule, A. Great altar of burnt sacrifice, I. Court of the Israelites. In other reconstructions, the Court of the Israelites is shown of a uniform width surrounding the courtyard with the temple and altar. W. Women's Court. In the section-drawing: The black area marks the rock; the dotted areas indicate fill. In Schmidt's reconstruction, the Holy of holies (C) is situated above the Holy Rock (cf. pp. 118f.). The semicircular stairs (between W and I) rise approximately four meters from the Women's Court to the next level. Even today, the gap is surmounted by a monumental staircase situated due east of 'Abd al-Malik's domed edifice (cf. *Plate IX*).

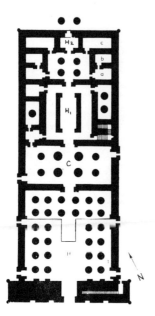

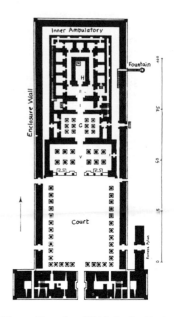

176. The Khonsu Temple of Ramses III (1197–1165 B.C.) at Karnak. The gradation of chambers of increasing sanctity is typical of Egyptian temple construction (C. Hall of Columns; H. Holy of Holies).

177. Horus Temple of Edfu in the Ptolemaic Period (V. Vestibule, C. Hall of Columns, H. Holy of Holies, N. *naos*).

statue of the deity *(162a, 229–30).*[41] As in Jerusalem, so too in Egypt there may be discerned a growing need to emphasize the increasing holiness of the graduated chambers. This was accomplished in part by increasing the number of spaces.[42] At the same time, however, the design invited entry. It sought "to captivate the visitor with magical power and to draw him ever further into the sanctuary."[43]

In the Canaanite sphere, the Baal temple of Ugarit *(178),* with its courtyard extending in front of the cov-ered(?) vestibule, is reminiscent of an Egyptian temple. That does not imply that it evidences Egyptian influence. The bent axis of the *cella* (the podium is not in line with the axis of the forecourt and vestibule) definitely detracts from the impression of axially differentiated rooms. By replacing the broad-room with a long hall, however, we arrive at

the temple configuration typical of the Jerusalem and later Syrian temples. In contrast to the Egyptian pattern, the god's house stands in isolation. One can-not stand before the god until one has passed through one or more courts situated on an axis. Thus in the Baal-Jupiter temple at Baalbek, there is a se-quence of colonnaded vestibule, hexag-onal courtyard, the great altar court, and finally the temple proper, set on a platform at the top of a monumental flight of stairs *(179).*

All these arrangements permit the faithful to ascend (in reality or in spirit) through ever holier precincts and up var-ious stairways to the mysteriously re-mote deity. In Jerusalem, the pilgrim—ideally approaching from the east (though there were entrances from south and north as well)—passed through the gate of the first court. The gate liturgy may have been performed at this point.

For that reason, the portals of the fore-court are called "Gates of Righteousness" (Ps 118:19; Isa 26:2). Once the pilgrim had crossed the first court, he ascended a stairway to the gate of the upper court. This may have been the "Yahweh Gate" [RSV: "gate of the LORD"] (Ps 118:20). After crossing the inner court he stood before the elongated temple building. At its opposite end arose the holy of holies, where Yahweh dwelt in darkness. The arrangement of the forecourts conveys the impression of the sublimity of Yahweh. The worshipper who had entered the courts reverently prostrated himself in the presence of the overpowering majesty of God (cf. 412–13).

The testimony of the psalms suggests, however, that in the temple courts the salutary power of Yahweh's blessing (cf. Pss 65:4; 84:2, 10; 94:13) was felt even more keenly than was his grandeur. This is attributable less to the architectural arrangement of the forecourts than to their appointments.

Pss 52:8 and 92:12 suggest that mag-

nificent olive trees, palms, and cedars of Lebanon stood in the temple courts. Their healthy green proclaims Yahweh's power of blessing. Mighty *trees* in general were considered to be "trees of God" (Pss 80:10; 104:16a). The expression "trees of God" is basically a superlative. The term may be explained, however, by the special relation of these trees to Yahweh (cf. Ps 104:16b). Vegetation throughout the entire country suffers as a result of the destruction of the temple and the departure of Yahweh (Hag 1:6, 10–11). In his shadow, however, vegetation flourishes as it does nowhere else. This notion is extremely ancient. A Sumerian hymn says of the Ninazu temple in Eshnunna: "Ninazu makes the plants grow luxuriantly round about you."[44] Another Sumerian hymn boasts of the Enki temple in Eridu: "the birds brood in its flourishing garden, which bears abundant fruits"[45] (cf. Ps 84:3 regarding birds). Temple gardens are attested throughout Mesopotamia, from Eridu and Uruk in the south to Assur in the north *(191, 202),* and also in Canaan *(182).*[46] Trees also were a feature of the temples in Egypt *(162a).* A love poem from the New Kingdom speaks of the trees which belong to the house of the glorious one (Re of Heliopolis).[47] Their planting was a ritual act.[48]

Fig. *180* shows Ur-Nammu of Ur (2060–1955 B.C.) offering a libation[49] to a tree which apparently represents the moon god Nanna, who sits enthroned behind it (cf. *239).* The beneficent power of the god is present in the tree (cf. *253–55).* The king, in strengthening the tree by a drink offering, enhances that power. In return, the tree dispenses life-giving water. Water-giving trees or gods appear quite frequently in Mesopotamian iconography and its Palestinian offshoots. A potsherd from Megiddo *(181)* shows a stylized tree with three pairs of goats. The presence of water (suggested by the two fish), which streams down from the crown of the tree, indicates that the symbol is one of fertility. The water symbolizes life, which is perceived in an almost material

178. In the Baal Temple of Ugarit, as in Egyptian temples, the court extends in front of the vestibule and the holy of holies. In contrast to Egyptian plans, however, the courtyard is not of a piece with the building proper. The bent-axis *cella* is also quite un-Egyptian.

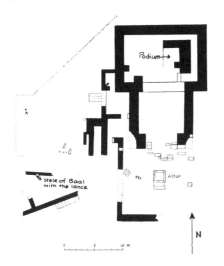

manner in the shade of holy trees (cf. Ps 121:5–6: "The LORD is your shade").

In the psalms, Yahweh himself is the source of all life. The river of delights emanates from him (Ps 36:8–9). In *his* shade one finds protection from the burning sun and from all kinds of other dangers (Pss 91:1; 121:5). The faithful are compared to the temple trees (Pss 52:8; 92:12–13), in which God's invisible, mysterious blessing is especially operative. The Sumerian king is celebrated as a "choice cedar which is an ornament in the court of the Ekur" (the principal temple of Nippur), "rooted in abundant waters," whose "shadow the land of Sumer humbly adores."[50]

Water, like trees, is a feature of the temple courts. It has been shown above that water is closely linked to trees. To be sure, the "bronze sea" (cf. 1 Kgs 7:23–26, 44; 2 Chr 4:2–10) is not mentioned in the psalms. However, it does play a part in the water symbolism of the psalms, and it must therefore be considered here. The term "sea" indicates that this is no mere wash basin (though it naturally fulfilled that function). Rather, its

water represents the harnessed, subdued Chaos from which the world arose. Whether it represents the heavenly or the subterranean ocean[51] is an irrelevant question, since both oceans (and the earthly ocean as well) originally and essentially belong together (cf. *37, 39*). The Babylonian *apsû* sometimes denotes an earthly entity, sometimes a subterranean entity, and sometimes a supercelestial one.[52] The bulls [RSV: "oxen"] which bear the bronze sea (1 Kgs 7:25; 2 Kgs 16:17) are symbols of fertility (cf. *290, 292, 294*). They are also found on a large cult basin from Cyprus (*183*). The two huge waterbasins in front of the temple of Muzazir (cf. *139*) are set on bulls' feet. The bulls of Fig. *183a*, however, may represent the closest analogy to the bulls of the bronze sea.[53]

The subdued primeval waters fecundate the earth (cf. Pss 46:4 with 46:3; 74:15 with 74:13–14; 104:10 with 104:6–9). In many temples we find not only basins, but sacred pools and lakes as well. In Egypt these were a source of water for the olive and myrrh plantations whose yields served the cultus. The

180. The tree in the vase-altar, like the Massebah on the Massebah-altar (*193*) is an em-

bodiment of the deity (cf. *253–55*).

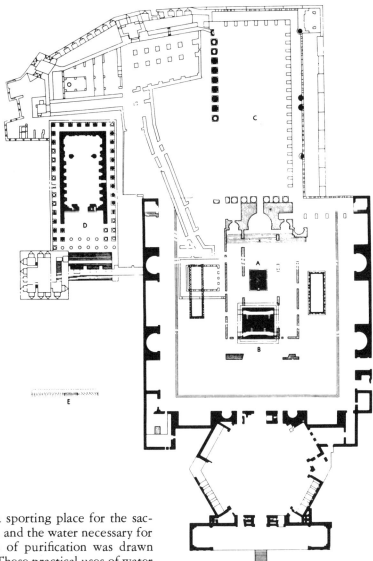

pools were a sporting place for the sacrificial geese, and the water necessary for various rites of purification was drawn from them. These practical uses of water proved no obstacle to the notion that here were indeed the holy, primeval waters from which the world emerged.[54] The same may have been the case in Jerusalem. The representation of the primeval sea did not exclude practical functions (2 Chr 4:10).

The symbolism of these basins sometimes suggests one thing, sometimes another. The sides of the temple pools at Baalbek (cf. 179) are decorated with sea motifs (184). A cult basin from the Assur temple in Assur[55] shows water-giving deities and priests of Ea (185)

179. "Enter . . . his courts with praise!" (Ps 100:4b).

In the Baal-Jupiter Temple at Baalbek, two courts, situated on an axis, extend in front of the temple proper (C). Two enormous altars (A and B; B was almost 20 meters high) were located in the second court; on either side of the altars lay two carefully bordered pools.

137

182. The upper part of this cultic stand from Meggido (1350–1150 B.C.) represents a temple surrounded by trees.

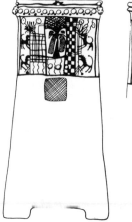

181. The divine powers attributed to trees such as the one pictured below are represented by two streams of water (with fish). Water is the equivalent of fertility and life (cf. 256 and 256a).

drawing holy water. The latter wear the skin of the symbolic animal of the god of rites and purifications (cf. 43, 91, and 285). Secretions from the holy trees increase the potency of the life-giving water (186); or perhaps the tree of life is brought to flower by sprinklings with the water (cf. 23–24). Fig. 187, from the mortuary temple of Seti I at Abydos, shows that the temple pools as well as the temple trees (cf. 180) were seen as a manifestation of the divine power present in the temple. A libation intended for the deity could be poured out to either.

Just as the great streams which water the earth flow forth from paradise (Gen 2:10–14), so too the blessing which emanates from the temple (Ps 133:3) will take concrete form in rivers which fructify the entire country. In the eschatological day of salvation, a wonderful stream will issue from the temple (Ezek 47:1; Joel 3:18; Zech 14:8; Rev 22:1–2; cf. 256a). Ps 46:4, however, speaks in the present of a river whose channels make glad the city of God (cf. Ps 65:9). Commentators generally agree that this stream makes Jerusalem a kind of paradise. Beyond that, the verse has given rise to the most diverse interpretations. Delitzsch speaks of the stream of grace.[56] Junker suggests that Yahweh is to Jerusalem what the Euphrates is to Babylon.[57] Gunkel interprets the entire psalm as a prophetic vision.[58] Kraus opposes that view and discerns instead very ancient cultic traditions transferred to Jerusalem.[59] In general, such cult traditions tend to attach themselves to specific features of temple furniture or—in the case of primary traditions—to be concretized in the same. There are a number of possibilities. Kraus quite

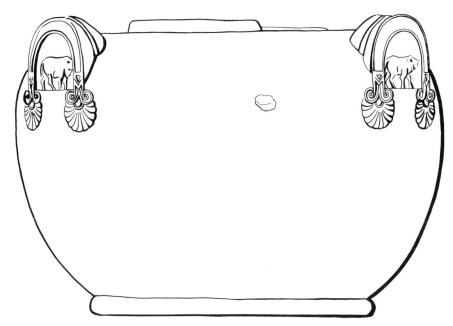

183. This limestone basin from Amathont on Cyprus measures 2.2 meters in diameter. The diameter of the Bronze Sea was almost twice as great. These dimensions, enormous by ancient standards, were in keeping with the concept that the basins contained the holy waters of the primeval sea.

183a. Pairs of lions, bulls, and similar animals served as bases for statues in the north Syrian region at the beginning of the first millennium B.C. The flat trough between the bulls pictured here, however, is not suited to such a function. C. L. Woolley, the archaeologist who discovered them (*Carchemish*, vol. 3, pp. 168f.), has suggested that these bulls, like those of the Solomonic temple, supported a huge water basin.

184. The temple pools at Baalbek *(179)* were decorated with sea motifs. Tritons and Nereids embody waves and wind.

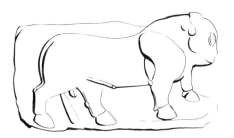

185. "A river flowed out of Eden to water the garden, and there it divided and became four rivers" (Gen 2:10).

"There is a river whose streams make glad the city of God" (Ps 46:4).

In these instances, "river" *(nhr)* may signify the primeval sea.

wrongly rejects any identification of the stream with the spring Gihon[60] which rises at the foot of the ancient city hill. Like Ps 46, Isaiah (8:6–7) contrasts raging, roaring waters to gently flowing waters. In Isaiah, the gently flowing waters are specifically identified as those of Shiloah, the conduit (or one of the conduits?) of Gihon. It should be noted that Ps 46:4 speaks not of the temple area, but of the city of God. Of course it is possible that in this instance "city of God" denotes only the temple area (cf. 2 Kgs 10:25 RSVm) and not Jerusalem as a whole. Perhaps the aqueduct from the time of Herod and Pilate was not the first to carry water to the sanctuary (cf. 202). It is interesting to note that in the Assyrian water system of Fig. 202 (early seventh century B.C.), the water in the temple area is divided, as in Ps 46:4, into several channels. Finally we should note that *nhr* (as has been shown with reference to Fig. 8) denotes not only running water, but frequently—especially in the psalms—the sea. From that point of view, the *nhr* could have been represented in cultic symbolism by the "bronze sea."

The waters divided (*plg* I means "to divide") from the sea (*ym, nhr*) would then have found concrete form in the lavers, which were of very imposing size. According to 1 Kgs 7:27–29, there were ten lavers in the temple at Jerusalem. The laver from Larnaka on Cyprus (*188*), like those of the Solomonic tem-

186. The god of the ground waters (cf. *91*) was a god of magic and healing. Here his priests are shown at the tree of life.

140

187. The Pharaoh pours a drink offering into the temple pools, thereby contributing to the preservation of their sacred powers.

ple (cf. 1 Kgs 7:29), is decorated with cherubim. Palms, bulls [RSV: "oxen"], and lions also appeared on the Solomonic lavers (1 Kgs 7:29, 36). Ezekiel (41:18) notes that a palm tree was always set between two cherubim.

The palm between two cherubim is merely a variation of the motif of the tree of life set between two animals, men, or divine beings (23, 24, 181, 186).[61] This motif, originating in Mesopotamia, became widespread in Palestine. It was carved on ivories, painted on vessels,[62] and cut into cylinder seals.[63] In the earlier period, the tree of life (frequently a more or less stylized palm) was usually flanked by goats (cf. 181) or oxen. In the second century B.C.,

188. Wheeled lavers adorned with cherubim were part of the inventory of the Solomonic temple. If the Bronze Sea is a cultic-symbolic representation of the River (*nhr;* Ps 46:5 MT; 46:4 RSV), the lavers may signify its branches (divisions).

189. The goats at the tree of life presage its vital powers, while the cherubs signalize its holiness. In the psalms, cherubim always appear in immediate proximity to the deity.

and especially in the first, cherubim began to replace them. Both variants appear together on an ivory from Nimrud *(189)*. The cherubim heighten the impression that the wondrous tree mediates mysterious powers. The gold lamella *(190)*, with its tree of life guarded by cherubim, was stitched to the breast of a deceased person. It was perhaps intended to mediate to him some of the inexhaustible powers of the tree of life. The homely sacramental symbol became a magical-mythical entity.[64]

A highly interesting wall painting from Mari *(191)* shows a rectangular space surrounded by a wall (not visible in Fig. *191*) and a spiral band (not visi-

ble). Within the space appears a date palm with a huge dove at its crown. The courtyard enclosed two additional rectangles set one above the other. They are flanked by two trees (or treelike emblems), four cherubim, and two bulls. One foot of each bull is planted on a mountaintop. The two mountains probably indicate that the center of the court is located on a mountain. The two fountain deities (cf. *153*) in the lower of the two smaller rectangles correspond to the two mountains. A stream with four branches (cf. Gen 2:10) rises from the vessels held by the deities. A stylized plant grows out of the stream. This is the place from which all life issues. In the center of this region, in the upper

190. Gold lamella with a flourishing tree of life and cherubim. These were buried with the deceased as an adornment and amulet.

191. "The righteous flourish like the palm tree, and grow like a cedar in Lebanon. They are planted in the house of the LORD, they flourish in the courts of our God. They still bring forth fruit in old age, they are ever full of sap and green, to show that the LORD is upright" (Ps 92:12–15a).

The presence of Yahweh in Jerusalem is manifested not so much in the magnificent trees as in the prosperity of the righteous.

rectangle, stands Ishtar, the goddess of fertility, love, and war. The palm is her tree and the dove is her bird (cf. *290*). Her right foot is set on a lion. The king stands in greeting before her. She appears to be presenting him with ring and staff.[65] In any case, the picture depicts all parts of an entire temple complex. The temple building is a broad-room with a wide antechamber (cf. *172–73, 207*). The anteroom and the forecourt incorporate all those features which characterize the temple as a sphere of life. We find these features repeated—almost without exception—in the Solomonic temple and in the description of paradise: the mountain (Ezek 28:13–16), the rivers, the trees, the cherubim. Even the bulls are present. In the Jerusalem temple they carried the bronze sea (1 Kgs 7:25). Belief in the presence of the *living* God supplied the temple forecourts with all the symbols which had already played a role in the Ishtar temple of Mari.

4. THE ALTARS

The altar, or rather, the altars also constitute part of the furniture of the forecourts. Altars also belong to the inventory of the temple building. Here they will be dealt with together. According to the magical-mythical conception of the world, man could not simply participate in the vital forces of the holy precincts without contributing his part to the preservation and renewal of the same. His contribution was sacrifice.

Figs. *180* and *187* quite clearly show how the king, as chief priest, sustains the life-force through his offerings. Sacrifice was widely understood as the supplying of food (*192*). Thus the evaporation of liquid, the desiccation of sacrificial offerings (*288*), their burning, or their enjoyment by sacred animals (*440*) may have reinforced the belief that they had been appropriated by the gods. A large portion of the sacrifices was also consumed by the priests, as stipulated in the legislation regarding sacrifice in Lev 1–9. In an addition to the Book of Daniel (Dan 14 [Bel and the Dragon]) this practice is set forth as a great fraud perpetrated by heathen priests.

Experience and knowledge of Yahweh's independence from the cosmic structure rendered sacrifice problematical in Israel (cf. Ps 50 and chap. 6.2). Nevertheless, it was provisionally retained, and it was reinterpreted only in certain respects.

If the sacrifice in and of itself represents a meal or gift for the deity and does not merely envision an interior act on the part of the worshipper, then it is obvious

192. Sometimes ingestion of nourishment by the deity was conceived of in a rather anthropomorphic fashion. This impression from an Anatolian cylinder seal seems to suggest such a view. The god of war, with his double axe, sits enthroned. The person making sacrifice is about to pour his libation directly into the god's cup (but cf. *375, 441–43*). Another worshipper, conducted by a tutelary goddess, brings forward a small male goat (cf. *435–36*). Ps 50:8–15 is directed against anthropomorphic conceptions of the nourishment of the Deity.

that the altar, as the place where the food or offering was set, must have been understood as the god's table, or as a representation of the deity himself. Subjectively or objectively, first one, then the other sense can come to the fore. The psalms repeatedly convey the impression that to the suppliant the altar was more a representation of Yahweh himself than simply a place of slaughter or some kind of table. That is the case, for example, when the suppliant circles round the altar singing the praises of Yahweh (Ps 26:6–7), or when going to the altar is parallel to appearing before God (Ps 43:4; cf. also Ps 118:27).

The altar is both a place of sacrifice and a representation of the deity, even when it consists of no more than a series of cavities or basinlike holes in a venerated, holy rock. The Holy Rock in Jerusalem may originally have been such an altar (154).

At first glance, those altars made of heaped up earth or uncut stones (Plates X and XI; Gen 31:46; Josh 8:31) seem to have had the character of a

193. ". . . I will go to the altar of God, to the God of my exceeding joy" (Ps 43:4).

podium, a slaughtering place, or a table. But the archaic prescriptions that the altar be built only of uncut stones and that one must not mount it on steps, "that your nakedness be not exposed on it" (Exod 20:25–26), intimate that even the stone-heap altar was understood to be more than a table. The altar of burnt sacrifice in the forecourt of the Yahweh temple at Arad (cf. 170 and 248) is built, in compliance with Exod 20:25, of uncut stones and without steps (Plate XI).

194. "Arrange the festal dance with branches, up to the horns of the altar" (Ps 118:27b,c AT).

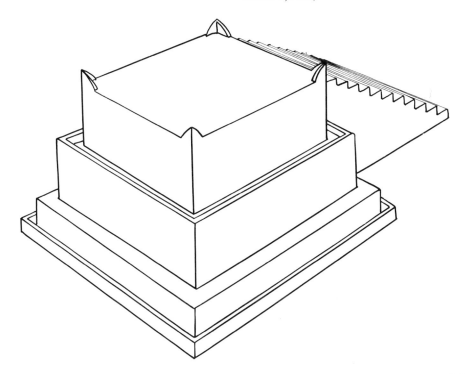

Its dimensions correspond to those specified in Exod 27:1 for the bronze-covered wooden altar of the tabernacle in the wilderness (5 × 5 × 3 ells [RSV: "cubits"] = ca. 2.25 × 2.25 × 1.35 meters). Thus, in the altar of burnt sacrifice at Arad, elements of *two* very different conceptions (Exod 20:25–26 and 27:1) take material form in a legitimate Yahweh altar.

The two functions of the altar (representation of the deity and "table") find their clearest expression in the Massebah altar typical of the Syrian-Phoenician cultural circle (*193*).[66] The Massebah altar shown in Fig. *193* is suited for offering sprinklings of blood, but not for burnt sacrifice. The horns at the four corners of the altar (cf. *195, 246*), a feature attested quite early in the Syrian-Phoenician sphere, may owe their origin to a quartered or quadruple Massebah which was first moved from the middle of the altar to the corners for practical reasons, perhaps to provide room for the burnt offering.[67] In any case, a great many OT texts indicate that the horns of the altar represent the deity in a very special way. The festal procession reached its goal at the horns of the altar (Ps 118:27); at them the man seeking asylum finds protection (1 Kgs 1:50; 2:28; Amos 3:14). The predication,

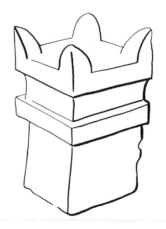

195. ". . . horn of my salvation" (Ps 18:3).

"horn of my salvation," accorded to Yahweh in Ps 18:3, may be connected with the power of protection offered by the horns of the altar. The blood of atonement is also applied to the horns of the altar (Lev 8:15; 16:18; etc.)

We are not certain of the appearance of the principal altar which stood before the Solomonic temple. It was in all probability cubical, built of wood (Exod 27:1–2) or stones, and in either case covered with copper (2 Kgs 16:14; 1 Kgs 8:64; 2 Chr 6:13; Exod 27:1–2). It was relatively small (1 Kgs 8:64; 2 Kgs 16:14). According to 2 Chr 6:13 it pos-

196. "I . . . go about thy altar, O LORD, singing aloud a song of thanksgiving, and tell-

ing all thy wondrous deeds" (Ps 26:6b–7).

sessed the canonical measurements (Exod 27:1–2) already encountered in the altar of burnt sacrifice of the temple at Arad *(Plate XI),* which continued in use into the Solomonic period. 1 Kgs 1:50 and 2:28 indicate that the four corners of the altar were provided with horns, which would also conform to the canonical requirements of Exod 27:1. A four-horned altar of carefully hewn stones (1.57 meters high) was recently discovered at Beersheba. Its stones had been reused in a wall dating from the eighth century B.C.[68] Since an altar of such modest proportions was too small for the greater solemnities (cf. Ps 66:15), the middle portion of the forecourt was used as a place of slaughter and sacrifice (1 Kgs 8:64).

Around 730 B.C., King Ahaz had the old copper altar replaced by a new, larger one (2 Kgs 16:10–16). It could be mounted by steps (2 Kgs 16:12; *193–94, 196).* King Ahaz built this altar after a model he had seen with the Assyrian king (?) in Damascus. Since there are no Assyrian step-altars, the prototype may have been Aramean.[69] De Groot[70] and Galling[71] conjecture that the altar of Ahaz corresponded in essentials to the Ezekiel altar. Three blocks measuring 8 × 8 × 1 meters, 7 × 7 × 2 meters, and 6 × 6 × 2 meters (Ezek 43:13–17) surmounted a base socle of approximately 9 × 9 × 0.5 meters. At the four corners of the altar were horns 0.5 meters in height. Steps led up to the altar from the east *(194; cf. 193 and 196).* The altar was large enough for doves, swallows, and sparrows to nest in it (Ps 84:3). This would be quite possible if the altar was built of uncut stones which in time developed numerous cracks and crannies. According to 2 Chr 4:1, an altar of the huge dimensions of the Ahaz-Ezekiel altar already existed in Solomonic times. However, that may be an instance of anachronism.

When the temple was destroyed by the Babylonians, the altar of burnt sacrifice was also destroyed. According to Ezra 3:3, however, it was rebuilt on its old foundations. That detail is confirmed by Hecataeus, who states that in the third century B.C. there stood before the temple an altar (approximately 4.5 meters high) of uncut stones built on a square foundation (with sides approximately 9 meters wide).[72] 1 Macc 4:47 confirms its construction of uncut stones. After Antiochus IV had desecrated the old altar, the Jews razed it. Then "they took unhewn stones, as the law directs, and built a new altar like the former one." Josephus also tells us that the altar was made of uncut stones.[73] In view of the size, one could hardly dispense with steps, despite Exod 20:26.

In Ps 84:3, altars are mentioned in the plural *(mzbḥwt).* The question of whether this plural refers to a plural number of places of sacrifice or is to be construed as a sacral plural, as in "mountains" (Pss 87:1 MT; 133:3) or "dwellings" (Pss 43:3 MT; 46:5 MT [RSV 46:4]; 84:2 MT [RSV 84:1]; 132:5, 7 MT) is probably to be resolved in favor of the latter sense. The texts cited above refer without exception to only one altar. The table for the showbread and the costly golden altar (1 Kgs 7:48) were in the interior of the temple and consequently could not provide the nesting place presupposed by Ps 84:3.

The golden altar of 1 Kgs 7:48 may have been an altar of incense. According to Exod 30:1–10, even the tabernacle in the wilderness was equipped with an altar of incense. It was approximately 90 centimeters high, and was furnished with four horns (cf. *195).*

The holy of holies of the Yahweh temple at Arad contained two incense altars *(248).* The larger of the two was approximately the same size as the horned altar of Megiddo *(195),* which may also have served as an incense altar. Approximately 150 incense altars from the Persian period have been found at Lachish. The inscription on one of them indicates that in postexilic Lachish, as well as in pre-exilic Arad, one sought to appease Yahweh's wrath *('p)* by soothing his nose *('p)* with incense *(197).*

Instead of an actual altar, a basin on a portable stand could also serve for burn-

197. The inscription on this altar from Lachish reads: "Incense (from) Y(a'u)sh, (the) son of Mech(ir) for Yah(weh), (our?) Lord."

198. Stand with a bowl for burning incense (cf. *199*). It was believed that the wrath of the gods could be appeased by fragrant odors pleasing to the nose *('ap),* for a characteristic sign of wrath is heavy breathing through the nose. For that reason, *'ap* could be used as a term for wrath (cf. Num 16:46–47). Ps 18:15 speaks of the wrathful blast of Yahweh's nostrils.

199. The offering of incense was an important part of expiatory sacrifices. On occasions of extreme necessity, the Canaanites and Phoenicians even sacrificed their own children. This fact is attested by Philo of Byblos (cited by Porphyry *De abstinentia* 2.56) and other writings. Lucian the Syrian supplements these reports with a further detail: the children were sometimes simply thrown or let fall from a lofty structure (*De dea Syria* 58). It is by no means certain, however, that the above illustration depicts this practice (*contra* P. Derchain, "Les plus anciens témoignages"). Here the Canaanites hold out a child to Ramses II; in precisely the same manner, the Philistines on their oxcarts hold out their children to Ramses III (H. H. Nelson et al., *Earlier Historical Records,* pl. 34; less clear in *ANEP,* no. 813). The arms, reaching downwards, set the children on the ground from the low oxcarts. Thus, it is not a matter of sacrifice, but of the giving of hostages. The same applies to the picture above (cf. also *86, 132a;* and O. Keel, "Kanaanäische Sühneriten").

ing incense (*198:* cf. 1 Kgs 7:50). Egyptian reliefs often show beleaguered Canaanites paying tribute to the Pharaoh, who storms upon them like a god of war (*132a, 300–302*); they attempted to placate him by offering incense (*132a, 199,* and cf. *86* and *162*). In doing so, they employed utensils quite similar to that shown in Fig. *198*. Some 1,000 years later, a similar incense burner appears in a relief on a Palmyrenian altar (*200*). The Aramaic inscription on the back of the altar informs us that such an instrument was called *ḥammān*.[74] In the OT, *ḥammānîm* were regarded as typically Canaanite, and were thus repudiated by the prophets (Isa 17:8; 27:9; Ezek 6:4, 6). It is therefore unlikely that such portable stands (or similarly portable incense coffers) were used for burning incense in the Jerusalem temple. Instead, as suggested in Exod 30:1–10 and 1 Kgs 7:48, a proper, albeit small altar was probably used. It would have been similar to those found at Arad and Lachish.

According to 1 Kgs 7:48, there was in the temple at Jerusalem another table besides the altar of incense: it was the table for the bread of the Presence (cf. 1 Sam 21:1–7). If the reference in 1 Kgs 6:20 is to be applied to it, it was made of cedar. According to Exod 25:23–30, it measured about 90 × 45 centimeters and was approximately 65 centimeters high. The show-bread table on the Arch of Titus quite accurately reflects these dimensions (cf. *460*). Ezekiel 41:21–22 calls for a table twice that size. Fig. *201* shows an Assyrian presentation table.

In Egypt, one presentation table is often placed next to another (cf. *196*). In Assyria, however, a single table is the rule (*373, 440*).[75] That apparently held true in the Canaanite-Mesopotamian region as well. There the gods were more consistently conceived of in anthropomorphic fashion than was the case in Egypt (cf. pp. 46, 326). As the OT demonstrates, that proved a lesser deterrent to an increasingly barren understanding of sacrifice than the more strongly dynamistic view of Egypt,

200. A portable incense stand, shown on the relief of an altar. The Aramaic inscription on the back of the altar informs us that the term for such a stand was *ḥammān*. *ḥammānîm* were apparently not used in the Jerusalem cultus, and were condemned by the prophets as a typically Canaanite implement.

where it was believed that the divine powers could be almost boundlessly augmented by increased sacrifices.

An Assyrian relief from the palace of Assurbanipal in Nineveh (*202*) very aptly summarizes what has been said thus far concerning the temple as region of life (cf. *162a, 191*): the entire temple complex rises on a mountain. The immediate vicinity of the temple is characterized by trees (*180–82*) and water (*183–88*). The water is remarkably supplied by an aqueduct,[76] which divides into several branches on the temple mount. The temple proper is not easily identified. At first glance, the arch at the left appears to be the entrance, and the pillared structure on the right the long-room, shown from the side (on the com-

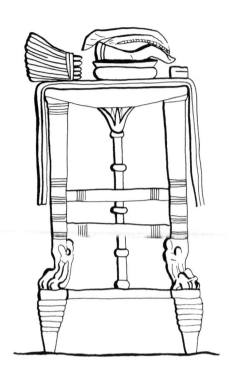

201. "If I were hungry, I would not tell you; for the world and all that is in it is mine" (Ps 50:12).

202. "How lovely is your dwelling place, O LORD of hosts! My soul yearns and pines for the courts of the LORD. My heart and my flesh cry out for the living God. . . . Happy they who dwell in your house! continually they praise you. Happy the men whose strength you are! their hearts are set on the pilgrimage. . . . I had rather one day in your courts than a thousand elsewhere" (Ps 84:2–3, 5–6, 11a NAB; cf. Ps 84:1–2, 4–5, 10a RSV).

bination of various aspects, cf. the gate and altar in Fig. *196*). This interpretation is seemingly reinforced by the presence of something like masonry between the pillars of the "long-room." Oddly enough, however, the vertical butt joints appear to be missing. However, this interpretation is seriously undermined by the fact that "up to the present there is no evidence from Syria of a temple plan with engaged columns, and that is precisely what we are faced with."[77] In consequence, we must probably take the supposed long-room to be the front of a *templum in antis* with two pillars,[78] and interpret the supposed masonry as the registers of a bronze portal or something of the kind. The supposed entrance, however, was probably a stele which actually stood in front of the temple and separate from it (cf. *440*). The stele bears the portrait of an Assyrian king in an attitude of worship (cf. *418*). The *via*

sacra with its little altar may have led in a straight line not only to the stele, but also to the very front of the temple which lay behind it.

S. Mowinckel assumes that the Jerusalem temple, like most great ancient Near Eastern sanctuaries, must have had its *via sacra*.[79] He takes *mslwt* of Ps 84:6 MT [RSV: 84:5] as an allusion to it. *mslh* is a paved street. The plural would have an intensive character, as in "mountains," "dwellings," and "altars."[80] Mowinckel assumes that the street would have led over the western hill to the temple mount (cf. *151* and *152*). It is more probable, however, that it led from Gihon (1 Kgs 1:38–39, 45), following at first the Kidron Valley, then approached the temple from the east, so that its last section merged with the extended axis of the temple complex.

5. THE HOUSE OF YAHWEH

The psalms use two principal terms for what we call the temple (or more precisely, the temple building): "house *(byt)* of Yahweh" (Pss 5:7; 23:6; 26:8; 27:4; etc.) and "palace *(hykl* [RSV: 'temple'], from the Sumerian *e-gal*, 'great house') of Yahweh" (Pss 5:7; 27:4; 48:9; 65:5; etc.). Neither *byt* nor *hykl* in themselves denote anything specifically cultic (as for instance our "temple" or "church"). The house or palace of Yahweh is therefore distinguished terminologically from other buildings only by its inhabitant or owner. The same is true of the term "dwelling place" *(mškn;* Pss 26:8 MT; 74:7); in a number of passages the plural [reflected in MT only] indicates the special quality of this particular dwelling place (Pss 43:3; 46:5 MT [RSV 46:4]; 84:2 MT [RSV 84:1]; 132:5, 7; cf. above p. 114).

There were two important types of houses in the ancient Near East. In both,

the basic shape was rectangular, but one had the entrance on the narrow side *(203)*, the other on the long side *(204)*. In the first type, in the case of a temple, the cult statue is usually placed on the narrow side opposite the entrance. This arrangement, like that of the later Christian basilicas, emphasizes the distance between the visitor and the god. The long-house may have originated in southern Russia.[81]

Two major variants of the second house-type are to be identified: in one, the entrance is located at the extreme end of the broad side *(205)*; in the other, it is placed at its center *(206)*. In the first instance, the visitor must turn ninety degrees upon entering in order to view the main portion of the room. This type is consequently called the bent-axis or "Around-the-corner" type. In passing by such a house, one sees nothing but the opposite wall near the door. The bent-

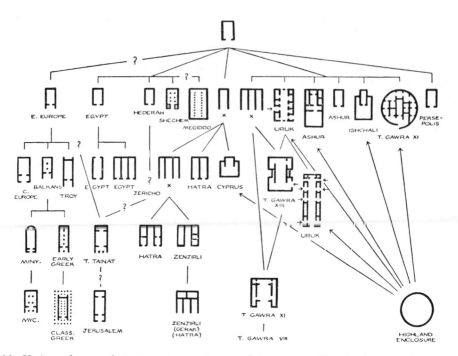

203. Various forms of the long-house. In temple structure, the long-house places distance between the visitor and the deity, whose image was located at the remote end of the narrow side. At the same time, however, the structure draws the worshipper toward the deity.

204. Various forms of the broad-house.

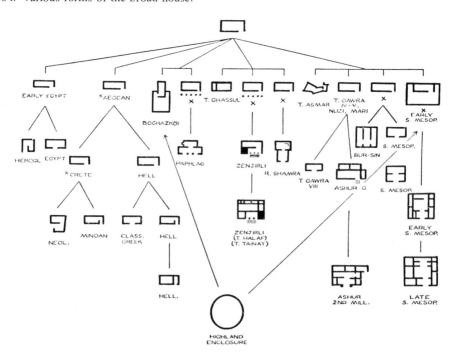

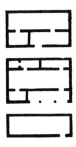

205. The broad-house with bent axis ("Around-the-corner" type; in the terminology of W. Andrae, *"Herdhaus"*) provides optimum separation between the occupant and the outside. Anyone passing by the exterior sees only a blank wall. A person entering must turn ninety degrees in order to survey the entire room.

the door; the cella, however, has a shaft through which light falls on the divine image. The graduated rooms evidence the need to establish, even in proximity to the deity, a certain distance between man and god. The image of the god, separated by the dark anteroom, yet illuminated from above, must have appeared to the beholder in a very mysterious light. To be sure, practical considerations as well as the desire to achieve distance may have played some part in the staggering of two rooms. The anteroom provided a place for votive offerings.

The Late Bronze temple at Hazor, while not actually deviating from the

axis type of house offers privacy and security. It has a strongly residential character. It may have originated along the eastern coast of the Mediterranean.[82]

At the end of the third century B.C., the bent-axis room was largely superseded in southern Mesopotamia by a broad-room, with its entrance located in the center of one broad side.[83] V. Müller[84] considers this type to be the result of a combination of the strictly symmetrical long-house with the bent-axis house. The entrance and—in the temple—the podium with the image of the god are moved to the center of the long side, rendering the image visible from outside, as in the long-house type *(203)*. In this case, however, the image does not appear far in the background of the room, as in the long-house. Instead, the visitor stands immediately opposite it. This type of building is usually linked by a central courtyard (cf. *170–73*). Thus, the deity is very close to anyone who pauses in the central court.

A model, or more correctly, a sketchy copy of a Sumerian temple was recently discovered in the vicinity of Uruk *(207)*. As in Figs. *172* and *173* (cf. also *191*), a second broad-room extends in front of the broad-room which contains the platform for the image of the god. Light could enter the anteroom only through

206. The broad-house, with its entrance located in the center of one of the longer sides, is often set in a courtyard and is therefore termed a courtyard house. A person entering the courtyard can see the image of the deity.

broad-room type, provided the best Canaanite example of "the cultic movement toward the long-room type" *(208)*.[85] Nevertheless, the temple at Hazor cannot be regarded as a precursor of the Solomonic temple, as has often been done, for the latter is not a broadroom structure. Its character is decidedly that of the long-room type.

The so-called fosse temple at Lachish *(208a)*, contemporary with Temple H at Hazor, evidences the same movement toward the long-room structure (without actually constituting a long-house). Subsequent additions to this typical bent-axis temple give it the character of a longroom. The entrance no longer leads directly into the main chamber, but into a vestibule (A). One cannot, however,

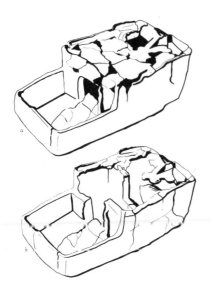

207. Sumerian temple model (a) with roof, and (b) with roof removed.

takable in Palestinian temple construction by the end of that period.

The temple at Jerusalem does not merely exhibit a certain tendency toward long-room construction, like the Late Bronze Age temples at Hazor and Lachish; it is decidedly a long-house structure. Every reconstruction based on OT information demonstrates that fact, however much the several reconstructions may differ in particulars *(209–13)*.

The long-house type represented by the Solomonic temple has not yet been attested in pre-Solomonic Palestine. To be sure, there is a kind of long-house temple from the late Middle Bronze Age (1650–1550 B.C.) at Sichem *(214)*, and one of perhaps a somewhat later date at Megiddo *(215)*. The Megiddo temple survived well into the Late Bronze Age. The ratio of the narrow side to the broad, however, is 1:3 in Jerusalem, whereas at Sichem it is 3:4 and at Megiddo only 6:7. The room thus approaches square proportions and cannot be considered typical of long-house construction.[87] It is noteworthy, however, that in its second phase the temple at Megiddo had a pedestal 1.10 meters high in front of the rear wall. An early

straightforwardly refer to Temple H at Hazor or the fosse temple at Lachish as long-room temples. And one certainly cannot speak of the general predominance of that type in Palestine of the Late Bronze Age,[86] even if a certain tendency toward the long-room is unmis-

208. The development of Temple H at Hazor in the Late Bronze period. The typical broad-room temple (II) dates from the 15th century B.C. In the 14th century it was augmented by an ante-*cella* with side chambers

and an anteroom (less wide than the main building) (IB). In the final phase (13th century B.C.) the ante-*cella* took the shape of a broad-room (IA).

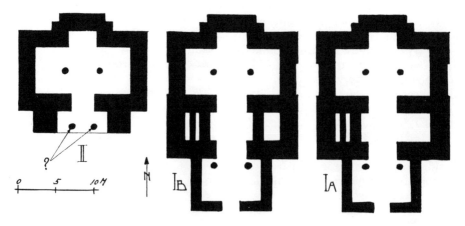

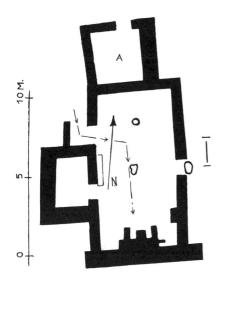

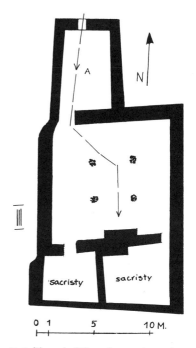

208a. The development of the "fosse temple" of Lachish in the Late Bronze period. Temple I, of the bent-axis type, was built at the end of the 15th or beginning of the 14th century B.C. Temple III no longer has a bent axis. It shows instead a certain movement toward the long-house type.

213. Attempted reconstruction of the Solomonic temple by G. E. Wright and W. F. Albright.

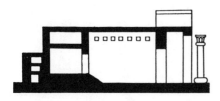

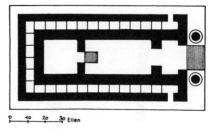

209. and 210. Attempted reconstruction of the Solomonic temple by C. Watzinger. The surrounding structure encompasses the vestibule, which is of a height equal to the rest of the building. The vestibule is flanked by towers. The holy of holies stands on a podium.

211. and 212. Attempted reconstruction of the Solomonic temple by T. A. Busink. The vestibule is not included in the surrounding structure. The level of the holy of holies is the same as that of the nave.

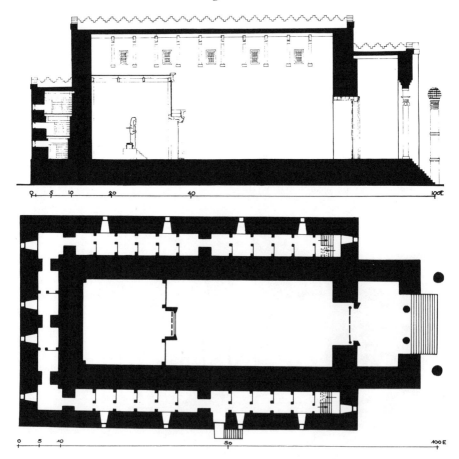

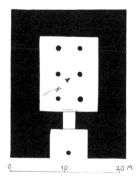
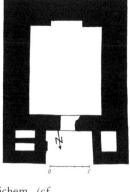

214. The fortress temple of Sichem (cf. *243*), built in the Middle Bronze period (ca. 1650 B.C.)

215. Temple at Megiddo dating from the Late Bronze period (ca. 1400 B.C.).

216. Early Iron Age temple at Beth-Shan (ca. 1100 B.C.).

Iron Age temple at Beth-Shan, which is decidedly of the long-room type, apparently also possessed a similar pedestal *(216)*. The entrance to that temple, however, is curiously off-center.

A holy of holies separated from the main room is also attested for the Late Bronze Age at Beth-Shan *(216a)*. It cannot be considered a parallel to the Jerusalem temple, however, because it is even less a long-house than the temples of Sichem and Megiddo. The long-house is typical of Assyrian temples *(217)*. W. Andrae,[88] A. Alt,[89] and recently, J. Hofer[90] attribute the long-house of the Jerusalem temple to Assyrian influence.

216a. Late Bronze Age temple at Beth-Shan (ca. 1300 B.C.). The holy of holies is clearly differentiated from the cult chamber.

217. Plan of the Sin-Shamash Temple at Assur (end of the 8th century B.C.).

218. The palace and temple of Tell Tainat in Syria (8th century B.C.).

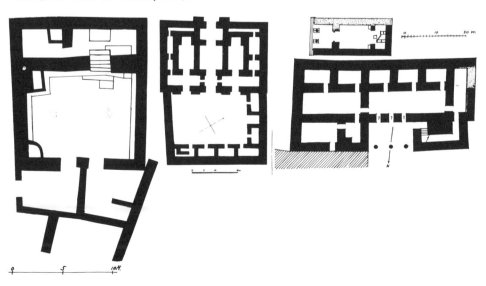

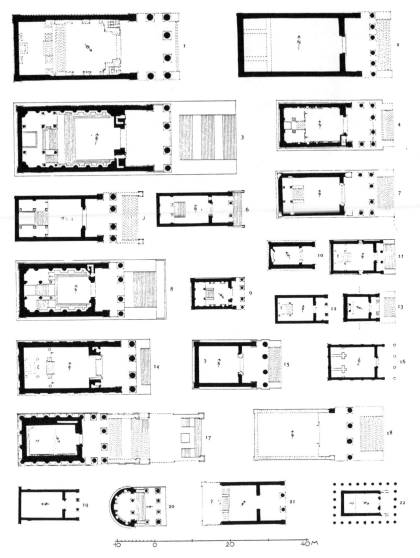

219. Roman temples in Lebanon and Syria: 1. Deir el-Kalaa, 2. Kalat Fakra, larger temple, 3. Niha, larger temple, 4. Kasr Naous, second temple, 5. Niha, smaller temple, 6. Hössn Sfire, smaller temple, 7. Kasr Naous, Helios Temple, 8. Hössn Niha, larger temple, 9. Bziza, 10. Akraba, 11. Januh, 12. Kasr el-Banat, 13. Hössn Niha, smaller temple, 14. Kasr Neba, 15. Beka, 16. Nebi Ham, 17. Hössn Soleiman, 18. El-Lebwe, 19. Hössn Soleiman, temple of the small district, 20. Hössn Soleiman, Exedra, 21. Kfar Zabad, 22. Kasr Nimrud.

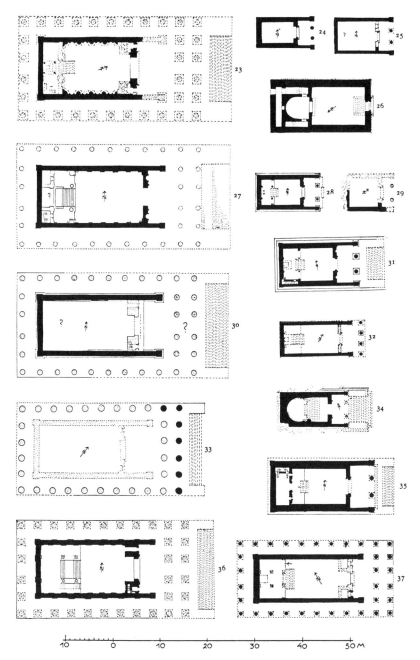

220. Roman temples in Lebanon and Syria. 23. Majdel Aanjar, 24. El-Knese, 25. Ain Libnaya, 26. Burkush, the so-called Mithraeum, 27. Deir el-Ashayr, 28. Ain Harsha, 29. El-Knese, 30. Nahle, 31. Hebbariya, 32. Zekweh, 33. Serain, 34. Nebi Safa, 36. Hössn Sfire, larger temple, 37. Beit Djalluk (cf. G. Taylor, *Roman Temples of Lebanon*).

159

220a. A representation of the sacred precincts of the goddess Neith from the Early Dynastic period. Two flags (cf. *162, 162a*), the symbol of the goddess (crossed arrows before a shield), and the chapel (cf. *229, 230*) are readily identified. In Egypt, two flags identify the entrance to the sacred sphere; in Syria, the entrance is sometimes marked by two Asherah-pillars (cf. *223–25;* and E. Porada, *Corpus,* vol. 1, no. 912 (where the dove links the pillar with Astarte); cf. *191, 225, 290, 475a*).

221. "His covert was in Salem, and his lair in Zion" (Ps 76:3 MT [translation by M. Dahood]; cf. Ps 76:2 RSV). A. side view; B. front view.

Busink,[91] however, has correctly emphasized that the Assyrian long-house, in contrast to the temples of Sichem, Megiddo, and Jerusalem, (1) does not represent a detached, single structure; (2) the vestibule, similar to that of a broad-room, extended in front of the entire complex and not only—as in Jerusalem—in front of the main chamber; and (3) in Jerusalem, the last chamber consisted of an enclosed wooden cube, whereas in Assur there was an elevated platform. The only real point of comparison between the Jerusalem and Assyrian temples lies in the pronounced long-house character of their principal chambers.

The long-room tendency is evidenced in the Late Bronze Age at Hazor and Lachish, and the incidence of structures approximating the long-house, such as the temples at Sichem and Megiddo,

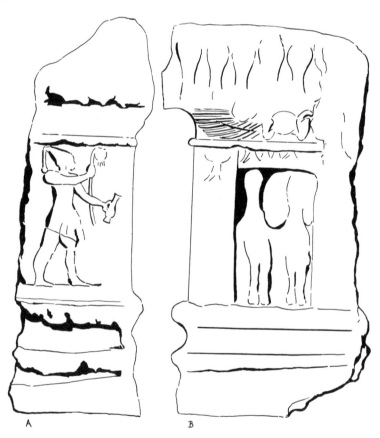

A   B

may provide sufficient grounds for understanding the long-house of the Jerusalem temple within the scope of autochthonous building traditions. In view of the fragmentary documentation, conclusive proof is hardly possible.

The temple at Tell Tainat (not far from the northernmost point of the Orontes), which dates only from the eighth century B.C. *(218),* has long been considered the closest analogy to the Solomonic temple. But in this case too, Busink has called attention to a number of differences: "At Tainat, the vestibule has an entrance open across the entire width of the building; at Jerusalem, the opening is flanked by sidewalls. Despite its partially open vestibule, the Solomonic temple is a closed shrine; the temple at Tainat is opened to the outside. The vestibule of the Jerusalem temple is a space which separates the *hêkāl* from the outer world; at Tell Tainat the vestibule forms a connecting link between the outer world and the interior of the sanctuary."[92] The surrounding structure, which encloses the Jerusalem temple on three sides, constitutes a second difference. It may have originated in the casemate walls (double walls connected by cross-walls, forming rooms).[93] Such walls are well attested for Solomon's time (cf. *159, 161*). They heighten the impression of seclusion and mystery. Further differences could be mentioned.

The most interesting element of the Jerusalem temple, however, is the holy of holies, the *dᵉbîr*. This too differs from the design of the Tell Tainat temple. At Tell Tainat, the *adyton* is removed from the main room by a partition wall, seen in the ground plan as a series of extensions. On the other hand, the *adyton* is connected to the main room by a wide opening which could scarcely be closed. In the Jerusalem temple, the holy of holies was a closed wooden cube located (perhaps on a dais) at the far end of the principal chamber. Only in Ezekiel's temple plan is it separated from the main room by a stone wall, as at Tell Tainat (Ezek 41:3).[94] For that reason, H. Schult[95] has advanced the hypothesis

that Solomon's temple was not a tripartite structure, but at most a bipartite one (vestibule and *hêkāl*), like Temple C at Megiddo, which dates from the Middle Bronze II period. The windowless "chamber of the god, built according to a quadratic plan,"[96] this "cube of cedar,"[97] was no more than a piece of furniture. An Egyptian inventory from the period between 1090 and 730 B.C. enumerates items made by the *gnwty*-craftsman. Without exception, they are wooden temple fixtures (litters, statues, barks and other implements of the gods). Included among these items is an object called *dbr,* defined more closely by the signs for "house" and "wood."[98] The *dᵉbîr* must therefore have been a kind of wooden chapel. In the Jerusalem temple it was cubical in form, with sides approximately ten meters long. A. Kuschke maintains, however, that such a large structure could scarcely be considered a fixture.[99] For Kuschke, the existence (Schult) or nonexistence (Noth) of a wooden or stone (Ezek 41:3) separating wall plays a limited role in the typological classification of the temple. In Kuschke's opinion, the temple is to be included under the "Syrian temple type" described by A. Alt.[100] Kuschke finds that the floor plans of thirty-seven Syrian temples *(219, 220)* from the Roman period correspond in general to the Jerusalem temple. "Constant . . . in all are, first, the ratio of the narrow sides of the temple to the long sides— approximately 1 : 2, with trifling variations; second, orientation toward the east (24 of 32 temples); and third, location of the habitation of the deity at or in front of the western rear wall."[101] A. Alt observed some thirty years ago that the proportions and orientation do not fall outside the range of "what is possible and usual elsewhere in Hellenistic-Roman architecture," and that "only in the interior does the peculiar character of the Syrian temple come to light."[102] Outside Syria, Hellenistic-Roman temples have no *adyton*. The *adyton* thus constitutes the principal characteristic of the Syrian temple type. Nevertheless,

Figs. *219* and *220* demonstrate how varied the form of the *adyton* can be. Kuschke takes the view that the proven existence of a divine habitation (of whatever form) at the rear wall of the *cella,* is sufficient reason to assign the Jerusalem temple to the Syrian temple type.

However that may be, the Solomonic *d^eḇîr* is in any case a god's chamber added to the completed *cella.* In that respect, it is comparable to the chapels of Egyptian gods *(229–30).* These were small chapels which contained the cult image. In earlier periods, they were built of wood, in later times, of stone. Their form is that of the early dynastic chapels *(220a).* The roof in particular harks back to construction of straw.[103] Reproductions of such temples have been found in Phoenicia *(221* and *222).* The band of hooded cobras which constitutes the upper termination is attributable to Egyptian influence, as are the winged sun, the lotus band, and many other features. The throne of the deity, on the other hand, appears to be typically Phoenician: borne by two animals (cherubim?), it almost completely fills the chapel *(221).* The Jerusalem *d^eḇîr* deviates from an Egyptian-Phoenician *naos* in form (cube), size (side length 10 meters), and in its position at the rear wall. The Egyptian *naoi* stand in the midst of the *cella.* Busink maintains the interesting opinion that the Jerusalem *d^eḇîr* is not primarily an imitation of the Egyptian-Phoenician *naos,* nor is it a structure analagous to the Syrian *adyton,* but is instead the direct successor of the tent which David pitched for the ark (2 Sam 6:17). The old tabernacle was received, as it were, into the temple, thereby accommodating the scruples aroused by the relocation from tabernacle to temple (cf. 2 Sam 7:1–7). The development was thus similar to that in Egypt, where the old chapels were taken over into the great temple complexes. In

222. ". . . he will hide me in his shelter in the day of trouble; he will conceal me under the cover of his tent" (Ps 27:5).

"Let me dwell in thy tent for ever! Oh to be safe under the shelter of thy wings!" (Ps 61:4).

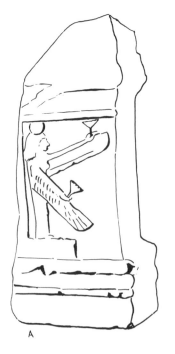

A

B

the priestly writings, the tent which housed the ark is reconstructed as a structure made up in part of a tent, in part of wood.[104] The compatibility of the two is thereby documented.

Busink[105] finds it rather odd that in the OT the $d^e b\hat{i}r$ is never referred to as a tent. He explains this fact by suggesting that '$\bar{o}hel$, when used with reference to a dwelling, invariably signifies the whole and not a constituent part. Where the term "tent" appears in the psalms (Pss 15:1, 27:5; 61:4; 78:60), it is applied by Busink to the temple as a whole—a questionable conclusion. The $d^e b\hat{i}r$ is, however, a relatively independent entity (naos), and not simply a chamber (cf. 1 Kgs 6:27: "the innermost house" [RSV: "the innermost part of the house"]). In Ps 27:5, "tent," as the dwelling place of God, stands parallel to "hut" [RSV: "shelter"] (sukkāh). It is the suppliant's hope that in the day of trouble, Yahweh will conceal him in his "hut" or "tent". A third parallel is found in a further action in the same verse: the suppliant will be set "high upon a rock." The context of the verse should be noted: the worshipper desires to dwell in the byt yhwh all the days of his life. The forecourts, of course, belong to the byt yhwh. The worshipper seeks his joy in the hykl, the palace [RSV: "temple"] of Yahweh (Ps 27:4). That is his hope in normal times. But in time of calamity, it is his hope that Yahweh will hide him in the holy of holies. Even if the holy of holies was not located on top of es-sahra,[106] it was cer-tainly built on a foundation of rock, and this rock base may have been the summit of Zion (cf. Isa 2:2; Mic 4:1). In Ps 28:1–2, at any rate, the suppliant addresses Yahweh as "my rock" while reaching out his hands in entreaty toward the $d^e b\hat{i}r$ [cf. Ps 28:2 RSVm]. It is the only passage in which the $d^e b\hat{i}r$ appears in the psalms. Ps 61:2 refers to the rock in a manner similar to Ps 27:5. It is too high for the suppliant, but he desires that Yahweh take him up upon it. Ps 61:4 speaks of the tent, and of shelter under the wings of God (cf. also Ps 31:20). The "wings of God" may allude to the cherub in the holy of holies (cf. Ps 18:10). In any case, the dark hut [RSV: "covering"] of Ps 18:11 is suggestive of the darkness in which Yahweh wishes to dwell (cf. the temple dedication text of 1 Kgs 8:12). Ps 76:2 calls Yahweh's "hut" [RSV: "abode"] in Jerusalem a "hiding place" [RSV: "dwelling place"] (m'nh). If the terms "tent," "hut," and "hiding place" are not termini technici for the $d^e b\hat{i}r$, but refer instead to the temple as a whole, still they describe the temple with a view to a single aspect which is concretized above all in the $d^e b\hat{i}r$. Similarly, the word "flesh" can signify the whole man, but precisely with reference to a single aspect which is manifested above all in his corporeal flesh and its frailty. In consequence, one can hardly say with Busink's certainty that the term "tent" is not attested in description of the $d^e b\hat{i}r$.

6. THE FURNISHINGS OF THE HOUSE OF YAHWEH

In 1 Kgs 7:13–51, we are told that the temple was equipped with a variety of metal objects. The first items mentioned are two pillars eight to nine meters tall (1 Kgs 7:15–22; cf. Jer 52:21–23), which were crowned by capitals at least two meters in height. These capitals bear a marked similarity "to the capitals on the miniature pillars from Arslan Tash [223], which appear to have been items of plunder from Syria, having originally served as furniture ornaments."[107] These ivory capitals bear no trace of the numerous pomegranates which adorned

224. This tripod from Ugarit indicates the manner in which a cultic implement could be decorated with pomegranates.

the two pillars of the Solomonic temple. However, pomegranates are well attested elsewhere as a decorative motif (224). Frequent reference to them in the Song of Solomon (4:3, 13; 6:7, 11; 7:12; 8:2) reveals their affinity to love and fertility motifs. Lotus blossoms can also be viewed as fertility symbols. They constitute the chief component of the capitals of the Solomonic temple and of the ivory capitals from Arslan Tash. The model of a small temple from Idalion (225) gives an indication of the function of the two pillars. The two free-standing pillars are crowned either by a lotus blossom or a crown of palm. They support a small porch roof and flank the entrance of the sanctuary. Their (modest) architectural function should provide no obstacle to comparison with the temple pillars, for that function is entirely unrelated to their symbolic value. Therefore we need not be concerned whether Jachin and Boaz continued to serve architectural purposes.[108] Two model shrines, one from Tell Far'ah (north) and one from Transjordan, have pillars with plant motifs on either side of the en-

trance. The two shrines, dating from the early Iron Age, resemble the shrine shown in Fig. 225.[109] In these shrines, however, the pillars apparently had no architectural function. On the model from Transjordan, a dove sits between the two pillars. A bird in flight also appears on a temple model from the Late Bronze Age sanctuary at Kāmid el-Lōz. In these temple models, the entrance is flanked by two pillars which terminate in capitals reminiscent of flowering papyrus. Any architectural function is excluded because the two pillars rise above the roof line.[110] No birds are to be seen in the temple model of Fig. 225, but the upper half of the model provides nesting holes for doves. The dove is the symbolic bird of Ishtar-Astarte (cf. 191, 290). It may not be as irrelevant as Noth imagines[111] to regard the two pillars as Asherahs (holy trees or tree symbols) in modified form (cf. the two trees which flank the Ishtar temple in Fig. 191).[112] They characterize the temple once more as a sphere of life. Even Noth[113] is struck by the degree of freedom evidenced in reporting the appearance of ancient Near Eastern-Canaanite fertility symbolism in the ornamentation of the great bronze objects of the Jerusalem temple. Kornfeld's interpretation[114] of the pillars as *djed* pillars, symbolizing stability, connects well with the names Jachin and Boaz. Once the two pillars had lost their relation to Ishtar-Astarte and vegetation, they would have readily been transformed into signs indicative of space in which the deity is present.[115]

Within the sanctuary at Jerusalem there were, besides the incense altar and the showbread table, one or more lampstands. According to 1 Sam 3:3, even in the temple at Shiloh there burned a "lamp of God." 1 Kgs 7:49 mentions ten lampstands in the Solomonic temple. Jer 52:19 also refers to a number of lampstands. We have no exact details regarding their appearance. The term *prh* ("bud," "blossom") used in this connection suggests that, as in the

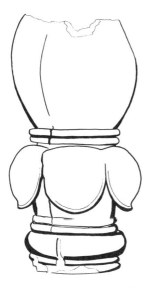

223. The configuration of the pillars Jachin and Boaz may have been roughly equivalent to that of this miniature ivory pillar.

226. Lampstand from Megiddo. Blossom motifs similar to those shown above may also have played a role in the decoration of the lampstands which illuminated the sanctum of the Solomonic temple.

lampstand from Megiddo *(226),* leaf and blossom ornamentation was employed.

The description of the seven-branched lampstand in Exod 25:31–40 (cf. 37:17–24) and in Josephus[116] may have applied to the principal lampstand of the postexilic temple (cf. Zech 4:2). The tripod and the seven upright arms seem to have been characteristic of it *(227;* cf.

225. The two pillars before this model of an Astarte temple may have been understood as Asherahs.

458). The lampstand seen on the Titus Arch in Rome *(228),* with its single, massive base and six curved branches, may trace back to the time of Herod.[117] The seven-branched candelabrum, frequently depicted in Jewish synagogues and tombs and on coins and ossuaries, was sometimes regarded as a symbol of God,[118] sometimes as a symbol of eternal life (cf. *257–58).*[119]

In addition to the incense altar, the showbread table, and the lampstands, the equipment of the sanctuary included many kinds of pots, cups, tongs, sprinkling-shells, firepans, and snuffers (cf. 1 Kgs 7:40, 50). In short, the divine household lacked nothing necessary to a substantial earthly household. Chapter 6.2 will treat more closely the details of these utensils. Here we have yet to consider the furnishings of the holy of holies.

227. The seven-branched lampstand of the postexilic period (cf. *181* and Zech 4:2).

228. The seven-branched lampstand of the Herodian temple.

The Solomonic holy of holies bears a certain resemblance to the chapels of Egyptian deities. In these chapels there was usually a cult image, which, judging from the illustrations in Figs. *229* and *230,* was approximately the size of an adult man. Like the *d^eb̂îr,* the chapels were windowless; and they were provided with a double door and bolt (1 Kgs 6:31–32). In Egypt, these doors were routinely closed. This may also have been the case in Jerusalem: the doors were opened only for specific cultic actions. One could then see the protruding poles of the ark of the covenant (1 Kgs 8:8). This observation does not prove that the *d^eb̂îr* was not dark inside.[120] Equally improbable is Noth's contention[121] that Solomon's speech at the dedication of the temple makes no reference to God's dwelling in the darkness of the *d^eb̂îr.* The passage reads: "The LORD has set the sun in the heavens [LXX], but he has said that he would dwell in thick darkness. I have built thee an exalted house, a place for thee to dwell in for ever" (1 Kgs 8:12–13). According to Noth, the first part is intended to contrast the sun god to the

storm god, Yahweh; the second part invites the storm god to take up residence in the temple. More probably, however, the verse is intended to explain why Yahweh dwells in darkness in the tent or the hutlike *d^eb̂îr* instead of manifesting himself radiant in the heavens like the sun god. In any case, the Massoretic text, which lacks the first half-verse concerning the sun, clearly understood the passage as an expression of Yahweh's will to dwell in the dark temple.

In Ps 18:9–10, "cherub" seems almost to be a figure of cloudy darkness. Ps 97:2 links "darkness" and "throne." "Clouds and thick darkness are round about him; righteousness and justice are the foundation of his throne."

Before we enter into detailed consideration of the cherub and throne as furniture elements of the *d^eb̂îr,* we must briefly examine the problems of the ark of the covenant. It appears once in the psalms, in connection with its actual transfer to Jerusalem (Ps 132:8). Maier is of the opinion that "the ark had no sacral-architectonic function in the Jerusalem temple."[122] At any rate, we have no basis for understanding it as a

166

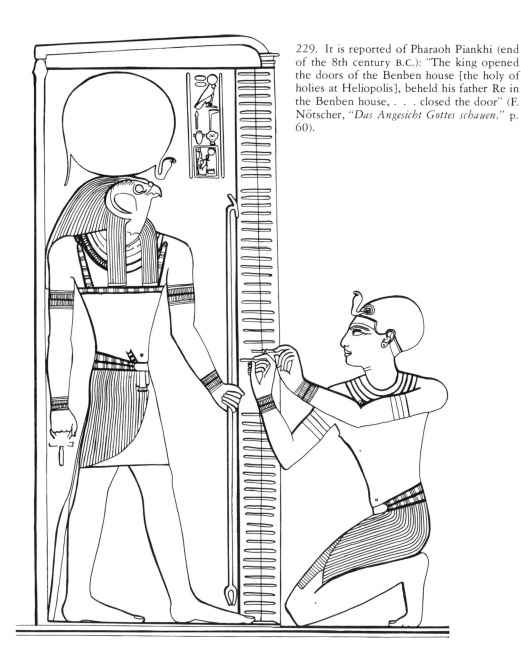

229. It is reported of Pharaoh Piankhi (end of the 8th century B.C.): "The king opened the doors of the Benben house [the holy of holies at Heliopolis], beheld his father Re in the Benben house, . . . closed the door" (F. Nötscher, *"Das Angesicht Gottes schauen,"* p. 60).

throne. More probably, it functioned as a footstool (cf. Pss 132:7; 99:5; 1 Chr 28:2; and *232–34, 236*).[123] According to Exod 37:1, the ark was approximately 1.25 meters long and 0.75 meters wide. Very probably it was placed parallel to the cherubim.[124] Thus, even if it took the function of a footstool, it lay at least in part beneath the wings of the cherubim.

The cherubim seem to have been major items in the inventory of the $d^e\underline{b}\hat{\imath}r$. 2 Kgs 19:14–15 (parallel to Isa 37:14–15) relates how Hezekiah took the threatening letter from the King of Assur into the house of Yahweh, there to unburden his need before him who is "enthroned above the cherubim." Yahweh is also addressed as one "en-

230. "As for me, I shall behold thy face in righteousness; when I awake, I shall be satisfied with beholding thy form" (Ps 17:15).

throned upon the cherubim" in Pss 80:2 and 99:1 (cf. 1 Sam 4:4; 2 Sam 6:2). A number of psalms, however, make mention of Yahweh's throne (Pss 9:4; 47:8; 93:2; 97:2). It is difficult to imagine the throne having been set in any place other than the *dᵉbîr* of the Jerusalem temple.

In a vision, Isaiah sees Yahweh sitting upon a throne, high and lifted up (Isa 6:1). Within the cube of the *dᵉbîr,* however, there would hardly have been room for the three-dimensional figures of two cherubim (1 Kgs 6:23) *and* a throne. While there is no reference to a

231. and 232. "The LORD reigns [as king]; let the peoples tremble! He sits enthroned upon the cherubim; let the earth quake!" (Ps 99:1).

throne in the description of the Solomonic temple (1 Kgs 6), nevertheless the enthronement of Yahweh in the dᵉbîr is well attested. We must therefore conclude that the two cherubim could be interpreted as a throne, as is suggested by the expression "enthroned upon the cherubim."

Fig. 221, and perhaps Fig. 222 as well, indicate that it was apparently a common Phoenician custom to furnish the *naos* with a cherubim throne. Regarding the two cherubim, we learn from the OT only that they stood parallel to each other, that their outer wings touched the wall, and that their wings touched

233. The king of Megiddo on his cherubim throne at a victory celebration. Here, in contrast to the previous illustration, the person enthroned does not sit directly on the wings of the cherubim. The cherubim provide only the support for the actual seat of the throne.

234. "Righteousness and justice are the foundation of his throne" (Ps 97:2b).

235. King Ahiram of Byblos on his cherubim throne.

each other (1 Kgs 6:27). The three-dimensional representation of Figs. *231* and *232* shows how that could have been accomplished. At Jerusalem, the outer wings of the cherubim may have been set at a less sharp angle, but that is not necessarily the case. The two inner wings formed a seat.

Figs. *233–36* demonstrate the great popularity of cherubim thrones in Canaan and Phoenicia during the Late Bronze and Early Iron Ages.[125] In all four illustrations, the cherubim provide only the base for the actual seat and back of the throne. In the throne model of Figs. *231* and *232,* however, these appear to be lacking. They may have been lacking in Jerusalem as well, which would explain why, on the one hand, cherubim are mentioned without reference to a throne, while on the other hand, Yahweh is represented as being enthroned.

The excavators of the terra-cotta model shown in Figs. *231–32* describe it as a "female figure sitting in a square armchair."[126] However, nothing is seen of this chair in the photographs, nor is it mentioned in the careful inventory of broken parts. Even if the description is correct, despite the photographic evidence to the contrary, the Jerusalem throne could have been constructed as

this one is, if only in appearance. The cherubim themselves could have formed the throne, and not merely have constituted the base which supported the throne proper, as in Figs. *233–36.* As the support *(mākôn)* of the throne, the cherubim guarantee its power and stability. Their composition from the body of a lion (panther, bull), a human head, and

236. "Thou who art enthroned upon the cherubim, shine forth before Ephraim, Benjamin and Manasseh!" (Ps 80:1c, 2a).

170

eagle's wings points to a union of the highest powers (strength, speed, sagacity). In his vision, Ezekiel sees the throne (analogous to Mesopotamian and not Canaanite-Phoenician prototypes) still more powerfully portrayed. The lapis lazuli throne of the deity rises above the firmament, which is borne by the four winds (Ezek 1). Yahweh is portrayed as Lord of the cosmos. The four creatures were first identified with cherubim by the redactor of Ezek 10, in order to make certain the identification of the cosmic Yahweh with the God of Jerusalem.[127]

In two passages in the psalms, however, it is stated that right order and right judgment (Pss 89:14; 97:2 [RSV: "righteousness and justice"]), rather than any natural forces, constitute the foundation (or support) of the divine throne. H. Brunner[128] has pointed out that in Egypt, especially in the Ramseid period, steps frequently led up to the divine or royal throne. Since these steps were enclosed by a side wall and were of a piece with the base, the foundation of the throne formed the sign, $m \} '.t$, "Maat," which is equivalent in meaning to the Hebrew $ṣdq$ (375).[129] Of course we cannot prove that this thought was reflected in furnishing the $d^{e} b \hat{i} r$.

7. THE SIGNIFICANCE OF THE TEMPLE

Not only the name "house (or palace) of Yahweh," but also the temple complex as a whole clearly points to the fact that it was conceived of as a dwelling place. In many details, however, it differs markedly from a conventional residence, and even from a royal palace.

The principal distinctions lie in the way in which the forecourts are adjoined to the house, and in the fact that this house encloses yet another house (the holy of holies) which is thought to be the dwelling place of God. Anyone entering the complex from the east had to pass through a series of gates and ascend a number of steps before he found himself (at least in spirit) before the holy of holies. This, with its darkness and isolation, was well suited to represent the mysterious God. It becomes clear, especially in Ezekiel's temple plan, that the axial arrangement of the several forecourts, chambers, and stairways (cf. Ezek 40:22, 34, 49) is intended to express the sublimity and holiness (cf. Ezek 43:1–12) of God (Pss 47:9; 97:9). Even more strongly than its architectural configuration, however, the location of the temple on Mount Zion (the highest

point of the city) characterized it as the entrance to the heavenly regions and as the link between heaven and earth. The temple is a part of earth which reaches into the heavens—or a part of heaven that touches the earth.

Even the towering height of the mountain is far surpassed by the loftiness of God, who is enthroned upon the mountain like an earthly king. Statements such as "Yahweh is great," "Yahweh is highly exalted" (cf. Pss 47:2, 9; 86:10; 95:3; etc.), and personal names such as Ramiah or Jehoram (Joram) ("Yahweh is lofty") were perhaps originally meant more literally than was the case at a later time (cf. Amos 4:13; 46 and 291).

Fig. 237 shows a badly damaged lead figurine of Jupiter Heliopolitanus. The god towers high above the huge temple building (cf. 179). At left and right are the half-figures of two enormous bulls. The god towers over them. The representation is reminiscent of Isa 6:1 and 1 Kgs 8:27. The latter passage expresses wonder that Yahweh, whom the highest heavens cannot contain, dwells in the temple. The immensity of Yahweh is also in mind when the temple gates are summoned to "lift up their heads" (Ps 24:7, 9), so that King Yahweh can enter in.

In Ps 24:7, the temple gates are designated *ptḥy 'wlm,* "gates of eternity" [RSV: "ancient doors"]. Because the psalm itself is very ancient, the term could hardly apply to the actual temple gates. Rather it might imply that the gates (of heaven), to which the temple gates give visible form, have been located at this place from time immemorial (as at Bethel). However, the election of Zion in history—an assertion repeatedly expressed in the psalms—would contradict the latter notion (cf. above, p. 120). In this instance, therefore, *'wlm* is to be understood as the sphere of God. Men pass away like shadows, but God abides for ever (*l'wlm;* Pss 102:12; 29:10; etc.). The temple complex naturally participates in his time. The temple gates (in Jerusalem, at any rate) are not particularly ancient; rather they are of continuous duration, unshakeable as

237. "His train filled the temple" (Isa 5:1).

Zion (Ps 125:1). They partake of the fixity of the heavens (cf. *19–20*). A temple in Sidon, or the city quarter defined by the temple, is called "high heaven."[130] In Egyptian temples, a sun flanked by hooded cobras or the winged sun mounted on the lintel (*221–22*) were often used to identify the temple gates as the gates of heaven. The plural number of gates (*238, 238a*) corresponds to the plural number of heavens (cf. *21, 30, 33*). As is shown in Fig. *238,* the seven gates were understood as a means of symbolizing the remote holiness of the deity.

In Egypt, the following formula was uttered at the daily opening of the *naos:* "The gates of heaven are opened."[131] The pertinent chapter bears the heading: "Utterance upon revealing the countenance of the god." A variant reads: "Utterance upon mounting the stairs" (which lead up to the *naos*).[132] When entering the *naos,* the officiant says: "I enter into heaven to behold N (name of the god)."[133] The temple of Heliopolis is called "the heaven of Egypt"; the temple of Karnak is "heaven on earth"; that at Dendera is "the heaven of Hathor."[134] The "farm of Neith" is "heaven in full form."[135] The temple, as the locus of the presence of God, is identical to heaven.[136] In the case of chthonic deities, the temple could naturally represent the earth and the interior earth as well. In the psalms, however, Yahweh appears nowhere as a chthonic deity. Accordingly, the temple is not depicted as a cave (cf. p. 181).

Mesopotamia also provides numerous examples of the identification of the temple with the heavenly regions. Fig. *239* shows King Nabuapaliddin of Babylon. Led by a priest and accompanied by a tutelary deity, he enters the sun temple of Sippar, his right hand raised in greeting. The emblem of the sun god stands on a tablelike platform. The sun god himself is seated behind it, under a baldachin composed of a serpent and a palm pillar. Above him, between the serpent and the pillar and over the ocean, are the emblems of three deities

238. "Can it indeed be that God dwells . . . on earth? If the heavens and the highest heavens cannot contain you, how much less this temple which I have built!" (1 Kgs 8:27 NAB).

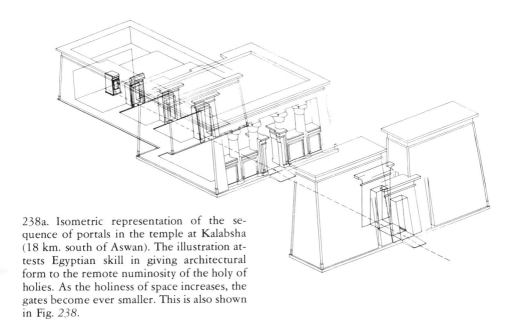

238a. Isometric representation of the sequence of portals in the temple at Kalabsha (18 km. south of Aswan). The illustration attests Egyptian skill in giving architectural form to the remote numinosity of the holy of holies. As the holiness of space increases, the gates become ever smaller. This is also shown in Fig. 238.

also mentioned in the text: they are Sin (= moon: horizontal crescent), Shamash (= sun: four-pointed star and clusters of flames), and Ishtar (= Venus: eight-pointed star). The "ocean" referred to is the heavenly ocean, above which the scene takes place. The four remaining planets (besides sun, moon, and Venus) are seen beneath the ocean. This picture merges temple interior and heaven in a manner quite similar to Isa 6. It is out of place to inquire whether the scene is set in the temple or in heaven.[137] The temple is on earth, but because Yahweh dwells in it, it is one and the same with heaven.

The temple is not merely a palace *(hykl)*, house *(byt)*, and habitation *(mškn)*, nor is the holy of holies *(dbyr)* simply a tent *('hl)*, hut *(skh)*, and hiding place *(m'nh)*. Because of him who occupies it, the temple is also a sanctuary *(mqdš, qdš)*. It is often unclear whether *qdš* should be translated "holiness" or "sanctuary, holy place." In Ps 60:6 (cf. Ps 108:7), the probable translation is: "God has spoken in his sanctuary." Similarly, Ps 150:1 should probably be translated: "Praise God in his sanctuary." But these verses may also be translated: "God has spoken in his holiness" (cf. RSVm; and Ps 89:35; Amos 4:2); and "Praise God in his holiness" (cf. Pss 29:2; 96:9 [RSV: "holy array"]). In the Israelite view, holiness is not inherent in any created thing. It receives the quality of holiness only through relation to Yahweh (cf. above, p. 151). Because this relation is presupposed in the temple and its furnishings, the holiness of Yahweh is positively visible in the temple.

The sense of the holiness of the temple finds its strongest expression in the concept that Yahweh himself established it. Just as the expression "trees of Yahweh" can be interpreted to mean that Yahweh planted them (Ps 104:16), so too can the expression "house of

239. "The LORD is in his holy temple, the LORD's throne is in heaven" (Ps 11:4).

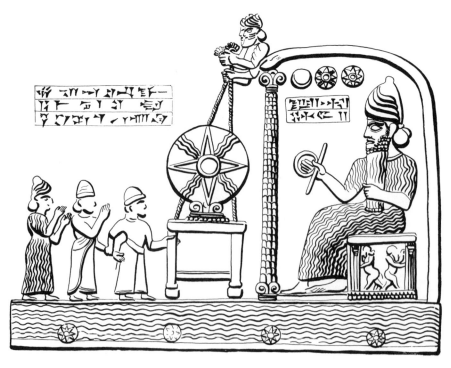

240. Yahweh chose ". . . Mount Zion, which he loves. He built his sanctuary like the high heavens, like the earth, which he has founded for ever" (Ps 78:68b, 69).

Yahweh" signify that God built the house (cf. Pss 78:69; 87:1; 147:2; Exod 15:17). The psalms couple positive assertions that Yahweh is the founder and builder of the temple (cf. Exod 25:9, 40) with complete silence concerning Solomon, the earthly builder.

In Mesopotamia too, the gods are looked on as founders (cf. the commentary on Fig. 3) and builders of the temples.[138] Fig. 240 depicts Marduk slaying an enemy who represents the power of Chaos. Another god raises his arms in triumph (or lamentation?). Six divinities (Anunnaki) are at work in the construction of the temple, built subsequent to the conquest of Chaos. One divinity at the lower right digs up the ground. Above him, another fills a wooden form with clay. A third, on a ladder, carries a basketful of bricks to the top of the rising walls, while a fourth stands ready to relieve him of his burden. A fifth figure is shown hefting building materials up to the sixth.[139]

Quite similar ideas are to be found in Egypt. According to the "Theology of Memphis," Ptah established the sanctuaries; according to the "Instruction for King Meri-ka-Re," they were founded by the sun god (cf. 364).[140]

In Israel's environment, the temple is the place where the ordered and enlivened world emerged after the conquest of Chaos. It stands on the spot from which Chaos was first banished. In the Third Dynasty at Ur (ca. 2050–1950 B.C.), this event was represented in a number of foundation figurines (sunk into the temple foundations). It is also depicted in a relief fragment (241) from the same period.[141] The relief fragment shows a god wearing a triple or quadruple horned crown. He is driving an enormous stake or spike into the ground in order to secure the building site. To the left of the god (241) may be seen a portion of the head and front paw of a huge leonine monster (cf. 43–45, 81). The divinely implanted stake keeps the monster at bay.

In Israel too, the foundation of the temple is occasionally related to the foundation of the earth (Ps 78:69). In the tradition as a whole, however, the foundation of the temple is clearly seen as a historical and not a primeval event (cf. p. 120). The solidity of Zion stands opposed to "Chaos" in Egypt (cf. Exod 15; Ps 78). It is the world of nations (Pss 46; 65; 76), not the floods of Chaos, which rage against Zion. Within the temple precincts, Yahweh grants his worshippers no mere vision of trees and water and other elements, but an experience of joyful, human fellowship (Pss 42:4; 55:14). Ethicization goes hand in hand with historicization and humaniza-

175

tion. In Ps 15 and Ps 24:3–6, natural-cultic purity is superseded by ethical sensibility.

In the Deuteronomic history, the temple is nothing more than "the place where one can call upon the name of Yahweh (that is the essential content of the prayer at the dedication of the temple in 1 Kgs 8:26–43), in such a way that prayer is made 'in this house' (which may signify the entire sacred precincts) (1 Kgs 8:33b), or in such a way that the worshipper, whether near or far, orients toward this house (1 Kgs 8:29b, etc.), thus making the house the point of 'prayer direction' (= Arabic: *qibla;* cf. Dan 6:11)."[142] In comparison with the significance of the temple in the Canaanite sphere, and probably also in the early monarchical period in Israel, such sentiments imply a substantial reduction in content.

Yet, even in the face of these and similar theological interpretations and devaluations, we must not overlook the fact that for large segments of the Jewish people, the temple and its appointments continued to possess a kind of sacramental power. Haggai, for instance, makes the productivity of the fields and lands dependent on reconstruction of the temple. But even more strongly than such individual voices, numerous reactions from strictly Yahwistic circles demonstrate that the deity was nonetheless considered to be present in power in the trees, water, and other elements of the temple. More cautiously, one could say that such misunderstandings were not excluded. Accordingly, the Septuagint usually renders the divine name

241. "When the earth totters, and all its inhabitants, it is I who keep steady its pillars" (Ps 75:3).

"rock" by *theos* (Pss [LXX; MT in brackets] 30 [31]:2; 61 [62]:2, 6–7; 70 [71]:3; 94 [95]:1; etc.). According to Hecataeus of Abdera (fourth century B.C.) the inner courtyard of the temple no longer had a sacred grove of trees.[143] The expression "to behold the face of God" is rendered in the Septuagint as "to appear before God" (Pss 16 [17]:15; 62 [63]:3; etc.).

CHAPTER IV
CONCEPTIONS OF GOD

The Israelite confederation of tribes borrowed from its long-established neighbors their conceptions of the cosmic system, the institutions of temple and kingship, and numerous cultic forms. Even though Israel imparted its own peculiar character to all these things, their foreign origin is nevertheless generally apparent. Consequently, the ancient Near Eastern iconography of temple, king, and cultus bears a remarkably close relation to corresponding statements in the psalms. The situation is entirely different, however, in the present chapter. Here we shall treat those aspects which have fundamentally codetermined the transformation of adopted institutions.

Israel brought with it from the desert experiences and conceptions of God which could not be easily harmonized with the various conceptions of God prevalent in the new environment. The result is reflected in the first and second prohibitions of the decalogue. The first commandment is grounded in the conviction of Yahweh's exclusiveness. The second prohibition is more difficult. The most plausible explanation may lie in the inaccessibility which is also reflected in the interpretation of the name of Yahweh in Exod 3:14: "I will be (there) as who I will be (there)" [cf. RSVm: "I WILL BE WHAT I WILL BE"] (on the form cf. Exod 33:19; Ezek 12:25). To be sure, one dare not exaggerate this inaccessibility. In the ark of the covenant and in all manner of "sacramental" rites, Yahweh was accessible to the desires and intentions of his worshippers. Far more than an image cast in human form, however, these things and processes preserved the character of mystery. This permitted less latitude to the notion that Yahweh himself, and not merely his beneficent inclination toward the devout, was fully present in them.

Nothing in the world—no king, no animal (bull!), no constellation of stars—can adequately embody Yahweh.

That is not to say, however, that every conception of Yahweh is illegitimate. The OT constantly advances such conceptions. Yet, again and again, voices are raised (Amos, Hosea, Isaiah, Jeremiah, Job, Qoheleth) against the superstition that God was fully apprehended in the image of father, shepherd, or king and could consequently be constrained in this human form with all its human consequences. Still, this protest by no means disallows every attempt to lend form and expression to the experience of God. Without that, and without a certain accessibility, a communion of the kind that existed between God and Israel (and between God and individual Israelites) would be inconceivable. The psalms are undoubtedly among the texts in which this covenant relation is most strongly expressed. Accordingly, the accessibility and positive presentation of Yahweh play a correspondingly large role in the psalms.

The material in this chapter is divided into three sections: "God in the Temple," "God in Creation," and "God in History." This division points to three areas of particular importance to the experience and conception of God as represented in the psalms. In making this division, the assignment of specific ideas to particular areas will frequently appear to be rather arbitrary. The Israelite was not so concerned as we to distinguish between the individual areas. The vital forces active in all creation are present—in a particularly intensive way—within the temple precincts. The foundation of the temple is the crown of the creative and (in Israel) historical activity of Yahweh (Ps 78). And even more difficult is the separation of creative and historical actions (cf. Ps 136). If one bears in mind that a specific concept (such as "Yahweh, my rock") can be deeply rooted in quite different spheres of thought, one will not attach too great significance to the present arrangement, at the same time allowing it some utility.

1. GOD IN THE TEMPLE

Throughout the entire period of its existence, the temple was for Israel one of the most important means of relation with God. One visited the temple to taste something of the sweetness and power of Yahweh (cf. Pss 27:4; 34:8). The worshipper's longing for God in Pss 42 and 84 is identical to the longing for the temple and its cult. The temple represents the deity. Fig. *242* shows two instances of libation to the moon god Nanna of Ur. In one, the drink offering is poured out into a vase-altar set before the god; in the other, it is poured out before the temple. In the Djemdet-Nasr period (2800–2700 B.C.) the deity was readily symbolized by his sanctuary. This was in accord with the religious reality. The later period, with greater theological precision, preferred to portray the deity himself (cf. *239*).[1]

The activity and nature of Yahweh are manifest in the temple and in the various characteristic features and appurtenances of the holy place. Strictly speaking, the present chapter should reexamine from this point of view the entire content of chapter 3. Because many details regarding symbolic content have already been considered, however, this section can be limited to a few particularly important points and supplementations.

a. The Rock

The Jerusalem temple stood on the highest point of the acropolis (cf. *157–58; Plate VII*). This location alone endowed it with considerable importance as a fortress. Very few temples were designed as bastions, like the so-called fortress-temple of Sichem, with its walls five meters thick and two huge towers flanking a single gate (*243*). But as a rule, temples were so substantially constructed that they could serve as places

242. "One thing have I asked of the LORD that I will seek after; that I may dwell in the house of the LORD all the days of my life, to behold the beauty of the LORD . . ." (Ps 27:4).

243. "Rescue me speedily! Be thou . . . for me, a strong fortress to save me!" (Ps 31:2).

of refuge in time of need (cf. Judg 9:46–49). When the suppliant of Ps 31:2 prays Yahweh to be for him an unassailable fortress *(byt mṣwdwt)*, his conception may have been inspired by the huge temple structure on Zion. The description of Yahweh as "a strong tower against the enemy" (Ps 61:3b) may be similarly understood. The tower may suggest a part of the acropolis (Ps 48:13; cf. Judg 9:51; 2 Chr 14:6) or some isolated tower in open country. Such isolated towers, as the smallest type of fortification (2 Kgs 17:9; 18:18), served as surveillance points or places of refuge in case of enemy attack (fortress of refuge). But these towers were also popularly used for presentation of offerings (2 Kgs 3:27; Jer 19:13; Zeph 1:5).[2] The oldest and most impressive example of such a tower is the massive edifice (12 meters high) from Neolithic Jericho *(244)*. One term is applied to Yahweh more frequently than "fortress" and "tower": he is often addressed as "height which offers refuge" *(mśgb* [variously translated in RSV]; twelve of sixteen occurrences in the OT are found in the psalms). In using the term, the Zion psalms 46 (vv. 7 and 11) and 48 (vv. 2–3) may have in mind Zion as acropolis.

In most cases, however, those passages which celebrate God as a high refuge, as an inaccessible mountain stronghold *(mṣwdh)*, or as a rock (of refuge) *(slʿ)* probably have in mind some natural feature of the landscape. Such eminences were of paramount importance in a territory repeatedly beset by military campaigns. In some parts of Palestine, in the regions east of the Dead Sea, and in the 'Araba, wadi beds, cut deep into the soft chalk or sandstone, have isolated, mighty rocks that could serve as natural strongholds *(Plate XII)*. In times of need, the population of the open country and of the smaller towns withdrew to these rocks of refuge (cf. Jer 4:29; 16:16; 49:16; 1 Sam 13:6). Some are mentioned by name in the OT: the rock of Rimmon ("pomegranite rock": Judg 20:47), the Wildgoats' Rocks (1 Sam 24:2), and [Jokthell] the rock of Edom (2 Kgs 14:7). The inaccessible places *(mṣwdwt* [RSV: "strongholds"]; cf. Job 39:28) to which David withdrew from time to time in his flights from Saul (1 Sam 22:4–5; 24:22) and the Philistines (2 Sam 5:17; 23:14) may have been similar rocks of refuge. A relief from the reign of Seti I depicts Canaanites retreating to one of these rocks. It is clear that, from the Egyptian point of view, even such a rock can provide no deliverance. One of the warriors is seen breaking his spear in despair *(245)*.

One may sense something of the "native quality of Israelite piety"[3] if the

244. "For thou art my refuge, a strong tower against the enemy" (Ps 61:3).

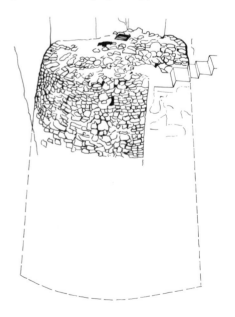

245. ". . . Lead thou me to a rock that is higher than I" (Ps 61:1c).
". . . he will set me high upon a rock" (Ps 27:5d).

suppliant has in mind particular features of the Palestinian mountain country when he addresses Yahweh as "my high place" (*mśgb* [RSV: "stronghold, fortress, refuge"]: Pss 18:2; 59:9, 16–17; 62:2,6; 94:22; 144:2), "my mountain fortress" (*mṣwdh* [RSV: "fortress"]: Pss 18:2; 31:4; 71:3; 91:2; 144:2), or simply as "my rock (of refuge)" (*slʿ:* Pss 18:2; 31:3; 42:9; 71:3; *ṣwr:* Pss 18:2, 46; 19:14; 28:1; 62:2, 6; etc.). It is no accident that confidence is expressed in autochthonous metaphors such as "my mountain fortress" or "my rock." In contrast to the prayers of ancient Mesopotamia and Egypt, the intense thematization of confidence is one of the principal characteristics of the psalms.[4]

One dare not ignore the features of the Palestinian landscape. Neither may we exclude the possibility that the suppliant regarded the temple precincts as the place of refuge *par excellence*. There, at the festivals of thanksgiving, he felt safe and sheltered; there, in lamentation, he directed his supplication toward the holy of holies (cf. Pss 28:1–2; 61:2). As was clearly demonstrated in the siege of A.D. 70, Zion had an excellent strategic position. In those texts where Yahweh the Rock appears as antipole to the forces of Chaos (Pss 18:2, 4; 61:2–4; 40:2), the Holy Rock of Zion (cf. *154*) is more likely to have provided the model

than some rock of refuge in the Judean desert.[5] In any case, the Holy Rock of Zion was very early understood as the cosmic cornerstone (Isa 28:16; cf. Mt 16:19) which forms the summit of the world-mountain (Ps 61:1c) and which restrains the rising waters of Chaos. With his own hands God set this stone in place (Job 38:6; cf. Pss 78:68; 87:1). It is easy to understand, on the basis of cosmic symbolism, that Yahweh is never called "my cave" or "my crevice," though *in concreto* these were resorted to for refuge as frequently as rocks and mountaintops (Judg 6:2; 1 Sam 13:6; 1 Kgs 18:4, 13; etc.; cf. *245a*). From the perspective of cosmic "geography," however, they belong to the realm of the nether world and are not suited for description of Yahweh, who is a God of life.

H. Schmidt writes in his small but interesting study of the Holy Rock: "In the most primitive times, the connection between the numen and the rock may have been understood as an indwelling, so that the stone and the deity were perceived to be very nearly identical."[6]

A hymn of thanksgiving for the "Peak of the West" *(dhnt imntt)* has been preserved from Deir el-Medinah, the artisans' colony in Upper Egypt *(Plate XIII).*[7] The stone pillars (Massebahs) which long played an important role as

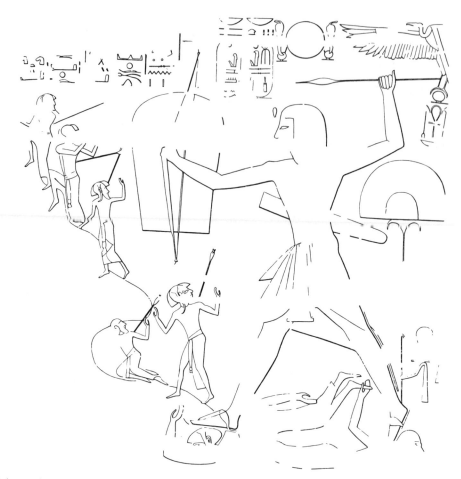

245a. Libyans, in flight before Ramses III, make haste to the mountains and hide themselves in caves. Rocks of refuge are a characteristic feature of the Palestinian landscape (especially as compared to Egypt and Mesopotamia), but they are not unique to Palestine.

Canaanite cult objects (246–47) were originally representative of such peaks. They were violently opposed by the later prophets and in Deuteronomy. The Massebah found in the holy of holies of the Yahweh temple at Arad indicates that for a time they were taken over by Yahwism (248).

Even in later periods the memory of the stone cult was alive in the characterization of God as "rock." In order to preclude any potential misunderstanding, the Septuagint simply translates ṣwr ("rock") as theos ("God"), and the rabbis derived ṣwr from yṣr, reading it as "shaper" or "creator."[8]

Despite such precautionary measures, many poets and suppliants, even in later periods, undoubtedly understood "mountain fortress" as a metaphor for "refuge," and "rock" as a metaphor for the unshakeable faithfulness of Yahweh. Upon this rock, one is safe from every onslaught of life-hating Chaos. The rock is not part of the transitory world, for the imperishability of Yahweh is present there. The suppliant of Ps 73 (v. 26 RSVm) spiritualizes the title of Yahweh, calling him the "rock of my heart" (= of thought and volition). One can "hold on to God," and this attribute is illustrated by the unyielding, indestructible firmness of rock.

b. Tests and Purifications

The experience of the immortal evokes in mortal man a sense of inferiority, impurity, and sin (cf. Ps 90; Isa 6). Where the holy is present sacramentally rather than in its primal power, the sense of sin is less spontaneously felt. The gate liturgy referred to in chapter 3.2 was intended to prevent one from approaching the holy in gross impurity, for then, far from receiving blessing, one would be struck with a curse. The gate liturgy is evidence not merely of human caution, but of the conviction that God tests man.

> The LORD is in his holy temple,
> The LORD's throne is in heaven;
> his eyes behold,
> his eyelids test [bḥn]
> the children of men.
> The LORD tests the righteous and the
>   wicked,

> and his soul hates him that loves violence
> . . .
> [Only] the upright shall behold his face.
>   (Ps 11:4–5, 7b)

Here the holy occupant of the temple appears as the great tester. The term (bḥn) employed in this text actually denotes the testing of metals. In antiquity, that could be reliably accomplished only by smelting. The Babylonian king Burnaburiash II (1367–1346 B.C.) writes in a letter to Amenophis IV: "Concerning the emissary whom you sent: the twenty minas of gold which he brought were not pure, for when it was put in the furnace, only five minas were produced."[9] For that reason, in the OT "to test" (bḥn)

246. "My God, my rock, in whom I take refuge" (Ps 18:2b).

Massebah in the forecourt of a temple at Byblos. It stands on or behind an altar with horns. The altar is covered with a metal grate (cf. Exod 27:4).

247. "So Jacob rose early in the morning, and he took the stone which he had put under his head and set it up for a pillar and poured oil on the top of it" (Gen 28:18).

The two Massebahs on this Tyrian coin are described as "anointed" with "ambrosia," that is, with butter, oil, or honey. A spring is shown beneath the inscription (cf. 183–88, 256). A tree stands to the right of the Massebahs (180–82, 253–55); at their left is an incense stand (197–200). The Massebahs function as temple, divine image, and altar. The little coin thus shows a sanctuary with all its appurtenances (cf. 191, 202).

248. "I cry out to you, my Rock" (Ps 28:1 [author's translation]).

Holy of holies in the Yahweh temple of Arad (cf. 170). Three steps lead up to the small chamber. Two incense altars stand on the topmost step (cf. 197). The only item found in the holy of holies was a beautifully hewn limestone stele painted red.

frequently stands parallel to "to smelt for refining" (srp) (Pss 17:3 [RSV: "try; test"]; 26:2 ["prove; test"]; 66:10 ["test; try"]). The testing can be accomplished only by the smelting process. That process, however, serves not only the purpose of testing, but also of refining and working the metal.

This is shown in Fig. 249.[10] At the left is seen an official weighing gold bars. A scribe makes a note of the amount delivered. At the right, six metalworkers fan the smelting-oven by blowing through reed tubes (?) tipped with fireproof clay. In Fig. 250, approximately 1,000 years later, bellows have replaced the archaic blowtubes. Two men (upper left) rhythmically shift their weight from one foot to the other. While one bellows is depressed, the other is pulled up by means of a cord, so that it can once more be filled with air. The man in the middle

feeds the fire. A heap of coals and a bucket of smeltable material (?) stand behind the fire. The scene below shows how a smelting-pot is removed from the fire. The continuation of the scene at the right depicts the casting of a gate. Two finished door panels may be seen at the upper right.

Like a metal smelter or smelting-furnace, Yahweh is present in the sanctuary. He who enters and remains unscathed may be reckoned as righteous. He may say that God has tried and purified him (Ps 17:3; cf. the purification of Isaiah in Isa 6:6). The suppliant who has spent even one night in proximity to the holy God (Ps 17:3aβ) is a righteous man who can be certain of divine assistance.

The suppliant of Ps 26 has not progressed so far. He asks first for that testing (v. 2a) which simultaneously implies purification (v. 2b). The worshipper asserts that he has fulfilled the requirements for entrance. He does not deserve to be swept away with the sinners (vv. 9–10). As a purified man, he can expect to find salvation in the sanctuary.

The experience of God as a consuming fire can purge a man from all his dross. So too can sufferings of every kind (Ps 66:10–12). In Ps 66:12, these sufferings are paraphrased by the merism "fire and water" (cf. Isa 43:2). Fire and water are the most important means of cultic purification (Num 31:23; cf. Ps 26:6). Here too the "testing" is viewed not simply as a process of assessment, but of refinement. Because the word of God has been refined, it is free of all dross, utterly pure (Ps 12:6) and desirable (Ps 119:140).

The situation is different in Ps 139. There the suppliant does not ask to be tested and purified like metal in a furnace. Instead he asks Yahweh to search him out (ḥqr) and—as a result of this process—to come to know him (v. 23; cf. v.1). Ideas of haruspicy may underlie this statement (and perhaps also Ps 7:9b) (251).[11] Haruspicy was highly developed in Babylon as early as the eighteenth century B.C.[12] The discoveries of an inscribed

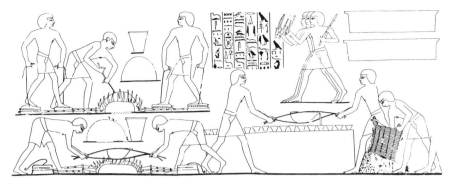

250. "For thou, O God, hast tested us; thou hast tried us as silver is tried" (Ps 66:10).

model liver in Temple II (208) at Hazor (252) and of another, uninscribed exemplar in Stratum VII at Megiddo[13] demonstrate that haruspicy was known in Palestine no later than the fifteenth century B.C. (cf. also Ezek 21:21). "The liver was regarded as the seat of feeling; therefore it was considered to be an appropriate mirror of future conditions. Furthermore, the livers of sacrificial lambs exhibited such diversity in structure that a multitude of opportunities for divination arose. The liver was believed to be a microcosm of the entire body. Indeed the whole environment was embodied in and assigned to portions of the liver. Not only was every possible part of the body included ('finger', 'mouth', 'genitals'); so were remoter entities, such as 'road', 'station', 'palace', and 'throne'."[14] The suppliant of Ps 139 expects from the testing of his inward parts some determination of the future, albeit in a different sense. It is his hope that God, having ascertained his blamelessness, will lead him into a bright future (vv. 23–24).

The steadfastness of Yahweh is graphically evident in the indestructability of the rock which forms the top of Zion. Man experiences God as one who tests and purifies. That experience is felt in the creaturely sense which overwhelms the dying man in the presence of

249. "Prove me, O LORD, and try me; test my heart and my mind" (Ps 26:2).

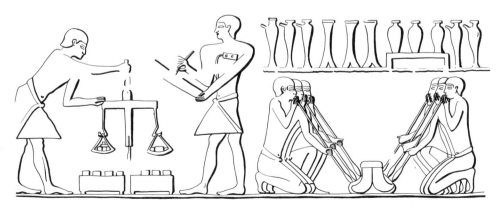

251. ". . . thou who triest the minds and hearts, thou righteous God" (Ps 7:9b).

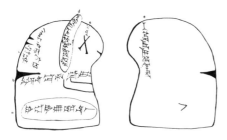

252. Model liver from Hazor. It helped inexperienced diviners (haruspices) to interpret the future by examination of the livers of sacrificial animals.

the holy God (Pss 130:3; 143:2), and also in the question regarding impurity and guilt posed in the gate liturgy. Yet in this process of purification, sweet fellowship with God plays a larger, more decisive role than purging uncleanness and guilt.

c. Tree, Fountain and Light

The suppliant of Ps 73 is wearied by temptations and troubled by oppressive doubts. Unscrupulous, greedy persons have become the objects of his wonderment and envy. But in the temple he comes to the realization that they stand on shaky ground. What really liberates him, however, is not the knowledge that "sin does not pay," but the experience of the "nearness of God" (cf. Ps 73:28). Only that is a sure defense against despair. This nearness means "life." The life offered by God on Zion (Ps 133:3) is manifested in the broad forecourts with their trees (253–55), in the water of the Bronze Sea and of the lavers, in the tree of life guarded by cherubim. In them is manifested the living (Ps 42:2; 84:2; 63:1), life-loving (Ps 30:5) God himself. With him is the "fountain of life" (cf. Ps 36:9; 256, 256a), and it lies within his power to permit one to take the "path of life" (Ps 16:11) and to dwell in the "land of the living" (Pss 27:13; 52:5; 116:9; 142:5). He is the giver of all life, which is concentrated and manifested in the temple precincts. Communion with him, in faithfulness and love, is therefore more important than life itself (Pss 63:3; 73:23–28). Only to upright and honest men, only to those who hold fast to Yahweh, does light rise up in the darkness (Pss 112:4; 97:11). For "in thy light do we see light" (Ps 36:9b). In this beautiful and puzzling statement, the "light" first mentioned may be the "light of his [i.e., God's] countenance" (Pss 4:6;

253. This Egyptian illustration and the two which follow it show how differently the relation between a tree and its goddess could be construed. To a great degree, the tree and the goddess could be seen as identical. Only the female breast (where the king drinks) and the arm which holds it indicate a personal being.

254. The goddess, in human figure, forms the trunk of the tree. She presents food (the round and oval flat cakes are breads) and drink to the man and woman.

"Blessed is he whom thou dost choose and bring near to dwell in thy courts! We shall be satisfied with the goodness of thy house" (Ps 65:4; cf. 90:14).

255. Here the tree and the nourishing deity appear to have no relation. But "Nut" written on the trunk of the tree and above the head of the goddess indicate that to the Egyptian, the two are identical. Israel did not identify the beauties of the holy precincts with Yahweh in the manner characteristic of Figs. 253–55. Nevertheless, those beauties were direct evidence of the blessing and vital power of Yahweh. The popularity of tree cults is reflected in Hos 14:8, where Yahweh compares himself to a cypress at which Israel might find refreshment: "How precious is thy steadfast love, O God! The children of men take refuge in the shadow of thy wings. They feast on the abundance of thy house, and thou givest them drink from the river of thy delights" (Ps 36:7–8).

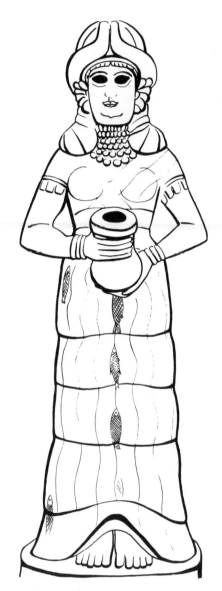

256. "For with thee is the fountain of life"
(Ps 36:9a).

A deity with a fountain-vessel from Mari.
This deity is female (cf. also *191*), but the
Mesopotamian deities which hold the vessel
are often male (cf., e.g., *185*).

44:3; 89:15). In that case, "of his
countenance" (that is, of his turning towards; *pnym:* "front, face") is an explica-
tive genitive. It equates "light" with
God's "turning." The second "light"
means simply "life," as implied by the
expression "light of life." "Of life," identifying light with life, is as much a genitive of explication as is "of his countenance." The dead see no light (Ps 49:19).
The sense of Ps 36:9b is therefore: "We
live by your good will." This meaning
fits very well the first half of the verse:
"For with thee is the fountain of life" (Ps
36:9a).

In Ps 27:1 (cf. also Ps 43:3), the
suppliant addresses God simply as "my
light." In Fig. *257,* each of the two Hellenistic paintings from Marissa shows a
lamp on a very high lampstand. Before
them appears a figure, hand raised in
greeting, leading a considerably smaller
figure. As S. Cook has indicated,[15] the
representation is strongly reminiscent of
Mesopotamian introduction scenes (cf.
272, 414). In that case, the lamp would
represent the deity, who is to be a light
to the deceased. The scenes were indeed
found in tombs.

Like "life," so too, "light" was manifest in the temple in the lamps of the
seven-branched lampstand *(255–26).* To
be sure, "Yahweh, my lamp" (Ps 18:29
MT; cf. 2 Sam 22:29; *Plate XIV*) is a less
lofty expression than "Yahweh, my
light," but it makes up in intimacy what
it lacks in loftiness. "Lamp" is much
more personal than "light" (cf. the
proper names "Neriah" = "Yahweh is
[my] lamp" and "Abner" = "the father
[God] is a lamp"). 2 Sam 22:29 reads,
"thou art my lamp, O LORD"; its parallel
in Ps 18:28 reads, "thou dost light my
lamp." This is tantamount to saying, "You
grant me a happy life" (cf. Prov 20:20;
24:20; Job 21:17; cf. 29:3). The metaphor can also describe the life one has
beyond death in one's progeny (1 Kgs
11:36; 15:4; 2 Sam 14:7).

Anyone who has experienced great
darkness knows what a small lamp can
mean. It relieves the whole weight of
the darkness. In Fig. *91,* a lamp set

256a. The text (not seen here) near the right hand of the god Amon reads: "We come before you to worship your beauty, Amon, king of gods. Life and happiness are in your hand. Water springs forth from beneath your feet." The continuation of the text designates the water as "Hapi," the innundation of the Nile which fecundates the land. Thus is ascribed to Amon a blessing originally attributed to Khnum (cf. *334*), the god of the first cataract. It was believed that he caused the Nile to flow forth from a secret cave in the vicinity of Aswan. Yahweh may also have taken over from local deities his function of dispensing water. Ps 36:9 praises Yahweh as the fountain of life, but the interest of the psalm is in life in general. There is no question of an actual fountain. Still, the term "fountain" has concrete implications. In Egyptian texts, as in Ps 36:9, there is found the association of a concrete phenomenon (Nile inundation) with a general one (life).

257. "In thy light do we see light" (Ps 36:9b).

258. "Thy word is a lamp to my feet and a light to my path" (Ps 119:105; cf. Prov 6:23).
259. Detail from Fig. *258*.

up at the left of the sick man banishes the demons. In Ps 119, many statements made earlier regarding God are carried over to the "word of God." Thus the suppliant describes it as a "lamp" to his feet and a light to his path (Ps 119:105). Perhaps the "imperishable light" (cf. Wis 18:4), seen in Fig. *258* in the gable of the Torah shrine (shrine for the scrolls of the Law), refers, in the sense of Ps 119, to the word of Yahweh as a lamp.[16]

d. The Wings of God

The predication of Yahweh as rock, shade, fountain, and light may be traced to the experience of the temple precincts. But it may also have originated in experiences of a much more general nature. The same may hold true of the "wings of God," beneath which the supplicant hopes to find shelter (Pss 17:8; 36:7; 57:1; 61:4; 63:7; 91:4). Kraus links the concept to the "wings of the cherubim extended over the ark."[17] That may well be. It should be borne in mind, however, that when the cherubim are directly mentioned in the psalms they appear as Yahweh's porters (Pss 18:10; 80:1; 99:1) and have no tutelary function (cf. *231-36*). In Ps 61:4, "wings" stand parallel to "tent." In the light of Figs. *221-22*, one might think of the wings which characterize the roof of the temple or *naos* as heaven (cf. *19, 21-24, 33*). In the final analysis, the image is drawn

260. "Keep me as the apple of the eye; hide me in the shadow of thy wings" (Ps 17:8; cf. 36:7; 61:4; 63:7).

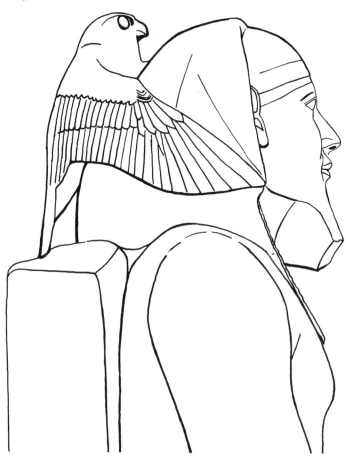

261. "In the shadow of thy wings I will take refuge, till the storms of destruction pass by" (Ps 57:1b).

262. "He will cover you with his pinions, and under his wings you will find refuge" (Ps 91:4). Cf. *238.*

from the bird which protectively spreads its wings over its young (Mt 23:37).

The protection bestowed on the Egyptian king by gods in the form of birds is quite naturally expressed by outstretched wings. The falcon god of Behedet, early identified with Horus, maintains this posture over Khefren (260). In many Egyptian representations, the falcon god appears as a falcon (Plate XXI), Amon appears as a goose (341), or Nekhebet appears as a vulture (425) hovering over the king.

Even at the outset of Egyptian history, wings were disassociated from the bird figure as a kind of hieroglyph for "protection." They can represent the feminine-motherly aspect of the sky in its protective function (cf. 19, 21, etc.). In the same way, wings serve to represent the protection afforded by two goddesses (misunderstood as gods on the Phoenician ivory in Fig. 261) to the newborn sun rising out of the lotus (261), and also the protection provided by Nephthys (and Isis) to Osiris (262), the "first among the dead." Thus the gesture of blessing with which Isis (right) greets Osiris is, for all practical purposes, synonymous with the wings of Nephthys (left) spread protectively behind him. This motif, which originated in Egypt, was adopted in Palestine and Syria (261) at the close of the second millennium and the beginning of the first; the Phoenicians carried it westward throughout the Mediterranean world and eastward via North Syria to northern Mesopotamia.

e. Ears That Hear and a Mouth That Speaks

The God who dwells on Zion tests and purifies the temple visitor. He who can stand before him participates in the blessing and life (Ps 24:5) that proceed from the living God (Ps 36:9) who is present there. To those who fear him, he is a rock of refuge and a lamp. They find shelter under his wings. But he is not only the source of life longed for by those who hunger and thirst in a dry and weary land (Pss 42:2–3; 63:1; 143:6). He is, more personally, one "who hears prayer" (cf.

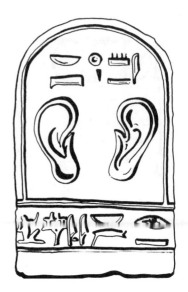

263. "I love the LORD because he has heard my voice in supplication, Because he has inclined his ear to me the day I called" (Ps 116:1b, 2).

Ps 65:2). In prayer, the afflicted one pours out his heart (Ps 102:praef.); he voices the thoughts and cares which torment him personally, in hopes that God may hear them. "Incline thy ear to me" (Pss 17:6; 31:2; 71:2; 86:1; etc.). "Give ear! Hear!" (cf. Pss 5:1; 17:1; 54:2; 55:2; etc.).

God does indeed hear. Therefore vows are repeatedly paid in the temple (Ps 107), and thanksgivings attest: "He inclined his ear to me" (Ps 116:2). This sentiment is expressed in stone by the two ears on the stele in Fig. 263. Above them appears the name of the god who has heard: "Amon-Re, the lord of heaven." Beneath the ears is the name of him who has been heard and who erected the memorial: "Neb-Mehit made (it)." Such memorial stones were to be found in every temple of the ancient world. Diogenes is reputed to have said to a visitor fascinated by the great number of these stones in the temple at Samothrace: "There would be far more if all those who were not saved had given them as well."[18] But the sentiment of Ps 116:2 cannot be so summarily dismissed. If one is to understand its basic inten-

264. "Out of the depths I cry to thee, O
LORD! Lord, hear my voice! Let thy ears be
attentive to the voice of my supplications!"
(Ps 130:1–2).

In most instances, the ears on Egyptian
stelae were intended to perpetuate petition
rather than thanksgiving. This is clearly evidenced by the inscription frequently attached
to such stelae: "Hear the prayer which X.Y.
has made." Attempt was made to render the
simple request more effective by means of
magic. As many ears as possible were included on the stele in order to represent the
divine audition and to compel hearing. On a
stele from Memphis there are no fewer than
376 ears (cf. M. H. P. Blok, "Remarques sur
quelques stèles," p. 134).

tion, one must remember that these
stones were the expression of individual
experiences and convictions. We are not
dealing in the realm of law—a point not
reflected in Diogenes' statement. Less
and more is at stake than Diogenes implies. These individual testimonies do
not express the conviction that the deity
obediently attends man's beck and call as
an ever-willing servant. Rather, they are
testimonies to the fact that in a moment
of extreme danger, one has thankfully
experienced existence as a profound gift.
As is graphically indicated by the two
ears on the memorial stone, ancient
Near Eastern man loved the concrete,
but to him the concrete was always simultaneously symbol.

The temple was a favorite place for
making petitions and lamentations, but
prayer could as well be made at any
other cherished spot. As was indicated in
the conclusion of chapter 3, the temple
was only a sacramental representation of
heaven as the dwelling place of God, and
as far as ancient man was concerned, the
heavens arched over the whole earth.
The ears of God, who dwells in heaven,
are accessible from any point on earth.
In Fig. 264, the hearing ears of the deity
appear amid the sun, moon, and stars.

It is in the sanctuary, however, that
Yahweh is present not only as silent
hearer and grantor, but also as articulate
speaker. "God *has spoken* in his
sanctuary. . . " (Pss 60:6, 108:8; cf.
35:3; 50:1; 62:11; 85:8; 89:19; etc.).
Only rarely did he speak in extraordinary epiphanies (e.g., Isa 6). As a rule,
he spoke by the mouth of his priests;
above all, he spoke through the cult
prophets who were more or less closely
associated with the temple.[19] On specific
occasions, they proclaimed salvation in
the name of God to the king, the people,
and the individual. They could also
threaten judgment and disaster (cf. Pss
50; 58; 81; 82; 95; *264a, 264b*).

These prophets presumably gained
their legitimacy to speak in the name of
Yahweh from their personal consciousness of mission (similar to the "free
prophets"), from their ties with Moses,

 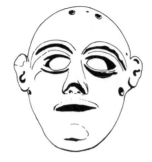 

264a. Three masks from (left to right) Hazor (first two) and Hebron. They are often described as cult masks despite the fact that they do not seem well suited for wearing. In isolated OT texts the term "teraphim" apparently denotes cult masks (1 Sam 19:13 RSVm; Judg 17:5; 18:17–20; Hos 3:4). The masks presumably qualified the wearer to speak in the name of the deity and to utter oracles (cf. Ezek 21:26; Zech 10:2). In the early period of the Jerusalem temple it is uncertain whether such masks were used by those who spoke in the name of Yahweh. Masks were not used in the later period, but there were in the Jerusalem cultus men who (without recourse to masks) spoke in the name of Yahweh.

265. "As a father receives his children with heartfelt love, so Yahweh receives with heartfelt love those who fear him" (Ps 103:13 [author's translation]).

Akhenaton, in the circle of his family, is shown kissing one of his daughters. The picture must be understood in relation to the luminous sun disc (Aton), whose salutary, life-giving power is incarnated in the action of the king (cf. 289). In the OT, the loving attitude of a father toward his children is seen not as a representation of cosmic life-forces, but as an image of the personal love of Yahweh.

194

264b. An Egyptian priest is shown wearing the mask of Anubis, god of the necropoleis (cf. 75). The mask evidently has no eyeholes. The practical usability of a mask apparently cannot be the basis for determining whether or not it was worn in the cultus. Egyptian pictures (cf. 70, 75) suggest that masks of the gods were not only worn for delivering oracles.

266. A charming scene on light blue chalcedony, from Elam (12th century B.C.). It bears the following inscription: "I, Shilhak-Inshushinak, the increaser of the kingdom, brought from the land of Puralish this chalcedony. I had it carefully worked and set, and to Bar-Uli, my beloved daughter, I gave it" (I. Seibert, Die Frau, pl. 42).

the lawgiver (cf. Num 11:16–17, 24–30), from religious traditions (cf. Pss 50; 81; 95), and from their participation in the official cultus. (Their declarations would have held for them and their contemporaries a force similar to the absolution uttered in the name of God in the Catholic confessional.)

f. Father and Mother, Host and Physician

The compassion (rḥmym, an abstract plural of rḥm, "mother's womb") accorded the suppliant in the temple has a personal structure similar to that of the hearing of prayer. It does not consist, however, in various mother-symbols and sacraments, but in the forgiveness of sins. The suppliant is assured of that forgiveness by means of various rites (Ps 51:1ff; cf. also 25:6–7; 40:11–13). God has pity on him, just as a father turns in love toward his child (265), forgiving

and reconciling the offense. He knows that weakness, more than wickedness, is the cause of most false steps (Ps 103:12–14). In the temple with Yahweh, one feels more securely sheltered than with one's own father and mother (Ps 27:10).

To be sure, such intimate imagery is rare in the psalms. Motherly love can be attributed to Yahweh only with considerable difficulty (but cf. Isa 49:15), and fatherly love is almost never represented in the art of the ancient Near East. Fig. 266 is quite unique. The sparing attribution of fatherly love to Yahweh is therefore not remarkable.

The psalms more frequently portray Yahweh as a magnanimous host who welcomes the temple visitor into his fellowship. He prepares the table for his guests, anoints their head with perfumed oils, and amply fills their cups (Ps 23:5; cf. 36:8; 63:5; 65:4; 103:5; 132:15). In some instances, he commands all this to be done by his servants (267–69). Fes-

195

267. "My cup overflows" (Ps 23:5bβ).

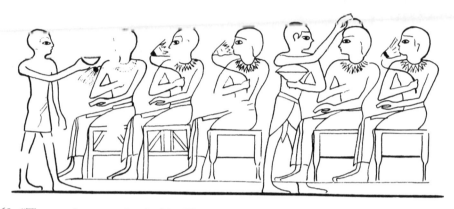

268. "Thou anointest my head with oil" (Ps 23:5bα; cf. 445).

269. "My soul is feasted as with marrow and fat" (Ps 63:5; 437–39a).

tive sacrificial meals at the temple form the basis of this conception.

Fig. 270 is related to banqueting scenes. It depicts an Egyptian physician whose servant offers a bowl containing a medicinal draught to a Caananite nobleman. The prince is accompanied by his wife. The servants of the prince bring the honorarium for the physician's services. If sickness is equivalent to weakness (cf. p. 62), healing is to be taken as strengthening. This explains the relation between the portrayal of a banquet and medical treatment. There were, of course, many diseases and infirmities which could not be healed by medical

270. ". . . who heals all your diseases [literally: "weaknesses"]" (Ps 103:3b; cf. 6:2; 30:2; 41:4; 147:3).

Nebamon, the chief physician, deceased, sits at table, while his brother presents him with a bouquet of flowers. This scene from the cult of the dead is coupled with an incident from the physician's life. A Syrian noble has come seeking treatment. One of Nebamon's servants hands him a medicinal draught. The boat (cf. 86) and the oxcarts in the bottom register indicate the length of the journey the man has undertaken in order to consult the famous physician. The servants of the patient bring costly vessels as remuneration (cf. 408). The children may also be part of the compensation. Syrian slaves were much valued in Egypt (cf. 132a). But the Syrian is accompanied by his wife. It is therefore possible that the children are those of the noble (?) couple, and that the servants are merely tending them during the interview (compare this scene to the story of Naaman the Syrian in 2 Kgs 5).

270a. The doorkeeper Ramu, shown here at sacrifice, has a deformed leg. Physicians have diagnosed the deformity as *pes equinus,* the typical result of poliomyelitis. The deity to whom sacrifice is offered is not shown (an exception to the rule), only named: "Ishtar of Syria" (upper horizontal line). In Egypt, she was regarded as a goddess of healing. The stele depicting Ramu's affliction and his sacrifice were intended to induce the goddess to free him from his malady.

means. In cases such as that shown in Fig. *270a,* the deity remained the only hope.

In the ancient Near East, even in modern times, more significance attaches to hospitality than is the case in the West. Its implications are not restricted to the realm of feeling. It also has consequences which may be characterized as juridical (cf. Ps 41:9; 1 Cor 10:20 ff.).[20] One who provides hospitality to another commits himself to concern for every aspect of his guest's well-being (cf. Gen 19). Above all, that includes safe conduct, such as is promised to the departing pilgrims in Ps 121. The trusting supplicant asks for guidance and escort (Pss 5:8; 61:2; etc.). God is obligated to provide such protection because the supplicant knows himself to be threatened by enemies (Pss 5:8; 27:11) and because, as host, God must maintain his own good name (Pss 23:3; 31:3).

271. The suppliants of Ps 49 (v. 15) and Ps 73 (v. 24) hope to be "taken" by Yahweh. They do not have in mind a fantastic assumption like Etana's; but they do look forward (in a real, actual sense) to being received by Yahweh and thus enabled to share in his eternity.

g. "He will take me"

The suppliant of Ps 73 has experienced in the temple the nearness and loving guidance of God. This experience nourishes the hope that God will not permit such fellowship to end in death, but instead will "take" (*lqḥ* [RSV: "receive"]) him (Ps 73:24). The ancient traditions of Enoch and Elijah are democratized in this hope. Of both it is said that they walked with God and finally were "taken" (Gen 5:24; 2 Kgs 2:3). The *terminus technicus* "translation" is often used with reference to the "taking" of Enoch and Elijah. This term, however, is not appropriate in this context. There is no question here of a miraculous assumption, as in the case of the Mesopotamian hero who was borne to heaven by an eagle so that he might fetch the herb of birth *(271).* In Ps 73:24 (cf. also Ps 49:15 [RSV: "ransom"] and Ps 16:10–11, where the term "to take" does not appear) the supplicant hopes that in the end God will accept him wholly and for ever. That implies, primarily, a personal act (acceptation) which secondarily means life beyond the allotted time.

This "taking," coupled with the theme of guidance, is reminiscent of one of the Pyramid Texts[21] in which the air god Shu is commanded: "Take the king by the arm, take him to heaven so that he may not die on the earth." Yet the external similarity is deceptive. Here the process is not personal. The wind is to bear the king from the mortal realm into the immortal.

More closely related to our text are the introduction scenes popular on Mesopotamian cylinder seals from the Akkadian period onwards *(272, 414, 426),* or the illustrations from New Kingdom papyri of the Book of the Dead *(273).* In both instances, however, one deity conducts while another receives the worshipper or the deceased, and only in Egypt is this accomplished definitively and for all time. The deceased asks the lord of the nether world: "Suffer me to remain at your side"[22] (cf. Ps 73:23). "Lo, I come to behold you and I refresh myself on your beauty"[23]

272. "Oh send out thy light and thy truth, let them lead me, let them bring me to thy holy hill and to thy dwelling" (Ps 43:3).

In the psalms, the attributes of Yahweh take the place of the tutelary goddesses who conduct and escort the suppliant (cf. 40).

273. "Teach me thy way, O LORD, and lead me on a level path because of my enemies" (Ps 27:11).

In the psalms, the suppliant hopes to avoid giving human enemies an opportunity to dispose of him. In this Egyptian papyrus, the deceased hopes to be conducted past the "devourer of the dead" and to be brought safely to Osiris.

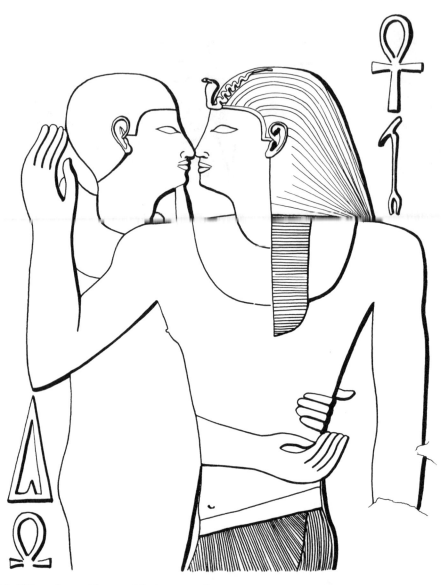

274. "Thou dost guide me with thy counsel, and afterward thou wilt receive me to glory" (Ps 73:24).

(cf. Ps 16:11b). But these lovely phrases are embedded in magical equations. The deceased passes himself off as Horus and approaches his father as the same, more demanding than hopeful. The speaker here is not a man who hopes, on the strength of his experience of God's nearness in the temple, to be taken one

day into the fulness of the divine fellowship. *That* hope is found only in the psalms. While this hope does not share the magical tendencies and the exclusivity of the Egyptian royal cultus, it does possess something of the intimacy and jubilation with which the gods receive the king, now in the temple *(274)*, someday in the beyond, in order to bestow on him eternal life (cf. Ps 103:5).[24]

The experience of God in the temple is described as "seeing God" or "the face of God" (Pss 42:2; 63:2; 84:7). Just as "seeing" can connote an experience in the widest sense (cf. Ps 16:10; Isa 38:11; Ps 44:15), so too, "God" or "the face of God" can encompass diverse realities. Yet, in addition to their extensive transferred meanings, in this context, "God" and "the face of God" often possess a very precise sense. In Egypt (cf. *229–30*),[25] as in Mesopotamia (cf. *239*),[26] the expression could be understood literally as a gazing upon the image or emblem of the deity. The same may also have been the case on occasion in the psalms (e.g. Pss 17:15; 68:24). But in all three cultural realms, "to see God" could likewise denote the experience, in the setting of the great temple festivals, of an elevating joy and happiness that was perceived as the ultimate reality of life.

2. GOD IN HIS CREATION

It was stated at the beginning of this chapter that individual themes would of necessity be assigned somewhat arbitrarily to one of the three sections. Fig. *274* and the illustration of the falcon god *(260)* demonstrate that this arbitrariness extends still further, and that much of

275. "For thou didst form my inward parts, . . . my frame was not hidden from thee, when I was being made in secret . . ." (Ps 139:13a, 15).

the material included in this chapter could just as well stand in chapter 5 ("The King") or chapter 1 ("Conceptions of the Cosmos"). Intense attention was paid to the action of God as it relates to the king. Many conceptions which resulted from this intellectual activity and many expressions which were forged in this connection later became common property.[27] Nevertheless, it remains probable that much of what was applied in a special sense to the king had always also applied, in less intensive form, to a broader generality of men. Such is the case, for example, with regard to the beginning of new life.

a. Generation and Birth

Even to prenational Israel, it was quite clear that the deity granted or denied progeny (cf. Gen 18:10–14; 25:21; 29:31; 30:1–2). In the case of the Egyptian king, this general notion appears in a concentrated form: the deity himself (in the figure of the king) begets the future ruler (cf. *333*). Goddesses assist at his birth *(336)*, and it is they who suckle him.

In the psalms, an unknown individual acknowledges that Yahweh shaped and formed him in his mother's womb (Ps 139:13, 16; cf. 33:15; 94:9). The only iconographic representation of this process known to the author *(334)* may derive from the birth-narrative of the

276. Yahweh appears as midwife in the following verse: "Yet thou art he who took me from the womb . . ." (Ps 22:9a).

him into being. He ought not now permit him to die destitute.

The individual reminded God of the divine assistance provided at his birth. In the same way, the nation, under assault by hostile peoples or suffering military occupation and the attendant outrages, recalled to God his role in the creation of the earth. At that time, God conquered the forces of destruction in a great battle. He ought not allow the result of his victory to be so easily wrested from him (Pss 74:12–18; 89:10–13). This extrapolation back from national history to the history of the earth is facilitated by the fact that the Hebrew '*rs* stands for both "earth" and "land" or "country." Mythological language, according to which the world is the result of the divine victory over the powers of darkness, occurs fairly frequently in the psalms as compared to the remaining books of the OT. Even in the psalms, however, it is not the rule.

Egyptian king. Should that be the case, the assertion of Ps 139 may be no more democratized than a suppliant's recollection elsewhere that God took him from his mother's womb (Pss 22:9a; 71:6; 276) and sheltered him on his mother's breast (Pss 22:9b; 277).

Small sculptures such as those shown in Figs. 275–77, which were donated as votive offerings, had a function in petition (cf. 270a) and in thanksgiving (307a).[28] The magical understanding of the world imputed to these plastic representations of pregnancy, birth, and suckling the power to guarantee and assist the processes they portray. In the ancient Near East, one could not conceive of these processes without more or less direct, intense cooperation of higher powers. In Israel—and elsewhere—this fact is nicely attested by the character of proper names, which often take the form of miniature songs or hymns of thanksgiving. Names frequently include the element *ntn*, "to give" (cf. Jonathan = "Yahweh has given"; Nathaniel = "God has given"; etc.). If a woman had been barren for a prolonged period, only God could make her a "joyous mother" (Ps 113:9). The reference to his divine role at the suppliant's birth is intended to remind God of his responsibility for his creature. God brought

277. ". . . thou didst keep me safe upon my mother's breasts" (Ps 22:9b).

The newborn child was laid on its father's knees (cf. 339). By accepting it he legitimized it as his child. By laying it on its mother's breast, he expressed his will to preserve its life (cf. Job 3:12).

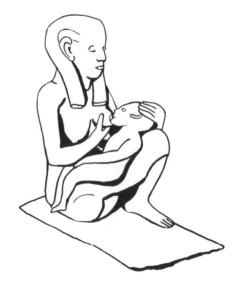

277a. "Naked I came from my mother's womb, and naked shall I return" (Job 1:21).

The concept that individual parts of the cosmos came into being by generation, birth, and the like (cf., e.g., Ps 90:2, and the Mother Earth which brings forth man in Ps 139:15) has drastically receded into the background and is discernible only in a few ill-preserved, fossilized remains. Fig. 277a depicts Mother Earth, the great bearer, mistress of the earth-mountain (Ninhursag), mistress of bearing (Nintu). At her left and right are crouched two fetuses. Two infants' heads project from her shoulders,

just as rays shoot forth from the shoulders of the sun god (9, 53, 286) and water and fish leap forth from the shoulders of Ea (43, 285). At her breast, the goddess gives suck to a child (shown only by its head and one arm). The symbol on either side of the goddess has been interpreted as a swaddling band,[29] or as the uterus of a cow, the mother animal *par excellence*.[30] In the OT, in addition to Ps 139:15, the famous prayer of Job (1:21) alludes to the concept of Mother Earth as the bearer of men and, in general, of all living things. Return to the womb of the earth presupposes emergence from it.

Though it does not depict the goddess in human form, Fig. 277b portrays the great Sumerian Mother as mistress of birth. In the archaic pictography of Uruk, the hut which gives birth to the two calves[31] has the sound-value *tut (tur),* "birth."[32] The staff-and-ring symbol above the hut is the sign of the goddess. The approximate meaning of the entire composition is that the mistress or goddess of birth brings forth the cattle. In Ps 144:13–14, Yahweh is discreetly portrayed as the giver of many strong, future generations of large and small livestock. As a whole, however, "creation" as "birth" plays a small role in the psalms which treat creation. Usually God is portrayed as *deus faber,* as craftsman, or as commander in chief, who by his all-powerful word calls obedient creatures into being. Thus, in its understanding of God (and that necessarily includes also its understanding of the

277b. "Our sheep bring forth thousands and increase to ten thousands in our fields. Our cattle are big with young, and there is no mischance, no miscarriage, and no cry of distress in our streets. Happy the people for whom things are thus, happy the people whose God is Yahweh" (Ps 144:13b–15 [author's translation]).

world), the OT differs markedly from its cultural milieu, where categories of generation and birth played a large part in representation of the world and its origin (cf., e.g., *25, 31*).

b. Deus faber

The best-known of those terms which describe God's creative activity as the work of a craftsman is *yṣr*, "to form, fashion, shape, create." As the potter (*yuṣr*) is free and sovereign over his vessels *(278),* so God's works are completely in his hands (cf. also Jer 18:1–10). This aspect is much more important in the psalms than are the technical processes of forming clay. The notion of fashioning the "eye" and the "heart" is readily conceivable, but when "summer" and "winter" (Ps 74:17) or "the dry land" (Ps 95:5) appear as objects created by God, "fashioning" can be understood only as a hieroglyph for "sovereign designing." This aspect is explicitly expressed in Ps 104, when God "forms" the feared sea monster Leviathan in order to "play" with him (v. 26).

Besides *yṣr* there appears a whole series of essentially similar concrete terms which describe or suggest the work of God in terms of craftsmanship. Thus, in Ps 144:12b, the comparison of the daughters of Israel with pillars, or even with Caryatids *(278a),* evokes the image of God as sculptor. According to Pss. 24:2; 89:11; 102:25; 104:5, God lays the foundations of the earth—an extremely difficult undertaking, for there existed no firm basis. He stretches out the heavens like a tent (Ps 104:2), gathers the waters as in a skin (Ps 33:7 [RSV: "bottle"]), hammers out the broad earth (Ps 136:6), plants cedars (Ps 104:16; cf. 94:9; *280*), and weaves man like a fabric (Ps 139:15; *279*).[33] But the frequently used terms such as *yṣr* tend to lose their concrete background. The verb "to establish, set firm," is used with widely differing objects, such as stars, sun and moon (Pss 8:3; 74:16), earth (Pss 24:2; 119:90), and men (Ps 119:73). It is used quite generally to underscore the reliability of the divine creation (Ps 33:4).

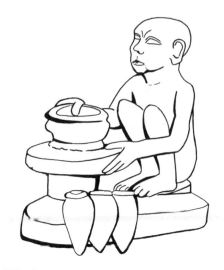

278. "I too was formed from a piece of clay" (Job 33:6b)

278a. "Our daughters [are] like corner pillars cut for the structure of a palace" (Ps 144:12b).

The frequently used verb "to make" is even less related to a specific act of craftsmanship. God "made" heaven and earth—in a word, everything (Pss 115:15; 121:2; etc.). He is the author of the universe, and, in consequence, is also its owner (Pss 95:4–5; 100:3). They are

279. ". . . when I was . . . wrought [like a colorful, woven fabric] in the depths of the earth" (Ps 139:15c).

280. "From his lofty abode he waters the mountains. . . . The trees of the field are satisfied, the cedars of Lebanon which he planted" (Ps 104:13a, 16 [author's translation]).

does not lead to a coalescence with the cosmos. It points instead beyond the cosmos to its author (cf. Ps 19:1–4).

c. Command and Wisdom

The experience of the utter contingency of the world is expressed most strongly in those passages which describe the processes of creation in terms of command and execution: "He spoke, and it came to be; he commanded, and it stood forth" (Ps 33:9; cf. 33:6; 148:5). Like a disciplined army which moves forward at a single command or trumpet call (281–82), the world obeys the word of the invisible God. He who determined the number of the stars calls them all by their names (Ps 147:4).

Although the works of God are infinite in number, all are created "in wisdom," which means in keeping with a definite and sensible order (Job 28:25–27; Ps 104:24; cf. 136:5; 147:5). That wisdom, which is continually discernible in the structure of created things, is one of the chief attributes of the Canaanite El. The "creator of creatures"[34] and the "creator of the earth"[35] is regarded as an exemplar of wisdom ("wise as El").[36] His wisdom is related to his great age.[37]

Israel adopted by and large the understanding of God which had taken form in El. El was identified with the God of Abraham and with Yahweh.[38] In Ugarit,

"his works" (Pss 104:31; 145:9, 17) or—in an intensification of God's personal action and sovereignty—the "work of his hands" (Pss 19:1; 102:25). Once, the heavens are even called the "work of his fingers" (Ps 8:3). God must have engaged himself carefully and quite personally in a work of such surpassing grandeur. The objective, prosaic understanding of the world as a creation, as something made and constructed, is ill-disposed toward any kind of pantheizing mysticism, but it by no means excludes a certain joyful enthusiasm (Pss 8:1–3; 104:24, 31; 139:14, 18; 148). Yet, this

281. "By the word of the LORD the heavens were made, and all their host by the breath of his mouth. Let all the earth fear the LORD, let all the inhabitants of the world stand in awe of him! For he spoke, and it came to be; he commanded, and it stood forth" (Ps 33:6, 8–9).

282. "Praise him, you highest heavens, and you waters above the heavens! Let them praise the name of the LORD! For he commanded and they were created" (Ps 148:4–5)

283. "He determines the number of the stars, he gives to all of them their names. Great is our LORD, and abundant in power; his understanding is beyond measure" (Ps 147:45; cf. 42).

284. "Of old thou didst lay the foundation of the earth, and the heavens are the work of thy hands. They will perish, but thou dost endure; they will all wear out like a garment. Thou changest them like raiment, and they pass away; but thou art the same, and thy years have no end" (Ps 102:25–27).

El was portrayed as an amiable old man (283–84, cf. 42). His long, ceremonial garment (Ps 104:1b, 2a) and his sitting posture (Ps 29:10) characterize him as the point of repose (Pss 90:1; 102:12, 24–27). He has one hand raised in blessing (cf. Ps 145:9). His headgear is reminiscent of the Egyptian atef-crown, a combination of the tall crown of Upper Egypt and the feather crown, supplemented by a pair of horns (cf. 369). The horns of the figure in Fig. 284 have been lost, but above the ears may be seen the holes into which they were fitted. The king, wearing the Egyptian uraeus-serpent on his brow, stands before the horned El of Fig. 283, who is holding a small incense bowl (?) in his right hand.

The king holds in his right hand a scepter, in his left a ewer for a drink offering. As king of the gods, El bears a certain resemblance to the earthly king (cf. the Ugaritic Keret epic).

d. The Judge

Like the earthly king, El is not only the author of order, but also its preserver. Whenever strife arises among the gods, they turn to El for arbitration. He is regarded as judge, inasmuch as it is he who balances the claims of the sea (ym) and the dry land (b'l), the rainy winter (b'l) and the arid summer (mwt).

Because the ancient Near East made use of "judgments" in the most diverse proceedings, various deities could bear the title of judge. In Mesopotamia, for example, Ea, god of wisdom and ruler of the ground-waters, can be predicated and portrayed as judge (285). He may be identified by the water streaming down from his shoulders. Two lesser deities conduct a bird-man before him for trial. It is the Zu-bird,[39] who is manifested in the raging tempest (cf. 92–93; Ps 55:8–9). A god appears as plaintiff. The plow laid over his shoulder identifies him as a god of vegetation. The scene as a whole represents judgment on the destructive typhoon—a vital issue to the farmers of Mesopotamia.

Though Ea here plays an important role as judge, for Mesopotamia as a whole "the judging god is simply Shamash (the sun god)."[40] He hates and dispels the darkness and every dark thing (cf. 53–55); he lifts into the light the form and order of all things; he surveys everything, knows everything, and reaches everything. The great hymn to Shamash begins with these words: "Illuminator of the earth, judge of the heavens, illuminator of the darkness, . . . above and below. . . Your radiant beams hold the land like a net."[41] In Fig. 286, Shamash is seated on a throne formed by mountains. A man, identified as an aide of the sun god by the beams radiating from his shoulders, conducts a lion-headed demon (cf. 94, 99–100) to trial. Another man assists. In Fig. 53, the same process, the subjugation of darkness by light, is interpreted as a battle. Like the judicial activity of Shamash, God's judicial activity appears in the psalms as an alternate form of his aggressive engagement on

285. "At the set time which I appoint I will judge with equity. When the earth totters, and all its inhabitants, it is I who keep steady its pillars. . . . It is God who executes judgment, putting down one and lifting up another" (Ps 75:2–3, 7).

286. "Rise up, O judge of the earth; render to the proud their deserts! O LORD, how long shall the wicked, how long shall the wicked exult?" (Ps 94:2–3).

behalf of right and righteousness (Pss 35:1–3, 23–24; 54:1, 5; 74:13–14, 22).

Like Shamash, the God of the psalmists is also a *universal* judge. In Ps 82, he condemns to death those gods responsible for injustice and violence. He is the "judge of the earth" (Ps 94:2), whose function it is to establish justice for all the nations of the earth (Ps 82:8; 96:13; 98:9). In Ps 84:11, the avenging God is hailed as "sun" (cf. Ps 121!). The Babylonian Shamash is almost exclusively judge.[42] The Egyptian sun god's sphere of activity is much wider. As governor of the world he is the guardian of justice. He exercises his office much in the manner of an earthly ruler. "Surrounded by a (royal) household, he sits enthroned in the bark in which he crosses the heavenly ocean" (287; cf. 16, 32).[43] The most important members of his household are Horus, the falcon-headed sky god, and Hathor, the mother goddess and goddess of love, shown with the cow's horns. The sun god is enthroned beneath his baldachin. The scribal god Thoth, with the ibis-head, appears before him to make report. Immediately behind the crouching pilot stands Maat, her feather on her head. She is the embodiment of the legitimate world order (cf. the commentary on Fig. 32).

Yahweh too has his heavenly household (Pss 29:1; 82; 89:5–8; 95:3; 96:4–5; 97:9).[44] In contrast to the Egyptian household (cf. also 332), the names of individual gods do not appear in it. Yahweh is the only figure with sharp contours. Re, on the other hand, exercises the office of world administration in close cooperation with other divine powers. Thus, he rules, looking down upon the earth from the height of heaven (Pss 11:4; 14:2; 102:19), always intent to preserve the condition of Maat and to ward off every disturbance of order. His concern extends to things both great and small. Even the simple, pious man may venture to submit the grievances he suffers to Re, "the righteous judge [cf. Pss 7:11; 9:4] who takes no bribe."[45]

e. The God of Life

When Re came to be linked with the primeval creator-god Atum, his role as creator and sustainer of the world assumed greater importance for the Egyptians than his role as world governor and judge. "For in the sun, which generates light and warmth, the basic conditions of life and indeed, life itself, Re is legitimized in immediate, daily experience as creator. It is not without reason that the hymns to the sun[46] emphasize this aspect of his activity, which is at once the most striking and convincing."[47] In Mesopotamia, on the other hand, these attributes play little or no part in defining Shamash. The natural phenomenon alone does not produce an image of divinity.[48]

The sun god was most impressively celebrated and portrayed as the life-giving sun disc (Aton) during the Amarna period (1377–1368 B.C.). The close relationship between Ps 104 and the great hymn to Aton from Amarna has been repeatedly noted. G. Nagel[49] has emphasized, however, that the Aton hymn and similar poems place the accent on the deity's everyday activity to sustain the world, while in Ps 104 Yahweh's work of creation stands in the foreground. That the Aton hymn was directly taken up by the Israelites is inconceivable. Phoenicia probably played a mediating role. That would explain not only the differences, but also the obvious delight of both hymns in picturesque detail, together with their common assertion that Aton, or respectively, Yahweh has brought forth life and preserves it even in its most minute ramifications.

From the Aton hymn of Amarna:

Thou settest every man in his place,
Thou suppliest their necessities:
Everyone has his food, and his time of life
   is reckoned. . .
The world came into being by thy hand,
According as thou has made them.
When thou hast risen they live,
When thou settest they die.
Thou art lifetime thy own self,
For one lives (only) through thee.[50]

From Ps 104:

These all look to thee
to give them their food in due season.
When thou givest to them, they gather it
   up;
when thou openest thy hand, they are
   filled with good things.
When thou hidest thy face, they are
   dismayed;
when thou takest away their breath, they
   die and return to their dust.
When thou sendest forth thy Spirit, they
   are created;
and thou renewest the face of the ground.
   (vv. 27–30)

The two texts demonstrate the potential for close convergence of differing religious statements, one bearing the im-

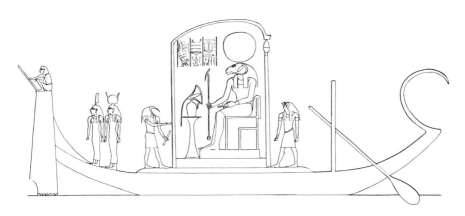

287. "Let the heavens praise thy wonders, O LORD, thy faithfulness in the assembly of the holy ones. For who in the skies can be compared to the LORD? who among the sons of gods [RSVm] is like the LORD, a God feared in the council of the holy ones, great and terrible above all that are round about him?" (Ps 89:5–7).

288. "Give us life, and we will call on thy
name! . . . O Lord God of hosts! let thy face
shine, that we may be saved!" (Ps 80:18b,
19).

Perceptions of creation are as much a basis
of this text from Ps 80 (a national lament) as
they are of the texts of Ps 74:13–17 or Ps
89:9–13.

press of the experience of nature, the
other standing firmly within Yahwism.

Fig. 288 shows the sun disc, whose
rays, forming hands, convey life (the loop
with the "cross") to the king and queen
by way of their noses. The conceptions
associated with the Egyptian sun god are
characteristically universal (289). They
are by no means limited to Aton. A hymn

to Amon-Re reads in part: "It is you who
have placed the breath of life in *every*
nose, so that what your two arms have
created may remain in life."[51] The relation with the natural phenomenon of the
sun is not always clear, but it is always
preserved.

In contrast to the Egyptian sun god,
the storm and vegetation deity of North

289. "At daybreak, when thou risest on the horizon, . . . Thou drivest away the darkness and givest thy rays . . . Washing their bodies, taking (their) clothing, Their [men's] arms are (raised) in praise at thy appearance. All the world, they do their work. All beasts are contented with their pasturage; Trees and plants are flourishing, The birds which fly from their nests, Their wings are (stretched out) in praise to thy *ka* [i.e., your person, you]. All beasts spring upon (their) feet. Whatever flies and alights, They live when thou hast risen (for) them" (*ANET,* p. 370).

"When the sun rises, they [predatory animals] get them away and lie down in their dens. Man goes forth to his work and to his labor until the evening. . . . Thou [Yahweh] dost cause the grass to grow for the cattle, . . . the trees of the LORD are watered abundantly. . . . In them the birds build their nests; the stork has her home in the fir trees. . . . These all look to thee [Yahweh], to give them their food in due season" (Ps 104:22–23, 14a, 16a, 17, 27).

Syria, northern Mesopotamia, and Asia Minor does not bestow life directly, but rather by means of his influence on the weather and vegetation. By the beginning of the second millennium, he was known in Mesopotamia by the name Hadad or Adad, a name probably related to the Arabic word *hadda*, "to thunder," "to crash." In Ugarit, Hadad was identified with the Hurrite god Teshub. From the middle of the second millennium at the latest, he was identified almost exclusively by the title Baal (possessor, lord). In the earlier period, his most important attribute was the thunder-club (*290;* cf. *46*). The obvious implication is that he uses it to make the heavens rumble. But in a Ugaritic text closely related to Ps 29, he thunders with his voice and not by means of a club:

Baal lets his holy voice resound,
Baal repeats the utterance of his lips [in the echo of the thunder];
his voice rang out, and the earth trembled. . .
the hills of the earth leapt [cf. Ps 29:6].
The enemies of Baal crept into the woods.
Then said Aliyan Baal:
Why does the enemy of Hadad flee?
Why does he flee before the weapon of the *dmrn?*
[Indeed] the eye of Baal anticipates his hand
when the cedar drops before his right hand.[52] (cf. Ps 29:5)

On the basis of this text and Ps 29 it is possible that the club was less an instrument of thunder than of combat against those enemies whom Baal battled in the storm. One could conclude from Ps 18:4–15 that the Chaos waters are the foe. Figs. *42* and *46* support that view.

In Fig. *290,* Baal wears a horned helmet. A suppliant stands before him. Between them is seen the Egyptian life-sign and, on a pedestal, the bull, cult symbol of Baal. They indicate that for which the suppliant is indebted to the god: life and fertility. The entire scene is set beneath the Egyptian winged sun. The god's consort stands behind him. The eight-pointed star relates her to the Mesopotamian Ishtar. Her concern is the

god, toward whom she extends the sign of life. The stele in Fig. *291* shows the deity in an attitude quite similar to that portrayed on the cylinder seal of Fig. *290.* Two rich locks emphasize his youthful strength and beauty. He *stands,* by way of contrast with the seated El, who inclines to leisure. Instead of the long garment of rank (cf. Gen 37), he wears the short work-apron. His lance, topped by a sprouting tree, is of particular interest. It may explain the peculiar statement of Ps 135:7 (quite similar to that of Jer 10:13; 51:16): "He it is. . . who makes lightnings for the rain and brings forth the wind from his storehouses." Just as Yahweh brings forth the wind, so the lightnings (iconographically, the lance) create a path for the rain. The rain, in turn, makes possible the growth of vegetation (iconographically, the sprouting tree). If the sprouting lance portrays the sequence of lightning-rain-vegetation, perhaps we ought not exclude the possibility that the club symbolizes the thunder which rocks the heavens and facilitates the downpour of rain.

We must not forget the fact, however, that in Figs. *42* and *46* the lance plays a role in the battle against Chaos. The stele may portray not simply the sequence lightning-rain-vegetation, but the longer sequence, conquest of Chaos-lightning-rain-vegetation. In the myth, the conquest of Chaos precedes the rule of Baal. Quite similarly, Ps 65 celebrates Yahweh's victory over Chaos (Ps 65:7–8) before the earth is visited with rain showers (Ps 65:9–13). Like Ps 65, the Ugaritic Keret epic celebrates the significance of Baal's rain for vegetation:

The rain [*mṭr*] of Baal was present for the earth,
and for the fields the rain [*mṭr*] of the exalted one;
delicious [*n'm*] to the earth was the rain of Baal
and to the fields the rain of the exalted one.
The fountain [was] a delight to the wheat.
Emmer wheat [grew] in the newly plowed land,
grain [*ṭrṭr*] in the furrows.[53]

290. "The God of glory thunders" (Ps 29:3b).

Psalm 65 similarly celebrates the God of Israel as the giver of rain:

Thou visitest the earth and waterest it,
thou greatly enrichest it;
the river of God [cf. Ps 46:4] is full of
water;
thou providest their grain,
for so thou hast prepared it.
Thou waterest its furrows abundantly,
settling its ridges,
softening it with showers,
and blessing its growth.
Thou crownest the year with thy bounty;
the tracks of thy chariot drip with fatness.
The pastures of the wilderness drip,
the hills gird themselves with joy,
the meadows clothe themselves with
flocks,
the valleys deck themselves with grain,
they shout and sing together for joy. (Ps
65:9–13; cf. 68:10)

The relation between the god of vegetation and the storm god is shown more clearly in Figs. *292* and *293* than in the two preceding illustrations. On the stele dating from the eighth century B.C. *(292)*, found approximately 30 kilometers northeast of Aleppo, the storm god wears a long, Assyrian-style garment. He holds in his left hand the lightning (shown as a somewhat undulating trident) with which he controls the bull.

291. "He it is who makes the clouds rise at the end of the earth, who makes lightnings for the rain and brings forth the wind from his storehouses" (Ps 135:7).

Like Baal, Yahweh commands the storms which are essential to the fertility of the land. But Baal, together with his clouds and winds and rain showers, must periodically enter the arid realm of Mot (cf. J. Aistleitner, *Texte,* p. 16), whereas Yahweh is the absolute, eternal lord and master.

213

The bull symbolizes the threatening darkness and the roaring of the thunderstorm. Here too, the deity directs the storm by means of lightning. As in Fig. *291,* the full sequence of lightning-rain-fertility is represented here. Indeed, the bull embodies not only the thunderstorm, but also the fertility which it engenders. The primary indicator of fertility may well be the object which the god holds in his right hand. There have been attempts to identify it as a large leaf, a pineapple, or a cluster of grapes.

In any case, there is agreement that it represents a plant symbolizing the god as bestower of vegetation.[54]

The relief from the Taurus mountains *(293)* dates from the same century as the stele of Fig. *292.* In his left hand, the god holds four ears of grain. They have overly long stalks reminiscent of the guide-rope in Fig. *292.* In fact, the accompanying text indicates that we are dealing here with the same god (Tarhuna) as in Fig. *292.* He grasps with his right hand the end of a vine twining round his body. He is the provider of bread and wine (Ps 104.14c, 15a, cf. 81:16a).

Two functions of the storm god are clearly discernible in the iconography: he subdues the powers of Chaos and grants fertility to the fields. The latter function

292. "The earth has yielded its increase; God, our God has blessed us" (Ps 67:6).

293. ". . . that he may bring forth food from the earth, and wine to gladden the heart of man" (Ps 104:14c, 15a; cf. 81:10, 16).

is predominantly expressed in Figs. *291–93*. In Figs. *42, 46, 49–50,* we encounter him as battler against Chaos. This aspect emerges more strongly in the psalms than does the role of bestowing fertility. It is more easily integrated into the strongly historical experience of the God of Israel. In order to deliver the nation (Ps 77:16–19), Jerusalem (Ps 46:6b), or the king (Ps 18:7–15) from the power of the enemy, Yahweh appears in the psalms with features of the battling storm god. The same occurs in representation of Yahweh's actual battle with Chaos (Pss 74:13–14; 89:9–10). These have the function (cf. *142, 144*) of mobilizing Yahweh's mighty power against human-historical enemies.

Like a hero awakening from the intoxication of wine (Ps 78:65), the god of Fig. *294* rages against his enemies. With one foot aggressively planted on the head of the animal, he flings his lightning bolts. He wears a long sword at his side, and another weapon (bow? quiver?) is visible over his left shoulder.

Fig. *295* has a remarkable number of features in common with Ps 18:9–10, 12–14. The rudimentary bird-figure,[55] indicated by the fanned tail, suggests a storm deity. This fact does not alter the identification of the figure as Assur, the national god of the Assyrians. In Egypt, wings were suggestive of "protection" from the beginning of the historical period. In Mesopotamia, on the other hand, wings symbolize the wind which flies fast as an arrow, or the hurricane which spreads its shadow over the land (cf. Imdugud, Fig. *164;* Zu, Fig. *285;* Pazuzu, Fig. *93*). The impression of a bird-figure is strengthened by the presence of a pair of wings. Nevertheless, it is not quite clear whether they are part of the god or part of the disc behind him. In the latter context, wings were introduced from Egypt into Mesopotamia under Mitannian influence in the fifteenth century B.C. Curved wings can represent the sky. Ps 18 pictures Yahweh bowing the heavens and thus descending at his coming (v. 9a). The second half-verse ("thick darkness was under his feet") indicates that the "heavens" signify the stormy sky. That may also hold true of the wings in Fig. *295*. It is not simply a picture of the heavens, but of the dark, moving thunderstorm. Thus, the Egyptian conception has been completely absorbed into the Mesopotamian conception of the storm-bird.[56] As early as 2000 B.C., Ningirsu, closely related to the war god Ninurta, appears to Gudea of Lagash as a huge man "who had a head as of a god, wings as of the Imdugud-bird, and a belly as of a hurricane."[57] In Ps 18, Yahweh *flies* and swoops down (like a bird of prey) on the wings of the wind (Ps 18:10b). In doing so, he is seated on the cherub, like Baal on his clouds (Ps 18:10a). According to Ps 18:11, dark, water-laden clouds surround Yahweh like a hiding place. In Fig. *295,* sacklike clouds filled with rain and hail (cf. Ps 33:7; Job 26:8) hang on either side of the god. The flaming brightness which surrounds the deity is also present in Ps 18 (v. 12). Finally, the lightnings of Ps 18 and Fig. *295* are understood as arrows which the god shoots from a mighty bow (v. 14; cf. Pss 77:17; 144:6). To be sure, the lightning-arrow is absent in Fig. 295, but it is clearly seen in other representations *(296)*. The trident-shape of the arrowhead leaves no doubt that lightning is intended (cf. *292* and *294*). In order to portray the zigzag path of the lightning, the psalmist has Yahweh scatter his arrow-shots. Fig. *295* shows, in addition to the god and the clouds, the head of a man. Similar depictions indicate that the head may be that of a charioteer, for the bow-shooting god within the disc seems to have increasingly manifested himself in battle rather than in the raging of the thunderstorm (cf. *Plate XX*).

In Fig. *297,* Assur hands over to the king the bow which he wields as god of storm and war. The inscription states that Assur and other deities presented "their mighty weapons and their magnificent bows to his sovereign hand."[58] This concept also seems to underlie Ps 18:34b.[59] Attempts have been made to

294. "Clouds and thick darkness are round about him. . . . Fire goes before him, and burns up his adversaries round about. His lightnings lighten the world" (Ps 97:2a, 3, 4a).

"Fire" or "fire of God" are common OT terms for lightning (cf. Pss 29:7; 50:3; 104:4; 148:8). The "fork" with curving prongs is a representation of fire stylized in an Anatolian-North Syrian-Assyrian manner (cf. *Plate V* and P. Jacobsthal, *Der Blitz*, pp. 7ff.).

295. "He bowed the heavens, and came down; thick darkness was under his feet. He rode on a cherub, and flew; he came swiftly upon the wings of the wind. He made darkness his covering around him, his canopy thick clouds dark with water. Out of the brightness before him there broke through his clouds hailstones and coals of fire. The LORD also thundered in the heavens, and the Most High uttered his voice. . . . And he sent out his arrows, and scattered them; he flashed forth lightnings, and routed them" (Ps 18:9–14).

296. "Flash forth the lightning and scatter them, send out thy arrows and rout them!" (Ps 144:6).

297. "Who . . . laid the brazen bow in my arms" (Ps 18:35b MT [author's translation]; cf. Ps 18:34b RSV; on the translation, cf. M. Dahood, *Psalms,* vol. 1, p. 155; on the iconography, cf. H. Seyrig, "Représentations de la main divine").

relate the winged disc, as it appears in Fig. *297,* to the winged sun disc, and in fact it did originally represent it. The arrows could therefore suggest sunbeams. They constituted an appropriate weapon for the sun god in his function as judge and requiter (cf. Pss 64:7; 121:6). Yet, to the author's knowledge, Shamash is never represented as an archer in Mesopotamia—a fact which stands in the way of this interpretation. Besides his representation in autochthonic symbols, he appears in the winged disc, a form derived from Egypt. The disc is sometimes shown with a garland of feathers passing through the underside, sometimes with a tail, but invariably without weapons or the torso of a man wielding weapons.[60]

f. Eruption and Transcendence

The storm god as god of war brings us to the boundaries of section 2. Before entering into the theme "God in History," however, we must briefly consider a natural phenomenon which has distinctively shaped Israel's conception of God. Its influence is particularly marked in the psalms.

The pillar of smoke [RSV: "cloud"] by day and the pillar of fire by night (Exod 13:21–22; 14:19–20 J; etc.; cf. Ps 105:39) and the Yahwistic account of the Sinai theophany (Exod 19:18) have long promoted the consideration that volcanic phenomena might have influenced the conception of Yahweh. The smoke of Sinai rises like the smoke of a smelting-

298. "Then the earth reeled and rocked; the foundations also of the mountains trembled. . . . Smoke went up from his nostrils, and devouring fire from his mouth; glowing coals flamed forth from him" (Ps 18:7–8).

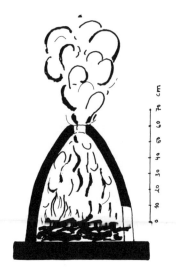

299. ". . . who touches the mountains, and they smoke" (Ps 104:32b; cf. 144:5b).

oven (298). In the world of the ancient Near East, it would have been difficult to find a better simile for a volcano. When, in a typical Yahwistic text (Gen 15:17), Yahweh passes by as a smoking *tannûr* (299), it is again reminiscent of a volcano. The land of Midian (east and southeast of the Gulf of Aqaba), where Moses first encountered Yahweh, had active volcanos up through the late Middle Ages.[61] Like every experience of the divine, the experience of Yahweh was not solely determined by experience of the world. Worldly experience was, however, a codeterminative factor. Mesopotamian theophany accounts are marked throughout by storm phenomena such as tempest, lightning, fire, thunder, and rain.[62] On occasion, an earthquake motif also plays a role.[63] Storm phenomena were *transferred* to *Yahweh* primarily in contention with the cult of Baal (Pss 29 and 65; the Elohistic

Sinai theophany in Exod 19:16). Volcanic phenomena, on the other hand, were apparently regarded as manifestations of Yahweh from the very beginning. In the psalms, they serve as visualizations of the appearance of Yahweh: "The earth reeled and rocked. . . . Smoke went up from his nostrils, and devouring fire from his mouth; glowing coals flamed forth from him" (Ps 18:7–8). "The mountains melt like wax before the LORD" (Ps 97:5). The only comparable Mesopotamian text known to the author is the following passage from a hymn to Inanna: "A flaming fire, that. . . am I, a flaming fire which is kindled in the midst of the mountain country: [I am] she who rains fire and ashes on the rebellious land."[64] In a delightful, almost playful manner, the following phrase predicates Yahweh's power: "[He] touches the mountains, and they smoke" (Ps 104:32b; cf. 144:5b). The image preserves the impression of the volcanoes in the wildest parts of Midian, whose smoke, visible from a great distance, rises suddenly in the marvelously clear air of the Arabian Peninsula. The volcanic phenomena associated with Yahweh from the very beginning permit a far stronger expression of the experience of that which is holy and wholly other than do the routine phenomena of the thunderstorms. The wrath, jealousy, and demanding power of Yahweh may also derive their emotional impact from volcanic phenomena. In the historical period, however, the manifestation of Yahweh was experienced not in volcanic eruptions, but in other events. Volcanic elements served only to make evident that power of Yahweh which, it was felt, was experienced in them. Among the most important of these events was victory in battle.

3. YAHWEH IN HISTORY

The dividing line between Yahweh's activity in the temple and in creation is *fluid;* so too is the line between his action in creation and in history. Thus, births, like wars, can be seen as nonrecurring historical events or as eternally recurrent natural events. The Israelites of the early prenational period seem to have perceived God's sovereign rule most vividly in these two life experiences. In both instances, man gives his utmost. Yet again and again, in both instances (even to the present day), man gains the impression that the result (the child or the victory) transcends his effort and cannot finally be explained by it. Ancient Near Eastern man quite naturally perceived here the mighty operation of the hand of God. It is no accident that the sovereignty formula ("He kills, he makes alive, he exalts, he humbles, etc.") occurs with great frequency in contexts explicitly concerned with life and death, such as birth (Ps 113:7–8; 1 Sam 2:6; Lk 1:52–53) and war (Ps 18:27; Deut 32:39; cf. also Ps 118:22–23). Hilma Granqvist, a physician who lived for a long time in the Near East, reports that women who had just given birth to their first child improvised little songs along the following lines:

> He brings to life
> and he sends to death.
> He makes rich
> and he makes poor.
> He gives and he denies.
> All things come from God,
> to God be thanks and praise![65]

Birth is a decisive moment in the life of the individual.

a. The Warrior

Dramatic climaxes in national and international history often erupt in war, which, like birth, produces new circumstances. In view of this fact, it is not surprising that antiquity experienced in war a very specific, divine power. In the northwest Semitic sphere, this power bears the name Reshef. In contrast to Baal, who represents the noble cosmic battle of life against Chaos and death, Reshef embodies the darker aspect of (historical) war. In the OT, *rešep* means "flame" (Ps 76:3 [RSV: "flashing"] and "plague" (Ps 78:48 [RSV: "thunderbolts"]). The god is portrayed as a grim warrior *(300–2)*. Reshef appears to-

300. "The LORD, strong and mighty, The LORD, mighty in battle!" (Ps 24:8).

301. "Contend, O LORD, with those who contend against me; fight against those who fight against me! Take hold of shield and buckler, and rise for my help! Draw the spear and javelin against my pursuers!" (Ps 35:1–3).

219

302. "Then the LORD awoke as from sleep, like a strong man shouting because of wine. And he put his adversaries to rout; he put them to everlasting shame" (Ps 78:65–66).

gether with Deber (pestilence) in the psalm of Habakkuk 3 (v. 5). This psalm depicts the god as a retainer of Yahweh, who marches forth in ominous power to save his own. But just as, in the priestly account (cf. Exod 13:15 P with 12:23 J), Yahweh himself assumed the role of the destroyer in the passover, so too Yahweh appears very early as the god of war. He first proved himself a "man of war"

(Exod 15:3) in the exodus from Egypt. He is celebrated as the same in Ps 24:8. The strength accorded to him there also appears in the title borne by Reshef in Egypt: "lord of strength among the Hennead."[66]

As god of war, Yahweh fights on behalf of the tribes centered round the ark of the covenant.[67] The procession of the ark into the sanctuary is to be understood as the background of Ps 24.[68] The concept of a war god who fights for his people is boldly individualized in Ps 35, and thus made effective for the individual believer. In verses 2 and 3, the suppliant calls upon Yahweh to take up his shield and to make ready his javelin [RSV: "spear"] and $s^e g \bar{o} r$. Attempts have been made to interpret *sgr* by means of the Scythian-Persian double axe (*sagaris*).[69] In Egyptian representations, Reshef sometimes does carry an axe as well as a shield and spear (302). Large numbers of axes of this sort have been found as votive offerings in the Reshef temple of Byblos. According to the War Scroll from Qumran,[70] however, $s^e g \bar{o} r$ signifies not an axe, but the end of a javelin. In Ps 35:3, this would stand metonymically for javelin.[71] But because a javelin is not normally handled by its end, the metonymy is somewhat peculiar. Equally peculiar, however, is the fact that in Figs. *300* and *301* Reshef wields his weapon far back toward its end. In Fig. *301,* at any rate, the weapon is a short javelin *(ḥnyt);* the shield and the long spear *(rmḥ)* are held in the other hand. But while the god of war is occasionally shown with two spears or with spear and axe, he never carries more than *one* shield. In consequence, Ps 35:2a can hardly be rendered "shield and target" (Kraus) or "small and large shield" (Deissler) [cf. RSV: "shield and buckler"]; it must be taken as hendiadys for "protective shield." This suggests that *ḥnyt wsgr* is also to be interpreted as hendiadys. The actual meaning of the verb in verse 3a is "to lay bare." Chariots are known to have been equipped with a kind of quiver for javelins. As a hendiadys, "to lay bare the javelin and the end of the shaft" [RSV: "Draw the spear and javelin"] simply means "to make the javelin quite ready".

In the Greek period, Reshef was consistently identified with Apollo. Originally, Apollo was anything but a radiant god of light. He was, indeed, the great god of healing and the warder-off of plagues (a role which can also be played by Reshef).[72] But there is always a strange aura about him. His most important attribute is the bow (303). "With his arrows he suddenly sends men mysterious diseases and unexpected death."[73] In Ugarit,[74] then later on a Cypriote inscription dated 341 B.C., Reshef is known as the lord of the arrow *(ḥṣ).*[75] The arrows in Ps 76:4 MT are "Reshef(s) of the bow" [cf. Ps 76:3 RSV: "flashing arrows"]. In Ps 38:2–3, Yahweh, like Reshef/Apollo, has struck the suppliant with disease-bearing arrows.

One of Israel's great achievements was its ability to integrate into Yahwistic faith the broadest possible range of ancient Near Eastern experiences of the divine without producing a hodgepodge of incoherent ideas. The intimate relation which the suppliant usually enjoyed with God served, by and large, to prevent disturbing features from developing into demonic ones. Where

303. A sick man laments: ". . . thy arrows have sunk into me, and thy hand has come down on me. There is no soundness in my flesh . . ." (Ps 38:2–3).

It is said of transgressors: ". . . God will shoot his arrow at them, they will be wounded suddenly" (Ps 64:7).

304. "You are my [wall of] protection and my shield!" (Ps 119:114a [author's translation]).

305. "O Israel, trust in the LORD! He is their [the individual Israelite's] help and their shield" (Ps 115:9).

that happened nonetheless, as in Job or Ps 89, believing Israel lodged a most vociferous protest.

b. "My Shield"

In war, the suppliant's intimacy with Yahweh found its most moving expression in the entreaty that Yahweh serve as

306. "The LORD is my strength and my shield; in him my heart trusts" (Ps 28:7).

the suppliant's shield-bearer (Ps 35:2). Strictly speaking, "shield-bearer" implies a subordinate position. The Assyrian general in Fig. 304 is protected by two shield-bearers. One holds the huge siege-shield—actually more a protective wall than a shield. The *ṣṛḥ* in Ps 91:4 may denote such a portable wall. Holding a (common) round shield *(mgn)*, the other bearer protects the contending general against missiles hurled from above. To summon Yahweh as shield-bearer presupposes that intimacy which permits one to ask a friend to perform a lowly service without in any way offending him.

The frequent predication of Yahweh as the suppliant's shield bears testimony to a strong relation of trust ("my shield": Pss 7:10; 18:2; 28:7; "our shield": Pss 33:20; 59:11; "their shield": Ps 115:9–11). This is probably a democratization of a confidence motif which originally

307. "Thou dost cover him [the righteous] with favor as with a [standing-] shield" (Ps 5:12).

pertained to the king. Ishtar of Arbela, for example, addresses an Assyrian king as follows: "Asarhaddon, in Arbela I am your gracious shield."[76] The connection of this promise to the cultic site Arbela gives rise to the conjecture that the statement may have been prompted by the shields which adorned the temples of many localities (cf. 139 and 1 Kgs 14:26–27). However that may be, the function of shields in the psalms is clearly protective and not decorative.

Above all, in *sieges* the shield protected the warrior from missiles of all kinds (305). A stately shield such as that carried by the Assyrian warrior in Fig. 306 could heighten the general sense of security. This was especially true when the shield afforded protection not only from the front but also from the sides, like the heavy Assyrian standing shield of Fig. 307. The standing shield (*ṣnh*), which went out of use in the seventh century B.C., is mentioned in formulalike con-

307a. Ps 107 and the unique stele shown above indicate that war was not the only occasion for protection and deliverance by the deity. The donor Pataweret, attacked by a crocodile, miraculously escaped his deadly peril. The bottom register of the thanksgiving stele indicates that Pataweret attributed his deliverance to the intervention of the local god of his hometown Assiut. Like a warrior, the god drove the fierce animal back with a long lance. The middle register shows the thankful Pataweret pouring a libation to the god, shown here (as in the top register) in full jackal form. In the uppermost scene, the rescued man presents a bouquet to the god's processional image.

texts in Pss 5:12; 35:2; and 91:4. In some psalms, "shield" remains no more than an ideogram for protection and security. In such uses, the realm of the concrete is occasionally abandoned. In Ps 3:3, the supplicant praises God as a shield "about me" (or "for me"?). "An ordinary shield provides cover from only *one* side, but Yahweh protects from every side."[77] But the question in this passage is whether "shield" is to be understood concretely or whether it has become a thoroughly abstract expression for "protection" (cf. the piling-up of images in Ps 5:12). In that case, one could no longer contrast "shield" and "Yahweh."[78]

As already indicated at the beginning

of this section, war can be regarded as either a natural or a historical event. Just as there is a time to be born and a time to die, a time to plant and a time to pluck up what is planted (Qoh 3:2), so too there is a time when kings go forth to battle (2 Sam 11:1). War, however, as a dramatic eruption of smouldering conflicts, seems more likely to make its mark upon the memory than other events which regularly recur in the community, for war is a final, irreversible event. Thus, history as a consciously experienced and transmitted entity begins in Egypt with the military conquest of the Delta by the inhabitants of the Nile Valley (cf. 397). The history of the confederation begins with a war of independence. The conflict with Pharaoh and the deliverance out of Egypt occupy a central position in the consciousness of Israel.

In the life of the individual, too, dramatic victories and deliverances are quite likely to be registered in some way and to be kept in remembrance as isolated events which determined the future (307a).

c. Leading

There is comparatively little reference in the psalms to the history of Israel as it is reflected in the Pentateuch or in the Deuteronomic history. Only fifteen or so of the one hundred and fifty psalms deal in any way with the formative events of the early Israelite period.[79] Most refer in an actualizing manner to a single event. Ps 95:7–11 warns the hearers not to be obdurate like their forefathers in the wilderness. Ps 50 is an actualization of the Sinai theophany. Ps 44:1 entreats God to preserve Israel in danger from enemies, for it was indeed *He* who gave the land to them of old. Only Pss 78, 105, 106, 135, and 136 describe a larger part of Yahweh's history with Israel. Ps 105 begins its survey with the promise of land to Abraham; the other four (Pss 78, 106, 135, and 136) begin with the exodus from Egypt. All but Ps 135 go on to tell of God's leading in the wilderness and of the "giving of the

land." Pss 105, 135, and 136 end there. Ps 78 goes further, up to the election of David, and Ps 106 continues as far as the exile.

None of the five psalms makes any reference to the Sinai theophany. That omission need not find its justification in the fact that the exodus and Sinai events originally derived from completely different experiences and traditions. It could also be related to the fact that the exodus and the giving of the land were actualized in the cultus in a different manner than was the Sinai event (cf. Ps 50). The saving acts of the period from exodus to entry into the land were briefly rehearsed (cf. the "previous" history in the covenant formula). The Sinai event, however, was more intensely actualized (cf. the declaration of intention, exclusive vocation, calling of witnesses, and curse and blessing in the covenant formula).[80] Ps 105 concludes its survey of the saving acts of God with the commentary that all these things happened so that Israel might keep the statutes of God. This concluding verse can be understood as a transition to the actualization of the revelation at Sinai.

Just as Ps 105 forms a transition to the actualization of the Sinai theophany, so Ps 78 leads up to the actualization of Nathan's prophecy, as represented in Ps 132 and—in a time of crisis—Ps 89. In illustrating the historical psalms, we shall not attempt to present the entire range of archaeological and iconographic material which might be adduced to elucidate the history and tradition of Israel from the time of Abraham through the exile. That has already been accomplished in L. Grollenberg's pictorial atlas,[81] and in similar works. Here we shall consider only a few conceptions typical of the psalms which are not found thus formulated—or are found only by way of exception—in the great narrative histories.

Of the promises made to the patriarchs, only the promise of the land appears in the psalms (Ps 105:11). While they did not yet possess the land, they did experience the working of God: for

308. "When they were few in number, of little account, and sojourners in it [the land], wandering from nation to nation, from one kingdom to another people, he allowed no one to oppress them; he rebuked kings on their account, saying, 'Touch not my anointed ones, do my prophets no harm!'" (Ps 105:12–15).

The group comprises a single row (cf. the dotted line a–b). Men form the vanguard and the rear guard. The women travel in the middle, between the asses which represent the herds.

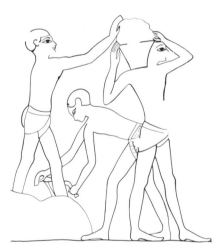

309. "I relieved his shoulder of the burden, his hands were freed from the basket" (Ps 81:6).

despite the fact that they were a small, defenseless group, they were not molested by any of the peoples among whom they passed on their restless journeyings. God had declared them "untouchable" (cf. 2 Sam 1:14), like prophets (cf. Gen 20:7) and anointed ones (Ps 105:15). This is an allusion to the accounts of the dangers suffered by the female forebears (Gen 12:9–20; 20:1–18; 26:1–13). The nomads believed that their women were regarded as fair game by the settled peoples (cf. also Gen 34). For that reason, the famous nomadic group of Beni Hasan travels with its women placed protectively in the middle (308). In Ps 105:12–15, the protection afforded the patriarchs in this danger is stylized in a degree equal to the untouchability of men of God.

226

In the same psalm (105:18), Joseph's imprisonment (Gen 39:20) is intensified to close, fettered confinement (cf. 77 and 134). In Ps 81:6, deliverance from Egypt (Ps 78:12, 43 mentions Zoan, not cited in Exodus) is described in the striking image of release from the pannier used to haul clay and finished bricks (309; cf. 240, 361, 362).

The most ancient song of thanksgiving for the annihilation of the Egyptians relates how Yahweh cast horse and chariot into the sea (Exod 15:21 [cf. Exod 15:1 RSVm]; 310; cf. 405). To a degree, that may approximate historical reality. The Egyptian chariot-troop apparently sank in the swamps of the Isthmus of Suez (cf. Exod 14:25). Isolated passages in the historical psalms carry forward this ancient tradition (Ps 106:11). In most passages, however, it is not the Egyptians, but the sea which appears as enemy. The deliverance at the Sea of Reeds becomes a victory over the Chaos monster, which is slain, divided, rent, and dismembered (Pss 66:6; 77:15–20; 78:13; 136:16; cf. 46–52, 142 and 144). As an aspect of the timeless battle of Yahweh against Chaos, the event has a timeless immediacy.

In the course of the migration in the wilderness, Yahweh nourished his people with manna. This is specifically described in Exod 16:14 and Num 11:7. In Pss 78:24–25 and 105:40 it becomes, by way of association with Exod 16:4, the grain of heaven, bread from heaven, angels' food. The elevation of the event into the realm of the miraculous counteracts that growing temporal distance which increasingly blurs the original impression. Such raising to the realm of the miraculous is one of the many processes by which the psalms make Yahweh's earlier saving acts effective in the present. This effort is frequently facilitated by the fact that a given notion is not exclusively historical in origin and can thus be transferred relatively easily from the timebound sphere to the realm of the cult or of creation. Thus, the concept of the deity who nourishes men has several roots: the sacrificial meal in the cultus; the gifts which the earth brings forth at God's command; and certain historical situations, such as the wanderings in the wilderness.

As already indicated, the giving of the land plays a dominant role in those psalms which make historical reference. In Ps 105:11, ḥbl is used as the term for the territory apportioned to Israel. ḥbl means "cord, rope" [RSV Ps 105:11: "portion"] (Josh 2:15). As is shown in

310. ". . . the horse and its chariot he has thrown into the sea" (Exod 15:1 RSVm).
"And the waters covered their adversaries; not one of them was left" (Ps 106:11; cf. 405).

Fig. *311*, cords were used in Egypt—and probably elsewhere—for measuring land. We may conclude that this was the custom in Israel from use of the word *ḥbl* to denote a portion of land (Pss 16:6 [RSV: "lines"] and 78:55 [RSV: "possession"]).

In the great apportionment of the land under Joshua, the Levites received no portion. Deuteronomy relates that

311. "For me the measuring lines have fallen on pleasant sites; fair to me indeed is my inheritance" (Ps 16:6 NAB).

312. "The LORD is my shepherd, I shall not want" (Ps 23:1; cf. Isa 63:14).

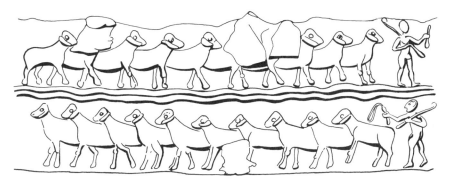

313. "He leads me in right paths [RSVm] for his name's sake. Even though I walk through the valley of deep darkness [RSVm], I fear no evil; for thou art with me: thy rod and thy staff, they comfort me" (Ps 23:3–4).

Yahweh is their inheritance (Deut 10:9). The priestly account reads: "I [Yahweh] am your portion and your inheritance" (Num 18:20). This statement, which is found in the context of a sober rule of maintenance, has material implications: the tribe of Levi receives its livelihood not from agricultural labor, but from portions of offerings and cultic taxes.[82] The proposition is less stringently interpreted in Ps 16. The suppliant, perhaps himself a Levite, sees in it not only a rule of maintenance, but "the offer of a completely distinctive community with God."[83] He participates in salvation history, not only by enjoying the fruits of the settlement made during the occupation of the land, but by making real the treasure of salvation and by shifting the accent from the gift to the giver.

In Pss 77:20; 78:52; and 95:7, God's activity in the period from the exodus to the giving of the land is compared to the activity of a *shepherd*. In Pss 78:52 and 95:7, Yahweh himself leads; in Ps 77:20 he leads by the hand of Moses and Aaron. God's shepherdlike concern for his people is represented above all in the national laments. The laments hope to move Yahweh to intervention in time of need by reminding him of his shepherdly duty. "The central elements of the shepherd motif are the shepherd's care

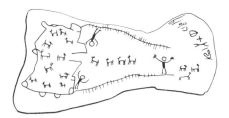

314. "He chose David his servant, and took him from the sheepfolds; from tending the ewes that had young he brought him to be the shepherd of Jacob his people, of Israel his inheritance" (Ps 78:70–71).

for the flock and the flock's trust in the shepherd."[84] The shepherd's power over the flock plays a more limited role. This is attested by many representations which show the shepherd laboring over his flock *(312)*.

All the passages cited above speak of Yahweh as the shepherd of his people. A shepherd tends a flock *(313)*, not a solitary sheep. Nevertheless, the suppliant of Ps 23 speaks of Yahweh as his personal shepherd. Here, as we have seen before, is an instance of individual appropriation of salvation history. In the case of the motifs of wing and shield, this process was accomplished by democratization; in the apportionment of the land it was accomplished by de-materialization (spiritualization). Here it occurs through individualization. In Ps 23, Yahweh no longer guides the flock, but the individual. Yahweh leads him; Yahweh's club (*šbṭ* [RSV: "rod"]) and staff *(mš'nt)* comfort him. Like Yahweh in Ps 23:4, the shepherd who leads the flock in the upper register of Fig. *313* carries a long staff for guiding the flock and a club for defense against predatory animals (cf. 1 Sam 17:34–36).[85] The iron *šbṭ* [RSV: "rod"], which shatters the potter's vessel in Ps 2:9, may denote a club or mace (cf. *358*). In Ps 45:6, it signifies the scepter. In Assyria the scepter was no more than a mace (cf. *418*). Many other passages suggest that *šbṭ* can designate a mace. It would be strange indeed for there to be no Hebrew word for a weapon that was so ancient and widespread in Asia Minor.

According to Ps 78:52–54, Yahweh, like a shepherd, leads his people out of Egypt into the land of Canaan. At the conclusion of this migration, Yahweh's office of shepherd is transferred, as it were, to David (Ps 78:70–72), a man fetched from the livestock pens. The pen is a small stockade *(314)* into which the flocks are driven at night and upon the appearance of robbers or predatory animals. The v-shaped entrance permits the flock to be brought quickly under protection and avoids the dangers of deflection posed by a narrow entryway. Psalm 78:70–72 makes a point of connecting David's shepherdship in Bethlehem with his shepherdship over Israel and God's shepherdship over his people. The OT tradition, like ancient Near Eastern iconography in general, cherishes such prefigurations, associations, and symbolic connections. This tendency would receive further confirmation if Gottlieb[86] proves correct in his theory that David was originally not a shepherd, but a warrior (1 Sam 16:18).

The remaining historical themes of the Psalter will be treated in other contexts. Among them is David's pains concerning a dwelling place for Yahweh (Ps 132). It is reminiscent of Gudea's efforts in building the Ningirsu temple (cf. chap. 5.3).

In the oracle of Ps 60:6–8 (= 108:7–9), Yahweh appears as a warrior who redistributes the territories conquered by David after the destruction of Samaria in 722 B.C.

A number of psalms refer to apostasy in the monarchical period (cf. the excursus on "Renunciation") and to the increasingly frequent foreign invasions (cf. chap. 2.3) which ravaged Israel and Judah in the waning days of the monarchy, finally bringing both kingdoms to an end. The last event of Israel's history directly referred to in the psalms is the exile (Pss 126; 137). Ps 137 contains the notorious statement: "Happy shall he be who takes your [Babylon's] little ones and dashes them against the rock!" (v. 9). Babylon is here personified as a queen. As is shown in Figs. *341* and *342,* neighboring peoples were subject to princes who were mere babes in the laps of their wet nurses. These infants manifested the endless continuance of the power of the dynasty. Their death meant the end of despotism.

The Psalter's survey of historical themes ends with the conclusion that God scattered Israel and sold his flock as sheep for slaughter (Ps 44:11–12). Scattered and oppressed, Israel hopes for return (Ps 126) and beseeches Yahweh to gather it from among the nations (Ps 106:47). The hope of return seems so utopian that it is awaited as an eschatological event resulting from Yahweh's intervention. Just as in wintertime the waterless, parched wadis of the Negev *(Plate XV)* are suddenly transformed into torrential watercourses (Ps 126:4), even so unexpectedly, it is hoped, will Yahweh redeem Israel.

EXCURSUS: RENUNCIATION

In hymns of praise, Yahweh is celebrated and portrayed as rock and light, as creator and judge, as shepherd and shield. These portrayals can be intensified by conjuring up negative, contrasting images.

> For the LORD will vindicate his people,
> and have compassion on his servants.
> The idols of the [other] nations are silver and gold,
> the work of men's hands. (Ps 135:14–15)

The lifeless, pompous *idols* serve as dark foils for the image of the living God, throwing that image into sharper relief. But reference to them clarifies another point as well: as the gods of other, generally stronger nations, they present an alternative to Yahweh. The suppliant's radical devotion to Yahweh leads him to disown the gods: to renunciation. Having given way to the impulse of praise (cf. 446), seized by its inherent autonomy, the psalmist must declare himself for Yahweh's exclusivity. Praise which does not reach this point has not attained anything unique, and has therefore found no object worthy of total commitment. It must stop half way. For the man who praises is set on giving himself completely to the object of his praise,[87] and he can do that only when he possesses the certainty that he is face to face with something incomparable and absolute. This characteristic feature of praise is so strong that in the polytheistic world of Mesopotamia, Sin, Shamash, Enlil, Marduk, and many other deities are simultaneously predicated as incomparable and superior to all other gods—an assertion which is absurd from a rational, logical standpoint.[88] To be sure, the experience and predication of a power as incomparable is short of a formal denial of other powers. As a result, it is not a renunciation in the strict sense. But no effective denial develops without the enthusiasm of the phrase, "who is like?"

In Israel, this enthusiasm was aroused by the exodus from Egypt, or more precisely, by the miracle at the Sea of Reeds. The resultant renunciation of other gods found its institutional *Sitz im Leben* in the covenant cult. In Josh 24, the people are presented with a choice unparalleled in the ancient Near East: they may serve the gods beyond the Euphrates, the gods of the Canaanites, or Yahweh. The people decide for Yahweh, which constitutes a denial of the other gods (Josh 24:21, 24 and Ps 81:9–10). In this action, Israel not only binds *itself* to Yahweh, but *Yahweh* to

315. "Their idols are silver and gold, the work of men's hands" (Ps 115:4).

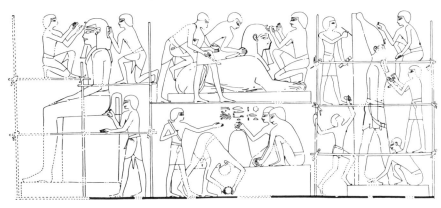

Israel. Israel's exclusive attachment to Yahweh obliges Yahweh to commit himself on Israel's behalf. He cannot disappoint the trust placed in him. Therein is shown, with utter consistency, the ultimate consequence of praise.

In what follows, we shall briefly sketch those powers which Israel liked to contrast to Yahweh. These powers are no match for Yahweh, and yet, Israel repeatedly threatened to lapse from him to them. As a result, the vehemence of the denial will often be proportionate to the fascination which the repudiated powers held for the suppliant. It is striking that the powers which the suppliant rejects as rivals of Yahweh are, for the most part, fabricated entities such as weapons or riches. Only rarely are they foreign gods. In Job 31:24–28, for example, the renunciation of gold and riches is juxtaposed to renunciation of the sun and moon.

In Ps 115:2, Israel is asked a mocking question regarding the whereabouts of its God in time of need. In verses 3–7 (cf. Ps 135:15–18), the question is answered explicitly with a denial of the heathen gods and implicitly with a confession of Yahweh. The nations worship the work of men's hands, silver and gold (Ps 115:4; 135:15). The "nations" were also aware of that fact. Fig. 315 provides a glimpse into a large workshop, where fifteen workers are busily engaged in completing two statues of Thut-mose III, a sphinx, and an offering table for the temple at Karnak. The workman at the upper left is attaching to the king's brow the cobra of the serpent goddess Uadshet. If the nations knew precisely who had made their divine images, why was Israel so insistent on the point? Quite simply because, in Israel's opinion, the nations did not appropriate the consequences of this knowledge. The deity was worshipped in these images. However subtly (or unsubtly) the individual Egyptian or Babylonian may have conceived of the relation between god and image,[89] the Israelite, looking on from the outside, probably had little opportunity of contact with such trains of thought, especially in their more refined form. He saw that these images of wood and stone, of silver and gold, were the center of an elaborate cultus (Ps 106:36; 433a, 440),[90] and that men came before them with petition and sacrifice. In military campaigns and conquests the images were a coveted prize, for the deity was apparently so essentially linked to its image that the protection and blessing of the deity represented could be gained by appropriating the image (cf. 1 Sam 5:1–2). Fig. 316 depicts Assyrian soldiers carrying off captured idols. The larger-than-life statue at the far left may repre-

316. "They have . . . feet, but do not walk, and they do not make a sound in their throat" (Ps 115:7).

317. "Their makers will end up like them, and so will anyone who relies on them" (Ps 115:8 JB).

318. "They made a calf in Horeb and adored a molten image; they exchanged their glory for the image of a grass-eating bullock" (Ps 106:19–20 NAB).

319. "For, lo, they that are far from thee shall perish; thou hast destroyed all them that go a whoring from thee" (Ps 73:27 KJV).

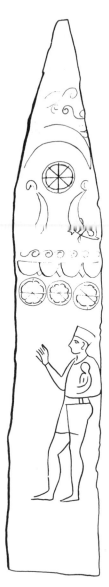

320. "They sacrificed their sons and their daughters to demons; they poured out innocent blood, . . . and the land was polluted with blood" (Ps 106:37–38).

sent Ninurta, the god of war. The bolt in the hands of the statue is as much a symbol of Ninurta[91] as the eagle, whose huge image is borne off by four other warriors. The woman who raises her hand in supplication is probably appealing to the Assyrian warriors and not to the gods who, like herself, are about to be led into exile. In the texts commemorating incidents of this kind it is said simply that so and so many *gods* (and not images of gods) were brought to Assur or Nineveh. From the point of view of their worshippers, they had to live there in exile (cf. Isa 46:1–2; Jer 48:7; 49:3).[92] The fact that the damaged images of these gods were buried like human dead indicates how closely they were bound up with human fate.[93]

In their brutality, the Assyrians occasionally executed deities. Such was the case with the god Chaldia after the conquest of Muzazir; perhaps they felt that the god had too long offered resistance to them or to their god.

Israel steadfastly rejected any extensive identification of Yahweh with any

kind of well-known phenomena (stars, men).[94] The ark, which during the early period represented Yahweh in a very immediate way, receded far into the background with the building of the

321. "Some boast of chariots, and some of horses; but we boast of the name of the LORD our God" (Ps 20.7, cf. Mic 1:13).

temple and was completely absent from the postexilic temple (Jer 3:16). Rejection of any representation of God was intensified by instances in which the godhead was represented in a manner which seemed, from Israel's point of view, to be especially inadequate. Worshipping the deity in the form of a bull [RSV: "ox"] is one such instance (Ps 106:20; 318; cf. 290, 433a).[95]

322. Hab 1:16 alludes to an actual cult of weapons: "[The wicked] sacrifices to his net and burns incense to his seine, for by them

The high importance attached by Canaanite religion to sexual potency and fertility is evidenced not only in the popularity of the bull, but also by the role which the sexual aspect generally played in Canaanite myth and ritual. The goddess of love was herself the model for the prostitutes who enticed clients from the windows of special buildings in the temple area (319).[96] In the OT, "playing

his portion is fat [RSVm] and his food is rich."

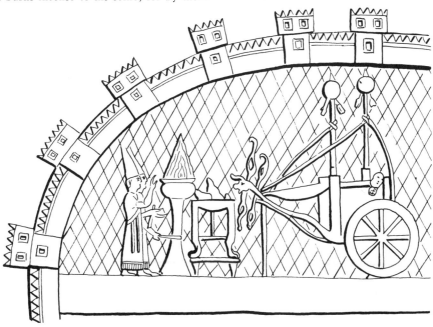

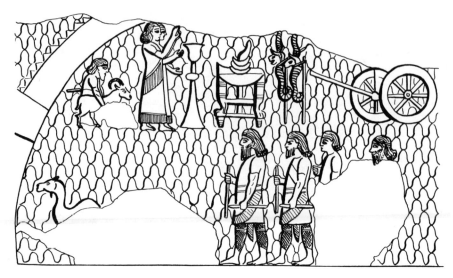

323. "At your reproof, God of Jacob, chariot and horse stand spellbound" (Ps 76:6 JB).

the harlot" became synonymous with "falling away from Yahweh" (Pss 73:27; 106:39).

The cult of idols, in which the deity seemed readily accessible to man and, in large measure, at man's disposal— indeed, in man's clutches—again and again proved a fascination to many Israelites, at least up to the time of the exile. The sensuous Canaaniate cultus remained a temptation even in later times. At last, the conviction prevailed that gods whose presence was bound to lifeless statues must themselves be lifeless and void. This conviction played a substantial role in the proclamation of Yahweh's uniqueness in Deutero-Isaiah (cf., e.g., Isa 40:18–20; 44:9–20; 46:6–7). The polemic against the service of idols was probably instrumental in wholly depotentizing heathen gods and in declaring them "things of nought" (Ps 96:4–5 NAB). They had long been regarded as subordinate to Yahweh (cf. p. 220; later these subordinated divinities were interpreted in part as angels). The later psalms (16:3–4 and 31:6) indicate, however, that their cultus remained attractive even after this down-playing. Apparently there were people who held

to these gods even after they had been seen through by the majority of the Judaic cult community. The worshippers felt compelled vigorously to disavow them. Whoever did not do so, but sacrificed to them instead, multiplied his wounds (Ps 16:4 [RSV: "sorrows"]; cf. 147:3).

The wounds envisioned here need not be spiritual torments. The psalmist may have in mind the self-inflicted wounds of the priests of orgiastic cults (cf. 1 Kgs 18:28; Zech 13:6),[97] or he may be thinking of still worse things. Ps 106:35–39 reproaches Israel for having mingled with the heathen and for having learned their ways. The consequence was this: "they sacrificed their sons and their daughters to the demons; they [thus] poured out innocent blood" (Ps 106:37–38). The psalmist senses that powers and forces which provoke such deeds can hardly be minimized as "nothings." The superstition that salvation could be gained by shedding innocent blood destroys communion with the holy God and consequently achieves superhuman, *demonic* proportions. The Carthaginian priest bearing a child to the sacrifice (*320;* cf. *199*) raises his hand in

236

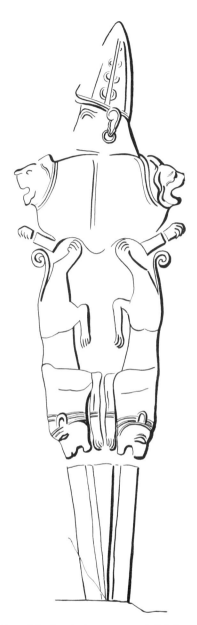

324. As a goddess of war, the Asiatic love goddess Astarte rides a horse.

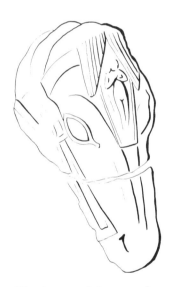

324a. The image of Astarte adorned the foreheads of horses.

323a. "Not by their own sword did they win the land" (Ps 44:3a).

as reverent a greeting as any other ancient Near Eastern suppliant (cf. *414, 415, 436*). He has even had his pious deed portrayed on a stele, so that the deity might remember it forever. The demonic consists in the delusion which demands such deeds as divine service. Ps 82 describes how Yahweh requires the

death of the gods responsible for iniquities on earth. Like the King of Babylon, they are to be cast from their lofty throne into the realm of the dead (Isa 14:12–20).[98]

The Canaanite or Assyrian-Babylonian deities are not the only entities in which Israel can place trust in a way destined to aggrieve Yahweh. *Military capability* can exercize a similar fascination. "Some boast of chariots, and some of horses, but we boast in the name of the LORD our God" (Ps 20:7; cf. 33:16–18; 44:3, 6–7; 147:10). Three of these four passages mention the war horse, which, as mount or chariot horse (cf. *382, 384, 405*), represented *the* costly, prestige weapon of the ancient Near East. A war chariot was worth twenty male slaves, a horse worth five (cf. 1 Kgs 10:29; Exod 21:32; Zech 11:12). Once the versatile two-wheeled war chariot was introduced in the sixteenth century B.C., it became a favorite posing-place for portraits of Egyptian, (cf. *381*), Canaanite *(321)* and later Assyrian kings *(Plate XX)* (cf. pp. 280–83). The richly robed Canaanite King of Megiddo *(321),* raised above his surroundings by the chariot, rides along controlling the concentrated power of his horses; but the vanquished must go naked before the horses, deprived of weapons and dignity, hands bound at their backs. The Canaanites had been using war chariots for centuries by the time the Israelites attempted to occupy the land (Judg 1:19; Josh 17:16–18). The Israelites, on the other hand, possessed none, and even in the time of David they knew little or nothing of how to handle any they might capture (Josh 11:6, 9; 2 Sam 8:4). But that was unimportant. It was the belief of ancient Israel that Yahweh had led the battle for them in settling the land (Josh 10:14, 42; Judg 4:14; 7:15; etc.). Israel performed only as auxiliaries (Judg 5:23). According to Ps 44:3, their part was of no consequence: "Not by *their own* sword did they win the land, nor did *their own* arm give them victory, but *thy* [Yahweh's] right hand and *thy* arm. . . ." The situation was fundamentally changed by the introduction of a standing army by David and a troop of chariots by Solomon (1 Kgs 9:19). War had become a matter of superior capability and cold calculation. Even after this far-reaching change, however, the prophets—especially Isaiah—demanded a thoroughgoing, confident trust in

Yahweh's control of history (Isa 7:8–9; 28:6; 30:15). The intense preoccupation with horses and chariots was to the prophets an expression of unbelief (Isa 30:16; 31:1–3).

Certain battle scenes from Egypt *(405)* or Assyria *(Plate XX)* create the impression that the king's overwhelming victory was entirely due to his chariot. It carried into battle not only the king, but also the standards of the gods *(332–33, 405a)*. The chariot was not only the royal throne; it was also a temple. In battle, it bestowed the dignity of throne and temple on the king and the deity, at the same time sharing in their dignity. In Egypt, the king's chariot was considered "a divine being; its constituent parts were considered to be animate, and their praises were sung in hymns."[99] Assyrian pictures show sacrifices being made before the standard-chariot *(322, 323)*.

The numinous power of the sword or of the intricately worked dagger held such repute in the Assyrian, North-Assyrian, and Hittite sphere that a deity could be represented in its form *(323a)*. The dagger stuck in the ground apparently symbolizes Nergal, the god of war and of the nether world. His logogram *U.GUR* is Sumerian for "sword."[100] In the face of such perceptions, proclamation of the view that the forefathers did not win the land by the sword (Ps 44:3) is not without significance.

With regard to Egypt, it may at first glance seem surprising that no divine honors were accorded the *horse* in the animal cult so prevalent in that country. But the horse had been introduced into Egypt (from interior Asia) too late for that. Yet, Astarte/Asiti, the Asiatic goddess of love and war (introduced into Egypt in the New Kingdom), bore the epithets "strong to horse" and "mistress of horses and chariots."[101] She is often depicted on horseback *(324)*. In North Syria in biblical times, the head-plates of bridle-gear were decorated with the image of the naked goddess. In this case, however, the mythical aspects serve only to heighten the military-technical factors. Their value is chiefly ornamental.

The admiration accorded the horse was based primarily on its military capabilities. It permitted surprise attacks and was much faster and more mobile than the war chariot, especially in difficult terrain (325). The Assyrian rider, cupping his hand to his mouth, calls out to his comrades across the hilly, wooded countryside. The horse is tricked out with a tasseled blanket and a headdress. They bear witness to the joy and admiration which the noble animal inspired in its rider. The same is evident in Fig. 326. The rider is as one with his mount. This confers on him superhuman strength and speed. Large numbers of Israelites were completely infatuated with these powerful horsemen (Ezek 23:13). Indeed, even images of "men portrayed upon the wall" (Ezek 23:14) transported them into wild raptures. The hymn, on the other hand, in its exultant approach to Yahweh, gives a decisive rebuff to this kind of pretension (327) and to the

325. "He makes grass grow up the hills. He gives to the beasts their food, and to the young ravens that cry. His delight is not in the strength of the horse" (Ps 147:8c–10a).

326. "A king is not saved by his great army; a warrior is not delivered by his great strength. The war horse is a vain hope for victory, and by its great might it cannot save" (Ps 33:16–17).

naked force of military capability (Pss 20:8; 33:16–18; 44:6–7; 147:10). When Yahweh appears, the hero's strength vanishes. Horse and chariot, which Yahweh once cast into the sea (Exod 15:1 RSVm), again lie stunned and useless (Ps 76:6). He breaks the bow and arrow (Pss 46:9b; 76:3a; cf. 37:15) and makes evident their worthlessness, as he did during Sennacherib's siege of Jerusalem (2 Kgs 19; Isa 36–37). In Fig. 328 (cf. 245), the Elamite officer Ituni, who is about to be executed, cuts his bow in pieces, thus acknowledging that his confidence in it was not justified. The Elamites were normally very proud of this weapon and were widely respected as excellent archers (Isa 22:6; Jer 49:35). What the Elamite officer does here to his bow, and thus to his confidence in it, is exactly what Yahweh will do to every earthly weapon and to all confidence in them. He will destroy them and put an end to brute force and power politics (Pss 46:9; 76:3–5; on the breaking of the bow cf. also Figs. 132a and 245).

More frequently than by renunciation of foreign gods and military capability, the turning to Yahweh is brought into relief by denial of human achievements (cf. Pss 52:7; 127:1–2) and by disavowal of exaggerated confidence in *men* (Pss 56:4, 11; 62:9; 116:11). In this connection, the psalmists effectively contrast the eternity of God with the transitoriness of man. In doing so, they make broad use of a simile which, like many others, lends a certain local color to the psalms. Man before God is like the spring grass, which the scorching east wind can wither in the space of a day (Pss 90:5–6; 102:11–12; 103:15–18; 129:6).[102] Man is utterly *transient* and *vulnerable,* whereas God abides forever. The image is typical of Palestine-Syria, where the ground, watered almost exclusively by the spring rains, dries up in a very short time. The situation is different in Egypt and Mesopotamia, which possess rivers.

Powerful men and princes, pursuing bold designs, are just as transient as common mortals. On that day when the vital spirit leaves them, it is finished even for such as they (Ps 146:3–4). "It is better to take refuge in the LORD than to put confidence in princes" (Ps 118:9). "Men. . . are a delusion; in the balances they go up; they are together lighter than a breath" (Ps 62:9). In the

240

327. ". . . neither delighteth he in any man's legs" (Ps 147:10b BCP; cf. Ezek 23:11–12).

Egyptian judgment of the dead, a man's heart is weighted against Maat (cosmic order, truth) (cf. 83). Normally, the heart of the deceased is able to muster the necessary weight. Maat presents no impossible demands. Should the man fail nevertheless, magic assists. Chapter 30 of the Book of the Dead is recited "so that the heart of the deceased be not re-jected." The gravity of the ethic is thus further weakened. Israel knew no such evasive measures. When the psalmist senses that all men are a delusion (Pss 62:9; 116:11), his perception is based not on "cosmic order," but on the holy, everlasting God. The suppliant continued to trust in God, even when all men seemed a delusion (Ps 116:10–11).

328. "He makes wars cease to the end of the earth; he breaks the bow, and shatters the spear, he burns the chariots with fire!" (Ps 46:9; cf. Hos 1:5; Jer 49:35; 245).

As long as this confidence holds, what can men, what can "flesh" do to him (Ps 54:4, 11)?

Decisive turning to God does not diminish the courage to face life. Rather, it provides an unshakable hold. It permits a sound approach to all that pertains to this world, and while not disdaining this-worldly possibilities it prevents overestimation of them. "Riches" are the expression of this-worldly possibilities. The OT views them as a gift of God (Prov 10:22; 11:16; 22:4). But whoever "trusts" in them and presumes too much (Ps 59:7; cf. 34:10; 62:10) will come to a miserable end, for he has misplaced his priorities. Only God is God (Ps 86:10), and there exists a salutary ordering and structuring of things which only he can sustain (Ps 71:16; cf. 83:18).

I. "For the pillars of the earth are the LORD's,
and on them he has set the earth" (1 Sam 2:8).

IA. There are many Egyptian representations of the sun god traversing the sky or the nether world in his bark (16, 19, 32, 287). The above impression of a cylinder seal, showing the Mesopotamian sun god in his boat, indicates that this concept, like certain others, existed simultaneously, yet without apparent dependency, in Mesopotamia and Egypt. The ship provides its own animation—something that is never the case (in this form) in Egypt. The bow takes the form of an oarsman, and the stern terminates in a serpent's head. The plow above the ship suggests the relation between the sun and the fertility of the earth. This chthonic reference to the sun and the sun boat is an aspect of the Sumerian culture within Mesopotamia. In southern Iraq, boats remain an important means of transportation to the present day. As Semitic influences prevailed, the idyllic sun boat disappeared from Mesopotamian iconography. It was superseded by the sun hero (Ps 19:5), mighty, strident (cf. 9), combatative (53, 90a), demanding rightousness (286, 390). Chthonic references were eliminated (cf. H. Frankfort, *Cylinder Seals*, pp. 108–10).

IB. The typification of the sky by a bird or the wings of a bird is characteristic of Egypt from the very beginnings of its culture (cf. 19, 21, 238). From Egypt, the symbol penetrated into Syria, Asia Minor, and Mesopotamia (cf. 22–24). On the Iranian helmet above, however, the concept greets us in a form apparently independent of Egyptian influence. The bird, with its wings extended over the *numen* of the earth-mountain, must almost certainly symbolize the sky.

II. "If it had not been the LORD who was on our side when men rose up against us, . . . then the flood would have swept us away, the torrent would have gone over us; then over us would have gone the raging waters" (Ps 124:2, 4–5; cf. Sir 40:13).

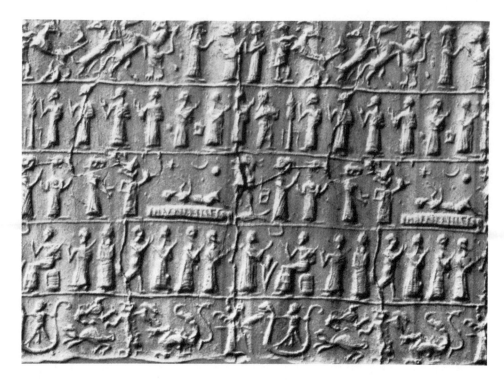

III. The faithless friends speak of the sick man: "A deadly thing has fastened on him; he will not rise again from where he lies [to die]" (Ps 41:8).

IV. This picture of two demons attacking one another is intended to induce intruding demons to do the same (cf. K. Frank, *Beschwörungsreliefs,* pp. 49–56).

V. "They set thy sanctuary on fire; to the ground they desecrated the dwelling place of thy name" (Ps 74:7).

"Thou [Yahweh] hast breached all his [the anointed one's] walls, thou hast laid his strongholds in ruins. All that pass by despoil him" (Ps 89:40–41a).

VI. "As the mountains are round about Jerusalem, so the LORD is round about his people" (Ps 125:2).

Some of the mountains which surround the ridges of Jerusalem may be seen in this photograph: the Mount of Olives (upper right); Mount Scopus (upper left); and the eastern slope of the Christian Zion (lower left). The Kidron Valley east of Ophel remains a deep wadi even today, but the Tyropöion Valley between Ophel and the western hill is almost completely filled. The lower portion is recognizable only as a slight depression; the upper portion is scarcely discernible. The location of the temple on a hill (cf. *Plate VII*) surrounded by hills (cf. *Plate IX*) conveys a sense of height and security.

VII. Mount Zion.

VIIA. The status of Mount Hermon as a holy mountain derives from remote antiquity. Its name, roughly translated as "mountain of the ban" is suggestive of holiness (cf. Haram, Harem). Ps 89:12 polemically denies any divinity to Hermon, making it praise the name of Yahweh. According to Ps 133:3, Yahweh has bestowed Hermon's abundant dew on Zion. The suppliant of Ps 42:7 hears the thundering of the underworld in the numerous rushing springs which rise at Hermon's foot (cf. 42).

VIIB. Zaphon, mountain of the gods of Ugarit, rises north of the city on the present Turkish-Syrian border. In Ugaritic mythology it plays a role similar to Olympus in Greek mythology. From a Jerusalemite point of view, it was located in the extreme north (ṣāpôn). Ps 48:2 claims the glory of this ancient holy mountain for Zion. It is here that the Great King of the gods holds sway. Here the destiny of the world is determined. The Canaanite Zaphon, like Hermon, proclaims the glory of its creator Yahweh.

VIII. The entrances to Assyrian palaces and temples were flanked by huge guardian demons. It was their function to prevent any evil powers from entering the protected precincts.

For the genius with the *situla:* "Purge me with hyssop, and I shall be clean; wash me, and I shall be whiter than snow" (Ps 51:7).

IX. View of the temple site from the Mount of Olives. Some exegetes and archaeologists (cf., e.g., *175*) locate the altar of burnt offering approximately at the spot marked by the little black dome (*qubbet es-silsile*), placing the holy of holies over the rock which is covered by the gilded dome. T. A. Busink, however, is of the opinion that the temple was situated somewhat north (right) of the domed structure.

X. Cult podium (*bāmāh*, "altar") approximately 1.25 m. in height, from Megiddo of the Early Bronze period.

XI. Courtyard of the Yahweh Temple of Arad (cf. *170*), with the altar of burnt offering (right; the covering is modern) and the steps to the holy of holies (cf. *248*) in the background.

XII. *Umm el hijjāra,* a classical rock of refuge, rises above the Petra basin.

XIII. On a memorial stone a necropolis worker named Nefer-abu records his sin against the Peak of the West, his prayer to it, and his healing by it: "I was an ignorant man, foolish; I did not know what is good and evil. I sinned against the mountaintop, and she chastened me, for I was in her hand by night as by day. . . I said to the mighty mountaintop of the west. . . 'See, I will say to the great and small who are among the workers: Beware of the mountaintop, for a lion is in the peak; she strikes, as a wild lion strikes, and pursues him who sins against her' [cf. Ps 51:14]. As I thus cried to my mistress I found that she came to me with sweet air . . . She made me forget the sickness . . . See, the peak of the west is gracious when one calls upon her" (A. Erman, "Denksteine," pp. 1099f.).

XIV. "Yes, you are my lamp, Yahweh; my God who lightens my darkness" (Ps 18:29 MT [author's translation]; cf. Ps 18:28 RSV; cf. 2 Sam 22:29).

XV. "Restore our fortunes, O LORD, like the watercourses in the Negeb!" (Ps 126:4).

XVI. Tutenkhamun hunting lions.   XVII. Tutankhamun vanquishes the Nubians.

XVIII. The upper register shows Eannatum of Lagash at the head of his troop. He holds a bent stick in his hand. He is not a god, but a hero; as champion he enters the battle first. The troop marches in columns of six and is armed with shields and spears. The corpses of dead enemies line the way.

In the lower register, Eannatum is more sharply set off from his troop, in that he alone rides in a chariot. Oddly, the forward rank of soldiers is shown in smaller scale than the rank behind. That rank is shown in scale roughly equivalent to that of Eannatum himself.

XIX. "All the horns of the wicked I will cut off,
but the horns of the righteous shall be exalted"
(Ps 75:10 RSVm).

XX. "Your sharpened arrows terrify the nations; the king's enemies lose courage" (Ps 45:6 MT [author's translation]; cf. Ps 45:5 RSV).

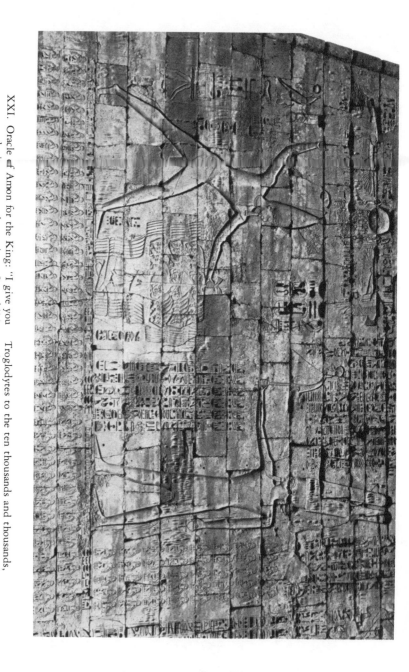

XXI. Oracle of Amon for the King: "I give you power and victory over the nations. I establish your might and set fear of you in all lands and terror of you unto the four supports of the heavens [cf. 28]. The great of all foreign lands are united in your fist; I myself stretch out my hands and bind them to you. I bind the Nubian Troglodytes to the ten thousands and thousands, and the peoples of the north to the hundred thousands, captive . . . as I then deliver the earth to you, as long and wide as it is, and the nations of the west and the nations of the east stand under your control" (A. Erman, *Literatur*, p. 319).

XXII. "Ask of me, and I will make the nations your heritage, and the ends of the earth your possession" (Ps 2:8; cf. 72:8; 89:25).

Viewed from the perspective of tradition history, this relief (like that of *Plate XXI*) concentrates three proceedings into *one* symbol: (1) The national god Amon presents the scimitar to the king, and with it bestows the right and power to conduct a war. This motif is first attested in the New Kingdom (cf. *405a,* scene 1). (2) The god delivers captive enemies to the king. This motif dates at least to the Old Kingdom (cf. *406,* and perhaps *397*). (3) The king, as victor, strikes down his enemies (only partly seen in *Plate XXII*). This motif dates from the early dynastic, perhaps even prehistoric period (cf. *395, 397, 398*). The antiquity of the various motifs demonstrates that the help of the gods played an ever larger role as time increased.

XXIII. Shalmaneser III (828–824 B.C.) receiving the tribute of Jehu of Israel. Jehu (or a representative) does proskynesis before the Assyrian king. The latter holds a shell in his raised hand (cf. 407, *Plate XXVI*), perhaps containing a libation for the gods (whose emblems are visible above Jehu) in thanksgiving for the subjugation of his enemies. The kissing of the feet may also have been part of the ritual of submission (cf. Ps 2:12).

XXIV. "I entrust the breath of my life to your power" (Ps 31:6a MT [author's translation]; cf. Ps 31:5a RSV).

"Make glad the life of your servant, for to you, Lord, I lift up my life" (Ps 86:4 [author's translation]).

XXV. A stele erected by Neb-Re for Amon in thanksgiving for the healing of a sickness (cf. *Plate XIII*). From the inscription: "Giving praise to Amon-Re, . . . Presiding over Karnak. . . . May he grant to me that my eyes look at his beauty [cf. Ps 27:4]. . . . I make adorations in his name; I give him praises to the height of heaven and to the width of the earth; [I] relate his power to him who travels downstream and to him who travels upstream [the Nile]. Beware ye of him! Repeat him to son and daughter, to great and small; relate him to generations of generations who have not yet come into being [cf. Pss 22:30–31; 102:18]. . . . Thou art Amon, the lord of the silent man, who comes at the voice of the poor man. If I call to thee when I am distressed, thou comest and thou rescuest me. Thou givest breath (to) him who is weak; thou rescuest him who is imprisoned. Thou art Amon-Re, Lord of Thebes who rescues him who is in the underworld [Pss 30:3; 89:48]. . . . He says: Though it may be that the servant is normal in doing wrong, still the Lord is normal in being merciful. The Lord of Thebes does not spend an entire day angry. As for his anger—in the completion of a moment there is no remnant [Ps 30:5] . . ." (*ANET*, p. 380).

XXVI. "What shall I render to the LORD for all
his bounty to me? I will lift up the cup of salvation and call on the name of the LORD" (Ps
116:12–13; cf. *Plate XXIII* and Fig. *407*).

XXVII. "Clap your hands, all peoples! Shout to God with loud songs of joy!" (Ps. 47:1; cf. 98:8).

XXVIII. "You will tread on the lion and the
adder, the young lion and the serpent you will
tread under foot" (Ps 91:13).

CHAPTER V
THE KING

328a. The highest dignitaries of the Egyptian empire march briskly in parade behind the king's three flail-bearers. First are the two eldest princes, wearing the prince's lock; then, alongside each other, come the viziers of Upper and Lower Egypt (cf. 392); next is the royal "scribe," with a scroll, followed by the "speaker," who carries a long staff as a mark of his dignity. Two officials who cannot be clearly identified bring up the rear. Israel adopted from Egypt the offices of scribe and speaker, but the viziership was apparently unknown, at least in the early monarchy.

The repudiation of all powers save Yahweh undergoes a special modification in the royal psalms.

It is possible to discern in the various strata of the Book of Judges (cf. especially 8:27–28; 9:7–15; 17:6; 18:1; 19:1; 21:25) and the two Books of Samuel the revolutionary nature of the introduction of monarchy into Israel. Even at a late stage it could be viewed as no more than a completely unwarranted aping of foreign customs (1 Sam 8:5; Deut 17:14).

In fact, the monarchy, since it was without tradition in Israel, was obliged to rely heavily on forms and institutions drawn from outside. Thus, for example, the official apparatus, in titles as well as in functions, was apparently modeled largely on the famous and venerable Egyptian apparatus (328a). The *swpr* corresponds to the Egyptian *šš*, "scribe, secretary"; the *mzkyr* corresponds to the Egyptian *whmw*, "speaker," etc.[1] There will be further discussion below of the influence of Egyptian institutions on the royal ritual and royal titulature (cf. also 146). Fig. 329 bears eloquent testimony to the high regard enjoyed in Egypt by the positions of official and scribe. It is also revealing that in Egypt war heroes were never deified, whereas scribes and other bearers of culture, like Imhotep and Amenhotep, the son of Hapu, were accorded that honor.[2]

In accentuating the dependence of Judaic-Israelite kingship on foreign models, we must not, however, disregard its independent features.[3] The epic literature is well aware that Israelite kingship, unlike the Sumerian-Akkadian or Egyptian kingship, did not descend from heaven in remote antiquity, but arose instead under specific historical circumstances. Without challenging Yahweh's part in it, the tradition records that the king was made king by the people (1 Sam 11:15; 2 Sam 2:4a; 5:3; 1 Kgs 12:1, 20). A large segment of the OT tradition (narrative books and Prophets) is very critical of kingship, if not entirely hostile toward it. The weaknesses and failures of the kings are mercilessly portrayed in a manner quite unusual in the ancient Near East.[4] Because Israel always cherished the memory of the prenational period (patriarchs, exodus, Sinai, settlement of the land), it never shared the Mesopotamian and Egyptian consciousness of kingship as an inevitable and inviolable necessity.

The royal psalms provide a marked

329. The positions of official and scribe were highly developed and much esteemed in Egypt from the period of the Old Kingdom onwards. Therefore, a certain Ramsesnakht, high priest of Amon of Thebes and holder of one of the most influential offices of the late period, can have himself depicted as a scribe. Just as the Horus falcon embraces Khefren the king (cf. 260), so here the baboon, animal of the scribal god Thoth (cf. 478a), is at one with Ramsesnakht. Thus, the scribe is shown to be fully inspired by the god whose powerful knowledge sustains the heavens (cf. 29). In other representations, Thoth himself (with the ibis-head) appears as scribe (349–50; 352; S. Schott, "Thoth als Verfasser").

331. ". . . I address my verses to the king" (Ps 45:1b).

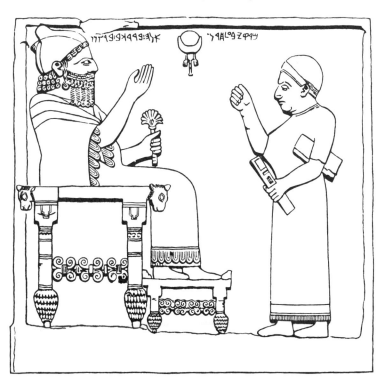

330. "My heart overflows with a goodly theme; . . . my tongue is like the pen of a ready scribe" (Ps 45:1a, c).

contrast to this specifically Israelite view of kingship. In them the king appears endowed with unprecedented power. He represents Yahweh. Relation to Yahweh is decided in relation to the king. To "serve Yahweh" means to submit to the king in Jerusalem (cf. Ps 2:11–12). It is true that the king is not unequivocally identified with God in

these psalms, nor does he become lord over the forces of nature or the object of cultic veneration.[5] Nonetheless, he bears a number of features of the divinized kings of Egypt or Akkad. That fact is also reflected in the relation between ancient Near Eastern iconography and the royal psalms.

The court was the circle in which the

unique dignity of the king was expressed and nurtured. The lips of the poet, inspired by the king, move like the stylus of a nimble scribe (Ps 45:1). In Egypt, and also in Assyria, such scribes were present on all important occasions (330). They wrote with brushes on parchment or papyrus (left), or with styluses on clay or wax-covered wood tablets (right).

The scribe-simile, the artful self-consciousness ("my verses"), and the aim to please the king all point to courtly circles. The royal official was maintained entirely by the good will of the king. Aside from the king's personal attitude toward him, the king's glory was his glory (cf. 1 Kgs 10:8; 331).

1. THE BIRTH AND INFANCY OF THE KING

The need for effective and competent leadership in the face of powerful enemies (Philistines) was an essential factor in furthering the rise of kingship in the OT. Military abilities and successes brought Saul (1 Sam 11) and David (2 Sam 5:2) to the throne (at an earlier stage, cf. Judg 11:8). In Mesopotamia and Egypt too, kingship may have originally achieved its plenitude of power on the basis of specific needs and functions. As late as the sixth century B.C., Ezekiel recognizes that the Pharaoh's power rests in the guarantee he affords for the construction and maintenance of the canals necessary to Egypt's existence (Ezek 29:3). The concrete, political basis of kingly power was importantly linked from the beginning, however, with a mythical-religious basis. The effective fullness of power could not be understood without reference to divine action. This applied, first of all, to the office which the king fulfilled,[6] but it was increasingly extended to his person. The practical consequences of this understanding were by no means so great as one might expect.[7] The myth of divine generation provided the Egyptians with their most consistent answer to the question of why one and not some other holds in his hand the fulness of power. A cycle of fifteen scenes, found almost entire in the temple of Hatshepsut (1501–1480 B.C.), represents the full history of her infancy. A similar cycle is

found in the temple of Amenophis III (1413–1377 B.C.) at Luxor.[8] Fragments of the cycle exist also at Medinet Habu and Karnak.[9]

In the Hatshepsut temple, the picture cycle begins with a portrayal of the assembly of the gods (332), at which Amon-Re makes known his love for the future queen mother (Scene 1). Amon's colossal size is a striking feature of the representation. He is more than twice the size of the twelve deities who have appeared before him, even though they are the most important of the Egyptian divinities. In the upper register (from right to left) are Osiris, Isis, Horus, Nephthys, Seth, and Hathor; in the lower register (also from right to left) are Mont, Atum, Shu, Tefnut, Geb, and Nut. At Luxor, the first scene shows the love goddess Hathor, who communicates to the queen mother Amon's intention to unite with her (Scene 1). In another picture (Scene 2), Amon himself communicates his intention to the king. Scene 3 depicts Amon on his way to the queen. The large picture (Scene 4; 333) depicts a preliminary high point, discreetly and delicately portraying the conception of the future king. The god and the queen are seated on the sign for "heaven" (cf. 11, 17, 21). The left hand of the god rests in the queen's right; her left hand tenderly supports his right, which extends the life-sign toward the queen's nose. Amon's feet are supported

247

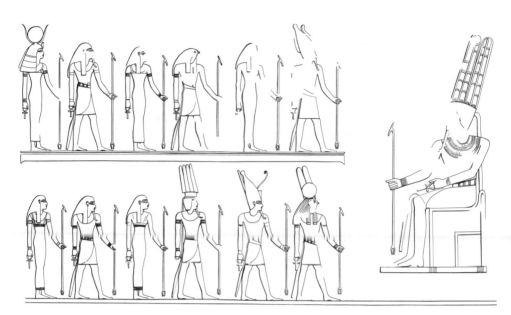

332. In the OT, the mark of a true prophet is his access to the circle in which God takes counsel with his heavenly company. Jeremiah queries in regard to his opponents: "Who among them has stood in the council [*swd*] of the LORD to perceive [him] and to hear his word?" (Jer 23:18).

In Ps 25:14, the privilege of the prophets is democratized: "The friendship [*swd*] of the LORD is for [all] those who fear him."

by the goddess Selket, who wears the symbolic scorpion on her head. In Mesopotamia too, the scorpion is the symbol of sacred marriage (cf. 388) and of love entering the body of the queen.[10] The queen's feet are upheld by Neith. The crossed darts and shield are a symbol which characterize Neith as a mighty protectress and goddess "who opens the paths."[11] The text indicates that Amon-Re enters the queen in the form of the reigning king.[12] That statement is important to the relation of experience and myth.

Ps 2:7 states that Yahweh begot the Israelite king (cf. Pss 109:3 LXX [cf. 110:3 RSV]; 89:26; and 2 Sam 7:14). The specification that it is *today* that Yahweh has begotten him, that is, on the day when the king proclaims it, precludes taking the statement literally. The term "adoption," frequently used in this context, is a bit too juridical. The same may be said of the term "vassal."[13] "Sonship" has emotional as well as legal

aspects. In consequence of this relation, the overlord subjects all peoples to the power of his new vassal king (Ps 2:8–11). In the pharaonic infancy narratives, kingly power is also the consequence of the divine fatherhood.[14]

The next scene of the cycle shows the ram-headed god Khnum receiving from Amon the charge to *form the body* of the future king (Scene 5). He executes this command (Scene 6) by "shaping" on the potter's wheel the body of the nascent king. The latter, in the manner of children, has a finger stuck in his mouth (334; cf. 31). Along with the body, Khnum forms the *ka*, the vital force or "soul" of the child (figure at the left). The cow- and mother-goddess Hathor, with the sun disc between her horns, is enthroned at the left of the scene. She extends the life-sign toward the fetus. The life-sign is usually held at the nose of the one who is to be quickened. In the present scene, this was ruled out on compositional grounds. In Egypt, a dif-

248

ferent deity is responsible for each phase of generation: for conception, Amon; for the shaping and vivification of the body, Khnum and Hathor; for birth itself, special birth divinities. In the OT, all these are concentrated in Yahweh. He "begets" (Ps 2:7); he forms the child in its mother's body (Ps 139:13, 16); and (at birth) he takes it from its mother's womb (Pss 22:9; 71:6; cf. *275–77*). This continuity made possible an essentially different trust relation than was possible under the discontinuity of divine actors in Egypt.

After the potter's scene, Thoth, messenger of the gods, announces to the

333. "You are my son, today *I* have begotten you" (Ps 2:7).

334. "Your hands have made me and solemnly ordained me" (Ps 119:73a [author's translation]).

335. Thoth, the messenger of the gods, announces to the queen that Amun is satisfied with the status of things and has granted her an elevation in rank.

queen an elevation in rank (Scene 7; 335). The formation of the fetus has made her queen mother. Like every woman in the ancient Near East, the queen attains full status by motherhood (cf. Ps 113:9). In the next scene of the cycle (Scene 8), the queen is conducted to the house of birth by Khnum and Hathor. The large cast present at the *birth* (Scene 9) characterizes it as the real climax of the cycle (336). The low degree of naturalism in rendering the scenes of generation and birth is probably less related to the delicate nature of the processes involved than to the fact that the reliefs are concerned to present a kind of "mystery play," and not the actual event. The moment depicted is scarcely reasonable under the circumstances: The enthroned queen is already holding the newborn infant in her arms. A female attendant kneels, ready to receive the child (or has just handed it to the queen?). Immediately behind the queen is a kneeling goddess, who apparently

336. The large cast of characters marks the birth of the future king as the most important scene of the entire cycle.

embodies the mountains of the horizon from which the newborn sun (cf. 337) has just arisen. Her name is signified by the twin-peaked mountain (cf. 10–13, 17–18). Behind her stand Nephthys and Isis, who are often associated with the sunrise (and sunset) (cf. 30, 37, 63). The god Heh (cf. 27a) is portrayed twice beneath the throne. He lifts up "length of days" and "life" to the newborn child. The remainder of the middle register is occupied by various tutelary genii holding life-signs. In the bottom register, the "souls" of the forefathers kneel, hailing the newborn king (cf. Ps 45:16). The s}-sign, signifying "protection," stands below the throne. It is flanked by two was-scepters (cf. 19). Bes and Thoeris, two fortune-bringing goddesses, are seen at the outer right. The frame in which the various figures are portrayed may originally have represented a bed decorated with lion-heads, viewed simultaneously from the side and from the top. It seems to have been misinterpreted at an early stage and understood as an artificial stand on which a throne, among other things, could be placed (cf. 333).[15] The birth goddess Meshenet, seated outside to the right, presides over what is taking place on the stand. The symbol which she wears on her head is a stylized cow-uterus (cf. 277a).

The birth of the god-king in Erment (337) is portrayed rather less discreetly than is the case in the two cycles from the early New Kingdom. Here the woman in labor is shown not enthroned, but in a realistic kneeling posture (cf. 31). The newborn child is seen coming forth from the womb. The scarab (ḫpr = "to become, to come into being") with the sun indicates that a new "sun" has come into being.

The two following scenes (10 and 11) show Amon acknowledging the newborn child as his son (338 and 339). In both

337. "Upon thee have I leaned from my birth; *thou* art he who took me from my mother's womb" (Ps 71:6; cf. 22:9).

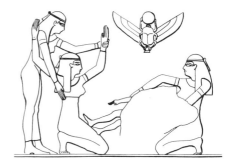

251

cases, it is the mother goddess Hathor who presents the child. Amon's greeting to his son consists in part of the words: "Welcome in peace, you son of my body. I grant you, like Re, to pass millions of years."[16] The adoption envisioned in Ps 2:7 may derive from this scene or the similar scene (14) of the installation of the crown prince (340). As opposed to Figs. 338 and 339, in Fig. 340 it is not the mother goddess Hathor, but the royal god, the sky god, who presents the crown prince to Amon.

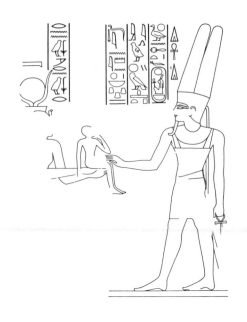

338. Hathor, the goddess of women, presents the newborn child to his divine father Amon.

339. "I will be his father, and he shall be my son" (2 Sam 7:14; cf. R. de Vaux, *Histoire ancienne d'Israel,* p. 226).

The suckling by divine wet nurses (Scene 12), the purification and presentation of the child before the palace gods (Scene 13), and the circumcision of the prince (Scene 15)[17] are not reflected in the psalms. The suckling of the Pharaoh by goddesses at the outset of every important stage of life, such as birth, accession to the throne, and death,[18] did penetrate into the Canaanite cultus.[19]

In Egypt, as in Pss 2:7–11; 89:26–29; and 110, the king's *lordship* is very closely related to his divine sonship. In the Hatshepsut cycle, Amon states at the conception of the future queen: "She is one who will reign over the two lands [Upper and Lower Egypt] while governing all living things. . . as far as every place over which I [as sun god] shine in my circuit."[20] Khnum promises while shaping her: "I give you. . . all flatlands; I give you all mountain lands and every nation that inhabits them."[21] Thus it is not surprising that Egypt's traditional enemies, the Nubians and Asiatics (with the full beards), are already set as a footstool beneath the feet of the future king, even as he sits as an infant on his nurse's lap (*341*). The cords which bind the enemies' necks are reminiscent of Ps 2:3; their posture, on the other hand, recalls Ps 110:1. Even more strikingly than

340. "He shall cry to me, 'Thou art my Father. . . .' And I will make him the first-born, the highest of all the kings of the earth" (Ps 89:26a, 27).

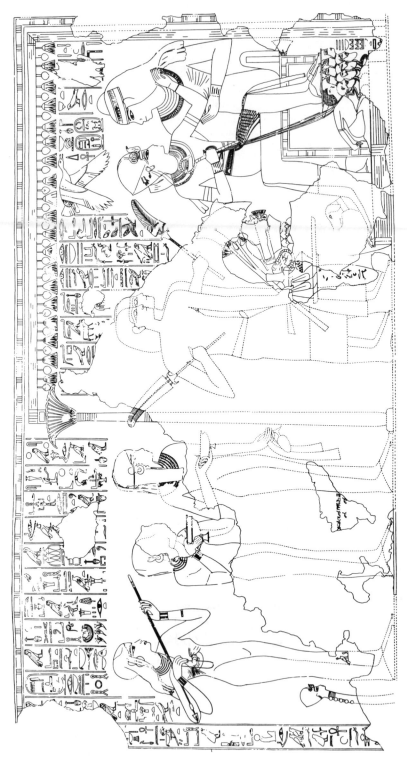

341. ". . . his enemies surrounded him [David] [with warfare], until the LORD put them under the soles of his feet" (1 Kgs 5:3).

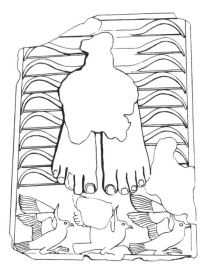

342. "Sit at my right hand, till I make your enemies your footstool" (Ps 110:1).

342a. The nine enemies beneath the king's feet (341, 342) must not be taken too concretely. This fact is demonstrated by the frequent variations on the theme. Here nine bows, rather than nine men, are placed under the soles of the king's feet. The *military capability* of the enemies takes the place of the *enemies* themselves (cf. *132a, 245, 328*). Similarly, the psalms of lamentation oscillate between the *wickedness* of sinners (Ps 7:9) and the *sinners* themselves (Ps 104:35).

Up to the period of the 18th Dynasty, the nine bows were symbolic of all the nations subjected to the king by inclusion in Upper and Lower Egypt (J. Vercoutter, "Les Haou-Nebout," pp. 109, 120). On a relief of Mentuhotep (11th Dynasty) on the island of Konosso, the gods themselves (the great "Henneiad" of Karnak, consisting of fifteen gods) appear in the form of fifteen bows laid under Amon-Min, the king of gods (*LD*, vol. 4, pl. 150c; P. Barguet, *Le Temple d'Amon-Rê*, p. 22). The nine bows became a symbol of the *countries* (regarded as hostile) surrounding Egypt only in the 19th Dynasty.

The three plovers, whose Egyptian name (*rekhjt*) also means "nation, subjects," carry approximately the same symbolic value as the thrice-three bows. There is a certain distinction in number. In Egypt, the plural is denoted by three examples of a given entity (cf. *395*), whereas three times three denotes a totality (cf. *429*). In Ps 83:6–8, Israel laments the fact that it is hard pressed by eight hostile neighbors plus mighty Assyria. Thus, Israel too has its nine bows/nations ("Gebal and Ammon" are to be read with the Syrian version as *gᵉbûl 'ammôn*, "the territory of Amon"). The plovers' crossed wings prevent them from flying away, indeed, from moving away at all, for the crossed wings make it impossible for them to maintain their equilibrium (B. Gunn, "An Inscribed Statue of King Zoser," p. 186). They lie helpless at the feet of the ruler.

in Fig. *341,* enemies appear as a footstool in Fig. *342.* As in Fig. *341,* here too appear the *nine* traditional enemy nations (cf. Ps 83:6–8 and *342a*).

In Ps 110, session at the *right hand of God* takes the place of sonship. The place at the right is the place of honor (Ps 45:9). "By his honorary position in the circle of divine power, the king partici-pates in the warlike, victorious power of Yahweh."[22] This sitting, however, pertains not to the realm of "infancy narrative," but to that of enthronement (cf. *352–55*). Here again, a concept which is in Egypt part of the "infancy narrative" of the Pharaoh is assigned in the psalms to the sphere of enthronement and adoption.

2. THE ENTHRONEMENT

Modern exegesis indicates that the en-thronement of the Davidic king may have been the original *Sitz im Leben* of Pss 2, 72, 101, and 110, and perhaps also of Pss 20 and 21.

In his study of the Judaic royal ritual, G. von Rad has shown that in many respects it may have been quite similar to the Egyptian.[23] To be sure, the documentation is so fragmentary that the overall course of the solemnities cannot be reconstructed with any degree of certainty, either for Israel[24] or for Egypt.[25] We must therefore underscore the hypothetical nature of this reconstruction before we proceed below to present the various scenes as part of a unified coronation rite.

Context frequently seems to indicate that the solemn purification of the king and the coronation are but an introduction to the monarch's cultic activity.[26] Before performing his filial duties, he is solemnly confirmed as son. It is therefore quite conceivable that this confirmation took place by a repetition of the actual enthronement process.[27] It is unclear whether other ceremonies, such as

343. "I have found David, my servant; with my holy oil I have anointed him" (Ps 89:20).

344. A Syrian vassal (cf. *408*) brings as tribute to the Pharaoh an ivory oil horn trimmed with a gold band (cf. O. Tufnell et al., *Lachish II,* pl. XV).

345. Before coronation the king is purified and sprinkled with the water of life. In Jerusalem, the coronation ceremonies began at the spring Gihon (1 Kgs 1:38; cf. *168* and

the carving of the name on the Ished-tree or the shooting of arrows, were part of the coronation events. Unfortunately, the royal ritual has not recently been subject to exhaustive investigation by Egyptologists.[28]

Even if the scenes treated below never constituted part of a self-contained process, they do have in common the function of establishing, legitimizing, and securing the Pharaoh's kingship. In that respect, their grouping is not entirely arbitrary.

Von Rad has set out a number of commonalities between the Egyptian and Judaic coronation rituals, but a further difficulty remains to be considered: nothing is known from Egypt of the central point of the Judaic kingly consecration, namely the *anointing* (cf. Pss 2:2; 18:50; 20:6; 45:7; 89:20; etc.).[29]

Plate VIII). In the consecration of the high priest, a rite partially analagous to the coronation, the candidate was solemnly washed at the beginning of the ceremony (Lev 8:6).

To be sure, we are informed that the king anointed vassal princes or divine images (377), but we have no information to indicate that the king himself was anointed. However, there has survived a small tablet from the Djemdet-Nasr period (343) which has been interpreted as an anointing.[30] Because the scene takes place before a temple, that is, before a deity (cf. 242), it undoubtedly has some religious significance. Whether it represents an anointing, however, and if so the anointing of a king, remains uncertain.[31] Anointing from an *oil-horn*

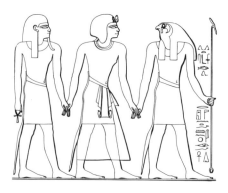

346. Atum (left) and Khonsu (right) lead the crown prince to his coronation before Amun, the god of the empire (on being led by the deity, cf. 272–74).

347. "Thou dost hold my right hand. Thou dost guide me with thy counsel" (Ps 73:23b–24a).

seems to have been distinctive to Syria-Palestine (1 Sam 16:13; 1 Kgs 1:39). Anointing horns, apparently of ivory decorated with gold bands, were brought to Egypt as tribute by Syrian princes (344).[32] Anointing confers glory and power. In Egypt, anointing was a means of increasing the beauty and power of the images of the gods (cf. 377) and of permitting vassals to participate in the glory of their overlord.[33]

According to 1 Kgs 1:38, the procession to Gihon preceded the anointing of Solomon. The enthronement ceremonial may have begun at a well because it was prefaced by cultic *purifications*. At any rate, that was the case in Egypt. There the enthronement, at which all the promises of birth were to be fulfilled, began with the candidate's purification by the water of life (345). Two priests dressed as the national deities Seth (left) and Horus (right) conducted the consecration. At this time Horus says: "I have purified [consecrated] you with life and strength so that you may endure even as Re [the sun god] endures."[34] There are some twenty-five examples of the scene, always associated with an ensuing coronation.[35] The psalms proclaim that Yahweh has consecrated (Ps 2:6) and blessed (Pss 21:6; 45:2) the king. In Ps 21:3, the blessing precedes the coronation. Kraus believes that Ps 110:7 may hark back to a sacramental draught from Gihon (cf. 1 Kgs 1:38), which would have constituted a part of the enthronement ceremonial. The draught permits the king to lift up his head in strength.

In Egypt, the newly consecrated king was led by two gods (left, Atum; right, Khonsu) *before the highest god* (346). This taking by the hand also plays a role in Babylonian and Hittite royal ritual. A saying on the clay cylinder inscription of Cyrus derives from the Babylonian tradition. It reads: "[Marduk] sought a righteous prince. . . , so that he might take his hand"[36] (cf. Isa 45:1). In several Hittite reliefs (347), a god of superhuman size places his arm about the king, grasps his hand, and thus escorts him in safety. In these instances, as opposed to

Figs. *272–73* and *346,* we are faced not with a presentation scene, but with the representation of a more general kind of leading.[37] In Ps 73:23, an otherwise unknown suppliant claims this gracious divine action for himself (cf. Ps 63:8 and *272, 273*).

The crowning may have constituted the initial climax of the enthronement solemnities. Of an entire series of scenes shown on an obelisk of Queen Hatshepsut in the temple at Karnak, the crowning was chosen to adorn the apex (*348*).

The queen kneels before Amon, who places the blue crown upon her head and causes "protection, blessing, and vital power to pour forth upon his daughter (the arms of the god form the hieroglyph *ka* = vital power)."[38] In Fig. *349,* the conferral of blessing is shown by the life-sign held in Amon's left hand. As signs of his newly granted dominion, the

king bears, in addition to the crown, the curved *scepter (ḥeḳaʾ* scepter), originally probably a shepherd's staff, and the so-called flail, originally perhaps a fly-whisk. The curved scepter is the determinative of the word "to rule."

In the psalms, as in the Egyptian pictures, the king is crowned directly by God (Pss 21:3b; 132:18; cf. also 89:39). The crown signifies the manifestation and completion (cf. Pss 5:12; 8:5; 103:4) of the king's election. In Egypt, the royal crown, and especially the royal serpent (uraeus) mounted on it, was felt to be a living being. A song to Thut-mose III says: "the serpent which is on your brow, which punishes them [the enemies of the king] with fire."[39] There may be a reminiscence of such ideas in Ps 21:9, which says of the king: "The LORD will swallow them [the enemies of the king] up in his wrath; and fire will consume them." The king bears the scepter, as well as the crown, at the divine behest (Ps 110:2; cf. 2:9; 45:6).

On the basis of 2 Kgs 11:12, von Rad[40] has characterized the crowning with the diadem and the presentation of the protocol as the most important moments of the enthronement.[41] The psalms also mention the giving of such a divine *protocol* (ordinance, covenant) to the king (Pss 2:7; 89:39).[42] In Ps 89:39, as in 2 Kgs 11:12, it stands side by side with the diadem. At the left side of Fig. *349,* the ibis-headed Thoth, scribe of the gods, is seen writing the protocol for the newly crowned king. In Fig. *350,* the scribe-god and the Pharaoh draft the document, assisted by the scribe-goddess Seshat. The participation of the Pharaoh in drafting his own deed of appointment typifies the self-understanding of Egyptian kingship. The principal content of the protocol is the "great name" (*351*; cf. 2 Sam 7:9; 1 Kgs 1:47), the fivefold *royal*

348. "For thou dost meet him with goodly blessings; thou dost set a crown of fine gold upon his head" (Ps 21:3).

349. While Amon crowns the king, the scribal god Thoth writes the protocol. Ps 89:39
accuses Yahweh: "Thou hast renounced the
covenant with thy servant [the Davidic king],
thou hast defiled his *crown* in the dust."

350. The king speaks: "I will tell of the decree of the LORD" (Ps 2:7a).

351. "I will make for you a great name" (2 Sam 7:9).

The illustration shows four of the five titles which constitute the "great name" of Sesostris I. At the upper left, the Horus (falcon) name stands inscribed in the palace facade (cf. *19*): "Life of Births" *('nḫ msw.t);* beneath it, in the cartouche, is the regnal name or "Name of the King of Upper [sedge] and Lower [bee] Egypt": "The Might of the Sun God Re Is Realized" *(ḫpr kʾ rʿ);* it is followed by the title: "Lord of the Two Lands" *(nb tʾwj).* At the upper right, in the second column, stands the so-called "Two Mistresses' name" (after the vulture goddess of Upper Egypt and the cobra goddess of Lower Egypt): "Life of Births" *('nḫ msw.t).* It is thus read in the same way as the Horus name and the Golden Horus name (not shown). The fourth name, the birth name or "Son of the Sun God name," is found in the second cartouche (right): "Man of the Strong One [a goddess]" *(s n wsr.t);* beneath it: "Like the Sun God in Eternity" *(mi rʿ ḏ.t)* (cf. A. H. Gardiner, *Egyptian Grammar,* p. 71).

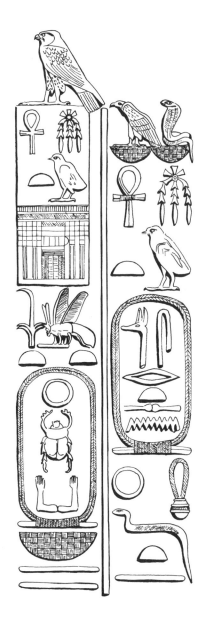

title received by the Pharaoh on accession to the throne. David himself apparently adopted a fivefold regnal name: "David [1], the son of Jesse [2], the man whom Elyon appointed [3], the anointed of the God of Jacob [4], the beloved of the Mighty One of Israel [5]" (cf. 2 Sam 23:1 NAB).[43] A. Alt[44] discerned some twenty years ago that noticeable remnants of such a title exist also in Isa 9:5.[45]

Ps 72:17 expresses a rather unusual wish with regard to the royal name. The correct translation is probably as follows:

May his [the king's] name endure for ever,
may his name flourish before the sun.

The *flourishing of the name* recalls the custom of writing the name of the newly enthroned Pharaoh on the leaves of the holy Ished-tree. W. Helck has gathered eighteen attestations of this name-writing scene.[46] They range in date from the period of Thut-mose III (1490–1436 B.C.) to the 22nd Dynasty (945–712 B.C.). The oldest example comes from the small temple at Medinet Habu.[47] On its right side is shown the enthroned Amon-Re, who writes the names of the king on the leaves of the Ished-tree (Persea, *Mimusops schimperi*). The king enters at the left, accompanied by Atum and Hathor. The legend reads: "Promenading of the king. Coming to the temple." Here, as Helck has shown, the most ancient understanding is reflected with relative purity. In it, the king would have discovered his throne names more or less by chance after they had been written (originally perhaps by Aton in Heliopolis) on the leaves of the holy Persea tree. Helck suggests the hypothesis that at one time the names may have been read out of the nervation of the leaves.

In Fig. *352,* the original sequence (writing and discovery of the name) is combined with two other concepts and, at the same time, reinterpreted. This is indicated by the words of Thoth, who now appears as writer: "I record for you years consisting of millions of Sed festivals; I have granted you eternity. . . ." Ptah (outer left) and the scribe-goddess Seshat (outer right) record the king's regnal years and jubilees on the palm panicle "year" (cf. *27a*), which terminates in the tadpole, the sign for 100,000. The enthroned Amon, using a similar palm panicle, presents to the kneeling Pharaoh a set of four ideograms signify-

ing the Sed festival. This great jubilee was usually celebrated for the first time in the thirtieth year of the sovereign's reign, and was then repeated at shorter intervals.

Nowhere is the wish for eternal rule made on behalf of the Judaic king, but there is indeed a desire that his name (Ps 72:17), his line, and his throne (Ps 89:36) might endure forever. Thus, the odd "before the sun" [RSV: "as long as the sun"] of Ps 72:17 (cf. 72:5) should probably be taken to mean "as long as the sun" (cf. Ps 89:36), and both may betray Egyptian influence.

In Fig. *348,* Hathor, standing behind Amon, expresses a wish for the newly crowned king: "As the sun [sun god] is, so may your name be; as the heaven is, so may your deeds be" (text under the right arm of Hathor). Such wishes are very common in the Egyptian enthronement texts.

In Egypt, the king's participation in the endless duration of the gods is expressed by his appearance in the midst of the gods as one of their own (cf. also *111*

352. "May his name endure for ever; may his name flourish as long as the sun [endures]"

(Ps 72:17 [author's translation]).

and 385). The situation is different in Mesopotamia.[18] There the king has access to the divine sphere only as an exception in the ceremonial of the Sacred Marriage (cf. 388).[49] In this context, he is occasionally shown enthroned beside a goddess.[50] In Egypt, on the other hand, *sitting at the right hand* is frequently attested not only in literature but in iconography as well. An illustration from Lepsius' *Denkmäler*[51] shows Amenophis not at the side of a goddess, however, but at the side of his mother Hatshepsut-Meryetra'. The frequently cited picture in Fig. 341 is also out of place here, for the king is sitting on his nurse's lap, and not at the right hand of a deity. In Fig. 353, however, a portraitlike representation of Pharaoh Horemheb shows him seated at the right hand of the king's god, Horus.[52]

In the psalms, the king normally sits *before* God (Ps 61:7), and his throne stands *before* the throne of God (Ps 89:36). It has been suggested that the psalmist may have understood Ps 110:1b, the wording of which is appar-

ently imported from Egypt, as an invitation for the king to "dwell" rather than to "sit" at the right hand of God.[53] *yšb* can mean both "to sit" and "to dwell." For all their differences, every attempted reconstruction situates the royal palace with its throne room on the south or right side (*ymyn,* "the right side; south") of the temple (354, 355).[54] It was later found offensive that God and king lived *threshold* to *threshold* (Ezek 43:8). In the

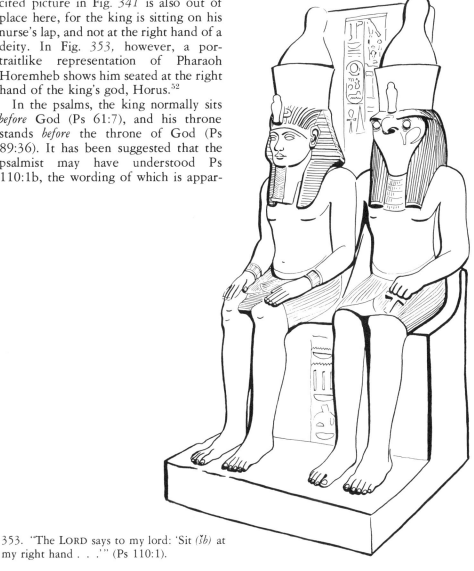

353. "The LORD says to my lord: 'Sit *(šb)* at my right hand . . .'" (Ps 110:1).

263

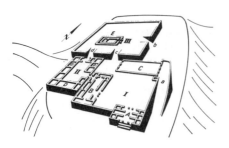

354. "Live (*šb*) at my right hand . . ." (Ps 110:1 [author's translation]). Reconstruction of the acropolis of Jerusalem in the time of Solomon, by K. Galling. I. outer palace court, II. inner palace court, III. temple court, A. hall of columns (entrance hall), B. audience hall, C."House of the Forest of Lebanon" (stable), D. private apartments, E. temple, a. ramp to the "House of the Forest of Lebanon", b. east gate of the temple (Gate of the People), c. outer and d. inner gates from palace to temple.

355. Reconstruction of the acropolis of Jerusalem in the time of Solomon, by T. A. Busink. 1. Temple, 2. Palace, 3. Queen's Palace, 4. Throne Room, 5. Stables (enlarged), 6. House of the Forest of Lebanon, 7. Holy Rock, I. Temple Court, II. Great Court, III. "Other" Court, IV. New Court.

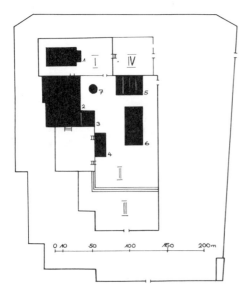

early period, the architectural unity of palace and temple was a monumental expression of the fellowship of God and king.[55] To Ezekiel, such fellowship had become unworthy of belief, and it was therefore necessary for him to take exception to the architectural expression of the concept.

The kingship of the newly crowned monarch was definitively manifested by his sitting on the *throne*. "To sit on the throne" means "to be king" (Ps 132:11–12; 1 Kgs 1:46). In Egypt, Isis, as mother of the king's god Horus, embodies the king's mother. Originally, Isis was none other than the throne, which she wore as her mark on her head well into the latest period (cf. 63). It is the throne which makes the king a king; it is his mother. When the king must be especially secure in his kingship, as in the administration of justice, he sits upon the throne (Ps 122:5; cf. 9:4, 7 and 285–86).

In order for the Davidic dynastic to rule "for ever," it must ever be furnished with new descendents (Ps 89:4a, 29a, 36a), and through all generations (Ps 89:4b) the throne of David must endure imperishable as the heavens (Ps 89:29b) or the sun (Ps 89:36b; cf. also 45:6). The distinctive quality of God's kingship is established by the notice that his throne is set in heaven (Pss 11:4; 103:19) and has endured since time immemorial (Ps 93:2).

If *world domination* is the most important consequence of divine generation (*341, 342*), it is even more the consequence of enthronement (cf. Pss 2:7–11; 45:2–5; 72:8; 110:1–2). In the Egyptian coronation ritual, that domination found expression in the shooting of arrows into the four quarters of the heavens (*356*). The king is assisted in this by Seth (cf. 2 Kgs 13:14–19). The wielding of the staff shown at the right probably has similar significance. There the falcon-headed Horus puts his arm around the Pharaoh's neck. The two posts with the crossed arrows are personified by the arms attached to them. They hold the *was*-scepter and the life-sign, indicating that a deity is represented. The two arrows are

356. "He [God] trains my hands for war
. . ." (Ps 18:34a).

357. ". . . my hand shall ever abide with
him, my arm also shall strengthen him" (Ps
89:21).

usually the symbol of the goddess Neith (cf. *333*). Because she was considered mistress of the arts of war and because it was she who opened the king's way in battle,[56] her presence would well suit this context. However, the signs set be-

neath the pair of arrows on the right are probably to be read as a short form for *nḫb.t ḥd.t nḫn,* "Nekhebet, the wise one of Nekhen."[57]

In Ps 18:34 (cf. 144:1), the king boasts that *Yahweh* trains his hands for

357a. The scene shows Amenophis III "shattering the red pots" *(sd dšrwt)*. They are symbolic of the deserts, the hostile foreign lands surrounding Egypt. They are characterized as red *(dšrt)* in contrast to the black (alluvial) soil of the Nile.

war. Yahweh made his way smooth (Ps 18:32); Yahweh supported him in the tumult of battle (Ps 18:35). Fig. *357* shows how the fierce war god Mont, related in some way to Seth, assists the king in the midst of battle. The rites of enthronement establish a reality which is henceforth effective every day.

The smashing of vessels and figurines inscribed with the names of royal and national enemies may have had a function similar to that of the shooting of arrows and the striking of blows into the four quarters of the heavens. To be sure, this portion of the rite has not yet been attested as part of the ancient Egyptian

266

358. "You shall break them with a rod of
iron . . ." (Ps 2:9a).

359. ". . . and dash them in pieces like a
potter's vessel" (Ps 2:9b).

360. Clay figure inscribed with the names of
enemy princes and nations. The figure was
ritually smashed.

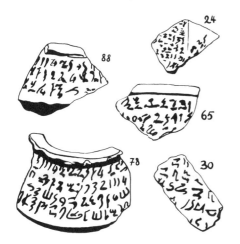

360a. "Now therefore, O kings, be wise; be warned, O rulers of the earth. Serve the LORD with fear, with trembling kiss his feet. . . . Blessed are all who take refuge in him" (Ps 2:10–11).

Fear before Yahweh is expressed here by submission to the king whom he has appointed. The Assyrian palace relief shows a scene which might have served as a model for Ps 2. The Assyrian king has conquered the Elamites and deposed the hostile king, Teumman. As agent of the Assyrian king, a general presents the nephew of the deposed Teumman for homage by the Elamite nobles. The nephew is friendly to Assyria (cf. Plate XXVII, part of the same scene). The first of the Elamite nobles is about to kiss the feet of the envoy of the Great King. Indeed, this homage before the new king is primarily a pledge of loyalty to the Great King who appointed him. Similarly, the homage of the "kings of the earth" before the Judaic king on Zion would be a tribute to Yahweh.

coronation solemnities, but it is clearly alluded to in verse 9 of Ps 2, which is an enthronement psalm. In Egypt, there is inscriptional and iconographic evidence for the rite as part of the cult of the dead[58] and the daily temple cultus (357a).[59] There have been numerous finds of pottery thus broken (359 and 360).[60] A dump containing approximately 3,600 potsherds was discovered at Mirgissa (15 kilometers south of Wadi Halfa) in 1962. The fragments may represent the remains of some 100 vessels. The fragments of the larger vessels bear star-shaped marks, indicating that they were smashed by maces.[61] The original background of the scene in Fig. 358 may have been a lively ball game for the entertainment of the goddess Hathor.[62] Like many other activities, it was later reinterpreted as an apotropaic rite. The leather ball became a clay globe representing the eye of Apophis, the enemy of the sun (cf. 55). It was ritually smashed.[63]

Traces of the rite of Fig. 357a are also found in the OT, for example in Jer 19:1–2a, 10–13.[64] In Ps 2:9, the potent, magical rite has become a mere simile.[65]

News of the coronation and triumph of the new king may have been delivered to the four quarters of the world by four rollers, pintail ducks, or other birds of passage (cf. the four birds in Fig. 233; Ps 68:11–13).[66] The enthronement may have concluded with the obeisance of the subjects (360a; cf. 410).

3. THE KING AS TEMPLE BUILDER AND PRIEST

An ancient Babylonian text describes as follows the creative activity of the god Ea:

He created the king to be custodian of the temple, he created mankind to discharge service of the gods.[67]

This statement is typical of the Mesopotamian tradition as a whole. It is not, to the knowledge of the present writer, attested in Egypt. To be sure, one of the fundamental duties of the Egyptian king was the building of temples and the offering of sacrifices, but he did not perform this function (at least not primarily) as the representative of mankind, for in the Egyptian view mankind was not created to this end.[68] He performs this function as son of the gods, who in a very special way have granted him life. "In return I will perform [their] rites everywhere, truly, steadfastly, and eternally; as long as they [the gods] exist on earth, I will perform them, I, the son of Re [the sun god]."[69]

This difference of view is also reflected in the iconography of the king as temple builder. In Mesopotamia, representations of the king as temple builder are found from the early Sumerian period through the late Assyrian period. Fig. *361* depicts Ur-Nanshe, the Ensi of Lagash (middle of the third millennium B.C.) carrying mortar. The temple-building hymn of his later successor Gudea suggests that this picture should be interpreted as the laying of the foundation stone:

He put the water of fortune in the frame of the brick-mold. . .
he lifted the holy pannier, approached the brick-mold.
Gudea put clay into the brick-mold, performed the obligatory rites. . .
He rapped on the brick-mold, brought the brick to light. . .
he took up the brick from the frame of the brick-mold,

[like] a crown which An wears, he carried the brick, carried it along. . .
made [more] bricks, brought them to the house.
laid out the plan of the house.
As to a little man building his [own] house anew,
Nisaba, who knows the interpretation of numbers,
suffers no sweet sleep come to his eye.[70]

Gudea's zeal is repeatedly stressed:

To build the house for his king
he does not sleep by night,
he does not slumber at midday. . .[71]

361. From the temple-building hymn of Gudea: "To build the house for his king, he does not sleep during the night, he does not slumber at midday . . ." (*SAHG*, p. 154).

269

362. Assurbanipal (668–626 B.C.) engaged in the lowly task of carrying the basket for his lord Marduk, the chief god of Babylon.

363. "Remember, O LORD, in David's favor, all the hardships he endured; how he swore to the LORD and vowed to the Mighty One of Jacob, 'I will not enter my house or get into my bed; I will not give sleep to my eyes or slumber to my eyelids, until I find a place for the LORD, a dwelling place for the Mighty One of Jacob'" (Ps 132:1–5).

364. The Pharaoh and the scribal goddess Seshat stake out the site for the temple.

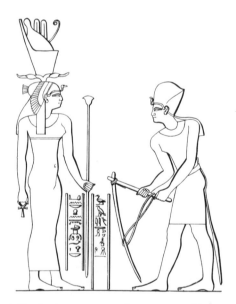

365. In the presence of Hathor, the Pharaoh lays out the course of the foundation trench (Hathor Temple of Dendera).

This latter declaration is strongly reminiscent of Ps 132:1–5, which relates that David had sworn not to grant sleep to his eyes nor slumber to his eyelids until he had found a dwelling place for

366. In the presence of Horus, the Pharaoh pours purified sand into the foundation trench (Horus Temple of Edfu). The temple must stand on pure ground.

368. The building sacrifice is offered. The "U" represents the excavation.

367. The Pharaoh presents the foundation gifts to Hathor: bars of gold, silver, and copper (Hathor Temple of Dendera).

369. In the presence of Hathor, the Pharaoh shapes the cornerstone of the temple (Hathor Temple of Dendera).

Yahweh. The king is portrayed as a zealous servant.

In iconography, the zeal of the devoted servant is portrayed by showing him carrying a basket. In the ancient Near East this task represented the most tedious, strenuous, and common form of labor. Mud was hauled in baskets; finished bricks were carried in baskets. Basket-carrying as such was not charac-

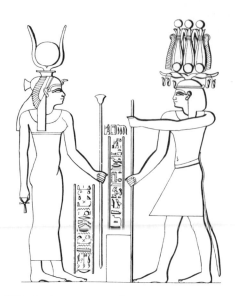

370. In the presence of Hathor, the Pharaoh sets the cornerstone (Hathor Temple of Dendera).

371. The Pharaoh presents the completed temple to Horus (Horus Temple of Edfu).

teristic of a definitive phase of labor (cf. 240). It was part of the building process from start to finish. It was a sign of servitude (Ps 81:6; 309). Yet, some 2,000 years after Ur-Nanshe, Assurbanipal had himself portrayed in this demeaning posture (362). And even where the royal temple builder is not shown in this ancient, traditional attitude, he nonetheless appears as the abject servant of the god for whom he toils (363).

Egyptian representations treating this theme are just as ancient as the Mesopotamian. They originated early in the third millennium B.C.,[72] although well-preserved, complete cycles have survived only from the Graeco-Roman period. The king's position in them is markedly different than in the Mesopotamian examples. He does not appear as servant of the gods. Rather, he acts on his own initiative and on his own responsibility. He builds as son for his father. As owner, he undertakes the critical tasks. Nowhere does he appear in the insignificant occupation of basket-carrying.

First, in collaboration with the scribal goddess Seshat, he lays out the base lines of the future temple, using four pegs and a line (364). Here, as often (cf. 111, 353, 385), the Egyptian king appears as equal among the gods. The four pegs (only two are visible in the picture) are firmly driven in. "Thus the four corners stand fast as the four pillars of the heavens."[73] Once the space has been staked out, the

372. It was necessary for the king to sustain the temple by endowing it with substantial real estate holdings. These provided support for the priests and provided a means for supplying the daily sacrifices. The illustration shows Pharaoh Shabaka donating lands (in the form of the hieroglyph "field") to Horus of Buto and his female partner Uto.

373. The sanctuary, its entrance flanked by two towers, is situated on a hill (cf. *202*). The deity is seated on a throne with a footstool. A worshipper stands before him, finger extended (cf. *418–19*). A show-table, a flaming censer, and a libation bowl are seen in front of the temple. The king is offering a libation. Behind him stands a servant with a large bowl. Another servant brings forward a sacrificial bull (cf. the scene in *440*).

374. "The LORD has sworn and will not change his mind, 'You are a priest for ever . . .'" (Ps 110:4).

375. The text reads: "Smoke and water pour forth for Amon. May he [Amon] give him [the king] life."

Pharaoh (symbolically) digs out the foundation trench with a hoe (365). This is done in the presence of the future owner of the temple (in this instance, Hathor of Dendera). Nonetheless, one does not gain the impression of a master-servant relationship.

The floor of the foundation trench is covered with a layer of pure sand (366). Then the foundation-offerings (bars of metal) are presented to the future lord (or mistress) of the temple (367), and drink offerings are poured out over the excavation (368). The king then forms

376. "I will come into thy house with burnt offerings; I will pay thee my vows. . . . I will offer to thee burnt offerings of fatlings, with

the smoke of the sacrifice of rams; I will make an offering of bulls and goats" (Ps 66:13, 15).

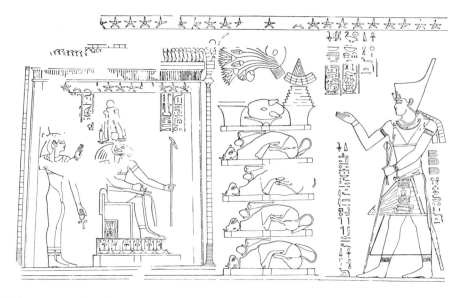

the cornerstone from clay (369) and sets it in place with the help of a rod (370). That action concludes the great foundation ceremony.

P. Montet[74] places the formation of the cornerstone (369) before the pouring of the sand (366), interpreting Fig. 369 as the dressing of the foundation trench which is to receive the sand. There is evidence for both sequences at Edfu: that of Montet appears in the second hall of columns; the sequence presented above appears on the exterior of the enclosure wall (cf. 177).

In an article entitled "Temple Building, a Task for Gods and Kings," A. S. Kapelrud finds a parallel to 1 Kgs 3–9 in Gudea's temple-hymn and deduces a common scheme of temple-building. That conclusion cannot be reached, however, without a number of improbable and imprecise readings of the text.

377. The anointing of the cult statue is part of the priestly service incumbent on the Pharaoh. Since there was no cult statue in the temple at Jerusalem, this duty was omitted. Instead, we learn that Yahweh anoints the suppliant (Ps 23:5) and especially the king (Ps 45:7) with the oil of gladness.

378. "May he [Yahweh] remember all your offerings . . ." (Ps 20:3a).

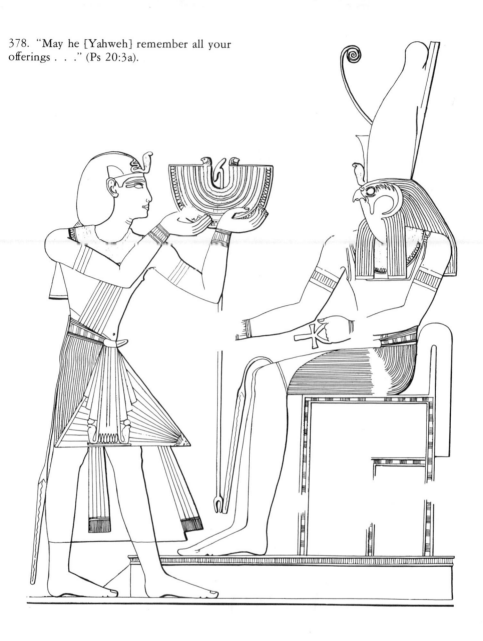

Solomon's dream at Gibeon (1 Kgs 3:2–15), for instance, has no relation at all to the dream in which Gudea is commanded to build a temple. On the contrary, in Israel the initiative for the building of the temple and for the institution of the monarchy appears to have come from the nation, and more specifically, from the king. Once Israel had finally become a settled people, there was re-luctance to leave the ark in the anachronistic, shabby tabernacle (2 Sam 7:2–3; cf. Ps 132:1–5). The permanent establishment of Yahweh in Jerusalem was intended to impart stability and permanency to the royal throne of David (2 Sam 7:13). The temple is a "pledge and guarantee of the well-being of the monarchy."[75] This impulse is clearly evident in Ps 2: nowhere but on Zion, the holy hill (v. 6) did Yahweh consecrate the king as king. Zion is made holy by the temple. From his temple on Zion, Yahweh sends forth the scepter of kingly might (Ps 110:2). With an utter disregard for history, Ps 78 (vv. 68–71) has *Yahweh* build the temple on Zion (cf. p. 120) and at the same time choose David as king. These actions are seen as the conclusion of the great saving event of the exodus. The temple of Yahweh and the throne of the house of David belong together (cf. Ps 122:1–5; cf. *354* and *355*). The importance of the spatial proximity of temple and palace must not be overstated, however, for that would degrade the temple to the status of a palace chapel.[76]

According to the Deuteronomic history, the building of the temple has an additional significance akin to an act of thanksgiving (1 Kgs 5:3–6). Thus, the OT understanding approximates the Egyptian view, which regarded the building of the temple primarily as the fulfillment of filial obligation.

Fig. *371* depicts the Pharaoh presenting the temple which he has built to the royal god Horus. Linked with the presentation of the temple is the summons to take possession of it (Ps 132:8).

As builder of the temple, the king is responsible for its maintenance (*372*) and for the cultus which is carried on in it. In the enthronement psalm 110, the Israelite king is awarded the priestly office in an oath sworn by Yahweh (v. 4). The concentration of the kingly and priestly offices in a single person places the Israelite king in the succession of the ancient kings of Jerusalem. The prototype is Melchizedek, who was simultaneously king and priest of the highest god (Gen 14:18 [RSV: "God Most

378a. In the reliefs which adorned the walls of Egyptian temples, there are countless representations of the king fulfilling his service to the gods. In reality, of course, this service was performed by numerous cult personnel—a fact attested by pictures from private tombs (*162, 162a*). But the king's participation in the sacred actions was not merely an ideal. That would have been out of accord with ancient Near Eastern notions. The king was present, if not personally, in the form of his statue. Here the statue is carried at the head of a procession by temple servants, who also bring fruits and breads from the daily offering. The statue holds in its hand a scepter, the determinative of the word *ḫrp,* "to control; to undertake [a thing]; to make sacrifice." In this context, the royal statue with the scepter signifies that it is the king who offers the sacrifice. A priest with a censer greets the procession at the entrance to the temple.

High"]). "The priestly activity of David and his successors is the subject of 2 Sam 6:14, 18; 24:17; 1 Kgs 8:14, 56. The king wears priestly attire (2 Sam 6:14), blesses the people, intercedes for the cult community, and presides over the rites. Indeed, he even offers sacrifice (1 Sam 13:9; 2 Sam 6:13, 17) and approaches God like the high priest.

Even in Ezekiel's concept of the 'prince,' he stands in the midst of the cultus (Ezek 44:3; 45:16, 22–25; 64:2–5)."[77]

Throughout the entire ancient Near East, but especially in ancient Sumer, cultic responsibilities devolve upon the king. The ancient Sumerian Ensi was as much priest as prince. He resides in the

379. "Do I eat the flesh of bulls, or drink the blood of goats? . . . What right have you to recite my statutes? . . . For you hate discipline. . . . He who brings thanksgiving as his sacrifice honors me; to him who orders his way aright I will show the salvation of God!" (Ps 50:13; 16b; 17a; 23).

temple and is responsible for the welfare of the city god. "The cult vase from Uruk places him at the head of a procession which appears before the goddess Inanna [cf. 62]. To be sure, only the train of his garment, borne by a servant, is preserved here."[78] As late as the Neo-Sumerian period, Ur-Nammu appears not only as temple builder (363), but also in a priestly capacity (180). Iconographic evidence for the priestly functions of Mesopotamian kings are extant well into the latest Assyrian epoch (373 and 440).

The priesthood of the king is much more strongly emphasized in Egypt than in Assyria. In the innumerable relief cycles from the temples of the New Kingdom and of the Graeco-Roman period, the king invariably appears as officiant (187, 229, 230, 374–79). This fact may be related to the obligations which devolve on the king as son of the gods. Beyond that, it is yet another indication that in Egypt the king played a much more central role than he did in Mesopotamia (cf. e.g., 19–24).

According to the relief cycles, it is the Pharaoh who daily opens the holy of holies and venerates the god, his father (229–30). It is Pharaoh who cleanses the throne (in Fig. 374, that of Osiris) and censes the cult statue, using an arm-shaped instrument (374) or a simple incense bowl (375). In Fig. 375, he also presents a drink offering with his right hand. The god Amon, to whom the offering is made, is seated on a throne whose base forms the sign for $m\}^{\prime}.t$ (right world order) (cf. p. 171).

The suppliant of Ps 66:13–15 speaks of rams, goats, and bulls which he desires to sacrifice. The original speaker may have been the king,[79] for the king may have been the only one who could have afforded such sacrifices.

An ancient Near Eastern meal did not consist merely of eating and drinking. Anointing with oil (Pss 23:5; 104:15; 133:2; 268, 445) was equally indispensible (377).

In addition to the daily veneration, purification, censing, libation, sacrifice, and anointing, the king was also responsible for providing the cult statue with clothing and ornaments (378). As was the case with a noble lord, not only support, but also entertainment had to be provided for the deity. Visits to other temples, song, music, dance (cf. chap. 6.3) and games of all kinds[80] served this purpose. These games frequently had erotic overtones. Since creation was largely understood in Egypt as generation, such games, like all aspects of the cultus, served to renew and sustain the creation.

Obviously, it was necessary for the king to delegate his priestly functions, except on special occasions. Still, the priests served under his commission. "It is the king who sends me to behold the god."[81] "The king gives the sacrificial gifts"[82] (cf. 378a).

Thus, in Ps 20:3, the king's sacrifices may be of the kind he personally offers (2 Sam 6:13, 17–18; 1 Kgs 8:5, 14, 62–64; 12:33; 2 Kgs 16:12–15). More probably, however, he has them presented by priests who act on his mandate. Undoubtedly Ps 61:8 was originally uttered by a king. Only the king, with the entire priesthood as his agent, can pay his vows "day after day."[83]

A peculiar scene frequently depicted in Egyptian temples is the "offering of Maat" (379) by the Pharaoh. Maat is shown as a sitting female figure with a feather in her hair. She embodies the rightness of individual things and aspects of the world (e.g., the cult; cf. Ps 132:9), and the rightness of the world as a whole. She is world order (cf. 32, 287). The gods are infused by Maat. By the offering of Maat, who becomes "in the act of presentation a kind of substance,"[84] the deity is supplied, as otherwise in sacrifice, with a power which constitutes his being.[85] While the cultic presentation of Maat may imply an ethical posture, it is nonetheless typical that in Egypt this attitude finds its highest expression in cultic-magical offerings. Quite the opposite is true in Israel. There the ethical-religious stance is not translated into reality in the cultus;

rather, the cultic is devaluated in favor of the ethical-religious (Pss 40:6–10, 50:14–15; 51:16–17; 69:30–31). In the view of the OT, the king (and man) cannot augment the righteousness of Yahweh. Righteousness and truth in the highest degree are inherent to Yahweh (cf., e.g., Pss 36:6, 10; 48:10–11; 85:10, 13; 89:16; etc.). The king receives righteousness from Yahweh (Ps 72:1–2). The

king can only make a solemn vow to hold fast to righteousness to the best of his ability. Ps 101 is such a vow of loyalty. The vow begins by praising the righteousness [RSV: "justice"] of Yahweh, then expresses the firm intention to strive for justice and right against injustice and transgression. This brings us to the king's responsibilities toward his people.

4. THE REPRESENTATION AND FURTHERANCE OF THE POWERS OF LIFE

The life and blessing inherent to the king from birth are bestowed in their fulness at the enthronement. These qualities are manifested in the display of royal splendor. The king is the fairest of all men, for God has blessed him (Ps 45:2; cf. v. 7). To be sure, the passage can also be taken to mean that God has blessed him because he is the fairest of men (cf. 1 Sam 10:23–24; 16:12, 18; 2 Sam 14:25). Both translations are grammatically possible, and it would be incorrect to eliminate one in favor of the other. Beauty presupposes blessing, and *vice versa*. The king is beautiful *ex officio*. Therefore he is invariably portrayed as such. Only rarely do the interests of portraiture (cf. *353*) displace the idealized image.

Nevertheless, to the ancient Near East, beauty consists not only in purity of form, but also in richness of color, light, and odor, and in display of wealth and power. A wide variety of status symbols plays an important role. One such status symbol was the war chariot.[86]

Though David rode on a mule (1 Kgs 1:33, 38; Zech 9:9; cf. *380*),[87] his sons expressed their claim to kingship by equipping themselves with horses, chariots, and bodyguards (2 Sam 15:1; 1 Kgs 1:5). The poet who desires to repre-

sent the king in all his glory bids him ascend his war chariot and ride forth (Ps 45:4). Here what was once foreign is no longer regarded as such. The beauty and splendor of the king are manifested in the concentrated strength of the bridled

380. The tribal princes of the period of the Judges rode on asses (Judg 5:10; 10:4); David rode on a mule (1 Kgs 1:33, 38). David's sons expressed their claim to kingship by acquiring horses and chariots (2 Sam 15:1; 1 Kgs 1:5). The future Messiah, however, was expected to come riding on an ass: "Rejoice greatly, O daughter of Zion! Shout aloud, O daughter of Jerusalem! Lo, your king comes to you; triumphant and victorious is he, humble and riding on an ass, on a colt the foal of an ass" (Zech 9:9).

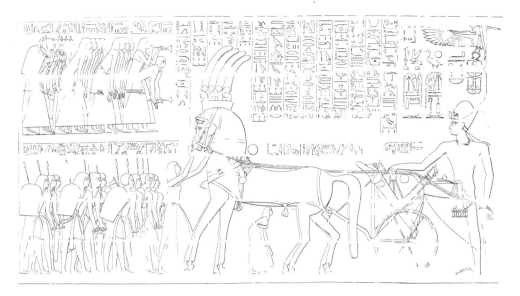

381. "Ride forth . . . let your right hand teach you dread deeds!" (Ps 45:4).

Ramses III mounts his chariot to ride forth in battle against the Libyans intruding on Egypt's western frontier. At the upper left, two trumpeters take turns in sounding the departure. The trumpeter whose turn it is to play holds under his arm the wooden core which was placed in the weak silver trumpet to prevent it from buckling on the march. The two silver trumpets of the Jerusalem temple (cf. 460–61) may be attributed to Egyptian influence.

horses and in mounting the elegant vehicle (381).[88]

Manifestation of the king's splendor is not merely an end in itself. It furthers the triumph of right order, of the defense of the helpless. Even the king's indulgence of his pleasure in the hunt (382) can be viewed as an aspect of his activity in establishing order. Dangerous predatory beasts are as much enemies of the king (Ps 45:5) as are the transgressors whom the king is sworn to eradicate (Ps 101:8). Assurbanipal relates the following in an inscription: "Since the time that I have sat on the throne of my father, my progenitor, Adad has loosed his downpours, Ea has opened his fountains, the forests have grown abundantly, the reeds have grown in the thickets so that no one can crowd in. The brood of lions flourished there, and they increased without number.

. . . They slay the cattle of the field, shed the blood of men. The shepherds, the overseers weep that the lions destroy everything. The dwelling places mourn day and night. The crimes of the lions were made known to me. In the course of my campaign I invaded their lairs, broke open their dens. . . . The people who inhabited the city I freed from danger."[89]

In Egypt, hunting scenes often present close parallels to the war scenes in which the Pharaoh vanquishes peoples hostile to Egypt (*Plates XVI* and *XVII*; cf. *111*). In a single breath, Amenemhet boasts of his successes in hunting and in war: "I overcame lions; I caught crocodiles. I subjugated the people of Wawat [region in the Sudan]; I carried off the Madjoi [a people in Egyptian Sudan]; I made the Asiatics do the dogwalk."[90] On a parade shield of Tutankh-

382. Assurbanipal: "The shepherds, the overseers, weep that the lions destroy everything. The dwelling places mourn day and night. The crimes of the lions were made known to me. In the course of my campaign I invaded their lairs, broke open their dens . . ." (*ANET,* p. 419).

383. Triumph over the enemy *(403)* is flanked by hunting scenes. A naked goddess looks on from the outer left of the scene. The bard of Ps 45 gives an account of the king's beauty before calling upon the queen to offer herself to him. Even so, greater emphasis is laid on his commitment to righteousness than on his purely military successes.

amun, the Pharaoh is shown striking down two lions instead of the traditional enemies of Egypt.[91] Similarly, on a set of ivory tablets from Ugarit, the scene of triumph over the enemy (cf. *403*) stands in immediate proximity to a hunting scene (*383*).[92]

In the hunt and in war, the king shows forth his glorious, victorious power as conqueror of all that is injurious and dangerous. But the chariot in which he sallies forth to his illustrious deeds also conveys him in parades, when there is no more at stake than a demonstration of his (and thus the nation's) splendor (*384*). A large troop of life-guardsmen

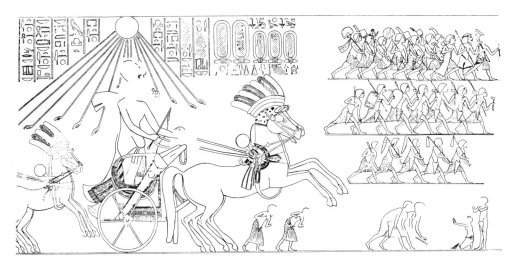

384. "You are the fairest of the sons of men; grace is poured upon your lips; therefore God has blessed you for ever" (Ps 45:2; cf. 1 Sam 9:2; 10:23; 16:12; 2 Sam 14:25–27).

385. "Hear, O daughter, consider, and incline your ear; forget your people and your father's house; and the king will desire your beauty. Since he is your lord, bow to him" (Ps 45:10–11).

runs stooped before the king (cf. 2 Sam 15:1; 1 Kgs 1:5). They clear the way. The public is represented by two persons (lower right), one of whom has fallen to his knees. Both hold their hands raised in homage.

The royal nuptials were one of the grandest occasions for display of kingly majesty and splendor. In Ps 45, the king mounts his chariot in order to fetch home his bride.[93] His warlike image in doing so corresponds to a knightly ideal of beauty and splendor (1 Macc 9:39; Song 3:6–8). In what was probably the most famous marriage in the ancient Near East, Ramses II (1301–1234 B.C.)

386. "Instead of your fathers shall be your
sons; you will make them princes in all the
earth" (Ps 45:16).

sent his entire army to fetch the daughter of the Hittite king Hattusilis III
(1282–1250 B.C.). The fact that Ramses
did not fetch her himself may be connected to the fact that she was officially
regarded as a kind of tribute.[94] Indeed,
the "being led" (*ybl*) in Ps 45:14 also
means "to be brought as gift." Fig. 385
shows the Hittite king dressed in a manner quite foreign to Egypt. In a worshipful attitude, he presents his daughter to
Ramses II. Ramses is enthroned between the gods Atum of Heliopolis and
Ptah of Memphis. Ps 45:6 (cf. RSVm) is
the only passage in which the Israelite
king is addressed as "god" or "divine."

In Ps 45:10–12, the psalmist addresses
the king's bride. Henceforth she is to
surrender herself to her royal lord. Fig.
386 depicts an intimate scene. From a
small vessel, the king pours a liquid into
the hand of the queen, who leans confid-
ingly against his knee. According to
Westendorf, the picture is to be read as a

hieroglyph, yielding: "hand" (*dr.t*), "to
pour" (*stj*), "liquid" (*mw*), "mouth" (*r}*),
and "to drink" (*shb*). To the Egyptians,
this clearly demonstrated the intimate
relation postulated by the picture.[95] Despite the intimate character of the scene,
the king and queen wear the full
trappings of office; for despite its intimate scope it is not a private scene.
What happens here serves the preservation of the dynasty: "Instead of your
fathers shall be your sons" (Ps 45:16).
Only after the succession has been se-
cured are the permanence, stability, and
prosperity of the kingdom guaranteed
(cf. p. 264 regarding the throne). In
addition to the scenes of triumph (403)
and of the hunt (383) juxtaposed on the
Ugaritic ivories mentioned above, there
appears also the intimate union of the
royal couple (387). The slightly rounded
stomach of the queen apparently indicates pregnancy (cf. 275).

In the view of the exponents of the

cult-mythical school, Ps 45 celebrates no ordinary marriage, but the sacred marriage of the king to a goddess of love. Mesopotamian evidence from various epochs indicates that the king united with Inanna/Ishtar within the scope of the spring New Year festival (388).[96] This union, sought by the goddess of love and fertility,[97] was intended to ensure the land's life and prosperity for the ensuing year. Inasmuch as the king always appears in this context as servant of the goddess, this action constitutes an element of the cultus (cf. 361 and 363).

387. "The LORD swore to David a sure oath from which he will not turn back: . . . sons of your body I will set on your throne" (Ps 132:11).

388. *Hieros gamos.* The couple lies on a bed covered with a costly spread. The scorpion of the goddess Ishshara is seen beneath the bed (cf. 333).

In Ps 45, however, there is talk neither of servitude on the part of the king, nor of the blessing of fertility which the union is supposed to effect. In Ps 72:16, to be sure, the king appears in connection with the fertility of the land (cf. also Gen 49:11–13, 25–26; Deut 33:13–16). However, this fertility is not the result of sacred marriage, but of intercessions made on the king's behalf because of his action in rescuing the innocent from the violent (vv. 14–15). When he stands up for the rights of the weak, he may consider the harvest blessing a part of his blessed rule (cf. 389, 389a).[98] The king's commitment to justice and righteousness is heavily emphasized in the psalms (cf. especially Pss 45:3–7; 72:2, 4, 12–14; and 101).

In the lands bordering Israel, especially in ancient Babylonia, concern for justice and righteousness is also part of the king's primary responsibility. Hammurabi is reminded in a letter: "Marduk, who loves you, has in truth created you so that you may help the right to triumph."[99] The correspondent thus makes an appeal to the great king's self-understanding. The latter had himself portrayed (390) receiving from the sun god (Shamash) the commission "to promote the welfare of the people, . . . to cause justice to prevail in the land, to destroy the wicked and the evil, that the strong might not oppress the weak, to rise like the sun over the black-headed [people], and to light up the land"[100] (cf. the psalm passages cited above). Legisla-

285

389. "May there always be grain in the land; may it rustle on the tops of the mountains! May its fruit shoot up like Lebanon, and may its stalks flower forth like the grass of the field" (Ps 72:16 [translation after Kraus]; cf. Ps 144:12–14).

In Ps 72, the hope of a wonderful growth of grain is formulated as an intercession for the righteous king who cares for the weak and the poor. The Pharaoh, however, attributes the bountiful harvests during his reign to his good (magic-cultic) relation to the grain god: "It is I who produced the grain, (because I was) beloved by the grain god. No one was hungry in my years" (Teaching of Amenemhet 1.11; cf. G. Posener, *De la divinité du Pharaon,* pp. 11f., 41f.; H. Gauthier, *Les fêtes du Min,* pp. 225–50. On the presentation of the sheaf, cf. Lev 23:9–14).

tive activity is here closely linked to "rescue" and "salvation."[101] In myth, either the sun god or Ea, lord of wisdom, appears as judge (cf. *285–86*). Just as they maintain the cosmic order by their judicial activity, so the king (after their example) protects the political cosmos from Chaos (cf. Ps 122:5).

In Egypt, the king's relation to (juridical) law is less emphasized. His chief justice, however, wears about his neck as a sign of office a figurine of Maat, the goddess of truth, justice, and world order.[102] When Maat and the king are placed in the same context, reference is usually to that world order which corresponds to the king's cosmic significance. According to the Kubban stele, Amon spoke thus at the birth of Ramses II: "It is I who have made him. In doing so, I again set justice in its place. The earth is established, heaven is pacified [cf. *21*]."[103] Nevertheless, the Pharaoh quite naturally had to concern himself also with legal order. Horemheb, for example, promulgated a series of laws "by which he accomplished Maat in the two lands. . . , in order to avert sin [*iŝf.t*] and to destroy falsehood."[104]

In addition to legislative and judicial activity in the narrower sense, the appointment of good officials, together with a broad variety of rewards for the good and punishments for the wicked, served to maintain the inherent order. In Ps 101, the king vows to keep those who are good and true at his side, but to drive away liars and slanderers. The goddess Maat stands behind the Pharaoh at the appointment of the vizier, the highest official.[105] From the 18th Dynasty onwards, there are frequent representations of the reward of deserving officials by the king (391). "King Horemheb stands beside a cushion-covered 'epiphany bench,' holding the Hekascepter and the flail in his left hand. His right arm rests on the cushion, the hand extended. Two attendants stand behind the king. Before him stands May, the master of the treasury. He holds a fan and a kerchief and extends his right hand towards the king. Behind him are two bowing officials in vizier's dress. They are identified as the governors of the southern and the northern city. Next to them are two servants, occupied in setting gold about the neck of the occupant of the tomb, and in anointing his body. Neferhotep lifts up his hands in joy. Finally he leaves the site of the festival, accompanied by another divine father of Amon named Parennefer. Both men wear the gold of reward about their necks. They are received and greeted by the father of the occupant of the tomb."[106]

The eradication of evildoers, as well as

389a. This illustration, like Fig. 389, depicts a fertility rite. The Pharaoh brings four vari-colored threshing-calves to the fertility god Min. According to the accompanying text, the rite is intended to increase the grain. It is not clear what significance attaches to the cleaving of the serpent, whose head and tail serve as staffs for the Pharaoh (cf. A. M. Blackman and H. W. Fairman, "The Significance").

390. "Give the king thy justice, O God, and thy righteousness to the royal son! May he judge the people with righteousness, and thy poor with justice!" (Ps 72:1–2).

the reward of the good, is an aspect of the duties of the king (Ps 101:8). Fig. *392* shows six policemen armed with staves hastening (upper right) to report to the chief of police (upper left) information concerning a dangerous incident. Since it is apparently still night or early morning, a coal fire has been lit. A chariot for the police chief stands ready at the center of the scene. He is in transit at the lower left. The glorious outcome of the expedition is depicted at the lower right. The police chief brings two captured nomads (?) and an Egyptian before the vizier, who is just emerging from the palace with his retinue. The expectation of divine help at morning (Pss 90:14; 143:8) probably has to do in part with the practice of administering justice in the morning.[107] In the final analysis, this

391. "I will look with favor on the faithful in the land, that they may dwell with me; he who walks in the way that is blameless shall minister to me" (Ps 101:6).

393. "May he defend the cause of the poor of the people, give deliverance to the needy, and crush the oppressor!" (Ps 72:4).

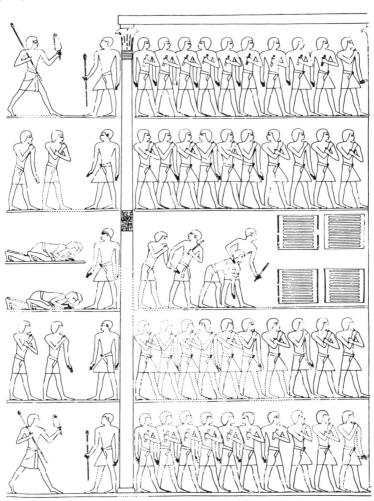

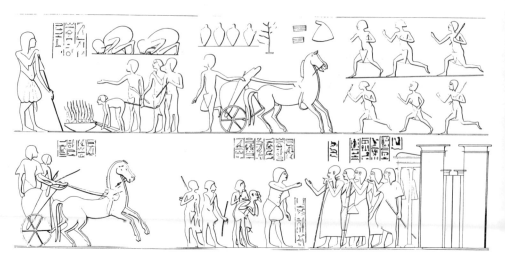

392. "Morning by morning I will destroy all
the wicked in the land, cutting off all the evildoers from the city of the LORD" (Ps 101:8).

custom may be attributable to the fact
that it is in the morning that the sun god
dispels all evil (cf. 53 and 286; Ps
104:22; Job 38:12–13), quite apart from
the fact that work is generally begun
early and that evildoers are often caught
at night.

Fig. 393 provides a glimpse into the
judgment hall. We must envision the vizier to the right of the picture. An inscription mounted above him denotes the
scene: "Session to hear complaints in the
judgment hall of the vizier." . . . "The
roof of the judgment hall is supported
by palm columns. The name of the
Pharaoh (Thut-mose III) and, beneath it,
that of the vizier (not likely in reality)
are engraved on a shield approximately
at the center of the column at the left."[108]
The king is the pillar of justice and righteousness (cf. 21). Before the vizier (not
visible) "the forty scrolls of the law lie on
four mats. Everyone is free to inspect
them. At the walls on either side stand
scribes; judicial officials stand along the

corridor. The center stands open for the
litigating parties, who must wait outside
until the bailiffs permit or compel them
to enter."[109] To be sure, this interpretation of the scene is not undisputed. N.
de Garis Davies[110] has suggested that the
forty items lying on the mats are not law
scrolls, but rather the staves of the forty
district governors who have been summoned to pay their duties. The staves,
tokens of their power, have been laid
down before the vizier as an expression
of subordination to him. Scrolls are
shorter and wound round with a cord.
Nevertheless, the picture does depict a
judgment scene, as stated in its title, for
appearance before the vizier was a means
of settling all kinds of disputes.

In Egypt, the vizier appears without
exception as the highest judge. In Israel,
however, that office is exercised by the
king himself (2 Sam 15:2–6; 1 Kgs
3:16–28). At least in the early monarchy, the office of vizier apparently
did not exist (cf. 328a).[111]

5. DEFENSE AGAINST ENEMIES

As stated at the beginning of this chapter, the Philistine menace was the primary reason which prompted Israel to transform its ancient, loose confederation of tribes into a monarchy. War did not universally play so decisive a role in the rise of kingship. But apart from a few exceptions (for instance, the Neo-Babylonian period), the king's spectacular martial functions are among those most frequently and impressively portrayed throughout the centuries. And it is in the war scenes that the differences between the national and prenational periods, and between Egyptian and Mesopotamian kingship come most strongly to the fore.[112]

The carvings on the ivory handle of a flint knife from the period before the founding of the Egyptian empire (ca. 3000 B.C.) depicts two warring groups (394). It shows the wild confusion of one-to-one combat. The better-armed troop of shorn warriors is at the point of victory over their long-haired adversaries. The dead between the two boats indicate, however, that it is a life-and-death battle even for the shorn warriors.

Such scenes disappear almost completely upon unification of the kingdom. First of all, from that period onwards it is usually the king, not a troop, who fights and is victorious. To be sure, he may be accompanied by a huge army, as in the battle scenes of the New Kingdom. But the king dominates the battle to such an extent that the entire army (as in the poem of Pentaur) appears as a body of servants whose utility is highly questionable.

Secondly, one can no longer really speak of battle. In his godlike superiority, the king annihilates his enemies, who cannot find the courage even to attempt resistance. This representation of war and battle is linked with the rise of kingship. It finds its strongest expression in the monumental hieroglyph which represents the striking down of enemies.

There are endless repetitions of this scene in Egypt, dating from the period of the unification of the kingdom down to the great Graeco-Roman temples (cf. the caption of Fig. 342a).[113]

A glance at the royal psalms is enough to show that in them the warring king is portrayed precisely as in Egyptian iconography. The figure of the king assumes monumental proportions. The army is insignificant; the king's superiority is absolute. He strikes down his enemies and treads them underfoot like dirt. The psalm verses attached to the Egyptian illustrations make clear the close relation of the two conceptions. The smiting motif is also determinative

394. Representation of a battle from predynastic Egypt.

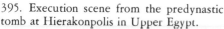

395. Execution scene from the predynastic tomb at Hierakonpolis in Upper Egypt.

396. Battle scene from the tomb at Hierakonpolis.

in the picture of the ruler in Num 24:17 J.[114] The prehistory of the Egyptian smiting motif may be traced to the prenational period. In the tomb of Hierakonpolis, there appears in addition to scenes of boating, hunting, and battle, an illustration of an execution (395). Three men bound together with a rope are bludgeoned with a mace. The figure with the mace is considerably larger than the other three, but he is not otherwise distinguished by any insignia. Scenes of actual battle (396) are found in addition to the execution scene in the tomb of Hierakonpolis. As stated above, the battle scenes disappear almost completely upon the dawning of kingship, while the execution scenes (or better, domination scenes) remain in high esteem for three millennia.

The Narmer palette (397) provides the oldest known example of the classical depiction of the scene. The name Narmer (n'r, "catfish"; mr, "chisel") is found on the upper edge of the palette, between two heads of Hathor. The colossal figure of the king fills the central section of the palette. He wears the crown of Upper Egypt. In his right hand he brandishes the mace; with his left hand he seizes an enemy by the forelock. In the psalms, the hairy crown of the head is also mentioned as an enemy characteristic (Ps 68:21). It is intended to signalize his animality and carnality.[115] With clenched fists, the captive awaits the death blow. He does not attempt resistance, nor does he beg for mercy. The hieroglyphs at his right identify him as the champion of the harpoon district in the Delta. The lower portion of the palette is taken up by two imploring, dying, or dead enemies. Hieroglyphs, which cannot yet be interpreted with any certainty, are assigned to each. Y. Yadin[116] has offered the conjecture that the sign at the right represents a Transjordanian forked corral (cf. 314). The king is barefooted. A servant holds his sandals, and also a water vessel, which may have been used for purification of the king (cf. 168). The king's bare feet indicate that he is standing on holy ground (cf. 411 and 424). The symbolic grouping at the upper right makes it clear that this smiting of an enemy is by no means a profane act. The chief elements of the grouping are a falcon and the hieroglyph for "land." The latter is more closely defined by six papyrus stalks; it terminates at the left in the head of a captive. The head closely resembles that of the captive held by the king. The symbolic grouping may be read: "The falcon-god Horus has taken captive the inhabitants of the papyrus land [i.e., the Delta]."[117] It is the god who has brought victory. The prisoners are his. The smiting of the enemies has a sacrificial character, the character of a ban.[118] This concept is also encountered in ancient Israel (cf. especially 1 Sam 15; Josh 6:17–18). In the psalms, however, this feature is completely lacking. Nowhere

397. "The LORD is at your right hand; he will shatter kings on the day of his wrath. He will execute judgment among the nations, filling them with corpses . . ." (Ps 110:5, 6a).

do we hear of the sacrificing of enemies. Yet, the belief that Yahweh delivers the enemies into the hand of the king continues with undiminished force (Pss 2:8; 110:1).

The Narmer palette may have been dedicated in the temple of Hierakon-polis as a thank offering for the decisive victory of Upper Egypt over the most important Lower Egyptian power. It was intended to perpetuate the king's gratitude, and to secure his own and the falcon god's victorious power. By no means, however, do all representations

of the smiting of enemies have the commemorative functions of the Narmer palette.[119]

With some exceptions, the practice of striking down enemy chieftains was discontinued rather early.[120] Nevertheless, the picture was repeatedly put forward. The view has often been taken that portrayal of the scene in endangered frontier districts like Aswan or the Sinai Peninsula (398) had more a propagandistic than a commemorative character. It was intended to set the might of the Pharaoh before the eyes of tribes greedy for invasion, and thus to drive out all aggressive desires.[121] In fact, however, the pictures were often placed where they could scarcely be seen. To be sure, from the site of the relief of Sekhemkhet (398), one overlooks the entire district of the Wadi Maghara; but the relief itself is very difficult to reach, and it is not visible from the valley.[122]

398. "But God will shatter the heads of his enemies, the hairy crown of him who walks in his guilty ways" (Ps 68:21).

The significance of these representations was not of a psychological-propagandistic nature, as has been thought in modern times. Rather, their function was to make magically present

399. "Your hand will find out all your enemies, your right hand will find out those who hate you" (Ps 21:8).

294

399a. Occasionally, especially in the early period, the king may have slain one or more enemy princes by his own hand (cf. F. Jesi, "Sacrifice humain"). For the most part, however, the scene of the smiting of enemies is to be viewed as a conceptual image, and not as a graphic picture. To "lift the mace" means "to overpower, conquer, take control." This interpretation of the king brandishing the mace makes sense of a representation of Mentuhotep which shows the two heraldic plants of Upper and Lower Egypt in place of cowering Nubians or Asiatics. Mentuhotep, the founder of the Middle Kingdom, did not "smite" the disorders which plagued the Two Lands during the First Intermediate Period; but he did bring those disorders under control.

400. The striking down of enemies, shown on scarabs found in Palestine (a. Beth-Shan, b. Beit Mirsim, c. Tell el-Far'ah).

a   b   c

in threatened territory the irresistible, victorious power of the Egyptian king.[123] This interpretation also accounts for the popularity of the theme. The more frequently the "magical picture" was displayed, the greater grew the Pharaoh's power to defend the land against every attack. This primary function does not exclude the fact that the representations preserve the memory of historical events, flatter the vanity of the ruler, and exercise a discouraging effect on potential invaders.

In representations of the striking down of enemies, the figure of the king underwent few changes in the course of the centuries. At the latter end of the pyramid period, however, a larger group of prisoners takes the place of the single captive.[124] The impression of Chaos is intensified by quantity (399). As is shown in Figs. 142 and 144, there exists in the associative thinking of the ancient Near East a profound relationship between national enemies and the power of Chaos. The old motifs continue in force alongside newer developments (scimitar instead of mace, group of prisoners in-

401. The smiting of an enemy, shown on a small ivory panel from Samaria.

402. Pharaoh Ahmose (1570–1545 B.C.) smiting an enemy.

403. The King of Ugarit (1400–1350 B.C.) strikes down an enemy.

stead of an individual, etc.). The symbolic nature of the motif is especially clear in Figs. *399a* and *132a,* and on a parade sheild from the tomb of Tutankhamun on which the king strikes down two lions instead of the customary enemies.[125]

Onwards from the middle of the second millennium B.C., the motif was diffused—probably through Phoenician mediation—throughout the Mediterranean world. It was not unknown in Palestine.[126] It is shown in miniature on scarabs from Tell el-Far'ah, Beit Mirsim, Lachish, Megiddo, Beth-Shan, and other sites *(400)*. Without exception, the

scimitar has replaced the archaic mace. In addition to scarabs, terra-cotta plaques[127] and ivory carvings *(401)* depicting the king's triumph have been found in Palestine.

In a variation of the motif only rarely attested in Egypt, the Pharaoh does not smite the captive, but *runs him through* instead. This variant is attested by a very carefully worked ivory panel which closely links Canaanite and Egyptian elements in its representation of various aspects of kingship (cf. *383* and *397*).[128] Thus, the Egyptizing portrayal of the king in the psalms may be traced in part to Canaanite mediation. The striking

296

404. "Thou didst give a wide place for my steps under me, and my feet did not slip. I pursued my enemies and overtook them; and did not turn back until they were consumed. I thrust them through, so that they were not able to rise; they fell under my feet. For *thou* didst gird me with strength for the battle; thou didst make my assailants sink under me" (Ps 18:36–39).

down of an enemy is perhaps not entirely foreign to Mesopotamia.[129] There, however, the motif did not achieve the degree of symbolic power and central importance which it did in Egypt. Accordingly, its power to influence larger circles was slight.

In Mesopotamia, the king, as servant of the gods, was never exalted above his environment to the degree characteristic in Egypt from the start. In the oldest important Mesopotamian war scene, the ruler Eannatum is portrayed not as a superhuman, solitary victor, but as a champion at the head of his troops, who are drawn in the same scale as the king

(Plate XVIII). The presence of troops prevails even in monuments from the Akkadian period (2350–2150 B.C.), when the kings who ruled Mesopotamia claimed for themselves a position which is otherwise typical of Egypt. To be sure, on the well-known stele of Naramsin *(Plate XIX)*, the role of the army is limited to admiration of the royal triumph. Nonetheless, the tradition is strong enough to guarantee at least the presence of troops. In Egypt, on the other hand, troops can be entirely absent *(404)* even in the New Kingdom (ca. 1610–1085 B.C.), a period which is otherwise fond of showing the king

405. "Thou didst make my enemies turn their backs to me, and those who hated me I destroyed. They cried for help, but there was none to save, they cried to the LORD, but he did not answer them. I beat them fine as dust before the wind; I cast them out like the mire of the streets" (Ps 18:40–42).

among his troops. In these representations, the king usually stands in his war chariot, a war machine which emerged at the beginning of the 18th Dynasty (ca. 1570–1345 B.C.). Like a god, he enters the tumult of battle (*405* and *Plate XVII*). Not a single enemy dares face him, none dares aim at him. Felled by his arrows, they lie before him, flee in horror, or stretch out their arms to beg for mercy (cf. *132a, 245, 245a*).

The appearance of the Assyrian king on the scene of battle is quite differently portrayed *(Plate XX)*. By way of contrast with the Egyptian king, he does not stand (quite unrealistically) alone in his chariot, but is accompanied by a shield-bearer and a charioteer. We know from literary sources that the Egyptian king also shared his chariot at least with a driver *(ktn)*. Egyptian chariots generally had a two-man crew. But portrayal of the driver would detract from the uniqueness of the king.

The difference between the two portrayals is shown even more clearly in the behavior of the enemies. The appearance of the Egyptian king arouses general panic, and not a one ventures to raise his arm against him. On the Assyrian relief, however, the enemy archers offer fierce resistance. Of course, their courage fails too at the approach of the king (Ps 45:5). The two archers at the far right have mightily drawn their bows, but the middle one seems unable to

298

muster the necessary strength. With a terrified defensive gesture, the one standing next to the king turns to flight. He hopes to avoid the fate of his comrade (under the Assyrian's horses), who is trying to crawl away after having been struck in the back by two arrows. This fourfold sequence demonstrates that resistance must be broken step by step. A real battle is being fought. The appearance of the Egyptian king, on the other hand, puts a sudden stop to all resistance.

A factor beyond the conception of kingship may be involved in the Egyptian representations, for in Egypt there prevailed a decidedly magical view of the picture itself. According to this view, the mere *portrayal* of an archer threatening the king could have dangerous consequences.

In the psalms it is sometimes the king (Ps 18:37–38), sometimes Yahweh (Ps 110:5–6) who shatters *(mḥṣ)* the skulls of his enemies. As a rule, the initiative lies with Yahweh.

In *Plate XX,* the god Assur hovers over the horses who draw the king's chariot. The god draws his bow in tandem with the king. The god, shown small, interprets the action of the king. The king fights as servant and viceroy of the god, under the aegis of the god, and on the god's behalf. The discreet manner of suggesting the deity's participation is striking. The scene is dominated by the historical element. In Egypt (and in Israel—insofar as elements remain unmodified by the adoptive conception), the theological element usually dominates. The *king* triumphs, inasmuch as he himself is god. The deity delivers up lands and peoples to the king, inasmuch as the king is the deity's son (cf. Ps 2 and 332–342).

Plate XXI shows Ramses III smiting his enemies. Opposite him stands Amon, the god of the realm, the scimitar in his hand. Beneath Amon's outstretched arm and beneath the feet of Amon and the king (on the circuits of stone which show the captive host) are inscribed the names of 249 peoples and cities which Ramses is said to have conquered and taken captive in the eighth year of his reign. As indicated in the marginal text, this composition depicts two proceedings: the god presents Pharaoh with the sword of victory (sometimes indicated simply by "victory"). With it the king triumphs over every foreign nation.[130]

This belief is expressed more clearly in *Plate XXII* than in *Plate XXI.* By means of two sets of cords, Amon leads to the Pharaoh five groups of Asiatic captives, thirteen to a row. As in *Plate XXI,* the captives are arranged on circuits of stone. The scene represents the outcome of the Palestinian expedition undertaken by Shishak I circa 925 B.C. (cf. 1 Kgs 14:25–26; 2 Chr 12:2–4). The depiction acknowledges that the cities taken (or more precisely, plundered) in the campaign were the gift of Amon and the district goddess of Thebes (Uaset). She is shown beneath Amon. Like him, she delivers to the king six rows of prisoners representing seventeen cities each. To the right of Amon and Uaset is a group of prisoners about to be struck down by the king. In eight scenes, the cycle of Fig. *405a* unfolds events which are concentrated into a single scene in *Plates XXI* and *XXII.*

The historico-theological concept of the god who delivers enemies into the hand of the king is very ancient (but cf. the discussion of war as "nature," p. 225). On the prehistoric palette shown in Fig. *135,* a goddess (upper right) is apparently delivering a captive enemy nation to the king. On the Narmer palette *(397),* the falcon god delivers up the papyrus land. As in *Plates XXI* and *XXII,* the scene is already connected to the scene of the striking down of enemies.

Magnificent renderings of the theme must have appeared at a very early time. On a relief fragment *(406)* from the pyramid complex of Sahu-Re (ca. 2480 B.C.) are seen the colossal form of the gods Seth (left) and Sopdu (right). Sopdu bears the title "lord of the mountainous foreign lands." With sol-

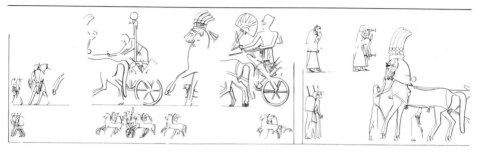

405a. In the Old and Middle Kingdoms, the striking down of enemies was widely used as a symbolic representation of the royal powers of defense and victory. In the New Kingdom, the triumphs of the king are portrayed in series of reliefs. Serial reliefs were already a customary feature of the foundation of a temple and of the royal festival of renewal (Sed festival). These reliefs bear impressive testimony to the fact that war, like all important events, was governed by religious ceremonies.

Upper Register (from right to left): (*a*) Amon, enthroned, presents the scimitar to the Pharaoh in the following words: "Take the sword, my beloved son, in order to strike the heads of the rebellious nations." The presentation of the sword legitimizes the war, and is at the same time a pledge of victory (cf.

297 and O. Keel, *Wirkmächtige Siegeszeichen,* pp. 11–88). (*b*) The king leaves the temple with the scimitar in his right hand, the bow in his left. The standards of four deities are carried before him: first is the standard of the warlike Upaut, "the opener of the way" (cf. *307a*); behind it are those of the Theban triad, Khons, Mut, and Amon (cf. *256a*). With a gesture of blessing, Mont, the god of war, follows the king (cf. *357*). (*c*) The king mounts his chariot to take to the field against the Libyans, who are harassing the western border of Egypt (cf. *381,* which shows this scene in detail). (*d*) The king and his army on march to the front. The king's tame lion is seen between the horses' feet (cf. *103*). The chariot with the standard of Amon (ram's head; cf. *162*) precedes the royal chariot.

emn tread, each leads to the Pharaoh two prisoners tethered on long ropes. The first prisoner (from the left) is an East African from Punt; the second is a Libyan; the fourth is an Asiatic. The third appears to be an Asiatic, but the identification cannot be made with certainty. In any case, we have here repre-

sentatives of the traditional enemies of Egypt. They are represented here not by ideogram (*397*), nor by city and national names (*Plates XXI* and *XXII*), but by racial type (Libyan, Asiatic, etc.). Sahu-Re does not relate the capture of foreign nations by the gods to the smiting-motif, but to the motif of the

300

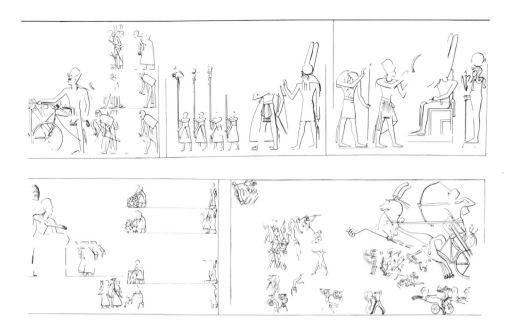

Lower Register (from right to left): *(e)* The concentrated power of the royal steeds stands in sharp contrast to the formless mass of fleeing and dying enemies (cf. *405, Plates XVI, XVII*). Within the mythical-timeless framework of antagonism between cosmos and chaos, the Egyptian army constitutes a narrative-historical element. Mercenary units have caught the Libyans in a pincer movement. This feature, however, carries little visual weight. *(f)* After the battle, the king addresses his officials and officers who are marshalled before an Egyptian citadel. His praise is less of their courage than of what *Amon-Re* has done for *him* in letting him appear before the enemy as a god. The army responds: "Happy is the heart of Egypt for ever, for its protector has a strong arm. . . ."

The severed hands and penises of the foe are piled in heaps before the king. The Libyans taken alive are brought bound before him. *(g)* The king returns to Thebes with the prisoners (between the feet of the horses) and his army. *(h)* The prisoners are delivered as temple slaves to Amon and his consort Mut. The king addresses them: "How powerful is that which you have done, lord of the gods; your thoughts and plans succeed, for it is you who have sent me forth in power. Your sword was with me . . ." (a translation of the texts accompanying these scenes exists in W. F. Edgerton and J. A. Wilson, *Historical Records,* pp. 4–19). Not all war cycles exhibit such intense theological and liturgical ramifications, but religious implications are never entirely lacking.

king as a lion (as in the battle scene of Fig. *135*) or lion-griffin (Sahu-Re) who annihilates the enemy.[131]

The representation of the city god of Lagash *(110)* is closely related to the preceding ones. He holds captive in a net the enemies of "his" king and slays them with the mace. A stele of Asarhad-don (680–669 B.C.; *407*) is an example of the motif of enemies led by a *rope*. The two enemies are Abdimilkutti of Sidon (or Ba'lu of Tyre) (standing) and the Nubian Pharaoh Usanahuru (kneeling) or his father Tirhaka, mentioned in the OT (2 Kgs 19:9; Isa 37:9). The king holds in his hand the mace, as did the

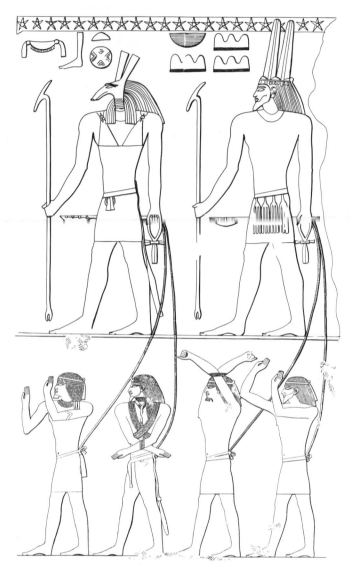

406. "The kings of the earth set themselves, and the rulers take counsel together, against the LORD and his anointed, saying, 'Let us burst their bonds asunder, and cast their cords from us.' He who sits in the heavens laughs; the LORD has them in derision" (Ps 2:2–4).

city god of Lagash in the representation made some 2,000 years earlier. Though it is the king who leads the enemy rulers captive and brandishes the mace, still the stele acknowledges the victory as the work of the gods. Asarhaddon raises the "cup of salvation" (Ps 116:13; cf. *Plates XXIII, XXVI,* and *444*) to the emblems of the gods (above, from left to right: seven stars, Assur, the queen of heaven, Sin, Shamash, an unidentifiable male deity, Adad, the star of Ishtar, Marduk, Nabu, Ea, Ninurta). The inscription, "which passes around the picture and continues on the obverse side, concludes with an instruction to anoint the memorial stone with oil and to give praise to the god Assur."[132]

In Egypt, god and king work together on the same plane, so to speak. In Mesopotamia, however, the two spheres are more sharply separated. Either it is the god who destroys the adversaries with net and mace (110), or it is the king who holds them in check with mace and rope. To be sure, the deity can act for the king, or the king can act with the aid of the gods. Yet, the two operate on different planes.

The pattern of the great Egyptian representations is found in Ps 2:8–9: Yahweh delivers the nations to the king, and the king dashes them in pieces like a potter's vessel. The chains with which the enemies are bound in Ps 2:2–3 are simultaneously Yahweh's and the king's. An unusual reversal of roles is found in Ps 149:8. There, in the eschatological day of salvation, Yahweh's faithful, at Yahweh's command, bind the kings of the earth in chains.

In addition to setting forth the inevitable triumph of the king on Zion, Ps 2 offers the kings and judges of the earth a means of escaping the threat of chains and execution: submission to Yahweh and his anointed. Homage (Pss 2:11–12; 18:44–45; 72:9, 11) and tribute (Ps 72:10; cf. 45:12; 68:29) are tokens of submission.

The title "king" was transferred to Yahweh. So was the hope that one day all peoples, laden with gifts, would come to do him homage (Ps 22:27; 47:9; 86:9; 96:7–10). In Egyptian burial chambers there are often scenes of neighboring peoples from near and far, appearing in long lines before the king or high officials to deliver their tribute. A group of Asiatics is shown in Fig. 408. The first three do homage; the others bear a quiver and vessels typical to Syria (and Crete). A child is also brought as tribute (cf. 132a, 270). The man with the oil-horn in Fig. 344 also belongs to this group. In Fig. 409, it is the Nubians, Egypt's southern neighbors, who approach with their treasures. Two of them bear plates with gold rings; two carry sacks filled to the brim with gold dust. Except for the third, over whose arm is draped a panther hide, each also bears two fronds. A young giraffe has been brought for the royal zoo.

An extraordinarily packed scene from Amarna (410) depicts delivery of the annual tribute by the southern (right) and northern (left) nations. The colossal figure of Amenophis IV (1377–1358 B.C.) is enthroned in the center, under a richly adorned baldachin. His queen, who is almost hidden by him, is at his side. Six naked princesses stand behind the couple. Almost three fourths of the register beneath the kiosk is taken up by the royal couple's chariots, litters, and the attendant personnel. Beneath them

407. ". . . to bind their kings with chains and their nobles with fetters of iron, to execute on them the judgment written! This is glory for all his faithful ones" (Ps 149:8–9).

408. "May those who dwell in the wilderness [east] bow down before him, and his enemies lick the dust! May the kings of Tarshish and of the isles [west] render him tribute . . . ." (Ps 72:9, 10a RSVm).

are seen the soldiers of the bodyguard, in a humble, bowed attitude (cf. 282). The outermost (left) quarter of the three lower registers is occupied, from top to bottom, by the Punt-people (Somaliland?); desert-dwellers, who have nothing to offer but ostrich plumes and eggs; and Cretans (or Hittites?). The Negroid peoples of the south (right of the kiosk) approach in a frenzy of motion, performing wrestling matches and joyful dances before the king; the Semitic peoples of the north (left of the king) approach in measured procession.

The most important gift of the southern peoples is gold (first, second, and third registers from the top); the north-ern peoples primarily bring weapons, chariots, horses, and vessels (first, second, and third registers from the top). Both sides also bring slaves (rebellious subjects?). Tame animals for the royal zoo are also seen on both sides.

The joyous dances of the Negroes indicate that the delivery of tribute was not so sad an occasion as one might think. The Pharaoh did not send the tribute-bearers home empty-handed. Furthermore, Egyptian sovereignty was capable of checking the never-ending feuds among the disunited city-states and tribes.

Some scholars doubt that these scenes are in fact concerned with the delivery of

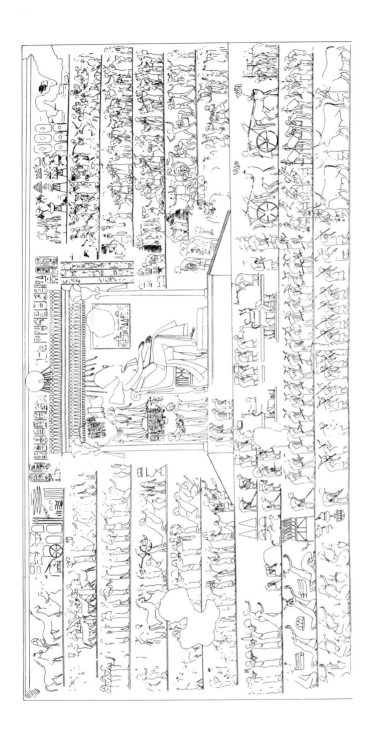

410. ". . . thou didst make me the head of the nations; people whom I had not known served me. As soon as they heard of me they obeyed me; foreigners came cringing to me" (Ps 18:43b, 44).

409. ". . . may the kings of Sheba and Seba [south] bring gifts! May all kings fall down before him, all nations serve him! For he delivers the needy when he calls, the poor and him who has no helper. He has pity on the weak and the needy, and saves the arms of the needy. From oppression and violence he redeems their life; and precious is their blood in his sight. Long may he live, may gold of Sheba be given to him! May prayer be made for him continually, and blessings invoked for him all the day!" (Ps 72:10b–15).

tribute.[133] In any event, it is probably best not to insist on the term "tribute" in interpreting these pictures. They seem to differentiate no more than does the Egyptian language between trading goods, occasional presents on special occasions (accession to the throne, New Year), and forced imposts (cf. p. 284).

In survey, it appears that in the ancient Near East there was eager expectation of a future time of salvation under the dominion of a powerful and righteous king whose beneficial sovereignty would encompass the entire world, excluding any further war. Within this general hope, Israelite expectation took a specific turn by stressing the importance of ethics—particularly concern for the poor and the weak (Ps 72!). The prophets, who acutely perceived the difficulty of maintaining a consistent ethical posture, added to this expectation the good news of a new creation of the human heart (cf. Ps 51:10–11). In the absence of this new disposition, which is to be effected solely by God, the prophets envision no possibility of an authentic time of salvation. This expectation of a radical, new intervention by God opened the way to authentic eschatological thinking, which is not content with the hope of the return of what has been, but is open to entirely new and unexpected horizons.[134]

306

CHAPTER VI

MAN BEFORE GOD

Body-soul dualism is unknown in biblical anthropology. Man has no existence without his body; man has no inner nature that is not expressed (cf. pp. 8–9).[1] Psychological concepts usually characterize parts of the body or particular features closely linked to these parts of the body. Thus, *npš* means throat, breathing, living being, life, desire; *'p* means nose, snorting, anger; *rḥm* means womb, and in the plural, compassion; *kbwd* means weight, (impressive) appearance, splendor, distinction; *g'wn* means height, loftiness, pride. In view of this tendency, it is not surprising that the (inner) relation of man to God is also viewed in terms of distinct manifestations and fixed postures, gestures, and actions.[2]

1. ATTITUDES OF PRAYER

a. *The Encounter with the Holy*

One of the most important of the verbs pertaining to the realm of prayer is the hithpael of *šḥh*. Though it appears to define only an exterior attitude, it provides at the same time a significant definition of the interior attitude of the Israelite suppliant.[3] It means "to prostrate oneself." It presupposes the experience of the holy. Religion does not begin with man's need and longing for something holy and absolute, as is so often assumed today. For us, religion may consist largely of yearning, because to us it is primarily a matter of remembrance. But that was not always so. In the tradition of Israel, religion manifestly begins with God's appearance and Israel's beholding of him. That may also be correct from a religious-historical point of view. One saw God in his deliverance of the nation from Egypt (Ps 95:5) and in his rescue of the individual from sundry plights (Pss 69:32; 107:24); one saw God in observing the night sky (Ps 8:3) and the cult in the temple at Jerusalem (Pss 48:8; 68:24). Man's entire religious activity is ultimately directed toward no other end than seeing God again and ever again (Pss 27:13; 63:2). The Sumerians of the Early Dynastic Period II furnished their portrait effigies with over-sized eyes. These were emplaced before the images of the gods so that no visible aspect of the divine splendor might elude them *(411)*.

411. "So I have looked upon thee in the sanctuary, beholding thy power and glory" (Ps 63:2).

A number of very different, intense experiences can be characterized as "seeing God." As is demonstrated by a passage from the story of Sinuhe and from other accounts, proskynesis was originally the spontaneous response to an *overwhelming* experience of the holy (cf. Pss 29:2; 96:9).

After a long sojourn in miserable Asia, the Egyptian Sinuhe was granted an audience with the Pharaoh. What he experienced in that audience is tantamount to a theophany:

"I found his majesty upon the Great Throne in a *recess* of fine gold. When I was stretched out upon my belly, I knew not myself in his presence, (although) this god greeted me pleasantly. I was like a man caught in the dark: my soul departed, my body was powerless, my heart was not in my body, that I might know life from death.

"THEN HIS MAJESTY SAID TO ONE OF THESE COURTIERS: 'Lift him up. Let him speak to me.' Then his majesty said: 'Behold, thou art come. Thou hast trodden the foreign countries *and made a flight. . . .*'" Sinuhe then answered: "'BEHOLD, I AM BEFORE THEE, THINE IS LIFE. MAY THY MAJESTY DO AS HE PLEASES.'"[4] (On the proskynesis before the king, cf. Pss 45:11; 72:11.)

A very similar scene takes place when the angel Gabriel appears to explain to Daniel the vision of the ram and the goat:

412. "O come, let us worship and bow down, let us kneel before the LORD, our Maker!" (Ps 95:6). "Bow down to Yahweh when the Holy One appears" (Ps 29:2b; 96:9a [translation by M. Dahood]).

309

413. "I bow down toward thy holy temple and give thanks to thy name . . ." (Ps 138:2).

"So he came near where I stood; and when he came, I was frightened and fell upon my face. . . . As he was speaking, I fell into a deep sleep with my face to the ground; but he touched me and set me on my feet" (Dan 8:17–18).

Proskynesis is at base a fear-response. Faced with the overpowering experience of the holy, man escapes into death. Regarded thus, falling down is equivalent to the death-feigning reflex well-known to behavioral research. Scripture formulates this response in terms of the famous maxim: No man can see God and live (cf. Exod 24:11; 33:22; Deut 4:33; Judg 13:22). Should a man live nonetheless, it is only due to the grace of God. In the two examples cited, being lifted up is an integral part of what takes place. When proskynesis pales into a conventional gesture, it becomes a gesture of greeting. It has the character of a *rite de passage*. It represents the passage from profane life into life before God or the king. Between the two spheres lies the weak swoon, "death." The prohibition of proskynesis before any god but Yahweh (Ps 81:9; 106:19) does not preclude certain civilities, but it does prohibit Israel from seeking the ultimate ground of its being anywhere but in Yahweh.

The gods (Pss 29:2; 96:6; 97:7), the Israelites (Pss 95:6; 132:7), and all nations (Pss 22:27, 29; 66:4; 89:8) have reason to bow down before Yahweh, for he subdued the waters of Chaos, established the earth, and created mankind. In some of the psalms, proskynesis is understood as the appropriate expression of creaturely feeling (Ps 95:6). Man is dust (Ps 103:14; Gen 18:27) animated by God (Gen 2:7). In the presence of the majesty of God, man is acutely aware of that fact, and he gives spontaneous expression to this consciousness by approaching Yahweh in fear and trembling (Pss 2:11; 5:7), falling down in the dust before him.

In the daily veneration of the divine images, the Egyptian touches the earth with his nose (*sn t*}) and lies on his belly (*rdjt ḥr ḫt*).[5] "The Sumerian Patesi Gudea prostrates himself (*ka-šu-gál*) in the temple before prayer. The words *ka* and *šu* indicate that in doing so, his mouth and hands touch the earth. In bilingual versions, this expression is regularly rendered as *labânu appa,* 'to make the nose flat.'"[6]

Fig. *412* (cf. *408*) nicely illustrates the Egyptian manner of kneeling, then throwing oneself down on the hands, at the same time keeping one knee drawn up (*413*) in order to facilitate rising. Proskynesis is not a sustained posture, especially not in daily practice. For a

414. "Blessed be he who enters in the name of the LORD!" (Ps 118:26a).

moment, man may perceive himself to be dust. Yet, he knows that by the grace of the deity he need not remain in that state.

As is shown in *Plate XXIII*, proskynesis was also known in Mesopotamia, but it appears less often in Mesopotamian iconography than it does in Egyptian. Sumer and Babylonia, on the one hand, and Assyria on the other, discovered their own respective forms for expressing and overcoming the sense of remoteness. The typical form in southern Mesopotamia is the introduction scene. A priest *(239)* or lesser deity *(414;* cf. also *272, 426)* leads the worshipper before the enthroned god. The suppliant dare not come alone nor speak.[7] He only raises his hand in greeting, as do the god and goddess conducting him. In return, the god on the throne lifts his forearm only slightly. The arms of the goddess

and the bald worshipper are sharply inclined. One sees the palm of the goddess's hand, since she has raised her left. The back of the suppliant's hand is seen, for he greets with his right. The statue in Fig. *436* shows the gesture clearly. The uplifted hand may be an expression of joyous excitement, of good will, and of blessing. Parrot[8] believes that the raised hand might also be intended to draw attention to the worshipper or to help carry the voice of his supplication to the divine throne. The latter is improbable, since the raised hand is not part of a prayer ritual, but is instead a greeting ritual typical to the iconography of scenes of introduction.

The fingers of the Babylonian worshipper's right hand *(420)* are positioned in a manner noticeably different from that of the Sumerian suppliant *(414, 426)*. The thumb and index finger are ex-

415. "But I through the abundance of thy steadfast love will enter thy house" (Ps 5:7).

416. The characteristic Egyptian attitude of prayer (arms raised, palms turned forward) is also found on this Egyptizing stele from Balu‘a in Transjordan (cf. *421*).

417. Prehistoric rock drawing from the vicinity of Aswan, showing a snake-charming.

tended, while the three remaining fingers are bent. The man is apparently about to kiss his outstretched finger, then throw the kiss to the god. R. Dussaud[9] regards the bowing of the knee and the throwing of kisses as gestures of prayer particularly typical to Syria-Palestine (cf. Job 31:27; 1 Kgs 19:18). The bronze statue of Fig. *420* is dedicated to the god Amurru, who penetrated into Babylon from Syria.

In blowing a kiss, one simultaneously

offers to the deity one's life's breath.[10] One's "soul" is lifted up to the deity, expressing the confidence that God will not let it be brought to shame (cf. Ps 25:1–2). Thus, it is not a gesture of sheer enthusiasm and veneration, as Job 31:27 gives to understand. The inscription on Fig. *420* describes the person represented as "suppliant."[11]

The cylinder seals of Figs. *272* and *414* indicate that the gesture of the raised hand was also known in the Canaanite sphere. The figure shown in Fig. *415* is from Hazor, in northern Palestine. In typical Mesopotamian fashion, he holds *one* hand raised. The position of the flat of the hand, however, is Egyptian. The posture of the Transjordanian prince on the Balu'a stele *(416)* is typically Egyptian. In other respects, the stele presents a curious mixture of local (headdress, profile and beard of the ruler, sun and moon symbols over his shoulders) and Egyptian (costume of the prince and costume and attributes of the two deities) influences. The characteristically Egyptian attitude

417a. "Look away from me . . ." (Ps 39:13).

The prisoner at the left attempts to ward off the Pharaoh's threatening might with the ancient gesture of two extended fingers (H. Schäfer, "Abwehren"); the prisoner at the right attempts to stave off disaster with upraised arms. The two gestures are parallel. A

passage from Amon's promise of victory to Thut-mose III attests the apotropaic effect of upraised arms: "The arms of your majesty are raised to ward off evil" ('*wj ḥm.ỉ ḥr ḥrt ḥr sḥrỉ ḏwt;* A. Erman, *Literatur,* p. 322; cf. Exod 17:8–13).

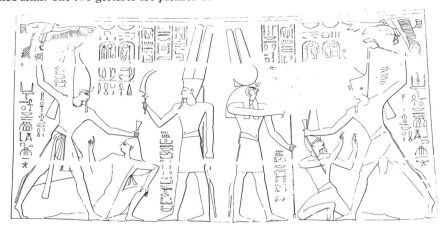

of prayer, arms raised with the palms forward (cf. *422*), may originally have had an exorcistic character *(417)*. Subsequently, depending on the circumstances, it developed a defensive, aversive significance *(417a, 103)* or a sense of protection, blessing, and praise *(132a, 256a, 262)*. The word designated by the gesture *i}w* can be rendered not only as "praise," but also as "salvation, blessing." Similarly, the Hebrew *b*e*rākāh* can mean not only "blessing," but also "praise" (cf. *eulogia* and *benedictio*). The gesture of raised arms with palms forward is as appropriate to aversion as to veneration. In the final analysis, it expresses the attempt to restrain a superior, numinous opposite by means of conjuring, thus rendering it serviceable or averting it. To the knowledge of the present writer, there is no basis in archaic iconography for deriving the gesture from a warrior's laying down of his arms in order to demonstrate the peaceful intention of his approach. Such an interpretation does nothing to explain the later use of the gesture as a sign of veneration and protection.

Strangely, words such as *tw}*, "to ask," and similar terms are also determined by the gesture of the raised hands. After all,

the goal of asking is receiving, for which palms turned inward is more appropriate *(Plate XXIV, 430)*. The Egyptian usage may be explained, however, by the fact that only rarely and by way of exception did the Egyptian approach his god with direct requests. As a rule, the Egyptian comes before his god with praise and blessing (cf. *132a*), even when he comes with petitionary intention. Only in a concise, concluding statement does he mention the end to which he has conjured up all of the numen's good attributes. Therefore, even in requesting the Egyptian stands before his god in an attitude of praise.[12]

The peculiar Assyrian gesture of the extended index finger *(418)* may have a significance similar to the Egyptian gesture of the raised hands. Schmoekel and others invest it with apotropaic significance.[13] Almost certainly, the extended finger of the figure at the right in Fig. *419* is intended to ward off the Chaos monster. In a prayer to the god Assur, the king complains of the machinations of his enemies: "In order to scatter the troops of Assur they extended their evil finger."[14]

Like the raised hands in Egypt, the Assyrian gesture may not have been of an

418. "Serve the Lord with fear . . ." (Ps 2:11).

419. The extended index finger may originally have been a conjuring gesture.

exclusively apotropaic character. Otherwise it would be difficult to understand its transformation into a gesture of greeting and prayer. It seems originally to have been credited with conjuring power in a general sense.[15]

The raised hands of the Egyptians and the extended index finger of the Assyrians appear to have primarily accompanied greetings of the deity and particularly active moments of the liturgy (cf. chap. 6.1.b). The twofold representation of Tukulti-Ninurta in Fig. *418* indicates that here, in any case, a *process* is involved. Index finger extended, the king approaches the symbol of Nusku-Nabu (a writing tablet with stylus[16]) and sits on his haunches before it.

It is noteworthy that Sumerian-Babylonian-Syrian suppliants, whose gestures seem so human, usually appear before the *deity* himself *(239, 272, 390, 414, 426)*, whereas Assyrian suppliants, especially those of the Middle and Neo-Assyrian periods (in instances where Babylonian influence had not grown too strong) are shown standing before the *symbol* of the deity *(23, 24, 407, 440)*. One can commend this Assyrian peculiarity as an expression of the sense of the deity's transcendence. The same facts can be construed, however, as a kind of fetishism (cf. the transcendence of God and sacramentalism in the priestly writings). In any event, the Assyrians had less human, intimate relations with the deity than did their neighbors to the south and west. Their preference in temple construction for the long-house with a high podium tends to

confirm this impression *(217)*.[17] In this context, the gesture of the extended finger conforms rather well to the interpretation adopted above.

b. Thanks and Praise

The gestures discussed thus far have been more or less exclusively gestures of first encounter with the holy. Kneeling, sitting, and standing are potential postures for longer tarrying in the deity's presence. The position of the hands is thus no longer so important. Fig. *421*, which shows the two knees in different positions, is reminiscent of proskynesis *(412–13)*, but the erect torso and the confidently raised head make known the god who raises man from the dust (Ps 113:7) and lifts up man's head (Ps 3:3).

Fig. *422*, like Fig. *418*, shows the suppliant sitting on his haunches. When he also places his hands on his knees, *(423)*, the position may be more accurately described as squatting. According to 2 Sam 7:18 (cf. 1 Chr 17:16), David entered the temple, sat before Yahweh, and uttered a humble, confident prayer (2 Sam 7:18–20, 25–29). "He sat" (*wyšb*) could describe the squatting posture shown in Fig. *423*. An Assyrian text which describes this posture treats it as sitting:

> Kneeling, Assurbanipal *sits* on his shanks, addresses himself repeatedly to his lord Nabu:
> 'I have grown to love you, Nabu. . .'[18]

As king, however, David could also have simply sat before God. It was a privilege of priests and high-ranking personages to sit in the presence of the deity *(424; cf. 167;* Ps 84:4 ["dwell" = "sit"]). The Sumerian ideogram for temple actually means "house of sitting for the priests."[19] Of course, "to sit" can mean "to dwell". Conversely, "dwelling" includes "sitting." The desire to be permitted to sit or to dwell in the temple (Ps 27:4) expresses the longing for an intimate relation with Yahweh and for participation in his glory. Standing before the (seated) deity expresses a very different relation between god and man. Like "sitting,"

420. "To thee, O LORD, I lift up my soul. O my God, in thee I trust" (Ps 25:1, 2a).

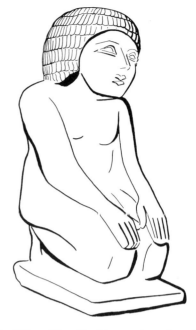

423. "Then King David went in and sat before the LORD and said: 'Who am I, Lord GOD, and who are the members of my house, that you have brought me to this point? Yet even this you see as too little, Lord GOD; you have also spoken of the house of your servant for a long time to come: this too you have shown to man, Lord GOD! What more can David say to you? You know your servant, Lord GOD!" (2 Sam 7:18–20 NAB).

"standing" also signifies more than the external attitude of the body. He who stands before the king (1 Kgs 1:2 KJV; 10:8) or before Yahweh (1 Kgs 17:1; Jer 7:10) is his servant.

Pss 134:1 and 135:2 mention those "who stand in the house of the LORD." The context makes it clear that the intended reference is to the priests and Levites who do service in the temple. "To stand" means "to be ready" to respond instantly to every inclination of the king (or the god) and to fulfill his wishes. In Israel's later history, God's will as expressed in the Torah became more and more *the* determinative of Is-

421. "Bless the LORD, O my soul; and all that is within me bless his holy name!" (Ps 103:1).

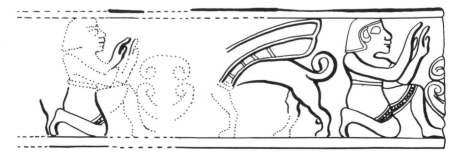

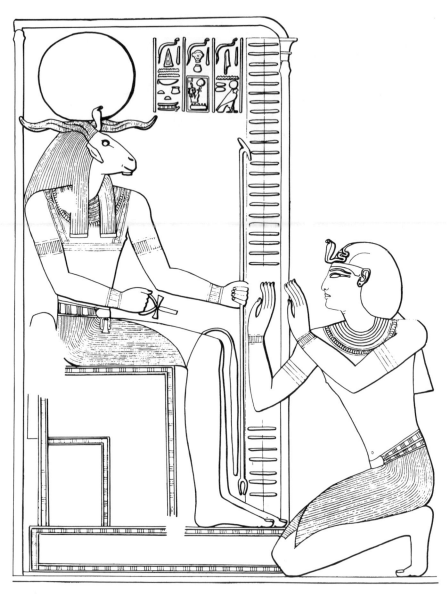

422. "Lift up your hands to the holy place,
and bless the LORD!" (Ps 134:2).

rael's experience of God. Therefore,
"standing" as it related to this experience
became the expression for divine service
in general. It could be said, even of
kneeling worshippers, that "they stood
up" (Neh 9:2–3; 1 Kgs 8:22, 54).[20]

In Egypt, the arms were held at the
side while standing (425), an attitude
equally expressive of passivity and read-

iness. In Sumer, the hands were generally folded (427), whether sitting (cf.
424) or standing (426). This gesture
produces an impression of recollection
and concentration. It represents a kind
of self-containment.

Because the magical effect of folding
the hands causes every activity to cease,
the huge eyes of the suppliant figures are

316

riveted on the divine effigy (cf. *411*). A beautiful personal name meaning "My eyes (are fixed) on Yahweh" occurs twice in postexilic texts (Ezra 10:22, 27 [Elioenai]; 1 Chr 26:3 [Elihoenai]; cf. 1 Chr 8:20 [Elienai]). The name may have been borrowed from Babylon, where names of the form *Itti-šamaš-înija* ("My eyes [are] with Shamash") occur with frequency: the names of other gods can appear in place of Shamash. Certain psalm verses are reminiscent of these Babylonian personal names: "My eyes are ever [directed] toward the LORD" (Ps 25:15); or "to thee I lift up my eyes, O thou who art enthroned in the heavens!" (Ps 123:1; cf. 121:1; 141:8).

424. "Blessed are those who dwell [sit] in thy house . . ." (Ps 84:4).

426. "Standing expresses deliberate passivity and willingness to serve" (F. Heiler, "Körperhaltungen," p. 176).

427. Folded hands represent a kind of self-binding. The suppliant surrenders himself to the deity, in the hope that the deity will guide his fortune for the good.

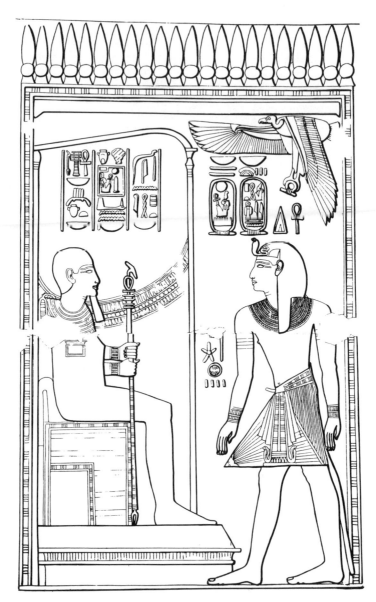

425. "Come, bless the LORD, all you servants of the LORD, who stand by night in the
house of the LORD!" (Ps 134:1).

The continuation of these verses, indicates, however, that it is not so much a
matter of contemplative-visionary *beholding* (as in Pss 17:15; 27:4, 13; 63:2) as of
a searching, imploring seeking-out. This
brings us to the third group of postures
for prayer.

c. Lamentation and Petition

The lamentation is found in its pure
form in the Qinah, the dirge (cf., e.g., 2
Sam 1:17–27; 3:33), which is arranged
according to the following pattern:
formerly everything was good; now all is
lost. This "lostness" is evident in a long

318

series of very specific gestures and postures: one crouched on the ground, threw dust on the head, rent the clothes, donned coarse apparel, abstained from nourishment (Pss 35:13–14; 69:10–11). In short, one imparted form to interior desolation and despair. The Egyptian female mourners of Fig. *428* cower on the ground, throw dust over themselves (?), hold their heads, and wail (as indicated by the half-opened mouths). There are manifold forms of expression in lamentation, corresponding to the chaotic emotions of grief and anguish.[21]

The pattern, "formerly everything was good; now all is lost," is also found in the psalms. There, however, it is always supplemented by the motif of confidence and petition. Thus, in Ps 89:19–37 Yahweh's gracious acts and promises to David are rehearsed in detail. Verses 38–45 then establish that with the fall of the Judaic monarchy, all this is lost. A dirge would end here. But in a concluding section, the psalmist asks Yahweh to remember his saving acts of old and to put an end to the malicious joy of the neighboring peoples.

In Fig. *428,* the cry for deliverance is suggested only by a helplessly outstretched arm. The composition of Fig. *429* creates a more powerful impression of need. There, lying on the ground is not an expression of creaturely feeling, as is the case in spontaneous proskynesis, nor is it a pointless expression of grief

428. "I went about as one who laments his mother, bowed down and in mourning" (Ps 35:14).

429. "Why dost thou hide thy face? . . . For our soul is bowed down to the dust; our body cleaves to the ground" (Ps 44:24a, 25).

and powerlessness, as in the pure lament. Its purpose is rather to manifest distress in order to establish a request (cf. Pss 7:5; 44:25; 119:25). As in Ps 89, the lamentation and its forms of expression are subordinated to the petition.

Lying on the back, as opposed to the stomach, appears nowhere as a simple expression of distress or of being overcome (proskynesis). Rather, it is the conscious expression of dependency and submission. One presents to the object of one's supplication the most vulnerable parts of the body (face, belly), thus exposing oneself in an attitude of utter defenselessness. Recognition of his own utter superiority is intended favorably to dispose the party entreated. It is no accident that the practice of lying on the back is attested in the Amarna letters,[22] which are brimful of requests.

The starving Asiatic and Libyan nomads of Fig. 429 apply to an Egyptian official for admission as protected aliens. So too, the suppliants of Pss 39:12 and

430. "Behold, as the eyes of servants look to the hand of their master, as the eyes of a maid to the hand of her mistress, so our eyes look to the LORD our God, till he have mercy upon us" (Ps 123:2).

119:19 turn to Yahweh as foreigners seeking protection. The attitude of total subservience, however, is foreign to the psalms. The Jewish inhabitants of Lachish *(Plate XXIV)* are in an even worse predicament than the Asiatics of Fig. *429,* "who know not how they may live."[23] They defied Sennacherib (upper right), king of the Assyrians, in the course of a long siege. Now they are led captive before the victor. In his presence, they fall on their knees, and finally (because they can no longer hold themselves erect?) fall completely to the ground (figure above the two kneeling figures). Their lives are forfeit. They are nothing but dust, ready to surrender the last spark of life to the king in hopes of receiving it from him anew. "Into thy hand I commit my spirit" (Ps 31:5). "Gladden the soul [life] of thy servant, for to thee, O Lord, do I lift up my soul [life]" (Ps 86:4; cf. 25:1; 143:8).

Unlike the suppliant of Fig. *420* (who throws a kiss), they do not put their lives in the king's hands out of trust in him. It is because no other way is left for them to preserve their lives. Only reluctantly, imploringly do they relinquish it. The two kneeling figures in particular are supplication personified. Their attitude is characterized by anxiety as well as entreaty. This fear may explain why their upper arms are held close to the body and not outstretched as might be expected for a gesture of entreaty (cf. such passages as Pss 28:2; 88:9; 143:6; 1 Kgs 8:54; and Fig. *429*). The Assyrian artist denies the Judeans the confidence necessary to voice their requests with hands outstretched. After all, they have rebelled against the king, and must plead their cause in repentance and contrition.

We have attempted above to explain why the palms of the hands were turned outwards in Egypt, even in petitionary prayer (cf. *429*). Palms turned inward are much more appropriate to petition, which is directed toward receiving. This is demonstrated by *Plate XXIV* and Fig.

431. "To thee, O LORD, I call; my rock, be not deaf to me, lest, if thou be silent to me, I become like those who go down to the Pit. Hear the voice of my supplication, as I cry to thee for help, as I lift up my hands to thy most holy sanctuary" (Ps 28:1–2; cf. 88:9; 143:6).

432. The inscription reads: "Lord Helios, because you rise as one who makes right, that one who insidiously laid snares for Kalliope ought not to escape you; no, send to him the sighs of those who have lost their life by violence. Kalliope the noble died at age 28" (F. Cumont, "Invocation au soleil," p. 393).

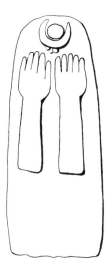

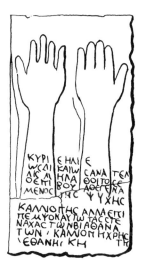

430. In Fig. 430, an Assyrian overseer distributes rations to two prisoners of war. They look expectantly toward his hand, while their own hand rises, as of its own volition, to receive (cf. Pss 104:27–28; 123:1–2; 145:15–16).

Quite apart from the position of the palms, the outstretched arms in Fig. 431 appear as a symbol for fervent prayer. The addressee of this prayer is an astral symbol, apparently the crescent moon with the sun disc or a sun-symbol on a kind of socle (cf. 416). The hands are extended in petitionary prayer because the suppliant finds himself in need. That means (as shown in chaps. 1 and 2) "in the depths" (Ps 130:1), whereas the deity is enthroned above (in heaven; in the holy of holies) (cf. Ps 22:3, 6). It is not particularly important whether the suppliant hopes to receive something in his outstretched hands or to be pulled up from the depths (cf. 245).[24] His primary object is contact with the living god, whatever concrete form that contact may take.[25]

In Fig. 432, the deity is called upon to manifest himself in the restoration of right order. The murderous sorcerer who has the life of young Kalliope on his conscience must not go unpunished.[26] The prayer is addressed to the sun god because in Anterior Asia he was an-ciently regarded as the omniscient, righteous judge (cf. 286). In the last analysis, his popularity is in part attributable to the fact that he is everywhere visible. The shepherd on the steppes, the caravaneers, the hunter in the mountains, the sailors on the sea, and even the wandering dead (who died by violence or were denied decent burial)—all lift up their hands to Shamash.[27]

The attempt to achieve contact with the deity also serves to explain the intention of the prayer. To the psalmists, God is not indeterminately omnipresent. He dwells in the temple, or in heaven. Therefore one lifts up one's hands toward the sanctuary (Ps 28:2; 1 Kgs 8:38, 48) or lifts up one's eyes (Ps 123:1) or hands toward heaven (1 Kgs 8:54). To do so, one need not be present at the sanctuary.[28] It can be done at sea, in the wilderness, in prison, or from the sick-bed (Ps 107; for an example of the latter instance, cf. 91 and Plate III). In far-off Babylon, Daniel prays toward Jerusalem (Dan 6:10). In doing so, he opens the window to facilitate contact.

Most of the pictures used to illustrate bodily postures in lamentation and entreaty have not shown a "man at prayer." But that is insignificant. In the presence of the king or a high official, one assumed the same posture as one did be-

433. "As a hart [or hind] longs for flowing streams, so longs my soul for thee, O God. My soul thirsts for God, for the living God" (Ps 42:1, 2a).

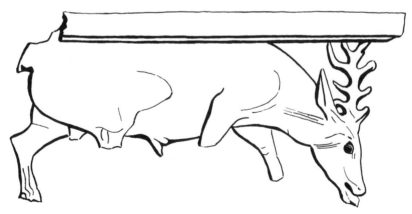

fore the deity; and especially in the cultus, the deity was generally understood by analogy to the king.

Figs. *431* and *432* are particularly demonstrative of the distance to be overcome in lamentation and petition. Lamentation and petition presuppose remoteness from something experienced. Only the hands, which formerly warded off the approach of the holy, can reach out in longing toward it. God is no more a product of necessity and longing than the sanctuary at Jerusalem, yearned for by the suppliant of Ps 42. The suppliant's desire is grounded in the rec-

ollection of blissful hours spent there (Ps 42:4). The depths of his longing are expressed not by a gesture, but by a simile. Just as the deer, parched with thirst in the dry summer, drag themselves with heavy head and hanging tongue over the barren hills, even so the suppliant of Ps 43:2–3 longs for the living God. In Ugarit, the thirst of the deer for water was proverbial.[29]

In the presence of such longing, great and joyous excitement was aroused by the cry, "Let us go to the house of the LORD" (Ps 122:1).

2. PROCESSIONS AND THE SACRIFICIAL CULT

Sacral processions are repeatedly alluded to in the psalms. There are at least two important types to be distinguished: the procession in which Yahweh himself participates (Pss 24:7–10; 47:5; 68:18, 24–25; 132); and the pilgrimage or simple temple visit, in which the people solemnly advance to the sanctuary (Pss 24:3–5; 84:7; 118; 122). There is talk of "going up" not only in the second type of procession (Ps 122:4) (which suggests the actual and cultic-mythological location of the temple on a mountain; cf. chap. 3.1), but also in the first (Pss 47:5; 68:18). Consequently, the transfer of the Ark to Zion obtrudes as the prototype of this kind of Yahweh procession. In Egypt, where the temple was regarded as an entity extant from the foundation of the world, one spoke on such occasions of the going out *(pr.t)* or epiphany of the deity *(ḫ'j)*. The essential feature was exit from the temple *(162, 433a, 434)*. The people had to "be made certain of their god. He who is otherwise remote from the laity, dwelling in the holy of holies, 'appears.' The faithful see 'the beauty of their lord,' become witnesses of his

glory, and experience his blessed nearness"[30] (cf. *307a, 450*).

Just as in Egypt, all kinds of cult symbols represented the deity, so too in Jerusalem the Ark may have mediated the nearness of God *(434, 434a)*. But in Jerusalem the entire process is characteristically linked with history (2 Sam 6:13–20). Yahweh was not always present there. He moved to Zion. His presence is not self-evident by nature (cf. p. 120). By analogy with Babylonian-Canaanite enthronement festivals, the "going up" may have been understood secondarily as a triumphant, victorious procession. As such, the victory over rival gods (e.g., those of the Philistines in 1 Sam 5) and hostile peoples is to some extent superseded by motifs from the battle against Chaos (cf. *45, 240*).

Visits to the temple by larger or smaller groups are to be distinguished from the Yahweh processions. These groups go to the temple because of Israel's statutory obligation to do homage to Yahweh (Ps 122:4). Three times a year, every Israelite is to behold the face of Yahweh (Exod 34:23) and, as stipulated in the same ancient law, no one is to appear empty-handed (Exod 34:20; cf. 23:15). The context suggests that the first fruits of the flocks and harvests were intended. These had to be surrendered at the temple in recognition of Yahweh's sovereignty. In the same manner, one delivered tribute to earthly princes or kings in token of one's loyalty (cf. *62, 408–410;* cf. Pss 68:29; 76:11; 96:7–9).

The occasion of the annual pilgrimages was also the customary time to pay vows (1 Sam 1:21) made on the last temple visit or in the grip of some trouble during the year (Pss 66:13, 14, 107, and chap. 2.1). Yahweh is a God who hears and to whom vows are therefore paid (Ps 65:1–2; cf. *263*). The vow, like many other cult practices, is the transference of a process from the realm of relations between men to that of relations between God and man. In necessity, a gift is promised to someone who might provide an escape from the precarious situation (or has already done so). When one has returned to normal life, thanks to the help supplied, one pays a visit to one's rescuer, delivers the promised gift, and solemnly thanks him once again.

Here the question of what the deity might do with a gift of a sheep *(435)* or a goat *(436)* plays a secondary role. One wanted to show one's gratitude and did so in the manner usual among men.

The psalmists recognize the problematical nature of this transference. First of all, we should note that the official sacrificial cultus with its immolations is hardly mentioned in the psalms.[31] On the other hand, there is quite frequent reference to votive thank offerings (Pss 22:25; 40:6–10; 50:14, 23; 56:12; 61:5, 8; 65:1; 66:19; 69:30–31; 100:praef; 107; 116:14, 18). In these instances, however, the hymn which accompanies the offering is often given prominence as the decisive factor (Pss 40:6–10; 50:14, 23; 69:30, 31). Mowinckel[32] has attributed this to a certain rivalry between the privileged sacrificial priests and the temple singers. The latter belonged to a lower caste of cult personnel, but according to Mowinckel, the authors of the majority of the psalms are to be found in their number. However, such sweeping expressions as "Sacrifice and [food-] offering thou dost not desire" (Ps 40:6; cf. 50) cannot be explained by such rival-

433a. A procession. The multiplicity of cult objects and manifestations of the deity is characteristic of Egypt. A priest with censer precedes the "white bull" with the sun between its horns. Here the bull and the statue are probably embodiments of the same god, namely, the ithyphallic Min. The life-size image of the fertility god is supported by two rods. Various kinds of fans and bouquets are carried before and after the image. A small statue of the king kneels in adoration before the effigy. The king himself strides across the picture.

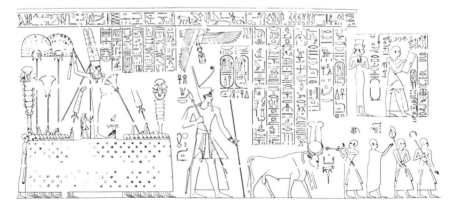

434. On the occasion of the beautiful festival of Opet (cf. W. Wolf, *Das Schöne Fest*), the great procession leaves the temple of Karnak to proceed to the temple of Luxor. The four flagpoles of the third pylon (of Amenhotep III) are apparently gilded only at the top, being otherwise rather roughhewn (on the flagpoles, cf. *162, 162a, 167a, 220a*). The gate itself is decorated with reliefs. The holy shrine *(naos; 221–22; 229–30)* is mounted on a ship. The shrine conceals the cult image. The ship apparently symbolizes the mobility of the deity. By the time this relief was made, the ship no longer had any practical significance. Twenty-four priests carry the *naos* and its ship on a platform. The bow of the bark is adorned with the head of the king. Its *naos,* containing an image of the deified king, is carried fourth in line, after those of Amun, Khons, and Mut. A man with a censer and a water vessel, and another man with a long-handled fan precede the bark. Aboard ship the king, in the form of small statues, performs his cultic service. As a sphinx, he watches at the bow; he cools the image of the deity with an ostrich-feather fan; and he holds fast the wing-shaped cover which protectively surrounds the *naos;* he also supports the pillars of the *naos.*

ries. The statement is sweeping even if it is intended to include only private thank offerings and not the official sacrifices.[33] The deeper reason for the tendency of the *song* of thanksgiving to render the accompanying offering unreal may have lain precisely in the apersonal ambiguity of the offering, which did not do justice to the uniquely personal character of the deliverance to which the thank offering was a response.[34]

For the psalmists, as opposed to the prophets, it is not a matter of shifting the accent from cultic sacrifice to knowledge of God and justice and righteousness (Amos 5:21, 24; Hos 6:6; Isa 1:10–17; Jer 7:21–23; etc.). Rather, emphasis is shifted from bloody sacrifice to the confession which accompanies it. Ps 69:30–31 expresses the conviction that the song (*šyr*) will please Yahweh more than a bull (*šwr* [RSV: "ox"]). The wordplay *šyr-šwr* gives linguistic form to the substitution of one for the other. The final clause, "a bull with horns and hoofs," suggests fattened cattle with over-large hoofs and horns *(437).*

In Egypt, the sacrifices could not be large and fat and numerous enough. There they were not primarily a means

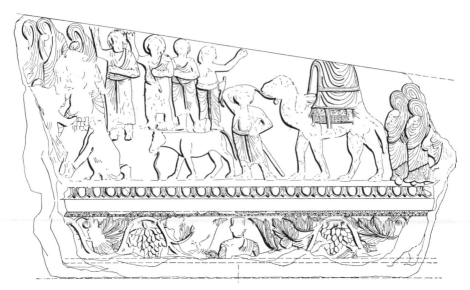

434a. Representation of a procession from the oasis of Palmyra. The driver of the camel which carries the portable sanctuary walks proudly behind a rather small horse. The shrine may have consisted of a leather or wooden container in which a holy object (e.g., a stone) was kept. A red covering is thrown over the chest (ark). Three veiled women appear behind the symbol of the deity, and again at the upper left. Four men greet the god with upraised arms. In its ascendancy, Palmyra harbored a large Arab population. The cults of Allat, Azizu, Arsu, and other Arabian deities indicate that these Arabs preserved, at least in part, the ancestral religion which they brought with them from the desert. The shrine on the camel's back, reminiscent of the Israelite ark, may derive from this heritage.

of showing forth the personal power of the Pharaohs,[35] but rather of augmenting, by the multiplication of sacrifices (cf. *196*), the life-forces of the gods, which were essential to the well-being of the land. This process was further strengthened by the identification of the sacrifices with the enemies of the gods and of the land. In Fig. *437,* the carved, wooden head of a Nubian has been placed between the horns of the ox, and the addition of two hands has transformed the horns of the ox into arms uplifted in entreaty. On the Narmer palette, two slain enemies have been marked as sacrifices by placing bull-masks on them.[36] Thus, not only are the vital forces augmented by sacrifice; at the same time, the powers of death and destruction are diminished.

In Israel, Yahweh, who could be identified with no earthly entity, was seen early on to be independent of any earthly means of sustenance. Ps 50 vehemently rejects the erroneous notion that Yahweh might feed on the flesh and blood of the sacrifices *(438, 439)*. This is perhaps the second, more general reason for replacing bloody sacrifice with the song of thanksgiving.

As was suggested in the discussion of the altar (cf. especially Figs. *192, 201*) and the priestly service of the king (pp. 277–79), the conception that the gods were nourished by the sacrifices was also prevalent in Mesopotamia. The anthropomorphic-personal conception of the gods, stronger in Mesopotamia than in Egypt, has already been evidenced in the Mesopotamian cosmic

326

view. This had the effect of preventing an inordinate multiplication of sacrifices. In Fig. *440,* as always in Mesopotamian offerings (cf. *373*), there is but *one* vessel to receive the drink offering, *one* table for the regular offerings, and *one* stand for the offering of incense. The sacrifice is intended for the war gods Ninurta and Nergal,[37] represented by the two standards. Large portions of the sacrifice are cast into Lake Van, on whose shore the two gods led the king in his triumphant progression. In obedience to a foreign will, zoologically unidentifiable animals snap at the sacrificial portions. The animals most probably represent in some way the two gods, or some local divinities to whom the sacrificer wished to show gratitude. The picture also shows one way of visualizing the appropriation of the sacrifice by the gods (cf. p. 144).

The king is preparing to pour wine or water from a libation cup into the vessel intended for such offerings. Two musicians provide musical accompaniment to the proceedings. Music accompanies the sacrifice, as it does a royal repast. The entire ceremony is related to the dedication of a monument which shows the king in the Assyrian attitude of veneration (cf. *418, 419*). Accordingly, the stele hewn in the rock wall is not primarily a monument to the king. Rather, it

436. "Offer to God a sacrifice of thanksgiving, and pay your vows to the Most High; and call upon me in the day of trouble; I will deliver you, and you shall glorify me" (Ps 50:14–15).

435. "Make your vows to the LORD your God, and perform them; let all around him bring gifts . . ." (Ps 76:11).

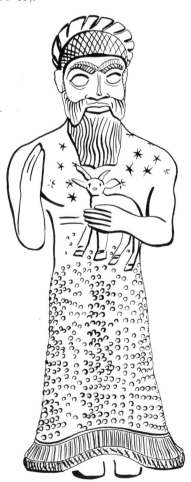

437. "I will praise the name of God with a song [*šîr*]; I will magnify him with thanksgiving. This will please the LORD more than an ox [*šôr*] or a bull with horns and hoofs" (Ps 69:30–13; MT vv. 31–32).

438. "Do good to Zion in thy good pleasure; rebuild the walls of Jerusalem, then wilt thou delight in right sacrifices, . . . then bulls will be offered on thy altar" (Ps 51:18–19).

The sacrificial animal has been laid on a mat for slaughter, and its feet have been bound together. The cutting-points are im-mediately purified with water. At the outer left, a priest (?) with a scroll in his hand watches the proceedings, so that the sacrifice will be performed in accordance with proper religious usage (on the slaughter itself, cf. A. Eggebrecht, *Schlachtungsbräuche*).

perpetuates the worship and thanks offered by the king to the gods in this remote place.

Similar hymns of thanks immortalized in stone were no rarity in the ancient Near East (*263, 307a, Plates XXV* and *XXVI*). Ps 40:6–10 mentions a scroll containing words concerning the suppliant. G. Bornhamm[38] has conjectured that this refers to a text telling of the suppliant's deliverance, brought by the suppliant to the temple. *mktm,* the

438a. The butcher holding the rear leg of the ox holds out a hand dipped in the blood of the sacrificial victim and says, "See the blood!" The man qualified to give an opinion on it is called an Iry-en-akhty; the title is composed of the elements "governor of the palace" and "priest of purification" or "purity" and "physician." He renders his pronouncement to the questioner: "It is clean!" The same formula is frequently found on the lips of the Israelite priests (cf. Lev 13:13, 17, 37, etc.).

439a. "My vows I will pay before those who fear him. The poor shall eat and be satisfied; those who seek him shall praise the LORD!" (Ps 22:25b, 26).

In Egypt the blood played no role in the cultic framework (cf. the washing away in Fig. 438); in the Semitic sphere, however, it was carefully collected and used for sprinklings, etc. (cf. Ps 16:4).

439. "I will offer to thee the sacrifice of thanksgiving and call upon the name of the LORD. I will pay my vows to the LORD in the presence of all his people" (Ps 116:17–18).

peculiar superscription of Pss 16 and 56–60, is translated in the Septuagint as *stēlographia*, "stele inscription." This, together with the request *'l tšḥt* ("do not destroy") subjoined to it in Pss 57–59, gives rise to the conjecture that these or the preceding psalms were engraved on stelae.[39] As indicated in Fig. 440, these stelae were dedicated within the context of a thank offering.

The confession of faith, whether sung or engraved on a stele, had long constituted an integral part of the sacrifice of thanksgiving. The place of the hymn of

thanks is recognizable in Ps 116:13. One cried out the name of Yahweh in lifting up the "cup of salvation." The cup may signify a libation. In Assyria (373, 440), Mari (441), and Egypt (442, 443), incense was frequently offered at the same time. On the Yehawmilk stele (*Plate XXVI*) from Byblos, the king lifts the cup with a gesture of greeting (cf. 415), but does not offer incense at the same time (cf. 407, *Plate XXIII*). The two Egyptian pictures make it quite clear that both animal sacrifice and libation originally were intended to effect a very

329

440. "With a freewill offering I will sacrifice to thee; I will give thanks to thy name, O LORD, for it is good. For thou hast delivered me from every trouble, and my eye has looked in triumph on my enemies" (Ps 54:6–7).

real increase in the deity's vital powers (cf. *180, 187*). In Fig. *442,* the vessels for receiving the drink offering are in the form of the hieroglyph, "heart." Wine gladdens the heart, and victuals strengthen it (Ps 104:15). There can be no doubt that the hearts in Fig. *442* are the hearts of the gods. In Fig. *443,* the vessel from which the king pours his drink offering has the shape of the hieroglyph, "life." That which the king provides for the god the deity returns to him (by his left hand). *Do ut des*. There is no such form of exchanging life in Israel. "Do I . . . drink the blood of goats?" (Ps 50:13). "He who brings thanksgiving as his sacrifice honors me" (Ps 50:23).

A shift of emphasis from animal sac-

441. Drink offerings of wine are ordered with some frequency in the Pentateuch (Exod 29:38–42; Num 15:5; 28:7–8, etc.). In the psalms, there is only one mention of a cup which can be interpreted as a libation cup (Ps 116:13). Libations of blood to foreign gods are cited once (Ps 16:4). The drink offerings were entirely the affair of the priests. The devotional collection represented by the Psalter, on the other hand, was appointed for use by the laity.

442. The vessels into which the Pharaoh pours his libation have the shape of the hieroglyph "heart." In the Egyptian understanding, the libation strengthens the heart of the god, just as food and drink strengthen the heart of man (Ps 104:15; cf. *192*).

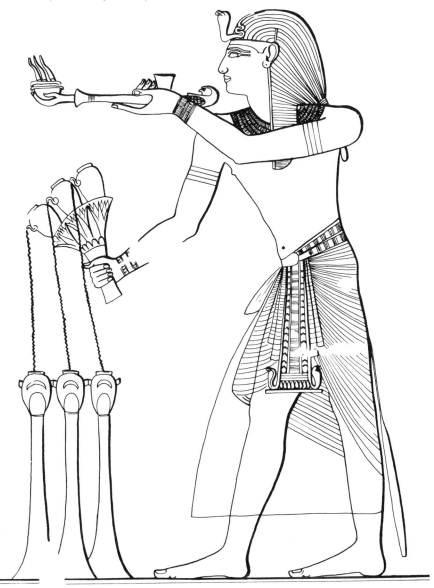

443. "Let my prayer be counted as incense before thee, and the lifting up of my hands as the evening sacrifice!" (Ps 141:2).

rifice to hymns of thanksgiving has already been discussed above. Animal sacrifices may have continued to be presented in connection with the offering of thanks. For even if the deity did not regale himself on the sacrifice, it was nonetheless necessary to the joyful repast which comprised a part of such festivals. At these times, even the poor could eat their fill (Ps 22:26).[40] But the hymn of thanksgiving superseded the sacrifice. That fact is indicated by the wordplay *šîr-šôr* and the association of "sacrifice" with "praise" (Ps 50:14, 23; cf. also Ps 27:6). More importantly, however, it is demonstrated by the priestly proclamation- and charge-formulae used in this connection. By means of these

444. The "cup of the saving acts of Yahweh" on a coin from the second year of the Jewish revolt against Roman domination (A.D. 66–70; cf. 460).

445. "Behold, how good and pleasant it is when brothers dwell in unity! It is like the precious oil upon the head . . ." (Ps 133:1–2; cf. 268).

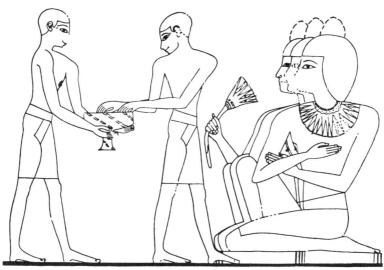

formulae, sacrificial offerings are declared to be unwanted (Pss 40:6; 51:16), and the hymn is pronounced well-pleasing (Ps 69:30–31; on such formulae cf. 438a).

In fact, the hymn of thanks even fulfills the *purpose of the sacrifice*. It aggrandizes the power of the deity to whom it is offered. The singer magnifies Yahweh (Ps 69:30). In being praised as deliverer, Yahweh is given weight (*kbwd*; Ps 50:15 [RSV: "glory"]). The singers of hymns confess the saving act of God in the presence of the whole congregation (Pss 9:14; 22:22, 25; 34:2; 40:9–10; 109:30; 111:1; 116:14, 18–19). God is great in Jerusalem and highly praised because songs of thanksgiving are incessantly sung there. There exists a relation between this singing of praise and the dwelling of the "name" (of good and great repute) and *kābôd* (the significance and glory) of Yahweh in Jerusalem.

Only a portion of the thank offering was presented to Yahweh; the rest was consumed by the party giving thanks and his associates. Thus, the thank offering not only increased the greatness of Yahweh; it also established community among those who shared the meal. The song of thanksgiving could also assume this function, at least to some degree. The hearers of the hymn were able to participate in the worshipper's wonderful experience and thus join themselves to his praise (Ps 22:26; 34:2–3). Community was no longer realized—at least not primarily—in the natural function of eating, but in common enthusiasm for Yahweh's salvific rule. In the great national-religious uprising against Rome in A.D. 66, during which it was necessary effectively to unite the people, God's "cup of salvation" adorned one of the coins of the rebellious forces (444). The sentiment thus expressed may have been

446. *"From you* comes *my shout* of joy in the great congregation" (Ps 22:26a MT [author's translation and italics; cf. Ps 22:25a RSV]; cf. Ps 51:15).

In Egypt, the power which opens the lips to the cultic cry of jubilation is called Mert. With her clapping hands, she is the embodiment of this jubilation.

based less on eating and drinking in common than on the common experience celebrated at the raising of the cup.

Sacrifice, meal, and song continued to belong together throughout the various shifts of emphasis from animal sacrifice to the song of thanksgiving, and the re-

sultant regard of the latter as the actual sacrifice. The sweet converse experienced by the suppliant of Ps 55:14 in the intimate circle *(swd)* in the house of Yahweh may have been related to the proceedings as a whole. Again and again the psalms demonstrate that it was the common *celebrations* of the goodness and love of Yahweh which leant fascination to the temple visit.

Thus, *celebration* and *community* were dependent on each other. The psalms can wax as eloquent about fellowship (133:1) as they can about praise of Yahweh (Ps 92:1–2). Without the community of those faithful to Yahweh, praise has no sounding-board, and without praise, the community has no established center. The community produces the atmosphere in which praise can flourish (Pss 42:4; 55:14).

In Ps 133:2, the effect of community is compared to the perfumed fat which was set on the heads of the guests at festive banquets (Pss 23:5; 92:10; 141:5). During the course of the meal, it melted on the head and gave forth a beguiling scent *(445)*. The atmosphere celebrated in Ps 133, however, was less related to everyday experience than to the sense of community experience in the cultus. The songs of thanksgiving, with their frequent biographical references, demonstrate that the solemn hours spent in the temple were entirely dependent on everyday experience (cf., e.g., Ps 107). What was solemnized in the temple was no more than the condensation, exaltation, and interpretation of these experiences. It is perhaps true that without the temple cultus everyday experiences could not have been elevated in this manner. If, however, the everyday were to have found no place in the temple, the cultus would have degenerated into lifeless, sterile ritual.

3. MUSIC AND SONG

a. *Dancing and Jubilation*

"Hallal" and similar combinations of phonemes appear in many languages as expressions of spontaneous, joyous excitement. The German *halali* or *hali halo* expresses the excitement of the hunt. The Arabic *tahlil* denotes the trilling cries of women arousing the men to battle; *'ahalla* is the cry of women greeting a newborn child; *tahallala* denotes joyful shouts in general.[41] The Hebrew *hll* denotes enthusiastic praise of a beautiful woman or man (cf. Ps 78:63 KJVm; Gen 12:15; Song 6:9), but it is far more frequently used in praise of God. In the presence of Yahweh's glory in the temple the suppliant shouts for joy *(yhll)*, just as one exults following a rich, festive meal (Ps 63:5). Sometimes God's action toward man is such that man cannot but rejoice. Then his mouth is filled with laughter and his tongue with shouts of joy *(rnh)* (cf. Pss 126:2; 65:8). The suppliant of Ps 22:25 makes the moving confession: "from thee [God] comes my praise [*thlh*]."

Jubilation can overtake a man as surprisingly as God's saving act itself. In Egypt, the experience of the arbitrary nature of jubilation found expression in the goddess Mert *(446)*. The goddess embodies cultic jubilation. In Fig. *446*, she is shown kneeling on the hieroglyph "gold" (necklace), clapping her hands. On her head she wears the garland of lilies typical of Upper Egypt. Like everything else in Egypt, cultic jubilation appears in two varieties, Upper and Lower Egyptian. Sometimes Mert, as the embodiment of temple music, is portrayed with a harp. Her characteristic posture, however, is with hands upraised for clapping and beating time. Women and children, clapping their hands in rhythm, follow after a band of musicians who play at the enthronement of Ummanigash *(Plate XXVII)*. The latter, a prince friendly toward Assur, was installed following Assurbanipal's victory over the Elamite king, Teumman. Ps 47:1 calls on all peoples to clap their hands in celebration of Yahweh's procession to Zion.

447. Detail from *Plate XXVII*. The woman beats her neck in order to impart rhythm to the high, extended tone. The original meaning of *hll* may refer to production of this trilling sound.

448. This Egyptian beats his breast (cf. *336*) in order to achieve the same effect as the woman in Fig. *447*.

449. "Thou hast turned for me my mourning into dancing; thou hast loosed my sackcloth and girded me with gladness" (Ps 30:11).

450. "The singers in front, the minstrels last, between them maidens playing timbrels: 'Bless God in the great congregation, the LORD, O you who are of Israel's fountain!'" (Ps 68:25–26).

Besides the cult objects, official reliefs of processions (cf. 433a, 434) show first and foremost the king, the priests and officials. This more modest stele shows a group of seven maidens as further participants in the procession: five beat tambourines, one plays the lyre, and one shakes a rattle. These latter two are apparently still children, for they are shown naked and of smaller stature than the others. (On sistrum-players and dancers in the great procession at the beautiful feast of Opet, cf. W. Wolf, *Das Schöne Fest*, pp. 16, 18f.; and O. Keel, *Die Weisheit 'spielt' vor Gott*, pp. 27–37).

On such occasions, the participants uttered long, loud shouts of joy. "The earth was split by their noise" (1 Kgs 1:40; cf. Josh 6:5, 20). The long-drawn-out cries were rhythmically broken by striking the neck with the hand (cf. the section from *Plate XXVII* in Fig. 447) or by beating the chest with the fist. The latter is shown in the Egyptian hieroglyph (448) which denotes *hjhnw*, "to shout for joy," and *hbj*, "to dance."[42] The rhythmic striking transforms the high, extended note into a trill. The root *hll* may originally have denoted this trill. The sound is still popular in the Near East today, and may often be heard at weddings and on similar occasions.

Like trilling, dancing is a spontaneous expression of overflowing joy. The close

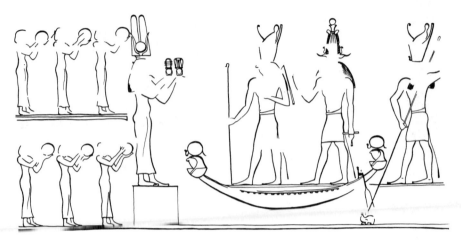

451. "Miriam . . . took a timbrel in her hand; and all the women went out after her with cymbals and dancing. And Miriam said to them: 'Sing to the LORD, for he has triumphed gloriously; the horse and his rider he has thrown into the sea'" (Exod 15:20–21; cf. Ps 149:3).

452. An Assyrian military band with tambourine, two kinds of lyres, and cymbals.

relation of the trill and the dance is indicated by the fact that the hieroglyph of Fig. 448 can denote both "to shout for joy" and "to dance." Dancing and singing, the women celebrate the victory of the men (Judg 11:34; 1 Sam 18:6–7).

When Yahweh is celebrated as victor, this dance assumes a decidedly cultic character (Exod 15:20; cf. Pss 68:25; 149:3). David dances as the Ark is transported to Zion (2 Sam 6:14–22), an event quite similar to a triumphal pro-

453. In contrast to the metal (and therefore costly) cymbal, the simple tambourine was a widespread popular instrument.

454. Goddess or priestess (?) with a tambourine.

cession. The clapping women and children of *Plate XXVII* bear witness to the great festivity of processions and pageants. It is not likely that our imaginations will exaggerate the festal joy of these occasions.

It would appear that even the regular, recurrent, hymnic praises of Yahweh included dancing (Pss 87:7; 150:4), at least on occasion. As shown by Ps 30:11, dance is even less likely to have been absent from the more private thanksgiving celebrations. Above all, the younger participants would have been moved to dancing by the singing and jangling of the tambourines. On the occasion of a great honor conferred on Ay by Amenophis IV, Ay's children gave vent to their joy in all kinds of leaps and dances *(449)*.

b. Percussion Instruments

The tambourine (*tōp* [RSV: "timbrel"]) accompanied songs of victory (Exod 15:20; Pss 68:25–26; 149:3). It was also apparently used on occasion in the praises at the sanctuary (Pss 81:2; 150:4). It played a rather important part in the Egyptian cultus *(450, 451)*. The context in which it is used in Fig. *451* is of special interest. On the right bank,

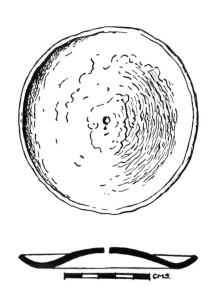

455. "Praise him with sounding cymbals; praise him with loud clashing cymbals!" (Ps 150:5).

339

Horus, the divine falcon and king of the gods, slays Seth, who appears as a tiny hippopotamus (in magical thinking, an imposing representation of the enemy is considered dangerous). That accomplished, Horus proceeds in triumph to the left bank, where he is received by Isis (the queen) and six princesses with tambourines. In the attached text, the women sing: "We hail you and we rejoice at your sight. We shout for joy, for we behold your triumph!"[43] The joy of the women after hours and days of uncertainty is similarly expressed in Exod 15:20–21; Judg 11:34; 1 Sam 18:6–7; and Ps 68:25, passages which describe events similar to that depicted in Fig. 451. The tambourine was also in widespread use in Assyria (452) and Canaan (453). In the Canaanite sphere, as in Babylon,[44] it is often played by women whom we may assume to be priestesses or goddesses (454). The tambourine was an instrument played typically by women. It seems to have been played by men only occasionally in military bands (452), or in bands of prophets (1 Sam 10:5) and similar closed associations. Because of its apparent close connection with the cult of female deities, it did not play a major role in the Jerusalem cultus. In the two Books of Chronicles it appears only in a single passage (1 Chr 13:8), and that passage is drawn verbatim from 2 Sam 6:5. Its omission cannot be accidental, for temple music otherwise plays an important role in the Chronicles, receiving frequent mention. At a later time, the tambourine was banned from the temple precincts, perhaps in the course of anti-Canaanite reforms (cf. p. 176) or because it no longer fulfilled the desires for a certain luxury. (The tambourine was made of a simple single- or double-sided frame of wood or clay, covered with skin.)

The cymbal (ṣlṣlym, mṣltym) gained considerably in importance in the later period. It is mentioned as a temple instrument thirteen times in the Chronicler's work. Elsewhere, it appears only in Ps 150 and 2 Sam 6:5. The latter is the only ancient reference to it. Nevertheless, archaeological finds from the Late Bronze and Early Iron Ages in Canaan indicate that it was apparently a widespread instrument at that time (cf. 455).[45]

It is not clear what is meant by sound-sounding cymbals (ṣlṣly šmʿ) and clashing cymbals (ṣlṣly trwʿh) of Ps 150:5. It may allude to two different methods of playing (perhaps restrained and vigorous) rather than two kinds of instrument (cf. Num 10:1–10). The rhythmic alternation of soft and loud playing of the individual instruments is keyed to the rhythm of respiration. Ps 150 concludes by summoning everything that has breath to the praises of God.

The timbrel or tambourine and the cymbals are the only percussion instruments mentioned in the psalms. The large, dark-toned kettledrums (cf. the second musician from the right in *Plate XXVII*) seem to have been very popular in Mesopotamia. There exists no literary or archaeological evidence for them in Palestine. On the other hand, it should be noted that drums built on a tambourinelike frame can reach considerable size, and would thus produce a heavy sound. It was rather difficult to hold these large drums. In Fig. 456, the man in the middle carries the frame on his shoulder, while two other musicians beat upon it.[46]

c. Wind Instruments

The following wind instruments are mentioned in the psalms: the horn (šwpr); a long, metal instrument without valves (ḥṣṣrh), which figures in translations as "trumpet" or "trombone"; and the flute (ʿwgb). For the most part, the *horn* was probably the ram's horn, as indicated by the occasional addition of hywbl ("of the ram") (Josh 6:4, 6, 8, 13). There is also the expression "to blow the ram" (mšk hywbl: Exod 19:13 MT). šwpr is itself derived from the Akkadian-Sumerian šlsapparu, "wild sheep," To be sure, the illustrations (456–58) hardly suggest a ram's horn. But we should bear in mind, especially in Fig. 458, the difficulty of the medium. Even on the basis

456. "Blow the *horn* at the new moon, at the full moon on the day of our feast, for it is a statute for Israel, a law from the God of Jacob" (Ps 81:5 MT [author's translation]; cf. Ps 81:3–4 RSV).

The "horn" dates the psalm in the pre-exilic or early postexilic period. Later the new moon was announced by blowing a *trumpet* (Num 10:10).

of Fig. *456,* it would probably be precarious to conclude that the horns of cattle were used for blowing.

The horn and the trumpet were as widely used as the tambourine and cymbals. As the most easily made instrument, the horn was in common use in Israel from the earliest times. According to one of the most ancient passages in the Bible (Exod 19:13, 16, 19 J/E), Yahweh himself blew the ram's horn [RSV: "trumpet"] on Sinai.[47] This could be connected to the volcanic elements of the Sinai theophany. According to Dio Cassius,[48] a "trumpet blast" was heard on the eruption of Vesuvius. This could describe the heavy, sustained sounds produced by escaping air.

Since Yahweh had once appeared amid torchlight [RSV: "lightnings"] and the blasting of the ram's horn (Exod 20:18), his presence could be ensured by blowing the ram's horn and burning torches (Judg 7:16). It is possible, of course, that in certain instances the reverse process took place, and that cultic elements were projected onto the

Sinai theophany. One ought not, however, represent that solution as the only possible explanation.[49] To do so does not do justice to the texts concerning the Sinai theophany (cf. *298–99*).

The ram's horn can produce but one or two resounding tones. It is therefore more suited for use as a signal than as an actual instrument of music. According to Ps 81:4 MT [RSV: 81:3], the day of the new, full moon is to be marked by blowing the ram's horn [RSV: "trumpet"] (cf. Num 10:10). The procession of Yahweh to Zion is also accompanied by the blowing of the horn (Ps 47:5). This may have something to do with the significance of the ram's horn at the coronation of the king (2 Sam 15:10; 1 Kgs 1:34, 39, 41–42; 2 Kgs 9:13). As noted above, Yahweh's ascent to Zion can be construed, at least secondarily, as the ascent to a throne. In Ps 98:6, the horn was also blown in the joyful obeisance before King Yahweh (cf. Ps 150:3).

Archaeological indications (cf. *457*) and the etymology of the word for the horn suggest that the horn may have

457. "Yahweh goes up with a cry of victory, Yahweh with the sound of horns" (Ps 47:6 MT [author's translation], cf. Ps 47:5 RSV).

erable cultic significance, lay in the fact that in the later period it no longer had a place in the temple service and was therefore free for use in the synagogue. Like the tambourine, the horn is mentioned in the Chronicles only in a passage taken verbatim from 2 Sam 6:5 (1 Chr 15:28), and once in connection with a covenant renewal (2 Chr 15:14).

The Chroniclers' favorite instrument was the trumpet, which replaced the horn. It is mentioned nineteen times in the Chronicles. The verb for trumpet-playing is used an additional six times. The trumpet may have been of Egyptian origin. To be sure, it is to be found once on a fragment of a steatite vessel from Bismaya (southeast of Nippur). The vessel dates from the second phase of the early Dynastic period (ca. 2500 B.C.).[50] But in Egypt, the trumpet is attested with some regularity from the middle of the third millennium B.C. onwards.[51] In the New Kingdom, it was used in the army as a signal instrument (282). During the reigns of Ramses II and III, trumpet-playing was very popular in the military and on state occasions.[52] The

been imported rather early from Mesopotamia into Palestine. As one of the oldest, most popular instruments, the horn alone survived into the synagogue service. It is frequently represented on the mosaic floors and capitals of synagogues (458). The chief reason for this adoption, beyond the horn's ven-

458. The horn is the only musical instrument that made its way into the synagogue.

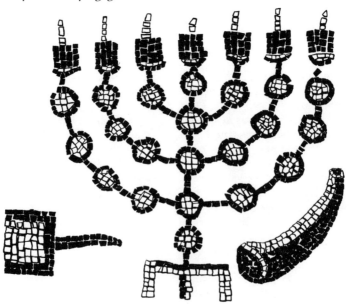

342

Baroque tendencies of these periods evidence a certain similarity to the world of the Chronicler. A stele from the time of Ramses II *(459)* shows a trumpet player standing in a worshipful posture, his trumpet under his arm, before the deified Ramses II (not visible in Fig. *459).* Perhaps he played as a trumpeter in the cult of the dead king.

The trumpet is mentioned only three times in OT texts which may be assigned with certainty to the pre-exilic period. At the coronation of Joash of Judah (836–797 B.C.), the trumpet replaces the horn (1 Kgs 1:34, 39, 41–42). In the reign of the same king, silver was collected for the purpose of making trumpets and other utensils for the temple (2 Kgs 12:13). According to Hos 5:8, the trumpet, as well as the horn, was used by the military as a signal instrument toward the end of the eighth century B.C.

In the psalms, the trumpet had apparently not yet won the place it later occupied in the Chronicles. It appears but a single time, in the obeisance made before King Yahweh (Ps 98:6). Even there, as in Hos 5:8, it appears together with the horn. A secondary priestly text (Num 10:1–10), together with the Books of Chronicles, show that it was only in postexilic times that the trumpet displaced the horn. In Num 10:10, the day of the new moon is no longer to be marked by the blowing of horns (as in Ps 81:4 MT [81:3 RSV: "trumpet"]), but by the blowing of trumpets. The two silver trumpets which Num 10:10 traces back to Moses played a very special role in the later period. On the Titus Arch in Rome, they appear among the pieces of booty carried from the second temple, beside the showbread table with the "cup of the salvation of Yahweh" *(460)*. The rebuilding of the temple was the primary goal of the Bar Kochba rebellion (A.D. 132–135). The importance of the two trumpets to the image of the second temple is demonstrated by the coinage of the rebellion. Besides the temple facade,[53] the

459. The metal trumpet was probably introduced into Israel from Egypt in the early monarchic period (cf. *381*).

460. "Sing praises to the LORD with the lyre, with the lyre and the sound of melody! With trumpets and the sound of the horn make a joyful noise before the King, the LORD!" (Ps 98:5–6).

461. The two trumpets ordered by Num 10:1–10 played an important role in the postexilic temple. Their significance is attested by their appearance on the coinage of the Bar Kochba Revolt.

coins depict a cult vessel,[54] the festal bouquet of the feast of Tabernacles,[55] two types of lyres,[56] and the silver trumpets[57] (cf. 461). The coin in Fig. 461 bears the inscription, "For the freedom of Jerusalem!" (l ḥrwt yrwšlm). According to Num 10:9, the trumpets also assumed the horn's function of realizing Yahweh's presence in battle, thereby ensuring victory.

In view of the late and scanty evidence from pre-exilic times, it is not likely that the trumpets were introduced into the cultus by David.[58] On the other hand, the trumpet was, and always remained a costly, kingly instrument. According to Num 10:8, it was the prerogative of the priests to blow the trumpet. The same is true in the War Scroll from Qumran, where the priests blow the trumpet and the Levites blow the horn.[59] In the Roman army, the *tuba* was the signal of the supreme command, while the horns served as signals for individual detachments.

The vertical flute ('wgb [RSV: "pipe"]) is the third instrument mentioned in the psalms. At no time does it seem to have achieved any great significance, and it is mentioned only once in the psalms (Ps 150:4). It was an ancient instrument. Jubal, the descendant of Cain, was regarded as its inventor (Gen 4:21). Bone playing-pipes from the fourth millennium B.C. have been found at Tepe Gawra in Assyria.[60] The flute is also attested in Egypt from the period of the Old Kingdom (462). Fig. 462 provides a charming glimpse of musical life in ancient Egypt: "With his right hand, the singer, identifi-

462. "Praise him with . . . [the] pipe!" (Ps 150:4).

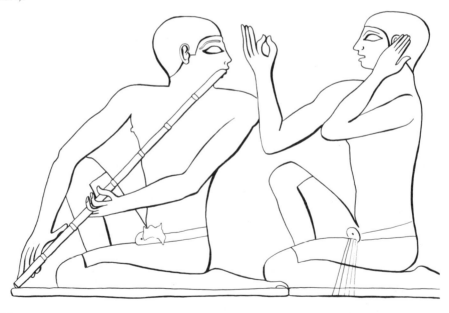

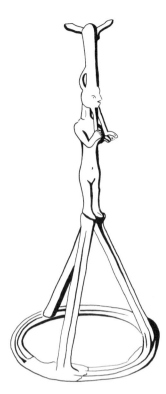

463. A number of examples of the double-flute *(ḥlyl)* have been discovered in Palestine. The instrument is not mentioned in the psalms.

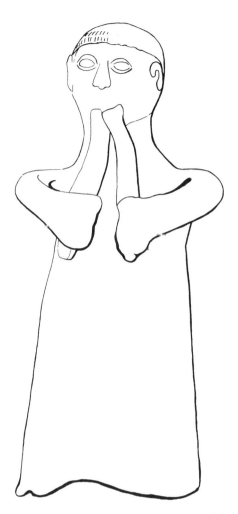

464. "You shall have a song as in the night when a holy feast is kept; and gladness of heart, as when one set out to the sound of the flute *(ḥlyl)* to go to the mountain of the LORD, to the Rock of Israel" (Isa 30:29).

able by his slightly parted lips, beats time for the accompanying flautist. The singer's left hand is placed at his ear, so that he can make use of head resonance in order better to control his own voice. The accompanist's turned head is a sign of his intense concentration. He fairly breathes with the singer."[61]

In Palestine, the bright-sounding double-flute *(ḥlyl; 463, 464)* is better attested than the dark-sounding vertical flute *('wgb)*. The piping female figure found at Megiddo *(463)*, whose deformity identifies her as a demon,[62] is of Phoenician provenance. Also Phoenician is the terra-cotta figure shown playing the *ḥlyl* in Fig. *464*. It was found at Achzib, 25 kilometers north of Haifa.

The shrill *ḥlyl* first surfaces in the OT in the ecstatic band of prophets mentioned in 1 Sam 10:5. It was played at exuberantly festive meals (Isa 5:12). It accompanies Solomon's procession from Gihon to Zion (1 Kgs 1:40) and the pilgrims on their way to Jerusalem (Isa 30:29), but it apparently was not used in the temple cultus, perhaps because of its connection with Phoenician heathen cults.

d. String Instruments

Many of the psalms are connected with celebrations of thanksgiving. The string instruments (*kinnôr* and *nēbel*) used on these occasions are often rendered as "harp," but this translation is probably not accurate. It is almost certain that *kinnôr*, cited thirteen times in the psalms, and *nēbel*, which occurs eight times, denote two different types of lyres.

The hallmark of the lyre is a yoke, "which is invariably lacking in the harp, be it curved [cf. *475*] or angular [Plate XXVII]."[63] To be sure, the harp was known both in Mesopotamia and Egypt by the third millennium B.C. But to the present day, not a single example of the harp has come to light from Syria-Palestine. The incidence of various kinds of lyres is attested, however, by relatively numerous examples (*233, 466, 468–70, 472–73*). The lyre undoubtedly originated in southern Mesopotamia. Magnificent lyres have been unearthed from the tombs of the First Dynasty of Ur (ca. 2500–2350 B.C.) (*465*). In the third millennium B.C., the lyre apparently made its way from Mesopotamia into the steppe regions between Mesopotamia and Egypt (*466–67*). Fig. *466*, dating from the second millennium B.C., shows a drawing in rock of two lyre players. It was discovered in the Negev. Similar representations from the same period have been found in Central Arabia.[64] The well-known portrayal of nomads from one of the tombs at Beni Hasan (*308, 467*) provides one of the earliest representations of the lyre on Egyptian soil. In the Middle Kingdom (2050–ca. 1770 B.C.) in Egypt, the lyre emerges here and there as an imported product. In the 18th Dynasty (1570–1345 B.C.) it became a fashionable instrument.[65] Egypt apparently took over the lyre from Canaan.[66] In any event, it was well-known in Egypt in the period of the New Kingdom (ca. 1610–1085 B.C.), as is indicated in the two illustrations from Megiddo (*233, 468*).

We cannot say with certainty whether the Israelites brought the lyre along out of the steppes or first became acquainted

465. The lyre apparently penetrated Syria-Palestine from Mesopotamia at a very early date.

466. Rock drawing from the Negeb showing two lyre players (second millennium B.C.).

468. Lyre players on a vase fragment from Megiddo (12th century B.C.).

467. ". . . I will go to the altar of God, to God my exceeding joy; and I will praise thee with the lyre, O God, my God" (Ps 43:4).

Philistine city of Ashdod. A comparison with *Plate XXIV* suggests that Fig. *470* may depict captive Judeans, perhaps from Lachish, or possibly from Jerusalem. The relief is from the palace of Sennacherib, who boasts of having received singers as tribute from Hezekiah.[67] The music of Judea was apparently not without fame in Mesopotamia (Ps 137:3).

kinnôr (41 times in the OT) seems simply to have meant "lyre." But *nēbel* (26 occurrences in the OT), which stands with *kinnôr* six times in the psalms (Pss 57:8; 71:22; 81:2; 92:3; 108:2; 150:3; only in Ps 144:9 does it stand alone), may also denote a lyre, as suggested by the close parallelism in Pss 71:22 and 92:3, and by the hendiadys in Ps 108:2. Moreover, archaeological evidence suggests that the fretted zither was as unknown in Palestine as the harp.[68] One may ask whether the clay figurine *(471)* found in a Hyksos stratum of Tell el-ʿAjjul (somewhat south of Gaza) repre-

469. Clay figurine of a lyre player from Ashdod (10th century B.C.).

471. Lute player (?) from Tell el-ʿAjjul (17th-16th centuries B.C.).

with it in Canaan. The cultural-historical note in Gen 4:20–21 seems to indicate that the Yahwistic source regarded the steppes as the original land of the lyre, or at least of the *kinnôr*. However that may be, the lyre enjoyed just as great popularity in Palestine of the first millennium B.C. as it did in the second millennium *(469, 470)*. Fig. *469* comes from the

sents a lute player. Perhaps the instrument mentioned in 1 Sam 18:6 *(šlyš)*, related somehow to the number three [cf. RSVm], denotes a three-stringed lute. In any event, "lute" is not a possible meaning of *kinnôr* and *nēbel*.

As the psalms and the Chronicles indicate, the *kinnôr* and *nēbel* always played an important role in the cultus at the

347

470. "On the poplars [RSVm] there [in exile] we hung up our lyres. For there our captors required of us songs, and our tormentors, mirth, saying, 'Sing us one of the songs of Zion!' How shall we sing the LORD's song in a foreign land?" (Ps 137:2–4).

474. "O God, I will sing you a new song, I will play to you on the ten-stringed lyre" (Ps 144:9 [author's translation]).

472. and 473. *nēbẹl* (472) and *kinnôr* (473) on coins of the Jewish revolt against Roman domination (A.D. 66–70).

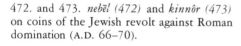

Jerusalem temple. Only lyres are seen, however, on those Bar Kochba coins which show instruments of temple music. Two types of lyre may be distinguished: the type with a jar-shaped sounding-box and curved yoke (472); and the type with a rounded bottom, which often had a simple sounding-

board and straight or only slightly curved yoke-arms (473). *nēbel*, however, can denote not only a type of lyre, but also a large storage jar (Lam 4:2; Isa 30:14). These jars (cf. the jar at the outer left of Fig. 233) often have a shape similar to that of the sounding-box of the lyre in Fig. 472 (cf. 474), or even to the lyre as a whole (cf. *233*). The obvious suggestion is that *nēbel* denoted this curved type of lyre. Because it was easily set on the ground, it also existed in large models *(474)* which could easily have been strung with the ten strings presupposed by Pss 33:2 and 144:9. The *nēbel* seems to have been a rarer, more solemn instrument than the *kinnôr*. Whereas the rectangular *(467)* or trapezoidal lyre *(466)* predominates in the steppes, the *nēbel* appears primarily in courtly contexts *(233, 474)*. In the psalms, the only instance in which *nēbel* does not stand with *kinnôr* as an implement of temple music is in a royal psalm (Ps 144:9). The *kinnôr* was in more common use (Ps 137:2). It was used by the ordinary worshipper in his hymn of thanksgiving (Ps 43:4).

In summary, we may say that the tambourine or frame-drum was used primarily in processions and in the women's songs of triumph (Ps 68:25, 27). The ram's horn was more a means of signaling than a musical instrument. It was used to announce holy times (Ps 81:3) and the coming of Yahweh (Ps 47:5) [RSV has "trumpet" in both instances]. It was replaced in postexilic times by the trumpet. The lyre was used to accompany hymns of thanksgiving (Pss 43:4; 57:8–9; 71:22). All these instruments, augmented by the flute, were played together at proskynesis before Yahweh. On the occasion of solemn sacrifices, they were combined in a choir of many voices (Pss 81:2–3; 98:5–6; 150:3–5). In the postexilic period, the clashing cymbals replaced the duller tambourine.

475. "I will sing praises to thee with the lyre, O Holy One of Israel. My lips will shout for joy, when I sing praises to thee" (Ps 71:22b, 23a).

475a. "I will sing to Yahweh my whole life long, I will play for my God as long as I live. May my composition be pleasing to him. I rejoice in Yahweh" (Ps 104:33–34 [author's translation]).

The motif of playing before God is also attested for Syria-Anatolia. Characteristically, it is here the lyre and not the harp which the worshipper plays before the deity (perhaps El; cf. 283–84).

476. "The right hand of Yahweh does mighty deeds; the right hand of Yahweh exalts" (Ps 118:15c, 16a [author's transla-tion]). "My God, I will highly exalt you" (Ps 118:28b [author's translation]).

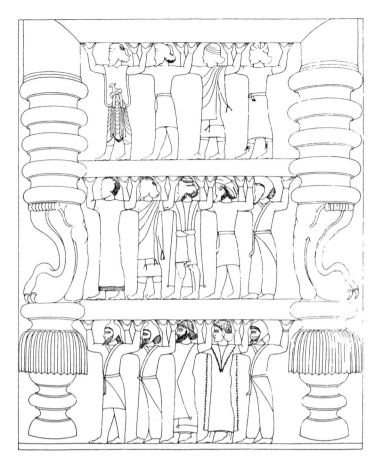

476a. "Yet thou art holy, enthroned on the praises of Israel" (Ps 23:3).

This relief from Persepolis presents a metaphor almost as striking as that of Ps 22:3. Fourteen representatives of the peoples of the Persian Empire bear the huge pedestal which supports the throne of the Persian king (not seen). Thus, the throne rests on the loyalty of the subjects. Their acceptance maintains the Great King in his lofty position. The feet of the pedestal do not touch the ground at any point (cf. the similar motif on the throne of Sennacherib in *Plate XXIV*). Just as the Persian king is enthroned on the loyalty of his subjects, so Yahweh is enthroned on the recognition and praise of Israel.

The purpose of singing and playing was to please Yahweh. Whether in the personal song of thanksgiving or in the many-voiced choir, one sang and played before Yahweh, for Yahweh (Pss 71:22; 104:33; 138:1; 144:9). Just as the Egyptian thought to please his god with cool water, flowers, music, and song *(475),* so too the Israelite hoped that his playing and singing would please Yahweh (Ps 104:34a). He was impelled to make music because he himself rejoiced in Yahweh (Ps 104:34b). In the final analysis, cultic music, like ululation and singing (Ps 22:25 [RSV: "praise"]), comes from Yahweh, for he is the source of the joy and rapture which cry out for musical expression. To be sure, music cannot be understood only as a response to the action of Yahweh. Yahweh's action can also be construed as a reaction to the music (2 Kgs 3:15; Num 10:9). Just as music can move a man to action, so, it was believed, it could induce God to intervene or to appear. This belief invested music with an almost sacramental significance. Stated differently, music partakes of the structure characteristic of praise in general.

4. WITH GOD

The worshipper exalts Yahweh (Pss 30:1; 118:28; 145:1 [RSV: "extol"]) because Yahweh has exalted him (Pss 9:13; 18:48; 118:16 [RSV varies]), and Yahweh has exalted the worshipper because he cherishes the high and holy name of Yahweh. Fig. 476 vividly demonstrates how praise exalts the one who praises. At the outer right, a servant of Amenophis IV kneels reverently before his lord; at the left, he is enthroned on the shoulders of his colleagues, having been exalted by the king. Fig. 476a shows the spontaneous occurrences of everyday life lifted up into the realm of the symbolic.

In worship, the believer becomes one with God and even perceives himself to be as strong and invulnerable as a god. With his God, he storms ramparts and leaps walls (Ps 18:29; 477). Less aggressive, more sympathetic effects of this bond are the fearlessness, independence, and joy mentioned in numerous psalms (Pss 3:6; 4:7; 27:3; 118:6; etc.).

In Ps 91, invulnerability is granted to *everyone* who puts his whole trust in Yahweh. In Mesopotamian and Egyptian myth, such invulnerability is granted only to certain figures. *Plate XXVIII* shows the youthful Horus, and Fig. 478 shows Shed, who was identified with the

478. "The LORD is on my side to help me; I shall look in triumph on those who hate me" (Ps 118:7).

477. "With you I storm walls; with my God I leap over ramparts" (Ps 18:30 MT [author's translation]; cf. Ps 18:29 RSV).

478a. "Blessed is the man . . . [whose] delight is in the law of the LORD, and on his law he meditates day and night" (Ps 1:1a, 2).

The juxtaposition of Ps 1:2 with this illustration may seem startling at first glance, but the combination is not so out of place as one might think. The Jewish reverence for scripture owes a great deal to the wisdom movement, which in itself was strongly affected by Egyptian influences. Above, an Egyptian wise man, under the tutelage of the scribal god Thoth, studies the latter's writings, believing that such study will ensure him a share in the salutary powers which uphold and rule the world. It was, after all, the wise Thoth who upheld the heavens by his statutes (29; cf. 27). In postexilic Judaism, the revaluation of the Mosaic law and the increasingly intense identification of the written instruction (law of Moses) with the cosmic law (cf. Sir 24) raised the study of scripture to the status of a means of salvation. In the end, it became indeed *the* means of salvation (cf. Jn 7:49). The Hermetic writings made a similar claim, but Hermes is no more than an *interpretatio Graeca* of the Egyptian Thoth.

former savior-god. Horus' mother Isis, out of fear of Seth, the murderer of her husband Osiris, was forced to raise her son in the swamps. But the serpents of the swamps could not harm him. Isis, knowledgeable in magic, gave him victory over the poisonous beasts. Horus stelae were intended, by means of picture and formula, to make this beneficial power available to any man. In Ps 91, trust in Yahweh accomplishes what the Horus stelae were intended to effect: trust in Yahweh protects against every deadly peril.

480. ". . . that yields its fruit in its season, and its leaf does not wither. In all that he does, he prospers" (Ps 1:3b).

479. "He is like a tree planted by streams of water . . ." (Ps 1:3a).

Jeremiah has another image for the fruit of trust in God: "Blessed is the man who trusts in the LORD. . . . He is like a tree planted by water, that sends out its roots by the stream, and does not fear when heat comes, for its leaves remain green, and is not anxious in the year of drought, for it does not cease to bear fruit" (Jer 17:7–8). The image of the tree is probably derived from Egypt (cf. *479, 480*). In Egyptian wisdom literature, it characterizes the "true silent ones."[69] In the psalms, it sometimes illustrates, as in Jeremiah, the condition of him who trusts in God (Ps 52:8); sometimes it describes the fate of the righteous (Ps

92:12–15). In both psalms, the courts of Yahweh take the place of the water. In this context, however, as was shown in chapter 3, the courts of Yahweh are tantamount to water (cf. also Ps 46:4). The unaltered image of the tree by the water occurs again in Ps 1, a late psalm. Here, however, it does not illustrate the condition and future of one who trusts in Yahweh or of one who is righteous. In Ps 1, that man is compared to a magnificent tree, such as those illustrated in Fig. *480*, for "his delight is the law of the LORD, and on his law he meditates day and night" (Ps 1:2; cf. *478a*).

EPILOGUE

Israel did not live in isolation. It engaged in an active intellectual exchange with the world around it. Not infrequently, this posed a catastrophic threat to Israel's particularity. However, it also permitted Israel's experiences and conceptions of God to be rounded out by those of neighboring peoples. Only thus did Israel achieve that mature fulness which never ceases to amaze those in a position to compare the Psalter with other ancient Near Eastern collections of prayers.

The adopted concepts and images, together with those created by Israel itself, are often reflected only allusively in the psalms, or as *membra disiecta*. The present work has attempted to indicate some of the systems of reference to which they belong or from which they depart. Individual images and symbols ought thereby to have become more intelligible and to have achieved clarity and color, so that they can be viewed with enjoyment.

Greater clarity, however, may have occasionally evoked surprise, for example, in the interpretation of the royal psalms with the aid of ancient Near Eastern royal iconography. In particular, the person who *prays* the psalms may have questioned how the realities addressed in the psalms can be related to the realities of his own existence if things were indeed so different at the time when the psalms were written.

We can legitimately doubt, however, that things were so fundamentally different when we observe the countless pictures from the ancient Near East which show its people being born and giving birth, bending over scrolls of writing, planning and erecting their buildings, falling in love, celebrating festivals, taking care for their sustenance, waging wars, taking sick, and dying. All these things they do not much differently than we.

The matter-of-fact manner in which the royal psalms regard the state as the representative of God may seem astonishing at first. But even in the OT, the close relation between God and king was not taken for granted. Prophetic circles often stood in criticism or rejection of such claims. The psalms, however, are not the expression of this prophetic theology, but of the official national pi-

ety. And it is not only in the ancient Near East that national piety has assigned a high value to the power of the state. Indeed, the ancient Near Eastern view, which is also reflected in the NT (Rom 13:1–7), may not be quite so wrongheaded as is generally assumed today. Ancient Near Eastern royal ideology frequently set forth an impressive picture of the just ruler. If a state functions, even to a degree, in accordance with the high ideals of the ancient Near Eastern model of kingship, it is no more out of place now than it was at the time of Paul to accept that state as a representation of God. The Roman state known to Paul, with its institutionalization of crass distinctions of class, was far less righteous in the biblical sense than a modern state based on law. Most persons, however, in attempting to come to terms with the meaning of the royal psalms, will prefer to adopt the NT solution, rather than to apply the ideology to a modern, though thoroughly anonymous executive branch. By means of the royal psalms, the NT transferred the ancient Near Eastern concept of the king, with all its titles and claims, to Jesus. According to the belief of the NT, only Jesus does justice to their enormous dimensions. He alone is *the* son. He alone has conquered all that is chaotic. Only for the coming of *his* kingdom can one pray as unconditionally as do the psalms. Quite unawares, the NT interpreted the nations' ancient discourse regarding the true king as an expression of the longing for Christ. This and similar considerations can also bring us closer to other ancient Near Eastern concepts and their application in the psalms. The reward for our pains may be the liberating recognition of certain basic structures which have withstood every change of form and coloration and are therefore able to let him who created them shine forth before us.

Of old thou didst lay the foundation of the earth,
and the heavens are the work of thy hands.
They will perish, but thou dost endure;
they will all wear out like a garment.
Thou changest them like raiment, and they pass away;
but thou art the same, and thy years have no end.
The children of thy servants shall dwell secure;
Their posterity shall be established before thee. (Ps 102:25–28)

ABBREVIATIONS

PERIODICALS, SERIALS, REFERENCE WORKS, AND INSTITUTIONS

AASOR — *Annual of the American Schools of Oriental Research*, (New Haven) Philadelphia 1919ff.

AfO — *Archiv für Orientforschung*, Berlin 1926ff.

AJA — *American Journal of Archaeology*, Baltimore 1885ff.

Alt *KS* — A. Alt, *Kleine Schriften zur Geschichte des Volkes Israel*, 3 vols., Munich 1959.

ANEP — *The Ancient Near East in Pictures Relating to the Old Testament*, ed. J. Pritchard, Princeton 1954 (^{2}1969).

ANEPS — *The Ancient Near East Supplementary Texts and Pictures*, ed. J. Pritchard, Princeton 1969.

ANET — *Ancient Near Eastern Texts Relating to the Old Testament*, ed. J. Pritchard, Princeton ^{2}1955.

AOB — *Altorientalische Bilder zum Alten Testament*, ed. H. Gressmann, Berlin-Leipzig ^{2}1927.

AOT — *Altorientalische Texte zum Alten Testament*, ed. H. Gressmann, Berlin-Leipzig ^{2}1926.

ARW — *Archiv für Religionswissenschaft* (Freiburg-Tübingen), Leipzig 1898ff.

ASAE — *Annales du service des antiquités de l'Egypte*, Cairo 1900ff.

AT — The Complete Bible: An American Translation.

ATD — Das Alte Testament Deutsch, ed. A. Weiser, 25 vols., Göttingen 1951ff.

AuS — G. Dalman, *Arbeit und Sitte in Palästina* (6 vols.), Hildesheim ^{2}1964.

BCP — Psalter, The Book of Common Prayer, 1928.

BHH — *Biblisch-historisches Handwörterbuch*, ed. B. Reicke and L. Rost, 3 vols., Göttingen 1962–1966.

BIFAO — *Bulletin de l'Institut Français d'Archéologie Orientale*, Cairo 1901ff.

BK AT — Biblischer Kommentar Altes Testament, ed. M. Noth and W. Wolff, Neukirchen-Vluyn 1956ff.

BL — *Bibel-Lexikon*, ed. H. Haag, Einsiedeln-Zurich-Cologne ^{2}1968.

BM — British Museum.

BWANT — Beiträge zur Wissenschaft vom Alten und Neuen Testament (Stuttgart) Leipzig 1908ff.

BZAW — Beihefte zur *ZAW* (Giessen) Berlin 1896ff.

BZNW — Beihefte zur *ZNW* (Giessen) Berlin 1900ff.

CBQ — *Catholic Biblical Quarterly*, Washington 1939ff.

Eissfeldt *KS* — O. Eissfeldt, *Kleine Schriften*, 3 vols., Tübingen 1962–1966.

Ev Theol — *Evangelische Theologie*, Munich 1934ff.

FRLANT — Forschungen zur Religion und Literatur des Alten und Neuen Testaments, Göttingen 1903ff.

Galling *BRL* — K. Galling, *Biblisches Reallexikon* (HAT 1), Tübingen 1937.

HAT — Handbuch zum Alten Testament, ed. O. Eissfeldt, Tübingen 1934ff.

HUCA — *Hebrew Union College Annual*, Cincinnati 1914ff.

IEJ — *Israel Exploration Journal*, Jerusalem 1950ff.

IWB — *Illustrated World of the Bible Library*, ed. B. Mazar, 5 vols., New York-Toronto-London 1958–1961 (= *Views of the Biblical World*, Jerusalem-Ramat Gan 1958–1961).

JAOS — *Journal of the American Oriental Society*, New Haven 1843ff.

JB — Jerusalem Bible.

JBL — *Journal of Biblical Literature*, published by the Society of Biblical Literature (Philadelphia) Boston 1881ff.

JEA	*Journal of Egyptian Archaeology,* London 1914ff.
JNES	*Journal of Near Eastern Studies,* Chicago 1942ff.
KAI	H. Donner/W. Röllig, *Kanaanäische und aramäische Inschriften,* 3 vols., Wiesbaden 1962–1964, vol. 1: ²1966, vol. 2: ²1968.
KJV	Authorized (King James) Version.
LD	R. Lepsius, *Denkmäler aus Ägypten und Äthiopien* (12 vols.), Berlin 1849–1858; reprint Osnabrück 1969.
LdA	*Lexikon der Alten Welt,* Zurich-Stuttgart 1965.
MAOG	*Mitteilungen der Altorientalischen Gesellschaft,* Leipzig 1925ff.
MDAIK	*Mitteilungen des Deutschen Archäologischen Instituts, Abteilung Kairo,* Wiesbaden.
MIFAO	Mémoires de l'Institut Français d'Archéologie Orientale, Cairo 1907ff.
MIOF	*Mitteilungen des Instituts für Orientforschung,* Berlin 1953ff.
MT	Masoretic text.
NAB	New American Bible.
OIP	Oriental Institute Publications, Chicago.
OLZ	*Orientalistische Literaturzeitung,* Leipzig 1898ff.
Or Ant	*Oriens Antiquus,* Rome 1962ff.
OTS	*Oudtestamentische Studiën,* Leiden 1942ff.
PEQ	*Palestine Exploration Quarterly,* London 1869ff.
PSBA	*Proceedings of the Society of Biblical Archeology,* London 1878ff.
RB	*Revue Biblique,* Paris 1892ff, 1904ff.
RdE	*Revue d'Egyptologie,* Paris 1933ff.
RLA	*Reallexikon der Assyriologie,* ed. E. Ebeling and B. Meissner, Berlin 1928ff.
RSVm	Revised Standard Version, margin.
SAHG	A. Falkenstein/W. von Soden, *Sumerische und akkadische Hymnen und Gebete,* Zurich-Stuttgart 1953.
SBM	Stuttgarter Biblische Monographien, ed. J. Haspecker and W. Pesch, Stuttgart 1967ff.
SBS	Stuttgarter Bibelstudien, ed. H. Haag, N. Lohfink and W. Pesch, Stuttgart 1965ff.
TGI	K. Galling, *Textbuch zur Geschichte Israels,* Tübingen ²1968.
ThB	Theologische Bücherei: Neudrucke und Berichte aus dem 20. Jahrhundert, Munich.
UT	C. H. Gordon, *Ugaritic Textbook* (Analecta Orientalia 38), Rome 1965.
VA	Berlin, Staatliche Museen, Vorderasiatische Abteilung.
VT	*Vetus Testamentum,* Leiden 1951ff.
VTS	Supplements to VT, Leiden 1953ff.
ZA	*Zeitschrift für Assyriologie und vorderasiatische Archäologie,* (Leipzig) Berlin 1886ff.
ZÄS	*Zeitschrift für Ägyptische Sprache und Altertumskunde,* Leipzig 1863ff.
ZAW	*Zeitschrift für die alttestamentliche Wissenschaft* (Giessen) Berlin 1881ff.
ZDPV	*Zeitschrift des Deutschen Palästina-Vereins* (Leipzig), Wiesbaden 1878ff.
ZThK	*Zeitschrift für Theologie und Kirche,* Tübingen 1891ff.

NOTES

INTRODUCTION

1. Cf. K. Jaritz, *Schriftarchäologie der altmesopotamischen Kultur*.
2. On both terms, cf. W. Wolf, *Die Kunst Ägyptens*, passim.
3. Cf. R. Anthes, "Mythologie und der gesunde Menschenverstand in Ägypten."
4. On this, cf. H. Schäfer, *Von ägyptischer Kunst*, pp. 163f.
5. Cf. also O. Keel, *Feinde und Gottesleugner*, pp. 63–68.
6. Cf. O. Michel in *BHH*, vol. 3, col. 2161. E. Brunner-Traut has coined the term *"Aspektive,"* derived from the German word *"Aspekt,"* for this mode of perception (cf. her epilogue in Schäfer, *Von ägyptischer Kunst*, pp. 395–432; and also by Brunner-Traut, *Aspektive und die historische Wandlung der Wahrnehmungsweise*). E. Hornung, who more

acutely perceives the particular manner of viewing reality as a particular kind of logic, uses the term *"Komplementarität,"* current in modern multiple-valued logic (cf. idem, *Der Eine und die Vielen*, pp. 233–40).
7. Cf. Schäfer, *Von ägyptischer Kunst*, pp. 283–317.
8. On this, cf. ibid., p. 118.
9. For this reason, I find the terms *"Aspektive"* and *"Komplementarität"* (cited above, n. 6) less than ideal.
10. C. Westermann, *Genesis*, p. 29.
11. Cf. Keel, *Feinde*, pp. 85–90.
12. Cf. H. Schäfer, "Weltgebäude der alten Ägypter."
13. A. Moret, *Du caractère religieux de la royauté pharaonique*; H. Frankfort, *Kingship and the Gods*, pp. 3–12.

CHAPTER I

1. This division follows that of H. Schäfer in "Weltgebäude der alten Ägypter."
2. On this entire question, cf. H. Schott, "Voraussetzung und Gegenstand altägyptischer Wissenschaft."
3. W. von Soden, *Leistung und Grenze sumerischer und babylonischer Wissenschaft*.
4. E. Heinrich and U. Seidl, "Grundrisszeichnungen aus dem Alten Orient."
5. *SAHG*, pp. 137–82, 372–74.
6. Ibid., p. 142.
7. Ibid., p. 182
8. Ibid., p. 66.
9. P. Lampl, *Cities and Planning in the Ancient Near East*.
10. *SAHG*, p. 90.
11. A. Erman, *Die Literatur der Ägypter*, p. 261.
12. Cf. H. Schäfer, *Von ägyptischer Kunst*, pp. 94f.
13. On this, cf. ibid., pp. 148–52.
14. G. Goyon, "Le Papyrus de Turin dit 'des mines d'or' et le Wadi Hammamat."
15. A. Erman, "Denksteine aus der thebanischen Gräberstadt," p. 1099. Cf. *Plate XIII*.
16. Cf. E. D. van Buren, "Mountain-Gods." Cf. also Fig. *42* and chap. 3.1.

17. P. Grelot, "La géographie mythique d'Hénoch et ses sources orientales," p. 64.
18. H. J. Kraus; A. Deissler; M. Dahood.
19. H. and J. Lewy, "The Week and the Oldest West Asiatic Calendar."
20. E. Unger, *Babylon, die heilige Stadt nach der Beschreibung der Babylonier*, p. 257, n. 1. *Gilgamesh* 11.139. On the discussion as a whole see Grelot, pp. 64–68.
21. *Gilgamesh*, Tablet 9, 2.1–5, 9, 20. Cf. P. A. Schollmeyer, *Sumerisch-babylonische Hymnen und Gebete an Šamaš*, p. 37.
22. H. Gunkel; A. Weiser; H. J. Kraus; A. Deissler.
23. W. Westendorf, *Altägyptische Darstellungen des Sonnenlaufes auf der abschüssigen Himmelsbahn*.
24. Cf. Schäfer, "Weltgebäude der alten Ägypter," p. 91.
25. H. Schäfer, "Die Ausdeutung der Spiegelplatte als Sonnenscheibe."
26. Westendorf, *Altägyptische Darstellungen des Sonnenlaufes*, pp. 18f.
27. Cf. p. 20 above.
28. Schäfer, "Weltgebäude," p. 97.
29. Cf. *Plate I A*.
30. Cf. B. Pering, "Die geflügelte Scheibe

in Assyrien"; and P. Welten, *Die Königs-Stempel,* pp. 19–31.

31. H. Frankfort, *Cylinder Seals,* pp. 7, 182.

32. O. Eissfeldt, "Die Flügelsonne als künstlerisches Motiv und als religiöses Symbol," pp. 417ff.

33. *Gilgamesh,* Tablet 9, 2.1–9.

34. *BHH,* vol. 3, col. 2162.

35. H. A. Brongers, "Merismus, Synekdoche und Hendiadys in der Bibel-Hebräischen Sprache," pp. 102–5.

36. *Pyramid Texts,* Utterances 308, 604, 890, 1208ff.

37. Cf. W. Staudacher, *Die Trennung von Himmel und Erde.*

38. Cf. *AOB,* no. 265.

39. This will be dealt with in greater detail below.

40. A. Piankoff, "Une statuette du dieu Heka."

41. This has been overlooked by M. Weyersberg, who has assembled a wealth of material on this problem in "Das Motiv der 'Himmelsstütze' in der altägyptischen Kosmologie."

42. J. Vandier, "Le Dieu Shou dans le papyrus Jumilhac," pp. 268f.

43. *Pyramid Texts,* Utterances 285, 308, 474.

44. Ps 22:29 does not belong here, contra H. J. Tromp, *Primitive Conceptions of Death and the Nether World in the Old Testament,* p. 32. Cf. O. Keel, "Nochmals Ps 22, 28–32."

45. Cf. M. Delcor, "Les attaches littéraires, l'origine et la signification de l'expression biblique 'prendre à témoin le ciel et la terre.'"

46. A. Piankoff and N. Rambova, *Mythological Papyri,* p. 106.

47. H. H. Schmid, *Gerechtigkeit als Weltordnung.*

48. This is proved by Fig. 34, a fragment published by J. J. Clère.

49. Schäfer, "Weltgebäude," p. 87.

50. Westendorf, *Altägyptische Darstellungen des Sonnenlaufes,* p. 65, n. 8.

51. Erman, *Literatur,* p. 163.

52. *AOT,* p. 131.

53. W. Wolf, "Der Berliner Ptah-Hymnus," p. 32; *AOT,* p. 17.

54. Cf. F. Daumas, "Sur trois représentations de Nout à Dendera."

55. E.g., Piankoff and Rambova, *Mythological Papyri,* no. 30.

56. Cf. N. Rambova, "Symbolism."

57. On this, cf. B. H. Stricker, *De groote Zeeslang.*

58. A. Piankoff, "Une représentation rare sur l'une des chapelles de Toutânkhamon," p. 113, n. 1.

59. Wolf, "Ptah-Hymnus," p. 27.

60. Contra A. Moortgat, *Die Kunst des Alten Mesopotamien,* pp. 106f.

61. Contra Moortgat, ibid.

62. Cf. Moortgat, ibid., pl. 283.

63. *SAHG,* pp. 102f.

64. Cf. P. Amiet, "Notes sur le répetoire iconographique de Mari à l'époque du palais," pp. 219–21.

65. J. Aistleitner, *Die mythologischen und kultischen Texte aus Ras Schamra,* p. 18.

66. K. Frank, *Babylonische Beschwörungsreliefs,* p. 72.

67. Aistleitner, pp. 31, 40.

68. E. D. van Buren, "The Dragon in Ancient Mesopotamia," p. 17.

69. Frankfort, *Cylinder Seals,* pp. 102f.

70. Cf. G. R. Driver, "Mythical Monsters in the Old Testament."

71. Cf. Aistleitner, p. 14.

72. T. Solyman, *Die Entstehung und Entwicklung der Götterwaffen im alten Mesopotamien und ihre Bedeutung,* pp. 58, 110.

73. Contra *ANEP,* no. 691.

74. A. M. Gierlich, *Der Lichtgedanke in den Psalmen.*

75. L. I. J. Stadelmann, *The Hebrew Conception of the World,* pp. 7f.; cf. G. Posener, *De la divinité du Pharaon,* pp. 56f.; Hos 2:23f. evidences a train of thought similar to the passages cited by Posener.

76. Von Soden, *Leistung und Grenze,* pp. 29–50.

77. "Die Weisheit Salomos."

78. "Hiob 38 und die altägyptische Weisheit."

79. "Eine 'Naturlehre' in den Sargtexten."

80. *AOT,* p. 16.

81. Frankfort, *Kingship and the Gods,* p. 159.

82. A. Barucq, *L'Expression de la louange divine et de la prière dans la Bible et en Egypte,* pp. 212–15.

83. Cf. Keel, "Nochmals Ps 22."

CHAPTER II

1. K. Seybold, *Das Gebet des Kranken im Alten Testament*, pp. 20–23. In his very careful investigation of the problem, Seyboldt accepts only Pss 38, 41, and 88 as psalms with positive reference to the sickness or healing of the suppliant (idem, pp. 98–117). He concedes a probable reference to sickness and healing to Pss 30, 39, 69, 102, 103, and Isa 38:9–20 (idem, pp. 123–53).

2. K. Kenyon, *Archaeology in the Holy Land*, pl. 38.

3. G. Quell, *Die Auffassung des Todes in Israel*, pp. 17ff.

4. H. Bonnet, *Bilderatlas zur Religionsgeschichte*, p. 76.

5. J. Vandier, *Manuel d'archéologie égyptienne*, vol. 3, pp. 471–74.

6. N. H. Ridderbos, "'*pr* als Staub des Totenortes."

7. N. J. Tromp, *Primitive Conceptions of Death and the Nether World in the Old Testament*, p. 69.

8. Herodotus *History* 2.86.

9. G. Kolpaktchy, *Ägyptisches Totenbuch*, pp. 247ff.

10. E. Otto, *Das ägyptische Mundöffnungsritual*, vol. 2, pp. 80–87.

11. H. Brunner, "Die Strafgrube."

12. Cf. Tromp, *Primitive Conceptions*, p. 67.

13. For a critique of Tromp's book, cf. W. von Soden, "Assyriologische Erwägungen zu einem neuen Buch über die Totenreichvorstellungen im AT."

14. Cf. J. Spiegel, *Die Idee vom Totengericht in der ägyptischen Religion*.

15. On the weighing, cf. H. A. Ducros, "Étude sur les balances égyptiennes."

16. Cf. *AuS*, vol. 1, pt. 2, p. 528.

17. H. J. Kraus, *Psalmen*, p. 43.

18. O. Keel, *Feinde und Gottesleugner*, pp. 36–51.

19. Cf. H. Klengel, "Neue Lamaštu-Amulette aus dem Vorderasiatischen Museum zu Berlin und dem British Museum"; and B. Meissner, "Siegelzylinder mit Krankheitsbeschwörungen."

20. F. Thureau-Dangin, "Rituel et amulettes contre Labartu," p. 190.

21. H. Schmökel, *Ur, Assur und Babylon*, p. 119.

22. Cf. K. Frank, *Babylonische Beschwörungsreliefs*, p. 50.

23. J. Henninger, "Geisterglaube bei den vorislamischen Arabern," pp. 287ff.

24. W. S. Smith, *The Art and Architecture of Ancient Egypt*, pp. 3f.

25. A. Rowe, *The Four Canaanite Temples of Beth-Shan*, vol. 1, pl. 38A, no. 14.

26. O. Eissfeldt, "Zur Deutung von Motiven auf den 1937 gefundenen phönizischen Elfenbeinarbeiten von Megiddo," pp. 91f.

27. H. Torczyner, "A Hebrew Incantation against Night Demons from Biblical Time," p. 19.

28. M. Dahood, *Psalms*, vol. 2, p. 331.

29. Cf. H. Gese et al., *Die Religionen Altsyriens, Altarabiens und der Mandäer*, p. 180.

30. Cf. Keel, *Feinde*, p. 201.

31. *ANEP*, nos. 67, 276.

32. Cf. Keel, *Feinde*, p. 73.

33. Cf. B. Meissner, *Assyrische Jagden*, p. 6.

34. H. Ricke et al., *The Beit el Wali Temple of Rameses II*, plates 10 and 14.

35. O. Weber, *Die Dämonenbeschwörung bei den Babyloniern und Assyrern*, p. 11.

36. G. Roeder, *Urkunden zur Religion des alten Ägyptens*, p. 245.

37. *AOT*, p. 57.

38. *AuS*, vol. 6, p. 334.

39. S. N. Kramer, *History Begins at Sumer*, p. 125.

40. A. Erman, *Die Literatur der Ägypter*, p. 259.

41. R. Haase, *Die keilschriftlichen Rechtssammlungen in deutscher Übersetzung*, p. 16.

42. G. Posener, "La mésaventure d'un Syrien et le nom égyptien de l'ours."

43. Cf. Keel, *Feinde*, p. 202.

44. H. Gunkel, *Die Psalmen*, p. 34.

45. Meissner, *Jagden*, p. 8.

46. Cf. ibid.

47. *Le filet divin*.

48. M. Alliot, "Les rites de la chasse au filet aux temples de Karnak, d'Edfou et d'Esneh"; H. W. Fairman, "The Kingship Rituals of Egypt," pp. 89–92.

49. Keel, *Feinde*, p. 196.

50. B. Grdseloff, "Zum Vogelfang"; cf. also Vandier, *Manuel*, vol. 5, pp. 307–13.

51. G. R. Driver, "Hebrew *môqeš*, 'striker.'"

52. Cf. E. Vogt, "'Ihr Tisch werde zur Falle' (Ps 69, 23)." Such a snare, like a bar (Amos 1:5), can be broken (Ps 124:7; contra G. Dalman, *AuS*, vol. 6, p. 338).

53. *AuS*, vol. 6, pp. 320–24 and figs. 60–62.

54. Xenophon *Cyn.* 122; J. Lips, *Fallensysteme der Naturvölker,* p. 47, fig. 90.

55. Cf. *ANEP,* no. 186; A. Erman and H. Ranke, *Ägypten und ägyptisches Leben im Altertum,* p. 274.

56. Contra Vandier, *Manuel,* vol. 4, p. 747.

57. W. Guglielmi, *Reden, Rufe and Lieder auf altägyptischen Darstellungen der Landwirtschaft, Viehzucht, des Fisch- und Vogelfangs vom Mittleren Reich bis zur Spätzeit,* p. 29.

58. Cf., e.g., A. de Buck, *Egyptian Reading Book,* pp. 11f.

59. L. W. King, *Babylonian Boundary Stones and Memorial Tablets in the British Museum,* p. 47; on the identification of the symbols, cf. U. Seidl, "Die babylonischen Kudurru Reliefs."

60. K. Koch, "Gibt es ein Vergeltungsdogma im Alten Testament?"

61. Cf. E. Pax, "Studien zum Vergeltungsproblem der Psalmen."

62. Cf. S. Moscati, *Historical Art in the Ancient Near East,* p. 58.

63. Cf. O. Keel, "Kanaanäische Sühneriten auf ägyptischen Tempelreliefs."

64. Cf., e.g., P. Albenda, "An Assyrian Relief Depicting a Nude Captive in Wellesley College."

65. Cf. J. Leclant, "La 'Mascarade' de boeufs gras et le triomphe de l'Egypte"; S. Schott, "Ein ungewöhnliches Symbol des Triumphes über die Feinde Ägyptens"; M. Abdul-Ḳader, "The Administration of Syro-Palestine during the New Kingdom," pl. 1 (showing a Syrian being paraded in an animal cage); D. Wildung, "Der König Aegyptens als Herr der Welt? Ein seltener ikonographischer Typus der Königsplastik des Neuen Reiches."

66. The original is unfortunately lost.

67. D. J. Wiseman, *Chronicles of Chaldean Kings (626–556 B. C.) in the British Museum,* p. 51; *AOT,* pp. 450ff.

68. *ANEP,* no. 344; for the cutting down of fruit trees in military actions in Egyptian texts, cf. the extensive collection of passages in H. Grapow, *Studien zu den Annalen Thutmosis des Dritten und zu ihnen verwandten historischen Berichten des Neuen Reiches,* pp. 59f.

69. J. Wellhausen, *Reste arabischen Heidentums,* p. 150; A. Jaussen, *Coutumes des Arabes du pays de Moab,* p. 320.

70. Cf. *ANET,* p. 262 c.

71. Cf. H. G. Güterbock, "Narration in Anatolian, Syrian, and Assyrian Art," esp. p. 64.

CHAPTER III

1. K. M. Kenyon, *Jerusalem: Excavating 3000 Years of History,* pp. 58–59.

2. L. H. Vincent, *Jérusalem de l'Ancien Testament,* vol. 1, pp. 328–30.

3. Cf. A. de Buck, *De egyptische Voorstellingen betreffende den Oerheuvel;* A. Saleh, "The So-called 'Primeval Hill' and Other Related Elevations in Ancient Egyptian Mythology."

4. P. Barguet, *Le Temple d'Amon-Rê à Karnak,* pp. 29–33.

5. H. Bonnet, *Reallexikon der ägyptischen Religionsgeschichte,* pp. 847f.; H. Frankfort, *Kingship and the Gods,* pp. 151–54.

6. I. E. S. Edwards, *The Pyramids of Egypt,* p. 288.

7. F. Stolz, *Strukturen und Figuren im Kult von Jerusalem,* pp. 111–21.

8. Tablet 6.2.

9. *AOT,* p. 122.

10. A. Parrot, *Sintflut und Arche Noahs; Der Turm von Babel; Ninive und das Alte Testament,* p. 103.

11. *Gilgamesh* 11.156.

12. W. F. Edgerton and J. A. Wilson, *Historical Records of Ramses III,* p. 128.

13. H. J. Kraus, "Archäologische und topographische Probleme Jerusalems im Lichte der Psalmenexegese," p. 126.

14. Cf. J. Boehmer, "Tabor, Hermon und andere Hauptberge"; O. Mowan, "Quatuor Montes Sacri in Ps 89, 13?"

15. Cf. R. J. Clifford, *The Cosmic Mountain in Canaan and the Old Testament.*

16. Cf. M. Dahood, *Psalms,* vol. 1, p. 77.

17. *Itinerarium Burdigalense* 591.4

18. *Comm. in Matt.* 24.15.

19. T. A. Busink, *Der Tempel von Jerusalem,* vol. 1, *Der Tempel Salomos,* pp. 1–20.

20. E. Vogt, "Vom Tempel zum Felsendom."

21. R. de Vaux, *Ancient Israel,* p. 318.

22. R. A. S. Macalister, *The Excavation of Gezer,* vol. 2, pp. 400–402; G. Schumacher, *Tell el-Mutesellim,* vol. 1, pp. 154–60.

23. Cf. J. Schreiner, *Sion-Jerusalem: Jahwes Königssitz.*

24. Cf. J. Jeremias, "Lade und Zion: Zur Entstehung der Zionstradition"; H. Gese, "Der Davidsbund und die Zionserwählung"; idem, "Natus ex Virgine."

25. "Ezechieltempel und Salomostadt."

26. W. Westendorf, *Das Alte Ägypten (Kunst im Bild),* p. 108.

27. A. Dessenne, *Le Sphinx,* pp. 176f.

28. C. F.-A. Schaeffer, *Ugaritica,* vol. 1, p. 21 and pl. 3.2. U. Schweitzer, in her monograph, *Löwe und Sphinx im alten Aegypten,* vigorously contested the function of these two figures as guardians (pp. 34, 36, 49f.), but her contentions have deservedly failed to gain any acceptance (Dessenne, *Le Sphinx,* pp. 176f.; R. de Vaux, "Les Chérubins et l'Arche d'alliance, les Sphinx gardiens et les trônes divins dans l'Ancien Testament," p. 237.

29. Cf. I. Fuhr-Jaeppelt, *Materialien zur Ikonographie des Löwenadlers Anzu-Imdugud.*

30. SAHG, p. 88.

31. Cf. K. Koch, "Tempeleinlassliturgien und Dekaloge"; K. Galling, "Der Beichtspiegel."

32. A. Erman, *Die Religion der Ägypter: Ihr Werden und Vergehen in vier Jahrtausenden,* p. 190; H. W. Fairman, "A Scene of Offering Truth in the Temple of Edfu"; H. Junker, "Vorschriften für den Tempelkult in Philae."

33. SAHG, p. 273.

34. Cf. Y. Shiloh, "The Four Room House: Its Situation and Function in the Israelite City."

35. Y. Aharoni, "Trial Excavation in the 'Solar Shrine' at Lachish: Preliminary Report," pp. 157–64.

36. G. Martiny, *Die Gegensätze im babylonischen und assyrischen Tempelbau,* pp. 3–11.

37. This is the opinion of Busink, *Der Tempel,* p. 146.

38. Cited by Josephus *Contra Apionem* 1.198. On the inertia of cultic installations, Cf. J. Hofer, "Zur Phänomenologie des Sakralraumes und sein Symbolismus im Alten Orient mit Berücksichtigung der Bauformen," pp. 5f., 204f.

39. Cf. S. Moscati, *Die Phöniker von 1200 vor Christus bis zum Untergang Karthagos,* pp. 104f.

40. W. S. Smith, *The Art and Architecture of Ancient Egypt,* p. 152; cf. p. 133.

41. Cf. Erman, *Religion,* pp. 167f.

42. Cf. Bonnet, *Reallexikon,* p. 783.

43. Hofer, "Phänomenologie des Sakralraums," p. 140, cf. pp. 132–40.

44. SAHG, p. 130.

45. Ibid., p. 135.

46. W. Andrae, "Der kultische Garten"; cf. F. Stolz, "Die Bäume des Gottesgartens auf dem Libanon."

47. S. Schott, *Altägyptische Liebeslieder,* pp. 48f.

48. H. Kees, *Der Götterglaube im Alten Ägypten,* p. 96.

49. Cf. K. Galling, *Der Altar in den Kulturen des Alten Orients,* IV.9-V.31.33f.

50. I. Seibert, *Hirt-Herde-König,* p. 21.

51. Cf. Busink, *Der Tempel,* pp. 335f.

52. Cf. *RLA* I:122–124.

53. Regarding other sacred water basins from the Mesopotamian-Syrian sphere, cf. Figs. *184–85* and Busink, *Der Tempel,* pp. 332–35.

54. Bonnet, *Reallexikon,* pp. 694f.

55. Cf. Busink, *Der Tempel,* pp. 333f.

56. F. Delitzsch, *Biblischer Kommentar über die Psalmen,* ad loc.

57. H. Junker, "Der Strom, dessen Arme die Stadt Gottes erfreuen," pp. 197–201.

58. H. Gunkel, *Die Psalmen,* ad loc.

59. H. J. Kraus, *Psalmen,* ad loc.

60. Ibid., p. 343.

61. De Vaux, "Chérubins," pp. 238–42; on the symbolism of the holy tree cf. H. Danthine, *Le palmier-dattier et les arbres sacrés dans l'iconographie de l'Asie occidentale ancienne,* vol. 1, pp. 136–64.

62. H. G. May and R. M. Engberg, *Material Remains of the Megiddo Cult,* pl. 40.

63. J. Nougayrol, *Cylindres-Sceaux et empreintes de cylindres trouvés en Palestine au cours de fouilles regulières,* pp. 23–25.

64. Cf. H. Frankfort, *The Art and Architecture of the Ancient Orient,* pp. 135–37.

65. Cf., however, M. T. Barrelet, "Une peinture de la cour 106 du palais de Mari," pp. 17–19; but cf. also H. Frankfort et al., *The Gimilsin Temple and the Palace of the Rulers at Tel Asmar,* pp. 202f., 215.

66. Cf. Galling, *Der Altar,* pp. 67f.

67. Cf. Ibid., pp. 59, 67; for a different interpretation see Barguet, *Le Temple,* p. 223, n. 2.

68. Y. Aharoni, "The Horned Altar of Beer-Sheba."

69. K. Galling, *BRL,* col. 21.

70. J. de Groot, *Die Altäre des salomonischen Tempels,* pp. 44f.

71. Galling, *Der Altar,* p. 69.

72. Josephus *Contra Apionem* 1. 198.

73. *Bellum Judaicum* 5.5–6.

74. *IWB* III: 164. It is not necessary to accept the opinion of H. Ingholt in "Le sens du mot hammān," that the *ḥammān* would have stood *upon* the block altar of Fig. *200.*

K. Galling ("Ba'al Ḥammon in Kition und die Ḥammanîm," pp. 68f.) rightly criticizes this hypothesis. The ḥammān depicted in Fig. 200 may, however, have stood beside the block altar. Nevertheless, Galling prefers to understand ḥammān as a designation for the small, four-footed incense coffers which emerged in Mesopotamia in the seventh century B.C. and soon spread into Palestine (idem, pp. 69f.).

75. Galling, *Der Altar,* pp. 42f.

76. On Assyrian aqueducts, cf. T. Jacobsen and S. Lloyd, *Sennacherib's Aqueduct at Jerwan.*

77. B. Hrouda, *Die Kulturgeschichte des assyrischen Flachbildes,* pp. 60f.

78. Cf. Frankfort, *The Art,* pp. 182f.

79. Cf. W. Andrae, *Alte Feststrassen im Nahen Osten.*

80. S. Mowinckel, *Psalmenstudien,* vol. 2, pp. 128–30.

81. V. Müller, "Types of Mesopotamian Houses," pp. 167f.

82. Ibid., p. 173.

83. Ibid., p. 157.

84. Ibid., pp. 176f.

85. Busink, *Der Tempel,* p. 591.

86. G. R. H. Wright makes this mistake in his recent study, "Pre-Israelite Temples in the Land of Canaan," p. 30.

87. Cf. A. Kuschke, "Der Tempel Salomos und der 'syrische Tempeltypus,' " contra H. Schult, "Der Debir im salomonischen Tempel."

88. W. Andrae, "Haus-Grab-Tempel in Alt-Mesopotamien," p. 1042; and idem, *Das Gotteshaus und die Urformen des Bauens im Alten Orient,* p. 25.

89. A. Alt, "Verbreitung und Herkunft des syrischen Tempeltypus," p. 114.

90. "Phänomenologie des Sakralraums," pp. 193–95.

91. Busink, *Der Tempel,* pp. 580f.

92. Ibid., pp. 561f.

93. Ibid., p. 611.

94. M. Noth, *Könige,* p. 119.

95. Schult, "Der Debir."

96. H. Schmidt, *Der heilige Fels in Jerusalem,* p. 43.

97. Ibid., p. 44.

98. Schult, "Der Debir," pp. 48f.

99. Kuschke, "Der Tempel Salomos," p. 128.

100. Alt, "Verbreitung und Herkunft."

101. Kuschke, "Der Tempel Salomos," p. 130.

102. Alt, "Verbreitung und Herkunft," p. 101.

103. Bonnet, *Reallexikon,* pp. 504f.

104. M. Noth, *Das zweite Buch Mose: Exodus,* p. 172.

105. *Der Tempel,* p. 609.

106. H. Schmidt, *Der Heilige Fels,* strongly advocates this view.

107. Noth, *Könige,* p. 152.

108. J. Oulette has recently expressed the view that they did in "Le vestibule du temple de Salomon était-il un *bit hilani?*"

109. S. Yeivin, "Jachin and Boaz," pls. 11.1 and 3.

110. A. Kuschke and M. Metzger, "Kumudi und die Ausgrabungen auf Tell Kāmid el-Lōz," p. 173 and pl. 6.

111. *Könige,* p. 154.

112. Cf. W. S. Smith, *Interconnections in the Ancient Near East,* p. 100; cf. also the caption of Fig. 220a.

113. *Könige,* p. 167.

114. W. Kornfeld, "Der Symbolismus der Tempelsäulen."

115. Yeivin, "Jachin and Boaz," pp. 102–4.

116. *Bellum Judaicum* 6.5.5.

117. Josephus *Antiquitates Judaicae* 3.6.7

118. E. R. Goodenough, *Jewish Symbols in the Greco-Roman World,* vol. 4, p. 95.

119. W. Wirgin, "The Menorah as Symbol of After-Life," pp. 102–4.

120. Contra Noth, *Könige,* p. 182.

121. Ibid., p. 181.

122. J. Maier, *Vom Kultus zur Gnosis,* p. 85.

123. De Vaux, "Chérubins," p. 234.

124. Maier, pp. 73–78.

125. Cf. H. Seyrig, "Trônes phéniciens flanqués de sphinx," which treats ten well known cherubim thrones; and de Vaux, "Chérubins," pp. 245–52.

126. E. Gjerstad, *The Swedish Cyprus Expedition, 1927–31,* vol. 2, p. 731.

127. L. Dürr, *Ezechiels Vision von der Erscheinung Gottes (Ez C. 1 und 10) im Lichte der vorderasiatischen Altertumskunde;* O. Keel, *Jahwevisionen und Siegelkunst.*

128. "Gerechtigkeit als Fundament des Thrones."

129. Cf. Schmid, *Gerechtigkeit.*

130. *KAI,* vol. 2, pp. 23f.

131. A. Moret, *Le rituel du culte divin journalier en Egypte d'après les papyrus de Berlin et les textes du temple de Sethi I à Abydos,* pp. 49f.

132. Ibid., p. 104.

133. Ibid., pp. 96f.

134. H. Grapow, *Vergleiche und andere bildliche Ausdrücke im Ägyptischen,* p. 15.

135. G. Roeder, *Die ägyptische Götterwelt,* p. 80.

136. Hofer, "Phänomenologie des Sakralraums," pp. 206–10.

137. Cf. H. Wildberger, *Jesaja,* pp. 245f.

138. *Enuma elish* 6.46–52; A. S. Kapelrud, "Temple Building, a Task for Gods and Kings."

139. Cf. D. Opitz, "Studien zur altorientalischen Kunst," pp. 61f.

140. *ANET,* pp. 5, 417.

141. R. S. Ellis, *Foundation Deposits in Ancient Mesopotamia.*

142. Noth, *Könige,* p. 193.

143. Josephus *Contra Apionem* 1.199.

CHAPTER IV

1. Cf. E. Heinrich, *Bauwerke in der altsumerischen Bildkunst,* p. 83.

2. J. Aistleitner, *Die mythologischen und kultischen Texte aus Ras Schamra,* 90, IK, lines 74–81.

3. J. Begrich, "Die Vertrauensäusserungen im israelitischen Klagelied des Einzelnen und in seinem babylonischen Gegenstück," p. 210.

4. On this, cf. O. Keel, *Feinde und Gottesleugner,* pp. 216–26.

5. The new studies of P. Hugger ("Jahwe, mein Fels") and D. Eichhorn *(Gott als Fels, Burg und Zuflucht: Eine Untersuchung zum Gebet des Mittlers in den Psalmen)* point in this direction.

6. H. Schmidt, *Der heilige Fels in Jerusalem,* p. 78.

7. A. Erman, "Denksteine aus der thebanischen Gräberstadt," pp. 1098–1100.

8. A. Wiegand, "Der Gottesname *ṣūr* und seine Deutung in dem Sinne Bildner oder Schöpfer in der alten jüdischen Literatur."

9. *Amarna Tablets,* no. 10, lines 17–20; cf. no. 7, lines 69–72.

10. There is a collection of similar scenes in H. Junker, "Die Hieroglyphen für 'Erz' und 'Erzarbeiter.' "

11. Cf. M. Dahood, *Psalms,* vol. 1, pp. xxixf.

12. *ANEP,* no. 594.

13. Ibid., no. 595.

14. B. Meissner, *Babylonien und Assyrien,* vol. 2, p. 267.

15. S. A. Cook, *The Religion of Ancient Palestine in the Light of Archaeology,* p. 41.

16. For similar depictions of the Torah shrine, cf. E. L. Sukenik, "Designs of the Torah Shrine in Ancient Synagogues in Palestine."

17. H. J. Kraus, *Psalmen,* p. 132; cf. also H. Gunkel, *Die Psalmen,* Ps 57.

18. Diogenes Laertius 6.2.59.

19. Cf. J. Jeremias, *Kultprophetie und Gerichtsverkündigung in der späteren Königszeit Israels.*

20. Cf. C. M. Doughty, *Die Offenbarung Arabiens,* p. 542; J. J. Hess, *Von den Beduinen des Innern Arabiens,* p. 94.

21. Utterance 604.

22. *Book of the Dead,* chap. 173.

23. Ibid., chap. 181.

24. A. Moret, "Sur le rite de l'embrassement."

25. Cf. F. Nötscher, *"Das Angesicht Gottes schauen" nach biblischer und babylonischer Auffassung,* pp. 60–62.

26. Ibid., pp. 62–84.

27. On this democratization, cf. H. Gunkel and J. Begrich, *Einleitung in die Psalmen,* pp. 147–49.

28. On this, cf. W. Spiegelberg, "Die Weihstatuette einer Wöchnerin."

29. E. D. van Buren, "A Clay Relief in the Iraq Museum," pp. 170f.

30. H. Frankfort, "A Note on the Lady of Birth."

31. On this interpretation, cf. P. Delougaz, "Animals Emerging from a Hut."

32. A. Falkenstein, *Archaische Texte aus Uruk,* no. 213.

33. On this, cf. O. Keel, *Die Weisheit "spielt" vor Gott,* pp. 9–11.

34. Aistleitner, Texte, 20, I AB 3–4, line 5.

35. *KAI* 26, III, 18.

36. Aistleitner, *Texte,* 41, II AB 4–5, 41.

37. Ibid., 41, II AB 4–5, 65.

38. Cf. O. Eissfeldt, "El und Jahwe."

39. T. Fish, "The Zu-Bird."

40. A. Gamper, *Gott als Richter in Mesopotamien und im Alten Testament,* p. 94, cf. pp. 76–87.

41. *SAHG,* p. 240.

42. P. A. Schollmeyer, *Sumerisch-babylonische Hymnen und Gebete an Šamaš,* pp. 5–7.

43. H. Bonnet, *Reallexikon der ägyptischen*

Religionsgeschichte, p. 628; J. Spiegel, "Der Sonnengott in der Barke als Richter."

44. Cf. H. W. Jüngling, *Der Tod der Götter: Eine Untersuchung zu Psalm 82*, pp. 38–69.

45. A. Erman, "Gebete eines ungerecht Verfolgten und andere Ostraka in den Königsgräbern," p. 27.

46. A. Scharff, *Ägyptische Sonnenlieder*.

47. Bonnet, *Reallexikon*, p. 626.

48. W. S. Smith (*The Art and Architecture of Ancient Egypt*, pp. 46, 68; *Interconnections in the Ancient Near East*, p. 147) takes the many scenes of animal and human life which decorate the sun temple of the Fifth Dynasty as an indication that the ornamentation of Old Kingdom tombs with similar scenes derives from the sanctuary of the sun at Heliopolis.

49. "A propos des rapports du Psaume 104 avec les textes égyptiens."

50. *ANET*, pp. 370–71.

51. A. Moret, *Le rituel du culte divin journalier en Egypte d'après les papyrus de Berlin et les texts du temple de Sethi I à Abydos*, p. 140.

52. Aistleitner, *Texte*, 45, II AB 7, lines 29–41.

53. Ibid., 101, II K 3, 5–11.

54. A. Vanel, *L'iconographie du dieu de l'orage dans le proche-orient ancien jusqu'au VIIème siècle avant J.-C.*, p. 148.

55. Cf. B. Pering, "Die gelügelte Scheibe in Assyrien," p. 284.

56. Cf. H. Frankfort, *The Art and Architecture of the Ancient Orient*, pp. 124f.

57. *SAHG*, pp. 141f.

58. *AOB*, text at no. 332.

59. Dahood, *Psalms*, vol. 1, p. 115.

60. Cf. Pering, "Die geflügelte Scheibe."

61. J. Koenig, "Aux origines des théophanies jahwistes."

62. J. Jeremias, *Theophanie*, pp. 87–90.

63. Ibid., p. 89.

64. *SAHG*, p. 230.

65. H. Granqvist, *Child Problems among the Arabs*, p. 35.

66. Bonnet, *Reallexikon*, p. 638.

67. Cf. G. von Rad, *Der Heilige Krieg im alten Israel;* R. Smend, *Jahwekrieg und Stämmebund*.

68. Cf. Kraus, Deissler, etc. ad loc.

69. Herodotus *History* 1.215; cf. also Kraus, *Psalmen*, p. 274.

70. *WR* 5.7.

71. Dahood, *Psalms*, vol. 1, pp. 210f.

72. D. Conrad, "Der Gott Reschef."

73. *LdA*, p. 213.

74. *UT*, no. 854.

75. *KAI*, no. 32, lines 3f.

76. *AOT*, p. 282.

77. Gunkel, *Psalmen*, p. 14.

78. Contra Gunkel.

79. Cf. F. N. Jasper, "Early Israelite Traditions and the Psalter," pp. 50f., where Ps 95:7–11 is to be added to the list.

80. On this, cf. K. Baltzer, *Das Bundesformular*, pp. 19–28.

81. *Bildatlas zur Bibel*.

82. G. von Rad, " 'Gerechtigkeit' und 'Leben' in der Kultsprache der Psalmen," p. 242.

83. Ibid.

84. H. Gottlieb, "Die Tradition von David als Hirten," p. 194.

85. *AuS*, vol. 6, p. 222.

86. "Die Tradition," pp. 190–93.

87. Cf. G. van der Leeuw, *Phänomenologie der Religion*, pp. 488–91.

88. C. J. Labuschagne, *The Incomparability of Yahweh in the Old Testament*, pp. 33–34.

89. On this, cf. G. Posener, *De la divinité du Pharaon*, pp. 16f.; H. D. Preuss, *Verspottung fremder Religionen im Alten Testament*, pp. 42–49.

90. Cf. A. L. Oppenheim, *Ancient Mesopotamia*, pp. 183–98; Moret, *Rituel*.

91. U. Seidl, "Die babylonischen Kudurru Reliefs," pp. 132f.

92. Cf. Meissner, *BuA*, vol. 2, pp. 126–30.

93. O. Keel, "Das Vergraben der 'fremden Götter' in Genesis XXXV 4b," pp. 322ff.

94. Cf. G. von Rad, "Aspekte alttestamentlichen Welverständnisses."

95. Cf. K. Jaroš, *Die Stellung des Elohisten zur kanaanäischen Religion*, pp. 351–88.

96. W. Fauth, *Aphrodite Parakyptusa*.

97. Apuleius *Metamorphoses* 8.

98. On the criticism of the gods, cf. Preuss, *Verspottung fremder Religionen*.

99. G. Posener et al., *Knaurs Lexikon der ägyptischen Kultur*, p. 198.

100. Cf. H. G. Güterbock, "A Votive Sword with Old Assyrian Inscription," p. 101.

101. Bonnet, *Reallexikon*, p. 56.

102. Cf. Dalman, *AuS*, vol. 1, pt. 2, pp. 314–29.

CHAPTER V

1. Cf. J. Begrich, "Sōfēr und Mazkīr"; R. de Vaux, "Titres et fonctionnaires égyptiens à la cour de David et Salomon"; M. Noth, *Könige,* pp. 63–66; T. N. D. Mettinger, *Solomonic State Officials.*

2. H. Bonnet, *Reallexikon der ägyptischen Religionsgeschichte,* pp. 856–60; E. Otto, "Gehalt und Bedeutung des ägyptischen Heroenglaubens."

3. Cf. M. Noth's famous essay, "Gott, König, Volk im Alten Testament" and K. H. Bernhardt, *Das Problem der altorientalischen Königsideologie im Alten Testament.*

4. Bernhardt, *Königsideologie,* pp. 114–77.

5. Ibid., p. 176.

6. H. Goedicke, *Die Stellung des Königs im Alten Reich,* pp. 87–91.

7. G. Posener, *De la divinité du Pharaon.*

8. Cf. H. Brunner, *Die Geburt des Gottkönigs* and, for the late period, F. Daumas, *Les mammisis des temples égyptiens.* E. Brunner-Traut ("Pharao und Jesus als Söhne Gottes") substantially covers the parallels between the pharaonic birth narratives and the infancy narratives of the gospels. The OT genealogy of the NT birth narratives is nicely presented by H. Gese ("Natus ex Virgine"). Gese seems, however, to underemphasize somewhat the indirect influence which Egyptian royal ideology exerted on the birth narratives via the royal psalms.

9. Cf. G. A. Gaballa, "New Evidence on the Birth of Pharaoh."

10. Cf. Brunner, *Geburt,* p. 45.

11. Bonnet, *Reallexikon,* p. 513.

12. Brunner, *Geburt,* p. 45.

13. On the characterization of the overlord as "father" and the vassal as "son," cf. E. Lipinski, *Le Poème royal du Psaume LXXXIX 1–5.20–38.*

14. Brunner, *Geburt,* p. 46.

15. Ibid., pp. 38f.

16. Ibid., p. 119.

17. On the circumcision, cf. C. de Wit, "La circoncision chez les anciens Egyptiens."

18. Cf. H. Ranke, "Ein ägyptisches Relief in Princeton"; J. Leclant, "Le rôle du lait et de l'allaitement d'après les textes des pyramides"; W. Vycichl, "L'allaitement divin du Pharaon expliqué par une coutume africaine"; J. Leclant, "Les rites de purification dans le cérémonial pharaonique du couronnement," p. 49.

19. W. A. Ward, "La déesse nourricière d'Ugarit"; W. Orthmann, "Die säugende Göttin: Zu einem Relief aus Karatepe."

20. Brunner, *Geburt,* p. 43.

21. Ibid., p. 72.

22. H. J. Kraus, *Psalmen,* p. 757.

23. G. von Rad, "Das judäische Königsritual."

24. Kraus, *Psalmen,* pp. 755f., 762 et al.

25. Bonnet, *Reallexikon,* p. 396.

26. Cf. P. Barguet, "La structure du temple Ipet-Sout d'Amon à Karnak du Moyen Empire à Amenophis II."

27. Cf., e.g., A. W. Shorter, "Reliefs Showing the Coronation of Rameses II."

28. This point is also made by Leclant, "Les rites de purification," p. 48. Summaries of the coronation rites are found in the works of A. Moret (*Du caractère religieux de la royauté pharaonique,* pp. 75–113), H. Frankfort (*Kingship and the Gods,* pp. 105–9), H. W. Fairman ("The Kingship Rituals of Egypt," pp. 77–85), and in an Egyptian text, the coronation inscription of Haremhab (A. H. Gardiner, "The Coronation of King Ḥaremḥab").

29. Bonnet, *Reallexikon,* p. 649.

30. Cf. I. Seibert, *Hirt-Herde-König,* p. 31.

31. Cf. ibid., pp. 31–38.

32. Cf. the illustration of a similar anointing horn from Megiddo of the Late Bronze period in *IWB* II: 135.

33. Bonnet, *Reallexikon,* p. 649.

34. Moret, *Royauté,* pl. 2.

35. Cf. A. H. Gardiner, "The Baptism of Pharaoh"; for supplementation and certain criticisms of Gardiner, cf. Leclant, "Les rites de purification."

36. *AOT,* p. 639; cf. Z. W. Falk, "Gestures Expressing Affirmation."

37. Cf. H. Otten, "Zur Datierung und Bedeutung des Felsheiligtums von Yazilikaya," p. 239.

38. W. Westendorf, *Das Alte Ägypten,* p. 101.

39. A. Erman, *Die Literatur der Ägypter,* p. 319.

40. "Das judäische Königsritual," pp. 207f.

41. Cf. also R. de Vaux, *Ancient Israel,* p. 103.

42. For a critical analysis cf. G. Jones, "The Decree of Yahweh, Ps 2,7."

43. Cf. H. Cazelles, "La titulature du roi David."

44. "Jesaia 8,23–9,6: Befreiungsnacht und Krönungstag," pp. 218f.

45. Cf. the more recent studies of W. Zimmerli, "Vier oder fünf Thronnamen des messianischen Herrschers von Jes IV 5b.6"; and K. D. Schunck, "Der fünfte Thronname des Messias."

46. W. Helck, "Die Szene des Aufschreibens des Namens auf dem *išd*-Baum."

47. *LD*, vol. 5, pl. 37; Helck, ibid., fig. 1.

48. Cf. Frankfort, *Kingship*, p. 11.

49. *SAHG*, pp. 73, 118.

50. Ibid., p. 98.

51. *LD*, vol. 5, pl. 62b; cited by H. Gunkel, *Die Psalmen*, p. 482.

52. J. de Savignac, "Théologie pharaonique et messianisme d'Israel," p. 83, cites other similar examples.

53. H. J. Kraus, *Gottesdienst in Israel*, p. 259.

54. K. Homburg, "Psalm 110,1 im Rahmen des judäischen Krönungszeremoniells."

55. N. Poulssen, *König und Tempel im Glaubenszeugnis des Alten Testaments*, p. 29.

56. Bonnet, *Reallexikon*, p. 513.

57. Cf. H. Kees, "Horus und Seth als Götterpaar," pp. 21f.; and on the rite as a whole, cf. O. Keel, *Wirkmächtige Siegeszeichen im Alten Testament*, pp. 113–21.

58. *Pyramid Texts*, Utterance 249b; L. Borchardt, "Bilder des 'Zerbrechens der Krüge.'"

59. A. Moret, "Le rite de briser les vases rouges au temple de Louxor."

60. Cf., e.g., K. Sethe, *Die Ächtung feindlicher Fürsten, Völker und Dinge*; G. Posener, *Princes et pays d'Asie et de Nubie;* idem, "Les empreintes magiques de Gizeh et les morts dangereux."

61. A. Vila, "Un dépot de textes d'envoûtement du moyen empire."

62. C. E. de Vries, "A Ritual Ball Game?"; O. Keel, *Die Weisheit "spielt" vor Gott*, pp. 23–25.

63. J. F. Borghouts, "The Evil Eye of Apopis."

64. Cf. G. Fohrer, *Die symbolischen Handlungen der Propheten*, pp. 38–40; A. Bentzen, "The Ritual Background of Amos 1,2–2,16."

65. A. Kleber, "Ps 2,9 in the Light of an Ancient Oriental Ceremony."

66. Cf. O. Keel, *Vögel als Boten*, 109–41.

67. P. Garelli and M. Leibovici, *Schöpfungsmythen*, p. 148.

68. S. Sauneron, J. Yoyotte, et al., *Schöpfungsmythen*, pp. 95–98.

69. Moret, *Royauté*, p. 117, cf. pp. 115–30; Erman, *Literatur*, p. 81.

70. *SAHG*, pp. 155f.

71. Ibid., p. 154, cf. pp. 143, 145.

72. R. 'Engelbach, "A Foundation Scene of the Second Dynasty"; L. Borchardt, "Jubiläumsbilder."

73. Moret, *Royauté*, p. 133.

74. "Le rituel de fondation des temples égyptiens."

75. Poulssen, *König und Tempel*, p. 52.

76. T. A. Busink, *Der Tempel von Jerusalem*, vol. 1, pp. 618–37, 642–46.

77. Kraus, *Psalmen*, p. 760.

78. H. Schmökel, *Kulturgeschichte des Alten Orients*, p. 86.

79. H. Gunkel and J. Begrich, *Einleitung in die Psalmen*, pp. 147ff.

80. Cf. Keel, *Die Weisheit "spielt" vor Gott*, pp. 23–37.

81. A. Moret, *Le rituel du culte divine journalier en Egypte*, pp. 43, 55.

82. Ibid., pp. 9f., 16, 19, 21, 37, etc.

83. Cf. the vows of the Egyptian king, p. 269 above.

84. H. H. Schmid, *Gerechtigkeit als Weltordnung*, p. 58.

85. Bonnet, *Reallexikon*, p. 431.

86. On its military significance, cf. p. 238 above.

87. Cf. Noth, *Könige*, p. 15.

88. A scarab of Amenhotep II (1436–1413 B.C.) demonstrates the degree to which horses and love of horses were part of the kingly life: Amenhotep is shown feeding a prancing horse (H. R. Hall, *Catalogue of Egyptian Scarabs in the British Museum*, no. 1640). Beside the display window at Medinet Habu, Ramses III is shown inspecting his stallion (H. H. Nelson, *Later Historical Records of Ramses III*, pl. 109.

89. B. Meissner, *Assyrische Jagden*, p. 23.

90. *ANET*, p. 419.

91. Keel, *Wirkmächtige Siegeszeichen*, fig. 49.

92. On the theme in general, cf. D. Opitz and M. Wolff, "Jagd zu Pferde in der altorientalischen und klassischen Kunst," pp. 352–59.

93. De Vaux, *Ancient Israel*, pp. 33f.

94. *ANET*, pp. 257f.

95. W. Westendorf, "Bemerkungen zu den Namen der Könige Djer-Athotis und Neferka," p. 141.

96. Cf. S. N. Kramer, *The Sacred Marriage*.

97. Frankfort, *Kingship*, p. 297.

98. L. Dürr, *Ursprung und Ausbau der israelitisch-jüdischen Heilandserwartung*, pp. 94–105.

99. Ibid., p. 78.
100. *ANET*, p. 164.
101. Cf. A. Gamper, *Gott als Richter in Mesopotamien und im Alten Testament*, pp. 45–55.
102. B. Grdseloff, "L'insigne du grand juge égyptien"; G. Möller, "Das Amtsabzeichen des Oberrichters in der Spätzeit."
103. A. Erman and H. Ranke, *Ägypten und ägyptisches Leben im Altertum*, p. 59.
104. Schmid, *Gerechtigkeit*, p. 52.
105. *BHH*, vol. 2, cols. 887f.
106. A. Radwan, *Die Darstellungen des regierenden Königs und seiner Familienangehörigen in den Privatgräbern der 18. Dyn.*, pp. 32f.
107. J. Ziegler, "Die Hilfe Gottes 'am Morgen.' "
108. W. Wreszinski, *Atlas zur altägyptischen Kulturgeschichte*, vol. 1, pl. 331.
109. Ibid.; cf. Erman and Ranke, *Ägypten*, pp. 157f.
110. *The Tomb of Rekh-mi-rēʿ*, vol. 1, pp. 31f.
111. Cf. Begrich, "Sōfēr und Mazkîr," p. 95.
112. Cf. Frankfort, *Kingship*, pp. 3–12.
113. Cf. H. Schäfer, "Das Niederschlagen der Feinde"; Keel, *Wirkmächtige Siegeszeichen*, pp. 53f.
114. K. Seybold, "Das Herrscherbild des Bileamorakels Num 24,15–19."
115. Cf. Gunkel, *Psalmen*, p. 285.
116. "The Earliest Record of Egypt's Military Penetration into Asia?"
117. Cf. A. H. Gardiner, *Egyptian Grammar*, p. 7
118. Cf. F. Jesi, "Rapport sur les recherches relatives à quelques figurations du sacrifice humain dans l'Egypte pharaonique."
119. On this, cf. J. H. Breasted, *A History of Egypt*, pp. 156f.; A. H. Gardiner, *Egypt of the Pharaohs*, pp. 199f.
120. Gardiner, *Egypt*, p. 253.
121. J. de Morgan, *La préhistoire orientale*, vol. 2, pp. 240, 246; A. H. Gardiner et al., *Inscriptions of Sinai*, vol. 2, p. 27.
122. G. Gerster, *Sinai: Land der Offenbarung*, p. 44.
123. Cf. W. Helck, "Zu den ägyptischen Sinai-Inschriften," p. 423.
124. Schäfer, *Das Niederschlagen*, pp. 173ff.
125. Keel, *Wirkmächtige Siegeszeichen*, fig. 49.
126. Cf. S. Moscati, "Un avorio di Ugarit e l'iconografia del nemico vinto."
127. S. Ronzevalle, "Tablettes égyptiennes."
128. C. F.-A. Schaeffer, "Les fouilles de Ras Shamra-Ugarit," *Syria* 31 (1954), pp. 14–67, especially pp. 40–42.
129. H. Frankfort, *Cylinder Seals,* nos. 38d, 42f; E. Porada, *Corpus of Ancient Near Eastern Seals,* vol. 1, nos. 382, 877.
130. Keel, *Wirkmächtige Siegeszeichen*, pp. 51–76.
131. Cf. L. Borchardt, *Das Grabdenkmal des Königs Sahure*, vol. 2, p. 18.
132. *AOB*, text at nos. 143 and 144.
133. Cf. C. Aldred, "The 'New Year' Gifts to the Pharaoh."
134. Cf. H. Gross, *Die Idee des ewigen und allgemeinen Weltfriedens im Alten Orient und im Alten Testament*, pp. 172–78.

CHAPTER VI

1. Cf. W. Schmidt, "Anthropologische Begriffe im Alten Testament," p. 381.
2. Cf. A. H. Gardiner, *Egyptian Grammar*, p. 4.
3. Herrmann, *Theologisches Wörterbuch zum Neuen Testament* 785, 34–40.
4. *ANET*, pp. 21–22.
5. A. Moret, *Le rituel du culte divin journalier en Egypte*, pp. 56–67.
6. F. Heiler, "Die Körperhaltung beim Gebet," pp. 171f.
7. E. Dhorme, *Les Religions de Babylonie et d'Assyrie*, pp. 249f., 257.
8. A. Parrot, "Gestes de la prière dans le monde mesopotamien," p. 180.
9. R. Dussaud, *Les Religions des Hittites et des Hourrites, des Phéniciens et des Syriens*, p. 383.
10. Ibid.
11. E. Sollberger, "Old Babylonian Worshipper Figurines." In a recent study, G. Amad (*Le baiser rituel: Un geste de culte méconnu*) has suggested that the gestures of the suppliants in Figs. *239, 279, 390, 418,* etc. are to be interpreted as representations of the cultic kiss. This seems scarcely probable.
12. On this entire question, cf. O. Keel, *Wirkmächtige Siegeszeichen im Alten Testament*, pp. 95–103.

13. H. Schmökel, *Ur, Assur und Babylon,* p. 282.

14. *AOT,* p. 264.

15. On this, cf. Keel, *Wirkmächtige Siegeszeichen,* pp. 108f.

16. On this, cf. D. Opitz, "Ein Altar des Königs Tukulti-Ninurta I von Assyrien," pp. 83–90.

17. Cf. H. Frankfort, *The Art and Architecture of the Ancient Orient,* pp. 132f., 137f.

18. *SAHG,* p. 293.

19. K. Jaritz, *Schriftarchäologie der altmesopotamischen Kultur,* p. 532.

20. Cf. D. R. Ap-Thomas, "Notes on Some Terms Relating to Prayer," pp. 225–28.

21. Cf. M. Werbrouck, *Les pleureuses dans l'Egypte ancienne;* E. Lüddeckens, *Untersuchungen über religiösen Gehalt, Sprache und Form der ägyptischen Totenklagen.* Figurines of mourners beating their hands above their heads have been found in graves of Tell Aitun near Lachish. The figures date from the twelfth to eleventh centuries B.C. (T. Dothan, "A Female Mourner Figurine from the Lachish Region"; cf. Jer 2:37).

22. Nos. 64.4–7, 65.4–6.

23. *ANET,* pp. 250f.

24. Cf. A. Greiff, *Das Gebet im Alten Testament,* p. 39.

25. Cf. Ap-Thomas, "Notes," pp. 298f.

26. F. Cumont, "Invocation au soleil accompagnée des 'mains supines.' "

27. *AOT,* pp. 245f.

28. Contra H. J. Kraus, *Psalmen,* p. 229.

29. *UT* 67 I 16f.; J. Aistleitner, *Die mythologischen und kultischen Texte aus Ras Schamra,* p. 15.

30. H. Bonnet, *Reallexikon der ägyptischen Religionsgeschichte,* p. 610.

31. Cf. L. Rost, "Ein Psalmenproblem."

32. S. Mowinckel, *Psalmenstudien,* VI, pp. 57f.

33. G. Bornkamm, "Lobpreis, Bekenntnis und Opfer," p. 54.

34. Cf. H. J. Hermission, *Sprache und Ritus im altisraelitischen Kult,* pp. 30f.

35. K. Galling, *Der Altar in den Kulturen des Alten Orients,* p. 15.

36. Cf. *ANEP,* no. 297.

37. *AOB,* text at no. 534.

38. "Lobpreis," pp. 53–58.

39. L. Delekat, *Asylie und Schutzorakel am Zionheiligtum,* pp. 14f.

40. Cf. G. Dalman, *AuS,* vol. 6, p. 71; R. Paret, *Symbolik des Isalm,* p. 29.

41. T. Nöldecke, "Halleluja."

42. Cf. H. Frankfort, *Kingship and the Gods,* p. 98.

43. G. Roeder, *Mythen und Legenden um ägyptische Gottheiten und Pharaonen,* p. 138.

44. J. Rimmer, *Ancient Musical Instruments of Western Asia,* pp. 23f.

45. G. Loud, *Megiddo,* vol. 2, pl. 185; Y. Yadin et al., *Hazor,* vol. 1, pl. 162.2,3; IWB, vol. 4, p. 252.

46. K. Galling, *BRL,* col. 392.

47. H. Seidl, "Horn und Trompete im alten Israel unter Berücksichtigung der 'Kriegsrolle' von Qumran," p. 589.

48. Dio Cassius 66.23.

49. Contra W. Beyerlin, *Herkunft und Geschichte der ältesten Sinaitraditionen.*

50. Frankfort, *The Art,* pp. 39f.

51. H. Hickmann, *Ägypten,* pp. 40f.

52. Ibid., p. 122.

53. Y. Meshorer, *Jewish Coins of the Second Temple Period,* nos. 165, 178–81, 199–201.

54. Ibid., nos. 166–69, 190–92, 202.

55. Ibid., nos. 165, 178–81, 199–201; cf. Ps 118:27.

56. Ibid., nos. 172, 177, 185–88, 193f., 205, 209, 212.

57. Ibid., nos. 182, 302.

58. Contra Seidl, "Horn und Trompete," p. 593.

59. *War Scroll* 8.2,8–12.

60. *ANEP,* no. 194.

61. W. Sameh, "Der Alltag im alten Ägypten," p. 38.

62. *AOB,* text at no. 654.

63. Galling, *BRL,* col. 390.

64. E. Anati, *Rock-Art in Central Arabia,* vol. 1, pp. 102–106.

65. H. Hickmann, *45 siècles de musique dans l'Egypte ancienne,* p. 12.

66. A. Erman, *Die Literatur der Ägypter,* p. 244.

67. *TGI,* p. 69.

68. Galling, *BRL,* col. 390.

69. *AOT,* p. 39.

BIBLIOGRAPHY

Abdul Hak, S., *Die Schätze des National-Museums von Damaskus* (Veröffentlichungen der Generaldirektion der Antiken und Museen), Damascus n.d.

Abdul-Ḳader M., "The Administration of Syro-Palestine during the New Kingdom," *ASAE* 56 (1959) 105–137.

Aharoni Y., "Trial Excavation in the 'Solar Shrine' at Lachish: Preliminary Report," *IEJ* 18 (1968) 157–169.

—"The Horned Altar of Beer-Sheba," *Biblical Archaeologist* 37 (1974) 2–6.

Aimé-Giron M. Noël, "Un naos phénicien de Sidon," *BIFAO* 34 (1934) 31–42.

Aistleitner J., *Die mythologischen und kultischen Texte aus Ras Schamra,* Budapest ²1964.

Akurgal E./Hirmer M., *Die Kunst der Hethiter,* Munich 1961.

— *Orient und Okzident: Die Geburt der griechischen Kunst,* Baden-Baden 1966.

Albenda P., "An Assyrian Relief Depicting a Nude Captive in Wellesley College," *JNES* 29 (1970) 145–150.

Albright W. F., *The Excavations of Tell Beit Mirsim,* vol. 1 (*AASOR* 12), New Haven 1932.

— *The Archaeology of Palestine,* Harmondsworth, Middlesex 1960.

Aldred C., "The 'New Year' Gifts to the Pharaoh," *JEA* 55 (1969) 73–81.

Alliot M., "Les rites de la chasse au filet aux temples de Karnak, d'Edfou et d'Esneh," *RdE* 5 (1946) 57–118.

Alt A., "Die Weisheit Salomos," in: idem, *KS,* vol. 2, pp. 90–99.

— "Verbreitung und Herkunft des syrischen Tempeltypus," in: idem, *KS,* vol. 2, pp. 100–115.

— "Jesaia 8,23–9,6: Befreiungsnacht und Krönungstag," in: idem, *KS,* vol. 2, pp. 206–225.

Amad G., *Le baiser rituel: Un geste de culte méconnu,* Beirut 1973.

Amarnatafeln Die El, ed. J. A. Knudtzon (2 vols.), Aalen ²1964.

Amiet P., "Notes sur le répertoire iconographique de Mari à l'époque du palais," *Syria* 37 (1960) 215–232.

— *La glyptique mesopotamienne archaïque,* Paris 1961.

— "Un vase rituel," *Syria* 42 (1965) 235–251.

Amiran R./Aharoni Y., *Ancient Arad: Introductory Guide,* Tel Aviv 1967.

Anati E., "Les gravures rupestres dans la région du Néguev," *Bible et Terre Sainte* 22 (1959) 6–14.

— *Palestine Before the Hebrews,* New York 1963.

— *Rock-Art in Central Arabia* (2 vols.; Bibliothèque du Muséon 50), Louvain-Leuven 1968.

Andrae W., "Haus–Grab–Tempel in Alt-Mesopotamien," *OLZ* 30 (1927) 1033–1042.

— *Das Gotteshaus und die Urformen des Bauens im Alten Orient,* Berlin 1930.

— *Kultrelief aus dem Brunnen des Assurtempels zu Assur* (Wissenschaftliche Veröffentlichungen der Deutschen Orientgesellschaft, no. 53), Leipzig 1931.

— *Das wiedererstandene Assur,* Leipzig 1938.

— *Alte Feststrassen im Nahen Osten,* Leipzig 1941.

— "Der kultische Garten," *Die Welt des Orients* 1 (1947/52) 485–494.

Anthes R., "Das Bild einer Gerichtsverhandlung und das Grab des Mes aus Sakkara," *MDAIK* 9 (1940) 93–119.

— "Mythologie und der gesunde Menschenverstand in Ägypten," *Mitteilungen der Deutschen Orientgesellschaft zu Berlin* 96 (1965) 5–40.

Ap-Thomas D. R., "Notes on Some Terms Relating to Prayer," *VT* 6 (1956) 225–241.

Arias P. E./Hirmer M., *Tausend Jahre Griechische Vasenkunst,* Munich 1960.

Baltzer K., *Das Bundesformular* (Wissenschaftliche Monographien zum Alten und Neuen Testament), Neukirchen ²1964.

Barguet P., "La structure du temple Ipet-Sout d'Amon à Karnak du Moyen Empire à Amenophis II," *BIFAO* 52 (1953) 145–155.

— *Le Temple d'Amon-Rê à Karnak: Essai d'exégèse,* Cairo 1962.

Barnett R. D., "The Nimrud Ivories and the Art of the Phoenicians," *Iraq* 2 (1935) 179–210.

— *A Catalogue of the Nimrud Ivories with Other Examples of Ancient Near Eastern Ivories in the British Museum*, London 1957.

— /Forman W., *Assyrische Palastreliefs*, Prague 1959.

— /Falkner M., *The Sculptures of Assur-Nasir-Apli II (883–859 B. C.), Tiglath-Pileser III (745–727 B.C.), Esarhaddon (681–669 B.C.) from the Central and South-West Palaces at Nimrud*, London 1962.

— "New Facts about Musical Instruments from Ur," *Iraq* 31 (1969) 96–103.

Barrelet M. T., "Une peinture de la cour 106 du palais de Mari," *Studia Mariana* 1950, 9–35.

— "Etudes de glyptique akkadienne: l'imagination figurative et le cycle d'Ea," *Orientalia* 39 (1970) 213–251.

— "Peut-on remettre en question la 'restitution matériélle de la Stèle des Vautours'?," *JNES* 29 (1970) 233–258.

Barrois A. G., *Manuel d'archéologie biblique* (2 vols.), Paris 1939–1953.

Barta W., "Das Götterkultbild als Mittelpunkt bei Prozessionsfesten," *MDAIK* 23 (1968) 75–78.

— "Der Königsring als Symbol zyklischer Wiederkehr," *ZÄS* 98 (1970) 5–16.

Barth C., *Die Errettung vom Tode in den individuellen Klage- und Dankliedern des Alten Testamentes*, Zollikon 1947.

Barucq A., *L'Expression de la louange divine et de la prière dans la Bible et en Egypte* (Institut Français d'Archéologie Orientale, Bibliothèque d'Etude 33), Cairo 1962.

Beek M. A., *Atlas of Mesopotamia*, London-Edinburgh 1962.

Begrich J., "Sōfēr und Mazkīr," in: idem, *Gesammelte Studien zum Alten Testament* (ThB 21), Munich 1964, pp. 67–98.

— "Die Vertrauensäusserungen im israelitischen Klagelied des Einzelnen und in seinem babylonischen Gegenstück," in: idem, *Gesammelte Studien zum Alten Testament* (ThB 21), Munich 1964, pp. 168–216.

Bénédite G., "Scribe et babouin," *Monuments et mémoires publiés par l'Académie des Inscriptions et Belles-Lettres* 19 (1911) 5–42.

Bentzen A., "The Ritual Background of Amos 1,2–2,16," *OTS* 7 (1950) 85–99.

Benzinger I., *Bilderatlas zur Bibelkunde*, Stuttgart ²1913.

Berger S., "A Note on Some Scenes of Land Measurement," *JEA* 20 (1934) 54–56.

Berlinger M. (ed.), *Plants of the Bible*, Haifa 1969.

Bernhardt K. H., *Das Problem der altorientalischen Königsideologie im Alten Testament* (VTS 8), Leiden 1961.

Beyerlin W., *Herkunft und Geschichte der ältesten Sinaitraditionen*, Tübingen 1961.

von Bissing W., *Das Re-Heiligtum des Königs Ne-woser-re (Rathures)* (3 vols.), Berlin 1905–1928.

Bittel K./Naumann R./Otto H., *Yazilikaia: Architektur, Felsbilder, Inschriften und Kleinfunde* (Wissenschaftliche Veröffentlichungen der Deutschen Orientgesellschaft, no. 61), Leipzig 1941, reprint Osnabrück 1967.

Blackman A.M./Apted M.R., *The Rock Tombs of Meir* (6 vols.), London 1914–1953.

— /Fairman H. W., "The Significance of the Ceremony ḥwt bḥsw in the Temple of Horus at Edfu," *JEA* 35 (1949) 98–112 and 36 (1950) 63–81.

Blok M. H. P., "Remarques sur quelques stèles dites 'à oreille,'" *Kemi* 1 (1928) 123–135.

Boehmer J., "Tabor, Hermon und andere Hauptberge," *ARW* 12 (1909) 313–321.

Boehmer R. M., *Die Entwicklung der Glyptik während der Akkad-Zeit*, Berlin 1965.

Boese J., *Altmesopotamische Weihplatten: Eine sumerische Denkmalsgattung des 3. Jt.s v. Chr.*, Berlin 1971.

Bonnet H., *Bilderatlas zur Religionsgeschichte: Ägyptische Religion*, Leipzig 1924.

— "Die Bedeutung der Räucherungen im ägyptischen Kult," *ZÄS* 67 (1931).

— *Reallexikon der ägyptischen Religionsgeschichte*, Berlin 1952.

Bonomi J./Sharpe S., *Alabaster Sarcophagus of Oimeneptah I*, London 1864.

Borchardt L., *Das Grabdenkmal des Königs Sahure* (2 vols.), Leipzig 1913.

— "Jubiläumsbilder," *ZÄS* 61 (1926) 30–51.

— "Bilder des 'Zerbrechens der Krüge,'" *ZÄS* 64 (1929) 12–16.

Borghouts J. F., "The Evil Eye of Apopis," *JEA* 59 (1973) 114–150.

Bornkamm G., "Lobpreis, Bekenntnis und Opfer," in: *Apophoreta: Festschrift für Ernst Haenchen* (BZNW 30), 1964, pp. 46–63.

Bossert H. T., *Altanatolien*, Berlin 1942.

— *Altsyrien*, Tübingen 1951.

Botta P. E., *Monuments de Ninive* (5 vols.), Paris 1849–1850.

Bouriant U. et al., *Monuments pour servir à l'étude du culte d'Atonou en Egypte*, vol. 1 (MIFAO 8), Cairo 1903.

Breasted J. H., *A History of Egypt*, London 1905.
— "Second Preliminary Report of the Egyptian Expedition," *The American Journal of Semitic Languages* 25 (1908) 1–110.
— *Geschichte Ägyptens*, Zurich 1936.
Brongers H. A., "Merismus, Synekdoche und Hendiadys in der Bibel-Hebräischen Sprache," *OTS* 14 (1965) 100–114.
Brunner H., "Die Strafgrube," *ZÄS* 80 (1955) 73f.
— "Gerechtigkeit als Fundament des Thrones," *VT* 8 (1958) 426ff.
— "Eine Dankstele an Upuaut," *MDAIK* 16 (1958) 5–17.
— *Die Geburt des Gottkönigs* (Ägyptologische Abhandlungen 10), Wiesbaden 1964.
Brunner-Traut E., "Pharao und Jesus als Söhne Gottes," *Antaios* 2 (1961) 266–284.
— *Ägypten*, Stuttgart ²1966.
— *Aspektive und die historische Wandlung der Wahrnehmungsweise* (Stuttgarter Privatstudiengesellschaft), Stuttgart 1974.
Bruyère B. "Sur le dieu Ched," in: *Rapport su les fouilles de Deir el Médineh* (1935–1949) (Fouilles de l'Institut Français du Caire XX.3), Cairo 1952, pp. 138–170.
de Buck A., *De egyptische Voorstellingen betreffende den Oerheuvel*, Leiden 1922.
— "La fleur au front du grand prêtre," *OTS* 9 (1951) 18–29.
— *Egyptian Reading Book*, Leiden ³1970.
Budge E. A. W., *Assyrian Sculptures in the British Museum: Reign of Ashur-Nasir-Pal, 885–860 B. C.*, London 1914.
Bühlmann W./Scherer K., *Stilfiguren der Bibel: Ein kleines Nachschlagewerk* (Biblische Beiträge 10), Fribourg 1973.
Buhl M. L., "The Goddesses of the Egyptian Tree Cult," *JNES* 6 (1947) 80–97.
van Buren, E. D., "A Clay Relief in the Iraq Museum," *AfO* 9 (1933 = 1934) 165–171.
— *The Flowing Vase and the God with Streams*, Berlin 1933.
— "Mountain-Gods," *Orientalia* 12 (1943) 78–84.
— "Concerning the Horned Cap of the Mesopotamian Gods," *Orientalia* 12 (1943) 318–327.
— "The Dragon in Ancient Mesopotamia," *Orientalia* 15 (1946) 1–45.
— "An Enlargement on a Given Theme," *Orientalia* 20 (1951) 15–69.
— "Foundation Rites for a New Temple," *Orientalia* 21 (1952) 293–306.
— "How Representations of Battles of the Gods Developed," *Orientalia* 24 (1955) 24–41.

Busink T. A., *Der Tempel von Jerusalem*, vol. 1, *Der Tempel Salomos*, Leiden 1970.
Calverley A. M./Broome M. F./Gardiner A. H., *The Temple of King Sethos I at Abydos* (4 vols.), London-Chicago 1933–1958.
Castellino D. G., *Le lamentazioni individuali e gli inni in Babilonia e in Israele*, Turin 1939.
Cazelles H., "La titulature du roi David," in: *Mélanges Bibliques rédigés en l'Honneur d'André Robert* (Travaux de l'Institute Catholique 4), Paris n.d. (1955?), pp. 131–136.
Chabas F. J., "Horus sur les crocodiles," *ZÄS* 6 (1868) 99–106.
Champdor A., *Les ruines de Palmyre*, Paris 1953.
— *Thèbes aux cent Portes*, Paris ²1953.
— *Le Livre des Morts: Papyrus d'Ani, de Hunefer, d'Anhai du British Museum*, Paris 1963.
Champollion J. F., *Monuments de l'Egypte et de la Nubie* (4 vols.), Paris 1835–1845.
Chassinat E., *Le temple d'Edfou* (14 vols.), Cairo 1928–1934.
— *Le temple de Dendara* (6 vols.), Cairo 1934–1952.
Clère J. J., "Fragments d'une nouvelle représentation egyptienne du monde," *MDAIK* 16 (1958) 30–46.
Clifford R. J., *The Cosmic Mountain in Canaan and the Old Testament*, Cambridge, Mass. 1972.
Collart P./Coupel P., *L'autel monumental de Baalbek*, Paris 1951.
Conrad D., "Der Gott Reschef," *ZAW* 83 (1971) 157–183.
Contenau G., "Mission archéologique à Sidon (1914)," *Syria* 1 (1920) 16–55.
— *Manuel d'archéologie orientale depuis les origines jusqu'à l'époque d'Alexandre* (4 vols.), Paris 1927–1947.
Cook S. A., *The Religion of Ancient Palestine in the Light of Archaeology*, London 1930.
Cornfeld G., *Von Adam bis Daniel: Das Alte Testament und sein historisch-archäologischer Hintergrund*, Würzburg 1962.
— /Botterweck G. J., *Die Bibel und ihre Welt*, Bergisch-Gladbach 1969.
Crowfoot J. W./Crowfoot G. M., *Ivories from Samaria*, London 1938.
Crüsemann F., *Studien zur Formgeschichte von Hymnus und Danklied in Israel* (Wissenschaftliche Monographien zum Alten und Neuen Testament 32), Neukirchen-Vluyn 1969.
Cumming C. G., *The Assyrian and Hebrew Hymns of Praise*, New York 1934.

Cumont F., "Invocation au soleil accompagnée des 'mains supines,'" *Syria* 13 (1932) 385–395.

Dahood M., *Psalms* (3 vols.; The Anchor Bible), New York 1966–1970.

Dalman G., *Arbeit und Sitte in Palästina* (6 vols.), Hildesheim ²1964.

Danthine H., *Le palmier-dattier et les arbres sacrés dans l'iconographie de l'Asie occidentale ancienne* (2 vols.), Paris 1937.

Daressy G., "Une flottille phénicienne d'après une peinture égyptienne," *Revue archéologique* 27(1895) 286–291.

—*Ostraca* (Catalogue général du musée de Caire 1) Cairo 1901.

Daumas F., "Sur trois représentations de Nout à Dendera," *ASAE* 51 (1951) 373–400.

—*Les mammisis des temples égyptiens,* Paris 1958.

Davies Nina M./Gardiner A. H., *Ancient Egyptian Paintings* (2 vols.), Chicago 1936.

—"Some Representations of Tombs from the Theban Necropolis," *JEA* 24 (1938) 25–40.

—"Two Pictures of Temples," *JEA* 41 (1955) 80–82.

—/Gardiner A. H., *Tutankhamun's Painted Box,* Oxford 1962.

Davies Norman de Garis, *The Rock Tombs of El Amarna* (6 vols.; Archaeological Survey of Egypt, Memoirs 13–18), London 1903–1908.

—/Gardiner A. H., *The Tomb of Huy* (No. 40), London 1926.

—*Two Ramesside Tombs at Thebes,* New York 1927.

—*The Tomb of Kenamūn* (2 vols.), New York 1930.

—/Davies Nina, *The Tombs of Menkheperrasonb, Amenmose, and Another* (The Theban Tombs Series 5), London 1933.

—*The Tomb of Nefer-Hotep at Thebes* (2 vols.), New York 1933.

—*The Tomb of Rekh-mi-rēʿ* (2 vols.), New York 1943.

—/Faulkner R. O., "A Syrian Trading Venture to Egypt," *JEA* 33 (1947) 40–46.

—*The Temple of Hibis in el Khārge Oasis,* "Part III: The Decoration," New York 1953.

Davis T. M., *The Tomb of Siptah, the Monkey Tomb and the Gold Tomb,* London 1908.

Decamps de Mertzenfeld C., *Inventaire commenté des ivoires phéniciens et apparentés découverts dans le Proche Orient,* Paris 1954.

Deissler A., *Die Psalmen* (3 vols.; Kleinkommentare zur Heiligen Schrift), Düsseldorf 1963–1965.

Delcor M., "Les attaches littéraires, l'origine et la signification de l'expression biblique 'prendre à témoin le ciel et la terre'," *VT* 16 (1966) 8–25.

Delekat L., *Asylie und Schutzorakel am Zionheiligtum,* Leiden 1967.

Delitzsch F., *Biblischer Kommentar über die Psalmen,* Leipzig ²1894.

Delougaz P./Lloyd S., *Presargonid Temples in the Diyala-Region* (OIP 58), Chicago 1942.

—*Pottery from the Diyala Region* (OIP 63), Chicago 1952.

—"Animals Emerging from a Hut," *JNES* 27 (1968) 184–197.

Derchain P., "Les plus anciens témoignages de sacrifices d'enfants chez les sémites occidentaux," *VT* 20 (1970) 331–355.

Dessenne A., *Le Sphinx: Etude iconographique,* vol. 1, *Des origines à la fin du second millénaire,* Paris 1957.

Dhorme E., *Les Religions de Babylonie et d'Assyrie,* Paris 1949.

Dikaios P., *A Guide to the Cyprus Museum,* Nicosia 1961.

Dothan M., "Ashdod: Preliminary Report on the Excavations in Seasons 1962/1963," *IEJ* 14 (1964) 79–95.

— "A Female Mourner Figurine from the Lachish Region," *Eretz Israel* 9 (1969) 42–46.

Doughty C. M., *Die Offenbarung Arabiens,* Leipzig 1937.

Driver G. R., "Hebrew *môqeš,* 'striker,'" *JBL* 73 (1954) 131–136.

—"Mythical Monsters in the Old Testament," in: *Studi orientalistici in Onore di Giorgio Levi della Vida,* vol. 1, Rome 1956, pp. 234–249.

Duchesne-Guillemin M., "L'Oliphant dans l'Antiquité, *Berytus* 18 (1969) 113–118.

Ducros H. A., "Etude sur les balances égyptiennes," *ASAE* 9 (1908) 32–53.

Dürr L., *Ezechiels Vision von der Erscheinung Gottes (Ez C. 1 und 10) im Lichte der vorderasiatischen Altertumskunde,* Würzburg 1917.

—*Ursprung und Ausbau der israelitisch-jüdischen Heilandserwartung,* Berlin 1925.

Dussaud R., "Note additionnelle aux rapports de MM. Dunand et Pillet," *Syria* 8 (1927) 113–125.

—"Temple et cultes de la triade héliopolitaine à Baʿalbeck," *Syria* 23 (1942/43) 33–77.

—*Les religions des Hittites et des Hourrites, des Phéniciens et des Syriens,* Paris 1949.

Edel E., "Zu den Inschriften auf den Jahreszeitenreliefs der Weltkammer aus dem

Sonnenheiligtum des Niuserre," in: *Nachrichten der Akademie der Wissenschaften in Göttingen aus dem Jahre 1961 und 1964,* resp. pp. 209–255, 87–217.

Edgerton W. F./Wilson J. A., *Historical Records of Ramses III: The Texts in Medinet Habu Volumes I and II,* Chicago 1936.

Edwards I. E. S., *The Pyramids of Egypt* (Pelican Book A 168), Harmondsworth, Middlesex ²1961.

Eggebrecht A., *Schlachtungsbräuche im alten Ägypten und ihre Wiedergabe im Flachbild bis zum Ende des Mittleren Reiches,* Munich 1973.

Ehrlich E. L., *Die Kultsymbolik im Alten Testament und im nachbiblischen Judentum* (vol. 3 of *Symbolik der Religionen*), Stuttgart 1959.

Eichhorn D., *Gott als Fels, Burg und Zuflucht: Eine Untersuchung zum Gebet des Mittlers in den Psalmen* (Europäische Hochschulschriften) Bern 1972.

Eisen G. A., *Ancient Oriental Cylinder and Other Seals with a Description of the Collection of Mrs. William H. Moore* (OIP 47), Chicago 1940.

Eissfeldt O., "Die Flügelsonne als künstlerisches Motiv und als religiöses Symbol," in: idem, *KS,* vol. 2, pp. 416–419.

—"Gabelhürden im Ostjordanland," in: idem, *KS,* vol. 3, pp. 61–66.

—"Noch einmal: Gabelhürden im Ostjordanland," in: idem, *KS,* vol. 3, pp. 67–70.

—"Zur Deutung von Motiven auf den 1937 gefundenen phönizischen Elfenbeinarbeiten von Megiddo," in: idem, *KS,* vol. 3, pp. 85–93.

—"El und Jahwe," in: idem, *KS,* vol. 3, pp. 386–397.

Elisofon E./van der Post L., *The Nile,* New York 1964.

Elliger K., *Das Buch der zwölf Kleinen Propheten,* vol. 2 (ATD 25), Göttingen 1950.

Ellis R. S., *Foundation Deposits in Ancient Mesopotamia* (Yale Near Eastern Researches 2), New Haven–London 1968.

Emery W. B., *Archaic Egypt* (Pelican Book A 462) Harmondsworth, Middlesex ²1963.

L'Encyclopédie de tous les pays du monde: Le Million, vol. 6, *Asie du Sud-Ouest,* Paris-Geneva-Brussels 1971.

Engelbach R., "An Alleged Winged Sun-Disk First Dynasty," *ZÄS* 65 (1930) 115f.

—"A Foundation Scene of the Second Dynasty," *JEA* 20 (1934) 183f.

Erman A., "Gebete eines ungerecht Verfolgten und andere Ostraka in den Königsgräbern," *ZÄS* 38 (1900) 19–41.

—"Denksteine aus der thebanischen Gräberstadt," *Sitzungsberichte der kgl. preuss. Akademie der Wissenschaften* 49 (1911) 1086–1110.

—*Die Literatur der Ägypter,* Leipzig 1923.

—/Ranke H., *Ägypten und ägyptisches Leben im Altertum,* Tübingen 1923.

—*Die Religion der Ägypter: Ihr Werden und Vergehen in vier Jahrtausenden,* Berlin-Leipzig 1934.

Fairman H. W., "The Kingship Rituals of Egypt," in: S. H. Hooke (ed.), *Myth, Ritual and Kingship,* Oxford 1958, pp. 74–104.

—"A Scene of Offering Truth in the Temple of Edfu," *MDAIK* 16 (1958) 86–92.

—*The Triumph of Horus: An Ancient Egyptian Sacred Drama,* London 1974.

Falk Z. W., "Gestures Expressing Affirmation," *Journal of Semitic Studies* 4 (1959) 268–269.

Falkenstein A., *Archaische Texte aus Uruk,* Leipzig 1936.

Faniel S./Levallois P./Gilou A., *Les merveilles du Louvre,* vol. 1 (Collection Réalités 2), Paris 1960.

Faulkner R. O., *The Ancient Egyptian Pyramid Texts* (2 vols.), Oxford 1969.

Fauth W., *Aphrodite Parakyptusa: Untersuchungen zum Erscheinungsbild der vorderasiatischen Dea Prospiciens,* Wiesbaden 1967.

Fechheimer H., *Die Plastik der Ägypter* (vol. 1 of *Die Kunst des Ostens*), Berlin 1922.

Fish T., "The Zu-Bird," *Bulletin of the John Rylands Library* 31 (1948) 162–171.

Fohrer G., *Die symbolischen Handlungen der Propheten* (Abhandlungen zur Theologie des Alten und Neuen Testaments 54), Zurich ²1968.

Foucart G./Baud M./Drioton E., *Tombes Thebaines: Necropole de Dirâ' abû'n nága; Le tombeau de Panehsy* (MIFAO 57.2), Cairo 1932.

Frank K., *Babylonische Beschwörungsreliefs* (Leipziger semitische Studien III.3), Leipzig 1908.

Frankfort H. et al., *The Cenotaph of Seti I at Abydos* (2 vols.), London 1933.

—*Sculpture of the Third Millennium B.C. from Tell Asmar and Khafājah* (OIP 44), Chicago 1939.

—et al., *The Gimilsin Temple and the Palace of the Rulers at Tell Asmar* (OIP 43), Chicago 1940.

—*More Sculpture from the Diyala Region* (OIP 60), Chicago 1943.

—"A Note on the Lady of Birth," *JNES* 3 (1944) 198–200.

—*Stratified Cylinder Seals from the Diyala Region* (OIP 72), Chicago ²1964.

—*Cylinder Seals,* Farnborough ²1965.

—et al., *Before Philosophy: The Intellectual Adventure of Ancient Man: An Essay on Speculative Thought in the Ancient Near East* (Pelican Book A 198) Harmondsworth, Middlesex ⁷1969.

—*Kingship and the Gods,* Chicago-London ⁶1969.

—*The Art and Architecture of the Ancient Orient* (The Pelican History of Art), Harmondsworth ⁴1970 (Paperback).

Fuhr-Jaeppelt I., *Materialien zur Ikonographie des Löwenadlers Anzu-Imdugud,* Munich 1972.

Furtwängler A., "Über ein auf Cypern gefundenes Bronzegerät: Ein Beitrag zur Erklärung der Kultgeräte des salomonischen Tempels," *Sitzungsberichte der philos.-philol. und der hist. Klasse der königlich bayerischen Akademie der Wissenschaften zu München 1899* 2 (1900) 411–433.

Gaballa G. A., "New Evidence on the Birth of Pharaoh," *Orientalia* 36 (1967) 299–304 and pls. 63–65.

Galling K., *Der Altar in den Kulturen des Alten Orients,* Berlin 1925.

—"Der Beichtspiegel: Eine gattungsgeschichtliche Studie," *ZAW* 47 (1929) 125–130.

—*Biblisches Reallexikon* (HAT 1), Tübingen 1937.

—"Beschriftete Bildsiegel des ersten Jahrtausends v. Chr. vornehmlich aus Syrien und Palästina: Ein Beitrag zur Geschichte der phönikischen Kunst," *ZDPV* 64 (1941) 121–202.

—"Ba'al Hammon in Kition und die Hammanîm," in: *Wort und Geschichte: Festschrift K. Elliger* (Altes Testament und Alter Orient 18), Neukirchen 1973, pp. 65–70.

Gamper A., *Gott als Richter in Mesopotamien und im Alten Testament,* Innsbruck 1966.

Gardiner A. H., "An Unusual Sketch of a Theban Funeral," *PSBA* 35 (1913) 229 and pl. 46.

—"The Baptism of Pharaoh," *JEA* 36 (1950/51) 3–12 and 37 (1952) 111.

—/Peet T. E./Černy J., *Inscriptions of Sinai* (2 vols.), London 1952–1955.

—"The Coronation of King Haremhab," *JEA* 39 (1953) 13–31.

—*Egyptian Grammar,* London ³1957 (1969).

—*Egypt of the Pharaohs,* Oxford ⁴1964.

Garelli P./Leibovici M., *Schöpfungsmythen:* see Sauneron.

Gaster T. H., "A Canaanite Magical Text," *Orientalia* 11 (1942) 41–79.

Gauthier H., *Les fêtes du dieu Min,* Cairo 1931.

de Genouillac H., *Fouilles françaises d'El-'Akhymer,* vol. 2, Paris 1925.

Gerster G., *Nubien: Goldland am Nil,* Zurich-Stuttgart 1964.

—*Sinai: Land der Offenbarung,* Zurich ²1970.

—"Ein sumerisches Tempelmodell," *Neue Zürcher Zeitung* 190 (26 April 1970) 57.

Gese H., "Der Davidsbund und die Zionserwählung," *ZThK* 61 (1964) 10–26; also in: idem, *Vom Sinai zum Zion,* Munich 1974, pp. 113–129.

—"Natus ex Virgine," in: *Probleme biblischer Theologie: Gerhard von Rad zum 70. Geburtstag* (ed. H. W. Wolff), Munich 1971, pp. 73–89; also in H. Gese, *Vom Sinai zum Zion,* Munich 1974, pp. 130–146.

—/Höfner M./Rudolph K., *Die Religionen Altsyriens, Altarabiens und der Mandäer,* Stuttgart 1970.

Gierlich A. M., *Der Lichtgedanke in den Psalmen* (Feiburger Theologische Studien 56), Freiburg 1940.

Giveon R., *Les Béduins Shosou des documents égyptiens,* Leiden 1971.

Gjerstad E., *The Swedish Cyprus Expedition 1927–31* (4 vols.), Stockholm 1934–1962.

Goedicke H., *Die Stellung des Königs im Alten Reich* (Ägyptologische Abhandlungen 2), Wiesbaden 1960.

Goodenough E. R., *Jewish Symbols in the Greco-Roman Period* (12 vols.), New York 1953–1965.

Gottlieb H., "Die Tradition von David als Hirten," *VT* 17 (1967) 190–200.

Goyon G., "Le Papyrus de Turin dit 'des mines d'or' et le Wadi Hammamat," *ASAE* 49 (1949) 337–392.

Granqvist H., *Child Problems among the Arabs,* Helsingfors-Copenhagen 1950.

Grapow H., *Vergleiche und andere bildliche Ausdrücke im Ägyptischen,* Leipzig 1920.

—*Studien zu den Annalen Thutmosis des Dritten und zu ihnen verwandten historischen Berichten des Neuen Reiches* (Abhandlungen der Deutschen Akademie der Wissenschaften zu Berlin, Phil.-hist. Klasse 1947, no. 2), Berlin 1949.

Grdseloff B., "Zum Vogelfang," *ZÄS* 74 (1938) 52–55, 136–139.

—"L'insigne du grand juge égyptien," *ASAE* 40 (1940) 185–202.

Greiff A., *Das Gebet im Alten Testament,* Münster 1915.

Grelot P., "La géographie mythique d'Hénoch et ses sources orientales," *RB* 65 (1958) 64–68.

Griffith F.L./Newberry P. E., *El Bersheh,* vol. 2 (Archaeological Survey of Egypt 4), 1895.

Grollenberg L. H., *Bildatlas zur Bibel,* Gütersloh 1957.

de Groot J., *Die Altäre des salomonischen Tempels,* Stuttgart 1924.

Gross H., *Die Idee des ewigen und allgemeinen Weltfriedens im Alten Orient und im Alten Testament* (Trierer Theologische Studien 7), Trier ²1967,

Guglielmi W., *Reden, Rufe und Lieder auf altägyptischen Darstellungen der Landwirtschaft, Viehzucht, des Fisch- und Vogelfangs vom Mittleren Reich bis zur Spätzeit,* Bonn 1973.

Gunkel H., "Ägyptische Parallelen zum AT," in: idem., *Reden und Aufsätze,* Göttingen 1913, pp. 136f.

—"Agyptische Danklieder," in: idem., *Reden und Aufsätze,* Göttingen 1913, pp. 141–149.

—/Begrich J., *Einleitung in die Psalmen* (HAT suppl.), Göttingen 1933.

—*Die Psalmen,* Göttingen ⁵1968.

Gunn B., "An Inscribed Statue of King Zoser," *ASAE* 26 (1926) 177–196.

Güterbock H. G., "A Note on the Stela of Tukulti-Ninurta II Found Near Tell Ashara," *JNES* 16 (1957) 123.

—"Narration in Anatolian, Syrian, and Assyrian Art," *AJA* 61 (1957) 62–71.

—"A Votive Sword with Old Assyrian Inscription," in: *Assyriological Studies* 16 (Festschrift for B. Landsberger), Chicago 1965, pp. 197–198.

Haase R., *Die keilschriftlichen Rechtssammlungen in deutscher Übersetzung,* Wiesbaden 1963.

Habachi L., "King Nebhetepre Menthuhotep: His Monuments, Place in History, Deification and Unusual Representations in the Form of Gods," *MDAIK* 19 (1963) 16–52.

Hall H. R., *Catalogue of Egyptian Scarabs in the British Museum,* London 1913.

Hamilton R. W., "Excavations at Tell Abu Hawām," *The Quarterly of the Department of Antiquities in Palestine* 4 (1935) 1–69.

Hamza M., "Excavations of the Department of Antiquities at Qantîr," *ASAE* 30 (1930) 45–51.

Heiler F., "Die Körperhaltung beim Gebet: Eine religionsgeschichtliche Skizze," *Mit-*teilungen der vorderasiatischen-ägyptischen Gesellschaft 22 (1917) 168–177.

Heinrich E., *Kleinfunde aus den archaischen Tempelschichten in Uruk,* Berlin 1936.

—*Bauwerke in der altsumerischen Bildkunst,* Wiesbaden 1967.

—/Seidl U., "Grundrisszeichnungen aus dem Alten Orient," *Mitteilungen der Deutschen Orientgesellschaft* 98 (1967) 24–45.

Heintz J. G., *Le filet divin* (Mémoire de l'Ecole Biblique), Jerusalem 1965.

Helck W., "Die Szene des Aufschreibens des Namens auf dem îŝd-Baum," *ZÄS* 82 (1957) 117–140.

—"Zu den ägyptischen Sinai-Inschriften," *OLZ* 53 (1958) 421–426.

Henninger J., "Geisterglaube bei den vorislamischen Arabern," in: *Festschrift Paul J. Schebesta,* Vienna-Mödling 1963, pp. 279–316.

Hermisson H. J., *Sprache und Ritus im altisraelitischen Kult* (Wissenschaftliche Monographien zum Alten und Neuen Testament 19), Neukirchen-Vluyn 1965.

Hess J. J., *Von den Beduinen des Innern Arabiens,* Zurich-Leipzig 1938.

Hickmann H., *45 siècles de musique dans l'Egypte ancienne,* Paris 1956.

—*Ägypten* (vol. 2, pt. 1 of *Musikgeschichte in Bildern*), Leipzig 1961.

Hill G. F., *A Catalogue of the Greek Coins of Phoenicia,* Bologna 1965.

Hofer J., "Zur Phänomenologie des Sakralraumes und sein Symbolismus im Alten Orient mit Berücksichtigung der Bauformen" (Diss. Vienna) 1969.

Homburg K., "Psalm 110,1 im Rahmen des judäischen Krönungszeremoniells," *ZAW* 84 (1972) 243–246.

Hornung E., "Chaotische Bereiche in der geordneten Welt," *ZÄS* 81 (1956) 28–32.

—"Zur geschichtlichen Rolle des Königs in der 18. Dynastie," *MDAIK* 15 (1957) 120–133.

—*Der Eine und die Vielen,* Darmstadt ²1973.

Horst F., "Habakkuk," in: T. H. Robinson/F. Horst, *Die Zwölf Kleinen Propheten* (HAT 14), Tübingen ³1964.

Hrouda B., "Zur Herkunft des assyrischen Lebensbaumes," *Baghdader Mitteilungen* 3 (1964) 41–51.

—*Die Kulturgeschichte des assyrischen Flachbildes,* Bonn 1965.

Hugger P., "Jahwe, mein Fels," in: *"Laeta dies": 50 Jahre Studienkolleg St. Benedikt,* Münsterschwarzach 1968, pp. 143–160.

Ingholt H., "Les sens du mot ḥammān," in:

Mélanges syriens offerts à R. Dussaud, vol. 2, Paris 1939, pp. 795–802.

Ions V., Egyptian Mythology, Feltham, Middlesex ²1968.

Isserlin B. S. J., "Psalm 68, Verse 14: An Archaeological Gloss," PEQ 103 (1971) 5–8.

Jacobsen T./Lloyd S., Sennacherib's Aqueduct at Jerwan (OIP 24), Chicago 1935.

Jacobsthal P., Der Blitz in der orientalischen und griechischen Kunst, Berlin 1906.

Jaritz K., Schriftarchäologie der altmesopotamischen Kultur, Graz 1967.

Jaroš K., Die Stellung des Elohisten zur kanaanäischen Religion (Orbis Biblicus et Orientalis 4), Fribourg–Göttingen 1974.

Jasper F. N., "Early Israelite Traditions and the Psalter," VT 17 (1967) 50–60.

Jastrow M., Bildermappe zur Religion Babyloniens und Assyriens, Giessen 1912.

Jaussen A., Coutumes des Arabes du pays de Moab, Paris 1908.

Jéquier G., Les frises d'objets des sarcophages du Moyen Empire (MIFAO 47), Cairo 1921.

Jeremias A., Handbuch der altorientalischen Geisteskultur, Leipzig 1913.

—Das Alte Testament im Lichte des Alten Orients, Leipzig ³1916.

Jeremias J., Theophanie (Wissenschaftliche Monographien zum Alten und Neuen Testament 10), Neukirchen-Vluyn 1965.

—Kultprophetie und Gerichtsverkündigung in der späteren Königszeit Israels (Wissenschaftliche Monographien zum Alten und Neuen Testament 35), Neukirchen-Vluyn 1970.

—"Lade und Zion: Zur Entstehung der Zionstradition," in: Probleme biblischer Theologie: Gerhard von Rad zum 70. Geburstag (ed. H. W. Wolff), Munich 1971, pp. 183–198.

Jesi F., "Rapport sur les recherches relative à quelques figurations du sacrifice humain dans l'Egypte pharaonique," JNES 17 (1958) 194–203.

Jirku A., Altorientalischer Kommentar zum AT, Leipzig 1923.

Jochims U., "Thirza und die Ausgrabungen auf dem Tell el-Fār'a," ZDPV 76 (1960) 73–96.

Johl C. H., Altägyptische Webestühle und Brettchenweberei in Altägypten (Untersuchungen zur Geschichte und Altertumskunde Ägyptens 8), Leipzig 1924.

Johns C. N., "Discoveries in Palestine Since 1939," PEQ 80 (1948) 81–101.

Jones G., "The Decree of Yahweh, Ps 2, 7," VT 15 (1965) 336–344.

Jüngling H. W., Der Tod der Götter: Eine Untersuchung zu Psalm 82 (SBS 38), Stuttgart 1969.

Junker H., "Die Hieroglyphen für 'Erz' und 'Erzarbeiter,' " MDAIK 14 (1956) 89–103.

—"Vorschriften für den Tempelkult in Philae," in: Studia Biblica et Orientalia, vol. 3, Oriens Antiquus (Analecta Biblica 12), Rome 1959, pp. 151–160.

—"Der Strom, dessen Arme die Stadt Gottes erfreuen," Biblica 43 (1962) 197ff.

Kaiser W., Ägyptisches Museum in Berlin (West), Berlin 1967.

Kantor H. J., "Syro-Palestinian Ivories," JNES 15 (1956) 153–174.

—"Narration in Egyptian Art," AJA 61 (1957) 44–54.

—"A Bronze Plaque with Relief Decoration from Tell Tainat," JNES 21 (1962) 93–117.

—"Landscape in Akkadian Art," JNES 25 (1966) 145–152.

Kapelrud A. S., "Temple Building, a Task for Gods and Kings," Orientalia 32 (1963) 56–62.

Kaplony P., "Eine Vogeljagdszene aus dem Grab des Mttj," Orientalia 39 (1970) 264–268.

Keel O., Feinde und Gottesleugner: Studien zum Image der Widersacher in den Individualpsalmen (SBM 7), Stuttgart 1969.

—"Nochmals Ps 22, 28–32," Biblica 51 (1970) 405–413.

—"Das Vergraben der 'fremden Götter' in Genesis XXXV 4b," VT 23 (1973) 305–336.

—Wirkmächtige Siegeszeichen im Alten Testament: Ikonographische Studien zu Jos 8,18.26; Ex 17,8–13; 2 Kön 13,14–19 und 1 Kön 22,11 (Orbis Biblicus et Orientalis 5), Fribourg-Göttingen 1974.

—Die Weisheit "spielt" vor Gott: Ein ikonographischer Beitrag zur Deutung des mᵉsaḥäqät in Spr 8,30f., Fribourg 1974.

—"Kanaanäische Sühneriten auf ägyptischen Tempelreliefs," VT 25 (1975) 413–469.

—Jahwevisionen und Siegelkunst: Eine neue Deutung der Majestätsschilderungen in Jes 6; Ez 1 und 10; und Sach 4 (SBS 84/85), Stuttgart 1977.

—Vögel als Boten: Studien zu Ps 68, 12–14; Gen 8, 6–12; Koh 10, 20 und dem Aussenden von Botenvögeln in Ägypten (Orbis Biblicus et Orientalis 14), Fribourg-Göttingen 1977.

Kees H., "Horus und Seth als Götterpaar" (pt. 1), Mitteilungen der vorderasiatisch-ägyptischen Gesellschaft 28 (1923) 3–72.

—*Der Götterglaube im Alten Ägypten* (*Mitteilungen der vorderasiatisch-ägyptischen Gesellschaft* 45), Leipzig 1941.

Keimer L., *Histoires de serpents dans l'Egypte ancienne et moderne*, Cairo 1947.

Kenyon K. M., *Digging up Jericho*, London 1957.

—*Jerusalem: Excavating 3000 Years of History*, New York 1967.

—*Archaeology in the Holy Land*, New York ³1970.

King L. W., *Babylonian Boundary Stones and Memorial Tablets in the British Museum*, London 1912.

—*Bronze Reliefs from the Gates of Shalmaneser, King of Assyria B.C. 860–825*, London 1915.

Kleber A., "Ps 2:9 in the Light of an Ancient Oriental Ceremony," *CBQ* 5 (1943) 63–67.

Klebs L., *Die Reliefs des Alten Reiches (2980–2475 v. Chr.), Material zur ägyptischen Kulturgeschichte*, Heidelberg 1915.

—*Die Reliefs und Malereien des Mittleren Reiches (7.–17. Dynastie, ca. 2475–1580 v. Chr.)*, Heidelberg 1922.

—*Die Reliefs und Malereien des Neuen Reiches (18.–20. Dynastie, ca. 1580–1100 v. Chr.)*, Heidelberg 1934.

Klengel-Brandt E., "Ein Pazuzu-Kopf mit Inschrift," *Orientalia* 37 (1968) 81–84.

Klengel H., "Neue Lamaštu-Amulette aus dem Vorderasiatischen Museum zu Berlin und dem British Museum," *MIOF* 7 (1959/60) 334–355.

—"Weitere Amulette gegen Lamaštu," *MIOF* 8 (1963) 24–29.

Koch K., "Gibt es ein Vergeltungsdogma im Alten Testament?" *ZThK* 32 (1955) 1–42.

—"Tempeleinlassliturgien und Dekaloge: Studien zur Theologie der alttestamentlichen Überlieferungen," in: *Festschrift G. von Rad*, Neukirchen 1961, pp. 46–60.

Koenig J., "Aux origines des théophanies jahwistes," *Revue de l'Histoire des Religions* 169 (1966) 1–36.

Kolpaktchy G., *Ägyptisches Totenbuch*, Munich-Planegg 1955.

Kon M., "The Menorah of the Arch of Titus," *PEQ* 82 (1950) 25–30.

Kornfeld W., "Der Symbolismus der Tempelsäulen," *ZAW* 74 (1962) 50–57.

Kramer S. N., *History Begins at Sumer*, New York ²1959.

—*The Sacred Marriage: Aspects of Faith, Myth, and Ritual in Ancient Sumer*, Bloomington-London 1969.

Kraus H. J., "Archäologische und topographische Probleme Jerusalems im Lichte der Psalmenexegese," *ZDPV* 75 (1959) 125–140.

—*Psalmen* (BK AT XV/1 and 2), Neukirchen ²1961.

—*Gottesdienst in Israel*, Munich ²1962. [E. T. *Worship in Israel*, Oxford 1966.]

Krencker D./Zschietzschmann W., *Römische Tempel in Syrien* (Archäologisches Institut des Deutschen Reiches, *Denkmäler antiker Architekur* V), Berlin-Leipzig 1938.

Kuschke A., "Der Tempel Salomos und der 'syrische Tempeltypus,' " *BZAW* 105 (1967) 124–132.

—/Metzger M., "Kumudi und die Ausgrabungen auf Tell Kamid el-Lōz," in: VTS 22 (1972) 143–173.

Labuschagne C. J., *The Incomparability of Yahweh in the Old Testament* (Pretoria Oriental Series 5), Leiden 1966.

Lambert W. G., "A Phoenician Statuette," *AfO* 23 (1970) 51.

Lamon R. S./Shipton G. M., *Megiddo*, vol. 1, *Seasons of 1925–34: Strata I–V* (OIP 42), Chicago 1939.

Lampl P., *Cities and Planning in the Ancient Near East*, New York 1968.

Landsberger B./Tadmor H., "Fragments of Clay Liver Models from Hazor," *IEJ* 14 (1964) 201–218.

Lange K./Hirmer M., *Ägypten: Architektur, Plastik, Malerei in drei Jahrtausenden*, Munich ⁴1967.

Lanzone R. V., *Dizionario di Mitologia egiziana*, Turin 1883.

Latte K., *Römische Religionsgeschichte*, Munich 1960.

Layard A. H., *The Monuments of Niniveh from Drawings Made on the Spot* (2 vols.), London 1849/1853.

Leclant J., "Le rôle du lait et de l'allaitement d'après les textes des pyramides," *JNES* 10 (1951) 123–127.

—"La 'Mascarade' de bœufs gras et le triomphe de l'Egypte," *MDAIK* 14 (1956) 128–145.

—"Astarté à cheval d'après les représentations égyptiennes," *Syria* 37 (1960) 1–67.

—"Les rites de purification dans le cérémonial pharaonique du couronnement," in: *Proceedings of the XIᵗʰ Congress of the International Association for the History of Religions*, vol. 2, Leiden 1958, pp. 48–51.

van der Leeuw G., *Phänomenologie der Religion* (Neue Theologische Grundrisse), Tübingen ²1956.

Legrain L., *Seal Cylinders* (Ur Excavations X), London 1951.

Legrain M. G., *Statues et statuettes de rois et de particuliers* (3 vols., Catalogue général du musée de Caire vols. 30, 49, 71), Cairo 1906–1914.

Leibovitch J., "Une scène de sacrifice rituel chez les Anciens Egyptiens," *JNES* 12 (1953) 59f.

Lenzen H. J., "Mesopotamische Tempelanlagen von der Frühzeit bis zum zweiten Jahrtausend," *ZA* 51 (1955) 1–36.

Lepsius R., *Denkmäler aus Ägypten und Äthiopien* (12 vols.), Berlin 1849–1858; reprint Osnabrück 1969.

Lessing E., *Die Bibel: Die Geschichte Israels und seines Glaubens,* Freiburg 1969.

Lewy H./Lewy J., "The Week and the Oldest West Asiatic Calendar," *HUCA* 17 (1942) 10–25.

Lhote A., *Les chefs-d'œuvre de la peinture égyptienne,* Paris 1954.

de Liagre-Böhl F. M. T., "Hymnisches und Rhythmisches in den Amarnabriefen aus Kanaan," in: idem, *Opera Minora,* Groningen-Djakarta 1953, pp. 375–379.

Liebowitz H. L., "Horses in New Kingdom Art and the Date of an Ivory from Megiddo," *Journal of the American Research Center in Egypt* 6 (1967) 129–134.

Lipinski E., *Le Poème royal du Psaume LXXXIX 1–5.20–38* (Cahiers de la Revue Biblique 6), Paris 1967.

Lips J., *Fallensysteme der Naturvölker,* Leipzig 1926.

Loud G., *The Megiddo Ivories* (OIP 52), Chicago 1939.

—*Megiddo,* vol. 2, *Seasons of 1935–39* (OIP 62), Chicago 1948. (For vol. 1 see Lamon.)

Lüddeckens E., *Untersuchungen über religiösen Gehalt, Sprache und Form der ägyptischen Totenklagen* (MDAIK 11), Berlin 1943.

Luschan F. von, *Ausgrabungen in Sendschirli* (5 vols.), Berlin 1893–1943.

Macadam M. F. L., *The Temples of Kawa* (2 vols.), London-Oxford 1949–1955.

Macalister R. A. S., *The Excavation of Geser* (3 vols.), London 1912.

Maier J., *Vom Kultus zur Gnosis* (Kairos: Religionswissenschaftliche Studien 1), Salzburg 1964.

Maisler B., *The Excavations at Tell Qasîle: Preliminary Report,* Jerusalem 1951.

Mallowan M. E. L., *Nimrud and Its Remains,* London 1966.

Mariette A., *Dendérah: Description générale du grand Temple de cette ville* (6 vols.), Paris 1870–1875.

—*Abydos* (2 vols.), Paris 1869–1880.

Martiny G., *Die Gegensätze im babylonischen und assyrischen Tempelbau* (Abhandlungen für die Kunde des Morgenlandes 21.3), Leipzig 1936.

Matthiae P., *Ars Syra: Contributi alla storia dell'Arte figurativa, siriana nell'età del Medio e Tardo Bronzo,* Rome 1962.

—"Empreintes d'un cylindre paléosyrien de Tell Mardikh," *Syria* 46 (1969) 1–43.

May H. G./Engberg R. M., *Material Remains of the Megiddo Cult* (OIP 26), Chicago 1935.

—"The Sacred Tree on Palestine Painted Pottery," *JAOS* 59 (1939) 251–259.

Mazar B., *Views of the Biblical World* (5 vols.), Jerusalem–Ramat Gan 1958–1961 (=IWB).

McCown C. C., *Tell en-Naṣbeh Excavated under the Direction of the Late William Frederic Badè,* vol. 1, *Archaeological and Historical Results,* Berkeley–New Haven 1947.

Meier G., *Die assyrische Beschwörungssammlung Maqlû* (AfO 2), Berlin 1937.

Meissner B., *Assyrische Jagden: Auf Grund alter Berichte und Darstellungen geschildert* (Der Alte Orient 3.2), Leipzig 1911.

—"Palästinensische Städtebilder aus der Zeit Tiglatpilesers III," *ZDPV* 39 (1916) 261–263.

—*Babylonien und Assyrien* (2 vols.), Heidelberg 1920–1925.

—"Siegelzylinder mit Krankheitsbeschwörungen," *MAOG* 8 (1934) 14–26.

—"Neue Siegelzylinder mit Krankheitsbeschwörungen," *AfO* 10 (1935/36) 160–162.

Mekhitarian A., *Ägyptische Malerei* (Die grossen Jahrhunderte der Malerei), Geneva 1954.

Meshorer Y., *Jewish Coins of the Second Temple Period,* Chicago 1967.

Mesnil du Buisson R., *Les peintures de la synagogue de Doura Europos,* Rome 1939.

—"Une tablette magique de la région du Moyen Euphrat," in: *Mélanges syriens offerts à M. René Dussaud,* vol. 1, Paris 1939, pp. 421–434.

Mettinger T. N. D., *Solomonic State Officials: A Study of the Civil Government Officials of the Israelite Monarchy,* Lund 1971.

Metzger M., "Himmlische und irdische Wohnstatt Jahwes," in: *Ugarit-Forschungen,* vol. 2, Neukirchen 1970, pp. 139–158.

Möller G., "Das Amtsabzeichen des Oberrichters in der Spätzeit," *ZÄS* 56 (1920) 67–68.

Moftah R., "Die uralte Sykomore und andere Erscheinungen der Hathor," *ZÄS* 92 (1966) 40–47.

Montet P., "Le rituel de fondation des temples égyptiens," *Kemi* 17 (1964) 74–100.

Moorey P. R. S., "A Bronze 'Pazuzu' Statuette from Egypt," *Iraq* 27 (1965) 33–41.

Moortgat A., *Vorderasiatische Rollsiegel,* Berlin ²1966.

—*Die Kunst des Alten Mesopotamien,* Darmstadt 1967.

Morenz S., "Eine 'Naturlehre' in den Sargtexten," *Wiener Zeitschrift für die Kunde des Morgenlandes* 54 (1957) 119–129.

—*Ägyptische Religion,* Stuttgart 1960.

—*Altägyptischer Jenseitsführer: Papyrus Berlin 3127,* Frankfurt am Main 1966.

Moret A., *Le rituel du culte divin journalier en Egypte d'après les papyrus de Berlin et les textes du temple de Sethi I à Abydos* (Annales du Musée Guimet 14), Paris 1902.

—*Du caractère religieux de la royauté pharaonique* (Annales du Musée Guimet 15), Paris 1902.

—"Sur le rite de l'embrassement," *Sphinx* 11 (1907/1908) 26–30.

—"Le rite de briser les vases rouges au temple de Louxor," *RdE* 3 (1946) 167.

de Morgan J., *La préhistoire orientale,* vol. 2, *L'égypte et l'afrique du nord,* Paris 1926.

Moscati S., *Geschichte und Kultur der semitischen Völker,* Einsiedeln-Zurich-Cologne 1961.

—"Un avorio di Ugarit e l'iconografia del nemico vinto," *Or Ant* 1 (1962) 3–7.

—*Historical Art in the Ancient Near East* (Studi Semitici 8), Rome 1963.

—*Die Phöniker von 1200 vor Christus bis zum Untergang Karthagos,* Zurich 1966.

Mowan O., "Quatuor Montes Sacri in Ps 89,13?," *VD* 41 (1963) 11–20.

Mowinckel S. *Psalmenstudien* (6 vols.), Oslo 1921–1924; reprint 2 vols., Amsterdam, 1961.

—*The Psalms in Israel's Worship,* Oxford–New York, 1962.

Müller V., "Types of Mesopotamian Houses: Studies in Oriental Archaeology III," *JAOS* 60 (1940) 151–180.

Mueller W. M., *Egyptological Researches* (3 vols.), Washington 1906–1920.

Murray M. A., "Ritual Masking," in: *Mélanges Maspero,* vol. 1, *Orient Ancien* (MIFAO 66.1), Cairo 1934, pp. 251–255.

Nagel G., "A propos des rapports du Psaume 104 avec les textes égyptiens," in:

Festschrift für A. Bertholet, Tübingen 1950, pp. 395–403.

Naville E., *Das ägyptische Todtenbuch der XVIII. bis XX. Dynastie aus verschiedenen Urkunden zusammengestellt und herausgegeben* (3 vols.), Berlin 1886.

—*The Temple of Deir el Bahari* (6 vols., Memoirs of the Egypt Exploration Society nos. 13, 14, 16, 19, 27, 29), London 1895–1908.

Nelson H. H. et al.: *Earlier Historical Records of Ramses III: Medinet Habu,* vol. 1 (OIP 8), Chicago 1930.

—*Later Historical Records of Ramses III: Medinet Habu,* vol. 2 (OIP 9), Chicago 1932.

—*The Calendar, the "Slaughterhouse" and Minor Records of Ramses III: Medinet Habu,* vol. 3 (OIP 23), Chicago 1934.

—*Ramses III's Temple within the Great Inclosure of Amon,* pt. 1, *Reliefs and Inscriptions at Karnak,* vol. 1 (OIP 25), Chicago 1936.

—*Ramses III's Temple within the Great Inclosure of Amon,* pt. 2, *Ramses III's Temple in the Precinct of Mut: Reliefs and Inscriptions at Karnak,* vol. 2 (OIP 35), Chicago 1936.

—*Festival Scenes of Ramses III: Medinet Habu,* vol. 4 (OIP 51), Chicago 1940.

Neugebauer O./Parker R. A., *Egyptian Astronomical Texts,* vol. 1, *The Early Decans,* London 1960.

Newberry P. E., *Beni Hasan* (2 vols.; Archaeological Survey of Egypt 1 and 2), London 1893–1894.

Nims C. F., *Thebes of the Pharaohs,* New York 1964.

—et al., *The Eastern High Gate: Medinet Habu,* vol. 8 (OIP 94), Chicago 1970.

Nöldecke T., "Halleluja," BZAW (1918) 375–380.

Noth M., *Die israelitischen Personennamen im Rahmen der gemeinsemitischen Namengebung* (BWANT III.10), Stuttgart 1928.

—"Gott, König, Volk im Alten Testament," in: idem, *Gesammelte Studien zum Alten Testament* (ThB 6), Munich 1960, pp. 188–229. [E. T. in: Noth, *The Laws in the Pentateuch and Other Essays,* New York 1966, pp. 145–178.]

—*Die Welt des Alten Testaments,* Berlin 1962. [E. T. *The Old Testament World,* Philadelphia 1966.]

—*Das zweite Buch Mose: Exodus* (ATD 5), Göttingen³ 1965. [E. T. *Exodus* (Old Testament Library), London-Philadelphia 1962.]

—*Könige* (BK AT IX), Neukirchen-Vluyn, 1965–1968.

Nötscher F., *"Das Angesicht Gottes schauen"*

nach biblischer und babylonischer Auffassung, Darmstadt ²1969.

Nougayrol J., *Cylindres-Sceaux et empreintes de cylindres trouvés en Palestine au cours de fouilles regulières* (Bibliothèque Archéologique et Historique 33), Paris 1939.

Özguc N., *The Anatolian Group of Cylinder Seal Impressions from Kültepe*, Ankara 1965.

Opitz D., "Studien zur altorientalischen Kunst," *AfO* 6 (1930/31) 59–65.

—"Ein Altar des Königs Tukulti-Ninurta I von Assyrien," *AfO* 7 (1931) 83–90.

—/Wolff M., "Jagd zu Pferde in der altorientalischen und klassischen Kunst," *AfO* 10 (1935/36) 317–359.

Oppenheim A. L., *Ancient Mesopotamia: Portrait of a Dead Civilisation*, Chicago 1964.

Oppenheim M. von, *Tell Halaf*, Paris 1939.

—et al., *Tell Halaf* (4 vols.), Berlin 1943–1962.

Orthmann W., "Die säugende Göttin: Zu einem Relief aus Karatepe," *Istanbuler Mitteilungen* 19/20 (1969/70) 137–143.

von der Osten H. N., *Ancient Oriental Seals in the Collection of Mr. Edward T. Newell* (OIP 22), Chicago 1934.

Otten H., "Zur Datierung und Bedeutung des Felsheiligtums von Yazilikaya," *ZA* 58 (1967) 222–240.

Otto E., "Gehalt und Bedeutung des ägyptischen Heroenglaubens," *ZÄS* 78 (1943) 28–40.

—*Ägypten: Der Weg des Pharaonenreiches*, Stuttgart ³1958.

—*Das ägyptische Mundöffnungsritual* (2 vols.; Ägyptologische Abhandlungen 3), Wiesbaden 1960.

—/Hirmer M., *Osiris und Amun*, Munich 1966.

Ouellette J. "Le vestibule du temple de Salomon était-il un *bit hilani?*" *RB* 76 (1969) 365–78.

Paget R. F. E./Pirie A. A., *The Tomb of Ptah-Hetep*, London 1898.

Paret R., *Symbolik des Islam* (vol. 2 of *Symbolik der Religionen*), Stuttgart 1958.

Parrot A., "Acquisitions et inédits du Musée du Louvre. 5. Antiquités 'mésopotamiennes'," *Syria* 31 (1954) 1–13.

—"Les fouilles de Mari. 9ᵉᵐᵉ campagne (Automne 1953)," *Syria* 31 (1954) 151–171.

—*Sintflut und Arche Noahs; Der Turm von Babel; Ninive und das Alte Testament* (Bibel und Archäologie 1), Zollikon-Zurich 1955.

—"Gestes de la prière dans le monde mesopotamien," in *Maqqēl shâqēdh: La Branche d'Amandier: Hommage à Wilhelm Vischer*, Montpellier 1960, pp. 177–180.

—*Assur: Die mesopotamische Kunst vom XIII. vorchristlichen Jahrhundert bis zum Tode Alexanders des Grossen*, Munich 1961.

—*Le temple de Jérusalem* (Cahiers d'archéologie biblique 5), Neuchâtel ²1962.

—*Sumer: Die mesopotamische Kunst von den Anfängen bis zum XII. vorchristlichen Jahrhundert*, Munich ²1962.

—*Sumer/Assur: Ergänzung 1969*, Munich 1970.

Paterson A., *Assyrian Sculptures: Palace of Sinacherib*, The Hague 1915.

—*Assyrian Sculptures*, Haarlem–London n.d.

Pax E., "Studien zum Vergeltungsproblem der Psalmen," *Studii Biblici Franciscani Liber Annuus* 2 (1960/61) 56–112.

Pedersen J., *Israel: Its Life and Culture, I–IV* (2 vols.), London–Copenhagen ⁴1959.

Pering B., "Die geflügelte Scheibe in Assyrien: Eine religionsgeschichtliche Untersuchung," *AfO* 8 (1932/33) 281–296.

Perrot G./Chipiez C., *Histoire de l'art dans l'antiquité*, vol. 3, Paris 1885.

Perrot N., *La représentation de l'arbre sacré sur les monuments de Mesopotamie et d'Elam*, Paris 1937.

Petrie F., *Ancient Gaza*, vol. 3 (Tell el Ajjul), London 1933.

—*Ancient Gaza*, vol. 4 (Tell el Ajjul), London 1934.

—*Ceremonial Slate Palettes*, London 1953.

Piankoff A., "Une statuette du dieu Ḥeka," in: *Mélanges Maspero*, vol. 1, *Orient Ancien* (MIFAO 66.1), Cairo 1934, pp. 349–352.

—"Une représentation rare sur l'une des chapelles de Toutânkhamon," *JEA* 35 (1949) 113–116.

—*Les chapelles de Tout-Ankh-Amon* (2 vols.; MIFAO 72), Cairo 1951/52.

—/Rambova N., *The Shrines of Tut-Ankh-Amon* (vol. 2 of *Egyptian Religious Texts and Representations*), New York 1955.

— / —*Mythological Papyri* (2 vols.; vol. 3 of *Egyptian Religious Texts and Representations*), New York 1957.

Pirenne J., *Histoire de la Civilisation de l'Egypte ancienne* (3 vols.), Neuchâtel-Paris 1961–1963.

Poinssot L./Lantier R., "Un sanctuaire de Tanit à Carthago," *Revue de l'Histoire des Religions* 87 (1923) 32–68.

Porada E., *Corpus of Ancient Near Eastern Seals in North American Collections*, vol. 1, *The Collection of the Pierpont Morgan Library*, New York 1948.

Posener G., *Princes et pays d'Asie et de Nubie: Textes hiératiques sur des figurines d'envoûtement du moyen empire*, Brussels 1940.

—"La mésaventure d'un Syrien et le nom égyptien de l'ours," *Or Ant* 13 (1944) 193–204.

—"Les empreintes magiques de Gizeh et les morts dangereux," *MDAIK* 16 (1958) 252–270.

—*De la divinité du Pharaon* (Cahiers de la société asiatique 15), Paris 1960.

—/Sauneron S./Yoyotte J., *Knaurs Lexikon der ägyptischen Kultur*, Munich–Zurich 1960.

Pottier E., *L'art Hittite* (2 vols.), Paris 1926–1931.

Poulssen N., *König und Tempel im Glaubenszeugnis des Alten Testamentes* (SBM 3), Stuttgart 1967.

Preuss H.D., *Verspottung fremder Religionen im Alten Testament*, Stuttgart 1971.

Prinz H., *Altorientalische Symbolik*, Berlin 1915.

Pritchard J. B., *The Bronze Age Cemetery at Gibeon*, Philadelphia 1963.

Quell G., *Die Auffassung des Todes in Israel*, Darmstadt ²1967.

Quibell J. E., "Slate Palette from Hieraconpolis," *ZÄS* 36 (1898) 81–84.

von Rad G., *Der Heilige Krieg im alten Israel* (Abhandlungen zur Theologie des Alten und Neuen Testaments), Zurich 1951.

—"Das judäische Königsritual," in: idem, *Gesammelte Studien zum Alten Testament* (ThB 8), Munich 1961, pp. 205–213. [E. T. in: von Rad, *The Problem of the Hexateuch and Other Essays*, Edinburgh-London 1966, pp. 222–231.]

—"'Gerechtigkeit' und 'Leben' in der Kultsprache der Psalmen," in: idem, *Gesammelte Studien* (ThB 8), pp. 225–247. [E. T. in: *The Problem of the Hexateuch*, pp. 243–266.]

—"Hiob 38 und die altägyptische Weisheit," in: idem, *Gesammelte Studien* (ThB 8), pp. 262–271. [E. T. in: *The Problem of the Hexateuch*, pp. 281–291.]

—"Aspekte alttestamentlichen Weltverständnisses," *Ev Theol* 24 (1964) pp. 57–73. [E. T. in: *The Problem of the Hexateuch*, pp. 144–165.]

Radwan A., *Die Darstellungen des regierenden Königs und seiner Familienangehörigen in den Privatgräbern der 18.Dyn.* (Münchner Ägyptologische Studien 21), Berlin 1969.

Rambova N., "Symbolism," in: A. Piankoff/N. Rambova, *Mythological Papyri*, vol. 1, New York 1957.

Ranke H., "Istar als Heilgöttin," in: *Studies Presented to F. L. Griffith*, London 1932, pp. 412–418.

—"Ein ägyptisches Relief in Princeton," *JNES* 9 (1950) 228–236.

Ransom C. L., "A Late Egyptian Sarcophagus," *The Metropolitan Museum of Art Bulletin* 9 (1914) 112–120.

Reifenberg A., *Ancient Hebrew Seals*, London 1950.

—*Ancient Jewish Coins*, Jerusalem ⁵1969.

Ricke H./Hughes G. R./Wente E. F., *The Beit el Wali Temple of Rameses II*, Chicago 1967.

Ridderbos N. H., "'pr als Staub des Totenortes," *OTS* 5 (1948) 174–178.

Riemschneider M., *Die Welt der Hethiter*, Stuttgart ⁵1961

—"Urartäische Bauten in den Königsinschriften," *Orientalia* 34 (1965) 312–335.

Rimmer J., *Ancient Musical Instruments of Western Asia*, London 1969.

Roeder G., *Urkunden zur Religion des alten Ägypten*, Jena 1915.

—*Die ägyptische Götterwelt*, Zurich-Stuttgart 1959.

—*Mythen und Legenden um ägyptische Gottheiten und Pharaonen*, Zurich-Stuttgart 1960.

—*Kulte, Orakel und Naturverehrung im alten Ägypten*, Zurich-Stuttgart 1960.

Ronzevalle S., "Tablettes égyptiennes," *Mélanges de l'Université St. Joseph* 3 (1909) 791f.

Rost L., "Ein Psalmenproblem," *Theologische Literaturzeitung* 93 (1968) 241–246.

Rowe A., *A Catalogue of Egyptian Scarabs, Scaraboids, Seals and Amulets in the Palestine Archaeological Museum*, Cairo 1936.

—*The Four Canaanite Temples of Beth-Shan*, vol. 1, Philadelphia 1940.

Rudolph W., *Jeremia* (HAT 12), Tübingen ²1958.

Sabourin L., "Un classement littéraire des Psaumes," *Sciences ecclésiastiques* 16 (1964) 23–58.

Saleh A., "The So-called 'Primeval Hill' and Other Related Elevations in Ancient Egyptian Mythology," *MDAIK* 25 (1969) 110–120.

Saggs H. W. F., "Pazuzu," *AfO* 19 (1959/60) 123–127.

Sameh W., "Der Alltag im alten Ägypten," *DU* 240 (February 1961) 1–40.

Sauneron S./Yoyotte J./Garelli P./Leibovici M. et al. *Schöpfungsmythen* (Quellen des Alten Orients), Einsiedeln-Zurich-Cologne 1964.

Säve-Söderbergh T., *Four Eighteen Dynasty Tombs* (vol. 1 of *Private Tombs at Thebes*), Oxford 1957.

de Savignac J., "Théologie pharaonique et messianisme d'Israel," *VT* 7 (1957) 82–90.

Schäfer H., "Die Ausdeutung der Spiegel platte als Sonnenscheibe," *ZÄS* 68 (1933) 1–7.

— H./Andrae W., *Die Kunst des Alten Orients*, Berlin 1925.

—"Weltgebäude der alten Ägypter," in: idem, *Ägyptische und heutige Kunst*, Berlin 1928, pp. 83–122.

—"Eine nordsyrische Kultsitte?," *ZÄS* 73 (1937) 54ff.

—"Abwehren und Hinzeigen," *MDAIK* 9 (1940) 151–154.

—"Das Niederschlagen der Feinde: Zur Geschichte eines ägyptischen Sinnbildes," *Wiener Zeitschrift für die Kunde des Morgenlands* 54 (1957) 168–176.

—*Von ägyptischer Kunst* (ed. E. Brunner-Traut), Wiesbaden ⁴1963.

Schaeffer C. F. A., "Les fouilles de Minet el-Beida et de Ras Shamra: Quatrième campagne (Printemps 1932): Rapport sommaire," *Syria* 14 (1933) 91–127.

—"Les fouilles de Ras Shamra-Ugarit: Septième campagne (Printemps 1935): Rapport sommaire," *Syria* 17 (1936) 105–48.

—"Les fouilles de Ras Shamra-Ugarit: Huitième campagne (Printemps 1936): Rapport sommaire," *Syria* 18 (1937) 125–54.

—*Ugaritica*, vol. 1, Paris 1939.

—"La coupe en argent encrustée d'or d'Enkomi-Alasia," *Syria* 30 (1953) 51–64.

—"Les fouilles de Ras Shamra-Ugarit: Quinzième, seizième et dixseptième campagnes (1951, 1952 et 1953)," *Syria* 31 (1954) 14–67.

—"Le vase de mariage du roi Niqmad d'Ugarit avec une princesse égyptienne," *Ugaritica*, vol. 3, Paris 1956, pp. 164–168.

—"Götter der Nord- und Inselvölker in Zypern," *AfO* 21 (1966) 59–69.

—"Nouveaux Témoignages du culte de El et de Baal à Ras Shamra-Ugarit et ailleurs en Syrie-Palestine," *Syria* 43 (1966) 1–19.

Schapiro M./Avi Yonah M., *Israel: Frühe Mosaiken*, Paris 1960.

Scharff A., *Ägyptische Sonnenlieder*, Berlin 1921.

—/Moortgat A., *Ägypten und Vorderasien im Altertum*, Munich 1950.

Schmid H. H., *Gerechtigkeit als Weltordnung*, Tübingen 1968.

Schmidt H., *Der heilige Fels in Jerusalem*, Tübingen 1933.

Schmidt V., *Levende og Døde i det gamle Aegypten: Album til ordning Sarkofager, Mumiekister, Mumiehylstre o.lign.*, Copenhagen 1919.

Schmidt W., "Anthropologische Begriffe im Alten Testament," *Ev Theol* 24 (1964) 374–388.

Schmökel H., *Kulturgeschichte des Alten Orients*, Stuttgart 1961.

—*Ur, Assur und Babylon*, Zurich ⁶1962.

Schollmeyer P. A., *Sumerisch-babylonische Hymnen und Gebete an Šamaš*, Paderborn 1912.

Schott S., *Altägyptische Liebeslieder*, Zurich ²1950.

—"Voraussetzung und Gegenstand altägyptischer Wissenschaft," in: *Jahrbuch der Akademie der Wissenschaft und der Literatur*, Mainz 1950, pp. 277–295.

—"Ein ungewöhnliches Symbol des Triumphes über die Feinde Ägyptens," *JNES* 14 (1955) 97–99.

—"Zum Weltbild der Jenseitsführer des neuen Reiches" (*Nachrichten der Akademie der Wissenschaften in Göttingen. Philologisch-historische Klasse I*), Göttingen 1965, pp. 185–197.

—"Aufnahmen vom Hungersnotrelief aus dem Aufweg der Unaspyramide," *RdE* 17 (1965) 7–13 and pls. 1–4.

—"Thoth als Verfasser heiliger Schriften," *ZÄS* 99 (1972) 20–25.

Schreiner J., *Sion-Jerusalem: Jahwes Königssitz* (Studien zum Alten und Neuen Testament VII), Munich 1963.

Schult H., "Der Debir im salomonischen Tempel," *ZDPV* 80 (1964) 46–54.

Schumacher G., *Tell el-Mutesellim* (2 vols.), Leipzig 1908.

Schunck K. D., "Der fünfte Thronname des Messias (Jes IX. 5–6)," *VT* 23 (1973) 108–110.

Schwegler T., *Probleme der biblischen Urgeschichte*, Munich 1960.

Schweitzer U., *Löwe und Sphinx im alten Aegypten* (Aegyptologische Forschungen 15), Glückstadt 1948.

Seele K. C., "Horus on the Crocodiles," *JNES* 6 (1947) 43–52.

Seibert I., *Hirt-Herde-König* (Deutsche Akademie der Wissenschaften zu Berlin. Schriften der Sektion für Altertumswissenschaft 53), Berlin 1969.

—*Die Frau im alten Orient*, Leipzig 1973.

Seidl H., "Horn und Trompete im alten Israel unter Berücksichtigung der 'Kriegsrolle' von Qumran," in: *Wissenschaftliche Zeitschrift der Karl-Marx-Universität*, Leipzig 1956/57, pp. 589–599.

Seidl U., "Die babylonischen Kudurru Reliefs," *Bagdader Mitteilungen* 4 (1968), Berlin 1969, 7–220.

Sellin E., "Die Ausgrabung von Sichem: Kurze vorläufige Mitteilung über die Arbeit im Frühjahr 1926," *ZDPV* 49 (1926) 229–236, 304–320.

Sethe K., *Die Ächtung feindlicher Fürsten, Völker und Dinge auf altägyptischen Tongefässscherben des Mittleren Reiches* (Abhandlungen der Preussischen Akademie der Wissenschaften, Jahrgang 1926. Phil.-hist. Klasse no. 5), Berlin 1926.

Seybold K., *Das Gebet des Kranken im Alten Testament: Untersuchungen zur Bestimmung und Zuordnung der Krankheits- und Heilungspsalmen* (BWANT 99), Stuttgart 1973.

—"Das Herrscherbild des Bileamorakels Num 24,15–19," *Theologische Zeitschrift* 29 (1973) 1–19.

Seyrig H., "La triade héliopolitaine et les temples de Baalbek," *Syria* 10 (1929) 314–356.

—"Antiquités syriennes 17: Bas reliefs monumentaux du temple de Bêl à Palmyre," *Syria* 15 (1934) 155–186.

—"Représentations de la main divine," *Syria* 20 (1939) 189–194.

—"Cylindre représentant une tauromachie," *Syria* 33 (1956) 169–174.

—"Trônes phéniciens flanqués de sphinx," *Syria* 36 (1959) 51f.

—"Antiquités syriennes 86: Quelques cylindres syriens," *Syria* 40 (1963) 253–260.

Shiloh Y., "The Four Room House: Its Situation and Function in the Israelite City," *IEJ* 20 (1970) 180–190.

Shorter A. W., "Reliefs Showing the Coronation of Rameses II," *JEA* 20 (1934) 18f and pl. III.

Siegler K. G., "Die Tore von Kalabsha," *MDAIK* 25 (1969) 139–153.

Simpson W. K., *Papyrus Reisner I: The Records of a Building Project in the Reign of Sesostris I*, Boston 1963.

Smend R., *Jahwekrieg und Stämmebund* (FRLANT 84), Göttingen 1963.

Smith W. S., *Interconnections in the Ancient Near East*, New Haven–London 1965.

—*The Art and Architecture of Ancient Egypt* (Pelican History of Art) Harmondsworth, Middlesex 1965.

von Soden W., *Leistung und Grenze sumerischer und babylonischer Wissenschaft* (Libelli 142), Darmstadt 1965.

—"Assyriologische Erwägungen zu einem neuen Buch über die Totenreichvorstellungen im AT," *Ugarit-Forschungen* 2 (1970) 331f.

Sollberger E., "Old Babylonian Worshipper Figurines," *Iraq* 31 (1969) 90–93.

Solyman T., *Die Entstehung und Entwicklung der Götterwaffen im alten Mesopotamien und ihre Bedeutung,* Beirut 1968.

Spiegel J., *Die Idee vom Totengericht in der ägyptischen Religion,* Glückstadt 1930.

—"Der Sonnengott in der Barke als Richter," *MDAIK* 8 (1939) 201–206.

Spiegelberg W., "Die Weihestatuette einer Wöchnerin," *ASAE* 29 (1929) 162–165.

Stadelmann L. I. J., *The Hebrew Conception of the World* (Analecta Biblica 39), Rome 1970.

Stadelmann R., *Syrisch-palästinensische Gottheiten in Ägypten,* Leiden 1967.

Staudacher W., *Die Trennung von Himmel und Erde: Ein vorgriechischer Schöpfungsmythos bei Hesiod und den Orphikern,* Tübingen 1942.

Steinmetzer F., "Babylonische Parallelen zu den Fluchpsalmen," *Biblische Zeitschrift* 10 (1912) 133–142, 363–369.

Stolz F., *Strukturen und Figuren im Kult von Jerusalem* (BZAW 118), Berlin 1970.

—"Die Bäume des Gottesgartens auf dem Libanon," *ZAW* 84 (1972) 141–156.

Stricker B. H., *De groote Zeeslang* (Mededelingen en Verhandelingen No 10 van het vooraziatisch-egyptisch Genootschap "Ex oriente lux"), Leiden 1953.

—"The Origin of the Greek Theatre," *JEA* 41 (1955) 34–47.

Strommenger E./Hirmer M., *Fünf Jahrtausende Mesopotamien: Die Kunst von den Anfängen um 5000 v. Chr. bis zu Alexander,* Munich 1962.

Stummer F., *Sumerisch-akkadische Parallelen zum Aufbau alttestamentlicher Psalmen,* Paderborn 1922.

Sukenik E. L., "Designs of the Torah Shrine in Ancient Synagogues in Palestine," *Palestine Exploration Fund Quarterly Statement* 63 (1931) 22–25.

—*The Ancient Synagogue of Beth Alpha,* Jerusalem 1932.

Tallqvist K., *Sumerisch-akkadische Namen der Totenwelt* (Studia Orientalia V. 4), Helsingfors 1934.

Taylor G., *The Roman Temples of Lebanon: Pictorial Guide,* Beirut 1967.

Thomas E., "Terrestrial Marsh and Solar Mat," *JEA* 45 (1959) 38–51.

Thomas W. D. (ed.), *Archaeology and Old Testament Study,* Oxford 1967.

Thureau-Dangin F., "Rituel et amulettes contre Labartu," *Revue d'Assyriologie et d'Archéologie Orientale* 18 (1921) 161–168.

—/Barrois A./Dossin G./Dunand M., *Arslan Tash* (2 vols.; Bibliothèque archéologique et historique 16), Paris 1931.

—/Dunand M., *Til Barsib,* Paris 1936.

Torczyner H., "A Hebrew Incantation against Night Demons from Biblical Times," *JNES* 6 (1947) 18–29.

Tournay R., I/Saouaf O., "Stèle de Tukulti-Ninurta II," *Annales archéologiques de Syrie* 2 (1952) 169–190.

Tournay R., *Les Psaumes,* Paris 1964.

Tromp N. J., *Primitive Conceptions of Death and the Nether World in the Old Testament* (Biblica et Orientalia 21), Rome 1969.

Tufnell O. et al., *Lachish,* vol. 2, *The Fosse Temple,* London 1940. *Lachish,* vol. 3, *The Iron Age,* London 1953. *Lachish,* vol. 4, *The Bronze Age,* London 1958.

Unger E., *Babylon, die heilige Stadt nach der Beschreibung der Babylonier,* Berlin-Leipzig 1931.

Vandier J., *Manuel d'archéologie égyptienne* (5 vols.), Paris 1952–1969.

—"Le Dieu Shou dans le papyrus Jumilhac," *MDAIK* 15 (1957) 268–273.

Vanel A., *L'iconographie du dieu de l'orage dans le proche-orient ancien jusqu'au VIIème siècle avant J.-C.* (Cahiers de la Revue Biblique 3), Paris 1965.

de Vaux R., "Titres et fonctionnaires égyptiens à la cour de David et Salomon," *RB* 48 (1939) 394–405.

—*Ancient Israel: Its Life and Institutions,* London–New York 1961.

—"Les Chérubins et l'Arche d'alliance, les Sphinx gardiens et les trônes divins dans l'Ancien Testament," *Mélanges de l'Université St. Joseph* 37 (1960/61) 91–124; cited from, idem, *Bible et Orient,* Paris 1967, pp. 231–259.

—*Histoire ancienne d'Israel,* Paris 1971.

Vercoutter J., "Les Haou-Nebout," *BIFAO* 46 (1947) 125–158 and 48 (1949) 107–209.

Vigneau A./Ozenfant A., *Encyclopédie photographique de l'art* (2 vols.), Paris 1935–1937.

Vila A., "Un dépot de textes d'envoûtement du moyen empire," *Journal des Savants* 1963, 135–160.

Vincent L. H., *Jérusalem de l'Ancien Testament: Recherches d'archéologie et d'histoire* (3 vols.), Paris 1954–1956.

Vogt E., "'Ihr Tisch werde zur Falle' (Ps 69,23)," *Biblica* 43 (1962) 78–82.

—"Vom Tempel zum Felsendom," *Biblica* 55 (1974) 23–64.

de Vries C. E., "A Ritual Ball Game?," in: *Studies in Honor of John A. Wilson,* Chicago 1969, pp. 25–35.

Vycichl, W., "L'allaitement divin du Pharaon expliqué par une coutume africaine," *Genève-Afrique* 5 (1966) 261–203.

Wächter L., *Der Tod im Alten Testament* (Arbeiten zur Theologie II, Series 8), Stuttgart 1967.

van de Walle B. "Les rois sportifs de l'ancienne Egypte," *Chronique d'Egypte* 26 (1938) 234–257.

Walser G., *Die Völkerschaften auf den Reliefs von Persepolis: Historische Studien über den sogenannten Tributzug an der Apadanatreppe,* Berlin 1966.

Wanke G., *Die Zionstheologie der Korachiten* (BZAW 97), Berlin 1966.

Ward W. A., "La déesse nourricière d'Ugarit," *Syria* 46 (1969) 225–239.

Ward W. H., *Cylinders and Other Oriental Seals in the Library of J. Pierpont Morgan,* New York 1909.

Warmington B. H., *Carthage* (Pelican Book A 598) Harmondsworth, Middlesex 1964.

Watzinger C., *Denkmäler Palästinas: Eine Einführung in die Archäologie des Heiligen Landes* (2 vols.), Leipzig 1933–1935.

Weber O., *Die Dämonenbeschwörung bei den Babyloniern und Assyrern* (Der Alte Orient VII.4), Leipzig 1906.

—*Altorientalische Siegelbilder,* Leipzig 1920.

Weiser A., *Die Psalmen* (ATD 14/15), Göttingen ⁵1959.

Wellhausen J., *Reste arabischen Heidentums,* Berlin ³1961.

Welten P., *Die Königs-Stempel: Ein Beitrag zur Militärpolitik Judas unter Hiskia und Josia,* Wiesbaden 1969.

Werbrouck M., *Les pleureuses dans l'Egypte ancienne,* Brussels 1938.

Westendorf W., "Bemerkungen zu den Namen der Könige Djer-Athotis und Neferka," *OLZ* 61 (1966) 533–541.

—*Altägyptische Darstellungen des Sonnenlaufes auf der abschüssigen Himmelsbahn* (Münchner Ägyptologische Studien 10), Berlin 1966.

—"Bemerkungen zur 'Kammer der Wiedergeburt' im Tutanchamungrab," *ZÄS* 94 (1967) 139–150.

—*Das Alte Ägypten (Kunst im Bild)*, Baden-Baden 1968.

Westermann C., *Das Loben in den Psalmen*, Göttingen ³1963. [E. T. *The Praise of God in the Psalms*, Richmond, Va. 1965.]

—*Genesis* (BK AT I), Neukirchen-Vluyn, 1966ff.

Weyersberg M., "Das Motiv der 'Himmelsstütze' in der altägyptischen Kosmologie," *Zeitschrift für Ethnologie* 86 (1961) 113–140.

Widengren G., "The Accadian and Hebrew Psalms of Lamentation as Religious Documents" (Diss. Uppsala 1936), Stockholm 1937.

Wiegand A., "Der Gottesname *ṣūr* und seine Deutung in dem Sinne Bildner oder Schöpfer in der alten jüdischen Literatur," *ZAW* 10 (1890) 85–97.

Wiegand T./Schulz B./Winnefeld H., *Baalbek: Ergebnisse der Ausgrabungen und Untersuchungen in den Jahren 1898–1905* (2 vols.), Berlin-Leipzig 1921.

Wildberger H., *Jesaja* (BK AT X), Neukirchen-Vluyn 1965–1970.

—/Wolgensinger M. und L., *Biblische Welt*, Zurich n.d.

Wildung D., "Der König Ägyptens als Herr der Welt? Ein seltener ikonographischer Typus der Königsplastik des Neuen Reiches," *AfO* 24 (1973) 108–116.

Wilkinson C. K., "Art of the Marlik Culture," *The Metropolitan Museum of Art Bulletin* 24 (1965/66) 101–109.

Wirgin W., "The Menorah as Symbol of After-Life," *IEJ* 14 (1964) 102ff.

Wiseman D. J., *Chronicles of Chaldaean Kings (626–556 B.C.) in the British Museum*, London 1961.

—/Forman W. and B., *Götter und Menschen im Rollsiegel Westasiens*, Prague 1958.

de Wit C., *Le rôle et le sens du lion dans l'Égypte Ancienne*, Leiden 1951.

—"La circoncision chez les anciens Egyptiens," *ZÄS* 99 (1972) 41–48.

Wolf W., "Der Berliner Ptah-Hymnus," *ZÄS* 64 (1929) 17–44.

—*Das Schöne Fest von Opet: Die Festzugsdarstellungen im grossen Säulengang des Tempels von Luksor*, Leipzig 1931.

—*Die Kunst Ägyptens*, Stuttgart 1957.

—*Kulturgeschichte des Alten Ägypten*, Stuttgart 1962.

Woolley C. L./Lawrence T. E., *Carchemish: Report on the Excavations at Djerablus on Behalf of the British Museum* (3 vols.), London 1914–1952.

—*Excavations at Ur*, London 1955.

Wreszinski W., *Atlas zur altägyptischen Kulturgeschichte* (3 vols.), Leipzig 1923–1938.

Wright G. R. H., "Pre-Israelite Temples in the Land of Canaan," *PEQ* 103 (1971) 17–32.

Yadin Y., "The Earliest Record of Egypt's Military Penetration into Asia?," *IEJ* 5 (1955) 1–16.

—"Solomon's City Wall and Gate at Gezer," *IEJ* 8 (1958) 80–86.

—*The Art of Warfare in Biblical Lands in the Light of Archaeological Study* (2 vols.), New York 1963.

—*Masada: Herod's Fortress and the Zealots' Last Stand*, New York 1966.

—et al. *Hazor* (4 vols. in 3 vols.), Jerusalem-Oxford 1958–1961.

Yeivin S., "Jachin and Boaz" (Hebrew), *Eretz Israel* 5 (1958) 97–104; E. T. in *PEQ* 91 (1959) 6–22.

—"The Date of the Seal 'Belonging to Shema' (the) Servant (of) Jerobeam,'" *JNES* 19 (1960) 205–212.

Ziegler J., "Die Hilfe Gottes 'am Morgen,'" *Bonner Biblische Beiträge* 1 (1950) 281–288.

Zimmerli W., "Ezechieltempel und Salomostadt," *VTS* 16 (1967) 398–414.

Zimmerli W., "Vier oder fünf Thronnamen des messianischen Herrschers von Jes IV 5b.6," *VT* 22 (1972) 249–252.

CATALOGUE OF THE ILLUSTRATIONS

The drawings in this book frequently omit, in whole or in part, the texts which originally accompanied the pictures. In Egyptian pictures, the text is usually subjoined to the scene; in Mesopotamian stelae and similar objects, the text often runs across the scene. Omissions of text are not specially noted. Unless otherwise noted, the drawings have been taken from the first source listed. Drawings with an asterisk (*) are by O. Keel; those with a double asterisk (**) by H. Keel-Leu.

Dates are based on the chronology used by A. Schaff and A. Moortgat in *Ägypten und Vorderasien im Altertum* (Munich, 1950). In this chronology, dates set within the third millennium and the first half of the second may tend to be somewhat early.

The technical data provided for the individual illustrations is not always as complete as the author would have wished. In view of the purposes of this study, however, it would be difficult to justify the expenditure of time necessary to provide fuller information. What is lacking can always be found, with a little effort, by reference to the information supplied.

1. Fragment of a clay tablet, 9.1 × 6.2 cm.: Nippur, Ur III Period (2050–1950 B.C.); Baghdad. E. Heinrich and U. Seidl, "Grundrisszeichnungen," pp. 33f. There is reference to extensive literature on Egyptian building plans in W. K. Simpson in *Papyrus Reisner*, vol. 1, p. 63, n. 10.*

2. Drawing reconstructed from Fig. *1*. E. Heinrich and U. Seidl. "Grundrisszeichnungen," p. 33.

3. Diorite statue, h. 93 cm.: Lagash (Tello), Ur III Period (2050–1950 B.C.); Louvre (Gudea-Statue B). S. N. Kramer, *History*, pl. 7; cf. *ANEP*, no. 749. A. Parrot, *Sumer*, fig. 253. M. A. Beek, *Atlas of Mesopotamia*, fig. 135.*

4. Clay tablet, 18 × 21 cm.: Nippur, 1500 B.C.; Hilprecht Collection, Jena. *BHH*, vol. 3., col. 1849f. *ANEP*, no. 260. For additional fragments of city plans, see E. Unger, *Babylon*, pp. 252–54.

5. Plan of the excavation of Nippur. *BHH*, vol. 3, col. 1849. On ancient Near Eastern city plans cf. P. Lampl, *Cities and Planning*.

6. Papyrus, Egyptian, 19th Dynasty (1345–1200 B.C.); Turin, Egyptian Museum. G. Goyon, "Le Papyrus de Turin," pl. 1. G. Posener et al., *Knaurs Lexikon*, p. 87. *IWB*, vol. 4, p. 119.

7. Drawing reconstructed from Fig. 6. G. Goyon, "Le Papyrus de Turin," p. 378.

8. Clay tablet 8 × 12 cm. with a drawing 8 × 8 cm.: Sippar, 6th–5th c. (probably derived from a prototype from the first Babylonian dynasty, 1850–1530 B.C.); BM 92687. E. Unger, *Babylon*, pp. 20–24, 254–58. P. Grelot, "La géographie," pp. 64–68. *IWB*, vol. 4, p. 118.*

9. Cylinder seal, Mesopotamian, Akkadian Period (2350–2150 B.C.); BM 89110. *AOB*, p. 319. H. Frankfort, *Cylinder Seals*, pl. 18a.*

10. Papyrus (Book of the Dead), New Kingdom (1570–1085 B.C.); Royal Museum, Leiden. E. Naville, *Todtenbuch*, vol. 1, pl. 28. H. Schäfer, "Weltgebäude," p. 101.

11. Papyrus of Nefer-Renpet, New Kingdom (1570–1085 B.C.); Brussels. A. Piankoff and N. Rambova, *Mythological Papyri*, p. 33.

12. Papyrus (Book of the Dead), New Kingdom (1570–1085 B.C.); Trinity College, Dublin. E. Naville, *Todtenbuch*, vol. 1, pl. 28. H. Schäfer, "Weltgebäude," p. 101.

13. Papyrus (Book of the Dead), New Kingdom (1570–1085 B.C.); BM 9901. E. Naville, *Todtenbuch*, vol. 1, pl. 28. H. Schäfer, "Weltgebäude," p. 101.

14. *(left)* Tomb painting (diameter of the threshing floor ca. 80 cm.): West Thebes, Deir el Medinah: Tomb of Amennakht (No. 266), 19th Dynasty (1345–1200 B.C.). N. de G. Davies, *Two Ramesside Tombs*, p. 56, pl. 40. B. H. Stricker, "Origin of the Greek Theatre," p. 42, fig. 5.

(right) Relief: El-Kâb: Tomb of Paheri, 18th Dynasty (1570–1345 B.C.). B. H. Stricker, "Origin of the Greek Theatre," p. 43, fig. 6c.

15. Tomb painting: Valley of the Kings: Ramses X (ca. 1085 B.C.). A. Piankoff and N. Rambova, *Mythological Papyri*, p. 31. H. Schäfer, "Weltgebäude," p. 89 (simplified).

16. Papyrus of Khonsu-mes, h. ca. 12 cm.; Paris, Bibliothèque nationale, EG no. 153. A.

Piankoff and N. Rambova, *Mythological Papyri*, no. 30, text 214.**

17. Papyrus of Ani, 18th Dynasty (1570–1345 B.C.); BM. S. Schott, "Weltbild," p. 185. W. Westendorf, *Sonnenlauf*, pl. 6.

18. Papyrus (Book of the Dead), New Kingdom (1570–1085 B.C.); Dublin, Trinity College. E. Naville, *Todtenbuch*, vol. 1, pl. 27.

19. Ivory comb with the name of King Djet: Abydos, First Dynasty (2850 B.C.); Cairo. W. Westendorf, *Sonnenlauf*, pl. 8. R. Engelbach, "An Alleged Winged Sun-Disk," pl. 8. H. Bonnet, *Reallexikon*, p. 88. H. Frankfort, *Kingship*, fig. 17. On the *was*-scepter, cf. G. Jéquier, *Frises*, pp. 176–80.

20. Tomb of King Sahure, seen from the south: Fifth Dynasty (2480–2350 B.C.). L. Borchardt, *Grabdenkmal*, vol. 1, p. 45. B. H. Stricker, *Zeeslang*, p. 14, fig. 2a.

21. Sandstone relief, Edfu: exterior of the western portion of the enclosure wall, second register, scene 38 (237–257 B.C.); E. Chassinat, *Edfou*, pl. 626.**

22. Stone relief, h. 75 cm.: Yazilikaya near Boghazköi: Tudhaliyas IV (1250–1220 B.C.). K. Bittel et al., *Yazilikaya*, pp. 92f., pl. 24.2. M. Riemschneider, *Welt der Hethiter*, pl. 37. H. Frankfort, *Cylinder Seals*, p. 275.**

23. Cylinder seal, limestone, 6.8 × 1.8 cm.: Assyrian, ca. 10th c. B.C. H. N. von der Osten, *Collection of Mr. E. T. Newell*, no. 416. H. Frankfort, *Cylinder Seals*, p. 213.**

24. Cylinder seal, Assyrian, 9th c. B.C. H. Frankfort, *Cylinder Seals*, pl. 33e. S. A. Cook, *Religion of Ancient Palestine*, p. 48, pl. 13.4. K. Galling, "Beschriftete Bildsiegel," no. 154. O. Eissfeldt, *KS*, vol. 2, pp. 418f., plates 4, 5.**

25. Papyrus Barker 210 III, 21st Dynasty (1085–950 B.C.); BM 10008.3; V. Ions, *Egyptian Mythology*, p. 46.**

26. Relief, yellow sandstone, w. 10.25 m.: Cenotaph of Seti I (Osireion) at Abydos: western half of the ceiling of the sarcophagus chamber of Seti I (1317–1301 B.C.). H. Frankfort et al., *Cenotaph of Seti I*, vol. 1, pp. 27, 72–75, pl. 81. O. Neugebauer and R. A. Parker, *Astronomical Texts*, vol. 1, pp. 36–94, plates 30–32. Drawing: W. B. Emery.

27. Papyrus Greenfield, h. ca. 0.4 m. (length of entire scroll, 37.5 m.): Deir el Bahri, 21st Dynasty (1085–950 B.C.); BM 10554.87. *ANEP*, no. 542. G. Posener et al., *Knaurs Lexikon*, p. 93.**

27a. Hieroglyph. A. H. Gardiner, *Grammar*, p. 449, no. C.11.**

28. Painting on a mummy-case, New Kingdom (1570–1085 B.C.); Louvre. R. V. Lanzone, *Dizionario*, p. 407, pl. 158.1. J. H. Breasted, *Geschichte Ägyptens*, p. 60. A. Erman and H. Ranke, *Ägypten*, p. 295. The picture is reversed in order to facilitate comparison with representations of the same motif.

29. Papyrus (Book of the Dead) of Nisti-ta-Nebet Taui, 21st Dynasty (1085–950 B.C.); Cairo. A. Piankoff and N. Rambova, *Mythological Papyri*, no. 8.**

30. Relief: Philae: Ptolemy IX (107–88 B.C.). *LD*, vol. 9, pl. 35b. H. Schäfer, "Weltgebäude," p. 106.

31. Ostracon, Egyptian, New Kingdom (1570–1085 B.C.); Cairo. H. Bonnet, *Bilderatlas*, fig. 7. H. Schäfer, *Von ägyptischer Kunst*, p. 130.

32. Papyrus, New Kingdom (1570–1085 B.C.); Louvre. A. Piankoff, "Une statuette," pl. IC. R. V. Lanzone, *Dizionario*, vol. 3, fig. 7. H. Schäfer, "Weltgebäude," p. 105.**

33. Relief on a sarcophagus cover (diameter of the disc, 43.5 cm.; total height, 88 cm.): Necropolis of Sakkarah, 30th Dynasty (378–341 B.C.) or Ptolemaic Period (after 300 B.C.); Metropolitan Museum, New York. C. L. Ransom, "A Late Egyptian Sarcophagus," p. 117. W. Westendorf, *Sonnenlauf*, pl. 27. H. Schäfer, "Weltgebäude," p. 86. G. Posener et al., *Knaurs Lexikon*, p. 187.

34. Limestone block, 3 fragments: h. 57 cm., w. 43 cm. (original diameter of the disc, ca. 75 cm.): antiquities dealer in Cairo, 1947–1948, end of the New Kingdom or somewhat later (ca. 700 B.C.); Cairo (?). J. J. Clère, "Fragments," p. 32. On the cool waters of Horus, cf. E. Edel, "Zu den Inschriften," pp. 111–15.

35. W. Barta, "Königsring," p. 6 (freehand drawing).

36. Painted relief: Dendera: Temple of the New Year, Roman Imperial Period (1st–2nd c. A.D.). E. Chassinat, *Dendara*, vol. 4, pl. 315. B. H. Stricker, *Zeeslang*, fig. 2c. W. Westendorf, *Sonnenlauf*, pl. 26.*

37. Sarcophagus relief: Abydos: Seti I (1307–1301 B.C.). J. Bonomi and S. Sharpe, *Alabaster Sarcophagus*, pl. 15. A. Champdor, *Livre des Morts*, p. 89. H. Schäfer, "Weltgebäude," p. 108.

38. Painting on an Egyptian coffin; Vatican Museum. V. Schmidt, *Levende og Døde*, p. 154. B. H. Stricker, *Zeeslang*, pp. 12f., fig. 4b.

39. Papyrus of Heruben, h. 18 cm., 21st Dynasty (1085–950 B.C.); Cairo 133. B. H. Stricker, *Zeeslang*, p. 11, fig. 3a. A. Piankoff

389

and N. Rambova, *Mythological Papyri,* no. 1.
G. Posener et al., *Knaurs Lexikon,* p. 150.

40. Wood with gold chasing: Valley of the Kings: Tutankhamun (1358–1349 B.C.); Cairo. A. Piankoff, "Une réprésentation." Idem, *Les chapelles,* pl. 4. Idem and N. Rambova, *Shrines,* pp. 120f., fig. 41, pl. 48. B. H. Stricker, *Zeeslang,* pp. 7, 10, fig. 2d.

41. Kudurru, limestone, h. 54 cm.: Susa, Late Kassite Period (12th c. B.C.); Louvre. A. Moortgat, *Kunst,* p. 106, pl. 231f. U. Seidl, *Kudurru Reliefs,* no. 40. A. Vigneau and A. Ozenfant, *Encyclopédie photographique,* fig. 266f.**

42. Cylinder seal, white stone, h. 6.5 cm.: Mari, Akkadian Period (2350–2150 B.C.); Damascus M 2734, H. J. Kantor, "Landscape," pl. 14, fig. 1. A. Parrot, *Sumer,* p. 228. Idem, "Les fouilles de Mari," p. 153, pl. 15.1. A. Vanel, *Iconographie,* pp. 73ff., fig. 30. Drawing by H. J. Kantor.

43. Cylinder seal, stone, h. 3.35 cm., diam. 2.4 cm.: Ur, Akkadian Period (2350–2150 B.C.); Baghdad. H. Frankfort, *Cylinder Seals,* pp. 102f., pl. 18k. Idem, *Kingship,* fig. 52. *ANEP,* no. 684. A. Parrot, *Sumer,* fig. 240. M. T. Barrelet, "Etudes de glyptique," p. 233, n. 3.**

44. Cylinder seal, shell, h. 3.35 cm., diam. 2 cm.: Akkadian Period (2350–2150 B.C.); Pierpont Morgan Collection, New York. H. Frankfort, *Cylinder Seals,* pp. 18f., pl. 22a. R. M. Boehmer, *Entwicklung der Glyptik,* pl. 31, fig. 373. A. Vanel, *Iconographie,* p. 175, fig. 5. *ANEP,* no. 689. A. Parrot, *Sumer,* fig. 227.*

45. Cylinder seal, steatite, h. 3.7 cm.: Assyrian, first half of the first millennium; Pierpont Morgan Collection, New York. E. Porada, *Corpus,* vol. 1, no. 689. A. Parrot, *Assur,* fig. 195. Cf. O. Weber, *Siegelbilder,* no. 311.*

46. Cylinder seal, Syrian, 18th–17th c. B.C.; Collection of W. H. Moore. G. A. Eisen, *Collection of Mrs. W. H. Moore,* no. 158. P. Amiet, "Une vase rituel," p. 245, fig. 6. A. Vanel, *Iconographie,* pp. 78f., 177, fig. 35.*

47. Cylinder seal, yellow frit, glazed: h. 2.5 cm., diam. 1 cm.: Assyrian, 9th–8th c. B.C.; Berlin, VA 7951. A. Moortgat, *Vorderasiatische Rollsiegel,* no. 691, cf. 689f., 692–95. H. Frankfort, *Cylinder Seals,* pl. 34g. O. Weber, *Siegelbilder,* no. 349.

48. Cylinder seal, serpentine, h. 1.7 cm.: Assyrian (Nineveh), 8th–7th c. B.C.; Pierpont Morgan Library, New York. E. Porada, *Corpus,* vol. 1, no. 688. O. Weber, *Siegelbilder,* no. 347. A. Jeremias, *Handbuch,* fig. 127. *IWB,* vol. 4, p. 41.

49. Cylinder seal, Assyrian, 8th–7th c. B.C.; BM. *AOB,* no. 374a. O. Weber, *Siegelbilder,* no. 348. A. Jeremias, *Handbuch,* fig. 174.

50. Limestone relief, h. 43 cm., w. 158 cm.: Malatya: Relief H, 8th c. B.C. or earlier; Ankara, Hittite Museum. *ANEP,* no. 670. A. Vanel, *Iconographie,* pp. 123, 183, fig. 64. P. Amiet, "Notes sur le répetoire," pp. 217f. *IWB,* vol. 3, p. 53.*

51. Shell plaque, h. 4 cm.: provenience unknown, possibly Akkadian (2350–2150 B.C.); Collection of E. Borowski, Basle. *ANEP,* no. 671.*

52. Cylinder seal, gray stone, h. 3.2 cm., diam. 2.2 cm.: Tell Asmar, Akkadian Period (2350–2150 B.C.); Baghdad. II. Frankfort, *Cylinder Seals,* p. 122, pl. 23j. *ANEP,* no. 691. *IWB,* vol. 4, p. 41.*

53. Cylinder seal, Akkadian Period (2350–2150 B.C.); Paris, Bibliothèque Nationale. O. Weber, *Siegelbilder,* no. 364. H. Frankfort, *Cylinder Seals,* pl. 18h.**

54. Painting: Valley of the Kings: Tomb of Siptah (1214–1208 B.C.). T. M. Davis, *Tomb of Siptah,* pl. 3. H. Bonnet, *Bilderatlas,* fig. 18. Cf. *LD,* vol. 6, pl. 134a.*

55. Papyrus of Heruben, h. ca. 18 cm., 21st Dynasty (1085–950 B.C.); Cairo. A. Piankoff and N. Rambova, *Mythological Papyri,* no. 2.**

56. Babylonian conception of the universe, after a sketch by W. Schwenzner in B. Meissner, *Babylonien und Assyrien,* vol. 2, p. 109.

57. Ancient Near Eastern conception of the universe, after a drawing by Alexandra Schober in T. Schwegler, *Probleme,* pl. 1.

58. Limestone relief: Karnak: Festival Temple of Thut-mose III (south wall of the small hall of columns, north of the holy of holies), 1502–1448 B.C. W. Wreszinski, *Atlas,* vol. 2, pl. 31.**

59. Cylinder seal, Akkadian Period (2350–2150 B.C.); Boston, Museum of Fine Arts 34.199; R. M. Boehmer, *Entwicklung der Glyptik,* fig. 721. H. Frankfort, *Cylinder Seals,* p. 140, fig. 36. Cf. H. J. Kantor, "Landscape."**

60. Cylinder seal, chalcedony, Neo-Assyrian Period (9th–7th c. B.C.); BM 89023. D. J. Wiseman and W. and B. Forman, *Götter und Menschen,* no. 63. I. Seibert, *Hirt-Herde-König,* pp. 63–65, fig. 56.*

61. Cylinder seal, Assyrian, 9th–8th c. B.C.; Berlin, VA 693. A. Moortgat, *Vorderasiatischen Rollsiegel,* no. 612. I. Seibert, *Hirt-Herde-König,* fig. 53.*

62. Alabaster vase, h. 1.1 m.: Uruk, Djemdet-Nasr Period (2800–2700 B.C.); Baghdad 19606. E. Heinrich, *Kleinfunde,* pp. 15f., plates 2, 3, 38. ANEP, no. 502. H. Schmökel, *Ur, Assur,* pl. 10. A. Parrot, *Sumer,* figs. 87–90.**

63. Papyrus of Anhai, 20th Dynasty (1200–1085 B.C.); BM 10472. H. Frankfort, *Kingship,* fig. 36, cf. pl. 18. A. Champdor, *Livre des Morts,* p. 124.*

64. Longitudinal section of a tomb of the Early Bronze Period: Tell en-Naşbeh, 3rd millennium B.C. C. Watzinger, *Denkmäler Palästinas,* vol. 1, pl. 12, fig. 27.

65. Cross section and longitudinal section of a tomb of the Middle Bronze Period (first half of the 2nd millennium B.C.). O. Tufnell et al., *Lachish,* vol. 3, p. 241, fig. 29.

66. Longitudinal section of a tomb of the Late Bronze Period (second half of the 2nd millennium B.C.) (possibly already in use in the Middle Bronze Period). J. B. Pritchard, *Bronze Age Cemetery,* p. 11, no. 10A.

67. Section of two tombs of the Late Bronze Period (second half of the 2nd millennium B.C.) (possibly already in use in the Middle Bronze Period). J. B. Pritchard, *Bronze Age Cemetery,* p. 64, nos. 59 (left) and 60 (right).

68. Longitudinal section of a Phoenician shaft tomb: Sidon. S. Moscati, *Phöniker,* p. 474, fig. 5.

68a. Limestone relief, h. ca. 80 cm., w. 2.50 m.: Amarna: Tomb of Ekhnaton, burial chamber of Meketaten: Amenophis IV (1377–1358 B.C.). U. Bouriant et al., *Monuments,* vol. 1, pp. 19f., pl. 6.

69. Limestone ostracon, Sheikh 'abd el-Qurna, 18th Dynasty (1570–1345 B.C.); Ashmolean Museum, Oxford. A. H. Gardiner, "An Unusual Sketch," H. Schäfer, *Von ägyptischer Kunst,* p. 133, fig. 99.

70. Funerary papyrus of Neb-ked, 18th Dynasty (1570–1345 B.C.); Louvre. G. Posener et al., *Knaurs Lexikon,* p. 95. H. Schäfer, *Von ägyptischer Kunst,* p. 133. H. Frankfort, *Kingship,* fig. 22.**

71. Papyrus (Book of the Dead), New Kingdom (1570–1085 B.C.); BM. E. Naville, *Todtenbuch,* vol. 1, pl. 104.

72. Papyrus of Amenemsaf; Louvre. A. Champidor, *Livre des Morts,* p. 118. E. Naville, *Todtenbuch,* vol. 1, pl. 104.

73. Hebrew tomb inscription, 1. 1.32 m.: Silwan, near Jerusalem, ca. 700 B.C.; BM 125205. ANEP, no. 811. KAI, no. 191.*

74. Painting on the sarcophagus of Djebastitefonch, Late Period (715–332 B.C.);

Hildesheim, Pelizaeus-Museum. G. Posener et al., *Knaurs Lexikon,* p. 55. Cf. ANEP, no. 642; IWB, vol. 1, pp. 122f.**

75. Tomb painting: Deir el Medinah, grave no. 2: Khabekhet, 20th Dynasty (1200–1085 B.C.). A. Lhote, *Peinture égyptienne,* pl. 10.**

76. Papyrus (Book of the Dead) of Hunefer, h. 23 cm.: Seti I (1317–1301 B.C.); BM 9901. ANEP no. 640. E. Naville, *Todtenbuch,* vol. 1, pl. 2. A. Champidor, *Livre des Morts,* pp. 148f.**

76a. Limestone relief, w. 2.25 m: Sakkarah, Necropolis of the Pyramid of Teti: middle of the reign of Ramses II (ca. 1270 B.C.); Cairo. R. Anthes, "Bild einer Gerichtsverhandlung," pl. 17.*

77. Relief: Khorsabad, Hall VIII, 18: Sargon II (721–705 B.C.); lost. P. E. Botta, *Monuments,* vol. 2, pl. 119.**

78. Cross section of typical cisterns. C.C. McCown, *Tell en-Naşbeh,* vol. 1, p. 129, nos. 304, 370.*

79. Cross section of cisterns. C.C. McCown, *Tell en-Naşbeh,* p. 216, nos. 156, 160.

80. Leather bucket. G. Dalman, *AuS,* vol. 6, fig. 45.

81. Cylinder seal, h. ca. 1.8 cm.: beginning of the First Babylonian Dynasty (ca. 1800 B.C.); BM. W. H. Ward, *Cylinders,* fig. 453. Cf. H. Frankfort, *Cylinder Seals,* pl. 27g; A. Parrot, *Sumer,* fig. 386. After a photograph in the British Museum.*

82. Papyrus (Book of the Dead) of Hunefer: Seti I (1317–1301 B.C.); BM 9901. E. Naville, *Todtenbuch,* vol. 1, pl. 136. A. Champidor, *Livre des Morts,* pp. 164f. ANEP, no. 639.**

83. Papyrus of Khonsu-mes, h. 15.3 cm.: 21st Dynasty (1085–950 B.C.); Kunsthistorisches Museum, Vienna. A. Piankoff and N. Rambova, *Mythological Papyri,* no. 17.**

84. Relief, alabaster (length of section, ca. 2.4 m.): Khorsabad: Sargon II (721–705 B.C.); Louvre. P. E. Botta, *Monuments,* vol. 1, pl. 34. Sections: ANEP, no. 107; A. Parrot, *Assur,* figs. 48, 267.**

85. Orthostat, rose limestone, h. 60–80 cm., w. 45–55 cm.: Tell Halaf: exterior wall of the temple palace: beginning of the first millennium B.C.; BM. M. von Oppenheim et al., *Tell Halaf,* vol. 3, pl. 43a. M. von Oppenheim, *Tell Halaf,* p. 163, pl. 22b. Cf. A. Parrot, *Assur,* pp. 83–97.*

86. Tomb painting: West Thebes, Dra Abu'l Naga: Tomb of Kanamon (no. 162): probably from the period of Amenophis III

(1413–1377 B.C.); destroyed. N. de G. Davies and R. O. Faulkner, "A Syrian Trading Venture," pl. 8. G. Daressy, "Une flotille phénicienne." L. Klebs, *Reliefs und Malereien des Neuen Reichs,* pp. 231–33. *ANEP,* no. 111. Drawing by N. de G. Davies.

87. Painting on stucco, 11th–9th c. B.C.; Cairo. W. Wresinski, *Atlas,* vol. 1, pl. 417. G. Posener et al., *Knaurs Lexikon,* p. 77. A. Erman, *Religion,* p. 272.**

88. Limestone relief: Sakkarah: causeway to the pyramid of Unis, 5th Dynasty (2480–2350 B.C.). S. Schott, "Aufnahmen vom Hungersnotrelief." *ANEP,* no. 102. *IWB,* vol. 1, p. 108, W. Wolf, *Kunst,* p. 186. E. Otto, *Weg des Pharaonenreiches,* pl. 8.**

89. Painting: Beni Hasan: Grave no. 15, 11th Dynasty (2052–1991 B.C.). P. E. Newberry, *Beni Hasan,* vol. 2, pl. 4; cf. pl. 13. J. F. Champollion, *Monuments,* vol. 4, pl. 382.**

90. Papyrus of Chenut-ta-wi, h. ca. 14 cm.; BM 10018. S. Schott, "Weltbild," pl. 4; cf. p. 187, n. 37. R. V. Lanzone, *Dizionario,* pl. 159.**

90a. Cylinder seal, marble, h. 3.2 cm.: Ur, late Akkadian Period (ca. 2200 B.C.). H. Frankfort, *Cylinder Seals,* pp. 175f., pl. 18d. R. M. Boehmer, *Entwicklung der Glyptik,* pl. 29, no. 340.*

91 and 92. Assyrian bronze tablet, obverse and reverse, h. (including head) 3.5 cm.: purchased in Palmyra, beginning of the first millennium B.C.; Clerq Collection, Paris. K. Frank, *Babylonische Beschwörungsreliefs,* plates 1 and 2, relief A. *AOB,* no. 387. *ANEP,* no. 658. A. Jeremias, *Handbuch,* p. 68, fig. 45. A. Parrot, *Assur,* fig. 130. Cf. H. Klengel, "Neue Lamaštu-Amulette"; idem, "Weitere Amulette"; F. Thureau-Dangin, "Rituel et amulettes." 91.* 92.**

93. Bronze statuette, h. 14.5 cm., 7th c. B.C.; Louvre. H. Schmökel, *Ur, Assur,* pl. 81. *AOB,* no. 383. *ANEP,* no. 659. A. Parrot, *Assur,* fig. 131. Cf. E. Klengel-Brandt, "Ein Pazuzu-Kopf"; P. R. S. Moorey, "A Bronze 'Pazuzu' "; H. W. F. Saggs, "Pazuzu."**

94. Plaque, yellow alabaster, w. ca. 4.5 cm.: Nebuchadnezzar II (604–562 B.C.); Metropolitan Museum, New York, 86.11.2. *ANEP,* no. 657.*

95. Papyrus of Hunefer: Seti I (1317–1301 B.C.); BM 9901. A. Champidor, *Livre des Morts,* p. 166.**

96. Cylinder seal, hematite, h. 2.5 cm., diam 1.7 cm.: Tell el-'Ajjul, 15th–12th c. B.C.; Jerusalem, Palestine Museum 35.4011. F. Petrie, *Ancient Gaza,* vol. 4, pp. 4f., pl.

12.1. J. Nougayrol, *Cylindres-Sceaux,* pp. 54f., pl. 9.**

97. Ivory, h. 13 cm., w. 5–6 cm.; Megiddo, 13th–12th c. B.C.; Oriental Institute, Chicago. G. Loud, *Megiddo Ivories,* pl. 5, no. 4. O. Eissfeldt, "Zur Deutung der Motiven," pp. 91f.

97a and b. Obverse and reverse of a gypsum tablet, h. 8.2 cm., w. 6.7 cm.: Arslan Tash, 8th–6th c. B.C.; Aleppo, no. 1329. R. Mesnil du Buisson, "Une tablette magique," plate facing p. 422. T. H. Gaster, "A Canaanite Magical Text," p. 77. *ANEP,* no. 662 (obverse only). Cf. H. Torczyner, "A Hebrew Incantation." On the representation of a similar demon, cf. A. Rowe, *Four Canaanite Temples,* pl. 39, no. 11.**

98. Figurine, crystaline limestone, h. 9 cm.: Susa, beginning of the third millennium B.C.; Guennol Collection, Brooklyn Museum, New York. A. Parrot, *Sumer,* fig. 97. M. A. Beek, *Atlas of Mesopotamia,* fig. 121.**

99. Terra-cotta figurine, h. 13 cm.: Tello, Ur III Period (2050–1950 B.C.); Louvre. A. Parrot, *Sumer,* fig. 298. Idem, *Assur,* fig. 312. S. Moscati, *Semitische Völker,* pl. 16. A. Vigneau and A. Ozenfant, *Encyclopédie photographique,* vol. 1, p. 251 A.**

100. Relief, gypsum: Nineveh: probably from the northern palace of Assurbanipal (668–626 B.C.); BM. After a photograph in the British Museum.**

101. Sandstone relief on a column: Musawarât eṣ-Ṣofra (at the pinnacle of the sixth cataract), southeastern temple (liontemple): Meroite, Early Ptolemaic Period (3rd c. B.C.). *LD,* vol. 10, pl. 74b.

102. Basalt statue, unfinished: Babylon: palace of Nebuchadnezzar II (604–562 B.C.). H. Schmökel, *Ur, Assur,* pl. 117.*

103. Sandstone relief, w. ca. 3 m.: West Thebes, Medinet Habu: eastern high gate, entrance through the middle tower, north wall: Ramses III (1197–1165 B.C.). C. F. Nims et al., *The Eastern High Gate,* pl. 622, text 12. On the theme, cf. M. Hamza, "Excavations." Drawing by A. Floroff.

104. Cylinder seal (section), h. 2 cm., diam. 0.9 m.: Beirut, 14th c. B.C. H. Seyrig, "Cylindre," p. 170, fig. 2.*

105. Slate palette, height of the fragment, 26 cm.: Egypt, Archaic Period (before 2850 B.C.); Louvre. J. Vandier, *Manuel,* vol. 1, pt. 1, pp. 592–94. *ANEP,* nos. 291f. W. Wolf, *Ägypten,* pp. 81, 84. W. B. Emery, *Archaic Egypt,* p. 166, pl. 3b.**

106. Ceramic object, h. 23.5 cm.: Tell

Asmar: small sanctuary: Isin-Larsa Period (ca. 1960-ca. 1860 B.C.); Baghdad (?). P. Delougaz, *Pottery,* pp. 121f., Frontispiece, plates 128, 129. *IWB,* vol. 3, pp. 238f.*

107. Relief, l. ca. 90 cm., h. (at the highest point) ca. 23.5 cm.: Nineveh: palace of Assurbanipal (668–626 B.C.); BM 124880. Photograph, British Museum.**

108. Relief, h. 14.4 cm.: Meir (ca. 35 km. south of Melawi): tomb of Ukh-ho-tep, Middle Kingdom (2052–1778 B.C.). A. M. Blackman and M. R. Apted, *Rock Tombs of Meir,* vol. 2, pl. 8. J. Vandier, *Manuel,* vol. 4, pt. 1, p. 811, fig. 455.*

109. Sandstone relief: Thebes: Luxor Temple, second pylon, western tower, exterior wall, south (rear) side: Ramses II (1301–1254 B.C.). W. Wreszinski, *Atlas,* vol. 2, plates 66f. *IWB,* vol. 2, p. 255. Cf. M. Burchardt, "Die Einnahme von Satuna," *ZÄS* 51 (1913): 106–9.

110. Limestone stele, h. (of both fragments) 75 cm.: Tello: Eannatum (ca. 2500 B.C.); Louvre. *ANEP,* no. 298 (cf. no. 307). A. Parrot, *Sumer,* figs. 163, 165f. M. T. Barrelet, "Peut-on remettre en question."**

111. Sandstone relief: Edfu: Temple, eastern enclosure wall, interior side, first register, first scene: Ptolemaic (237–57 B.C.). E. Chassinat, *Edfou,* vol. 14, plates 585f.**

112. Wall painting, Beni Hasan, Middle Kingdom (2052–1778 B.C.). B. Grdseloff, "Zum Vogelfang," pp. 52–55. P. E. Newberry, *Beni Hasan,* vol. 2, plates 6, 14.

113. Rock trap from northern Galilee. G. Dalman, *AuS,* vol. 6, fig. 60.

114. Wooden bird trap. G. Dalman, *AuS,* vol. 6, fig. 60.

115. Painting: Sheikh 'abd el-Qurna: Tomb of Nakht: Thut-mose IV (1442–1413 B.C.). A. Lhote, *Peinture égyptienne,* figs. XV, 85. H. Schäfer, *Von ägyptischer Kunst,* fig. 267.**

116. Modern net trap from Galilee. G. Dalman, *AuS,* vol. 6, fig. 63.

117. Reconstruction of an Egyptian drawnet by P. Montet, in J. Vandier, *Manuel,* vol. 5, pt. 2, p. 323.

118. Painting: Thebes: Tomb C, 18th Dynasty (1570–1345 B.C.); Berlin 18540. W. Wreszinski, *Atlas,* vol. 1, pl. 33. *AOB,* no. 181. J. Vandier, *Manuel,* vol. 5, pt. 2, fig. 144.3.**

119. Relief, w. 168 cm., h. 62–74.5 cm.: Nineveh: palace of Assurbanipal (668–626 B.C.); BM 124827. B. Meissner, *Assyrische Jagden,* p. 15, fig. 3. R. D. Barnett and W. Forman, *Assyrische Palastreliefs,* fig. 101. Cf. J.

Vandier, *Manuel,* vol. 4, pt. 1, p. 803, fig. 452.2. After a photograph in the British Museum.**

119a. Drawing on rock, w. 168 cm., Upper Egypt, ca. 3000 B.C. E. Anati, *Rock-Art,* vol. 1, p. 107, fig. 70. Cf. idem, "Les gravures rupestres."

120. Tomb painting: Sheikh 'abd el-Qurna: Tomb of Menena (no. 69): Thutmose IV (1422–1423 B.C.). N. M. Davies and A. H. Gardiner, *Paintings,* vol. 2, pl. 54. Cf. P. Kaplony, "Eine Vogeljagdszene."*

121. Basalt relief, h. 1.62 m.: Khorsabad: Sargon II (721–705 B.C.); Louvre. A. Parrot, *Assur,* figs. 66f. A. Moortgat, *Kunst,* fig. 274. Cf. *ANEP,* no. 185; M. A. Beek, *Atlas of Mesopotamia,* fig. 197.**

122. Limestone stele, Ras Shamra, 14th c. B.C.; Aleppo, National Museum. C. F. A. Schaeffer, "Les fouilles de Ras Shamra-Ugarit," *Syria* 17 (1936), pl. 14. *ANEP,* no. 608.*

123. Relief on yellow limestone, h. ca. 20 cm.: Nimrud: throne room of Shalmaneser III (858–824 B.C.); Baghdad 65574. M. E. L. Mallowan, *Nimrud,* fig. 371d. Drawing by A. Aebischer.

124. Painting: West Thebes: unidentified grave, 18th Dynasty (1570–1345 B.C.); BM 37982. A. Lhote, *Peinture égyptienne,* fig. 80. G. Posener et al., *Knaurs Lexikon,* p. 253. *IWB,* vol. 3, pp. 210f. S. Berger, "A Note on Some Scenes," pp. 54–56.*

125. Kudurru relief, black limestone, h. 56.5 cm., w. 20 cm.: 10th year of King Marduk-nadin-ahhe (1116–1101 B.C.); BM 90840. U. Seidl, "Kudurru Reliefs," no. 80. L. W. King, *Babylonian Boundary Stones,* pp. 42–45, pl. 43; cf. plates 44, 46, 48, 50. Drawing after a photograph in the British Museum.**

126. Kudurru relief, h. 61 cm., w. 26.7–27.9 cm.: Melishipak (1191–1177 B.C.); BM 90827, face A. L. W. King, *Babylonian Boundary Stones,* pl. 18. U. Seidl, "Kudurru Reliefs," no. 25.*

127. Tomb painting: Deir el Medinah: Tomb of Sennudjem (no. 1), east wall: 19th Dynasty (1345–1200 B.C.). A. Mekhitarian, *Ägyptische Malerei,* p. 149. E. Otto and M. Hirmer, *Osiris und Amun,* p. 115.**

128. Tomb painting: Deir el Medinah: Tomb of Sennudjem (no. 1), east wall: 19th Dynasty (1345–1200 B.C.). E. Otto and M. Hirmer, *Osiris und Amun,* p. 115. W. Sameh, "Alltag," p. 16.**

129. Tomb painting: Sheikh 'abd el-Qurna: Tomb of Nakht, 18th Dynasty

(1570–1345 B.C.). A. Lhote, *Peinture égyptienne*, fig. 78. *AOB*, no. 167. A. Erman and H. Ranke, *Ägypten*, p. 532, fig. 220.**

130. Limestone relief: Luxor: first court of columns, first year of Ramses II (1301–1234 B.C.). W. Wreszinski, *Atlas*, vol. 2, plates 71f.

131. Bronze relief, h. ca. 28 cm.: Balawat: Shalmaneser III (858–824 B.C.). L.W. King, *Bronze Reliefs*, pl. 21. *ANEP*, no. 362. A. Parrot, *Assur*, fig. 127. R. D. Barnett and W. Forman, *Assyrische Palastreliefs*, fig. 159.**

132. Relief: Nimrud: central palace of Tiglath-pileser III (745–727 B.C.); BM 118903 and 115634. R. D. Barnett and W. Forman, *Assyrische Palastreliefs*, figs. 40f. R. D. Barnett and M. Falkner, *Sculptures*, pp. 14ff., plates 37–40."

132a. Relief, w. ca. 1.70 cm.: Beit el-Wali (ca. 50 km. south of Aswan): entrance hall of the temple, north wall, second scene from the east: Ramses II (1301–1234 B.C.). H. Ricke et al., *Beit el Wali Temple*, pl. 12, cf. pl. 10, text 13. H. Schäfer, *Von ägyptischer Kunst*, pp. 238f., pl. 36. W. Wreszinski, *Atlas*, vol. 2, pl. 163. Drawing by J. F. Foster.

133. Wall painting (section): Tell 'Ahmar, 8th c. B.C.; destroyed; copy, L. Cavro, Paris. A. Parrot, *Assur*, figs. 116 (section), 117.**

134. Relief: Nineveh: palace of Sennacherib, Room 33 (704–681 B.C.); BM 124801. R. D. Barnett and W. Forman, *Assyrische Palastreliefs*, fig. 130.**

135. Slate palette, ca. 25 × 20 cm.: late prehistorical period (before 2850 B.C.); BM 20791. F. Petrie, *Ceremonial Slate Palettes*, p. 14, pl. E. W. Wolf, *Kunst*, fig. 46. *IWB*, vol. 3, p. 110.**

136. Bronze gate, h. 28 cm. Tell Balawat: Shalmaneser II (858–824 B.C.); BM. L. W. King, *Bronze Reliefs*, pl. 50. *IWB*, vol. 3, pp. 232f.**

137. Relief, Nineveh, Sennacherib (704–681 B.C.); BM 124822. Drawing by A. Aebischer from a photograph by the author. Cf. A. H. Layard, *Monuments*, pl. 15.

138. Stele, width of section ca. 65 cm.: funerary temple of Merneptah: Amenophis III (1413–1377 B.C.); Cairo. W. Westendorf, *Ägypten*, p. 107. Cf. J. Leclant, "La 'Mascarade' "; S. Schott, "Ein ungewöhnliches Symbol."**

139. Relief, Khorsabad, Sargon II (721–705 B.C.); lost. P. E. Botta, *Monuments*, vol. 2, pl. 141. *AOB*, no. 136. *ANEP*, no. 370. *IWB*, vol. 3, p. 66. Cf. M. Riemschneider, "Urartäische Bauten," pp. 325–28.**

140. Bronze relief, h. ca. 28 cm.: Tell Balawat, Shalmaneser III (858–824 B.C.); BM. L. W. King, *Bronze Reliefs*, pl. 8.*

141. Limestone relief: Luxor: first court of columns, exterior of the west wall: Ramses II (1301–1234 B.C.). W. Wreszinski, *Atlas*. vol. 2, pl. 65. W. Wolf, *Kunst*, fig. 574.

142. Basalt stele, h. 90 cm.: near Tell Ashara (Terqa), Tukulti-Ninurta II (888–884 B.C.); Aleppo. H. Schmökel, *Ur, Assur*, pl. 83. Cf. R. J. Tournay and S. Saouaf, "Stèle de Tukulti-Ninurta II," pp. 169–90; H. G. Güterbock, "A Note on the Stela," p. 123.*

143. Orthostatic relief, h. of section ca. 65 cm.: Alaça Hüyük, 15th c. B.C.; Ankara, Hittite Museum. E. Akurgal and M. Hirmer, *Kunst*, pl. 94. M. Riemschneider, *Hethiter*, pl. 54. *IWB*, vol. 3, p. 31.**

144. Sandstone relief: Edfu: Temple, western enclosure wall, interior, first register, 12th scene: Ptolemy IX/Alexander I (107–88 B.C.). E. Chassinat, *Edfou*, vol. 13, pl. 513, G. Roeder, *Mythen*, fig. 28.**

145. Proto-Ionic capital: Jerusalem: probably from the time of Solomon (970–932 B.C.). K. M. Kenyon, *Jerusalem*, pl. 20.**

146. Monolith of Silwan, Jerusalem, 8th c. B.C. L. H. Vincent, *Jérusalem*, vol. 1, pp. 328–30, pl. 71.

147. Various forms of the primeval hill. Freehand drawing. Cf. H. Frankfort, *Kingship*, pp. 152–154.**

148. Sculpture, h. 35 cm, 19th Dynasty (1345–1200 B.C.); Florence. H. Frankfort, *Kingship*, p. 33.**

149. Pyramid of Djoser, 109 × 124 m., h. 62 m.: Sakkarah, Third Dynasty (2650–2600 B.C.). *ANEP*, no. 764. W. Westendorf, *Ägypten*, p. 29.*

150. Busink's reconstruction of the "Tower of Babel," in A. Parrot, *Sintflut*, p. 92, fig. 15.

151. Plan of Jerusalem at the time of Solomon (970–932 B.C.). K. M. Kenyon, *Jerusalem*, p. 81.

152. Diagram of the north-south line of Ophel, drawn from Fig. *151*. Drawing by U. Winter.

153. Relief, gypsum, h. 1.36 m.: Assur: fountain of the Assur temple: second half of the second millennium B.C.; Berlin, VA 1358 W. Andrae, *Kultrelief*, pl. 1. A. Moortgat, *Kunst*, pp. 115f., pl. 236. *ANEP*, no. 528. A. Parrot, *Assur*, fig. 9.**

153a. Ivory inlay: figure of the mountain deity, ca. 14. cm. high: Assur: New Palace, ca. 1500 B.C.; Berlin, Staatliche Museen. W. Andrae, *Kultrelief*, pp. 5f., pl. 6a. A. Moortgat, *Kunst*, fig. 243.**

154. The Holy Rock at Jerusalem. Drawing by H. Schmidt in *Der heilige Fels,* pp. 102f., fig. 1; cf. fig. 2. T. A. Busink, *Tempel,* vol. 1, p. 11, fig. 5.

155. Rock at Gezer. R. A. S. Macalister, *Excavation of Geser,* vol. 2., p. 401, fig. 490.

156. Rock at Megiddo. G. Schumacher, *Tell el-Mutesellim,* vol. 1, fig. 226, pl. 49. *AOB,* no. 409. K. Galling, *BRL,* cols. 17f., figs. 1, 2.

157. Limestone relief: Karnak: Temple, exterior of the south wall of the great hall: Ramses II (1301–1234 B.C.). *LD,* vol. 6, pl. 145c. W. Wreszinski, *Atlas,* vol. 2, pl. 58. *AOB,* no 102. *ANEP,* no. 334 (greatly simplified). Cf. Fig. 199.**

158. Relief, gypsum, h. 1.06 m.: Nimrud: Tiglath-pileser III (745–727 B.C.); BM 118908. R. D. Barnett and M. Falkner, *Sculptures,* pl. 70. *AOB,* no. 133. *ANEP,* no. 366. M. A. Beek, *Atlas of Mesopotamia,* fig. 190. B. Meissner, "Palästinensische Städtbilder," pp. 261–63.**

158a. Relief, sandstone: Soleb (ca. 600 km. south of Aswan): Temple, west side of the northern tower of the second pylon: Amenophis III (1413–1377 B.C.). J. H. Breasted, "Second Preliminary Report," pp. 89–92, fig. 51; cf. fig. 50 (the drawing is greatly simplified; e.g., the king is seen at every gate, and not merely at two of them). A section appears in *LD,* vol. 5, pl. 83c. A. Moret, *Royauté pharaonique,* fig. 32.

159–161. Tenaille gates at Hazor, Megiddo, and Gezer. Y. Yadin, "Solomon's City Wall," pp. 84f.

162. Wall painting: West Thebes: Dra Abu'l Naga: tomb of Panehsi (no. 16): Ramses II (1301–1234 B.C.). G. Foucart et al., *Tombeau de Panehsy,* p. 31, fig. 16. A section appears in W. Wreszinski, *Atlas,* vol. 1, pl. 114. Drawing by M. Baud.

162a. Wall painting, w. ca. 1.70 cm.: West Thebes: Choche: Tomb of Neferhotep (no. 49), right side of the north wall of the inner chamber: period of Eje (1349–1345 B.C.). N. Davies, *Tomb of Nefer-Hotep,* vol. 1, pp. 28–32, pl. 41; vol. 2, plates 3, 6. Drawing by N. de G. Davies.

163. Granite statue, length of base, 2.11 m.: Soleb (Sudan), whence it was brought to Gebel Barkal: Amenophis III (1413–1377 B.C.); BM. W. Westendorf, *Ägypten,* p. 108.**

164. Bronze relief, l. 2.37 m., h. 1.07 m.: Tell Obeid: first half of the third millennium B.C.; BM. A. Parrot, *Sumer,* fig. 187. H. Schmökel, *Ur, Assur,* pl. 40. M. A. Beek,

Atlas of Mesopotamia, fig. 93. Cf. *ANEP,* no. 599.**

165. Three-dimensional figure, fired clay: Tell Harmal, near Baghdad: beginning of the second millennium, B.C. A. Parrot, "Acquisitions," p. 10, fig. 6. Idem, *Sumer,* figs. 354, 356.

166. Lion orthostat, basalt: Hazor: Temple: pavement of the burial quadrant 2161, stratum 3: Late Bronze Period (15th–13th c. B.C.); Jerusalem, Israel Museum. Y. Yadin et al., *Hazor IV–V,* pls. 120, 2, 328. *ANEP,* no. 856.**

167. Fragment of a ceramic shrine, Gezer. R. A. S. Macalister, *Excavation of Geser,* vol. 2, p. 437, figs. 517–19.

167a. Relief: East Thebes: Luxor Temple, Great Court of Ramses II, southwest wall: Ramses II (1304–1238 B.C.). E. Otto and M. Hirmer, *Osiris und Amun,* pl. 33.**

168. Bronze figures (section of a model 60 × 40 cm.): Susa: Shilhak-Inshushinak (12th c. B.C.); Louvre. A. Parrot, *Sumer,* figs. 408f. *AOB,* no. 468. *ANEP,* no. 619.**

169. Plans of houses at Tell el-Far'ah, Iron Age (10th c. B.C.). U. Jochims, "Thirza und die Ausgrabungen," p. 87, fig. 4.

170. Temple at Arad. R. Amiran and Y. Aharoni, *Ancient Arad,* fig. 19. Y. Aharoni, "Trial Excavation," p. 158. T. A. Busink, *Tempel,* vol. 1, p. 593, fig. 169.

171. Temple at Lachish. Y. Aharoni, "Trial Excavation," p. 158. O. Tufnell et al., *Lachish,* vol. 3, pl. 121.

172. Plan of the Enki Temple of Amarsin: Ur, ca. 2000 B.C. A. Moortgat, *Kunst,* p. 64., fig. 44.

173. Plan of the Ninmach Temple: Babylon, 8th–7th c. B.C. A. Moortgat, *Kunst,* p. 161, fig. 114.

174. Reconstruction of Ezekiel's temple plan. I. Benzinger, *Bilderatlas,* p. 293. *BHH,* vol. 3, cols. 1943f.

175. Reconstructed plan of the Herodian temple. H. Schmidt, *Der heilige Fels,* figs. 11, 11a.

176. Khonsu Temple, Karnak, 20th Dynasty (1200–1085 B.C.). J. Vandier, *Manuel,* vol. 2, pt. 2, p. 941, fig. 440.

177. Horus Temple, l. 137 m.: Edfu, 237–57 B.C. W. Wolf, *Kunst,* p. 606, fig. 609.

178. Baal Temple, Ugarit, ca. 2000 B.C. C. F. A. Schaeffer, "Les fouilles de Ras Shamra-Ugarit," *Syria* 15 (1934): 122, fig. 14. Cf. T. A. Busink, *Tempel,* vol. 1, pp. 478–80.

179. Plan of the temple at Baalbek, 1st–

2nd c. A.D. P. Collart and P. Coupel, *L'autel monumental de Baalbek,* pl. 3.

180. Section of a limestone stele (height of section, 32 cm.): Ur, Urnammu (ca. 2050 B.C.); Philadelphia, University Museum. *ANEP,* no. 306. A. Parrot, *Sumer,* figs. 279–282. H. Schmökel, *Ur, Assur,* pl. 54.**

181. Ceramic fragment, h. 15 cm.: Tell Far'ah (Negev, ca. 30 km. WNW of Beersheba), 19th Dynasty (1345–1200 B.C.). H. G. May and R. M. Engberg, *Material Remains,* pl. 40b. I. Seibert, *Hirt-Herde-König,* p. 38, fig. 17. Cf. H. G. May, "The Sacred Tree."

182. Cultic stand, painted clay, h. 106 cm.: Meggido (1350–1150 B.C.); Loud, *Meggido,* vol. 2, pl. 251.**

183. Limestone basin, h. 1.85 m., diam. 2.2 m.: Amathont (Cyprus), probably 6th c. B.C.; Louvre. G. Perrot and G. Chipiez, *Histoire de l'art,* vol. 3, p. 280, fig. 211. H. T. Bossert, *Altsyrien,* nos. 281f. Cf. A. Parrot, *Le temple de Jérusalem,* pp. 99f.**

183a. Basalt sculpture, l. 2.40 m., h. 1.10 m.: Carchemish: temple court: 9th c. B.C.; Ankara. C. L. Wooley and T. E. Lawrence, *Carchemish,* vol. 3, pl. B47, pp. 168f. Orthmann, *Späthethische Reliefs,* pl. 25c.**

184. Relief: Baalbek: great court of the Jupiter Temple, east side of the north water basin: Roman Period (2nd c. A.D.). T. Wiegand et al., *Baalbek,* pl. 111.*

185. Dolerite relief, h. 1.17 m.: Assur: fountain of the Assur Temple: 8th–7th c. B.C.; Berlin, VA. W. Andrae, *Das wiedererstandene Assur,* p. 155, pl. 2b. A. Parrot, *Assur,* p. 74, fig. 82.**

186. Cylinder seal, carnelian, h. 3.7 cm., diam. 1.7 cm.: 9th–8th c. B.C.; Pierpont Morgan Library, New York. *ANEP,* no. 706. M. A. Beek, *Atlas of Mesopotamia,* fig. 252. Cf. H. Frankfort, *Cylinder Seals,* pl. 34b.**

187. Limestone relief, Abydos, temple of Seti I (1317–1301 B.C.). A. M. Calverley et al., *Abydos,* vol. 1, pl. 3.**

188. Portable kettle, bronze: Larnaca (Cyprus), Late Mycenean Period (1400–1200 B.C.); Berlin. A. Furtwängler, "Über ein . . . Bronzegerät," p. 411. *AOB,* no. 505. *IWB,* vol. 2, p. 217. Cf. *AOB,* no. 506; *ANEP,* no. 587.**

189. Ivory, Nimrud, 9th–8th c. B.C. R. D. Barnett, *Catalogue,* pl. 33f. *BL,* col. 1031, fig. 67, fig. 2.**

190. Gold lamella, l. 20 cm.: Enkomi-Alasia: grave no. 2: Neo-Cypriot Period (1430–1350 B.C.). C. F. A. Schaeffer, "La coupe en argent," pp. 57f.*

191. Wall painting, l. 2.5 m., h. 1.75 m.: Mari: period of Hammurabi (1728–1686 B.C.); copy (after the original) in the Louvre. A. Parrot, *Sumer,* pp. 279f., fig. 346. M. T. Barrelet, "Une peinture de la cour 106," pl. 1. Cf. A. Moortgat, *Kunst,* p. 74.**

192. Cylinder seal (impression) from Kültepe, 19th–18th c. B.C.; Ankara, Inventory No. Kt. a/k 462. N. Ozgüç, *Anatolian Group,* no. 67 (cf. nos. 49 and 71).**

193. Step-altar, hewn sandstone, with *massebah:* Petra: El-Meesara. K. Galling, *BRL,* cols. 17f., fig. 4. *AOB,* no. 449.*

194. Attempted reconstruction of the altar of Ezekiel by E. Avi-Yonah. *IWB,* vol. 3, p. 201. Cf. *BHH,* vol. 1, col. 64.

195. Limestone altar, h. 54.5 cm.: Megiddo, near the sacred precincts: 10th–9th c. B.C.; Jerusalem, Palestine Museum. H. G. May and R. M. Engberg, *Material Remains,* pp. 12f., pl. 12. *ANEP,* no. 575. After a photograph by the author.**

196. Relief: Amarna: Tomb of Panhesi: Amenophis IV (1377–1358 B.C.). N. de G. Davies, *Amarna,* vol. 2, pl. 18. J. Vandier, *Manuel,* vol. 4, pt. 1, p. 683, fig. 379.

197. Incense altar with an Aramaean inscription, Lachish, 5th–4th c. B.C.; Jerusalem, Palestine Museum. O. Tufnell et al., *Lachish,* vol. 3, pp. 286, 358f., pl. 49.3. Y. Aharoni, "Trial Excavation," pp. 163f., pl. 10a.*

198. Incense stand, ceramic, h. 67 cm.: Megiddo, 1150–1100 B.C.); Chicago, Oriental Institute A 20830. H. G. May and R. M. Engberg, *Material Remains,* pp. 20–23, pl. 20. *ANEP,* no. 583.**

199. Section of the relief in Fig. 157.

200. Relief on an incense altar, Palmyra, 85 A.D.; Oxford, Ashmolean Museum. *IWB,* vol. 3, p. 164. H. Ingholt, "Le sens," figs. 1, 2.**

201. Relief: Nineveh: palace of Assurbanipal, Room S (668–626 B.C.); BM 124886. R. D. Barnett and W. Forman, *Assyrische Palastreliefs,* fig. 98.**

202. Relief, w. 1.32 m., h. 0.93 m.: Nineveh: palace of Assurbanipal (668–626 B.C.); BM 124939A. R. D. Barnett and W. Forman, *Assyrische Palastreliefs,* fig. 134. A. Jeremias, *Das AT im Lichte des AO,* fig. 18. *BHH,* vol. 3, cols. 1385f. Drawing after a photograph in the British Museum.**

203. Long-house types. V. Müller, "Types," p. 179, pl. 1. *ANEP,* no. 752.

204. Bent-axis house types. V. Müller, "Types," p. 180, pl. 2. *ANEP,* no. 753.

205. Bent-axis house. W. Andrae,

"Haus-Grab-Tempel," col. 1037.

206. Courtyard house. W. Andrae, "Haus-Grab-Tempel," col. 1037.

207. Clay model, l. ca. 60 cm.: ca. 15 km. northeast of Uruk. G. Gerster, "Ein sumerisches Tempelmodell."**

208. Temple plans from Hazor, Late Bronze Age (1550–1200 B.C.). T. A. Busink, *Tempel,* vol. 1, p. 398, fig. 100.

208a. Plan of the Mortuary Temple I and III at Lachish (I: ca. 1480 B.C.; III: ca. 1325–1230 B.C.). O. Tufnell et al., *Lachish II,* plates 66, 68. T. A. Busink, *Tempel,* vol. 1, pp. 405–11.

209–213. Attempted reconstructions of the Solomonic temple at Jerusalem (970–932 B.C.).

209–210. Longitudinal section and ground plan. C. Watzinger, *Denkmäler Palästinas,* vol. 1, pl. 16.

211–212. Longitudinal section and ground plan. T. A. Busink, *Tempel,* vol. 1, pp. 167, 165, figs. 49, 48.

213. Attempted reconstruction of Wright, Albright, and Stevens, in T. A. Busink, *Tempel,* fig. 15.

214. Plan of the temple at Sichem, Middle Bronze Age (ca. 1650 B.C.). E. Sellin, "Ausgrabung von Sichem," pl. 33. *ANEP,* no. 868. T. A. Busink, *Tempel,* vol. 1, p. 389, fig. 96A.

215. Plan of a temple at Megiddo, Late Bronze Age (ca. 1400–1150 B.C.). T. A. Busink, *Tempel,* vol. 1, p. 396, fig. 99. *ANEP,* no. 735.

216. Plan of a temple at Beth-Shan, Iron Age I (ca. 1200–930 B.C.). T. A. Busink, *Tempel,* vol. 1, p. 425, fig. 114.

216a. Plan of a temple at Beth-Shan, Late Bronze Age (ca. 1400–1300 B.C.). T. A. Busink, *Tempel,* vol. 1, p. 413, fig. 108. *ANEP,* no. 737.

217. Plan of the Sin-Shamash Temple: Assur: Sennacherib (704–681 B.C.). W. Andrae, *Das wiedererstandene Assur,* p. 156, fig. 57.

218. Plan of the palace and temple at Tell Tainat, according to McEwan, in T. A. Busink, *Tempel,* vol. 1, p. 599, fig. 166. *ANEP,* no. 739.

219 and 220. Plans of Roman temples in Syria. D. Krencker and W. Zschietzschmann, *Römische Tempel,* plates 117f.

220a. Ivory, w. of section, 4 cm.: Abydos: Early Dynastic royal tombs nos. B 18, 19: King Aha (ca. 2850 B.C.). J. Vandier, *Manuel,* vol. 1, pt. 2, pp. 836f., fig. 560.

221. White limestone *naos,* h. 60 cm., w. 32 cm.: Sidon (?): beginning of the 5th c. B.C.; Louvre, AO 2060. M. Noël Aimé-Giron, "Un naos phénicien," pl. 1f. S. Moscati, *Phöniker,* facing p. 139.*

222. Limestone *naos,* h. 65 cm., w. 36 cm.: Sidon: first half of the 5th c. B.C. M. Noël Aimé-Giron, "Un naos phénicien," pl. 4. *AOB,* nos. 519f.

223. Fragment of a columnar furniture ornament, ivory, h. 13.8 cm.: Arslan Tash: 8th c. B.C. F. Thureau-Dangin et al., *Arslan Tash,* vol. 1, pp. 129f; vol. 2, pl. 44, fig. 93.**

224. Bronze tripod, h. 12.1 cm.: Ras Shamra: 14th–13th c. B.C. H. T. Bossert, *Altsyrien,* no. 786. *ANEP,* no. 588. G. Cornfeld, *Von Adam,* p. 304.**

225. Clay model, h. 21 cm.: Idalion (Cyprus): Iron Age (8th–7th c. B.C.); Louvre. *AOB,* no. 523. H. T. Bossert, *Altsyrien,* no. 16. A. Vigneau and A. Ozenfant, *Encylopédie photographique,* vol. 2, p. 152A.**

226. Lampstand, gray limestone, painted, h. ca. 23 cm.: Megiddo: 5th c. B.C. (?). G. Schumacher, *Tell el-Mutesellim,* frontispiece, fig. 190. *AOB,* no. 467. T. A. Busink, *Tempel,* vol. 1, pl. 10, fig. 72.**

227. Wall painting, Synagogue at Dura Europos, 244 A.D. R. Mesnil du Buisson, *Les peintures,* p. 21, fig. 15. T. A. Busink, *Tempel,* vol. 1, p. 295, fig. 71.

228. Relief, Titus Arch, Rome, 70 A.D. *AOB,* no. 509. G. Cornfeld, *Von Adam,* p. 315. L. H. Grollenberg, *Bildatlas,* figs. 207f. Cf. M. Kon, "The Menorah of the Arch of Titus."**

229. Limestone relief, Abydos, temple of Seti I (1317–1301 B.C.). A. M. Calverley et al., *Abydos,* vol. 2, pl. 4.*

230. Limestone relief, Abydos, temple of Seti I (1317–1301 B.C.). A. H. Calverley et al., *Abydos,* vol. 2, pl. 4.**

231 and 232. Reddish-brown clay figure with light brown clay coating and black painting: height of the seated figure, 28.6 cm.; length of the cherub, 20 cm.: Ayia Irini: Cypriot-Archaic Period I (700–600 B.C.). E. Gjerstad, *Swedish Cyprus Expedition,* vol. 2, p. 731, pl. 233, figs. 10f. H. T. Bossert, *Altsyrien,* nos. 130f.**

233. Carved ivory, l. ca. 13 cm.: Megiddo: 1350–1150 B.C.; Jerusalem, Palestine Museum 38780. G. Loud, *Megiddo Ivories,* pl. 4, no. 2. *ANEP,* no. 332. For the other half, cf. Fig. *321;* cf. B. S. J. Isserlin, "Psalm 68, Verse 14."*

234. Ivory model of a throne, h. 2.6 cm., w. 1.7 cm.: Megiddo: 135–1150 B.C.);

Chicago, Oriental Institute. G. Loud, *Megiddo Ivories*, pl. 4, no. 3. O. Eissfeldt, "Zur Deutung von Motiven," pl. 5, fig. 3.**

235. Stone sarcophagus, length of section, 33 cm.: Byblos: Tomb 5: late second millennium B.C.; inscription ca. 1000 B.C.; Beirut. *ANEP*, no. 458; cf. nos. 456f., 459. *KAI*, no. 1.*

236. Stele with relief: Hadrummetum (Sousse). S. Moscati, *Phöniker*, fig. 35, cf. fig. 9. B. H. Warmington, *Carthage*, fig. 8a.**

237. Lead figurine, Baalbek, Roman Imperial Period. H. Seyrig, "La triade," pl. 84, fig. 1. Cf. R. Dussaud, "Temples et cultes," p. 47, fig. 7.*

238. Relief: Meroë: Begrawiya: Lepsius' Pyramid Group C, Pyramid 15: west wall of the chapel of Prince Taktıdamani, ca. 15 B.C.–15. A.D. *LD*, vol. 10, pl. 54e. A similar representation is found in the Osiris Chapel at the interior of the eastern *temenos*-wall at Karnak: 23rd Dynasty (middle of the 8th c. B.C.). Cf. C. F. Nims, *Thebes*, p. 107.

238a. Isometric representation of the sequence of portals in the sandstone temple at Kalabsha, l. 72 m., w. 35.5 m.: formerly ca. 56 km. south of Aswan; since relocation in 1962–1963, 18 km. south of Aswan: Late Ptolemaic-Augustan Period. K. G. Siegler, "Die Tore von Kalabscha," fig. 7. Drawing by U. Rombock.

239. Stone tablet with inscription, 18 × 30 cm. (scene, 18 × 10 cm.): Sippar (40 km. southwest of Baghdad): Nabuapaliddin (885–850 B.C.); BM 91000. *AOB*, no 322. *ANEP*, no. 529. A. Parrot, *Assur*, fig. 215. M. A. Beek, *Atlas of Mesopotamia*, fig. 37. Cf. M. Metzger, "Himmlische und irdische Wohnstatt," pp. 141–44.**

240. Cylinder seal, h. 4 cm., Akkadian-Period (2350–2150 B.C.); private collection. R. M. Boehmer, *Entwicklung der Glyptik*, no. 915, fig. 353. H. Frankfort, *Cylinder Seals*, pp. 131f., pl. 22k. D. Opitz, "Studien zur altorientalischen Kunst," pl. 3.2. *ANEP*, no 690. Cf. E. D. van Buren, "Representations of Battles."*

241. Fragment of a relief, limestone, h. 57 cm. (figure, ca. 38 cm.): Susa, Pazur-Šušinak (second half of the third millennium B.C.); Louvre. A. Parrot, *Sumer*, fig. 293. A. Moortgat, *Kunst*, pl. 158. R. S. Ellis, *Foundation Deposits*, fig. 16.**

242. Votive tablet, limestone, h. ca. 20 cm.: Ur, ca. 2500 B.C.; BM 188561. C. L. Woolley, *Ur*, p. 115. *ANEP*, no. 603. E. Heinrich, *Bauwerke*, p. 83, fig. 101.**

243. Reconstruction of the Fortress Tem-

ple at Sichem, 21.3 × 23.6 m.; corner tower 7 × 5 m., walls 5.2 m. thick; the temple stands on a platform: 1650 B.C. T. A. Busink, *Tempel*, vol. 1, pp. 388–94, figs. 96–98. Cf. Fig. 214.

244. Tower of refuge, h. 12 m., diam. 9 m.: Jericho: preceramic Neolithic Age (7th millennium, B.C.). K. M. Kenyon, *Digging Up Jericho*, pl. 25. *ANEP*, no. 863. H. Wildberger and M. Wolgensinger, *Biblische Welt*, fig. 40.*

245. Limestone relief: Karnak: exterior of the north wall of the great hall, east projection: Seti I (1317–1301 B.C.). W. Wreszinski, *Altas*, vol. 2, plates 34, 35a, 39f., 42. *AOB*, no. 95. *ANEP*, nos. 327, 329. R. Giveon, *Les Bédouins Shosou*, pp. 39–60.**

245a. Relief, w. ca. 2 m.: Karnak: temple of Ramses III in the forecourt of the Amon Temple, exterior of the west wall, north end: Ramses III (1197–1165 B.C.). H. H. Nelson, *Reliefs and Inscriptions at Karnak*, vol. 2, plates 81, 82. Drawing by D. N. Wilbur.

246. Bronze coin, Byblos, Emperor Marcrinus (A.D. 217–218); BM. Inscription: "(Coin) of holy Byblos *(hieras byblou)*." S. A. Cook, *Religion of Ancient Palestine*, pp. 160f., pl. 33, no. 5. *AOB*, no. 521. R. Dussaud, "Note additionnelle," p. 133ff.**

247. Coin, bronze, diam. ca. 3 cm., ca. 3 g.: Tyre, 3rd–4th c. A.D. G. F. Hill, *Catalogue*, pl. 33.14.**

248. Holy of holies, view to the northwest: steps, two altars and a painted stele (without image): h. of the taller incense altar, 51 cm.: Arad, 10th–8th c. B.C.; Jerusalem, Israel Museum. *BL*, pl. 21. *ANEP*, no. 872.*

249. Limestone relief, h. ca. 25. cm.: Sakkarah: tomb of Mereruka: Teti (6th Dynasty, 2350–2200 B.C.). *ANEP*, no. 133. H. Schäfer, *Von ägyptischer Kunst*, fig. 183a.**

250. Tomb painting, h. ca. 60 cm.: Abd el-Qurna: tomb of Rekhmire (no. 100): Thut-mose III (1502–1448 B.C.). N. de G. Davies, *Tomb of Rekh-mi-rē'*, vol. 2, pl. 52. W. Wreszinski, *Atlas*, vol. 1, pl. 316. G. Posener et al., *Knaurs Lexikon*, p. 45.*

251. Terra sigillata, Roman; Archäologisches Institut der Universität Tübingen. K. Latte, *Römische Religionsgeschichte*, p. xvi, fig. 25.**

252. Liver model, clay, ca. 7.7 cm.: Hazor: burial area H: Jerusalem, Israel Museum. B. Landsberger and H. Tadmor, "Fragments of Clay Liver Models," p. 206f. Y. Yadin et al., *Hazor III–IV*, pl. 315. *ANEP*, no. 844.

253. Tomb painting: Valley of the Kings: tomb of Thut-mose III (1502–1448 B.C.). A.

Mekhitarian, *Ägyptische Malerei,* p. 38. G. Posener et al., *Knaurs Lexikon,* p. 167. Cf. M. L. Buhl, "The Goddess of the Egyptian Tree Cult"; R. Moftah, "Die uralte Sykomore."**

254. Tomb painting, Deir el Medinah: tomb of Sennudyem (no. 1): 19th Dynasty (1345–1200 B.C.). W. Westendorf, *Ägypten,* p. 191. E. Otto and M. Hirmer, *Osiris und Amun,* p. 115.*

255. Papyrus of Nesi-pa-ka-shuty, h. 19 cm.; Louvre E 17401. A. Piankoff and N. Rambova, *Mythological Papyri,* no. 9.**

256. Limestone statue, h. ca. 1.5 m.: Mari: palace, 18th c. B.C.; Aleppo 1659. A. Parrot, *Sumer,* figs. 399f. *ANEP,* no. 516. H. Schmokel, *Ur, Assur,* pl. 63.**

256a. Relief: Karnak: Temple of Amon. great hall of columns, interior of the west wall: Ramses II (1301–1234 B.C.). H. H. Nelson, *Reliefs and Inscriptions at Karnak,* vol. 1, p. ix; vol. 2, pl. 80C.**

257. Tomb painting: Marissa: tomb no. 2, inner chamber: Hellenistic Period (3rd c. B.C.). L. H. Vincent, *Jérusalem,* vol. 2, p. 412, fig. 127.**

258. Mosaic floor: Beth Alpha (Hepzibah): Synagogue: early 6th c. A.D. M. Schapiro and M. Avi Yonah, *Israel: Frühe Mosaiken,* pl. 6. E. L. Sukenik, *Ancient Synagogue,* pp. 22f., plates 8, 9.**

259. Detail from Fig. 258.**

260. Statue, dark gray diorite, height of section, ca. 42 cm.: Gizeh: Khefren (4th Dynasty, 2600–2480 B.C.); Cairo. J. H. Breasted, *Geschichte Ägyptens,* pl. 53. W. Wolf, *Kunst,* pp. 143f. *ANEP,* no. 377. G. Posener et al., *Knaurs Lexikon,* p. 45.*

261. Ivory carving, h. 8.4 cm., w. 9.8 cm.: Arslan Tash (ca. 40 km. east of Carchemish), whence it was brought to Damascus as booty: 8th c. B.C.; Louvre. F. Thureau-Dangin et al., *Arslan Tash,* vol. 1, p. 93; vol. 2, pl. 19, fig. 1. Cf. H. Frankfort, *Art and Architecture,* pp. 318f.*

262. Papyrus of Konshu-Renep, h. ca. 15 cm.: 21st Dynasty (1165–1085 B.C.); Cairo. A. Piankoff and N. Rambova, *Mythological Papyri,* no. 11. Cf. V. Schmidt, *Levende og Døde,* p. 154.**

263. Memorial stone; Berlin 7354. A. Erman, *Religion,* p. 145, fig. 53.**

264. Stele, limestone, h. 58 cm., w. 40 cm.: Tell Defenneh (southwest of Pelusium): Persian Period (525–332 A.D.). W. M. Müller, *Egyptological Researches,* vol. 1, p. 30, pl. 40. *AOB,* no. 354. *IWB,* vol. 3, p. 143.**

264a. (From left to right) Ceramic mask, h. 16.3 cm.: Hazor: Area D: Late Bronze Period II (1450–1200 B.C.); Jerusalem, Israel Museum. Y. Yadin et al., *Hazor,* vol. 1, p. 138, pl. 163.*

Ceramic mask, h. 14.7 cm.: Hazor: Area C: Late Bronze Period II (1450–1200 B.C.); Jerusalem, Israel Museum. Y. Yadin et al., *Hazor,* vol. 2, pl. 183. *ANEP,* no. 843.*

Limestone mask: vicinity of Hebron; private collection. *L'Encyclopédie de tous les pays,* vol. 6, p. 275.*

An additional cult mask from Palestine is noted in R. A. S. Macalister, *Excavation of Geser,* vol. 2, p. 233, fig. 383.

264b. Relief: Dendera: Hathor Temple: chambers on the roof: south side, first chamber, north wall: 1st c. A.D. A. Mariette, *Dendérah,* vol. 4, pl. 31. Cf. M. A. Murray, "Ritual Masking," p. 255.

265. Relief, limestone, h. 32 cm.: commercial (Amarna?), ca. 1355 B.C.; West Berlin, Aegyptisches Museum, Inv. no. 14145. A. Erman, *Religion,* p. 120, fig. 51. W. Kaiser, *Aegyptisches Museum,* no. 749. K. Lange and M. Hirmer, *Ägypten,* pl. 184.

266. Engraving on light blue chalcedony, w. ca. 4 cm., h. ca. 3 cm.: Elamite, 12th c. B.C.; BM 113886. I. Seibert, *Frau,* pl. 42.**

267. Ivory carving, h. 5.6 cm: Megiddo: 1350–1150 B.C.; Oriental Institute, Chicago. G. Loud, *Megiddo Ivories,* pl. 32, no. 160.**

268. Tomb painting: Abd el-Qurna: tomb of Thot-nofer (no. 80), right transverse chamber: Amenophis II (1448–1422 B.C.). W. Wreszinski, *Atlas,* vol. 1, pl. 258.**

269. Tomb relief: Gizeh: tomb no. 24: 4th Dynasty (2600–2480 B.C.); Berlin. *LD,* vol. 3, pl. 21.*

270. Tomb painting, w. ca. 2.20 m.: West Thebes: Dra 'abu'l naga: tomb of Nebamon (no. 17): Amenophis II (1448–1422 B.C.). T. Säve-Söderberg, *Four Tombs,* pp. 25–27, pl. 23. W. Wreszinski, *Atlas,* vol. 1, pl. 115. *IWB,* vol. 4, p. 275. J. Vandier, *Manuel,* vol. 4, p. 588. W. S. Smith, *Interconnections,* fig. 41. Drawing by N. de G. Davies.

270a. Stele, limestone, h. 26.5 cm.: 18th–19th Dynasty (ca. 1570–1200 B.C.); Glyptothek Ny Carlsberg, Copenhagen. H. Ranke, "Istar als Heilsgöttin," pl. 66.**

271. Cylinder seal, serpentine, h. 5.05 cm.: Akkadian Period (2350–2150 B.C.); Berlin, VA 3456. A. Moortgat, *Vorderasiatische Rollsiegel,* no. 234. A. Parrot, *Assur,* fig. 359. H. Schmökel, *Ur, Assur,* pl. 48. *ANEP,* no. 695.**

272. Cylinder seal, green slate, h. 5.4 cm.,

diam. 3.2 cm.: Urnammu (ca. 2050 B.C.); BM 89126. D. J. Wiseman and W. and B. Forman, *Götter und Menschen*, fig. 40.**

273. Papyrus of Dirpu, h. 23.5 cm.: Deir el-Bahari, 21st Dynasty (1165–1085 B.C.); Cairo. A. Piankoff and N. Rambova, *Mythological Papyri*, no. 6.**

274. Limestone relief, h. ca. 65 cm.: Karnak: Seostris I (1971–1930 B.C.); Cairo. H. Fechheimer, *Plastik*, no. 146. W. Wolf, *Kunst*, p. 363, figs. 308f.**

275. Clay statuette, Achsib, 6th–5th c. B.C.; Jerusalem, Palestine Museum. Photograph by the author. Cf. W. G. Lambert, "A Phoenician Statuette." At least three examples of this statuette are known.**

276. Terra-cotta group, from the sanctuary of a birth goddess near Lapithos, Cyprus: 6th or early 5th c. B.C.; Cyprus Museum, Nicosia. P. Dikaios, *A Guide to the Cyprus Museum*, pp. 204f., pl. 31, no. 2. G. Cornfeld and G. J. Botterwerk, *Bibel und ihre Welt*, fig. 230. Cf. H. T. Bossert, *Altsyrien*, no. 156.*

277. Cast figure, bronze, h. 13 cm.: 12th Dynasty (1991–1778 B.C.); Berlin, Staatliche Museen. G. Roeder, *Mythen*, pl. 13. W. Westendorf, *Ägypten*, p. 78.*

277a. Clay relief, h. 11 cm.: Larsa Period (ca. 1960–1860 B.C.); Baghdad (doublet in the Louvre). E. D. van Buren, "A Clay Relief," p. 166, fig. 1. H. Frankfort, *Art and Architecture*, p. 112.**

277b. Projection of a circular relief on a stone vessel, h. ca. 11 cm.: small temple IX, Khafayeh: ca. 3000 B.C.; Baghdad. P. Delougaz, "Animals Emerging from a Hut," p. 87, fig. 6. Idem and S. Lloyd, *Pre-Sargonid Temples*, fig. 98. Drawing by H. J. Kantor.

278. Limestone statue, h. 13.3 cm.: beginning of the 5th Dynasty (2480–2350 B.C.); Chicago, Oriental Institute. *IWB*, vol. 3, p. 114. W. Wolf, *Kunst*, p. 167, fig. 133.**

278a. Statue, basalt, height of the goddess, 2.73 m.; height of the lioness, 1.92 m.: Tell Halaf, 9th c. B.C.; Aleppo. M. von Oppenheim et al., *Tell Halaf*, vol. 2, pp. 55, 68, pl. 11; vol. 3, plates 123b, 127–29, 133–35. M. von Oppenheim, *Tell Halaf*, pl. 1.**

279. Painting, height of the figure, 24 cm.: Beni Hasan: tomb no. 3, principal chamber, west wall: Middle Kingdom (2052–1778 B.C.). C. H. Johl, *Webestühle*, fig. 21. *ANEP*, no. 143. Drawing by N. de G. Davies.

280. Painting, h. ca. 30 cm.: Thebes: tomb of Ipui (no. 217): Ramses II (1301–1234 B.C.). G. Posener et al., *Knaurs Lexikon*, p. 38. *ANEP*, no. 95. Cf. *AOB*, no. 175; cf. J. F.

Champollion, *Monuments*, vol. 2, pl. 185.3; *IWB*, vol. 1, p. 266.**

281. Cylinder seal, carnelian, h. 2.5 cm. (?): Persian Period (5th c. B.C.); Draper Collection, U.S.A. K. Galling, "Beschriftete Bildsiegel," no. 171. O. Weber, *Siegelbilder*, no. 532.*

282. Relief, h. ca. 1.5 m.: Amarna, Amenophis IV (1377–1385 B.C.). N. de G. Davies, *Amarna*, vol. 3, pl. 30.

283. Stele, serpentine, h. 47 cm.: Ugarit, 14th c. B.C.; Aleppo. C. F. A. Schaeffer, "Les fouilles de Ras Shamra-Ugarit," *Syria* 18 (1937), pl. 17; cf. p. 129, fig. 1. *ANEP*, no. 493. *BHH*, vol. 1, cols. 387f. Cf. C. F. A. Schaeffer, "Götter."*

284. Bronze figure with gold overlay, h. 13.8 cm.: Ugarit, southern city: second half of the 2nd millennium B.C.; Damascus 23394. C. F. A. Schaeffer, "Nouveaux Témoignages," p. 7, fig. 3, pl. 2. *ANEP*, no. 826. Drawing by M. Kuss.

285. Cylinder seal, black and green variegated serpentine, Akkadian Period (2350–2150 B.C.); BM 103317. D. J. Wiseman and W. and B. Forman, *Götter und Menschen*, fig. 36. Cf. H. Frankfort, *Cylinder Seals*, plates 23d, f. A. Moortgat, *Vorderasiatische Rollsiegel*, nos. 223–26. Cf. M. T. Barrelet, "Etudes de glyptique akkadienne."*

286. Cylinder seal, Akkadian Period (2350–2150 B.C.); Leningrad, Hermitage 6587. R. M. Boehmer, *Entwicklung der Glyptik*, no. 461.**

287. Relief: Wadi Sebua: Holy of holies in the temple of Ramses II (1301–1234 B.C.). *LD*, vol. 7, pl. 181. A. Erman, *Religion*, p. 18, fig. 6. H. Bonnet, *Reallexikon*, p. 783, fig. 176.

288. Limestone relief, h. 1.05 m.: Amarna: portion of the balustrade of a temple ramp: Amenophis IV (1377–1358 B.C.); Cairo. E. Elisofon and L. van der Post, *The Nile*, p. 218. *ANEP*, no. 408. *BHH*, vol. 1, col. 44, fig. 4.**

289. Limestone relief, Amarna, Amenophis IV (1377–1358 B.C.) U. Bouriant et al., *Monuments*, vol. 1, pl. 1. A. Erman and H. Ranke, *Ägypten*, p. 462, fig. 184. *AOB*, no. 546. *IWB*, vol. 4, p. 47.

290. Seal impression, ceramic, height of the scene, 7.3 cm.: Tell Mardikh, ca. 1725 B.C.; Damascus/Aleppo. P. Mattiae, "Empreintes d'un cylindre," p. 5, fig. 1, plates 1, 2. Cf. A. Moortgat, *Vorderasiatische Rollsiegel*, no. 523.

291. Limestone stele, h. 1.42 m., w. 0.47–0.5 m.: Ugarit: large western temple

(cf. Fig. *178*): first half of the 2nd millennium
B.C.; Louvre AO 15775. C. F. A. Schaeffer,
"Les fouilles de Minet el-Beida et de Ras
Shamra," *Syria* 14 (1933), pl. 16. H. Schäfer,
"Eine nordsyrische Kultsitte?", pl. 7a. *ANEP,*
no. 490.*

292. Stele, gray volcanic basalt, h. 1.62
m.: Jekke (ca. 30 km. northeast of Aleppo):
8th–7th c. B.C.; Aleppo 2459. *ANEP,* no.
500. A. Vanel, *Iconographie,* fig. 70.**

293. Rock relief, h. of the deity, ca. 4.2
m.: Ivriz (southeastern Anatolia): second half
of the 8th c. B.C. H. T. Bossert, *Altanatolien,*
no. 796. *AOB,* no. 343. *ANEP,* no. 527. M.
Riemschneider, *Hethiter,* pl. 45. E. Akurgal
and M. Hirmer, *Kunst,* pl. 24. A. Vanel,
Iconographie, pp. 146f., fig. 69.**

294. Basalt stele, h. 1.35 m.: Arslan Tash:
Tiglath-pileser III (745–727 B.C.); Louvre.
ANEP, no 501. L. H. Grollenberg, *Bildatlas,*
fig. 219. J. Vanel, *Iconographie,* pp. 149f., fig.
21.**

295. Enameled seal, h. 28 cm.: Assur:
Tukulti-Ninurta II (888–884 B.C.); BM
115706. *AOB,* no. 333. *ANEP,* no. 536. A.
Parrot, *Assur,* fig. 282.*

296. Relief, Nimrud, Assurbanipal II
(883–859 B.C.); BM. B. Meissner, *Babylonien
und Assyrien,* vol. 2, p. 40, fig. 10. E. A. W.
Budge, *Assyrian Sculptures,* pl. 18.1. B. Pering, "Die geflügelte Scheibe," pl. 4.2.

297. Obelisk relief, h. ca. 30 cm.,
Nineveh: 11th–10th c. B.C.; BM 118898.
AOB, no. 332. *ANEP,* no. 440. A. Moortgat,
Kunst, fig. 252. A. Parrot, *Assur,* fig. 40c.*

298. Reconstruction of a copper smelting
oven: Tell Qasîle (north of Tel Aviv): 11th c.
B.C. B. Maisler, *Excavations at Tell Qasîle,* fig.
3. *ANEP,* no. 134. *IWB,* vol. 3, p. 178.

299. Drawing of a baking-oven: eš-šobak
(north of Petra). G. Dalman, *AuS,* vol. 4, fig.
17.3.

300. Bronze statue, h. 13 cm.: Megiddo:
tomb no. 4: Late Bronze Period (1350–1200
B.C.); Jerusalem, Palestine Museum. H. G.
May and R. M. Engberg, *Material Remains,*
pp. 33ff., pl. 34, fig. 357. *ANEP,* no. 348.**

301. Limestone stele, Horbet (Nile Delta), 19th Dynasty (1345–1200 B.C.); Hildesheim, Pelizäus Museum 1100. *AOB,* no.
348.**

302. Limestone stele, New Kingdom
(1570–1085 B.C.); Chicago, Oriental Institute 10569. *ANEP,* no. 476. *IWB,* vol. 3, p.
274.*

303. Vase painting on a goblet: Orvieto,
ca. 460 B.C.; Louvre G 341. P. E. Arias and
M. Hirmer, *Tausend Jahre,* pl. 175.**

304. Relief, h. 91 cm.: Nimrud: central
palace: Tiglath-pileser III (745–727 B.C.);
Bombay. R. D. Barnett and M. Falkner,
Sculptures, p. 14, pl. 32.**

305. Limestone relief: Luxor: first hall of
columns, exterior of the west wall, south of
the side entrance: first year of Ramses II
(1301–1234 B.C.). W. Wreszinski, *Atlas,* vol.
2, pl. 71.**

306. Relief, Nineveh, Assurbanipal
(668–626 B.C.). M. A. Beek, *Atlas of
Mesopotamia,* fig. 230.**

307. Relief: Nineveh: palace of Assurban-
ipal (668–626 B.C.): Room C: 668–626 B.C.);
BM 124860. R. D. Barnett and W. Forman,
Assyrische Palastreliefs, fig. 76.**

307a. Stele, limestone, h. 49 cm.: probably from Assiut: tomb of Shalkana: 19th–
20th Dynasty (1345–1085 B.C.); BM 1632.
H. Brunner, "Dankstele," pl. 3.*

308. Wall painting, h. of figures, ca. 50
cm.: Beni Hasan: tomb of Khnum-Hotep III
(no. 3): Sesostris II (1897–1879 B.C.). P. E.
Newberry, *Beni Hasan,* vol. 1, pl. 31. *LD,*
vol. 4, pl. 131, cf. pl. 132. *AOB,* no. 51.
ANEP, no. 3. *IWB,* vol. 1, p. 26.

309. Tomb painting, h. ca. 48 cm.: Abd
el-Qurna: tomb of Rekh-mi-Re (no. 100):
Thut-mose III (1502–1448 B.C.). *ANEP,* no.
115. A. Lhote, *Peinture égyptienne,* pl. 99. A.
Mekhitarian, *Ägyptische Malerei,* p. 48.**

310. Relief: Nineveh: southwest palace:
Assurbanipal (668–626 B.C.); BM. *ANEP,*
no. 204. M. A. Beek, *Atlas of Mesopotamia,*
fig. 226.*

311. Tomb painting: Abd el-Qurna: tomb
of Menena (no. 69), transverse chamber, left
entrance wall: late 18th Dynasty (1570–1345
B.C.). W. Wreszinski, *Atlas,* vol. 1, plates
231f. A. Lhote, *Peinture égyptienne,* pl. 77. Cf.
S. Berger, "A Note on Some Scenes."**

312. Limestone relief, h. 38 m.: Sakkarh:
tomb of Tji: 5th Dynasty (2480–2350 B.C.).
W. Wolf, *Kunst,* p. 228, fig. 195. A. Mekhitarian, *Ägyptische Malerei,* p. 11. W. Westendorf, *Ägypten,* p. 55.**

313. Cylinder seal, yellow limestone, h.
5.7 cm., diam. 5 cm.: beginning of the third
millennium B.C.; Berlin, VA 7234. H.
Frankfort, *Cylinder Seals,* pl. 5e. A. Moortgat,
Vorderasiatische Rollsiegel, no. 4. H.
Schmökel, *Ur, Assur,* pl. 4.*

314. Inscriptional stone, l. 40 cm., h. 20
cm.: cenotaph of Hani (15 km. east of Pump
Station H 5, on the road between El Mefraq
and Baghdad): 1st c. B.C. O. Eissfeldt, *KS,*
vol. 3, pl. 1, fig. 2.**

315. Tomb painting: Abd el-Qurna: tomb

of Rekh-mi-Re (no. 100): Thut-mose III (1502–1448 B.C.). N. Davies, *Tomb of Rekh-mi-rē'*, pl. 60. J. Vandier, *Manuel,* vol. 3, p. 7, fig. 3.

316. Relief: Nineveh: southwest palace: Sennacherib (704–681 B.C.); lost. R. D. Barnett and M. Falkner, *Sculptures,* p. 17, pl. 7. A. H. Layard, *Monuments,* vol. 1, pl. 67A.**

317. Relief, Khorsabad, Sargon II (721–705 B.C.). P. E. Botta, *Monuments,* vol. 2, pl. 114. *IWB,* vol. 3, pl. 215. B. Meissner, *Babylonien und Assyrien,* vol. 2, p. 129.**

318. Orthostatic relief, granite, h. 1.26 m.: Alaça Hüyük: 15th c. B.C.; Ankara, Hittite Museum. E. Akurgal and M. Hirmer, *Kunst der Hethiter,* pl. 92. H. T. Bossert, *Altanatolien,* no. 510. *ANEP,* no. 616.**

319. Ivory carving, Nimrud, 9th–8th c. B.C.; Baghdad. *IWB,* vol. 2, p. 172. Cf. *ANEP,* no. 131; F. Thureau-Dangin et al., *Arslan Tash,* plates 45–59.**

320. Stele, Carthage, 4th c. B.C.; Tunis, Bardo Museum. L. Poinssot and R. Lantier, "Un sanctuaire," pl. 4.2, p. 47. S. Moscati, *Phöniker,* fig. 40 (facing p. 200). G. Cornfeld and G. J. Botterweck, *Bibel und ihre Welt,* fig. 650. B. H. Warmington, *Carthage,* fig. 8b.**

321. Ivory carving, l. ca. 13 cm.: Megiddo: 1350–1150 B.C.; Jerusalem, Palestine Museum 38780. G. Loud, *Megiddo Ivories,* pl. 4, fig. 2. *ANEP,* no. 332. On the date, cf. H. L. Liebowitz, "Horses." For the other half of the ivory, cf. Fig. *233.***

322. Relief, Nineveh, Sennacherib (704–681 B.C.). A. H. Layard, *Monuments,* vol. 2, pl. 24. *AOB,* no. 538.**

323. Relief, Nineveh, Sennacherib (704–681 B.C.). A. H. Layard, *Monuments,* vol. 2, p. 469. A. Paterson, *Assyrian Sculptures,* pl. 94. B. Meissner, *Babylonien und Assyrien,* vol. 2, p. 89.**

323a. Relief, h. 3.39 m.: Yazilikaya: east wall of the smaller chamber: second half of the 13th c. B.C. K. Bittel et al., *Yazilikaya,* pp. 101–4, plates 29–31. E. Akurgal and M. Hirmer, *Kunst,* plates 81–83. H. Frankfort, *Art and Architecture,* pp. 228f. Cf. H. G. Güterbock, "A Votive Sword."**

324. Clay shard, h. 9.5 cm.: Thebes: 19th Dynasty (1345–1200 B.C.); Berlin A 21826. *ANEP,* no. 479. *AOB,* no. 274. Cf. J. Leclant, "Astarté à cheval," pp. 1–67.**

324a. Stone sculpture, life-size: Sendshirli: 9th–8th c. B.C.; Berlin. F. von Luschan, *Ausgrabungen in Sendschirli,* vol. 4, p. 337, fig. 249. H. J. Kantor, "A Bronze Plaque," p. 94, fig. 2.**

325. Relief, gypseous alabaster, h. 1.29 m.: Nineveh: Assurbanipal (668–626 B.C.); Louvre. A. Parrot, *Assur,* fig. 57. Cf. M. A. Beek, *Atlas of Mesopotamia,* fig. 221.**

326. Wall painting, h. 35 cm. Tell 'Ahmar: 7th c. B.C.; original destroyed; after a copy from the original by L. Cavro in the Louvre. A. Parrot, *Assur,* fig. 340. A. Moortgat, *Kunst,* p. 158, fig. 111.**

327. Wall painting, Tell 'Ahmar, 8th c. B.C.; destroyed; copy by L. Cavro in the Louvre. A. Parrot, *Assur,* fig. IV.**

328. Relief, Nineveh, Assurbanipal (668–626 B.C.); BM 128941. R. D. Barnett and W. Forman, *Assyrische Palastreliefs,* fig. 128. *IWB,* vol. 3, p, 150.**

328a. Sandstone relief: Medinet Habu: first forecourt, interior of the south wall: Ramses III (1197–1165 B.C. H. H. Nelson, *Later Historical Records,* pl. 62.

329. Sculpture from gray granite, h. 80 cm.: Karnak: Temple of Amon: 20th Dynasty (1200–1085 B.C.); Cairo Museum 42162. M. G. Legrain, *Statues,* vol. 2, p. 29, pl. 26.**

330. Wall painting, h. 1.4 m.: Tell 'Ahmar: palace: Hall 24: 8th c. B.C.; destroyed; copy by L. Cavro in the Louvre. A. Parrot, *Assur,* fig. 348. *ANEP,* no. 235.**

331. Dolerite, h. 1.12 m.: Zinjirli: second half of the 8th c. B.C.: Berlin VA 2817. *BHH,* vol. 3, cols. 1719f. F. von Luschan, *Ausgrabungen in Sendschirli,* vol. 4, pl. 60. E. Akurgal and M. Hirmer, *Kunst,* pl. 131. *ANEP,* no. 460.

332. Relief, w. ca. 3 m.: Deir el-Bahri: temple of Hatshepsut: central hall of columns, north wall: 1501–1480 B.C. E. Naville, *Deir el Bahari,* vol. 2, pl. 46. In the original, a long speech of Amon is inserted in the space between Amon and the twelve assembled deities, making the distance between them considerably greater than what is shown here. A Babylonian assembly of the gods is illustrated in M. Jastrow, *Bildermappe,* fig. 173. On the Hittite assembly of the gods, see K. Bittel et al., *Yazilikaia.***

333. Relief, Luxor, temple of Amenophis III (1417–1377 B.C.). H. Brunner, *Geburt,* pl. 4. E. Otto and M. Hirmer, *Osiris und Amun,* pl. 30.

334. Relief, Luxor, temple of Amenophis III (1417–1377 B.C.). H. Brunner, *Geburt,* pp. 90–106, plates 6, 20. E. Otto and M. Hirmer, *Osiris und Amun,* pl. 32. *ANEP,* no. 569. Drawing by J. Dittmar.

335. Relief, Luxor, temple of Amenophis III (1417–1377 B.C.). H. Brunner, *Geburt,* pl. 7. Drawing by J. Dittmar.

336. Limestone relief, w. ca. 3 m.: Deir el-Bahri: temple of Hatshepsut, central hall of columns, north wall, lower register: 1501–1480 B.C. E. Naville, *Deir el Bahari,* vol. 2, pl. 51.**

337. Relief: Erment (20 km. south of Luxor, West Bank): Ptolemy XV (Caesar) (47–30 B.C.). *LD,* vol. 9, pl. 60a. J. F. Champollion, *Monuments,* vol. 2, pl. 145.7, fig. 2. A. Moret, *Royauté pharaonique,* p. 68, fig. 11.**

338. Relief, Luxor, temple of Amenophis III (1413–1377 B.C.) H. Brunner, *Geburt,* pl. 10. Drawing by J. Dittmar.

339. Relief, Luxor, temple of Amenophis III (1413–1377 B.C.) H. Brunner, *Geburt,* pl. 11. Drawing by J. Dittmar.

340. Relief, Luxor, temple of Amenophis III (1413–1377 B.C.). H. Brunner, *Geburt,* pl. 14. Drawing by J. Dittmar.

341. Painting: Abd el-Qurna: tomb of Kanamon (no. 93): Amenophis II (1448–1422 B.C.). N. de G. Davies, *Tomb of Kenamūn,* vol. 1, pp. 19–21, pl. 9. N. M. Davies and A. H. Gardiner, *Egyptian Paintings,* vol. 1, p. 29. *LD,* vol. 5, pl. 62c. W. Wreszinski, *Atlas,* vol. 1, pl. 298. *AOB,* no. 59.

342. Painting: Abd el-Qurna: tomb of Hekaerneheh: Thut-mose IV (1422–1413 B.C.). *LD,* vol. 5, pl. 69a. J. Vandier, *Manuel,* vol. 4, fig. 293.

342a. Base of a statue, limestone, l. 66.3 cm.: from the exterior of the southern *temenos*-wall of the Djoser Pyramid at Sakkarah: 3rd Dynasty (2650–2600 B.C.); Cairo. B. Gunn, "An Inscribed Statue," pl. 1A.*

343. Stone tablet, Kish, Djemdet-Nasr Period (2800–2700 B.C.); Brussels 0711. H. de Genouillac, *Fouilles françaises d'El-'Akhymer,* pl. 1.1. I. Seibert, *Hirt-Herde-König,* fig. 10. E. Heinrich, *Bauwerke,* p. 43, fig. 39.*

344. Painting, height of the entire fragment, 1.32 m., w. 1.12 m.: Thebes: tomb no. 63: Thut-mose IV (1422–1413 B.C.); BM 37991. *ANEP,* no. 47. *IWB,* vol. 2, p. 135. Cf. M. Duchesne-Guillemin, "L'Oliphant."**

345–346 and 349. Relief: Karnak: Great Temple, hypostyle, west side: Seti I (1317–1301 B.C.). *LD,* vol. 6, pl. 124d. A. Moret, *Royauté pharaonique,* pl. 2. H. Bonnet, *Reallexikon,* p. 397. On Fig. 345 cf. A. H. Gardiner, "The Baptism of Pharaoh."

347. Relief, height of the deity, 1.64 m.: Yazilikaya (ca. 3 km. east of Boghazköi): middle of the 13th c. B.C.; copy in Berlin, Staatliche Museen. K. Bittel et al., *Yazilikaya,* vol. 1, pp. 98–101, frontispiece,

and pl. 28. E. Akurgal and M. Hirmer, *Kunst,* plates 84–85. *AOB,* no. 342. *ANEP,* no. 541. M. Riemschneider, *Hethiter,* pl. 36. Cf. H. Otten, "Zur Datierung," p. 239.*

348. Relief (peak of the obelisk of Queen Hatshepsut), rose granite: Karnak: Hatshepsut (1501–1480 B.C.). W. Westendorf, *Ägypten,* p. 100. A. Champidor, *Thèbes,* p. 26.**

349. See 345.

350. Relief: Semneh: Temple, exterior of the east wall: 18th Dynasty (1570–1345 B.C.). *LD,* vol. 5, pl. 55b.

351. Limestone relief, h. ca. 95 m.: Karnak, small temple: Sesostris I (1971–1930 B.C.); reconstructed in 1937–1939. L. H. Grollenberg, *Bildatlas,* p. 39. W. Wolf, *Kunst,* p. 306, fig. 241.*

352. Sandstone relief: complex of Ramses III at Medinet Habu: exterior of the first pylon, north of the entrance: period of Ramses IV (ca. 1165 B.C.). H. H. Nelson, *Later Historical Records,* pl. 119B, p. 84. Cf. the well-known representation of the same theme in *LD,* vol. 6, p. 169; *AOB,* no. 101.

353. Statue, white limestone, h. 1.52 m, base 73 × 75 cm.: Horemheb (1345–1318 B.C.); Vienna, Kunsthistorisches Museum. J. Vandier, *Manuel,* vol. 3, pp. 369f., pl. 120.5. Drawing after a photograph in the Kunsthistorisches Museum, Vienna, Inv. no. 8301.**

354. Reconstruction of the acropolis of Jerusalem by K. Galling in *BHH,* vol. 3, cols. 1363f.

355. Plan of Solomon's citadel by T. A. Busink in *Tempel,* vol. 1, p. 160, fig. 47.

356. Relief, Karnak (C 7), Thut-mose III (1502–1448 B.C.). *LD,* vol. 5, pl. 36b. A. Moret, *Royauté pharaonique,* p. 155, fig. 21. *AOB,* no. 53. *IWB,* vol. 2, p. 274. G. Roeder, *Götterwelt,* p. 253.

357. Wood covered with linen and stucco, h. 86 cm.: Thebes: Tomb of Thut-mose IV (1422–1413 B.C.); Cairo. W. Wreszinski, *Atlas,* vol. 2, pl. 1. *AOB,* no. 62. *ANEP,* nos. 315–316 (greatly simplified).**

357a. Relief: Luxor: Temple: Room XVII, interior of the east wall, second register: Amenophis III (1413–1377 B.C.); from a photograph released to the author for publication by Dr. G. R. Hughes, the Director of the Oriental Institute, Chicago. Cf. A. Moret, "Le rite de briser les vases."**

358. Relief: Edfu: Temple: exterior east wall of the *naos:* 237–57 B.C. E. Chassinat, *Edfou,* vol. 4, pl. 93.**

359. Potsherds, Thebes, 11th–13th Dynasties (2052–1770 B.C.). K. Sethe, *Die Ächtung feindlicher Fürsten,* pl. 33.*

403

360. Clay statuette, h. 33 cm.: Sakkarah: 12th–13th Dynasties (1991–1770 B.C.); Brussels, Royal Museums. *BHH,* vol. 1, pl. 2a. *ANEP,* no. 593.*

360a. Relief, gypsum: Nineveh: Assurbanipal (668–626 B.C.); BM. A. Paterson, *Assyrian Sculptures,* plates 76, 77.**

361. Limestone relief, h. of section, ca. 25 cm.: Tello: Ur-Nanshe (ca. 2500 B.C.); Louvre, AO 2344. A. Parrot, *Sumer,* fig. 159. *ANEP,* no. 247. H. Schmökel, *Ur, Assur,* pl. 29.*

362. Stone stele, h. 38.6 cm.: Babylon: Assurbanipal (668–626 B.C.); BM 90864. *ANEP,* no. 450. H. Schmökel, *Ur, Assur,* pl. 105.*

363. Limestone stele, h. of section, ca. 30 cm.: Ur: Ur-Nammu (ca. 2050 B.C.); Philadelphia, University Museum. A. Parrot, *Sumer,* fig. 282. C. L. Woolley, *Ur,* pp. 63, 65.**

364. Sandstone relief: Edfu: Temple: second hypostyle hall, south wall, right side, third scene: 237–57 B.C. E. Chassinat, *Edfou,* vol. 12, pl. 369. Cf. *LD,* vol. 6, pl. 148a; cf. A. Moret, *Royauté pharaonique,* fig. 25; cf. R. Engelbach, "A Foundation Scene"; L. Borchardt, "Jubiläumsbilder."**

365. Relief: Dendera: Great Temple: Roman Period (1st c. A.D.). A. Mariette, *Dendérah,* vol. 1, pl. 20. A. Moret, *Royauté pharaonique,* fig. 26. Cf. J. F. Champollion, *Monuments,* vol. 1, pl. 48; cf. L. Borchardt, "Jubiläumsbilder."

366. Relief: Edfu: Temple: second hypostyle hall, west wall, first register, first scene: 237–57 B.C. E. Chassinat, *Edfou,* vol. 12, pl. 374. Cf. L. Borchardt, "Jubiläumsbilder."**

367. Relief: Dendera: Great Temple: Hall B: Roman Period (1st c. A.D.). A. Mariette, *Dendérah,* vol. 1, pl. 22. A. Moret, *Royauté pharaonique,* fig. 28.

368. Relief: Abusir: Re Temple: Ne-user-Re (5th Dynasty, 2480–2350 B.C.); Berlin. H. Bonnet, *Bilderatlas,* fig. 75. H. Schäfer, *Von ägyptischer Kunst,* fig. 97a. Cf. L. Borchardt, "Jubiläumsbilder."

369. Relief: Dendera: Great Temple: Hall B: Roman Period (1st c. A.D.). A. Mariette, *Dendérah,* vol. 1, pl. 21a. A. Moret, *Royauté pharaonique,* fig. 27.

370. Relief: Dendera: Great Temple: Hall B: Roman Period (1st c. B.C.). A. Mariette, *Dendérah,* vol. 1, pl. 21b. A. Moret, *Royauté pharaonique,* fig. 29.

371. Relief: Edfu: Temple: second hypostyle hall, east wall, first register, third scene: 237–57 B.C. E. Chassinat, *Edfou,* vol. 12, pl.

378. Cf. A. Moret, *Royauté pharaonique,* fig. 31.**

372. Upper portion of a limestone stele, w. 22.5 cm.: Buto (?): Shabaka (ca. 715–698 B.C.); New York, Metropolitan Museum 55.144.6. After a photograph in the Metropolitan Museum.**

373. Obelisk, limestone, h. 3.5 m.: Nineveh: Assurbanipal I (?) (1047–1029 B.C.). *AOB,* no. 533. *ANEP,* no. 624. M. A. Beek, *Atlas of Mesopotamia,* p. 139. Cf. B. Hrouda, *Kulturgeschichte,* p. 60.

374. Relief, Abydos, temple of Seti I (1317–1301 B.C.). A. M. Calverley et al., *Abydos,* vol. 1, pl. 6. Cf. G. Roeder, *Kulte,* p. 109.**

375. Wall painting: Deir el-Bahri: temple of Hatshepsut, rear wall of the Hathor Chapel: Hatshepsut/Thut-mose III (1501–1448 B.C.); Cairo. E. Otto and M. Hirmer, *Osiris und Amun,* p. 113.**

376. Temple relief: El-Kharge Oasis: Hibis: Amon Temple: Darius I (521–486 B.C.). N. Davies, *Temple of Hibis,* pt. 3, pp. 24f., pl. 31. Several columns of text between the Pharaoh and the sacrificed cattle have been omitted.

377. Relief, Abydos, temple of Seti I (1317–1301 B.C.). A. M. Calverley et al., *Abydos,* vol. 2, pl. 5.**

378. Relief: Abydos: temple of Seti I: Horus Chapel, south wall: Seti I (1317–1301 B.C.). A. M. Calverley et al., *Abydos,* vol. 1, pl. 33.**

378a. Sandstone relief, w. ca. 2.20 m.: West Thebes: Medinet Habu: exterior of the south wall, west of the entrance, lowest register: Ramses III (1197–1165 B.C.). H. H. Nelson, *The Calendar,* pl. 168.

379. Relief, Abydos, temple of Seti I (1317–1301 B.C.). A. M. Calverley et al., *Abydos,* vol. 4, pl. 10. Cf. *AOB,* nos. 103f.; *ANEP,* no. 572; H. W. Fairman, "A Scene of Offering."**

380. Painted relief, Serabit el Khadem (Sinai) Amenemhet III (1840–1792 B.C.). W. S. Smith, *Interconnections,* fig. 12. G. Gerster, *Sinai,* p. 49. *IWB,* vol. 1, p. 66. Cf. A. H. Gardiner et al., *Inscriptions of Sinai,* vol. 1, plates 37, 39, 44.

381. Sandstone relief: Medinet Habu: north end of the west wall, exterior: Ramses III (1197–1165 B.C.). H. H. Nelson et al., *Earlier Historical Records,* pl. 16.

382. Wall painting, length of section, 2.1 m.: Tell 'Ahmar: 7th c. B.C.; copy by L. Cavro in the Louvre. A. Parrot, *Assur,* fig. 345. F.

Thureau-Dangin and M. Dunand, *Til Barsib,* plates 53, 27e.*

383. Ivory panel, h. ca. 24 cm.: Ugarit: 1400–1350 B.C.; Damascus. W. H. Ward, "La déesse nourricière," p. 237, fig. 4.*

384. Relief, Amarna (C 6), Amenophis IV (1377–1358 B.C.). N. de G. Davies, *Amarna,* vol. 1, pl. 10. *AOB,* no. 72.

385. Relief on a stele, Abu Simbel, Ramses II (1301–1234 B.C.). *LD,* vol. 7, pl. 196. W. S. Smith, *Interconnections,* fig. 46. *ANEP,* no. 339; text: *ANET,* pp. 257f. There is a copy of the scene in the museum of the Oriental Institute, Chicago, no. 13545. On similar scenes from Mesopotamia, cf. L. W. King, *Bronze Reliefs,* plates 27–29, 34.**

386. Wooden chest with gold chasework, h. of section, 15 cm.: Valley of the Kings: tomb no. 62: Tutankhamun (1358–1349 B.C.); Cairo. W. Westendorf, *Ägypten,* p. 155.**

387. Ivory tablet, h. ca. 24 cm.: Ugarit: 1400–1350 B.C.; Damascus. C. F. A. Schaeffer, "Les fouilles de Ras Shamra-Ugarit," p. 57, pl. 9. *ANEP,* no. 818. S. Abdul Hak, *Schätze des National-Museums,* pl. 10.**

388. Cylinder seal, limestone, h. 2 cm., diam. 1.2 cm.: Tell Asmar: middle of the third millennium B.C.; Baghdad. *ANEP,* no. 680. H. Frankfort, *Cylinder Seals,* pl. 15 l.*

389. Relief: Edfu: chamber of Khmin, south wall, first register, second scene: 237–57 B.C. E. Chassinat, *Edfou,* vol. 12, pl. 332.**

389a. Relief: Karnak: Khons Temple: propylon: Ptolemy II (Euergetes I) (246–221 B.C.). *LD,* vol. 9, pl. 12a. A. Moret, *Royauté pharaonique,* p. 157.**

390. Relief, diorite stele, h. ca. 65 cm.: Susa: Hammurabi (1728–1686 B.C.); Louvre. *AOB,* no. 318. *ANEP,* nos. 515, 246. H. Schmökel, *Ur, Assur,* pl. 64.**

391. Tomb painting: Abd el Qurna: Tomb of Nefer-hotep (no. 50): transverse hall, left wall: Horemheb (1345–1318 B.C.). A. Radwan, *Darstellungen des regierenden Königs,* pl. 24. J. Vandier, *Manuel,* vol. 4, fig. 369.**

392. Relief: Amarna: Tomb of Mahu: Amenophis IV (1377–1358 B.C.). N. de G. Davies, *Amarna,* vol. 4, pl. 25f. J. Vandier, *Manuel,* vol. 4, p. 708, fig. 394.

393. Painting: Abd el Qurna: Tomb of Rekh-mi-Rc (no. 100): linear chamber, left side wall: Thut-mose III (1502–1448 B.C.). N. Davies, *Tomb of Rekh-mi-re',* vol. 1, pp. 31f., vol. 2, pl. 25. W. Wreszinski, *Atlas,* pl.

331. A. Erman and H. Ranke, *Ägypten,* p. 158.

394. Ivory handle of a flint knife, h. of handle, 9.5 cm.: Gebel el-'Arak: period of the unification of the Kingdoms (ca. 3000 B.C.); Louvre E 11517. W. Westendorf, *Ägypten,* p. 21. *ANEP,* no. 290.*

395 and 396. Tomb painting, h. ca. 15 cm.: Hierakonpolis (Nekhen): shortly before the period of the unification of the Kingdoms (ca. 3000 B.C.). H. Schäfer and W. Andrae, *Kunst des Alten Orients,* p. 178. W. Wolf, *Kunst,* figs. 39a, d. J. Vandier, *Manuel,* vol. 1, pt. 1, p. 563, fig. 375. Drawing by O. Camponovo.

397. Slate palette, h. 64 cm.: Hierakonpolis (Kom el-'Ahmar): Narmer (period of the unification of the Kingdoms, ca. 2850 B.C.); Cairo. J. E. Quibell, "Slate Palette," pl. 13. *AOB,* no. 27. *ANEP,* no. 296. J. Vandier, *Manuel,* vol. 1, pt. 1, pp. 595–599. A. H. Gardiner, *Grammar,* p. 7.

398. Relief, h. 62 cm.: Maghara (Sinai): Sekhemkhet (third king of the 3rd Dynasty) (ca. 2650–2600 B.C.). A. H. Gardiner et al., *Inscriptions of Sinai,* vol. 1, pl. 1, no. 1a. G. Gerster, *Sinai,* pp. 40, 44f.*

399. Ostracon, Ramses III (1197–1165 B.C.); Brussels, Royal Museums. *IWB,* vol. 4, p. 28.*

399a. Relief, limestone, h. 2.11 m.: Dendera: Chapel of Mentuhotep: north wall: Mentuhotep Nebhetepre (2052–1991 B.C.); Cairo Museum 46068. L. Habachi, "King Nebhetepre," p. 22, fig. 6.

400 a). Scarab, steatite, whitish-yellow, h. 1.4 cm.: Beth-Shan: 19th Dynasty (1345–1200 B.C.); Jerusalem, Palestine Museum I 3801. A. Rowe, *Catalogue of Egyptian Scarabs,* no. 671.*

b). Scarab: Tell Beit Mirsim: towards the end of the period of Ramses II (1301–1234 B.C.). W. F. Albright, *Tell Beit Mirsim,* p. 51, fig. 9. C. Watzinger, *Denkmäler Palästinas,* vol. 1, p. 40, figs. 3f.*

c). Scarab, steatite, light brown, h. 1.8 cm.: Tell el-Far'ah: 19th Dynasty; Jerusalem, Palestine Museum I 9771. A. Rowe, *Catalogue of Egyptian Scarabs,* no. 670.*

401. Ivory with inlay (lost): Samaria: first half of the 9th c. B.C. J. W. and G. M. Crowfoot, *Ivories from Samaria,* pl. 14.1.

402. Axe made of wood, bronze, gold, etc., length of blade, 13.5 cm.: Thebes: Ahmose (1570–1545 B.C.); New York, Metropolitan Museum. H. Schäfer and W. An-

drae, *Kunst des Alten Orients,* pl. 402.5. *ANEP,* no. 310. *IWB,* vol. 2, p. 133.**

403. Ivory, h. ca. 24 cm., w. ca. 12.5 cm.: Ugarit: 1400–1350 B.C.; Damascus. C. F. A. Schaeffer, "Les fouilles de Ras Shamra-Ugarit," *Syria* 31 (1954), p. 57, pl. 10. S. Abdul Hak, *Schätze des National-Museums,* pl. 9. *ANEP,* no. 817. Cf. Fig. 383.**

404. Relief: Abu Simbel: hall of columns of the great rock temple: Ramses II (1301–1234 B.C.). W. Wreszinski, *Atlas,* vol. 2, pl. 182. W. Wolf, *Kunst,* fig. 575. A. Champidor, *Thèbes,* p. 146. G. Posener et al., *Knaurs Lexikon,* p. 136.**

405. Relief: West Thebes: Ramesseum: second pylon, west side, lower scene: Ramses II (1301–1234 B.C.). *LD,* vol. 6, pl. 165.

405a. Greatly simplified drawing of the reliefs on the western (a, b, c) and northern (d, e, f) exterior and the eastern interior (g, h) of the second forecourt of the temple at Medinet Habu: Ramses III (1197–1165 B.C.). H. H. Nelson et al., *Earlier Historical Records,* vol. 1, plates 13, 14, 16, 17, 18, 22, 24, 26.**

406. Limestone relief, h. of the prisoner, ca. 35 cm.: Abusir: pyramid installation of Sahure: ca. 2500 B.C.; Berlin 21782. L. Borchardt, *Grabdenkmal,* vol. 2, plates 5–7; text pp. 18–21. Cf. *ANEP,* no. 1; cf. H. Fechheimer, *Plastik,* pp. 122f.**

407. Stele, h. 3.46 cm.: Senjirli: Asarhaddon (680–669 B.C.); Berlin VA. *BHH,* vol. 1, col. 135. *AOB,* no. 144. *ANEP,* no. 437. H. Schmökel, *Ur, Assur,* pl. 98.

408. Wall painting, h. 1.32 m.: Abd el Qurna: tomb no. 63.: Thut-mose IV (1422–1413 B.C.); BM 37991. N. M. Davies and A. H. Gardiner, *Paintings,* vol. 1, pl. 42. A. Champidor, *Thèbes,* p. 133. *ANEP,* no. 47.*

409. Tomb painting: Abd el Qurna: Tomb of Huy (no. 40): Tutankhamun (1358–1349 B.C.). N. de G. Davies and A. H. Gardiner, *Tomb of Huy,* pl. 27. G. Gerster, *Nubien,* p. 53. J. Vandier, *Manuel,* vol. 4, p. 606.**

410. Relief: Amarna: Tomb of Meryra II: east wall: Amenophis IV (1377–1358 B.C.). N. de G. Davies, *Amarna,* vol. 2, pl. 37, cf. plates 38–40, 98. For representations of the delivery of tribute in Mesopotamia, cf. G. Walser, *Völkerschaften,* pp. 11–19.

411. Statuette, gypsum, pupils of black limestone, eyes shell set in asphalt, h. 40 cm.: Abu Tempel: Tell Asmar: first half of the 3rd millennium B.C. (Early Dynastic Period II); Oriental Institute, Chicago. H. Frankfort, *Sculpture of the Third Millennium B.C.,* plates 21–23, 25. Idem, *More Sculpture,* plates

89–90. Idem, *Art and Architecture,* pp. 46–48.**

412. Sketch on limestone, New Kingdom (1570–1085 B.C.). A. Erman and H. Ranke, *Ägypten,* p. 477, fig. 188.

413. Papyrus (Book of the Dead) of Heruben, h. ca. 5 cm.: 12th Dynasty (1085–950 B.C.); Cairo, no. 133. A. Piankoff and N. Rambova, *Mythological Papyri,* no. 1. G. Posener et al., *Knaurs Lexikon,* p. 137.**

414. Cylinder seal, jasper, h. 3.2 cm., diam. 2 cm.: Ur III Period (2050–1950 B.C.); New York, Pierpont Morgan Library. M. A. Beek, *Atlas of Mesopotamia,* fig. 133. *ANEP,* no. 700.**

415. Bronze plaque, h. 9.4 cm.: Hazor: Late Bronze Period (1500–1200 B.C.); Hazor. Y. Yadin et al., *Hazor III–IV,* pl. 339.1. *ANEP,* no 772.**

416. Stele, black basalt, h. 1.83 m.: Balu'ah (between Arnon and Kerak): inscription, end of the third millennium B.C.; relief, 11th–12th c. B.C.; Amman. *ANEP,* no. 488. *BHH,* vol. 2, col. 1230.*

417. Drawing on rock: vicinity of Aswan: prehistoric (before 3000 B.C.). L. Keimer, *Histoires de serpents,* p. 2, fig. 1.

417a. Relief, sandstone, w. ca. 4.40 m.: West Thebes: Medinet Habu: column on the south side of the first forecourt: Ramses III (1197–1165 B.C.). H. H. Nelson, *Later Historical Records,* pl. 121C.

418. Altar relief, gypsum, h. 57.5 cm.: Assur: Ishtar Temple: Tukulti-Ninurta I (1243–1207 B.C.); Berlin VA 8146. A. Parrot, *Assur,* fig. 8. *ANEP,* no. 576.**

419. Cylinder seal, jasper: Assyrian. A. Jeremias, *Handbuch,* p. 27, fig. 17; cf. p. 273, fig. 173.

420. Bronze statue, hands and face gilded, h. 19.6 cm.: probably from Larsa: Hammurabi (1728–1686 B.C.); Louvre AO 15704. *ANEP,* no. 622. H. Schmökel, Ur, *Assur,* pl. 66. Cf. E. Sollberger, "Worshipper Figurines."**

421. Small ivory casket: Hazor: period of the Israelite Monarchy (after 1000 B.C.). Y. Yadin et al., *Hazor,* vol. 1, pl. 155. *IWB,* vol. 4, p. 113.**

422. Relief: Abydos: mortuary temple of Seti I (1317–1301 B.C.). A. M. Calverley et al., *Abydos,* vol. 2, pl. 14.

423. Granite figure, h. 39 cm.: Memphis: 2nd Dynasty (2850–2650 B.C.; possibly later); Cairo. W. Westendorf, *Ägypten,* p. 26. Cf. A. Parrot, *Sumer,* fig. 104.**

424. Sculpture, black volcanic stone, h. ca. 39 cm.: probably from Lagash: Early

Dynastic Period: possibly Ur-Nanshe (ca. 2500 B.C.); Baghdad. *ANEP,* no. 229. M. A. Beek, *Atlas of Mesopotamia,* fig. 110.**

425. Relief: Abydos: mortuary temple of Seti I: niche between the chapels of Re-Harakhti and Ptah: Seti I (1317–1301 B.C.). A. M. Calverley et al., *Abydos,* vol. 4, pl. 33.**

426. Cylinder seal, ironstone, h. 2.9 cm.: Ur III Period (2050–1950 B.C.); formerly Berlin VA 538. A. Moortgat, *Vorderasiatische Rollsiegel,* no. 256. H. Schmökel, *Ur, Assur,* pl. 55b. M. A. Beek, *Atlas of Mesopotamia,* fig. 228.*

427. Portion of a diorite statue of Gudea, h. of the hands, ca. 5 cm · Lagash: Neo-Sumerian Period, 22nd c. B.C.; Louvre. A. Parrot, *Sumer,* fig. XXXIIA.**

428. Tomb painting: Abd el Qurna: Tomb of Userhet (no. 51): 19th Dynasty (1345–1200 B.C.). A. Mekhitarian, *Ägyptische Malerei,* p. 135.**

429. Limestone relief, h. ca. 53 cm.: Sakkarah: Tomb of Horemheb (1345–1318 B.C.); Leiden, Rijksmuseum. *AOB,* no. 87. *ANEP,* no. 5. W. Wolf, *Kunst,* fig. 499. Text: *ANET,* pp. 250f.**

430. Relief, gypseous alabaster, h. of the register, 20 cm.: Nineveh: north palace, chamber T: Assurbanipal (668–626 B.C.); Louvre. *ANEP,* no. 168.**

431. Stone stele, h. 46 cm.: Hazor: stelae sanctuary: Late Bronze Period (1500–1200 B.C.). W. F. Albright, *Archäologie,* pl. 23. Y. Yadin et al., *Hazor,* vol. 1, pl. 29.1.2. G. Cornfeld, *Von Adam,* p. 83. *ANEP,* no. 871.*

432. Relief, marble: Enkomi (Cyprus). F. Cumont, "Invocation au soleil," p. 388, fig. 1.*

433. Ivory carving: Arslan Tash: first half of the first millennium B.C.; Louvre. F. Thureau-Dangin et al., *Arslan Tash,* pl. 36, fig. 62, cf. fig. 61. S. Moscati, *Phöniker,* fig. 21. G. Cornfeld, *Von Adam,* p. 373.*

433a. Sandstone relief: Medinet Habu: interior of the north wall of the second forecourt: Ramses III (1197–1165 B.C.). H. H. Nelson, *Festival Scenes,* plates 196D, 226.

434. Relief: East Thebes: Luxor Temple: colonnade of Amenhotep III, northwest corner, second scene: Tutankhamun (1358–1349 B.C.). W. Wolf, *Das schöne Fest,* pl. 1, scene 2.

434a. Limestone relief, Palmyra, middle of the 1st c. B.C. H. Seyrig, "Antiquités syriennes 17," pl. 19. A. Champidor, *Palmyre,* pp. 65, 86f.

435. Mother of pearl, h. ca. 8 cm.: Mari:

Temple of Ninhursag: third millennium B.C.; Aleppo. S. Moscati, *Semitische Völker,* pl. 15. M. A. Beek, *Atlas of Mesopotamia,* fig. 147. *ANEP,* no. 850.*

436. Statue, h. 6.3 cm.: Susa: Elamite: middle of the 2nd millennium B.C.; Louvre. A. Parrot, *Sumer,* fig. 404a. *IWB,* vol. 3, p. 68. E. D. van Buren, "An Enlargement on a Given Theme."**

437. Relief, Kawa (Sudan), Tutankhamun (1358–1349 B.C.). M. F. L. Macadam, *Temples of Kawa,* vol. 2, plates 1, 40c. J. Leclant, "La 'Mascarade'," p. 131, fig. 8.

438. Tomb painting: Abd el Qurna: Tomb of Menna (no. 69): Thut-mose IV (1422–1413 B.C.). A. Lhote, *Peinture égyptienne,* pl. 15.**

438a. Relief, limestone: Sakkarah· Mastaba of Ptah-Hotep: 5th Dynasty (2480–2350 B.C.). R. F. E. Paget and A. A. Pirie, *Tomb of Ptah-Hetep,* p. 31, pl. 36. J. Leibovitch, "Une scène de sacrifice," p. 59, fig. 1.

439. Ivory carving, h. 3.3 cm., w. 7 cm.: Mari: Shamash Temple: middle of the third millennium B.C.; Damascus. A. Parrot, "Les fouilles de Mari," pl. 18.1. Idem, *Sumer,* fig. 171 B. *ANEP,* no. 845.**

439a. Relief: Nineveh: palace of Sennacherib (704–681 B.C.). *BHH,* vol. 3, col. 1698. A. Paterson, *Assyrian Sculptures,* pl. 85.

440. Bronze relief, h. ca. 8 cm.: Tell Balawat: Shalmaneser III (858–824 B.C.); BM. R. D. Barnett and W. Forman, *Assyrische Palastreliefs,* pl. 170. *AOB,* no. 534. *ANEP,* no. 625. A. Parrot, *Assur,* fig. 138.**

441. Wall painting: Mari: hall 132, field 4: ca. 200 B.C. A. Moortgat, *Kunst,* pp. 77–79. A. Parrot, *Sumer,* fig. 348b.**

442. Relief: Abydos: mortuary temple of Seti I (1317–1301 B.C.). A. M. Calverley et al., *Abydos,* vol. 4, pl. 6. Cf. H. Bonnet, "Die Bedeutung der Räucherungen."**

443. Wall painting: Thebes: Valley of the Kings: Seti I (1371–1301 B.C.). E. Elisofon and L. van der Post, *The Nile,* p. 191.**

444. Silver coin, diam. 2.2 cm.: A.D. 67 (second year of the rebellion). L. H. Grollenberg, *Bildatlas,* fig. 305. Y. Meshorer, *Jewish Coins,* no. 151. A. Reifenberg, *Ancient Jewish Coins,* no. 139.*

445. Painting: Abd el Qurna: Tomb of Rekh-mi-Re (no. 100): linear chamber, right side wall: Thut-mose III (1502–1448 B.C.). N. Davies, *Tomb of Rekh-mi-rē',* vol. 2, pl. 66. W. Wreszinski, *Atlas,* vol. 1, pl. 333.

446. Limestone relief, Abydos, temple of

Seti I (1317–1301 B.C.) A. M. Calverley et al., *Abydos,* vol. 4, pl. 28.**

447. Detail of Plate XXIII. Limestone: Nineveh: southwest palace: Assurbanipal (668–626 B.C.); BM 124802. J. Rimmer, *Musical Instruments,* pl. 14b. *ANEP,* no. 204. M. A. Beek, *Atlas of Mesopotamia,* fig. 226. A. Parrot, *Assur,* fig. 392.**

448. Freehand drawing. Cf. A. Gardiner, *Grammar,* 445 A 32; N. Davies, *Tomb of Rekh-mi-rēʿ,* vol. 2, pl. 92.*

449. Relief: Amarna: southern group of tombs: tomb no. 1: entrance wall, right side (B): Amenophis IV (1377–1358 B.C.). *LD,* vol. 6, pl. 104. N. de G. Davies, *Amarna,* vol. 6, pl. 29. *AOB,* no. 80.

450. Stele, h. 46 cm., w. 37 cm.· Abydos (Kom es-Sultân). Ramses II (1301–1234 B.C.). A. Mariette, *Abydos,* vol. 2, pl. 52b. On the representation of the bark, cf. *LD,* vol. 5, pl. 14; *AOB,* no. 497. Compare the girls with tambourines to *ANEP,* no. 211.**

451. Sandstone relief: Edfu: Temple: western portion of the enclosure-wall, interior, first register, tenth scene: Ptolemy IX/ Alexander I (107–88 B.C.) (possibly somewhat later). E. Chassinat, *Edfou,* vol. 13, plates 509f. Cf. G. Roeder, *Mythen,* p. 135, fig. 26.**

452. Relief, gypseous alabaster, h. ca. 38 cm.: Nineveh: Assurbanipal (668–626 B.C.); Louvre. A. Parrot, *Assur,* fig. 391, cf. fig. 61. *ANEP,* no. 502.**

453. Terra-cotta figure, h. 21 cm.: Achsiv: ca. 450 B.C.; Jerusalem, Palestine Museum; photograph by the author. C. N. Johns, "Discoveries," pp. 88f. E. Lessing, *Die Bibel,* pl. 56.*

454. Terra-cotta figure, h. 12 cm.: Megiddo: stratum V. G. Schumacher, *Tell el-Mutesellim,* vol. 1, p. 102, fig. 156.*

455. Cymbals, Tell Abu Hawām, Late Bronze Period (between 1500 and 1200 B.C.). R. W. Hamilton, "Excavations at Tell Abu Hawām," p. 60, no. 369. On similar cymbals from the Late Bronze and Early Iron Ages at Megiddo cf. G. Loud, *Megiddo,* vol. 2, pl. 185.

456. Basalt relief, h. 90 cm., w. 130 cm.: Carchemish: 9th–8th c. B.C.; BM 117810, Ankara 141. C. L. Woolley and T. E. Lawrence, *Carchemish,* vol. 2, plates B, 18b. *ANEP,* no. 201. K. Galling, *BRL,* col. 390.**

457. Painting on plaster stucco, h. 40 cm.: Mari: 18th c. B.C. A. Parrot, *Assur,* fig. 389.**

458. Mosaic: Huldah: Synagogue: end of the 6th c. A.D. M. Schapiro and M. Avi Yonah, *Israel: Frühe Mosaiken,* pl. 28.*

459. Relief stele, Tell Khorbet, Ramses II (1301–1234 B.C.); Hildesheim, Pelizäus Museum, stele no. 397. H. Hickmann, *Musikgeschichte,* vol. 2, pt. 1, p. 123, fig. 89. On the discovery of trumpets at Beth-Shan, cf. A. Rowe, *Four Canaanite Temples,* pl. 69 A 6.**

460. Relief: Rome: Titus Arch: A.D. 70. *AOB,* no. 509. L. H. Grollenberg, *Bildatlas,* figs. 407f. E. Lessing, *Die Bibel,* pl. 113.*

461. Silver coin, diam. 1.9 cm.: Bar Kochba Rebellion (A.D. 132–135). A. Reifenberg, *Ancient Jewish Coins,* no. 186. Y. Meshorer, *Jewish Coins,* no. 208.*

462. Painted relief: Sakkarah: Tomb of Nenkhftka: 5th Dynasty (2480–2350 B.C.); Cairo. H. Hickmann, *Musikgeschichte,* vol. 2, pt. 1, pp. 26f. W. Sameh, "Alltag," p. 38.**

463. Bronze tripod, h. 36 cm.: Megiddo: Iron Age I (ca. 1200–900 B.C.). G. Schumacher, *Tell el-Mutesellim,* vol. 1, pp. 85f., pl. 50. *AOB,* no. 654.**

464. Terra-cotta figure, h. 18 cm.: Achsiv: 5th c. B.C.; Jerusalem, Palestine Museum. E. Lessing, *Die Bibel,* pl. 56.*

465. Mosaic, shell, lapis lazuli, red limestone, w. 47 cm., h. 20 cm. (entire standard): Ur, ca. 2500 B.C.; BM 121201. A. Parrot, *Assur,* fig. 366. H. Schmökel, *Ur, Assur,* pl. 39. Cf. R. D. Barnett, "New Facts about Musical Instruments."**

466. Rock drawing, Central Negev, second millennium B.C. E. Anati, *Palestine before the Hebrews,* p. 210. Idem, *Rock-Art,* vol. 1, p. 106, fig. 68.

467. Section of Fig. *308.*

468. Vase painting, Megiddo, 12th c. B.C. G. Loud, *Megiddo,* vol. 2, pl. 76.1. G. Cornfeld and G. J. Botterwerk, *Bibel und ihre Welt,* fig. 547.**

469. Terra-cotta figure, Ashdod, 8th–7th c. B.C. M. Dothan, "Ashdod: Preliminary Report," plates 22f. Idem, *"kan hmngnym m'šdwd,"* *Qadmonioth* 3 (1970): 94f., pl. III.*

470. Relief, gypseous alabaster, w. 101 cm., h. 98.5 cm.: Nineveh: palace of Sennacherib (704–681 B.C.); BM 124947. *AOB,* no. 151. *ANEP,* no. 205. H. Schmökel, *Ur, Assur,* pl. 101. A. Parrot, *Assur,* fig. 393. M. A. Beek, *Atlas of Mesopotamia,* fig. 219.*

471. Stone figure, h. 7.7 cm.: Tell el-'Ajjul: Hyksos Period (17th–16th c. B.C.). F. Petrie, *Ancient Gaza,* vol. 3, pl. 16, no. 39.

472. Bronze coin, diam. 2.3 cm.: Bar Kochba Rebellion (A.D. 132–135). A. Reifenberg, *Ancient Jewish Coins,* no. 205. Y. Meshorer, *Jewish Coins,* no. 212.*

473. Bronze coin, diam. 2.5 cm.: Bar

Kochba Rebellion (A.D. 132–135). A. Reifenberg, *Ancient Jewish Coins,* no. 192. Y. Meshorer, *Jewish Coins,* no. 172.*

474. Relief, Amarna, Amenophis IV (1377–1358 B.C.). N. de G. Davies, *Amarna,* vol. 3, pl. 5.

475. Painted wooden stele of Zedhonsuantankh: 19th–20th Dynasties (1345–1085 B.C.); Louvre. A. Champidor, *Thèbes,* p. 33. J. Pirenne, *Histoire,* vol. 3. fig. 66.**

475a. Cylinder seal, haematite, h. 1.4 cm., diam. 0.77 cm.: Anatolian-Syrian: ca. 1900 B.C.; Baltimore, Walters Gallery; after a photograph in the Walters Gallery, made available to the author for publication by Dr. J. V. Canby, curator of the ancient Near Eastern and Egyptian division of the Gallery. On the theme, cf. H. Frankfort, *Cylinder Seals,* pl. 45c.**

476. Relief, Amarna, Amenophis IV (1377–1358 B.C.). N. de G. Davies, *Amarna,* vol. 1, pl. 8.

476a. Relief, h. ca. 3.60 m.: Persepolis: Hall of a Hundred Columns: western portal in the south wall, eastern doorjamb: Xerxes I (486–465 B.C.) and Artaxerxes I (464–424 B.C.). G. Walser, *Völkerschaften,* pp. 63–67, fig. 6. Drawing by E. Herzfeld.

477. Relief, Nimrud, Tiglath-pileser III (745–727 B.C.). A. H. Layard, *Monuments,* pl. 62.2. *AOB,* no. 134. *ANEP,* no. 369. R. D. Barnett and M. Falkner, *Sculptures,* pl. 62.

478. Limestone stele, h. 30 cm.: Deir el Medinah: Ramses II (1304–1238 B.C.). B. Bruyère, "Sur le dieu Ched," pp. 141f., fig. 18.

478a. Statuary grouping, dark gray schist, h. 19.4 cm.: Hermopolis (?): Amenophis III (1413–1377 B.C.); Louvre 11154. G. Bénédite, "Scribe et babouin," pl. 1. G. Posener et al., *Knaurs Lexikon,* p. 262.**

479. Painting on stucco: Deir el Medinah: Tomb of Amenakht (no. 218): 19th–20th Dynasties (1345–1085 B.C.). A. Lhote, *Peinture égyptienne,* p. 138.**

480. Painting: Deir el Medinah: Tomb of Sennudjem (no. 1): 19th Dynasty (1345–1200 B.C.). W. Wolf, *Kunst,* p. 590, fig. 592. W. Sameh, "Alltag," p. 5. G. Posener et al., *Knaurs Lexikon,* p. 269.**

Concluding vignette: Tomb painting, height of the figure, ca. 1.05 m.: West Thebes: Sheikh abd el Qurna: tomb no. 226: Amenophis III (1413–1377 B.C.). N. Davies, *Tombs of Menkheperrasonb,* pp. 39f., pl. 30, fragment E.

PLATES

I. Gorge of the Arnon River, near the point at which it empties into the Dead Sea. Photograph by the author (1965).

IA. Cylinder seal, shell, h. 3.6 cm., diam. 2.1 cm.: Tell Asmar: Late Akkadian Period (ca. 2200 B.C.); Chicago, Oriental Institute A 11396. H. Frankfort, *Cylinder Seals,* pp. 108–10, pl. 19e. R. M. Boehmer, *Entwicklung der Glyptik,* pl. 40, fig. 477. Photograph: Oriental Institute, Chicago.

IB. Bronze helmet with gold and silver decoration over pitch, h. 16.5 cm., w. 22.1 cm.: Northwest Persia, from the district of the Safid River: ca. 1000 B.C.; New York, Metropolitan Museum of Art 63.74, Fletcher Fund, 1963. Photograph: Metropolitan Museum, New York. C. K. Wilkinson, "Art of the Marlik Culture," p. 107, fig. 9.

II. Part of the gorge which leads to Petra: Photograph by the author (1965).

III. Cylinder seal, h. 7.2 cm.: Assyrian: first half of the first millennium; Louvre. Photograph by M. Chuzeville. A. Vigneau and A. Ozenfant, *Encyclopédie photographique,* vol. 2,

p. 96, fig. 142. B. Meissner, *Babylonien und Assyrien,* vol. 2, fig. 39. Cf. B. Meissner, "Siegelzylinder"; idem, "Neue Siegelzylinder."

IV. Relief, Nineveh, Assurbanipal (668–626 B.C.). Photograph: BM. *AOB,* no. 384.

V. Relief, l. 94 cm., w. 63 cm.: Nineveh: palace of Assurbanipal: chamber above chamber S: Assurbanipal (668–626 B.C.); BM 124919. Photograph: BM. R. D. Barnett and M. Forman, *Assyrische Palastreliefs,* pl. 132. L. H. Grollenberg, *Bildatlas,* p. 83.

VI. Upper portion of Ophel and the Temple site. Aerial photograph by WSW; Photograph: W. Braun, Jerusalem.

VII. Jerusalem, scene from the Wadi *en-nār* north towards Ophel and the south wall of the Temple area. Photograph by the author (1969).

VIIA. Hermon (Jebel esh-Sheikh), 2814 m. above sea level, seen from the east. Photograph: P. Giegel, Zurich.

VIIB. Zaphon (Latin name: Mons Casius; Arabic: Jebel el-'Aqra), 1729 m. above sea level, seen from the south. Photograph: G. Eichholz, *Landschaften der Bibel,* Neukirchen, 3rd ed., 1972, p. 27 (color).

VIII. Relief, ca. 4.5 × 4.5 m.: Khorsabad: Sargon II (721–705 B.C.). Photograph: BM. H. Schmökel, *Ur, Assur,* pl. 96. Cf. H. Frankfort, *Art and Architecture,* pp. 146–49.

IX. Jerusalem, Temple site seen from the Mount of Olives. Telephoto by the author (1969).

X. Podium constructed of unhewn stones, h. ca. 1.25 m., diam. ca. 7 m.; to its right a temple (with podium) from the beginning of the second millennium B.C.: Megiddo, stratum 16 (3rd millennium B.C.). Photograph by the author (1969).

XI. Altar: Court of the temple with the altar of burnt sacrifice, seen from the east (cf. Fig. *170*); in the background are the steps to the holy of holies (cf. Fig. *248*). Photograph by the author (1969).

XII. Umm el-Biyara (1060 m.) above the floor of Petra. Photograph: W. Baier, Aarau. *BL,* pl. XVIb.

XIII. The Pinnacle of the West. Photograph: Prof. C. F. Nims, Oriental Institute, Chicago (1972).

XIV. Oil lamp, 12.8 cm. × 12.2 cm.: Late Bronze Period; Author's collection. Photograph by the author.

XV. Dry watercourse northwest of Beersheba. Photograph by the author (1961).

XVI. Painted wooden casket (with gesso coating), height of the scenes, 26.5 cm., w. 6. cm.: Tomb of Tutankhamun (1358–1349 B.C.); Cairo Museum, no. 324. N. M. Davies and A. H. Gardiner, *Tutankhamun's Painted Box,* pl. IV. Photograph: Oriental Institute, Chicago.

XVII. Ibid., pl. II: Photograph: Oriental Institute, Chicago.

XVIII. Limestone stele, fragment, h. 75 cm.: Lagash: Eannatum (ca. 2400 B.C.); Louvre. Photograph: M. Chuzeville. *AOB,* no. 32. *ANEP,* no. 300. A. Parrot, *Sumer,* fig. 164.

XIX. Sandstone stele, h. ca. 2 m.: Susa: Naramsin (ca. 2250 B.C.); Louvre. Photograph: M. Chuzeville. *AOB,* nos. 41, 43. *ANEP,* no. 309. A. Parrot, *Sumer,* fig. 213. H. Schmökel, *Ur, Assur,* pl. 46. A. Moortgat, *Kunst,* pl. 155.

XX. Relief, Nimrud, Assurbanipal II (883–859 B.C.); BM 124540. Photograph: BM. H. Frankfort, *Kingship,* fig. 8.

XXI. Relief: Medinet Habu: first pylon: Ramses III (1197–1165 B.C.). Photograph: A. Gaddies, Luxor. A. Champidor, *Thèbes,* pp. 156f.

XXII. Relief: Karnak: Amon Temple: exterior of the south wall: Sheshonk I (ca. 930 B.C.). Photograph: A. Gaddis, Luxor. *AOB,* no. 114. *ANEP,* no. 349.

XXIII. Black obelisk, h. (entire) 2.02 m.: Nimrud: Shalmaneser III (858–824 B.C.); BM 118885. Photograph: BM. *AOB,* no. 123. *ANEP,* nos. 351–55. H. Schmökel, *Ur, Assur,* pl. 90.

XXIV. Relief, gypseous alabaster, h. 1.37 m., w. 1.75 m.: Nineveh: palace of Sennacherib (704–681 B.C.); BM 124911: Photograph: BM. *AOB,* no. 138. *ANEP,* no. 371. A. Parrot, *Assur,* no. 49.

XXV. Stele of Neb-Re, h. 67 cm., w. 39 cm.: West Thebes: Amon Temple: 19th Dynasty (1345–1200 B.C.); Berlin, stele 23077. Photograph: Staatliche Museen, Berlin. A. Erman, "Denksteine," pp. 1087–97, pl. 16.

XXVI. Limestone stele, h. 1.13 m.: Byblos: fifth or early fourth c. B.C.; Louvre. Photograph: M. Chuzeville. *AOB,* no. 516. *ANEP,* no. 477. *KAI,* no. 10.

XXVII. Relief, gypseous alabaster, h. 0.39 m., l. 1.45 m.: Nineveh: Assurbanipal (668–626 B.C.); BM 124802. Photograph: BM. *AOB,* no. 152. *ANEP,* no. 204. A. Parrot, *Assur,* fig. 392. M. A. Beek, *Atlas of Mesopotamia,* fig. 226.

XXVIII. Steatite stele, h. ca. 20 cm.: ca. 400 B.C.; BM 36250. Photograph: BM. Cf. F. J. Chabas, "Horus sur les crocodiles"; K. C. Seele, "Horus on the Crocodiles."

INDEX OF BIBLICAL REFERENCES

OLD TESTAMENT

414

50:11 *144*
50:12 *42, 144, 150*
50:13 *144, 278, 330*
50:14 *144, 280, 324, 327, 332*
50:15 *144, 280, 327, 333*
50:16 *126*
50:16b *278*
50:17–21 *126*
50:17a *278*
50:23 *278, 324, 330, 332*

51:1ff *194*
51:7 *81*
51:8 *66*
51:10–11 *306*
51:15 *59, 334*
51:16 *59, 280, 333*
51:17 *59, 280*
51:18 *18, 120, 328*
51:19 *328*

52:5 *186*
52:7 *240*
52:8 *125, 135, 136, 354*

53:5 *66*

54:1 *208*
54:2 *192*
54:4 *242*
54:5 *208*
54:6–7 *330*
54:11 *242*

55:2 *192*
55:4–9 *97*
55:14 *175, 334, 335*
55:20 *95, 96*
55:23 *66, 67, 72, 96*

56 *329*
56:4 *240*
56:5–7 *97*
56:11 *240*
56:12 *324*
56:13 *53, 66*

57 *329*
57:1 *28, 190*
57:1b *191*
57:6 *89*
57:8 *347, 349*
57:9 *349*
57:10 *31, 33*
57:11 *27, 30, 31, 43*

58 *193, 329*
58:2 *97*
58:3 *97*
58:4 *51, 87, 88, 97*
58:5 *97*
58:6 *86, 97*
58:7 *97*

58:8 *65, 66, 97*
58:9 *97*

59 *329*
59:6 *85, 87*
59:7 *242*
59:9 *181*
59:11 *222*
59:13 *39, 42*
59:14 *87*
59:15 *85, 198*
59:16–17 *181*

60 *100, 329*
60:1–3 *100*
60:6 *101, 174, 193, 230*
60:7 *101, 230*
60:8 *101, 230*
60:10 *100, 101*
60:11 *101*

61:1c *181*
61:2 *24, 25, 28, 39, 76, 112,
        118, 163, 176, 181, 198*
61:3 *28, 181*
61:3b *186*
61:4 *28, 162, 163, 180, 181,
        190*
61:5 *324*
61:6 *176, 181*
61:7 *176, 263*
61:8 *279, 324*

62:2 *181*
62:3 *101, 102, 176*
62:6 *181*
62:9 *73, 240, 241*
62:10 *242*
62:11 *193*

63:1 *76, 186, 192*
63:2 *201, 308, 318*
63:3 *186*
63:5 *195, 196, 335*
63:7 *190*
63:8 *259*
63:10 *66, 76, 103*

64:3–4 *94*
64:5 *89*
64:7 *217, 221*

65 *175, 212, 218*
65:1 *324*
65:2 *192, 324*
65:4 *128, 135, 187, 195*
65:5 *151*
65:6 *49*
65:7 *48, 49, 53, 71, 107, 212*
65:8 *22, 23, 39, 48, 212, 335*
65:9 *29, 48, 212, 213*
65:10–13 *29, 212, 213*

66:4 *310*
66:6 *21, 227*
66:10 *184, 185*
66:11 *184*
66:12 *184*
66:13 *274, 279, 324*
66:14 *279, 324*
66:15 *147, 274, 279*
66:19 *324*

67:5 *39*
67:6 *39, 214*
67:7 *39, 125*
67:8 *42*

68:6c *76*
68:10 *213*
68:11–13 *268*
68:15 *116*
68:16 *116, 120*
68:18 *323*
68:21 *292, 294*
68:22 *23*
68:22b *74*
68:23 *103*
68:24 *201, 308, 323*
68:25 *323, 337, 338, 339, 340,
        349*
68:26 *337, 339*
68:27 *349*
68:29 *303, 324*

69:1 *71*
69:2 *29, 70, 71*
69:10 *319*
69:11 *319*
69:12 *122*
69:14 *71*
69:15 *39, 71, 72*
69:21 *80*
69:22 *91*
69:27 *97*
69:28 *97*
69:30 *59, 280, 324, 325, 328,
        333*
69:31 *59, 280, 324, 328, 333*
69:34 *35, 56*

70:3 *176*

71:2 *192*
71:3 *181*
71:6 *202, 249, 251*
71:16 *242*
71:20 *35*
71:22 *347, 349, 351*
71:22b *349*
71:23a *349*

72 *26, 256, 286, 306*
72:1 *280, 288*
72:2 *280, 285, 288*
72:4 *285, 289*

APOCRYPHA

NEW TESTAMENT